W9-CAY-802

DATE DUE GET A

IN

Europe

Cheryl Matherly and Robert Sanborn

PLANNING/COMMUNICATIONS

River Forest, Illinois

For quantity discounts and permissions, contact the publisher:

PLANNING/COMMUNICATIONS

7215 Oak Avenue, River Forest, Illinois 60305

Phone: 708/366–5200

http://jobfindersonline.com

email: info@planningcommunications.com

Cover design by Salvatore Concialdi

Front cover photo of Venice by Daniel Lauber. Copyright 2003.
All rights reserved. Used by permission.

Produced using Corel Ventura 10

Disclaimer of All Warranties and Liabilities

While every effort has been taken to assure the accuracy and timeliness of the information contained in this book, the authors and publisher make no warranties, either expressed or implied, with respect to the information contained herein. The authors and publisher shall not be liable for any incidental or consequential damages in connection with, or arising out of, the use of materials in this book.

PUBLISHER'S CATALOGING–IN–PUBLICATION

Matherly, Cheryl

How to Get a Job in Europe / Cheryl Matherly and Robert Sanborn. — 5th ed.

p. cm.
Includes bibliographical references and index.
LCCN: 2003103396
ISBN: 1–884587–28–3 (paperback)
ISBN: 1–884587–29–1 (hard cover)

1. Employment in foreign countries. 2. Americans—Employment—Europe. 3. Job hunting—Europe.
I. Sanborn, Robert. II. Title.
HF5549.5.E45M26 2003   650.14

Contents

Acknowledgments

This fifth edition of *How to Get a Job in Europe* would never have been possible without the hard work, creativeness, and perseverance of several contributors. Lauren Alexander performed admirably as a research assistant, diligently rooting out information via the Internet, the library, and the telephone. We recognize Anderson Brandao for all his help and diligence in helping us produce the original edition of the book. Also providing hard work through the years were Ann Peterson, J.R. Smiljanic, Don Kindred, Linda Breed, Alan Ying, Victoria Mejia, Tam Truong, Rebecca Durrer, Claire Saxton, Kristin Baker, Ariel Strichartz, Biff Clay, Andi Galt, and Sandra De Los Santos. We both thank the staff of the Rice University Career Services Center for their assistance and want to express our appreciation for the superb editing and proof–reading done by Jennifer Atkin of Planning/Communications. Bob thanks his strongest support system, his wife Ellen and his lovely daughter Virginia Elisabet. Cheryl adds her heartfelt thanks to her husband Steven Wilson, her sometimes research assistant and always best friend.

Note to Our Readers

We have made every effort to provide the most useful, up-to-date information available to help you find the job you want. Our staff of fact checkers has verified every name, address, phone number, email address, and URL. But offices move and people change jobs, so we urge you to call or write before you visit. And if you think we should include information on companies, organizations, or people that we've missed, write to us at the address below.

Drop Us a Line!

Among the features in this edition are short notes from working travelers like yourself, recounting their experiences in Europe. For this feature to be a success in future editions, we need your input. So if you've crushed wine with your bare feet in Italy, au paired in Austria, penned copy on Fleet Street, or have any other experiences you think fellow readers might be interested in, please write to us in care of our publisher Planning/Communications. Not only might your experiences be published, but your story may help your fellow travelers in their searches for jobs and experiences in faraway lands. Send your stories Cheryl Metherly at:

Email: matherly@planningcommunications.com

or

Europe Stories
Planning/Communications
7215 Oak Ave.
River Forest, IL 60305

Part I

Getting a Job in Europe

Chapter 1

So You Want To Get a Job in Europe

How to get the most out of this book. Myths about international work debunked. Books on working and living in Europe. Addresses of chambers of commerce.

Rome, Paris, London — yes, Americans are fascinated with Europe. Many Americans have lived and worked in Europe before moving on to greater things. Thomas Jefferson and Benjamin Franklin both worked in Europe during their careers. Ernest Hemingway spent part of his career in Spain. Jim Morrison spent some time in Paris. President Bill Clinton studied in England. International work has long been a ticket to glamour, adventure, and career advancement.

You can work in Europe in jobs ranging from investment banking in Frankfurt to teaching English in Prague to bartending in a London pub. These jobs and many more are available or can be created to satisfy your desire for a European work experience. This book offers a variety of options and resources for Americans seeking work in Europe.

How much do you know about international work? A European job may not entail constant travel (if any), and you will often be expected to work for less money than in the United States. You may have to speak a foreign language, and your two years of high school French may do little more than allow you to converse with kindergartners. You will likely be living in accommodations that are more cramped than you are used to in the U.S. — unless you are moving from Manhattan!

Chances are, however, that if you are reading this book, you are ready for all that. It's the adventure — both good and bad — that is motivating you to find international work.

Myths About International Work

1. Foreign languages get you a job

Many Americans think that knowing a foreign language means they are qualified for an international job. We have met countless students and graduates who want to work abroad and think it shouldn't be a problem to locate international work because they have majored in a foreign language. This is the equivalent of saying, "If you speak English, you can get any job in the United States." Foreign languages can, and certainly do, help Americans land a job in Europe. Fluency (or at least a willingness to become fluent) in the language of the country in which you wish to work is a must, but it is not the sole factor in your eligibility for a position. Employers look for skills and experience. Knowledge of a foreign language is taken for granted.

2. Classes on Europe and similar topics help you get a job

Most college students have the opportunity to take courses on European history, current events, and international relations. Many people assume that having several international affairs classes under their belt has prepared them to work abroad. An understanding of current and historical events in your country of interest is needed, but as with foreign language experience, it will be taken for granted. You should take these courses and have this knowledge, but don't expect to sell employability based on the knowledge acquired through your international relations course work.

3. My American MBA degree will not be useful in Europe

Many Americans think that technical graduate degrees such as an MBA don't count for much in Europe. The reality is that Europeans regard an American MBA quite highly. Many European schools (see Chapter 2) now offer MBA degrees based on the American model. An American MBA, coupled with fluency in an European language and knowledge of the job market, will open doors for you in Europe. Thanks to the growing presence of American businesses in Europe, possessing an MBA degree can only enhance your chance of getting hired there.

4. American subsidiaries hire lots of Americans

Europeans run and staff most American firms in Europe. It is true that Americans are hired by American subsidiaries in Europe. These are most likely to be people, however, who have skills that are needed in Europe and who have worked with a particular company for quite a while during which they have proven their value to the company. If you want to get a job with an American company in Europe, you must prove you have the right skills, know the right people in the company, or simply be in the right place at the right time — or all of the above.

5. If you go to Europe, you're bound to find something

Americans, especially American college students, often go to Europe under the risky assumption that once they arrive, some type of job opportunity will simply materialize. Without planning, you are likely to end up unemployed with few work prospects. Looking for a job once you are in Europe can be done, but it is not as easy as hopping the next plane and reading the help wanted ads. Most countries require you to arrive with a work permit, although notable exceptions to this rule are the student programs sponsored by BUNAC and the Council for International Educational Exchange. Chapter 4 outlines the steps you should follow before leaving America.

One American's path to a career in Europe

Michael Yeaman is an American with the good fortune of working professionally in London. How did he do it? The hard way, some might say. After receiving his undergraduate and masters degrees in geophysics from Stanford University, he worked in the United States for a number of years in Amoco Oil's international division. After about eight years, the U.S. office of an Australian oil firm hired him due to the skills and knowledge he developed at Amoco. In less than a year, the firm transferred him to London. Paid moving expenses, a professional position, good salary — this is what many people dream of when contemplating a successful transfer to Europe. In Michael's case, it took nine years to get there. As you will learn here, there is more than one path to a career in Europe.

About This Book

We have written this book to provide an accurate and honest assessment of your opportunities to work abroad. Anyone who thinks that a European job search will be easy will soon learn otherwise. Europe is a tough place to find employment, some countries more than others. Getting a good job — especially a permanent one — involves a great deal of work. For those who work hard, network, use the resources presented here, and have a lot of gumption, the rewards of international work can be well worth the effort.

The book will be most useful when read in its entirety, but it is organized so that you can skip to the chapters that are most relevant to your particular search. We cover the best ways to get to Europe, how to prepare for your job search, and tips for uncovering potential employers.

Chapter 2 focuses on the qualifications needed to get hired in Europe and provides insight into educational opportunities in Europe and in the United States that best prepare you for an international career. Chapter 3 reports on the European economy and the political and economic upheavals that affect job seekers. These changes in Europe suggest opportunities and challenges for Americans looking for work abroad. Chapter 4 provides a step–by–step strategy for finding work in Europe. Chapter 5 gives details and samples of resumes and cover letters for the international job search. Chapter 6 offers tips on effective interviewing. Chapter 7 details the role of placement organizations in your search. Chapter 8 explores how to prepare for a professional career in Europe. It covers international banking, positions with the United States federal government, working as a correspondent with a major newspaper, and a whole lot more. Chapter 9 covers strategies for finding summer jobs or internships. Chapter 10 looks at alternatives for teaching English abroad.

Each chapter in Part II focuses on one or more European nations and the employment opportunities each offers. We do not cover some European countries, specifically the Balkan nations and the former member states of the Soviet Union. We decided to leave them out because, at the time of this writing, economic and political conditions were so volatile there that it was impossible to provide relevant and current advice for job seekers. You can find resources for finding jobs in those countries in the *International Job Finder* described on page 7.

Periodicals for the International Job Seeker

Preparation is the key to an international job search, and your research can make the difference between success and failure. A number of books and periodicals provide useful background information to help direct your efforts.

The Economist is a weekly magazine that examines business and current events in Europe. It is probably the single best source of information on current political and economic happenings — making it a must for the prospective job seeker who wants to learn more about the current scene in Europe. It is widely available at bookstores as well as by subscription.

The Economist is also available online at www.economist.com. The online edition publishes all articles from the print edition (including those printed only in British copies) plus a searchable archive of all *The Economist's* articles back to June 1997. Also included are "Country Briefings" (articles, background profiles, forecasts and statistics, market and currency updates, newswires, and links for 60 countries at www.economist.com/countries), "Cities Guide," "Global Executive" (career guidance and job postings for senior international businesspeople), and more.

You can subscribe to the print edition at the magazine's website or by mail. For delivery in North America ($129/annual U.S. subscription; $189/annual Canada or Mexico subscription), contact *The Economist*, Subscription Department, P.O. Box 58524, Boulder, CO 80322–8524, Tel.: (800) 456–6086, Fax: (303) 504–7455. For delivery outside North America, visit the website to get subscription rates and to place your subscribe online.

These daily business newspapers can also give insight into current business conditions in Europe and ongoing employment trends:

The Financial Times of London	**The Wall Street Journal**
Business Information Limited	Tel.: (800) JOURNAL
Towerhouse, South Hampton Street	
London WC2E 7HA, England	www.wsj.com
US Tel.: (800) 628–8088	(Also publishes a European edition)

A number of business weeklies are published in both the United States and Europe and provide coverage of European business and economic activity:

Bloomberg

Tel.: (212) 318–2000

www.bloomberg.com

Business Week

Tel.: (888) 878–5151

www.businessweek.com

Forbes

Tel.: (800) 888–9896

www.forbes.com

Fortune

www.fortune.com

Red Herring

Tel.: (800) 627–4931

www.redherring.com

The *International Herald Tribune,* published jointly by *The Washington Post* and *The New York Times,* is the only pan–European English daily offering broad coverage of daily business and political events in Europe. You can place a domestic subscription at: *International Herald Tribune*, 850 Third Ave., New York, NY 10022, Tel.: (212) 752–3890, Fax.: (212) 755–8785, www.iht.com. For delivery in Europe, contact: *International Herald Tribune*, 6 bis, rue des Graviers, 92521 Neuilly Cedex, France, Tel.: [33] 1 41 43 93 00, Fax: [33] 1 41 43 92 12.

You will also want to read European newspapers that are primarily devoted to events within their own country. They are often available at large bookstores or newsstands. If you intend to job search and live in one particular country or region of Europe, these newspapers may be your best job–search resource. Chapters 11 through 21 include lists of newspapers and periodicals for each country.

Books on Working Abroad

Bookstore tend to stock only a few international career books — some truly helpful, some only so–so. In case you cannot find a particular book at your local bookstore, we have provided contact information on their publishers. The following titles are particularly informative.

Adventure Careers. Alex Hiam and Susan Angle. Career Press, 180 Fifth Avenue, P.O. Box 34, Hawthorne, NJ 07507. Not specifically on working abroad, but a thoughtful guide to those pondering international or other non–traditional career paths. $11.99, 288 pages, 1995.

Alternative Travel Directory. Clay Hubbs. Transitions Abroad Publishing. Reports on online and offline resources for short–term and long–term employment overseas. Also describes over 2,000 schools, specialty travel tours and programs, and key information sources for independent travelers. Available from Planning/Communications — see the "Resource Center" beginning on page 472. $19.95, 293 pages, 2002.

The Back Door Guide to Short–Term Job Adventures. Michael Landes. Ten Speed Press. Available from Planning/Communications — see the "Resource Center" beginning on page 472. A guide to internships, extraordinary experiences, seasonal jobs, and volunteering for everyone from college students to senior citizens. One section lists 200 programs overseas. $21.95, 420 pages, 2002.

Best Resumes and CVs for International Jobs. Ron Krannich and Wendy Enelow. Available from Planning/Communications — see the "Resource Center" beginning on page 472. Over 100 sample resumes and CVs provide concrete examples of the principles the authors espouse for tailoring your resume or CV to get hired in a job abroad. $24.95, 248 pages, 2002.

Directory of Jobs and Careers Abroad. Dan Boothby. Distributed in the U.S. by Globe Pequot Press, P.O. Box 480. Guilford, CT 06437, www.globe – pequot.com. Part I covers how to find work abroad. Part II offers detailed information on recruitment and sources of jobs for 35 different careers and volunteering. Part III reports on career opportunities, immigration and residency, costs and standards of living, health, welfare and education, and employment prospects in 50 countries, including all of Europe. $19.95, 415 pages. Published annually.

Key resource for finding international jobs

International Job Finder: Where the Jobs are Worldwide, by Daniel Lauber with Kraig Rice. Identifies the 1,200 most effective online and print resources for finding jobs worldwide and tells you everything each resource offers so you can decide which will help you find the international job of your dreams. In the book you will:

    ✓ Discover how to conduct a successful and safe online international job search, even if you are an Internet novice.

    ✓ See how to locate all the key resources on each website so you can quickly and easily use the job databases, resume banks, email job agents, directories of employers, salary surveys, links to other websites, and other job resources on each Internet site.

    ✓ Learn how to spot and avoid international job scams and troublespots.

    ✓ Find out which print resources will help you advance your international career.

The *International Job Finder* is available in bookstores and from Planning/Communications — see the "Resource Center" beginning on page 472. For more details, visit http://jobfindersonline.com. $19.95, 348 pages, 2002.

Directory of Websites for International Jobs. Ron and Caryl Krannich. Impact Publications. Available from Planning/Communications — see the "Resource Center" beginning on page 472. Capsule information on over 1,400 websites for the international job search. $19.95, 151 pages, 2001.

Global Resume and CV Guide. Mary Anne Thompson. John Wiley & Sons. Available from Planning/Communications — see the "Resource Center" beginning on page 472. A very thorough country–by–country guide to preparing resumes and cover letters. $17.95, 294 pages, 2000.

Job Surfing: Working Abroad. Princeton Review Staff. Available from Planning/Communications — see the "Resource Center" beginning on page 472. A practical guide to finding jobs abroad with hundreds of websites. $14.95, 352 pages, 2002.

International Jobs. Eric Kocher. Addison–Wesley Publishing Company, 202 Carnegie Center, Reading, MA 01867. A handbook of career opportunities around the world. $16.00, 321 pages, 1999.

Live and Work Abroad: A Guide for Modern Nomads. Huw Francis and Michelyne Callan. 2001. Vacation Work Publications, 9 Park End St., Oxford, England OX1 1HJ; www.vacationworks.com. Nuts–and–bolts guide to finding work overseas. £11.95, 256 pages, 2001.

Summer Jobs Abroad. Andrew James and David Woodworth, ed. Globe Pequot Press, P.O. Box 480, Guilford, CT 06437, www.globe–pequot .com. Covering 50 countries, including all European nations, this directory provides job descriptions and contact information for summer and temporary jobs in agriculture, hotel work and catering, industrial and office work, sports (courier, camping, ski resorts), work at sea, au pairs and nannies, family helps and exchanges plus voluntary work and archeology. $17.95, 297 pages, published annually.

Work Abroad: The Complete Guide to Finding a Job Overseas. Clay Hubbs, editor. Transitions Abroad Publishing. Available from Planning/Communications — see the "Resource Center" beginning on page 472. Valuable collection of essays on all aspects of working abroad: preparing your job search, a broad array of jobs, information on countries where these jobs are available, and a directory of key employers with full contact information. Includes chapters on internships and volunteering. $15.95, 250 pages, 2002

Work Overseas: How to Find a High–Paying Tax–Free Job. George Robinson. 2002. Robert D. Reed Publishers, 750 La Playa, Suite 647, San Francisco, California 94121. http://rdrpublishers.com. Job search strategies from someone who has lived the life he describes. $29.95, 186 pages, 2000.

Work Worldwide: International Career Strategies for the Adventurous Job Seeker. Nancy Mueller. 2000. John Muir Publications. Available from Planning/Communications — see the "Resource Center" beginning on page 472. Customs vary in each nation. In many European countries, for example, you should not boast about your accomplishments during your job interview. This step–by–step gem provides guidance for resumes, cover letters, interviewing, and networking for each nation, including all of Europe. $14.95, 231 pages, 2000.

Work Your Way Around the World. Susan Griffith. Published in odd–numbered years. Globe Pequot Press, P.O. Box 480, Guilford, CT 06437, www.globe–pequot.com. Written for the working traveler. Extremely thorough guide on finding temporary work in almost any country in the world. $19.95, 546 pages, 2003.

 Another outstanding resource for the European job search is the bimonthly magazine *Transitions Abroad*. Packed with information on work, study, and travel abroad, this magazine is especially targeted to students, although there are articles that will be of interest to anyone who is considering living abroad. Contact: Transitions Abroad; Transitions Abroad Publishing, Inc., 18 Hulst Road, P.O. Box 1300, Amherst, MA 01004, www.transitionsabroad.com.

Books on Living Abroad

The Adventure of Working Abroad. Joyce Sautters Osland. 1995. Jossey–Bass Publishers, 350 Sansome Street, San Francisco, CA 94104. Looks at experiences of expatriates. $25.00, 244 pages, 1995.

The Art of Crossing Cultures. Craig Sorti. 2001. Intercultural Press, P.O. Box 700, Yarmouth, ME 04096. Focuses on the personal challenges of living abroad. $16.95, 153 pages, 2001.

Culture Shock! Successful Living Abroad: Living and Working Abroad. Monica Rabe. Graphic Arts Center Publishing Co., 3019 NW Yeon, Portland, OR 97210; www.gacpc.com. Assists anyone contemplating a move to another country by giving tips to avoid the effects of culture shock. $13.95, 150 pages, 1997.

The Global Etiquette Guide to Europe. Dean Foster. John Wiley & Sons. Available from Planning/Communications — see the "Resource Center" starting on page 472. An in–depth look at communication styles and etiquette in each European nation: proper business attires, acceptable topics of discussion, acceptable and unacceptable gestures, public manners, customs, greetings and introductions, dealing with authorities, how women are treated, gift–giving etiquette, and more. $17.95, 390 pages, 2000.

The Expert Expatriate: Your Guide to Successful Relocation Abroad Moving, Living, Thriving. Melissa Brayer Hess and Patricia Linderman. Intercultural Press, P.O. Box 700, Yarmouth, ME 04096. Tips for first–time expatriates written by two American Foreign Service spouses. $19.95, 270 pages, 2002.

Gestures: The Do's and Taboos of Body Language Around the World. Roger Axtell. John Wiley & Sons, 111 River Street, Hoboken, NJ 07030, www.wiley.com. An entertaining primer on intercultural communications. $16.95, 256 pages, 1997.

International Travel Health Guide 2001. (12th ed.) Stuart Rose. Travel Medicine, Inc., 351 Pleasant Street, Suite 312, Northampton, MA 01060. Provides current information on health concerns for those traveling or living abroad. $24.95, 2001.

Survival Kit for Overseas Living. L. Robert Kohls. Intercultural Press, P.O. Box 700, Yarmouth, ME 04096. Focuses on the adaptations one has to make in adjusting to life in a foreign land. $15.00, 188 pages, 2001.

When Cultures Collide. Richard D. Lewis. Nicholas Brealey Publishing, 17470 Sonoma Highway, Sonoma, CA 95476. A cross–cultural guide that is a must–read for professionals living and working overseas; explores the cultural roots of national behavior. $19.95, 500 pages, 2000.

For a quick overview of whatever country or countries you might be interested in, *Culturegrams* are another option. These four–page summaries of essential information on customs, manners, and the like, cover dozens of cultures worldwide and are updated annually. Single copies are available, or you may purchase the entire set. Send inquires to Axion Press, CultureGrams, 333 South 520 West, Suite 360, Lindon, UT 84042. You can also purchase Culturegrams online at www.culturegrams.com.

Similar to Culturegrams is the U.S. government's *Background Notes* series. Each report gives an overview of the history, geography, culture, and foreign relations of a particular country. *Background Notes* are available online at www.state.gov/r/pa/ei/bgn/. Print versions may be ordered from the Superintendent of Documents, U.S. Government Printing Office, Washington, DC 20402.

Addresses of Chambers of Commerce

A chamber of commerce, whether located in the United States or in Europe, can offer information on businesses and organizations in the country of your choice. Often, information on economic trends and living conditions is also available. The following list provides the addresses for the major chambers of commerce for each country included in this book. Where possible, a U.S. location is specified. For more complete listings of chambers of commerce, please refer to the individual country chapters in Part II.

EUROPEAN–AMERICAN BUSINESS COUNCIL
1025 Connecticut Avenue NW
Washington, DC 20036
Tel.: (202) 728–0777
Fax: (202) 728–2937
www.eabc.org

AUSTRIA
United States–Austrian Chamber of Commerce
165 West 46th Street
New York, NY 10036
Tel.: (212) 819–0117
Fax: (212) 819–0345
www.usatchamber.com

BELGIUM
Belgian–American Chamber of Commerce in the U.S.
245 Park Avenue, 24th Floor
New York, NY 10167
Tel.: (212) 672–1632
Fax: (212) 672–1644
www.belcham.org

CYPRUS
Cyprus Trade Center

13 East 40th Street
New York, NY 10016
Tel.: (212) 213–9100
Fax: (212) 213–2918
www.cyprus–tradeny.org

CZECH REPUBLIC
Czech–U.S. Business Council
1615 H Street NW
Washington, DC 20062
Tel.: (202) 463–5460
Fax: (202) 463–3114
Email: eurasia@uschamber.com

DENMARK
Danish–American Chamber of
Commerce
885 Second Avenue, 18th Floor
New York, NY 10017
Tel.: (212) 980–6240
Fax: (212) 754–1904
www.daccny.com

FINLAND
Finnish–American Chamber of
Commerce
866 U.N. Plaza
New York, NY 10017
Tel.: (212) 821–0225
Fax: (212) 750–4418
www.finlandtrade.com

FRANCE
French–American Chamber of
Commerce in the U.S.
1350 Avenue of the Americas, 6th Floor
New York, NY 10019
Tel.: (212) 765–4460
Fax: (212) 765–4650
www.faccnyc.org

GERMANY
German–American Chamber of
Commerce
40 West 57th Street, 31st Floor
New York, NY 10019–4092
Tel.: (212) 974–8830
Fax: (212) 974–8867
www.gaccny.com

GREECE
Hellenic–American Chamber of
Commerce
960 Avenue of the Americas
Suite 1204

New York, NY 10001–2112
Tel.: (212) 629–6380
Fax: (212) 564–9281

HUNGARY
Hungarian–U.S. Business Council
1615 H Street, NW
Washington, DC 20062
Tel.: (202) 463–5460
Fax: (202) 463–3114
Email: eurasia@uschamber.com

IRELAND
Ireland Chamber of Commerce in the
U.S.
556 Central Avenue
New Providence, NJ 07974
Tel.: (908) 286–1300
Fax: (908) 286–1200
www.iccusa.org

ITALY
Italy–America Chamber of Commerce
730 Fifth Avenue, Suite 600
New York, NY 10019
Tel.: (212) 459–0044
Fax: (212) 459–0090
www.italchambers.net/newyork

LIECHTENSTEIN
Liechtenstein Industrie–und–
Handeslkammer
Postfach 232
Josef Rheinberger–Strasse 11
FL–9490 Vaduz. Liechtenstein
Tel.: [41] 75 237 55 11
Fax: [41] 75 237 55 12

LUXEMBOURG
Luxembourg Chamber of Commerce
825 Third Avenue, 36th Floor
New York, NY 10022
Tel.: (212) 888–6701
Fax: (212) 888–1162
www.luxembourgbusiness.org

MALTA
Malta Chamber of Commerce
Exchange Buildings
Republic Street
VLT05 Valletta, Malta
Tel.: [356] 233 873
Fax: [356] 245 223
www.chamber.org.mt

THE NETHERLANDS
The Netherlands Chamber of
Commerce in the U.S.
One Rockefeller Plaza, Suite 1420
New York, NY 10020
Tel.: (212) 265–6460
Fax: (212) 265–6402
www.netherlands.org

NORWAY
Norwegian–American Chamber of
Commerce
800 Third Avenue
New York, NY 10022
Tel.: (212) 421–1655
Fax: (212) 838–0374
www.nacc.no

POLAND
Polish–U.S. Business Council
1615 H Street NW
Washington, DC 20062
Tel.: (212) 463–5460
Fax: (202) 463–3114
Email: eurasia@uschamber.com
www.uschamber.com

PORTUGAL
Portugal–U.S. Chamber of Commerce
590 Fifth Avenue
New York, NY 10036
Tel.: (212) 354–4627
Fax: (212) 575–4737
www.portugal–us.com

ROMANIA
Romanian–U.S. Business Council
1615 H Street NW
Washington, DC 20062
Tel.: (212) 463–5460
Fax: (202) 463–3114
Email: eurasia@uschamber.com
www.uschamber.com

SLOVAK REPUBLIC
Slovak Chamber of Commerce and
Industry
Gorkého 9

816 03 Bratislava, Slovakia
Tel.: [421] 7 5443 32 72
Fax: [421] 7 5443 30 54
www.scci.sk

SPAIN
Spain–U.S. Chamber of Commerce
350 Fifth Avenue, Suite 2029
New York, NY 10118
Tel.: (212) 967–2170
Fax: (212) 564–1415
www.spainuscc.org

SWEDEN
The Swedish–American Chamber of
Commerce
119 Oronoco Street
Alexandria, VA 22314
Tel.: (703) 836–6560
Fax: (703) 836–6561
www.saccny.org

SWITZERLAND
Swiss American Chamber of Commerce
608 Fifth Avenue, Suite 309
New York, NY 10020
Tel.: (212) 246–7789
Fax: (212) 246–1366
www.amcham.ch

TURKEY
Union of Chambers of Commerce,
Industry, Maritime Commerce, and
Commodity Exchanges
Ataturk Bulvari 149
TR–06582 Bakanliklar, Ankara, Turkey
Tel.: [90] 312 125 561
Fax: [90] 312 118 1002

UNITED KINGDOM
British–American Chamber of
Commerce
52 Vanderbilt Avenue, 20th Floor
New York, NY 10017
Tel.: (212) 661–5660
Fax: (212) 661–1886
www.bacc.org

Safety for Americans Abroad

The issue of safety, while always a concern for Americans abroad, has assumed center stage as terrorists target western interests and the United States invades Iraq in March 2003. Even with these threats, Americans living or traveling abroad are much more likely to be the victim of a pickpocket or bad case of food poisoning than of a political extremist. Yet as long as the U.S. is at war with a specific country or terrorists in general, the prudent American expat will take cautionary steps to keep safe. The following tips can easily be summed up with the advice: *Be aware of what is going on around you!*

Tip #1. *Always be aware of current events in the country to which you are traveling.* Because the world situation can change quickly, it is important to read a newspaper, watch the TV news, or check Internet news outlets on a daily basis. The State Department issues travel safety warnings for Americans at its website (http://travel.state.gov). The "Latest Travel Warnings" provide current news about places deemed dangerous for American travelers. The "Public Announcements" list terrorist and other threats issued for Americans in specific countries. The U.K.'s Foreign & Commonwealth Office offers similar advice online at http://193.114.50.10. Select "Traveling Overseas" where you can pick "Country Advice." The savvy world traveler would be prudent to check both sites before traveling or moving to any country around the globe.

Tip #2. *Register with the American embassy.* The U.S. embassy is a source of safety and security information, as well as a point of contact if an emergency arises. The addresses for the U.S. embassy and consulates in each European nation are included in each chapter in Part II.

Tip #3. *Blend in.* Be observant. Pay attention to what locals do. Try to emulate their behavior as much as possible. Blending in completely is most often an impossibility, but avoiding clothing and behavior considered inappropriate or offensive in your host country will go a long way toward helping you be less noticeable. Don't draw attention to yourself as an American.

Tip #4. *Know your country, both home and host.* When abroad, many potentially dangerous situations can be avoided if you understand what is occurring. For example, political rallies are usually planned in advance. Be aware of them and avoid them. Know the local laws — ignorance is never an excuse. Keeping up with current events and the United States' actions within the world will help you know when it would be best to avoid travel and may help you tactfully field job interview questions about why America chooses certain political maneuvers, economic sanctions, etc.

Tip #5. *Speak the language of the host country whenever possible.* Nothing makes a person stick out more than speaking English where it is a foreign language. Even with other Americans, practice speaking in your host nation's native tongue. If you are in a group of people speaking English, speak softly. Most Americans talk at louder volumes than people of other nationalities, whether English–speaking or not.

Tip #6. *Avoid American hangouts.* It may be tempting to sink your teeth into a burger at the local American chain restaurant, but this makes you more identifiable as an American.

Tip #7. *Remember that anti–Americanism exists to varying degrees throughout the world.* While in most cases it is non–threatening, you would be prudent to avoid individuals who vocally criticize the United States and make you feel uncomfortable about your citizenry. When questions are directed at you, it helps to really know American policies and history very well. Calm explanations help diffuse anger and antagonism. Some people use anti–American statements as an opportunity to discuss the reality of living in America.

Like all Americans, we were deeply shocked, angered, and saddened by the September 11, 2001, attacks on New York City and Washington, D.C. It was impossible to write this book — and impossible to read it — without thinking about how much the world has changed since then. As the U.S. and the rest of the world engages in the war against terrorism, there will undoubtedly be some industries, such as security, that will benefit and others, such as tourism, that are likely to suffer for the foreseeable future. It is impossible, however, to make bold predictions about how world events will affect the job market for the international job seeker.

Yet we are confident in making this prediction: World politics will make international exchanges like those discussed here even more important. Rather than retreat behind our borders, it may be more important than ever for Americans to participate in cultural exchanges and become citizen ambassadors to the rest of the world. Working abroad can present opportunities far beyond mere professional development. It can contribute to global understanding.

Chapter 2

Do You Qualify to Work Abroad?

How to determine if an international job is really for you. Adapting to life in a foreign country. Employment regulations in Europe. Foreign language requirements for employment in Europe. Areas where Americans are most and least likely to find jobs. Higher education and international career preparation. Internships and temporary jobs.

Many factors affect whether you can get a job in Europe. You must have enough interest. You must be willing to work hard at finding a job. You need to be flexible enough to adapt to living in another culture. It helps if you speak another language and if your education or previous work experience have prepared you with marketable skills. Take a close look at what you have to offer an employer, and evaluate your qualifications to work abroad.

Adapting to International Living

People who have lived and worked overseas always have stories about the interesting, amusing, and outrageous incidents they have experienced. They like to gossip about the seemingly inexplicable behavior of people from the different country, perhaps to make sense of it or simply to entertain others. These stories often reveal how people who have lived and worked abroad inevitably question their basic assumptions about themselves, their culture, their interpersonal relationships, and their management style.

International living provides many stressors, both positive (such as adventure or novelty) and negative (feelings of inadequacy or language barriers). The cross–cultural setting can be so stressful that it demands that ordinary people respond in extraordinary ways and thereby discover strengths that they would have never developed in their own culture. Many people living

15

abroad challenge themselves, first to survive the differences and changes, then to be effective, and finally to develop explanations for the ambiguity of their new experiences.

Obviously, you do not have to leave the U.S. to undergo this type of growth, but there is no question that an international experience can be fertile ground for personal development. Still, not all people take advantage of this opportunity when they leave the country. Some people go abroad for a variety of reasons that have nothing to do with personal growth. They can be motivated by hardship, pay, and a reputedly glamorous lifestyle; some are polishing their resumes for future job–hopping; others grab international assignments as a way to escape personal, family, or even legal problems. Research suggests, however, that the people who are most successful living abroad are those who have a positive attitude about work and possess a strong sense of self. People with a grounded, stable personality have the wherewithal to handle the normal pressures of an international assignment without "going native" or turning to other coping mechanisms, such as drugs or alcohol. Additionally, people who are flexible, adaptable, and open–minded are best prepared for a cross–cultural experience.

European Employment Regulations

Each country in Europe has different laws regarding foreign workers. One unfortunate fact is true of all countries: It is difficult to get permission to work. Many countries mandate that you must secure employment before you can apply for a work visa, while employers require a work visa before they will hire you. Chapters 11 through 21 outline specific work visa regulations for each country. If you want to work for a large multinational corporation, the company itself can often obtain the documentation necessary for international employment. This process, however, is very time–consuming, labor–intensive, and expensive. Most companies won't do this unless you offer a very specific skill they cannot find in their European location. This is part of the reason that we stress the importance of identifying your most marketable skills.

Students often have an easier time of circumventing employment regulations. Several work exchange programs provide the necessary documents for American students seeking jobs and internships as explained in chapters 7 and 9. The Council on International Educational Exchange (CIEE) and British Universities North America Club (BUNAC) sponsor Americans to work overseas in casual jobs that can be ideal for students who want to work abroad for the summer. Other organizations, such as the International Association for the Exchange of Students for Technical Experience (IAESTE), can actually assist students with finding internships related to their academic major.

Many Americans seeking work in Europe don't bother with regulations and search for employment that ranges from grape–picking to working in a pub. While some people are successful at finding work without legal permission, this is risky. Many employers will not consider hiring you because they can be fined for violating their country's employment laws. Also, you have no recourse if you have trouble with your employer, such as a dispute over wages. Finally, if you are discovered to be working illegally in the country, you can be deported.

Foreign Language Requirements

Clearly, foreign language skills improve your employment opportunities in Europe. Although you may have studied a foreign language in high school or college, it may not be sufficient for the workplace. An employer may be impressed by your ability to translate medieval Spanish literature, but the company is still looking for employees who can read technical manuals and communicate with clients.

A good gauge of your language skills is your ability to use a foreign language to engage in small talk and basic conversations about the industry. If a potential employer contacts you by telephone in a foreign language, you should be able to respond and converse until you can gracefully shift into English. Only send a cover letter in a foreign language if you speak as fluently as your letter would indicate.

Fluency, although tremendously helpful, is not necessary when applying for an international job. You must, however, demonstrate a willingness to improve your language skills perhaps by enrolling in foreign language classes while you are job–searching. The best courses usually emphasize practical skills, such as business terminology, rather than a tourist–oriented vocabulary. Intensive conversational foreign language courses with qualified instructors are available at most community colleges and continuing education programs at universities. Commercial courses are more expensive, but often emphasize business language skills.

Some countries are more particular about your ability to speak the native language than others. For example, few companies in Denmark expect foreigners to learn Danish. In France, however, poor language skills are fatal to your job search. Chapters 11 through 21 examine this issue for each nation.

The Easiest Jobs To Find

Some international jobs are easier for Americans to find than others. Teaching English is a good way to work in some parts of Europe. Work permits are easier to come by for English teachers, and the demand is great, especially in Central Europe. Working in resort areas or in any hospitality–oriented business is another area where work is relatively easy to find. This is especially true in countries such as Greece, where English speakers are needed to cater to tourists from the British Isles and Scandinavia. Agriculture or other similarly low–skilled, manual labor jobs are available at the right time of year. For opportunities in these jobs to be available to outsiders, however, you should look in countries where unemployment is relatively low. Au pair work (childcare and housework) is also readily available for Americans. Chapter 9 discusses ways to find summer and temporary work. Nonprofit organizations can sometimes provide low–paid work if you arrange things before arriving in Europe. Opportunities with nonprofits are discussed in the country chapters and in Chapter 8.

Areas Where Jobs for Americans are Scarce

Americans will find that some areas offer few opportunities. Small European companies engaged in non–tourism or trade–related business, for instance, have little use for American workers. This type of company will only hire you if you provide some skill not readily available from local workers, such as computer programming.

The competition for the few positions with the United Nations or international government organizations is especially keen. These organizations have highly bureaucratic hiring processes and a surplus of applicants. You can enhance your odds of securing this kind of work by earning a graduate degree and allowing ample time, sometimes as much as two years, for your application to filter through the process.

U.S. firms operating abroad are usually not a good bet for the American job seeker. These companies prefer to hire local workers because they do not have to confront the legal issues associated with hiring foreign workers. You should approach American firms operating abroad strategically. Consider how to build a career with these organizations rather than just landing a job.

Higher Education and the International Career

The best way to work abroad is to get the right education that will provide you skills that will put you in high demand. Computer programming, accounting, and business are a few areas in which a graduate degree can significantly increase your odds of finding work. Although your political science and history classes won't get you a job, a graduate degree from a top school of international affairs can open many doors.

Top Graduate and Professional Schools of International Affairs

Columbia University
School of International and
Public Affairs (SIPA)
420 West 118th Street
New York, NY 10027
Tel.: (212) 854–5406
Fax: (212) 864–4847
www.sipa.columbia.edu

Georgetown University
Edmund A. Walsh School of Foreign
Service
301 Bunn InterCultural Center
37th & O Streets NW
Washington, DC 20057
Tel.: (202) 687–0100

www.georgetown.edu

Harvard University
John F. Kennedy School of Government
79 John F. Kennedy Street
Cambridge, MA 02138
Tel.: (617) 495–1100
www.ksg.harvard.edu

Johns Hopkins University
Nitze School of Advanced International
Studies (SAIS)
1740 Massachusetts Ave NW
Washington, DC 20036
Tel.: (202) 663–5700
Fax: (202) 663–7788

www.sais–jhu.edu

Princeton University
Woodrow Wilson School of Public and
International Affairs
121 Robertson Hall
Princeton, NJ 08544–1013
Tel.: (609) 258–4836
Fax: (609) 258–2095

www.wws.princeton.edu

Tufts University
Fletcher School of Law and Diplomacy
160 Packard Avenue
Medford, MA 02155–7082
Tel.: (617) 627–3700
fletcher.tufts.edu

A Master of Business Administration (MBA) degree from a school that offers a specialization in international business can make you marketable to an international employer. Many MBA programs offer this type of degree, with various emphases and specializations. Look at a variety of MBA programs to find one that best meets your objectives. (Be sure to inquire about the school's international placement success rates from its career center.)

Top International MBA Programs (U.S.)

Columbia University
Graduate School of Business
3022 Broadway
105 Uris Hall
New York, NY 10027
Tel.: (212) 854–5553
www.columbia.edu/cu/business

Harvard University
Graduate School of
Business Administration
MBA Admissions
Dillon House
Soldiers Field Road
Boston, MA 02163
Tel.: (617) 495–6127
Fax: (617) 496–9272
www.hbs.edu/mba

New York University
Stern School of Business Administration
Department of International Business
44 West Fourth Street
New York, NY 10012
Tel.: (212) 998–0100
www.stern.nyu.edu

Northwestern University
Kellogg School of Management
2001 Sheridan Road
Evanston, IL 60208
Tel.: (847) 491–3300
www.kelloggnorthwestern.edu

Thunderbird: The American Graduate School of International Management
15249 North 59th Avenue
Glendale, AZ 85306–6000
Tel.: (602) 978–7100
Fax: (602) 439–5432
www.t–bird.edu

University of California at Los Angeles
The Anderson School
110 Westwood Plaza
Los Angeles, CA 90095
Tel.: (310) 825–6944
www.anderson.ucla.edu

University of Michigan
Business School
701 Tappan Street
Ann Arbor, MI 48109–1234
Tel.: (734) 763–5796
Fax: (734)763–7804
www.bus.umich.edu

University of Pennsylvania
The Wharton School
420 Jon M. Huntsman Hall!
3730 Walnut Street
Philadelphia, PA 19104–6361
Tel.: (215) 898–6183
Fax: (215) 898–0120
www.wharton.upenn.edu

University of South Carolina
Graduate School, College of Business Administration
Program in International Business Studies

1705 College Street
Columbia, SC 29208
Tel.: (803) 777–2730
http://darlamoore.badm.sc.edu

European MBA Programs

A number of business programs in Europe grant an MBA degree. These programs are widely accepted in Europe and offer a quality education. Nearly all classes are taught in English, although many of these schools also offer bilingual instruction. At INSEAD, the most prestigious of the European schools, roughly 10 percent of the students are American. These schools can provide an ideal starting point for those interested in European business. The following schools are consistently ranked as the best MBA programs in Europe. INSEAD and IMD are arguably among the top ten MBA schools in the world.

IESE European Graduate School of Business and Management
Instituto de Estudios Superiores de la Empresa
Avenida Pearson 21
E–08034 Barcelona, Spain
Tel.: [34] 93 253 4200
Fax: [34] 93 253 4343
www.iese.edu

IMD International Institute for Management Development
MBA Information Service
Chemin de Bellerive 23
P.O. Box 915
CH–1001 Lausanne, Switzerland
Tel.: [41] 21 618 01 11
Fax: [41] 21 618 07 07
Email: info@imd.ch
www02.imd.ch

INSEAD The European Institute of Business Administration
Admission Office
Boulevard de Constance
F–77305 Fontainebleau Cedex, France
Tel.: [33] 1 60 72 40 00
Fax: [33] 1 60 74 55 00
Email: admissions@insead.fr
www.insead.fr

The London Business School
Sussex Place
Regents Park
London NWI 4SA, UK
Tel: [44] 20 7262 5050
Fax: [44] 20 7724 7875
www.lbs.lon.ac.uk

Manchester Business School
Booth Street West
Manchester M15 6PB, UK
Tel.: [44] 161 275 6333
Fax: [44] 161 275 6489
www.mbs.ac.uk/index.cfm

Rotterdam School of Management
Erasmus University Graduate School of Business
P.O. Box 1738
NL–3000 DR Rotterdam, Netherlands
Tel.: [31] 10–408 22 22
Fax: [31] 10–452 95 09
www.rsm.nl

SDOA Scuola di Direzione Aziendale
Via G. Pellegrino, 19
I–84019 Vietri sul Mare–Salerno, Italy
Tel.: [39] 89 761 166
Fax: [39] 89 210 002
www.sdoa.it

Internships

There are many programs for college students seeking international internships. These internships are often available for academic credit and may be unpaid. You do, however, receive valuable work experience that can be the ticket to launching your international career.

The best place to find out about internship programs is through the career center or the international programs office at the local university. Program details, such as the types of jobs offered, number of placements available, and application requirements, vary from year to year, so become familiar with your campus resources for international exchanges. The following books can also be helpful for identifying internships.

The Back Door Guide to Short–Term Job Adventures: Internships, Extraordinary Experiences, Seasonal Jobs, Volunteering, Work Abroad. Michael Landes. Ten Speed Press. Available from Planning/Communications — see the "Resource Center" beginning on page 472. Over 1,000 listings for offbeat opportunities, including many international internships. $21.95, 336 pages, 2002.

Directory of International Internships. Charles A. Gliozzo, Vernicka K. Tyson. 2002. Career Services and Placement Office of Michigan State University, 113 Student Services Building, East Lansing, MI 48824, Attn: Directory of International Internships. For a listing of internships across a wide spectrum of interests, see www.isp.msu.edu/InternationalInternships.

Internships 2004. Peterson's Guides. Available from Planning/Communications — see the "Resource Center" beginning on page 472. Concentrates mostly on opportunities in the United States, but also includes a chapter on the international arena. Published each July for the following year. For example, the 2004 edition was published in July 2003. $26.00, 744 pages.

Chapter 9 offers details on organizations that facilitate internships in more than one county, while the specific country–by–country chapters in Part II include information internships by European region.

Interning with Uncle Sam

Don't overlook the U.S. government for possible overseas opportunities. The Department of State, for example, offers spring, summer, and fall internships to upper–level undergraduates and graduate students. Although most of these positions are at the departments' Washington, D.C., headquarters, opportunities are available to serve as Junior Foreign Service Officers performing professional–level work in research, writing, computer science, and international law at U.S. embassies and consulates abroad. For more information, write to the Department of State, Attn: Student Programs, Recruitment Division, SA–1, 2201 C Street NW, Washington, DC 20520; Tel.: (202) 647–5225; www.state.gov. As with any bureaucracy, application processing takes time. Application deadlines are generally six to eight months before your internship begins.

Temporary Jobs

Jobs that don't require a formal education, such as au pair work, agriculture work, and manual labor, are relatively easy to obtain. Au pairs are in constant demand, and there are many agencies that place Americans in European homes. This work is time–consuming and often doesn't leave much free time for travel. Work camps and agricultural work are plentiful during specific seasons. During fruit–picking season, for example, laborers are in high demand. Working in resorts, as in agriculture, is also seasonal. Chapter 9 presents a rundown of possibilities for these and other temporary positions. Resources for temporary work are also included in the country–by–country reports included in Part II of this book.

Help us keep you current with free updates

We realize that companies move, go out of business, or start anew. We know that websites come and go. Many of the companies and websites listed in *How to Get a Job in Europe* could undergo change in the coming months and years.

You are the key to keeping this book current. If you would be so kind as to alert us to any changes to the job sources described in this book, we will post those changes on our free online Update Sheet at http://jobfindersonline.com.

When you find that a website described here no longer exists, has a new URL, has changed the job resources it offers — or if you have found any new European job resources you think we should add — send us an email that tells us the name of the job resource, its URL, and the page of this book on which the job source appears. Please tell us what has changed. We will confirm your information and post it online. Similarly, please tell us about any changes in print resources or company information so we can post the changes online.

Send your email with changes to:
europe_update@planningcommunications.com

To see the free Update Sheet which you can print from your web browser, visit http://jobfindersonline.com — the links to the free Update Sheet will be obvious on our home page.

Chapter 3

Key Employment Sectors in the New Europe

> Description and analysis of the economic trends and events transforming Europe and how they will affect Americans. The European single market, European monetary union, and European business expansion. Best opportunities for employment in E.U. countries.

In 1993, the 12 member countries of the European Union (E.U.) formed a single market, a market that some observers have referred to as a United States of Europe. This characterization, while not completely accurate, does capture the extent of cooperation among the member nations. The European Union, previously known as the European Community and the Common Market, features a unified economic system, increasing European economic power and mobility. This merger created common financial regulations, trade and labor standards, and free access to member products and jobs. Member nations remain independent, but trade, manufacturing, finance, and transportation have largely become pan–European efforts. With over 450 million potential consumers in the newly expanded trade bloc, the European Union surpasses the countries encompassed by the North American Free Trade Agreement as the world's largest market. The E.U. has grown from the original dozen to its current 15 members. Ten additional countries, including Latvia, Lithuania, and Estonia, which were republics of the Soviet Union just over a decade ago, have been invited to enter the E.U. in 2004.

The official objectives of the European Union are to:

✓ Promote economic and social progress among member countries (the single market was established in 1993; the single currency was launched in 1999);

✓ Assert the identity of the European Union on the international scene through European humanitarian aid to non–E.U. countries, common foreign and security policy, action in international crises, and common positions within international organizations;

✓ Introduce European citizenship, not to replace national citizenship but rather to confer a number of civil and political rights on European citizens;

✓ Develop an area of freedom, security, and justice linked to the operation of the internal market and more particularly the freedom of movement of persons;

✓ Maintain and build on established E.U. laws.

The Single Market

The E.U.'s primary objective is to create an internal market without restrictions on movement of goods, services, labor, and capital. Trade and movement in such a market are as open as among the states of the U.S. Foreign companies, too, are allowed to compete in previously protected areas. Opening trading lines and dismantling restrictions among the European countries create opportunities for expansion in the European marketplace. For example, Italian companies that formerly sold only merchandise in France can now market these goods throughout Europe without prohibitive restrictions, taxes, or national alterations to the product.

The E.U.'s recent decision to expand its trade bloc into the former Communist countries of Eastern Europe is a particularly significant development. In November 2002, the European Commission, the administrative body of the E.U., formally recognized Russia as a market economy. The move, acknowledging the progress Russia made in respect to market economy principles, meant that it would be subject to the same free trade rules that the E.U. imposes on other market economies. The leaders of the E.U. determined in December 2002 that 10 candidate countries (Cyprus, the Czech Republic, Estonia, Hungary, Latvia, Lithuania, Malta, Poland, the Slovak Republic, and Slovenia) met the political, economic, and administrative and judicial criteria to become full members in 2004. Bulgaria and Romania were encouraged to place an increased focus on judicial and administrative reforms in order to join the E.U. by 2007. (Turkey, despite its own protests and what was seen as heavy–handed lobbying by the U.S., was denied membership until it strengthened its democracy and the protection of human rights.)

The E.U. is a major trading partner with the United States. In 2001, exports of E.U. goods to the U.S. were valued at approximately €239.9 billion (24.4 percent of the total E.U. exports), while the imports from the U.S. to the E.U. were valued at €195.7 billion (19 percent of the total E.U. imports). Despite trade–related disputes that appear in the headlines from time to time, the U.S. and E.U. are committed to a politically and economically significant cooperation agenda. This is creating a new market in which American and European companies are just learning to compete.

Economists generally regard the single–market model as good for economic growth and standards of living in the E.U. as a whole, but this benefit will take time to develop fully. Since many companies are opening themselves up to a more competitive market, mergers between companies and expansions among the larger ones are now the rules of business, as national firms attempt to acquire international expertise and enter new markets. The initial competition among companies for market position in the E.U. creates lower prices but also unemployment. As the companies grow, expand, and profit, however, the single market is expected to create at least 2 million new jobs during the next decade.

Who's in the European Union?

Members as of 2003:
Austria, Belgium, Britain, Denmark, Finland, France, Germany, Greece, Ireland, Italy, Luxembourg, the Netherlands, Portugal, Spain, and Sweden.

Entering in 2004:
Cyprus, the Czech Republic, Estonia, Hungary, Latvia, Lithuania, Malta, Poland, Slovakia, and Slovenia.

A Common Currency

Beginning January 1, 1999, 12 members of the E.U. adopted a single European currency, the euro (€). For its first two years, the euro existed as a virtual currency. National currencies were pegged to the euro at fixed rates and ceased to be traded independently on the currency market. The francs, liras, and drachmas circulating in participating countries essentially became local versions of the euro. On January 1, 2002, amid great fanfare, the countries participating in this ambitious currency changeover officially retired their local currencies and began issuing euro notes and coins. The European Monetary Union (E.M.U.) members include Austria, Belgium, Finland, France, Germany, Greece, Ireland, Italy, Luxembourg, the Netherlands, Portugal and Spain. Voters in Britain, Denmark, and Sweden rejected participating in the monetary union.

The economic case for a single currency in Europe rests on three main claims: 1) that it lowers transaction costs for traders and travelers; 2) that it is necessary to complete the single market; and 3) that participants benefit from a strong, inflation–free currency with a reputation inherited from the deutschmark. Prior to the introduction of the euro, a tourist who successively changed $100 into the currency of member states would end up with roughly $50 after paying commission charges and adjusting for different exchange rates. Perhaps the strongest argument in the common currency's favor is the claim that the single European currency will usher in permanent low inflation. With low inflation, markets will work more efficiently, the quality of savings and investment decisions will improve, tax distortions can be removed, and incomes can be more evenly distributed. And, more to the point, jobs will be created.

Despite lingering concerns that eurozone countries are still too vulnerable to instabilities in global markets, most economists consider the adoption of a common currency to be a success. The eurozone has seen foreign direct investment increase by 384 percent to €601 billion since 2000. Over the same period, the increase in foreign direct investment into Britain, Sweden and Denmark, countries that did not adopt the euro, was one–eighth as much. Trade with other E.U. member countries increased by 4 percent annually in France and Germany while stagnating in Britain. And the increasing the economic integration between the eurozone countries has encouraged lower prices — prices of certain goods now vary by no more than 3 percent among eurozone cities, whereas the same goods cost at least 16 percent more in the U.K. A Ford Focus, for example, now costs 32 percent more in the U.K. than in the eurozone countries.

The relative success of the euro is giving pause to critics in the countries that had been ardent opponents of a common currency. According to a Eurobarometer poll conducted in the summer 2002, supporters of the euro in Sweden and Denmark now outnumber opponents.

 ### Euro bills and coins

Euro notes and coins officially began to circulate on January 2002. There are seven notes and eight euro coins. The notes are 500, 200, 100, 50, 20, 10, and 5 euro. The coins are 2 euro, 1 euro, 50 euro cent, 20 euro cent, 10 euro cent, 5 euro cent, 2 euro cent, and 1 euro cent.

Robert Kalina of the Austrian Central Bank designed the notes. They are strongly symbolic and closely related to the historical phases that make up Europe's architectural heritage. Windows and gateways dominate the front side of each banknote as symbols of the spirit of openness and cooperation in the E.U. The reverse side of each banknote features a bridge from a particular age, a metaphor for communication among the people of Europe and between Europe and the rest of the world. The notes differ in size and include a color spectrum of green, yellow, blue, mauve, and orange.

What European Business Expansion Means to Americans Seeking Jobs

With the expansion of American firms into the European market, you might assume that jobs for Americans would be abundant, but that is not necessarily the case. Basic regulations within each country ensure that a certain percentage of jobs will be held by the citizens of that country. Most of the jobs open to Americans in these countries are short–term, for those with specific skills, or for top–level executives.

Americans face another competitive disadvantage: Workers from E.U. countries are allowed to travel and work in other E.U. countries without any restrictions, including work permits. A worker from Italy can travel to Greece, for example, to locate employment without worrying about a visa or work permit. European workers can easily gain employment in any E.U. member country, providing employers with a large pool of European applicants to chose from before they have to consider Americans.

There are still, of course, many openings that Americans can fill after mastering the paperwork. Many American accountants, consultants, investment lawyers, and mergers–and–acquisitions specialists have settled in Europe's financial capitals to take advantage of the upcoming general business expansion.

Americans can overcome employment roadblocks by emphasizing their unique skills and intelligently marketing themselves to potential employers. Writing an effective international resume and highlighting the education, training, and experience desired by European employers are certainly keys. The most practical route to employment in Europe is to find a position in the U.S. and transfer abroad later. U.S.–based multinational manufacturers and exporters, internationally oriented consulting and law firms, and communication companies present opportunities for employment in Europe. Summer work and internships in Europe also serve to introduce a potential employer to an applicant's talents.

Language skills certainly help promote an American's employment opportunities in Europe. Within the E.U. bureaucracy, French and English are dominant, although German is spreading. English predominates at the lower levels, with French still important in the higher branches. In business, French and German are widespread, although a host country's language may range from Flemish to Portuguese to Magyar.

Employment Sectors in Europe

In the aftermath of corporate scandals, collapsing stock markets, the attack on September 11, 2001, and geo–political tensions in the Middle East, the U.S. government has sought to effect a policy–induced recovery through the lowering of interest rates, tax cuts, and other efforts at fiscal stimulus. It is unclear whether these measures will restore global confidence sufficient to increase the prospects for employment in the E.U. Yet, there is reason for optimism. After a contraction in 2001, the first in 20 years, international trade is expected to begin to grow slowly, accelerating to about 7 percent in 2004.

Employment creation in the E.U. is estimated to continue, albeit at a weak pace. The rise in the 2002 unemployment rate in the E.U. was slight, with Germany and Austria reporting a decline in unemployment. The eurozone unemployment rate is forecast at 8.3 percent in 2003, only marginally higher than 2002, but in several Member States (notably in the Netherlands and Portugal) the unemployment rate continues to increase more sharply. In November 2002, the European Commission reported improved performance in the overall E.U. labor markets despite the economic slowdown. In 2001, the E.U. saw strong employment growth with two million new jobs created. The overall E.U. unemployment rate came down from 8.2 percent in 2000 to 7.4 percent in 2001, while the long–term unemployment rate decreased from 3.7 percent in 2000 to 3.3 percent in 2001.

The pace of change and the degree of economic interdependency in the world market means that it is important that anyone seriously embarking on a job search in Europe stay abreast of global political and economic developments.

Agriculture. Food is big business in Europe. The E.U. is the world's largest importer as well as the world's second–largest exporter of agricultural products. Farming alone in the current E.U. nations is worth €220 billion a year and employs 7.5 million people. The food production industry is responsible for the jobs of another 2.6 million workers and is valued at €600 billion. Despite the priority placed on agriculture by the E.U., European farming and agriculture has had its share of problems in recent years. These are probably best exemplified by the highly publicized woes of the British beef industry — and the resulting bans and boycotts on the continent — brought on by mad cow disease and hoof–and–mouth disease. These problems have now been resolved and, while employment in agribusiness probably won't skyrocket anytime soon, low–skill seasonal employment in agriculture, especially in wine–producing regions, is generally abundant for Americans. Apart from mad cows, the widespread European resistance to the use of genetically modified organisms (GMOs) in food products indicates that there will be opportunities for people interested in employment, internships, or volunteer work with organic farms.

Education. Teaching jobs assume several forms: English language teaching is fairly common, especially in Central Europe; secondary and university education positions are usually unionized and difficult to acquire; American primary and secondary schools in Europe are quite common and offer numerous opportunities. If you speak English and have a college degree, you are usually qualified to teach English abroad. Competition for positions teaching English is stiff in countries that are part of the E.U., but there still remain good opportunities in Central and Eastern European countries. Teaching in an American school is not as easy. You must be certified to teach; usually a few years of experience are required.

Management consulting and finance. The word that would best describe the outlook for consulting and finance is caution. Financial services in the E.U. are increasingly globalized, due to the twin revolutions in deregulation and communication technology. The general uncertainty in the world's financial markets, brought on by the terrorist attacks in America and the global military response, has meant that many of the leading finance firms have lowered their hiring goals. Europeans are waiting to assess the full market impact brought on by the creation of the single market and the introduction of the euro. It is clear, however, that Britain's reluctance to adopt the euro has not affected London's traditional role as a leading European banking and financial center. London's nearest European rival is Frankfurt.

Despite this economic prognosis, the best candidates for financial industry positions in Europe possess an MBA and have begun their careers with major consulting firms in the U.S.

Manufacturing and trading. The global economic slowdown has had a strong impact on the E.U. manufacturing sector. The decline in the American computer industry, in particular, has resonated in European markets with companies such as Motorola announcing waves of layoffs worldwide. Europe's auto industry is similarly under pressure, due to a weakening economy and an overcrowded market. Indeed, established carmakers, such as Italy's Fiat and France's Renault, have reported that their market shares are steadily disappearing. The telecommunications equipment market apparently is nearing saturation, with European giants, such as cellular phone manufacturer Nokia, reporting earnings losses. The overall outlook is that the manufacturing and trading industries in Europe will present limited opportunities for Americans until the global economy trends up.

Nonprofit organizations. Nonprofit organizations in Europe may be found in Brussels and Strasbourg, the sites of the E.U. administration and the European Parliament, and in Geneva and Paris, where various United Nations agencies are based. Many global relief and development organizations are based in London and Rome. Environmental groups exist throughout the E.U., especially in Germany and Northern Europe, where industrialization and associated environmental degradation has been most severe. Specialized knowledge and experience along with familiarity with languages and cultures are the key to nonprofit jobs. Whenever a job seeker can offer a type of experience not easily found locally, the chances for getting that job increase substantially.

Retail. When the E.U. undertook the currency changeover, some change in price levels was inevitable as retailers aimed to keep the .99 price tickets to attract customers. At the same time, there was public concern that some retail businesses would use the euro introduction to mask price hikes. European consumers were particularly concerned that the voluntary agreements to keep prices at their pre–euro levels would be largely ignored. Now that the transition is mostly complete, however, it is generally accepted that retailing has benefited from the elimination of trade barriers and the resulting reductions in prices of goods.

Although European retailers are very active in the U.S., American retailers generally have yet to exploit fully the opportunities presented by the E.U.'s single market and unified currency. This means that there are real employment opportunities for Americans with suitable experience in retailing.

Travel and tourism. The travel and tourism industry has been especially impacted by the terrorist attacks in the U.S. and around the world. American's continued reluctance to fly, for example, devastated the airline industry and led American carriers to announce that they would eliminate more than 100,000 jobs. Many European carriers have followed suit. Alitalia announced plans to eliminate 3,500 jobs, and Swissair found its planes grounded as airline officials pleaded with Swiss banks for a fiscal bailout. The industry lost $50 billion globally in 2001. The reluctance of the E.U. to financially bail out ailing airlines means that these losses will not likely be stemmed soon.

The decline in airline travel has affected the entire tourist industry in the E.U. European tourist destinations, which are highly dependent upon American travelers, have reported sharp declines in visitors. Britain, for example, reported that the number of overseas visitors coming to the U.K. in 2001 fell by the largest margin in 20 years. Although the World Travel and Tourism Council projects that the decline in tourist activity will be short–lived, it is likely that as long as the American–led global war on terrorism continues, activity at Europe's tourist sites will remain low. There will be some demand for seasonal employees in the travel and tourist industry, but American job seekers may be expected to demonstrate that they possess special skills that are in demand by employers.

Chapter 4

The Nine-Step Job Search

> The nine steps to getting a job in Europe. How to organize
> your job search, research countries, use conventional and elec-
> tronic resources, and make contact with hiring authorities.

The good news is that anyone with gumption and gusto can successfully
find work abroad. The bad news is that no one is waiting in line to hand you
your dream international job. Successful job searching, especially for a job in
Europe, is hard work. It hinges on your ability to effectively develop a strategy
to reach the right employers. This chapter is devoted to helping you find the
right resources to get the best results from the time you invest in your job search.

Nine Steps to Getting a Job in Europe

STEP 1. Know why you want to work in Europe

Why do you want to work abroad? The answer to this question is key for
focusing your job search. You need to know if you are looking for an international career or an international job. An international job is work that you do
with the primary objective of supporting yourself while you live abroad. Your
job may or may not be related to your long–term career plans. For example,
you might work as an au pair for a year in Spain in order to improve your
Spanish. An international career, by contrast, may take several years and a
graduate degree to achieve. Most Americans working for multinationals in
Europe have international careers. Your objective for working abroad will direct the techniques you use to find a job. Here are a few other practical
matters to consider:

Where do you want to perform this job? Do you want to do this job in a
German– or an English–speaking country? Do you want to be in Western Europe, Central Europe, or Britain? Do you want to be on the beach, in the
mountains, or in the city?

What special skills do you possess that might interest an employer? As we've already discussed, employers will hire you because you have the particular skills they need. Think first about your academic preparation. An accounting or finance degree can make you very marketable. Consider also those hidden skills that you may not have used much in your jobs in the U.S. For example, if you are good with children, you might find an employer willing to hire you as a childcare worker. If you have strong grammar and are a clear speaker, you might try teaching English.

How strong are your language skills? If you speak another language or languages fluently, you may be qualified for certain jobs. For example, most jobs in the hospitality industry, regardless of the position, require that you speak fluently at least one other European language.

What kind of experience do you want from this job? Are you trying to build an international career or do you just want to support yourself in Europe?

How important is money? Be honest! Some of the most interesting and rewarding opportunities are with volunteer organizations.

STEP 2. Identify jobs that match your background

Think about your abilities, skills, areas of special knowledge, and your interests, particularly those you've developed through your education or previous jobs. Employers will expect that you bring a particular set of skills. Often an accounting, finance, or computer science degree may prepare you with what you need. You may also possess special abilities that can place you in demand. For example, if you like working outside, agricultural work might be a good fit. If you are an excellent cook, you might apply as a chef in a guesthouse or ski resort.

STEP 3. Research your target country

Your job search requires that you be completely familiar with the country in which you would like to work. The best place to begin is by reading local newspapers. Chapters 11 through 21 include lists of major newspapers in each country in Europe, often available at larger newsstands or university libraries. Additionally, many newspapers also maintain sites on the Internet.

The appropriate chambers of commerce, world trade centers, and consular offices can also be good sources of information about key industrial sectors, economic trends, and relevant employment laws. You will also need to do your homework to learn about crosscultural issues that will affect your job search.

The following list of directories can help with your research. Most of these are available in the reference section of any public or university library. A more complete list is included in the International Business section of Chapter 8.

Directories

Directory of American Firms Operating in Foreign Countries. Uniworld Business Directories, 257 Central Park West, Suite 10A, New York, NY 10024; tel.: (212) 496–2448; www.uniworldbp.com. Covers 2,600 American firms and 34,500 subsidiaries in 190 countries. $325, three 3 volumes, 4,200 pages. Updated on a semiregular basis.

Europe's 15,000 Largest Companies. Euroconfidential SA, 18, rue de Rixensart, 1332 Genval, Belgium, tel.: [32] 2 652 02 84; email: info@euroconfidential.com, www.euroconfidential.com. Companies are divided by category — industrial, trading or service — and full contact details are given. Individual information for each company includes rank, industry branch, sales, percentage change in sales, profits for the past two years, number of employees, assets and equity capital, equity capital as percentage of assets, year established, and name of chief executive officer. €385, 1,025 pages. Updated annually.

Major Chemical and Petrochemical Companies of Europe. Graham & Whiteside Ltd., available from Gale Group, 27500 Drake Road, Farmington Hills, MI 48331; tel.: (248) 699–4253, (800) 877–4253, www.galegroup.com. Provides detailed coverage of 2,800 of the top chemical and petrochemical companies of Europe, including the contact names of 15,000 senior executives. $510. Published annually.

Major Employers of Europe. Graham & Whiteside Ltd., available from Gale Group, 27500 Drake Road, Farmington Hills, MI 48331; tel.: (248) 699–4253, (800) 877–4253, www.galegroup.com. Identifies the top 10,000 companies in Europe by number of employees. Includes company contact information, names of managing directors and human resources directors, and a description of business activities. $295, 1,400 pages. Published annually.

Major Energy Companies of Europe. Graham & Whiteside Ltd., available from Gale Group, 27500 Drake Road, Farmington Hills, MI 48331; tel.: (248) 699–4253, (800) 877–4253, www.galegroup.com. Provides detailed coverage of 1,350 of the top energy–producing companies of Europe, including those in coal mining, electrical supply, fuel distribution, natural gas supply, nuclear engineering, and oil production and distribution. $510, 295 pages. Published annually.

Major Food and Drink Companies of Europe. Graham & Whiteside Ltd., available from Gale Group, 27500 Drake Road, Farmington Hills, MI 48331; tel.: (248) 699–4253, (800) 877–4253, www.galegroup.com. Provides detailed coverage of 3,800 of the largest food and drink companies in Europe, including the contact names of 19,000 senior executives. $510, 560 pages. Published annually.

Major Telecommunications Companies of the World. Graham & Whiteside Ltd.,available from Gale Group, 27500 Drake Road, Farmington Hills, MI 48331; tel.: (248) 699–4253, (800) 877–4253, www.galegroup.com. Provides detailed coverage of 3,500 companies in the telecommunications and Internet markets, including the contact names of 10,500 senior executives. $885, 1,000 pages. Published annually.

World Business Directory. Graham & Whiteside Ltd., available from Gale Group, 27500 Drake Road, Farmington Hills, MI 48331; tel.: (248) 699–4253, (800) 877–4253, www.galegroup.com. Profiles 134,000 small– and medium–size firms and local niche companies, including 50,000 in the U.K. and Europe. $645, 6,736 pages in four volumes. Published annually.

World Trade Centers

World trade centers can provide information on international businesses, regional job markets, and influential people in the international business world. Here is a list of world trade centers in major U.S. cities:

Atlanta
World Trade Center Atlanta
One Sun Trust Plaza
Lower Lobby, Suite 100
303 Peachtree Street NE
Atlanta, Georgia 30308–3252
Tel.: (404) 880–1550
Fax: (404) 880–1555
www.wtcatlanta.com

Boston
World Trade Center Boston
164 Northern Avenue
Executive Offices, Suite 50
Boston, MA 02210–2004
Tel.: (617) 385–5000
Fax: (617) 385–5033
Email: info@wtcb.com
www.wtcb.com

Chicago
World Trade Center Chicago
200 World Trade Center, Suite 1540
Chicago, IL 60654
Tel.: (312) 4670550
Fax: (312) 4670615
Email: info@wtcc.org
www.wtcc.org

Denver
World Trade Center Denver
1625 Broadway, Suite 680
Denver, CO 80202
Tel.: (303) 592–5760
Fax: (303) 592–5228
Email: wtcdenver@worldnet.att.net
www.wtcdn.com

Detroit/Windsor
1251 Fort Street
Trenton, MI 48183
Tel.: (313) 479–2345

Fax: (313) 479–5733
Email: email@ wtcdw.com
www.wtcdw.com

Houston
Houston World Trade Association
1200 Smith, Suite 700
Houston, TX 77002
Tel.: (713) 844–3637
Fax: (713) 844–0237
Email: pfoley@houston.org
www.houston.org

Indianapolis
54 Monument Circle, Suite 250
Indianapolis, IN 46204
Tel.: (317) 756–8102
Fax: (317) 756–8122
www.wtcin.com

Los Angeles
Los Angeles World Trade Center
Greater Los Angeles World Trade
Center Association
350 South Figueroa Street, Suite 172
Los Angeles, CA 90071
Tel.: (310) 680–1888
Fax: (310) 680–1878
Email: infola@wtcanet.org
www.wtcanet.org

Miami
World Trade Center Miami
777 NW 72nd Avenue, Suite 3BB65
Miami, FL 33126–3009
Tel.: (305) 871–7910
Fax: (305) 871–7904
Email: info@worldtrade.org
www.worldtrade.org

New York
World Trade Center New York

60 East 42nd Street, Suite 1901
New York, NY 10165
Tel.: (212) 432–2700
Fax: (202) 488–0064
Email: janet@wtca.org

Seattle
Seattle World Trade Center
Columbia Hospitality
2200 Alaskan Way, Suite 410
Seattle, WA 98121
Tel.: (206) 956–4590
Fax: (206) 374–0410
Email: info@wtcseattle.com
www.wtcseattle.org

St. Louis
World Trade Center St. Louis
St. Louis County Economic Council

121 South Meramec, Suite 1111
St. Louis, MO 63105
Tel.: (314) 615–8141
Fax: (314) 862–0102
Email: info@worldtradecenterstl.com
www.worldtradecenter–stl.com

Washington, D.C.
Ronald Reagan Building
and International Trade Center
1300 Pennsylvania Avenue, NW
Suite M–1100
Washington, DC 20004
Tel.: (202) 418–4224
Fax: (202) 418–4238
Email: hosethc@urbanretail.com
www.itcdc.com

World trade centers are also located in the following U. S.cities: Baltimore, Bridgeport, Charleston, Columbus, Fort Lauderdale, Honolulu, Irvine, Jacksonville, Kansas City, Las Vegas, Long Beach, McAllen, Milwaukee, New Orleans, Norfolk, Orlando, Oxnard, Phoenix, Pittsburgh, Portland, Raleigh–Durham, San Antonio, San Francisco, St. Paul, Tacoma, Tampa, Wichita, Wilmington. Check your phone book for contact information.

STEP 4. Write a resume and cover letter

Your international resume and cover letter resemble those you prepare for an American job search, but there are important differences. First, you should describe your education in a way that someone not familiar with the American educational system will understand. For example, instead of listing a GPA, use Grade Point Average or a class ranking, such as top 25 percent of the class. Do not use acronyms or abbreviations that would be unfamiliar to a European employer. Emphasize the specific, practical skills you offer an employer, such as programming or business skills. Include any previous international experience to assure the employer that you are familiar with working or living in a cross–cultural setting. If you are applying through a program such as BUNAC, which arranges your work permit, be sure to include that information.

Most European employers expect you to include personal information, such as your age, marital status, and health. Chapter 5 offers several examples of good resumes and cover letters. Mary Anne Thompson's *The Global Resume and CV Guide* (John Wiley & Sons) and *Best Resumes and CVs for International Jobs* by Ron Krannich and Wendy Enelow (Impact Publications) are solid all–around resources on writing resumes for international jobs. Both are described in Chapter 5 and are available from Planning/Communications. See Chapter 22 for details.

STEP 5: Use a variety of job search strategies

Generally, the more techniques you use to find job leads, the faster you'll find work. Job search strategies fall into three categories: identifying specific openings, mailing targeted letters, and building a network. Depending on your interests, some of these approaches may be more effective than others. For example, because nonprofit organizations frequently do not advertise job openings, networking is the best way to uncover these leads. On the other hand, the federal government is required to advertise every vacancy.

Job openings are advertised in a variety of locations, and you should take advantage of all of them. They include local newspapers, employment agencies, professional organization newsletters, and job bulletins. International positions are frequently advertised in *The Economist* and the *International Herald Tribune*. European employers, especially in the U.K. and Ireland, are increasingly listing jobs on the Internet. Each chapter in Part II identifies valuable websites for people seeking jobs in each country. The most complete collection of online and print resources for job openings in Europe appears in the *International Job Finder: Where the Jobs are Worldwide*, described on page 7.

Sources of International Job Openings

International Career Employment Weekly
1088 Middle River Road
Stanardsville, VA 22973
Tel.: (800) 291–4618
Fax: (434) 985–6828
www.internationaljobs.org
Includes advertisements for jobs in humanitarian assistance, health care, education, foreign policy, business, and engineering. A hard–copy newsletter listing jobs is published weekly ($26 for 6 weeks, $42 for 3 months, $149 for 1 year). It is also available via the web or by email. You may access some of the job listings online without subscribing. This company also publishes the *International Employment Hotline*, a monthly newsletter that includes all of the jobs featured in the weekly newspaper, as well as useful articles for the international job seeker. Subscriptions are available for 3 months for $21, 6 months for $39, and 1 year for $69.

International Employment Gazette
423 Townes Street
Greenville, SC 29601
Tel.: (800) 8229188

Fax: (864) 2353369
Email: info@intemployment.com
www.intemployment.com
Published every other week, this lists over 400 overseas jobs in each issue. Occupations featured in each issue include education, business, agriculture, science, construction, computers, health care, engineering, social services, transportation, and communication. Subscriptions are available for 1 month for $19.95, 3 months for $39.95, and 1 year for $99.95. Your subscription to the print journal gives you access to the online job listings.

Overseas Employment Newsletter
P.O. Box 460
Town of Mount Royal
Quebec, Canada H3P 2T1
Tel.: (514) 7391108
Fax: (514) 7390795
Every two weeks, Overseas Employment Services publishes this newsletter in which they "describe in detail at least 300 currently available jobs for a broad range of skills, careers and positions in many developing nations and industrialized countries around the world."

Useful Websites for European Job Listings

The good news is that an increasing number of European employers are listing jobs on the internet. Each chapter in Part II lists websites that target the specific country. The websites described here cover all of Europe.

Escape Artist

www.escapeartist.com

This is the first place that any international job seeker should begin. The site includes good information for the would–be expatriate, including tips on visas, relocation, taxation, and health insurance. The site also provides country–by–country listings of useful websites for job seekers.

Riley Guide

www.rileyguide.com/internat.html

This site, developed by former university librarian Margaret Riley Dikel, was the first Internet guide to online job search resources. It is widely recognized as the best resource for finding job search resources on the web. The international section, like the entire site, is regularly updated and provides links to most of the major websites that you will need for your job search.

Transitions Abroad Online

www.transitionsabroad.com

Transitions Abroad is a respected publisher of a bi–monthly magazine and books on working and studying abroad. The website is easy to navigate and a good resource for up–to–date listings of work abroad programs. It is organized by type of program (short–term work programs, internships, volunteer, and teaching) as well as by country. The site also includes information for special–needs travelers, such as people with disabilities or retirees.

ACCESS:
Networking in the Public Interest

www.accessjobs.org

ACCESS is a comprehensive resource for employment, internships, and career development for nonprofit organizations. The site is not exclusively for the international job seeker, but its fine search engine permits you to look for opportunities in different countries in Europe. For a $25 annual fee, you can also register to receive email announcements about job opportunities, free access to virtual job fairs, and discounts on consultation with career counselors who specialize in opportunities with nonprofit organizations.

Europages

www.europages.com

Europages, the European Business Directory, is a "business–to–business directory published in six languages." It includes links with the Yellow Pages in 30 different countries. You can search companies by name, country, or industry. In addition to contact information, each company profile includes a description of its products or services.

Job Monkey

www.jobmonkey.com

If you are looking for work as an entertainer at a resort in Mallorca or as an English teacher in Hungary, this is the site for you. Job Monkey claims to list the coolest jobs on earth. It certainly lists the most off–beat. It is a good resource for jobs in hospitality, entertainment, and teaching in Central Europe. Be forewarned, however, that many of the job listings are for European citizens.

JobPilot

www.jobpilot.net

JobPilot features sites for 14 European countries. Employers who regularly post on Job Pilot include all 30 companies listed in Germany's DAX share index as well as 21 companies in the EuroSTOXX 50 share index. Each of the 14 European sites use the local language.

Monster Global Gateway

http://globalgateway.monster.com

The name says it all — this is a monster job listing site. To access jobs, you indicate both your nationality and your target destination. (We found more than 5,000 jobs listed in Europe for companies interested in hiring Americans.) The site also includes thorough information on issues ranging from visas to relocating your family.

Overseasjobs
www.overseasjobs.com
Overseasjobs.com is part of a comprehensive recruitment network for high school and college students, resort and hospitality staff, expatriates and international job seekers, part–time workers, and adventure seekers. The easy–to–navigate search engine allows you to look for full–time jobs in most European

countries. The related sites, Summerjobs.com, Internjobs.com, and Resortjobs.com, also list international opportunities.

Top Jobs on the Net
www.topjobs.net

This U.K.–based site was among the first Internet employment sites in Europe. The job listings in the U.K. are its strength, but it is also a resource for professional and technical jobs throughout Europe. Jobs can be searched according to industry and geography.

Targeted mailings can be effective if done properly. A targeted mailing is not synonymous with a mass mailing. With a mass mailing, you might send a letter and resume to 50 or more employers. You will probably receive little response for the money you spend on postage. With a targeted mailing, however, you identify a select number of employers to whom you want to apply. Your criteria for setting up a targeted mailing might include: 1) Type of employer; 2) Geographic location; 3) Size of employer; 4) Hiring history (for example, have they hired Americans with your background?). Your advantage with a targeted mailing is that you work with a select number of companies to which you can write carefully drafted letters explaining your qualifications. You also can better manage effective follow–up.

Your initial list should include no more than 20 carefully selected employers. Try to get your package to a specific person who manages a department in which you would like to work. (You could also send the same package to the personnel department, although since their job is to process employment information, not make hiring decisions, they are less likely to be able to provide the kind of attention you need.) In each package, send an individualized cover letter (see the section on cover letters in Chapter 5) and a resume. Be prepared to follow up by telephone, letter, or email on every package you mail. To get an idea of which organizations and people to target, talk to your contacts, use library resources, directories, and chambers of commerce.

Searching for International Jobs Electronically

The Internet has made looking for an international job much easier and faster. Most aspects of your job search can be conducted on the web, and you will likely encounter few problems with using email to contact employers except in a few Eastern European countries. Here are some tips for using the web to look for work in Europe:

> Develop an electronic version of your resume that you can submit to an employer by email. An electronic resume resembles your regular resume except that all of the text embellishment, such as boldface, italics, or underlining, has been removed. You will email your electronic resume to employers, and you don't

want to lose your resume formatting.

⌗ Create a personal web page on which you can post your resume. If you are posting your resume on your family page, make sure the rest of the content is something you are willing to share with a potential employer!

⌗ Post your resume to online databases that are accessed by employers. Most of the major job boards include a place where you can post your resume. If you are only casually looking for work, this is a low–stress way to test the water.

⌗ Regularly review job ads on major bulletin boards. Many sites feature job search agents that you can configure to notify you by email of job postings that match your requirements.

⌗ Apply online to jobs advertised on the websites of major European employers. This is an easy and inexpensive way to apply to several companies. The same advice about targeting your resume and cover letter to the employer, however, apply even in cyberspace!

Finding your job online

I decided I wanted something other than the usual summer–abroad work experience of wait–staffing, bartending, or temping. I really wanted a job in the high–tech industry because my major in college is computer science, so I started looking for high–tech jobs in London. I didn't have too much luck with my international summer job search while only pursuing the usual job search routes, such as contacting alumni and computer companies listed in work–abroad books. As an alternative to these approaches, I decided to post my resume on about ten of the major online job banks, and I used the job banks to apply online to specific high–tech jobs posted on the Internet.

In a few weeks, I received a solicitation to interview with a London–based network administrator. That administrator became my boss in a few weeks. My job as a computer support analyst is still the best summer job I've ever had. My boss and I still keep in touch, and it's great to know that not only do I have an international friend, but I also have an international industry contact. —*Jyoti Gupta, Houston, Texas*

⌗ See *The Directory of Websites for International Jobs* (Impact Publications) and the *International Job Finder: Where the Jobs are Worldwide* to cut through the Internet clutter to zero in on important online employment resources. More details are available in the Resource Chapter, starting on page 472.

Surfing Safely

It was probably only a matter of time before unscrupulous people would find a way to use the Internet to take advantage of job seekers. Reports are now circulating about people who have become victims of identity theft after they responded to bogus ads posted on legitimate job boards.

The scam typically works like this: You submit your resume to an online job ad and then receive an encouraging email from an employer asking for additional information such as your age, height, weight, Social Security number, and bank account numbers. These scam artists have found just enough job seekers willing to share their personal history to make this fraud a growing method for identity theft.

The best way to protect yourself is to exercise common sense. Never disclose your Social Security number or bank account numbers to an employer before the interview, even if the employer insists it is needed for a background check. Look for clues that you have been contacted by a fraudulent employer, such as misspellings or grammatical errors in the email, or a request that you reply to a personal email address. And if you are in doubt, call the company directly to find out if it is legitimate.

STEP 6. Network

Networking, or talking with people who can help you in your job search, will generally yield your best results. Employers, especially those who have not previously hired Americans, are more likely to consider you if you have been referred by someone they trust. Potential contacts include friends, people you meet through professional organizations, relatives, alumni, speakers at on–campus events, professors, former employers, and many others. Find creative ways to expand the number of your contacts. Most networking happens informally. You meet someone at a party who knows someone working for a company in Paris in which you are interested. You can create occasions for spontaneous networking by telling many people about your job search.

Networking for a job on a different continent can be difficult, but it's not impossible. You will probably be surprised at how many people you already know who are able to provide you with leads, at least for other contacts. World trade centers also provide a good starting point, and international alumni from schools you attended can also be helpful. Use professional associations and international chambers of commerce as resources to make helpful contacts.

One assertive technique for making contacts in a particular field is the information interview. These are not the same as job interviews. You are not asking your contact for a job, rather for information about his or her company or industry. The purpose of the information interview is to teach you more about a particular career field and help you build a useful network. As you begin your international job search, conducting information interviews with local people can help you learn more about particular companies and find connections to helpful people living and working in Europe.

The following is a list of questions you may want to ask in an information interview. It is your responsibility to understand the nature of your visit (to get information, not a job), to know the basics about the organization ahead of time (so as not to waste time), and to take responsibility for the progress of the interview.

Alumni networking

Your university alumni association may be an excellent networking resource. Many alumni associations have contact services that can put you in touch with alumni overseas who are willing to help graduates of their alma mater. By no means will this ensure you a job, since the alumni abroad may have nothing to do with hiring, but your alumni contacts may help you open the door to many overseas companies. The individual alumnus may be able to provide information on the local job market, help you get an interview, help you find accommodations in an area you would visit for an interview, or perhaps even provide a place for you to stay during your visit.

Job Description

- What are your major duties and responsibilities?

- How does your position fit into the structure of the organization?

- With whom in the organization (superiors, subordinates, peers) do you have the most contact?

- Describe a typical day.

- What aspects of your job do you find most interesting?

- What aspects do you enjoy least?

- What changes do you see occurring in this field? Will the type and number of jobs change significantly over the next 10 years? What, if any, effect will changing technology have on the field?

Career Path

- What are the typical entry–level jobs in this field?

- What is the best way to find this job in Europe?

- What were the positions you had that led to this one?

- How long does it usually take to move from one step to the next in this field?

- Are there any specifically defined prerequisites for advancement — for example, years in service, examinations, advanced degrees, board interviews, and so on?

- ☐ What are the best jobs in this field for career advancement?
- ☐ Are there other areas of this field to which people may be transferred? What are they?

Preparation

- ☐ What are the academic and experience prerequisites for entry–level jobs in this field?
- ☐ Is the degree that I have or am pursuing suitable?
- ☐ What languages should I speak if I want to find a job in this field abroad?
- ☐ Are there any specific courses I might take that would be particularly useful?
- ☐ Are there any extracurricular or other experiences (work, volunteering, internships, etc.) that would enhance my chances of employment?
- ☐ What types of training do companies give employees entering the field?
- ☐ What advice would you give to someone planning to enter this field?

General

- ☐ What is the current demand for employees at entry level in this field? And higher?
- ☐ What are the salary ranges at various levels in the field?
- ☐ How many hours a week does someone typically work in this field?
- ☐ Where might I find job descriptions and other specifications for some of the positions in this field?
- ☐ Are the content and format of my resume appropriate for someone seeking a job in this field?
- ☐ Is there anyone else in the field with whom you would suggest I talk?

Don't let the information interview end without asking this last question. This is how you expand your network. Remember, your job search depends on who you know, and networking is the way you meet them.

STEP 7. Organize your job search

Approach your job search deliberately. Keeping records, a daily planner, and scheduling each day's activities will improve your job search's efficiency. Following the tips that follow will further enhance your job search.

Decide how to spend your time each day. An international job search can be very, very slow, and the long periods you will spend waiting for an employer to respond to your letters may zap your motivation. The successful job seekers, however, are persistent. Structure your job search tasks and plan to spend a regular amount of time each week working to accomplish them.

Keep a personal calendar for your appointments and for record–keeping. Whether you use a paper calendar or a PDA will depend on your personal style.

For each employer you contact, keep the following information:

- Name, address, phone number, fax, and email address of the employer.
- Brief description of the employer.
- Name and title of contact person(s) within the firm.
- Where you learned about the job opening (publication, professor, friend, etc.).
- Specific or possible openings.
- Date you sent initial resume.
- Follow–up by you or employer. (If the employer doesn't contact you within three weeks of your mailing, you should call or email.)
- Date of interview and other interview information (place, interviewer, information gleaned from the interview, and so on).
- Date you sent a thank–you letter.
- Resolution: What happened with this employer, and (to the best of your knowledge) why.

Use a personal information manager or contact program (such as *Act!, Microsoft Outlook, Lotus Organizer)*, database (such as *FileMaker Pro, Microsoft Access)*, or spreadsheet (like *Excel, Lotus 1–2–3,* or *Quattro Pro)* to manage your contact information. Many resume preparation applications like *WinWay Resume* (available from Planning/Communications; see Chapter 22) include a contact management module.

Don't expect immediate results. A job search in the U.S. takes six to nine months. An international job search can take much longer.

Develop a support system. Job searching can be frustrating, especially if you are receiving little response to your hard work. Know who among your friends and family can provide the encouragement to keep you motivated. Better yet, form a job–search group of friends who also want to work abroad.

Allow free time to do fun things, and give yourself breaks. Remember why you decided to seek work in Europe in the first place!

STEP 8. Follow up all calls and letters; keep talking to people

Employers, especially international employers, are more likely to treat you seriously if you promise to follow up on your initial calls or letters. They are less likely to shove your resume under a stack of personnel files if you make it clear that you will be calling back soon. Follow–up phone calls, faxes, and emails to Europe from the United States are a possibility and can indicate a true interest on your part in getting a particular job.

Improving response and follow up

Nothing is more frustrating than mailing letters and receiving little or no response. These three tips can help improve response rates.

First, many European companies make extensive use of faxing as a part of their day–to–day activities. While faxing unsolicited resumes or letters of inquiry isn't a good plan, you might better your chances for a prompt response if you include a fax number with your initial correspondence. A fax number also indicates to potential employers that you could speedily provide additional information..

Second, you might improve your chances not only of prompt follow up but of actual employment if you can tell employers you can arrange your own work permit. BUNAC, the Council on International Educational Exchange (CIEE), and the Association for International Practical Training (AIPT) are three organizations that can provide students or young professionals with short–term work permits for certain European countries (see Chapter 9). Many employers will not secure an employment permit for you.

Finally, be aware that smaller organizations — especially nonprofits — simply do not have the funds to respond to every inquiry they receive (including both unsolicited resumes and requests for information). By enclosing International Reply Coupons (IRCs), available from your local post office, with hard copies of your resume and cover letter, you incur the cost of the return mailing, not them. This is also the reason that, when possible, it is best to use the web to reach European employers.

STEP 9. Make personal contact with employers

There is no substitute for face–to–face interviews. No matter how professional your resume is, it can only help your chances of securing a job if you establish contact in person. By visiting the companies yourself, you will impress them with the seriousness of your interest in working with them. Also, if you have the opportunity to visit the organizations that interest you, you'll have a better idea of where you would or wouldn't feel comfortable working. Only plan to travel to Europe once you have established some solid job leads or firm appointments for interviews.

Of course, not everyone can afford a job search trip to Europe. Technology, such as video–conferencing, makes it possible to meet face–to–face with employers without boarding an airplane. Some particularly creative job seekers have designed custom business cards that actually are CD–ROMs. When played, these tech–savvy business cards feature a short personal introduction by the job seeker. Other job seekers have fallen back on the old–fashioned telephone as a tool by which to interview with an employer.

There are no magic spells to make an international job search move quickly. The requirements for success are rather mundane — persistence, organization, and aggressiveness. There are many resources to help you with your job search, but ultimately, success rests with you. And you will feel tremendous satisfaction knowing that you made it happen. *Bon chance!*

Study trips to Europe

Making personal contacts with companies is so effective that some educational organizations offer college students and recent graduates one– to two–week information trips to visit major companies in a foreign country. These trips frequently include tours of major companies that feature a chance to speak to human resources representatives about the organization's global hiring strategy. For a $1,975 fee, the Study Tour to Germany, sponsored by CDS International (www.cdsintl.org) provides a roundtrip flight from New York to Germany, nine nights in hotels, some dinners, all ground transportation, and visits with German companies such as BMW, Volkswagen, Robert Bosch, Deutsche Banc, and Lufthansa. The German Academic Exchange Service (www.daad.org) offers a summer program called "High Tech in Old Munich" that provides similar opportunities for company visits.

Chapter 5

The International Resume

The basics of the international resume. The resume format.
Contents of the international resume. List of verbs to use.
Sample international resumes. The importance of the cover
letter. Sample cover letters.

This chapter provides a basic overview on preparing a resume for international work. We do not intend to suggest that there is a single European resume format. In fact, there are unique cultural criteria that guide resume preparation for each European nation. If possible, it's a savvy move to have a knowledgeable native of your target country review your resume and offer suggestions about what employers expect to see. Although many European employers are familiar with American–style resumes, you will be more appealing if you present your employment history in a format that is typical for that country. Common complaints among hiring officials abroad are that American resumes are too aggressive and that they lack cultural sensitivity. French employers, for example, prefer handwritten cover letters because they have handwriting experts analyze them to identify the applicant's personality traits. Later in this chapter, we suggest several books that identify resume styles for jobs in different countries.

Regardless of the country in which you intend to work, the purpose of the resume remains the same, to concisely tell an employer:

☑ Who you are
☑ What you have done
☑ What you do now
☑ What you can do

Your resume is a key tool to get you a job interview. Although many of the components of an international resume are similar to those used domestically, there are important differences. European employers generally expect to see personal information, including marital status, age, and health information on the resume. (Note: This information is *not* included in resumes used in the U.S.) You will want to make sure you have clearly explained your background, especially your education, in terms that are meaningful to employers not familiar with the U.S. educational system. Most important, you must stress those points that make you unique in the international job market.

CV vs. Resume

CV or resume? Which is it? In most countries, the terms *resume* and *CV* (curriculum vita) are synonymous. They refer to a document that summarizes your professional and educational experience. When there is a difference, a CV is simply a lengthier version of your resume. It provides more details about your educational experience, accomplishments, and may include attachments. A CV is usually used for academic and research positions. Rule of thumb? When a job ad calls for a CV, your international resume will suffice.

Resume Formats

There is no single right style or format. Choose any format that works best for you and that you find appealing. These are the three most common formats:

Chronological. The chronological resume is the traditional style most often used in the workplace and job search. In this format, you list your experience in chronological order, beginning with your most recent experience and working backward. The advantage of this format is that it is familiar and easy for employers to read.

Functional. The functional resume is most common among career changers, people re–entering the job market after a lengthy absence, and those wishing to highlight aspects of their experience not related directly to employment. This format places the emphasis on the skills you possess rather than the places you obtained them. A functional skills resume is the most difficult to write but can be very effective at demonstrating to an employer what you know how to do. This is considered a non–traditional format, even in the U.S.

Combination. The combination resume combines the best features of a functional resume and a chronological resume. You can highlight skills and accomplishments while maintaining the somewhat traditional format of a re–verse chronological resume.

Length, Layout, and Appearance

Employers initially do not read your resume; they skim it. Make sure information is clear and concise. European employers are accustomed to receiving two–page resumes, so you may format your resume accordingly. Be honest about the information you have to present, however. Just because you can fill two pages does not mean you should. Employers can see when you are padding your resume. In general, follow these formating tips:

- Use one–inch margins on all sides.

- Place material in order of importance.

- Use a reverse chronological sequence (unless the norm in your target country is different).

- Highlight important points by selectively underlining or boldfacing key words.

- Use the jargon of your profession.

- Stress your assets; downplay your liabilities.

- Do not exaggerate. Be prepared to provide hard proof of your credentials (i.e., copies of certificates, diplomas, pay stubs from previous employment).

- Use the present tense for current experiences and the past tense for previous experiences.

- Write in telegraphic style that avoids using personal pronouns.

- Avoid abbreviations; write everything out in full. The recipient of your resume may not know what an abbreviation stands for.

- Proofread carefully for grammatical, spelling, or typographical errors.

- Have the draft of your resume reviewed by a friend, someone in the field, and a native from your target country before you make a final copy.

- Print your resume cleanly on good quality bond paper, preferably on European–sized A4 (21 x 29.7cm.) white paper.

- Use the same A4–size bond paper for your cover letter.

The Electronic Resume

The growing use of the Internet for hiring overseas makes it essential for you to produce an electronic as well as print resume. Many online job sites allow applicants to submit their resumes on the spot as an ASCII text file, a PDF file, or in a word processor format either as an email, attachment to an email, or by cutting and pasting your resume into an online form.

An electronic resume is similar to a conventional resume, but it is designed to be read by a computer that will be searching for "keywords." There are a few aspects to the electronic resume that distinguish it from your print resume or CV:

☑ You need to include "keywords" that you identify from company literature, job descriptions, or trade magazines.

☑ Place the list of keywords at the top of your resume. These are words for which a computer scans.

☑ List computer skills and other required job skills you possess.

☑ Use a font size between 10 and 14 points. Use an easily-scanned font like Times Roman or Arial.

☑ Avoid graphics, bolding, underlining, or other text embellishment — these make scanning more difficult.

☑ Leave a large margin all the way around the resume.

It would take an entire book to explain all the intricacies of electronic resumes. You would be prudent to consult at least one of these informative books for in-depth guidance on preparing electronic resumes:

e-Resumes. Susan Whitcomb and Pat Kendall. McGraw-Hill. Available from Planning/Communications — see the "Resource Center" beginning on page 472. $11.95, 208 pages, 2002.

Electronic Resumes & Online Networking. Rebecca Smith. Career Press, 3 Tice Rd. P.O. Box 687, Franklin Lakes, NJ 07417, www.careerpress.com. $13.99, 221 pages, 2000.

Cyberspace Resume Kit. Mary Nemnich and Fred Jandt. Jist Publishing, 8902 Otis Ave., Indianapolis, IN 46216–1033, www.jist.com. $18.95, 352 pages, 2000.

Resumes in Cyberspace. Pat Criscito. Barrons Educational Series, 250 Wireless Boulevard, Hauppauge, NY 11788. $14.95, 300 pages, 2000.

Remember that Internet access varies widely among European companies and employers. It is often a good idea to mail your print resume and cover letter as a follow-up to your emailed resume.

Contents of an International Resume

Resumes for international jobs — whether print or electronic — should include the following information.

Contact information. Your name, address, phone numbers (home, work, mobile), fax number, and email address should appear at the top of the page. If you list two addresses or phone numbers, label them appropriately. Include the area codes with your phone number and fax number. Include a phone number where employers can reach you or leave a message for you during their workday — keeping in mind the time difference between the U.S. and Europe. Also include the URL of your personal web page, if you have one.

Professional Objective. You do not have to include an objective, but if you do, write one that is concise, specific, and that makes sense in terms of the particular job for which you are applying. Tailor your career objective to the job for which you are applying. Include this objective in your resume if you are not also sending a cover letter. You may want to use a few different resumes, highlighting different objectives and perhaps tailoring each resume to a particular employer.

Education. Present your education in a format that an employer who is not familiar with the American system of education can easily understand. List your expected or earned degrees in reverse chronological order with the dates, names, and locations of the institutions and concentrations or major field(s) of studies. Current students and recent graduates should include their grade point averages if they enhance their presentations. If you do include grade point averages, be sure to indicate the range of the scale since these vary both domestically and internationally. (For example, write 3.5/4.0, not just 3.5.) If you include academic honors or special achievements, add a couple of words to explain them to an international employer. If you are counting on your educational background to get you a job, you may need to provide a brief description of your course of study. Remember, the amount of time it takes to complete a university degree can vary in other countries from three to five years.

Experience. This is probably the most important section of your resume. Use action words and avoid phrases like "my duties included" or "my responsibilities were." In addition to describing duties, mention special skills or accomplishments. Your work experience should be listed in reverse chronological order and should include job titles, dates of employment, names and locations of employers. Include volunteer work here only if it is career–related. Make sure that an employer reading your experience section can clearly identify your marketable skills.

International Experience. This section should include anything that will demonstrate your ability to work effectively in a foreign country. Potential employers are looking for your ability to adapt to different cultures and work environments.

Languages. Mention your language skills including your level of fluency — whether you have a working knowledge or simply studied a foreign language. Any exposure at all is a plus. Do not to exaggerate your language skills. You could be very embarrassed the first time your prospective employer calls on the phone and attempts to converse in that language.

Additional Information. Include hobbies, volunteer work, memberships, awards, travel, and so on. Be cautious, especially about your hobbies. An employer may be reluctant to hire someone who loves to spend weekends skiing because she may think you may be unavailable to work on weekends.

References. You may state that references are available upon request, but do not list references by name. Prepare a separate sheet that lists your references, including phone numbers and email addresses. Most European employers take past employer references very seriously. Because you are not European, the employer is less familiar with your background and may consider you a risky hire. Always obtain permission to use someone as a reference and give references advance warning that they may receive a call. If references know the nature of the job you are seeking, they can give you a more effective reference.

Active Verbs

Using these "active" verbs in your resume helps to convey your capabilities in a more vivid manner.

Administer: A department of people; programs; a specific activity, such as a test.

Analyze: Quantitative data; statistical data; human/social situations.

Appraise: Evaluate programs or services, judge the value of property, evaluate performance of individuals.

Budget: Outline costs of a project; assure that money will not be spent in excess of funds; use money efficiently and economically.

Compile: Gather numerical, statistical data; accumulate facts in a given topic area.

Control: Exercise financial control or environmental control; control a crowd, or children.

Coordinate: Numerous events involving groups of people; quantities of information; activities in several locations; events in a time sequence.

Create: Artistically (visual arts, etc.); new ideas for an organization; new ways to solve mechanical problems; invent new apparatus, equipment.

Deal with pressure: Risks toward self, physical and otherwise; risks toward others; time pressure or deadlines for getting work done.

Delegate: Distribute tasks to others, give responsibility to others on a work team.

Distribute: Products to people personally; market products or make them available to customers.

Edit: Newspaper; magazine pieces; book manuscripts, etc.

Estimate: Judge likely costs of an operation; project possibilities of future income; judge physical space accurately.

Evaluate: Assess a program to determine its success; judge the performance of an individual.

Imagine: New ways of dealing with old problems; theoretical relationship; artistic ideas or perspectives.

Initiate: Personal contacts with strangers; new ideas or ways of doing things; new approaches.

Interpret: Other languages; obscure phrases or passages in English; meaning of statistical data; relative importance of situations.

Interview: Evaluate applicants for organizations; obtain information from others.

Investigate: Seek information that may be hard to obtain; seek the underlying causes of a problem.

Listen: To conversations between others; to extended conversation from one person in order to help; to recording devices or other listening situations.

Manage: Be responsible for the work of others; have responsibility for the processing of information; guide activities of a team; have responsibility for meeting objectives of an organization or department.

Monitor: Follow progress of another person; observe progress of equipment or apparatus.

Negotiate: Financial contracts; between individuals or groups.

Plan: Anticipate future needs of a company or organization; schedule a sequence of events; arrange an itinerary for a trip.

Process: The orderly flow of data and/or information; introduce an individual to the routines and procedures of an organization; identify human interactions taking place in a group; channel information through a system.

Program: For computers; develop and arrange a sequence of events.

Promote: Through written media; on a personal level or one–to–one; arrange financial backing.

Recruit: Attempt to acquire the services of people for an organization.

Research: Extract information from library, archives, etc.; obtain information from other people (surveys); obtain information from physical data.

Review: Observe, inspect, summarize a collection of documents, information, etc.; assess effects of a program; assess performance of an individual.

Sell: Convince an individual or organization to purchase or accept a product, service, idea, or policy.

Speak: Address an audience, individual, or group, in person or through electronic media.

Supervise: Hold direct responsibility over the work of others, final responsibility; oversee the maintenance of a physical plant or building.

Teach: Instruct students in an academic setting; train individuals to perform certain tasks; familiarize or orient people in the context of a given system.

Translate: Express words of one language in another language; reduce sophisticated language to simpler terms.

Troubleshoot: Find sources of difficulty in human relations, systems, or physical apparatus.

Write: Copywrite for sales; creative writing; reports or memos.

Which language to use?

You will have to choose whether to submit your resume in English or the language of the country where your potential employer is located. Many multinational organizations will expect that you speak English as well as the local language. It is a good idea to prepare your resume in both languages to demonstrate your proficiency. The tips in this chapter are intended for people preparing English–language resumes. It is very important that someone who speaks the other language fluently and understands the nuances of the job search review your foreign language resume.

Even if you are preparing an English–language resume, you're not off the hook. You need to consider whether to use American or British English. As a general guideline, resumes sent to American companies in Europe should use American English, while those going to European companies should use British English. Fortunately, most word processing packages include a spell checker for both versions of English, although you may have to manually select the version you want to use.

Sample resumes

As noted earlier, use the resume format that best fits your specific needs. The first three sample resumes illustrate different ways to organize and format a chronological resume. The two samples that follow illustrate the functional and combination formats respectively.

Sample Chronological Resume

Bruce Fallstein

10 E. Shuffle Street   Telephone: (202) 555–0909
Asbury Park, New Jersey 07712   Email: bfallstein@rosalita.com

Date of birth: 23 September 1969 USA
Married, no children

EDUCATION	**Georgetown University**, Washington, D.C. M.B.A., Concentration in Marketing, May 2001 Extensive Coursework in International Business Chair of International Society
	Northern Illinois University, DeKalb, Illinois B.A. Economics, May 1995 Presidential Scholar, cum laude Coursework in International Relations and Spanish
EXPERIENCE	Management Consultant **Cap Gemini Ernst & Young**, Houston, Texas. Provided consulting services to the energy industry. Involved in developing an international client base. June 1995–1999
	Marketing Assistant **Health and Fitness Magazine**, Chicago, Illinois. Initiated a new marketing strategy to increase circulation of the magazine in the Chicago restaurant community. August 1994–April 1995.
	Computer Consultant **Northern Illinois University**, DeKalb, Illinois. Advised students in using Microsoft Word and other software programs for the Macintosh SE. January 1993–July 1994
INTERNATIONAL ACTIVITIES	Fluent in French and Spanish; elementary knowledge of Swedish. Have traveled throughout Western Europe and the Middle East.
LEADERSHIP ACTIVITIES	Youth City Representative, P.W. Williams Campaign for Governor President, Northern Illinois University Student Government Tutor, Student Volunteer Program
REFERENCES	References Available Upon Request

Sample Chronological Resume

Philip David Q. Bach

8423 South Heath Street   Home: (773) 555–5309
Chicago, IL 60608   Email: pdq_bach@classical.net

Birth: 30 December 1974; Single

Career Objective	Position in economic analysis and management with a multinational firm.
Education	**University of Northern South Dakota at Hoople**, School of International and Public Affairs. Master's degree in International Econometrics, May 1999. Specialization: Western Europe.
	Emory University, Atlanta, Georgia. Bachelor's degree in Econometrics, May 1997. **University of Tübingen**, Germany. Studies in International Affairs, 1995–96.
Relevant Course Work	Financial Management and Statistical Analysis. International Trade Analysis.
Experience	**Wahall Pembina Consulting**, Chicago, IL, 1999+ Perform analysis and design for Flash Financial Software. Assist client with identifying data inconsistencies and testing system issues. Provide client support, functional analysis and training of client users.
	Dresdner Bank, Frankfurt, Germany, Summer 1998. Assisted in Central Office, International Division, North America. Responsible for learning German and U.S. banking rules, Euromarket instruments and activities, and aiding team members on correspondence and investment banking projects dealing with U.S. banks and corporations.
	Emory University, Atlanta, Georgia, 1996–97. Teaching Assistant. Taught first semester micro– and macro–economics courses.
Additional Information	Knowledge of Excel, Lotus 1–2–3, SPSSP, C++
Languages	Fluent in German, fair knowledge of Italian.
References	References Available Upon Request

Sample Chronological Resume

Stephanie Speelberg

12929 Jurassic Parkway
Tel./Fax (765) 555–3748
Jones, Indiana 46938
Email: sspeelberg@et.com

Objective	Summer internship in banking

Experience

Schindler Energy, Sugarland, IN
Intern: Summer 2001
- Assisted with transitional issues for newly acquired steel mill ranging from defining accounting procedures to evaluating opportunities for hedging energy costs.

Close Encounters Hotels, Ltd., Brighton, U.K.
Intern: Summer 2000
- Analyzed cost and pricing structure of unprofitable hotel restaurant.
- Designed and executed audio/visual sales presentations to corporate clients.

Covenant Arc, A/S, Otterup, Denmark
Marketing Intern: Spring 2000
- Designed two–year strategy for welding machine sales to U.S. market.
- Promoted products at trade shows in U.S. and Europe.

AIESEC–Florida, International Exchange Program
President: 2000–2001
Director of Corporate Fundraising: Fall 1999
- Launched sales campaign resulting in 15 internships for foreign and American students.
- Raised $5,000 in corporate contributions.

Education

Florida State University, Tallahassee, Florida
Bachelor of Science: Marketing, May 2003
- National Merit Scholar
- Semester abroad: University of East Anglia, U.K.

Languages   Danish, Norwegian, beginning Japanese.

References   Available upon request

Jeanne Majel Roddenberry

111 Spock Lane   (823) 555–1313
Quark, Washington 98980   Email: jmrodenb@ds9.com

CAREER OBJECTIVE   Position as an English teacher.

AREAS OF EXPERTISE

Interpersonal/Communication Skills

- Conducted 20 to 30 parent–teacher conferences per month.
- Counseled individual students as needed.
- Supervised and advised one student teacher per semester for three years.
- Interviewed applicants for employment; provided supervision and training.
- Successfully sold and marketed merchandise to customers.
- Served in leadership capacity with educational association.

International

- Fluent in French and German.
- Volunteered for two months in Senegal.
- Lived in Paris for one year during high school.

Planning

- Initiated and executed seminars and meetings.
- Developed lesson plans for all subjects taught.
- Assisted with leadership goals of the school and district.
- Planned and developed educational programs for in–service teacher groups.

EXPERIENCE   Teacher, fourth grade, Ferenginar School District, Ferenginar, Washington, 1995–present.
Assistant Manager, The Limited, Seattle, Washington, 1993–1995 (summers).
Administrative Aide, Uhura Brothers, Bajor, Oregon, 1991–1992 (summers).

EDUCATION   University of Washington, Seattle, Washington
B.S., Elementary Education, 1995
Grade Point Average: 3.7/4.0

HONORS/ ACTIVITIES   Dean's List, six semesters (top 5 percent of students); Vice–President, Palmer Residential Hall

Sample Combination Resume

Raymona Kinsella

100 Miracle Max Avenue

Guilder, Texas 77306

www.pdq.net~kinsellafamily.html

Work: (713) 555–1000

Home: (281) 555–9700

Email: rkinsella@dreamfield.com

OBJECTIVE:

A computer programming–related position, preferably involving software–engineering skills.

EDUCATION:

Louisiana State University, Baton Rouge, Louisiana

B.S., Computer Science, May 1997

QUALIFICATIONS:

Career–related projects:

• Designed and implemented multi–tasking operating system for the IBM PC.

• Designed electronic mail system using PSL/PSA specification language.

Computer languages and operating systems:

• Proficient in Ada, Modula–2, Pascal, COBOL.

• Familiar with C++, Fortran, Lisp, Prolog, dBaseIII, SQL, QBE.

• Experienced in Linux, UNIX, MS–DOS, XENIX operating systems.

Hardware:

• IBM PC (MS–DOS, Xenix), Pyramid 90x (UNIX), Cyber 990 (NOS).

• Data General MV/10000 (UNIX, AOS/VS).

International:

• Speak Spanish and Portuguese.

• Traveled throughout Europe and South America.

• Lived in Madrid, Spain, for one year.

WORK EXPERIENCE:

Chisholm Programming Services, Houston, Texas. 10/97–Present

• *UNIX Programmer*: Responsible for porting MS–DOS database applications to IBM–PC/AT; running Xenix System V; system administration.

Moonlight Graham Arts Center, Houston, Texas 9/93–9/94

• *Computer Programmer*: Performed daily disk backup on Burroughs B–1955 machine. Executed database update programs and checks. Assisted customers with user problems.

PERSONAL:

Born: 1 December 1975

Single, no children

Interests: Travel, backpacking, cooking

The Cover Letter

Your resume and cover letter pack a one–two punch toward the same goal: to get a potential employer interested enough to want to interview you for the job. Your cover letter will be more effective if it is addressed to a particular person. It should be concise, no longer than one page, and designed to be read by someone who has limited time. Each of your cover letters should look like it was individually written for the job at hand.

To be most effective, your cover letter should be tailored to the job for which you are applying. Organize it around the requirements of the job. Use your cover letter to show exactly how your background, experience, and skills can be of value to the potential employer. Of course, some requirements are universal: intelligence, assertiveness, imagination, good interpersonal skills. These can be demonstrated either experientially (work) or inferentially (academic or extracurricular achievements, interests, hobbies).

Contact the American affiliate of a particular company, if possible by telephone, to find out exactly where and to whom your resume should be sent. You may also be able to find this information on the company's website. If you don't want your resume put immediately in the inactive file, you should include in your cover letter words to this effect: "I will be contacting you within three weeks regarding arrangements for an interview." In this way, you prompt a timely response, and if the employer does not respond, he or she can expect your follow–up.

Another method that often prompts a response is to send a copy of your letter and resume to the department head or manager within the division where you would like to work. This puts more responsibility on the recipient of your letter, letting him know that he will not be the only person in that organization to read it. This technique increases the odds that your resume will end up in the right hands.

Cover Letter Basics

First paragraph. This quick introduction should be designed to stir enough interest to get the recipient to continue to the second paragraph. It should convey who you are, why you are writing, how you heard of the opening, which position you seek, who suggested you write, or what it is about the organization that motivated you to write.

Middle paragraphs. Use a short paragraph or two to show what it is about you that makes you right for this job and how hiring you can benefit the employer. Refer to specific items in your work and/or academic history that demonstrate why you are both interested and qualified for the position, the organization, or the field. Do not simply repeat your resume; expand upon something in your background — briefly! It is better to highlight how well you did something than simply state what you did.

Final paragraph. Use the concluding paragraph to artfully ask for an interview. You have several options on how to manage this. You can await a written or phoned reply, or you can follow–up with a phone call or email. You are more likely to get an interview if you follow–up your correspondence. A phone call is particularly appropriate when applying to a local organization where travel to an interview will not be a problem. If you are applying to a distant company and are planning to be in the area, call to let the employer know this. Be aware, though, that few employers will pay for your to travel to a job interview. An increasing number of foreign employers interview applicants online or by telephone.

Format. When submitting a printed cover letter, use a ragged right margin — do *not* justify the text. Justification is a dead giveaway that your cover may be a mailmerge letter sent to many companies. At least a ragged right margin leaves the possibility open that your application is not simply a mass mailing. You would also be prudent to turn off automatic hyphenation which, when used, is another telltale sign of a computer–generated mass–produced letter.

Electronic applications. Include a cover letter even if you are applying for a job via email. The electronic cover letter is very similar to the paper version with one important difference: length. A cover letter accompanying an electronic resume should include all of the information listed above, but it should fit on a single computer screen. The reader should not need to scroll down to see the entire cover letter.

Email address. Use a dignified email address. You cannot imagine how much email addresses like bill@partyboy.com or ski_bum@hotmail.com turn off a potential employer.

The two cover letters that follow illustrate these principles. The first sample is directed to only one person. The second sample illustrates how to show you have sent the letter to more than one person at the company.

Sample Cover Letter

April 15, 2004
1949 Dread Pirate Roberts Drive
Ottumwa, Iowa 52501

Mr. Jacques C. Guroid
Manager, International Division
Fezzik and Vizzini, Ltd.
7, rue d'Argent
F–75631 Paris, France

Dear Mr. Guroid:

As a second–year graduate student at Rice University's Jones School of Business Administration, I was intrigued to learn about the expansion of your international division. (The Wall Street Journal, March 16, 2004.) I am writing to express an interest in joining your marketing department.

My MBA requirements have included intensive coursework in international marketing, accounting, and finance. These have given me a firm foundation from which to begin an international business career. In addition, I have held intern positions at JPMorgan Chase and AT&T, both of which strengthened my understanding of international markets and marketing practices. I am fluent in French and Spanish.

The enclosed resume provides a more detailed description of my qualifications. I hope you will agree that my academic and work experiences make me well–suited to contribute to Fezzik and Vizzini's future international expansion.

I will call you in a few weeks to discuss my application further. In the interim, feel free to reach me by telephone at (732) 555–5454 or email at inigom@fireswamp.com.

Thank you for your consideration.

Sincerely,

Inigo Montoya

Inigo Montoya

Sample Cover Letter

July 9, 2003
912 East 47th Street
Chicago, Illinois 60653
773/555–5454

Mr. Raymond Davies
Recruiting Coordinator
International Banc d'Argent
1929 Wall Street
New York, NY 10005

Dear Mr. Davies:

I am writing to inquire about opportunities with the foreign trading group at International Banc d'Argent. I received your name from Ms. Princess Buttercup, finance manager with IBA. I believe my substantial work experience in foreign trade will make me a valuable addition to your group.

I am currently a foreign trade analyst at BankOne in Chicago. At BankOne, I have focused on international finance. My work brings me into daily contact with the international aspects of trade, economics, and foreign policy analysis.

As my resume indicates, I also have extensive experience in a research environment and have successfully managed numerous projects involving the supervision of personnel and the elimination of kinks from the system.

Again, I would like to express my interest in a position with IBA and assure you of my proven ability to perform well. I look forward to hearing from you soon and giving you a chance to assess for yourself my qualifications.

I will call you within the next two weeks regarding the position.

Thank you for your time and consideration.

Sincerely,

Nichelle Nichol

Nichelle Nichol

cc: Ms. Princess Buttercup, Finance Manger, IBA

Preparing Culturally Appropriate Resumes, CVs, and Cover Letters

The tips in this section for preparing resumes and cover letters are, by necessity, pretty general. Remember, there is no single style for a "European" resume. However, an "American–style" resume or cover letter may actually undermine your job search. After all, who wants to hire someone who has not done enough homework to be familiar with the culture of the country in which the employer is located? You want your resume and cover letter to reflect that you are candidate ready to hit the ground running from day one.

So what do you do? You do your homework so you know what to emphasize or downplay in your job application documents. Evaluate your application according to the following criteria to determine if you have written a culturally appropriate CV:

Length. While most CVs and resumes should be two pages, the norm in some countries is longer resumes with attachments such as copies of the degrees you have earned.

Format. The biggest issue is typically whether to use a chronological or a reverse–chronological format for your resume. When in doubt, use reverse chronological. In many European countries, it is also common to attach a photo to your application and to include personal information.

Sweat the details, country by country

Two key resources to learn the nuances of resume and cover letter preparation for jobs in specific countries are:

The Global Resume and CV Guide. Mary Anne Thompson. John Wiley & Sons. Available from Planning/Communications — see the "Resource Center" beginning on page 472. An unrivaled resource for details on the unique job application practices for 20 European nations. Includes guidelines for each country's preferred resume and cover letter content and format as well as sample resumes, advice on interviewing, culture, work permits, and visas, plus a short directory of global experts in executive search and recruitment. Extremely thorough. $17.95, 294 pages, 2000.

Best Resumes and CVs for International Jobs: Your Passport to the Global Job Market. Ron Krannich and Wendy Enelow. Impact Publications. Available from Planning/Communications — see the "Resource Center" beginning on page 472. Includes several sample resumes for people applying for jobs in Eastern and Western Europe, graduating students seeking international opportunities, Americans seeking opportunities abroad, keywords for international resumes, and resume preparation forms. $24.95, 248 pages, 2002.

Education. Academic credentials and certifications are more important in some countries than others. For example, the degrees you have earned and their titles are very important in Germany where you will want to include any certifications you have completed (i.e. M.A., Ph.D., J.D., CFP).

Language. Whether you submit a CV written in English or a foreign language depends on the company to which you are applying. When applying to a multinational company, your English–language documents will suffice. When applying to smaller or European employers, use materials prepared in the language of the employer's country.

Accuracy. Make sure that your CV and cover letter do not have any grammatical or spelling errors — something easier said than done when writing in a foreign language. Use your word processor's spell check to make a first pass over your documents. Find a native speaker of the language in which your CV or cover letter is written to make a second check. There is one thing that employers the world over have in common: They frown upon misspellings and typographical errors.

Chapter 6

The International Interview

> The interview and how to prepare for it. The kinds of questions you will be asked. How you will be evaluated. Responding to job offers and rejections.

Getting a job in Europe sometimes may not necessitate interviewing at all. Since you live across the ocean, the employer might trust that your written credentials represent you well. If you are looking for work with a corporation with offices in the United States, a representative from their American office may interview you. A lucky few who are qualified for a professional position in Europe may be flown in for an interview, though this does not happen often. No matter how you are interviewed, you must be prepared to represent yourself in the best way possible.

The purpose of an interview is to give you and an employer the opportunity to evaluate each other. The interview should be an active two–way exchange of information. The interviewer wants to evaluate your personality in terms of the position and the organization. You can use the interview to find out if the position interests you, to sell yourself by highlighting your positive points, and to gain a job offer. Remember that the employer wants to hire you if you can convince him or her that you are right for the job.

Because of travel constraints in the international job search, an employer may choose to interview you by telephone. It is to your advantage to practice what you intend to say so that you will sound smooth and articulate over the phone: Your verbal communication skills will shape the impression that you make on prospective employer. You should have a quiet place to call from, with no noises, distractions, or potential interruptions to break the flow of your interview. It's a good idea to write down points you want to bring up in response to potential interview questions so you don't forget anything. Questions asked during the phone interview will probably be the same as those during a regular interview. You should also come up with a list of questions about the job or the company in case you're given the opportunity to ask questions.

Qualities on Which You Are Evaluated

These are some qualities on which a typical interviewer might evaluate you:

Personal appearance. You should look neat and professional. In Europe, however, what constitutes "professionalism" varies slightly from what you're accustomed to in the U.S. Depending on where you are, the standards may be more or less formal than in the States. If you're familiar with the standards of professional dress in the country in which you'll be interviewing, wear clothes that are appropriate. If you aren't familiar or aren't comfortable with professional dress habits abroad, don't let it bother you. Your potential employer should realize that standards of professional dress vary across cultures, and you will seldom go wrong if you present yourself well by American standards.

Work experience. Articulate your pertinent work experience, its value, and how it might relate to the job you are applying for. Even if the work experience is unrelated to your field, employers look upon any previous work experience as an asset.

Education. The importance of degrees and grades varies from job to job and from organization to organization. You should always be prepared, however, to answer questions about your academic background, special interests or achievements, or any possible deficiencies.

Verbal communication skills. Effective communication includes effective listening as well as the articulate, confident, and poised expression of ideas. Because verbal communication skills are so important, you should be careful to accurately portray your foreign language abilities on your resume. Unless the employer has indicated that foreign language skills are not required for the job, you will likely be interviewed in both English and the second language. Make sure you have basic business terminology at your fingertips so that you can discuss your interest in the position.

General personality qualities. Poise, sincerity, enthusiasm, self–confidence, maturity, and motivation are valued by most employers. Of course, depending on the personality of the organization and the available position, some of these qualities may be stressed more than others.

Skills. The interviewer will evaluate your skills for the job, such as organization, analysis, and research. It is important to emphasize the skills that you feel the employer is seeking and to give specific examples of how you developed them.

Goals/Motivation. Employers will assess your ability to articulate your short– and long–term goals. You should be ambitious, yet realistic about the training and qualifications needed to advance. You should demonstrate interest in the functional area or industry to which you are applying for work and a desire to succeed and work hard. Be prepared to thoroughly discuss your interest in working in Europe, in particular how this experience will relate to your long–term goals.

Before the Interview

☑ Identify your strengths, skills, goals, and personal qualities. This self–assessment is crucial to knowing what you have to offer an employer and conveying it effectively.

☑ Research the organization by reading its annual report, reviewing its web site, and examining other sources of information. This will demonstrate that you are sincerely interested in the position and also prepare you to ask intelligent questions. An interview is supposed to be a dialogue; you want to learn about them just as they want to learn about you.

☑ Rehearse what you plan to say during the interview. Practice answers to commonly asked questions and determine how you will emphasize your strengths and skills. Practice is especially important if you will be interviewing in a foreign language.

☑ Dress professionally and conservatively. If you make a negative first impression you may not be fairly considered for the job. Women should wear a tailored suit or dress. Limit jewelry and cosmetics and keep hair neat. Men should wear a suit and tie, with hair and beard or mustache trimmed.

☑ Be prepared for questions about the country in which you are working. It's a good idea to do some research about the region, its customs, people, political situations, and so on. You might want to pick up an English copy of a recent newspaper from the area so you will have a bit of small talk to draw from. Anything that will make you sound informed about the area will make you appear as a serious job candidate and give you an advantage.

During the Interview

☑ Make sure that you arrive for your interview on time or a few minutes early.

☑ Greet the interviewer by his or her last name, offer a firm handshake and a warm smile.

☑ Be aware of your non–verbal behavior. Wait to sit until you are offered a chair. Sit straight, look alert, speak in a clear, strong voice, and stay relaxed. Make good eye contact, avoid nervous mannerisms, and listen carefully to the questions the employer asks. Smile.

☑ Follow the interviewer's lead, but try to get the interviewer to describe the position and duties to you fairly early in the interview so that you can later relate your background and skills in context.

☑   Be specific, concrete, and detailed in your answers. The more information you volunteer, the better the employer can evaluate your qualifications for the position.

☑   Don't mention salary in a first interview unless the employer does. If asked, give a realistic range and add that the opportunity is the most important factor for you. Make sure you have correct information about salaries in Europe; they can be much lower than for comparable positions in the U.S.

☑   Offer examples of your work and references that will document your best qualities.

☑   Answer questions truthfully and candidly. Never appear to be glossing over anything, yet don't over–answer questions. The interviewer may steer the interview into sensitive political or social questions. Answer honestly, but try not to say more than is necessary.

☑   Never make derogatory remarks about present or former employers or companies.

Questions You May Be Asked During an Interview

Although it may appear differently, the employer has a reason for each question he or she asks. Try to put yourself in the interviewer's shoes and ask why you might be asked a particular question. This can help you focus your answer with the most relevant information. Direct your responses toward the particular position for which you are applying. What follows are some questions that employers often ask during interviews. Rehearse answers to these questions prior to your interview so you can appear relaxed and confident.

Ice breakers. These are designed to put you at ease and engage you in informal conversation. Be yourself, act natural, and be friendly.

- Did you have any trouble finding your way here?
- How was your plane flight?
- Can you believe this weather?
- I see you're from Omaha. Is this your first trip to Europe

Work history and education. These queries determine whether your background and skills are appropriate for the position. Be prepared to talk about your skills and relate them to the job to be filled. Give specific examples of how you used skills in the past. Questions concerning your past help the employer determine how you might make decisions in the future.

- Tell me about yourself.
- Tell me about the most satisfying job/internship you ever held.
- Tell me about the best boss you ever had. The worst.
- What have you learned from some of the jobs you've held?

- For what achievements were you recognized by your superiors at your last position?
- What are you looking for in an employer?
- What are you seeking in a position?
- Why did you choose to get a degree in the area that you did?
- In what activities have you participated outside of class?
- How did you finance your education?

Ambitions and plans. These questions evaluate your ambition, your goals and their feasibility, and how actively you seek to achieve those goals.

- Are you a joiner or a loner? A leader or a follower? A committee member or chairperson? Keep in mind that a ship full of captains will flounder as badly as a ship with none at all.
- What job in our company would you select if you were free to choose?
- What does success mean to you? How do you judge it?
- Assuming you are hired for this job, what do you see as your future?
- What personal characteristics do you think are necessary for success in this field?
- Will you fight to get ahead in your career?
- Are you willing to prove yourself as a staff member of our firm? How do you envision your role?
- Are you willing to work overtime?
- Where do you see yourself five years from now? Ten years?
- How much money do you hope to earn in five years? Ten years?

Company or organization. These questions determine if you have conscientiously researched the company and if you would be a good match for it. They also seek to identify your interest in the company.

- Do you prefer working for a small or large organization?
- Do you prefer a private or public organization? Why?
- What do you know about our organization?
- Why did you choose to interview with us?
- What kind of work are you interested in doing for us?
- What do you feel our organization has to offer you? What do you have to offer us?

Values and self–assessment. These queries help the interviewer get to know you better and to see how well you understand yourself.

- What kind of personal satisfaction do you hope to gain through work?

- If you had unlimited funds, what would you do? Where would you live?
- What motivates you?
- What are your strengths and weaknesses?
- How would you describe yourself?
- What do you do with your free time?
- What kind of people do you like to work with?
- How do you adapt to other cultures?

They want to know *what?*

Questions and practices that are considered discriminatory — and illegal — in the United States are perfectly acceptable and common in Europe. To begin with, you may be asked to submit a photograph with your resume or other application materials. In many European countries, this is standard. Both men and women are likely to be asked about their marital status, but for women seeking a potentially long–term position within a company, inquiries about their married life — for example, how long they've been married — may be a subtle way of finding out whether they intend to have children in the near future. (In some European countries, companies are obligated to pay a woman's salary while she is on an extended maternity leave; hence, this is a source of concern to a potential employer.) Some interviewees don't have any qualms about lines of questioning that are personal. If you think you'd likely take offense, though, be prepared. Knowing to expect personal questions and deciding ahead of time how to answer them will serve you in good stead.

Closing and Post–Interview

Don't be discouraged if the interviewer does not make a definite offer or discuss a specific salary.

- ☑ If you get the impression that the interview isn't going well and that you've already been rejected, don't let your discouragement show. Once in a while, an interviewer who is genuinely interested in you may try to discourage you just to test your reaction.

- ☑ Be prepared to ask questions at the end of the interview. If your questions were addressed during the interview, refer to them, saying afterward that they have now been answered to your satisfaction.

- ☑ When the interview ends, ask when a hiring decision will be made. This question not only reconfirms your interest in the position but also lets you know when to expect a response. Don't forget to thank your interviewer for his or her time and to make clear your interest in the position.

☑ Note areas to improve upon for your next interview and what went particularly well. Experience is only valuable to the extent that you're willing to learn from it.

Interviewing across cultures

Like resumes and cover letters, interviewing styles differ from country to country. Interviewing with a foreign employer is undeniably stressful. Each company will have its own criteria for evaluating candidates, and some of these will no doubt reflect cultural preferences and expectations. Here are some issues to consider with preparing for an international job interview:

◆ **Dress and appearance.** Determine if there is a standard interview outfit that people of that country typically wear. In some countries, such as Spain and Italy, the so-phistication of your interview attire is considered a re-flection of your sophistication as a person. In other countries, being too well–dressed may be perceived as arrogance.

◆ **Your role as an interviewee.** In an American–style interview, you are taught to "sell yourself," to assertively promote your best qualities and downplay your weak-nesses. In some cultures, this can be considered pushy and a turn–off. In Germany, for example, employers may focus exclusively on the facts of your employment history (dates, job responsibilities, etc.), and will not be interested in hearing self–promotion. As a general rule of thumb, follow the interviewer's lead and let him or her establish the tone.

◆ **Formality and etiquette.** Make sure you know how much emphasis a particular culture places on protocol and etiquette — this is sometimes as important as your previ-ous experience. Pay attention to the tone of the interview. In some cultures, job interviews are very serious, and if you crack a joke, the employer may assume that you will not take your job seriously. Never assume you may use someone's first name without asking permission.

◆ **The value of educational credentials.** In some coun-tries, employers place the most value on experiences that can be documented with diplomas, certificates, or written references. In other countries, placing too much emphasis on your academic credentials will merely prove that you are a "pointy–headed intellectual" not suited for the practical aspects of doing business.

Mary Anne Thompson's *The Global Resume and CV Guide* (see Chapter 22 for details) includes a valuable chapter on cultural differences in interviews.

☑   If you are interested in the position, type a brief thank–you letter to the interviewer, indicating your interest and appreciation.

☑   Accept or reject all job offers in writing.

After the Interview

The interview is over and now the waiting begins. There may be many reasons why a company is slow to reply to you after the interview. It could be that the interview process hasn't concluded or that other commitments have kept the company from making a decision. However, if much time has passed and you haven't heard anything from a company in which you are particularly interested, a telephone call or an email message asking about the status of your application is appropriate. This inquiry should be stated in a manner that is not pushy but shows your continued interest in the company. Remember that waiting is an integral part of the job hunt, but a demonstration of your continued interest is appropriate.

Soft–sell thank–you letters

Most job applicants in the United States view the thank–you letter not so much as an expression of simple thanks but as one more step in the self–marketing process. Letters are brief, snappy, and assertively confident. Candidates typically make mention of key points that were discussed during the interview, try to state one or two additional reasons why they would be an asset if hired, reiterate their continued interest in the possibility of employment, and, as if it isn't already obvious, close by indicating their desire for favorable consideration. This type of "hard sell" may not be so effective in Europe, where a more subtle approach is often the norm, and in some countries, the post–interview thank–you note isn't usually part of the employment process. In writing a thank–you letter for a European job interview, your best approach may be to compose something more along the lines of a genuine and simple expression of thanks rather than a Madison–Avenue blitz. If you mention your qualifications, say something truly substantive — for example, something relevant that didn't come up during the interview. Anything else may be viewed as an uncouth and unwelcome attempt to curry favor.

The Rejection

When you receive a rejection letter or phone call, as everyone does at one time or another in the job–hunting process, evaluate the reasons why. Were you not suited for the positions? Perhaps your job search should be more specifically designed and targeted. Are your personal and professional goals different from the company's? Make sure, as you prepare for each interview, that you have realistic expectations regarding initial positions and career paths.

Could it be that you simply did not interview well? Perhaps you were not well enough prepared or were a bit preoccupied that day. In that case, you could benefit from feedback regarding your interviewing skills. Try a mock interview with a career counselor. Don't let a rejection get you down; if you learn from one job interview, the next may be more successful.

The Offer

When your hard work finally pays off, make sure to get your offer in writing. Your employer should include your starting date, salary, responsibilities, location, and the date by which you must respond. Maintain a healthy skepticism even when celebrating the successful outcome of your hard work. Perhaps more than with an American job offer, closely evaluate your offer to make sure it is as great as it seems at first. The employer has made you an offer that is in the company's best interest; make sure it is fair to you as well.

Evaluating job offers. Take a close look at the salary and make sure it is reasonable for the city in which you will be living. Evaluate your base salary, housing allowances, and relocation benefits. Also calculate how much taxes and national health insurance will take from your paycheck. Ask questions about medical coverage and, depending on the length of time you'll be living abroad, contributions to pension plans.

Response date. Make sure the response date gives you time to complete negotiations with other employers if possible. Up to two weeks is generally considered a reasonable response time. Be very skeptical if an organization tries to rush your decision — they may have a reason why they don't want you to carefully evaluate its offer! You may have to make a decision before you have complete information on all possible job offers. However, you should only accept an offer if you really intend to stick with it. Remember, if the company to which you are applying is based in Europe, it will take longer for your acceptance letter to reach the organization within the acceptable time, so you may have to send it earlier or fax it.

Starting date. Companies with formal training programs have specific starting dates. However, with many other employers you can negotiate a start date that is mutually acceptable. If you want to take a vacation before starting, try to arrange it before accepting the offer.

Get everything in writing. Once you and your new employer have agreed to the terms of the job, make sure you get everything in writing.

Chapter 7

Placement Organizations & the International Job Search

What placement agencies can and cannot do for you. Executive search firms. Temporary job recruiters. Internet agencies and special services agencies. Lists of placement agencies in the U.S. and in Europe.

Placement organizations include executive search firms, recruitment agencies, and Internet services. Executive search firms are retained by companies to find the most suitable candidate for a particular job. These firms typically search for senior–level jobs for which the pool of appropriate, high–level candidates can be identified and targeted. Contingent recruiting refers to an arrangement in which the recruiting firm's fees are contingent upon the job placement being made. These recruitment firms tend to work on filling jobs at lower salary levels but can also focus on temporary or contract positions. They typically assist with positions ranging from secretarial to qualified accountants to sales and marketing professionals. Online recruiting has proliferated in recent years. The very best sites offer a mixture of automation (online registration and profile updating) and personalization (regular newsletters, information on relevant new opportunities, etc.).

Executive Search Firms

An executive search firm caters to business executives, engineers, or other professionals with specific skills and a good deal of experience. The company with the vacant position pays the search firm's fees. Executive search firms can give you an idea of your value in Europe and whether a placement is possible. Because they are paid by the hiring organization, they usually won't waste their time with someone they can't place. Be very leery of executive search firms that charge a fee; the most reputable organizations do not charge the job seeker.

Directories of Executive Search Firms

The following publications list executive recruiters in the U.S. and Europe.

Executive Search in France and Europe. 2002. Kennedy Information. One Phoenix Mill Lane, 5th Floor, Peterborough, NH 03458; tel.: (800) 531–0007; email: bookstore@kennedyinfo.com; www.kennedyinfo.com. Profiles 308 firms in 22 European countries, 75 in France alone. The directory is intended for people planning to look for jobs as executive search consultants, but it is also useful for job seekers needing detailed information about search firms in Europe. $520, 853 pages.

International Directory of Executive Recruiters. 2003. Kennedy Information. Available from Planning/Communications — see the "Resource Center" beginning on page 472. Lists full contact information for search firms in 60 countries. Provides tips for job seekers along with recommendations of books and other resources in career management and job–changing. $149, CD–ROM only, requires Microsoft Windows®

The Executive Grapevine: The International Directory of Executive Recruitment Consultants. Executive Grapevine International, New Barnes Mill, Cottonmill Lane, St Albans, AL1 2HA, U.K.; Tel.: [44] 1727 844 335; Fax: [44] 1727 844 779; email contact: info@askgrapevine.com; www.askgrapevine.com. Provides information on 1,736 executive search firms in over 80 countries. The 2002 edition includes biographies alongside each of company's profile so the reader may identify both the firm, and the each consultant's specialty. £199, 400 pages. Published annually.

Largest Global Executive Search Firms

The following are the largest executive search firms that operate in Europe. All of them maintain a strong presence in Europe and recruit on behalf of employers hiring executives for international positions.

Amrop Hever Group
Hunt Howe Partners LLC
One Dag Hammarskjold Plaza
34th Floor
New York, NY 10017
Tel.: (212) 758–2800
Fax: (212) 758–7710
ww.amrophever.com

Boyden
364 Elwood Avenue
Hawthorne, NY 10532
Tel.: (914) 747–0093
www.boyden.com

CONEX/Intersearch
150 East 52nd Street, 2nd Floor
New York, NY 10022
Tel:(212) 371–3737
Fax:(212) 371–3897

www.intersearch.org

Egon Zehnder International
350 Park Avenue, 8th Floor
New York, NY 10022
Tel.: (212) 519–6000
Fax: (212) 519–6060
www.zehnder.com

Heidrick & Struggles
Wall Street Office
40 Wall Street, 48th Floor
New York, NY 10005
Phone: (212) 699–3000
Fax: (212) 699–3100
www.heidrick.com

Horton International
Corporate Center West, Suite 327
433 South Main Street

West Hartford, CT 06110
Tel: (860) 521–0101
Fax: (860) 521–0140
www.horton–intl.com

A.T. Kearney Executive Search
153 East 53rd Street
New York, NY 10022
Tel.: (212)751–7040
Fax: (212) 350–3150
www.executivesearch.atkearney.com

Korn/Ferry International
1800 Century Park East, Suite 900
Los Angeles, CA 90067
Tel.: (310) 552–1834
www.kornferry.com

H. Neumann International
Guenthergasse 3
A–1090 Vienna, Austria
Tel: [43] 1 40 140 0
www.neumann–inter.com

Norman Broadbent International
2859 Paces Ferry Road, Suite 1400
Atlanta, GA 30339
Tel.: (770) 955–9550
Fax: (770) 980–9367
www.normanbroadbent.com

Ray & Berndtson
230 Park Avenue, Suite 1000
New York, NY 10169
Tel.: (212) 309–8710
Fax: (212) 309–8704
www.rayberndtson.com

Russel Reynolds Associates
200 Park Avenue, Suite 2300
New York, NY 10166–0002
Tel: (212) 351–2000
Fax: (212) 370–0896
www.russreyn.com

Spencer Stuart
277 Park Avenue, 29th Floor
New York, NY 10172
Tel.: (212) 336–0200
Fax: (212) 336–0296
www.spencerstuart.com

TranSearch International
Martin H . Bauman Associates (Affiliate)
375 Park Avenue, Suite 2002
New York, NY 10152
Tel.: (212) 752–6580
Fax: (212) 755–1096
www.transearch.com

Recruitment Agencies

Unlike executive search firms, recruitment agencies place workers in contract, temporary, and permanent assignments in a variety of industries. Industries ranging from law to nursing now rely on recruitment agencies.

The advantage to working with a recruiting agency is that you usually can be placed quickly, your work assignments are flexible, and it is a convenient way to get your foot in the door with a local business. Many recruitment agencies will not assist with work visas in foreign countries, so you will want to make sure you let the firm know if you have arranged your own working papers. If you are looking for temporary work, be sure to inquire about the agency's policies on accepting a permanent position with a company in which you've been placed. Many will charge the employer a hefty fee!

Major Recruitment Agencies

The following are major recruitment agencies that maintain a strong international presence. They have offices in most major European cities.

Adecco, Inc.
175 Broad Hollow Road
Melville, NY 11747

Tel.: (631) 844–7800
http://adecco.com

Greythorn Limited
125 High Holborn
London, U.K. WC1V 6QA
Tel.: [44] 20 7576 6000
Fax: [44] 20 7831 2233
www.greythorn.com

Robert Half International
2884 Sand Hill Road
Menlo Park, CA 94025
Tel.: (800) 474–4253
www.rhii.com

Kelly Services
999 West Big Beaver
Troy, MI 48084
Tel.: (248) 362–4444
Fax: (248) 244–5236
www.kellyservices.com

Kostals Consultancy
The Hawthorns

Staunton
Gloucester, U.K. GL19 3NY
Tel.: [44] 1452 840002
Fax: [44] 1452 840040
www.kostals.com

Manpower
5301 North Ironwood Road
P.O. Box 2053
Milwaukee, WI 53201–2053
Tel.: (414) 961–1000
www.manpower.com

Randstad Holding nv
P.O. Box 12600
1100 AP Amsterdam–Zuidoost
Netherlands
Tel.: [31]–(20)–569 59 11
Fax: [31]–(20)–569 55 20
www.randstad.com

Internet Resources

Headhunters are increasingly turning to the Internet to identify talent. The good news is that when you post your resume to these sites, thousands of potential recruiters will view it. Some of the following sites cater to experienced professionals and offer services similar to brick–and–mortar executive search firms.

BCEurope

www.bceurope.com

An executive search firm based in Europe, Bertram Consulting specializes in executive and senior placements for professionals in high tech, telecommunications, and information technology. There is a very limited listing of available jobs (the site cautions that most executive search agencies do not advertise their job openings,) but you can submit your CV online in order to begin working with a search consultant.

Brilliantpeople.com

www.brilliantpeople.com

Operated by the world's largest executive search and recruitment firm, Management Recruiters International (MRI), this site offers three sections: a job listings bulletin board, a database of MRI executive recruiters, and tools such as job search agents that will help you manage your search. Also available are

a resume builder and a skills assessment instrument.

Executivesonly.com

http://Executivesonly.com

This site offers two membership levels. Executive Membership provides access to an online database of executive–level positions paying at least $70,000 annually. The Private Career Search Assistance programs offer services ranging from individual career counseling, executive resume and cover letter writing, and resume distribution. All of this comes with a fee: Access to the job database begins at $185 for 24 weeks and a professionally written cover letter and resume will set you back $595.

JobServe

www.jobserve.com

This site features jobs posted by European (mostly U.K.) recruitment firms looking for professionals in fields such as IT, accounting, law, catering and hospitality. The jobs featured on this site are both permanent and contract. Candidates who complete a free registration receive daily emails listing new jobs for which they are qualified.

My.chief.monster.com

http://My.chief.monster.com
Managed by the aptly named employment site Monster.com, this is an online executive search service that caters to professionals earning at least $125,000. You must complete a registration and meet minimum criteria to access the site, but it is free and confidential. Chief.Monster provides access to senior–level opportunities from top employers, executive search firms and venture capital companies. It also offers tools for benchmarking your skills and compensation against peers.

Recruitersonline.com

www.recruitersonline.com
Over 8,000 executive search firms, employment agencies, and headhunters post jobs to this site. You can search jobs and post a resume for free. You can also search for executive recruiters that

represent over 150 industry specialties in different geographic locations.

Sixfigurejobs.com

http://sixfigurejobs.com
The name of this site should give you some idea of the job seeker it caters to. It is for professionals who possess the qualifications to command a high–income salary. Anyone who completes an application will be accepted into the online resume database, but you have to be accepted as a member to get access to the job postings and lists of headhunters. SixFigures.com also manages the site SixFigureMBA.com.

WorkingDay

www.workingday.com
This Swedish site is a traditional recruitment and headhunting firm that specializes in recruiting college graduates and young professionals with up to ten years of work experience. WorkingDay represents employers in business, engineering, and IT. Registration, which mostly consists of emailing your resume as a PDF document, is free.

Special Service Agencies

Chapter 9 lists agencies that place students in summer and temporary positions. These positions include au pair work, agricultural work, secretarial positions, positions teaching English, and work in vacation areas. Temporary recruitment agencies can be a good place to look for short–term clerical or retail assignments. Usually temporary agencies have a large number of positions to fill, and if you are not too picky or have excellent clerical skills, they can find you work quite quickly.

Most temporary recruitment agencies, however, do not provide job seekers assistance with work visas. If you are a student, there are two organizations that can help you obtain a work visa that will permit you to use the services of a recruitment agency. The Council on International Educational Exchange (CIEE) will arrange three– to six–month work permits in Ireland, France, and Germany. For more information, contact CIEE directly at 205 East 42nd Street, New York, NY 10017; (888) 268–6245; www.ciee.org. BUNAC (British Universities North America Club) can arrange work visas that permit Americans to work in the U.K. for up to six months. For more information, contact BUNAC at P.O. Box 430, Southbury, CT 06488; tel.: (203) 264–0901; email: enquiries@bunacusa.org; www.bunacusa.org. These are the only two organizations that can arrange work visas that do not require you to have a pre–arranged job.

Chapter

The International Professional Career

Jobs in business, law, media and communications, non-profits, U.S. federal government, and teaching. Survey of employment opportunities. Descriptions of work in each field. Lists of resources, publications, career guides, and professional organizations. Names and addresses of leading employers.

Building an international career is a long–term proposition. It usually requires a combination of the right education and appropriate work experience with a multinational corporation that has an international career track. This chapter contains information, resources, and employer listings for international business, law, media and communications firms, as well as for international nonprofit, federal government, and teaching opportunities in Europe. The following sections will give you a clear picture of an international career and the options that are available in Europe:

- ☑ International business, with subsections on:
  - ◆ Trade
  - ◆ Banking and finance
  - ◆ Economics
  - ◆ Consulting
- ☑ Law
- ☑ Media and communications
- ☑ International nonprofits
- ☑ U.S. federal government positions abroad
- ☑ International teaching

International Business

American job seekers can be very competitive on the international scene. American firms are expanding operations into the European Union, and European companies are actively engaged in international mergers and acquisitions as part of their own expansion plans. European companies are usually required to hire their own nationals unless the company can show that a foreigner has some special skill not readily available locally. Your best strategy might be to work first for the company in the U.S., prove your abilities, and request a transfer to Europe. Also, a graduate degree, especially an MBA, significantly increases your chances of successfully joining a company in Europe. See Chapter 2 for more information on graduate programs that will enhance your international career.

The following section summarizes general international business resources. The best way to find these directories is to begin with the reference section of your local public or university library. Many of the directories, such as *Hoover's Handbook*, can also be accessed online. Check with the publisher for current pricing.

International Business Resources

America's Corporate Families. Dun & Bradstreet Information Services, Three Sylvan Way, Parsippany, NJ 07054–3896; email: dnbmdd@dnb.com. Lists 11,000 U.S. parent companies and 76,000 foreign subsidiaries. Updated annually.

American Export Register. Thomas Publishing Co., International Division, Five Penn Plaza, New York, NY 10001; email: info@aernet.com. Covers 45,000 U.S. manufacturers and distributors in the export trade and service firms assisting foreign private and public customers. Lists company name, address, and product. Updated annually.

Directory of American Firms Operating in Foreign Countries. Uniworld Business Directories, 257 Central Park West, Suite 10A, New York, NY 10014–4110; www.uniworldbp.com. Information on 2,600 U.S. corporations operating abroad, cataloged by firm name and geographic location. Three volumes; updated annually.

Directory of E.U. Information Sources. Euroconfidentiel S.A., rue de Rixensart 18, B–1332 Genval, Belgium. Includes information on European Union institutions and related organizations. Updated annually.

Directory of Foreign Banks in the U.S. International Business Publishing Consultants, Inc., P.O. Box 422039, San Francisco, CA 94142–2039; www.ipbc.com. Lists more than 1,000 banks and subsidiaries in the U.S.

Directory of U.S. Importers and the *Directory of U.S. Exporters*. PIERS Publishing, Journal of Commerce Group, 33 Washington Street, Newark, NJ 07102–3180; www.pierspub.com. Includes 55,000 U.S. firms with import and export interests. Five volumes; updated annually.

East European Business Information. Headland Press, One Henry Smiths Terrace, Headland, Cleveland U.K. TS24 OPD. Information on organizations providing commercial and industrial information in Eastern Europe. Updated annually.

Europages: The European Business Directory. EUREDIT S.A., 9 av. De Friedland, F–75008 Paris, France; www.europages.com. Covers 150,000 companies in 18 countries. Available online. Published annually

The Europe Review. Kogan Page Ltd., 120 Pentonville Road, London U.K. N1 9JN. Key facts, indicator, country profile, business guide, and directory for countries in Europe. Updated annually.

European Companies Handbook. Euromoney Publications plc, Nestor House, Playhouse Yard, London, U.K. EC4V 5EX. Top 5,000 companies in Europe.

Europe's 15,000 Largest Companies. ELC Publishing, 109 Uxbridge Road, Ealing, London U.K. W5 5TL; email: elc@brg.co.uk. Lists 10,000 leading industrial, trading, insurance, and transportation companies, plus banks, hotels and restaurants, ad agencies, and other enterprises. Includes a ranking of Europe's 500 most profitable and, perhaps just as useful, the 125 least–profitable firms. Updated annually.

Faulkner & Gray's European Business Directory. Thomson Financial, One State Street Plaza, 30th Floor, New York, NY 10004. Lists 2,000 accountants, attorneys, consultants, commercial and investment banks, search firms, translators, and other firms in Europe and the United States engaged or interested in European business. Published annually.

Major Companies of Central and Eastern Europe and the Commonwealth of Independent States. Graham & Whiteside Ltd., available from Gale Group, 27500 Drake Road, Farmington Hills, MI 48331; tel.: (248) 699–4253, (800) 877–4253, www.galegroup.com. Lists 9,500 companies, including firms involved with international trade organizations, chambers of commerce, financial houses, and manufacturers in Eastern Europe and the CIS. $1,145, 1,600 pages. Published annually.

Major Companies of Europe. Graham & Whiteside Ltd., Graham & Whiteside Ltd., available from Gale Group, 27500 Drake Road, Farmington Hills, MI 48331; tel.: (248) 699–4253, (800) 877–4253, www.galegroup.com.. Lists 10,000 top firms and 190,000 key executives, including company name, address, phone numbers, names and titles of key personnel, number of employees, and other information. $295, 1,400 pages. Published annually.

Principal International Business Directory. Dun & Bradstreet Co., Three Sylvan Way, Parsippany, NJ 07054–3896. Presents up–to–date information on about 50,000 leading enterprises in 145 countries throughout the world. Published annually.

Standard & Poor's Register of Corporations, Directors and Executives. Standard & Poor's, 55 Water Street, New York, NY 10041–0003; www.cusip.com. Listings of manufacturers by special product and leading trade and brand names, as well as an alphabetical listing with addresses, information about branch offices, subsidiaries, and estimated capitalization. Updated annually.

Who Owns Whom: Continental Europe. Dun & Bradstreet Ltd., 50–100 Holmers Farm Way, High Wycombe, Buckinghamshire U.K. HP12 4UL; email: customerhelp@dnb.com. Available in the U.S. from Dun & Bradstreet Information Services, Three Sylvan Way, Parsippany, NJ 07054. Provides information on 202,000 parent companies and 513,000 domestic and foreign subsidiaries and affiliates for Western European nations. Updated annually.

General Business Publications

Hoover's Handbook of American Business. Hoover's Inc., 5800 Airport Blvd., Austin, TX 78752; www.hoovers.com. Profiles 750 of America's largest and most influential companies. Also includes lists on various themes such as the 20 largest airline companies in the world, 20 largest ad agencies in the U.S., and so on. $195, 1,752 pages, published each December.

Hoover's Handbook of World Business. Hoover's Inc., 5800 Airport Blvd., Austin, TX 78752; www.hoovers.com. Profiles 300 of the most influential companies based outside the U.S., many of which own venerable U.S. businesses. $165, 724 pages, published each January.

How to Find Information About Companies. Washington, DC: Washington Researchers Publishing. An excellent guide to sources; deals with federal government agencies that provide information, including organizations in both the legislative and executive branches, as well as non–governmental sources. Among government organizations cited are: the International Development Corporation Administration, the International Trade Commission, and the Department of Commerce. Non–government sources include trade and professional associations and unions, business databases, job–search services, and investigative services. $395 per volume.

Top 25 Companies in Europe

(2001, ranked by *Fortune* magazine)

European Ranking	Global Ranking	Company
1	5	DaimlerChrysler (Germany)
2	6	Royal Dutch/Shell Group (U.K./Netherlands)
3	7	BP (Britain)
4	14	TotalFinaElf (France)
5	17	AXA (France)
6	21	Volkswagen (Germany)
7	23	Siemens (Germany)
8	24	ING Group (Netherlands)
9	25	Allianz (Germany)
10	27	E.ON (Germany)

11	29	Deutsche Bank (Germany)
12	35	CGNU (Britain)
13	37	Carrefour (France)
14	38	Credit Suisse (Switzerland)
15	42	BNP Paribas (France)
16	46	Assicurazioni Generali (Italy)
17	47	Fiat (Italy)
18	57	HSBC Holdings (Britain)
19	58	Koninklijke Ahold (Netherlands)
20	59	Nestlé (Switzerland)
21	63	UBS (Switzerland)
22	69	ENI (Italy)
23	72	Unilever (Britain/Netherlands)
24	73	Fortis (Belgium/Netherlands)
25	74	ABN AMRO Holding (Netherlands)

International Trade

People who work in international trade can be employed by a variety of organizations. The U.S. federal government is a major employer in this field, and American state and local governments are also increasingly looking for experts in international trade. International organizations, such as the International Monetary Fund and the U.N., also hire for trade positions. You can find employment in the private sector with chambers of commerce or companies that specialize in import–export.

You will probably need a graduate degree to enter this field. Many people in international trade have a doctorate or master's degree in international affairs, economics, or public policy, although MBAs are becoming increasingly common. There are also opportunities for attorneys to work with companies and government agencies on trade laws and restrictions.

Some of the skills necessary to be successful in international trade include:

☑ Strong writing and research skills

☑ A solid background in international business and economics

☑ Fluency in a second language

☑ Detailed knowledge of a particular world region

☑ Strong leadership skills

Some of the best places to get work experience in international trade are with commodity trading companies, lobbyists with Capitol Hill offices, trade associations, consulting firms, and federal government agencies that deal with trade, such as the Department of Commerce. The Federation of International Trade Associations (www.fita.org) is a good place to learn more about careers in international trade.

Jobs in international trade are actually advertised in newspaper classifieds. The Thursday employment section of *The Wall Street Journal* is a good place to look for ads, as are the *International Herald Tribune*, the Sunday *New York Times*, and *International Opportunities Newsletter. The Economist* may have a few international trade position listings, and it also provides excellent coverage and analysis of international trade.

For leads on international trade openings, it is also worthwhile to write to these chambers of commerce:

International Chamber of Commerce
38 Cours Albert 1
F–75008 Paris, France
Tel.: [33] 49 53 28 28
Fax: [33] 49 53 28 262
www.iccwbo.org

U.S. Chamber of Commerce
1615 H Street NW
Washington, DC 20062
Tel.: (202) 659–6000
email: custsvc@uschamber.com
www.uschamber.org

The U.S. Department of Commerce is an important center for information about international trade in general and U.S. international trade in particular. From the website, you can access a global listing of trade events, international market research, and practical tools to help with every step of the export process. Some of the other resources available from the Department of Commerce are:

◆ *World Traders Data Reports.* Describes company financial references, activities, reputation, primary area of operation, date established, number of employees, and general profiles. Written by U.S. Commercial Service attaches abroad

◆ *Country Desk Offices.* Specific country files on U.S. and foreign businesses.

◆ *Export Counseling Service.* Coordinates information and consults with new export businesses through nationwide district offices, helping direct representation and sales to foreign government tenders.

◆ *Foreign Commercial Service.* Assists U.S. corporations through export promotions, market research, counseling, and liaison with foreign business leaders and government officials.

◆ *Trade Operations Program.* Specifies products, countries of interest, and opportunities through Foreign Service updates.

You can request U.S. import and export statistics from the U.S. Department of Commerce, International Trade Administration, 1401 Constitution Avenue, NW, Washington, DC 20230, tel.: (202) 482–2000, fax: (202) 482–2741; www.ita.doc.gov.

International Banking and Finance

Banking and finance have long been at the center of the international job market. Recent issues in the world of finance — the Latin American debt crisis, the Asian financial crisis, the trend of institutional mergers and acquisitions, the rise of technology, the introduction of the Euro — are reshaping the industry and its career opportunities. The good news is that most experts predict that career opportunities will continue for people with wide–ranging backgrounds in economics, politics, business, foreign languages, and international experience.

The kind of work you do in this field depends on whether you work for a commercial or investment bank. Although the distinction between the two forms of banks is sometimes blurry, commercial banks can be described broadly as being in the business of lending, while investment banks provide specialized services, such as deal–structuring assistance for mergers and acquisitions. In government and semi–public financial institutions, there is also a need for talented people who understand the complexities of the global financial markets and can analyze private–sector investment activities.

An MBA is not necessary to be considered by international businesses, but basic business knowledge is essential. Some of the skills necessary to build a career in international banking include:

☑ Strong accounting skills and experience.

☑ A thorough understanding of economics and finance.

☑ Substantial prior work experience.

☑ A familiarity with a foreign language, although most banks will not expect that you be fluent.

For more information about careers in international banking, see the Institute for International Banking (www.iib.org).

Many U.S. banks hire foreign nationals for their overseas subsidiaries, making it somewhat easier for a U.S. citizen to find a first job in the U.S. than abroad. Most international assignments are reserved for more senior positions, although good training and several successful domestic assignments might get you transferred abroad. You may find that the odds of going abroad are better if you first work for an international bank in the U.S. This is because international banks frequently have less structured recruitment policies.

Regardless of the specific area you want to work in, it is important to look at the needs of individual banks. Your prospects will be considerably enhanced if you can communicate how the combination of your language proficiency, international affairs knowledge, and business experience can directly contribute to a bank's specific growth objectives.

Selected Employers in International Banking and Finance

Bank of America
Bank of America Corporate Center
100 N. Tryon St.
Charlotte, NC 28255
Tel.: (800) 299–2265
Fax: (704) 386–6699
www.bankofamerica.com

Bear Stearns
383 Madison Avenue
New York, NY 10179
Tel.: (212) 272–2000
Fax: (212) 272–4785

www.bearstearns.com

Citigroup
399 Park Avenue
New York, NY 10043
Tel.: (212) 559–1000
Fax: (212) 793–3946
www.citigroup.com

Crédit Suisse First Boston
11 Madison Avenue
New York, NY 10010
Tel.: (212) 325–2000
Fax: (212) 538–3395

www.csfb.com

Goldman Sachs Group
85 Broad Street
New York, NY 10004
Tel.: (212) 902–1000
Fax: (212) 902–3000
www.gs.com

JPMorgan Chase
270 Park Avenue
New York, NY 10017–2070
Tel.: 212–270–6000
www.jpmorganchase.com

MBNA Corporation
1100 N. King Street
Wilmington, DE 19884–0131 ·

Tel.: (302)–453–9920
Fax: (302) 432–3614
www.mbnainternational.com

Merrill Lynch
4 World Financial Center
250 Vesey Street
New York, NY 10080
Tel.: (212) 449–1000
www.merrilllynch.com

Morgan Stanley
1585 Broadway
New York, NY 10036
Tel.: (212) 761–4000
Fax: (212) 762–0575
www.morganstanley.com

International Economics

International economists work in many fields: banking, finance, business, consulting, development, government, and trade. They also work in the related areas of security policy, human rights, and media. Most economists with an international specialization find positions in either private–sector finance or business. In the private sector, specialties for international economists include economic analysis, corporate profitability, securities, sales and trading, professional banking, community banking, and auditing. An advanced degree, such as a Ph.D., is usually required to find work in this field. You can increase your odds of getting a job by complementing your studies in economics with a specialty in accounting, finance, trade, development, or policy analysis.

Selected Employers of Economists

Agency for International Development (A.I.D.)
Ronald Reagan Building
1300 Pennsylvania Avenue NW
Washington, DC 20523–2700
Tel.: (202) 712–4810
Fax: (202) 216–3524
www.usaid.gov

Central Intelligence Agency (CIA)
Office of Public Affairs
Washington, DC 20505
Tel.: (703) 482–1739
Fax: (703) 482–1739
www.cia.gov

International Finance Corporation
2121 Pennsylvania Avenue NW
Washington, DC 20433
Tel.: (202) 473–7711

Fax: (202) 974–4384
www.ifc.org

International Monetary Fund (I.M.F)
700 19th Street NW
Washington, DC 20431
Tel.: (202) 623–7000
Fax: (202) 623–4661
Email: recruit@imf.org
www.imf.org

Office of Economic Cooperation and Development (O.E.C.D.)
OECD Washington Center
2001 L Street NW, Suite 650
Washington, DC 20036–4922
Tel.: (202) 785–6323
Fax: (202) 785–0350
www.oecdwash.org

Overseas Private Investment Corporation (O.P.I.C.)
1100 New York Avenue NW
Washington, DC 20527
Tel.: (202) 336–8400
Fax: (202) 408–9859
www.opic.gov

United Nations
Recruitment Programs Sections
Office of Personnel Services
1st Avenue & 46th Street
New York, NY 10017
www.un.org

U.S. Department of Commerce
Bureau of Economic Analysis
1441 L Street NW
Washington, DC 20230
Tel.: (202) 606 9900
www.bea.doc.gov

U.S. Department of Commerce
International Trade Administration
1401 Constitution Avenue NW
Washington, DC 20230
Tel.: (202) 482–2000
Fax: (202) 482–2741
www.ita.doc.gov

U.S. Department of Energy
Office of the Assistant Secretary
for International Affairs and
Energy Emergencies
Forrestal Building
1000 Independence Avenue SW
Washington, DC 20585
Tel.: (800) 342–5363
Fax: (202) 586–4403

www.energy.gov

U.S. Department of Labor
Bureau of International Labor Affairs
Frances Perkins Building
200 Constitution Avenue
Washington, DC 20210
Tel.: (866) 487–2365
www.dol.gov

U.S. Department of State
Bureau of Economic and
Business Affairs
2201 C Street NW
Washington, DC 20520
Tel.: (202) 647–4000
www.state.gov

U.S. Department of the Treasury
1500 Pennsylvania Avenue NW
Washington, DC 20220
Tel.: (202) 622–2000
Fax: (202) 622–6415
www.ustreas.gov

U.S. International Trade Commission
500 E Street SW
Washington, DC 20436
Tel.: (202) 205–2000
www.usitc.gov

World Bank
Career Information Center
1818 H Street NW
Washington, DC 20433
Tel.: (202) 473–1000
Fax: (202) 477–6391
www.worldbank.org

International Consulting

Consultants help companies solve a wide variety of business problems. Depending on the size and the firm's strategy, consulting activities can include researching a new market, designing and coding a large manufacturing control system, providing outplacement services, or assisting an organization in totally rethinking its strategy.

Consulting firms have diverse origins, outlooks, and focuses. Some of the leading firms began in accounting and expanded to meet the demand for management consulting services. Others were founded specifically for management or more technical consulting. Although a few firms boast several hundred employees worldwide and recruit intensively, many are small operations that emphasize the experience and high–level skills of their leaner staffs.

If you work as a consultant, your ability to work abroad will depend on the type of clients who hire the firm's services. You may not be relocated to an international office, but you may find yourself working with a foreign client and spending extended periods abroad while completing a project.

Management consulting firms, the type of consulting with which most people are familiar, can be categorized on the basis of their business focus:

☑ *Pure Strategy.* Provides overall corporate direction; hired directly by CEOs. Usually small, prestigious firms that hire MBAs.

☑ *Traditional.* Strategic but area–specific consulting, such as finance. More diversified than pure strategy consulting firms.

☑ *Accountancy.* Strong in information technology work; the fastest–growing type of management consulting firm.

☑ *Human resources.* Personnel management, including pay structures and pension plans; most political branch.

☑ *Specialists.* Area experts, such as information technology or data processing. Usually small firms.

There are opportunities to work as a consultant without a graduate degree. But since this is a field in which your marketable commodity is your knowledge, you will likely find that you have more opportunities if you complete an advanced degree. An MBA is most common, but consultants also hold graduate degrees in technical fields, or even in the humanities and social sciences.

Some of the skills necessary for finding work as a consultant include:

☑ An ability to quickly understand business situations

☑ An ability to systematically analyze problems

☑ Good skills in managing client–relations

☑ Common sense

☑ Communication skills

☑ Initiative and creativity

☑ Independent thinking

Technical expertise may not be required, especially if you are just starting out. Many consulting firms are known for their rigorous training programs. A specialization in an area such as MIS may be a ticket to help you get your foot in the door.

Selected International Consulting Employers

Accenture
161 North Clark Street
Chicago, IL 60601
Tel.: (312) 693–0161

www.accenture.com

Systems and consulting services, involving planning, design, and installation of information systems for management planning and control.

Bain and Co.
2 Copley Place
Boston, MA 02116
Tel.: (617) 572–2000
Fax: (617) 572–2427
www.bain.com
Consulting in business unit, organizational, and corporate strategy; distribution and logistics; mergers, acquisitions, and divestiture; sales and marketing strategy.

BearingPoint
1676 International Drive
McLean, VA 22102
Tel.: (703) 747–3000
Fax: (703) 747–8500
www.bearingpoint.com
Provides services in communications and content, consumer and industrial markets, financial services, high tech, and the public sector (formerly KPMG Consulting).

Booz, Allen, and Hamilton
8283 Greensboro Drive
McLean, VA 22102
Tel.: (703) 902–5000
Fax: (703) 902–3333
www.bah.com
The technology business unit covers such areas as defense and national security, the environment, transportation, and space. The commercial unit includes consumer and engineered products; communications, media, and technology; energy; and financial services.

Boston Consulting Group
Exchange Place, 31st Floor
Boston, MA 02109
Tel.: (617) 973–1200
Fax: (617) 973–1399
www.bcg.com
Best known for long–range strategic business planning. The firm specializes in industries including consumer goods, financial services, and telecommunications.

Cap Gemini Ernst & Young
5 Times Square
New York, NY 10036
Tel.: (212) 768–2066
www.us.cgey.com
The subsidiary of the French consultancy Cap Gemini offers management and IT consulting services, systems integration, technology development design, and outsourcing services.

Deloitte Consulting
1633 Broadway, 35th Floor
New York, NY 10019–6754
Tel.: (203) 492–4500
Fax: (203) 492–4743
www.dc.com
Areas of expertise include IT services, strategy and financial management, outsourcing, process, application integration, and human resources.

Hewitt Associates
100 Half Day Road
Lincolnshire, IL 60069–3342
Tel.: (847) 295–5000
Fax: (847) 295–7634
www.hewitt.com
Provides a variety of HR–related services, including organizational change management, talent and reward consulting, and benefits outsourcing.

A.T. Kearney
5400 Legacy Drive
Plano, TX 75201
Tel.: (972) 604–4600
Fax: (972) 543–7680
www.atkearney.com
Provides consulting on strategic analysis, operations and organization, and information technology. It also offers executive search services and publishes strategic briefings and white papers.

McKinsey and Co.
55 East 52nd Street
New York, NY 10022
Tel.: (212) 446–7000
Fax: (212) 446–8575
www.mckinsey.com
One of the world's top management consulting firms. Provides a full spectrum of consulting services (finance,

technology management, strategy), primarily to private companies.

Towers Perrin
One Stamford Plaza
263 Tresser Blvd
Stamford, CT 06901
Tel.: (203) 326–5400
Fax: (203) 326–5499
www.towers.com
Core focus is on human resources consulting.

Watson Wyatt
1717 H Street NW
Washington, DC 20006–3900
Tel.: (202) 715–7000
Fax: (202) 715–7700
www.watsonwyatt.com
One of the largest human resources consulting firms. Offers expertise in actuarial and benefits services, retirement consulting, and employee compensation and retention.

International Law

International law practice describes a scope of work rather than a specific kind of work. A career in international law involves practicing domestic or local law for foreign clients or counseling domestic clients on the legal aspects of transactions under the laws of a foreign territory. Most international lawyers work on domestic matters 90 percent of the time and on international matters just 10 percent of the time. Lawyers who practice internationally are expected to be familiar with business, trade, and corporate law, as well as the civil law system (which prevails in many European countries) and how it may conflict with the common law system (which prevails in the U.K. and the United States).

You can find many international lawyers working for the federal government. The departments of Justice, State, Commerce, and Labor, the Federal Trade and Federal Communications commissions, and the Office of U.S. Trade Representation in particular hire attorneys to work on international matters. Private firms hire attorneys to practice domestic law — securities, tax, real estate — or regulatory law — customs, food & drug, anti–boycott — for foreign clients. Corporations will hire in–house counsel to manage international business transactions.

Employers invariably cite excellent undergraduate and law school academic records as the primary hiring criteria. Other criteria for a career in international law include:

- ☑ Academic achievement
- ☑ Strong business skills
- ☑ Fluency in a foreign language (especially Spanish, French, and Japanese)
- ☑ Knowledge of international economics
- ☑ International work or study experience
- ☑ Sensitivity to other cultures

Few, if any, firms specifically hire international lawyers straight out of law school. A few years of successful domestic legal practice are normally required before a lawyer gets an international case. Individuals with international academic or employment backgrounds, however, do possess a competitive edge. They have a record of grades or other performance measures that give an employer confidence that the prospective lawyer has international business skills and knowledge of world affairs that would be an asset to the firm. Specialization in a particular area (such as Great Britain, the E.U., or Germany) might be helpful.

Large firms tend to dominate international law practice in the U.S. The geographic location of a firm often influences its practice: New York City and Chicago for international business; Washington, D.C., for international public affairs; San Francisco for the Pacific Rim; Houston for Latin America; and Miami for international financing. Some firms also maintain offices abroad, but that does not always mean that most attorneys in those firms practice internationally. In recent years, medium–sized firms have also begun to enter the international law market.

When you apply to law school, remember that international law is not actually a field of law, such as tax or environmental law, but merely a term that describes the practice of various types of law across national boundaries, not always involving travel. For more information on careers in international law, check out the American Bar Association (www.abanet.org); the Association of Student International Law Societies (www.asil.org); or the International Law Society of America (www.isil.org).

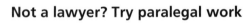

Not a lawyer? Try paralegal work

People with an interest in international law often find positions as legal assistants or paralegals within law firms that have large international practices. Working as a paralegal offers a number of benefits. It gives you the chance to view how a law office works from the inside. Also, you develop a valuable skill that can be highly sought after and well–paid. Paralegals work in the same locale as lawyers, do similar work, and can derive immense pleasure from their jobs. This can also be excellent work if you are thinking about seeking a law degree. Law firms in Europe, especially American firms, will sometimes consider hiring new college graduates as paralegals through programs such as the Association for International Practical Training's Americans Abroad program (see Chapter 9 for more details).

Selected Law Firms that Specialize in International Practice

Baker & McKenzie
One Prudential Plaza
130 East Randolph Drive
Chicago, IL 60601
Tel.: (312) 861–8000

www.bakerinfo.com

Covington and Burling
1201 Pennsylvania Avenue NW
Washington, DC 20004
Tel.: (202) 662–6000

Fax: (202) 662–6291
www.cov.com

Gibson, Dunn, and Crutcher
333 South Grand Avenue
Los Angeles, CA 90071–3197
Tel.: (213) 229–7000
Fax: (213) 229–7520
www.gdclaw.com

Jones, Day, Reavis & Pogue
222 East 41st Street
New York, NY 10017–6702
Tel: 212.326.3939
Fax: 212.755.7306
www.jonesday.com

Mayer, Brown & Platt
190 South LaSalle Street
Chicago, IL 60603
Tel.: (312) 782–0600
Fax: (312) 701–7711
www.mayerbrown.com

Sidley Austin Brown & Wood
1501 K Street, N.W.
Washington, D.C. 20005

Tel.: (202) 736–8000
Fax: (202) 736–8711
www.sidley.com

Skadden, Arps, Slate, Meagher & Flom
Four Times Square
New York, NY 10036
Tel.: (212) 735 3000
Fax: (212) 735 2000
www.skadden.com

Weil, Gotshal & Manges
767 Fifth Avenue
New York, NY 10153
Tel.: (212) 310–8000
Fax: (212) 310–8007
www.weil.com

White & Case
1155 Avenue of the Americas
New York, NY 10036–2787
Tel.: (212) 819–8200
Fax: (212) 354–8113
www.whitecase.com

International Media and Journalism

International journalism is very competitive. The largest employers of foreign correspondents are the wire services. The Associated Press, for example, has 200 reporters stationed around the world. *The New York Times* has the largest overseas staff of any newspaper by far, with more than 100 correspondents. *The Los Angeles Times, The Wall Street Journal, The Washington Post, Time* magazine, and *Newsweek* also have large overseas staffs. Other large metropolitan papers maintain overseas staffs of ten to 50. International publications, such as the *International Herald Tribune*, owned by *the* and *The New York Times*, and the *Christian Science Monitor*, employ many Americans abroad.

If you are hired by a wire service, you will probably be assigned first to a smaller office in the U.S. If you are good and make your interest in foreign reporting known, you may eventually be transferred to the foreign desk in New York, and then, with luck, overseas. Experienced, senior personnel are likely to occupy the desirable European capital bureaus. Another approach would be to work for an English–language paper overseas. They often need native English speakers as writers and editors.

Newspapers and magazines are less hierarchical than the large wire services, but you still must work up to the foreign jobs from within the organiza-

Fellowships for Journalists

In an increasingly interdependent world, many organizations believe it is important that journalists gain a strong global understanding. Organizations long associated with programs for academic researchers, such as the Fulbright Commission, also offer special programs for journalists to spend a brief period of time abroad, with the aim of deepening the journalist's global outlook. For more information on special programs for journalists, contact the following:

Fulbright Scholarships for Journalists
The Council for International Exchange of Scholars
3007 Tilden Street NW, Suite 5–L
Washington, DC 20008
Tel.: (202) 686–7877
Email: apprequest@cies.iie.org
www.cies.org

CDS International
The Robert Bosch Foundation Fellowship Program
871 United Nations Plaza, 15th Floor
New York, NY 10017–1814
Tel.: (212) 497–3500
Fax: (212) 497–3535
www.cdsintl.org

American Council on Germany
14 East 60th Street, Suite 606
New York, NY 10022
Tel.: (212) 826–3636
www.acgusa.org

tion. You may find that freelancing for several newspapers can give you the freedom to live overseas while you build your journalism career.

Whether you need a graduate degree to be a journalist is hotly debated. Many editors consider a journalism degree too narrow. They claim to prefer candidates who have a broad liberal arts background and possess wide knowledge of politics, history, and international affairs. Other editors claim that journalism school provides professional training essential for success in the field.

Some of the skills that all editors agree are important for the field include:

- ☑ Good writing, editing, and reporting skills
- ☑ Fluency in more than one language is helpful
- ☑ Substantial work experience
- ☑ A nose for a good story

For more information about careers in international broadcasting and media, check out the Society of Professional Journalists (www.spj.org).

Selected International Communications Employers

Broadcasting

American Broadcasting Company
77 West 66th Street
New York, NY 10023
Tel.: (212) 456–7777
Fax: (212) 456–1424
http://abc.go.com

AOL Time Warner
Time and Life Building
75 Rockefeller Plaza
New York, NY 10019
Tel.: (212) 484–8000
Fax: (212) 489–6183
www.aoltimewarner.com

Cable News Network (CNN)
Turner Broadcasting System Inc.
100 International Boulevard
One CNN Center
Atlanta, GA 30303
Tel.: (404) 827–1500
Fax: (404) 827–2437
www.cnn.com

CBS Television Network
51 West 52nd Street
New York, NY 10019
Tel.: (212) 975–4321
Fax: (212) 875–4516
www.cbs.com

MTV Networks
1515 Broadway
New York, NY 10036
Tel.: (212) 258–8000
www.mtv.com

National Broadcasting Company (NBC)
30 Rockefeller Plaza
New York, NY 10112
Tel.: (212) 664–4444
Fax: (212) 664–4085
www.nbc.com

Magazines

Business Week
1221 Avenue of the Americas
43rd Floor
New York, NY 10020
Tel.: (212) 512–2511
www.businessweek.com

The Economist
The Economist Building
111 West 57th Street
New York, NY 10019
Tel.: (212) 541–5730
www.economist.com

***Forbes*, Inc.**
60 Fifth Avenue
New York, NY 10011
Tel.: (212) 620–2200
Fax: (212) 620–2245
www.forbes.com

***Foreign Affairs* Magazine**
58 East 68th Street
New York, NY 10021
Tel.: (212) 734–0400

***Fortune* Magazine**
Time and Life Building
Rockefeller Center
New York, NY 10020
Tel.: (212) 522–1212
www.fortune.com

National Geographic Society
1145 17th Street NW
Washington, DC 20036–4688
Tel.: (202) 857–7000
Fax: (202) 775–6141
www.nationalgeographic.com

Motion Pictures/TV Production

Fox Filmed Entertainment
10201 West Pico Blvd.
Los Angeles, CA 90035
Tel.: (310) 277–2211
Fax: (310) 203–1558
www.foxmovies.com

Lucasfilm
P.O. Box 2009
San Rafael, CA 94912
Tel.: (415) 662–1800

Fax: (415) 662–2437
www.lucasfilm.com

Metro–Goldwyn–Mayer
2500 Broadway Street
Santa Monica, CA 90404
Tel.: (310) 449–3000
Fax: (310) 449–8857
www.mgm.com

Warner Brothers
1325 Avenue of the Americas
New York, NY 10019
Tel.: (212) 636–5000
Fax (212) 397–4736
www.warnerbros.com

Newspapers

Christian Science Monitor
One Norway Street
Boston, MA 02115
Tel.: (617) 450–2026
Fax: (617) 450–2031
www.csmonistor.com

Financial Times
One Southwark Bridge
London SE1 9HL, U.K.
Tel.: [44] 20 7873 3000
Fax: [44] 20 7873 3076
www.pearson.com/aboutus/ft/index.htm

Gannett Company
7950 Jones Branch Drive
McLean, VA 22107
Tel.: (703) 854–6000
Fax: (703) 854–2046
www.gannett.com

Hearst Corporation
959 Eighth Avenue
New York, NY 10019
Tel.: (212) 649–2000
Fax: (212) 765–3528
www.hearstcorp.com

International Herald Tribune
6 bis, rue des Graviers
F–92521 Neuilly Cedex, France
Tel.: [33] 141 43 93 00
Fax: [33] 141 43 93 38
www.iht.com

Knight–Ridder
50 W. San Fernando St.

San Jose, CA 95113
Tel.: (408) 938–7700
Fax: (408) 938–7755
www.kri.com

The New York Times
229 West 43rd Street
New York, NY 10036
Tel.: (212) 556–1234
Fax: (212) 556–7389
www.nytimes.com

The Wall Street Journal
Dow Jones and Co.
200 Liberty Street
New York, NY 10281
Tel.: (212) 416–2000
Fax: (212) 416–4348
www.dj.com

The Washington Post
1150 Fifteenth St. NW
Washington, DC 20071
Tel.: (202) 334–6000
Fax: (202) 334–4536
www.washpostco.com

News Services

The Associated Press
50 Rockefeller Plaza
New York, NY 10020
Tel.: (212) 621–1500
Fax: (212) 621–5447
www.ap.org

Foreign Press Association
11 Carleton House Terrace
London SW1Y 5AJ, U.K.
Tel.: [44] 20 7 930 0445
Fax: [44] 20 7 925 0469
www.foreign–press.org.uk

Reuters
85 Fleet Street
London EC4P 4AJ, U.K.
Tel.: [44] 20 7250 1122
Fax: [44] 20 7542 4064
www.reuters.com

United Press International
1510 H Street NW
Washington, DC 20005
Tel.: (202) 898–8000
Fax: (202) 898–8057
www.upi.com

International Nonprofits

Nonprofit organizations offer a wide array of opportunities for the professional in international affairs. Many people are attracted to a chance to contribute to socially relevant work. The opportunities range from analyst positions in think tanks to managerial positions in issue–specific nonprofits. Nonprofits are among the largest industries in the U.S., employing an estimated one–eighth of all professionals.

International nonprofit organizations can be loosely distinguished by their primary activity: whether they lobby government or provide direct services. It is probably more useful, however, to categorize nonprofits according to their mission or constituency, which may include the following: arts management; children and youth; faith–based work; environment; community organizing; gay, lesbian, and bisexual issues; housing and homelessness; labor; peace and conflict resolution; international relief; public policy research; public health; social work; and technology; to name only a few!

If you decide that you want to work in the nonprofit field, your first task is to decide the issues on which you want to focus. Your second task is to decide what kind of work you wish to do: fundraising, research, program planning, etc. A graduate degree related to your special area of interest, such as urban planning, may help with finding work with an international nonprofit, but it is not required. Instead, employers hiring for the nonprofit sector will expect that you have a specialized skill such as teaching, engineering, or fundraising.

Other criteria that employers typically look for includes:

☑ A passion for the issues that the nonprofit agency addresses

☑ Flexibility

☑ Ability to multi–task

☑ An appreciation of the unique culture of a nonprofit

A good resource for information on international careers with nonprofit organizations is Idealist (www.idealist.org). *International Career Employment Weekly* (www.internationaljobs.org, see chapter 4 for more details) is also a useful resource for learning more about nonprofit careers.

Selected International Nonprofit Employers

American Council on Germany
14 East 60th Street, Suite 606
New York, NY 10022
Tel.: (212) 826–3636
Fax: (212) 758–3445
www.acgusa.org

**American Enterprise Institute
for Public Policy Research**
International Programs
1150 17th Street NW

Washington, DC 20036
Tel.: (202) 862–5800
Fax: (202) 862–7177
www.aei.org

American Red Cross
431 18th Street NW
Washington, DC 20006
Tel.: (202) 639–3520
www.redcross.org

American–Scandinavian Foundation
58 Park Avenue
New York, NY 10016
Tel.: (212) 879–9779
www.amscan.org

American Society of International Law
2223 Massachusetts Avenue NW
Washington, DC 20008
Tel.: (202) 939–6000
Fax: (202) 797–7133
www.asil.org

Amnesty International of the U.S.A.
322 Eighth Avenue
New York, NY 10001
Tel.: (212) 807–8400
Fax: (212) 627–1451
www.amnesty–usa.org

Atlantic Council of the U.S.
910 17th Street NW, Suite 1000
Washington, DC 20006
Tel.: (202) 463–7241
www.acus.org

Business Council for International Understanding
1212 Avenue of the Americas
10th Floor
New York, NY 10036
Tel. (212) 490–0460
Fax: (212) 697–8526
www.bciu.org

CARE
151 Ellis Street
Atlanta, GA 30303
Tel.: (800) 521–2273
www.care.org

Center for Defense Information
1779 Massachusetts Avenue NW
Washington, DC 20036
Tel.: (202) 332–0600
Fax: (202) 462–4559
www.cdi.org

Committee for Economic Development
2000 L Street NW, Suite 700
Washington, DC 20036
Tel.: (202) 296–5860
Fax: (202) 223–0776
www.ced.org

Council for a Livable World
110 Maryland Avenue NE
Washington, DC 20002
Tel.: (202) 543–4100
www.clw.org

Doctors Without Borders U.S.A.
6 East 39th Street, 8th Floor
New York, NY 10016
Tel.: 800–638–8079
www.dwb.org

Foreign Policy Association
470 Park Avenue South
New York, NY 10016
Tel.: (212) 481–8100
Fax: (212) 481–9275
www.fpa.org

Hudson Institute
1015 18th Street NW, Suite 300
Washington, DC 20036
Tel.: (202) 223–7770
Fax: (202) 223–8537
www.hudson.org

Institute for Policy Studies
733 155th Street NW, Suite 1020
Washington, DC 20005
Tel.: (202) 234–9382
www.ips–dc.org

International Republican Institute
1225 Eye Street, Suite 700
Washington, DC 20005
Tel.: (202) 408–9450
Fax: (202) 408–9462
www.iri.org

National Democratic Institute for International Affairs
2030 M Street NW, 5th Floor
Washington, DC 20036–3306
Tel.: (202) 728–5500
Fax: (202) 728–5520
www.ndi.org

Nature Conservancy International
4245 North Fairfax Drive, Suite 100
Arlington, VA 22203–1606
Tel.: (703) 841–5300
www.tnc.org

Save the Children Federation
54 Wilton Road
Westport, CT 06880

Tel.: (800) 728–3843
www.savethechildren.org

U.S. Committee for UNICEF
Recruitment Programmes Section,
Room 2500
Office of Personnel Services
United Nations
New York, NY 10017
Tel.: (800) 367–5437

www.unicef.org

Women's International League for Peace and Freedom
1213 Race Street
Philadelphia, PA 19107
Tel.: (215) 563–7110
Fax: (215) 563–5527
www.wilpf.org

The U.S. Federal Government

The federal government of the United States is one of the greatest potential employers for individuals interested in working in Europe. Many U.S. government agencies will become involved with business and trade issues, as well as political concerns, in the expanding European Community.

The U.S. government presence in Europe includes the Foreign Service, Commerce Department, trade missions, and security and defense organizations. Finding a position in Washington can be a very good route to eventually transferring abroad. You should realize that most federal employers with international affairs offices aren't necessarily focused exclusively upon Europe, and you may not receive a European assignment.

Foreign–oriented agencies, such as the Central Intelligence Agency or the Department of State, generally conduct their own recruiting processes. Domestic–oriented agencies that are involved with international activities, such as the Department of the Treasury or the Department of Commerce, recruit through the Office of Personnel Management (OPM), which is the human resource office of the federal government. To learn more about applying for federal jobs, contact the Office of Personnel Management, 1900 E Street, NW, Washington, DC 20415–0001, tel.: (202) 606–1800, tel: (478) 757–3000 (Federal Employment Information), www.opm.gov.

Executive Branch Employers
Office of Management and Budget
Executive Office of the President
725 17th Street NW
Washington, DC 20503
Tel.: (202) 395–3080
Fax: (202) 395–3888
www.omb.gov
International Affairs Division includes Trade, Monetary, Investment Policy, Summer Internships.

Office of U.S. Trade Representative
600 17th Street NW
Washington, DC 20508
Tel.: (888) 473–8787

www.ustr.gov

Department of Agriculture
14th Street and Independence Ave SW
Washington, DC 20250
Tel.: (202) 720–2791
www.usda.gov

Department of Commerce
1401 Constitution Avenue NW
Washington, DC 20230
Tel.: (202) 501–0666
www.commerce.gov

Department of Defense
Office of the Assistant Secretary for
Security Affairs
The Pentagon
Washington, DC 20301–1155
www.defenselink.mil

Department of Education
400 Maryland Avenue SW
Washington, DC 20202–0498
Tel.: (800) 872–5327
Fax: (202) 404–0689
www.ed.gov

Department of Energy
1000 Independence Avenue SW
Washington, DC 20585
Tel.: (800) 342–5363
Fax: (202) 586–4403
www.energy.gov

Department of Health and Human Services
200 Independence Avenue SW
Washington, DC 20201
Tel.: (202) 619–0257
www.hhs.gov

Department of Housing and Urban Development
451 Seventh Street SW
Washington, DC 20410
Tel.: (202) 708–1112
www.hud.gov

Department of the Interior
1849 C Street NW
Washington, DC 20240
Tel.: (202) 208–3100
www.doi.gov

Department of Labor
Frances Perkins Building
200 Constitution Avenue NW
Washington, DC 20210
Tel.: (202) 487–2365
www.dol.gov

Department of State
2201 C Street NW
Washington, DC 20520
Tel.: (202) 647–4000
www.state.gov

Department of Transportation
Office of Policy and International Affairs
400 Seventh Street SW
Washington, DC 20590
Tel.: (202) 366–4000
www.dot.gov

Department of the Treasury
Office of the Assistant Secretary for
International Affairs
1500 Pennsylvania Avenue NW
Washington, DC 20220
Tel.: (202) 622–2000
www.treas.gov

The Foreign Service

The Department of State's Foreign Service has its own application procedure, consisting of a number of steps. (Certain specialist positions — for example, security officers, couriers, secretaries, doctors, nurses, summer employment, and internships — do not require this procedure.) The first is a written exam, usually offered in November, that lasts about four hours and includes a test of job–related knowledge, another test of English expression, and a biographic information questionnaire. The knowledge test is fairly wide–ranging and generally includes questions on world geography, the historical antecedents of international affairs, basic economic principles, U.S. history, contemporary cultural trends, and the like. The English expression test assesses one's knowledge of English grammar, punctuation, and spelling. The biographic information questionnaire is designed to compare personal characteristics of applicants with those of successful federal government professionals and administrators. There is no fee for taking the Foreign Service Exam. Registration for the written portion closes in early October. In recent

Department of Homeland Security

The new Department of Homeland Security combines all or parts of 22 existing federal agencies and employs some 170,000 people. It also represents the largest government reorganization since President Harry Truman combined the various military services to create the Department of Defense in 1947. DHS has four divisions, pooling resources from several groups:

- Border and transportation security (U.S. Border Patrol, Customs, Immigration and Naturalization Service, etc.)

- Emergency preparedness and response (Federal Emergency Management Agency)

- Chemical, biological, radiological and nuclear countermeasures

- Information analysis and infrastructure protection (Federal Bureau of Investigation).

What does this development mean for the international job seeker? First, many of the international career opportunities with the federal government will, for the foreseeable future, focus on issues of national security. Second, several of the agencies that will be brought under the new department are hiring a lot of personnel. The state department, border patrol, INS, and the FBI are among the organizations that have high recruiting targets.

As of this writing, the DHS was temporarily located at the Nebraska Avenue Center, a U.S. Navy facility in northwest Washington, D.C. More information can be obtained online as it becomes available at www.dhs.gov.

A good resource is the *Guide to Homeland Security Careers* by Donald Hutton and Anna Mydlarz. Barron's. Available from Planning/Communications — see the "Resource Center" beginning on page 472. Reports on qualifications, application process, strategies and tips, and job descriptions for over 100 career opportunities with this new federal department. $14.95, 264 pages, 2003.

years, the exam has been offered in alternate years.

Roughly 14,000 applicants worldwide take the written exam. Of those, about 3,000 are invited to participate in the next step in the process, the oral assessment. Normally conducted within nine months of the written exam, the oral assessment lasts a full day and consists of the following exercises: (a) a démarche (a role–playing exercise in which the candidate plays the part of a foreign service officer abroad and presents a position statement to two representatives of a foreign government, played by examination assessors), (b) a written report and analysis of the démarche, (c) an essay, (d) an oral exam consisting of three hypothetical questions, one each from three of the Foreign Services six functional fields (administrative, consular, economic, political, information/cultural, and commercial), and (e) a group exercise, structured as a budget meeting, designed to measure oral presentation, negotiating, and teamwork skills.

At the end of the day, participants in the oral assessment are given either a personal interview (if they pass) or an exit interview (otherwise). The personal interview is like a traditional job interview, wherein the assessors review your personal information (application forms and so on) and ask you questions. The number of applicants invited to continue in the process varies yearly, depending on the Foreign Service's hiring needs.

For those who successfully complete the personal interview, there are security and medical clearances to obtain (which can take many months), and then one's name is placed on a register. As positions become available, applicants who are on the register may be given an offer. Candidates remain on the register for 18 months.

Appointees are trained and oriented in Washington for two to 12 months, which is usually followed by a four-year probationary period. Initial assignments are entirely at the discretion of the respective divisions. You may not get an assignment in Europe. Advancement is highly competitive, dependent upon periodic review and evaluation.

For an application and information packet, contact the U.S. Department of State, Office of Recruitment, Examination and Employment, HR/REE, SA–1, 2401 E St, NW, 5H, Washington, D.C. 20522, tel: (202) 261–8888, fax: (202) 261–8841, www.careers.state.gov.

Selected U.S. Government Agencies with International Affairs Divisions

Most of these federal government agencies, like the Department of State, conduct their own recruitment. Employment news is generally available on the agencies websites, or you can contact them directly for information on how to apply for jobs.

Agency for International Development
Ronald Reagan Building
Washington, DC 20523–1000
Tel.: (202) 712–4810
Fax: (202) 216–3524
www.usaid.gov

Central Intelligence Agency
Office of Public Affairs
Washington, DC 20505
Tel.: (703) 482–1739
Fax: (703) 482–1739
www.cia.gov

Congressional Budget Office
Second & D Streets SW
Washington, DC 20515–6925
Tel.: (202) 226–2628
Fax: (202) 225–7539
www.cbo.gov

Customs Service
1300 Pennsylvania Avenue NW
Washington, DC 20229
Tel.: (202) 927–1000
ww.customs.gov

Defense Intelligence Agency
Civilian Staffing Operations Division
200 MacDill Boulevard

Civilian Personnel Division(DAH–2)
Washington, DC 20340–5100
Tel.: (800) 526–4629
www.dia.mil

Drug Enforcement Administration
Office of Personnel
2401 Jefferson Davis Highway
Alexandria, VA 22301
Tel.: (800) DEA 4288
www.usdoj.gov/dea

Environmental Protection Agency
Ariel Rios Building
1200 Pennsylvania Avenue, NW
Washington, DC 20460
Tel.: (202) 260–2090
www.epa.gov

Federal Communications Commission
445 12th Street SW
Washington, DC 20554
Tel.: (888) 225–5322
www.fcc.gov

Federal Maritime Commission
800 North Capitol Street NW
Washington, DC 20573
Tel.: (202) 523–5773
www.fmc.gov

Federal Reserve System
20th Street & Constitution Avenue NW
Washington, DC 20551
Tel.: (202) 452–3000
Tel.: (800) 448–4894 (24–hour jobline)
www.federalreserve.gov

Federal Trade Commission
Sixth Street & Pennsylvania Ave. NW
Washington, DC 20580
Tel.: (202) 326–2222
www.ftc.gov

General Accounting Office
441 G Street NW
Washington, DC 20548
Tel.: (202) 512–4800

www.gao.gov

House International Relations Committee
2170 Rayburn House Office Building
Washington, DC 20515
Tel.: (202) 225–5021
www.house.gov/international_relations

Immigration and Naturalization Service
425 I Street NW
Washington, DC 20536
Tel.: (800) 375–5283
www.ins.usdoj.gov

International Trade Commission
500 E Street SW
Washington, DC 20436
Tel.: (202) 205–2000
www.usitc.gov

National Aeronautics and Space Administration
300 E Street SW
Washington, DC 20546
Tel.: (202) 358–0000
www.nasa.gov

Securities and Exchange Commission
450 Fifth Street NW
Washington, DC 20549
Tel.: (202) 942–7040
www.sec.gov

Senate Foreign Relations Committee
Majority Office
Washington, DC 20510
Tel.: (202) 224–4651
http://foreign.senate.gov

Smithsonian Institution
Main Office of Human Resources
P.O. Box 50638
Washington, DC 20091
Tel.: (202) 275–1102
Jobline: (202) 287–3102
www.si.edu

International Teaching

Positions for American teachers can be found throughout Europe, and the demand remains constant. Small class sizes, historical settings, and diverse student populations — often multinational and multilingual — all provide for an intimate, stimulating, and rewarding teaching experience.

The biggest employers of teachers at the pre–university level in Europe are American–sponsored schools, international schools, and Department of Defense Dependents' Schools. American–sponsored schools are private schools that accept American and multinational students and are founded by American citizens but not controlled by the U.S. government. International schools are independent but usually feature an American– or British-inspired curriculum. Department of Defense Dependents' Schools are for the children of military and civilian employees working at overseas bases or other government facilities.

Fulbright Teaching Exchanges

Sponsored by the U.S. Department of State, the Fulbright Teacher and Administrator Exchange Program arranges direct one–to–one exchanges. In most cases, both teachers secure a leave of absence with pay from their home institutions and then trade classrooms for the school year. The program is open to educators from K–12 schools, two–year colleges, and four–year colleges.

The European countries participating in this exchange include: Bulgaria, Czech Republic, Finland, France, Germany, Greece, Hungary, Ireland, Italy, Norway, Poland, Romania, Slovakia, Spain, Turkey, and the U.K.

To be eligible, you must be a U.S. citizen, fluent in English, in your third year of teaching, and in a full–time position. In addition to the general eligibility requirements, you must also meet country–specific subject, level, and language requirements detailed in the application. There is no age limit. Educators with families are encouraged to apply and bring their families along.

For an application, contact the:
Fulbright Teacher Exchange Program
Attention: FCS
600 Maryland Ave. SW, Suite 320
Washington, DC 20024–2520
Tel.: (800) 726–0479
Fax: (202) 479–6806
Email: fulbright@grad.usda.gov
www.fulbrightexchanges.org

To teach at the elementary and secondary levels, most overseas schools require:

- ✓ A bachelor's degree
- ✓ A teacher certification
- ✓ At least two years of teaching experience.

Positions at most schools are filled months before the school year begins, so you should apply well ahead of time.

The Department of State maintains information on American–sponsored schools around the world, including fact sheets on the schools, as well as other information resources for teaching abroad. This information is accessible on-line at www.state.gov/m/a/os.

For information on international schools, see *The ISS Directory of Over-seas Schools*, compiled by International Schools Services Inc. The directory does not include schools sponsored by the Department of Defense, but it is a good resource for other international schools all over the world. Although the directory is aimed primarily at the prospective student, an address is included for each school, so you can write individual schools for more information. ISS also helps teachers find positions overseas, with annual recruitment fairs and monthly newsletters. The New Perspectives program places applicants who are certified but lack experience. If you use ISS facilities, you must pay an initial fee as well as a secondary fee if you are placed in a job. For information, contact International Schools Services, Educational Staffing, 15 Roszel Road, P.O. Box 5910, Princeton, NJ 08543, tel.: (609) 452–0990, fax: (609) 452–2690, email: iss@iss.edu, www.iss.edu.

Another useful directory for finding independent schools abroad is the *Schools Abroad of Interest to Americans* (2001, Porter Sargent Publications, 11 Beacon Street, Suite 140, Boston, MA 02108–3099; email: info@portersarget.com). The directory lists 650 elementary and secondary schools in 125 countries.

For specific job leads, the following publications can be helpful:

The International Educator
International Educators Institute
P.O. Box 513
Cummaquid, MA 02637
Tel.: (508) 362–1414
Fax: (508) 362–1411
email: tie@tieonline.com
www.tieonline.com

The Times Educational Supplement
TES Subscriptions
Tower House
Sovereign Park
Lathkill Street
Market Harborough LE19 9EF, U.K.
Tel.: [44] 1858 438805
www.tes.co.uk

Friends of World Teaching
P.O. Box 1049
San Diego, CA 92112–1049
Tel.: 800–503–7436
Fax 619–224–5363

email: director@fowt.com
www.fowt.com
Offers listings of English–language K–12 schools in over 100 countries. For $20, you receive school listings for three countries.

The International Employment Hotline
1088 Middle River Road
Stanardsville, VA 22973
Although not geared exclusively toward educators, it does list teaching and other education–related positions abroad and also provides information on upcoming recruitment fairs.

Transitions Abroad magazine
18 Hulst Road
P.O. Box 1300
Amherst, MA 01004

Another good resource on international teaching. Provides both general information and listings of program opportunities in specific countries when available.

The following organizations also sponsor international recruitment fairs:

Search Associates

P.O. Box 636

Dallas, PA 18612

Tel.: (570) 696–4600

Fax: (570) 696–9500

www.search–associates.com

To qualify as a Search Associate's regular teaching candidate, you should have a minimum of two years of recent, full-time teaching experience in a recognized K–12 program. There are some job fairs conducted by Search Associates through which candidates with less than two years experience are routinely placed.

University of Northern Iowa

Overseas Placement Service for Educators

SSC #19

Cedar Falls, IA 50614–0390

Tel.: (319) 273–2083

Fax: (319) 273–6998

Email: overseas.placement@uni.edu

www.uni.edu/placement/overseas/

The UNI Overseas Placement Service for Educators, operated by the UNI Career Center, connects international K–12 schools with certified educators year round. UNIs Overseas Recruiting Fair was the original international fair for educators. Only certified elementary and secondary educators may participate.

If you would like to work for a Department of Defense school, you must be prepared to be assigned anywhere worldwide, not just Europe. In addition to a teaching certification and work experience, you must pass physical examinations. For more information, contact the:

**Department of Defense
Dependents' Schools**

Teacher Recruitment Section

4040 North Fairfax Dr.

Arlington, VA 22203–1634

Ttel.: (703) 696–3067

Fax: (708) 696–2699

www.odedodea.edu.

Chapter 9

Internships, Volunteering, Summer, & Temporary Jobs

Work exchange organizations and internships. Sources for summer and temporary employment in Europe. Types of summer and temporary jobs available with addresses of employers and placement agencies. Sources of volunteer work.

First, the good news. There are many good summer and temporary jobs in Europe. In fact, these are often easier to obtain than permanent positions because they are plentiful and convenient for employers to fill with foreign workers.

Now, the bad news. Finding these summer and temporary jobs takes effort. In almost every country, you must have secured employment before a work permit will be issued, yet a work permit is required before you'll be allowed into the country to work. Most employers are relunctant to complete the vast amount of paperwork required to obtain the work visa necessary to hire a summer or temporary employee. This may make working overseas sound like a legal Catch–22, but it's not. College students in particular are eligible for a host of special programs that enable them to get around these restrictions. These programs aren't free, but they enable you to obtain work permits and can even place you into a job.

This chapter proffers sources for summer jobs, internships, other temporary employment, and volunteer opportunities throughout Europe. In addition, each of the individual country chapters covers sources for positions for that particular country. So be sure to look for additional resources in the chapters in Part II for the countries that interest you.

You may be able to find unofficial summer work and bypass the cumbersome bureaucratic procedures for gaining employment in Europe, and possibly avoid local taxes and deductions as well. Unfortunately, you also forfeit government labor regulations that protect against exploitative practices. You run the risk of working long hours at wages below the legal minimum, and if your employer fails to pay you, your options for recource are very limited. Be very cautious about working "under the table" in Europe.

Most organizations that assist students with short–term or temporary work operate on a one–to–one exchange: for every American sent to work in an European country, one person from that nation can work in the U.S. A limited number of organizations that don't rely on this reciprocal exchange basis will actually place you in a job or internship, usually for a fee. The jobs that these organizations arrange are frequently unpaid. Two organizations — BUNAC and the Council on International Educational Exchange — provide you with a work visa without requiring that you first arrange a job.

Work Exchange Organizations

AIESEC (International Association for Students in Economics and Business)

127 West 26th Street, 10th Floor
New York, NY 10001
Tel.: (212) 757–3774
Fax: (212) 757–4062
Email: aiesec@aisecus.org
www.aiesecus.org

AIESEC, a French acronym for the International Association of Students in Economics and Business Management, is a work–exchange program that focuses on placing undergraduate students interested in business, technology, and service–related careers in internships or "traineeships" with local companies. AIESEC is composed of about 735 student–run university chapters in 87 different countries. All candidates who apply to AIESEC are interviewed by a local review board, usually comprised of AIESEC student members, university faculty, and local business people. If you are selected as an AIESEC trainee, you will be placed in an internship within six months. There is a $500 application fee, $455 of which is refunded if you do not find an internship. The more flexible you are in terms of the type of work you will do or locations to which you will travel, the more likely you will obtain an AIESEC internship.

Association for International Practical Training (AIPT)

10400 Little Patuxent Pkwy., Suite 250
Columbia, MD 21044–3510
Tel.: (410) 997–2200
Fax: (410) 992–3249
email: aipt@aipt.org
www.aipt.org

The Association for International Practical Training may provide the best opportunities for professionals. AIPT is a non–governmental, nonprofit cultural exchange organization that manages programs that facilitate international placements for both students and experienced professionals. AIPT's "Prearranged Training Program" helps American professionals who have found jobs obtain the necessary visas and work permits. The "Americans Abroad" program assists students and early–career American professionals with finding a job overseas for up to two years. Applicants to the Americans Abroad program register to use AIPT's PINPOINT database of international job opportunities. People interested in hospitality careers will find this service particularly helpful. American professionals can train in any country that has an AIPT counterpart, which includes Austria, Finland, France, Germany, Ireland, Slovakia, Sweden, Switzerland, and the U.K. Fees vary depending on the country.

ASSIST (American Slavic Student Internship Service Training)

1535 SW Upper Hall
Portland, OR 97201
Tel./Fax: (503) 220–2535
email: assistusa@aol.com

ASSIST offers internships in the Commonwealth of Independent States (CIS) for undergraduate and graduate students specializing in Russian studies, Russian language, international business, international law, and international relations. Most positions require advanced Russian language skills, but this requirement can be waived for students who demonstrate competence in an area of particular interest to a CIS firm. Internships are available year–round and are offered in business, education, media, publishing, sports, and tourism. The majority of placements are in Moscow and St. Petersburg and usually last from one to three months, although some long–term internships are available.

BUNAC
(British Universities
North America Club)
16 Bowling Green Lane
London EC1R 0QH, England
Tel.: [44] 020 7251–3472
Fax: [44] 020 7251–0215
Email: enquiries@bunac.org.uk
www.bunac.org
or
P.O. Box 430
Southbury, CT 06489, USA
Tel.: (203) 264–0901
Fax: (203) 264–0251
Each year, BUNAC helps thousands of American students obtain special blue card work permits that allow them to work at both paid and unpaid jobs throughout Great Britain. BUNAC is also a resource and support center for American students participating in their programs. You are responsible for finding your own job using the resources available through the program or your own personal contacts. Most BUNAC participants arrive in the U.K. without a prearranged job, but participants rarely have a problem earning enough money to cover their living and travel expenses. BUNAC is an acronym for British Universities North America Club, although nobody refers to it by its full name.

CDS International
871 United Nations Plaza, 15th Floor
New York, NY 10017

Tel.: (212) 497–3500
email: info@cdsintl.org
www.cdsintl.org
CDS International was founded in 1968 to arrange internships in American companies and to exchange farmers between Germany and the U.S. Most of the CDS International programs are still in Germany, but the organization has expanded to include programs in Switzerland, Turkey, and Cyprus. CDS International directs a lot of programs, and each one has its own guidelines for application and eligibility. Here is a partial list of the CDS programs that place Americans in overseas internships and summer jobs:

◆ *The Robert Bosch Foundation Fellowship Program* provides young American professionals (ages 23 to 34) with executive–level internships in the German government;

◆ *Bavarian American Center Professional Internship Program* provides American graduates students with internships in the Bavarian State Ministries or the Bavarian State Chancellory;

◆ *Internship Program in Germany* places Americans and young professionals in paid internships in business, technical, and engineering positions;

◆ *Culinary Arts and Hospitality Internship Program* provides preaxial training opportunities in Switzerland for recent graduates in the fields of culinary arts or hospitality management;

◆ *Summer Internship Program in Turkey* provides training opportunities in Turkey and Cyprus for American students in the fields of business, international finance, hospitality, or MIS/IT management;

◆ *Gear Up! The Automotive Industry Internship Program in Germany for Engineering Students* places students in automotive internships in the Saxony region of Germany.

Center for Cultural Interchange
17 North Second Avenue
St. Charles, IL 60174

Tel.: (888) 227–6231
www.cci–exchange.com
Participants intern in a business or organization related to their course of study
while living with a screened host family.
All placements are unpaid. Interns
should expect to work 30 to 40 hours
per week. Placements are in England,
France, Ireland, Italy, and Spain.

Council on International Educational Exchange
633 Third Avenue
New York, NY 10017
Tel.: (800) 407–8839
Fax: (212) 822–2649
Email: work@ciee.org
www.ciee.org
The Council's Work Abroad Program is
a good bet for obtaining work permits
before locating a position. For a fee, the
organization will acquire a three– to six–
month work permit for you that will enable you to hold a temporary or summer jobs in Ireland, France, or
Germany. You also will receive a program handbook with general information on the country you have chosen to
visit, employment tips and contacts, and
suggestions for travel and housing.

Institute for the International Education of Students (IES)
33 North LaSalle Street, 15th floor
Chicago, IL 60602
Tel.: (800) 995–2300
Fax: (312) 944–1448
Email: info@IESabroad.org
www.IESabroad.org
IES offers study–abroad programs in
Austria, France, Germany, Ireland, Italy,
the Netherlands, Spain, and the United
Kingdom. Many include internships for
students studying political science, business, education, the arts and museums.
The internships have a strong academic
component that includes an academic
seminar, tutorial, or directed independent study, and an evaluative report from
the supervisor of the organization offering the internship. Each student must
complete a major written project.

International Cooperative Education
15 Spiros Way
Menlo Park, CA 94025

Tel.: (650) 323–4944
Fax: (650) 323 1104
Email: info@icemenlo.com
www.icemenlo.com
ICE arranges paid summer work in Belgium, Finland, Germany, and Switzerland. Jobs are available in a variety of
fields, including education, business,
hospitality, health science, banking, retail sales, and information technology.
Applicants must be between 18 and 30,
and some jobs require fluency in the
language. The application fee is $600.

International Association for the Exchange of Students for Technical Experience (IAESTE)
10400 Little Patuxent Pkwy., Suite 250
Columbia, MD 21044–3510
Tel.: (410) 997–2200
Fax: (410) 992–3249
Email: iaeste@aipt.org
www.iaeste.org
Affiliated with AIPT, IAESTE is a one–
to–one exchange program that provides
opportunities in 80 countries and the
United States for students in architecture, computer science, engineering, the
natural and physical sciences, and
mathematics. Juniors, seniors, and
graduate students are eligible for summer placements and for longer–term
placements from three to 12 months. To
apply, you should complete an initial
application and submit a $25
nonrefundable fee by January 1. In
early February you will receive a list of
available job vacancies. You must submit a resume, transcript, a certificate of
enrollment, language certification, an
essay, and an updated application that
lists your job preferences. Because there
are usually more applicants than positions, a selection panel nominates one
candidate for each job. The nomina-
tions are then forwarded to IAESTE's
overseas counterpart and the international employer for approval. Most applicants are notified by late April
whether or not they have been accepted.

InterExchange
161 Sixth Avenue
New York, NY 10013

Tel.: (212) 924–0446
Fax: (212) 924–0575
www.interexchange.org
All of InterExchange's programs require that you be at least 18 years old, a U.S. citizen, and a native English speaker. Most positions require some knowledge of languages. Fees vary depending on the program. InterExchange's programs include:

♦ *Teaching English Abroad*, available in Belgium, Spain, and Bulgaria;

♦ *Work & Travel Abroad*, offering casual jobs in Belgium and Norway;

♦ *Internships Abroad*, a year–long professional program in England and France;

♦ *Au Pairing Abroad*, available in France, Germany, the Netherlands, and Spain;

♦ *Volunteering Abroad*, available in Russia and the Newly Independent States.

I know what you did last summer... as a state department intern

During the summer of 2002, I lived and worked in Vienna, Austria, as an intern with the Economic and Political Department of the U.S. Embassy. This full–time, unpaid internship offered through the U.S. State Department gave me valuable insight into the everyday work of Foreign Service officers. I had many opportunities to contribute to the work of the embassy. In my first week, I composed the Ambassador's introductory remarks for a conference on Security and Strategy. I also researched and wrote reports on Austrian technology exchange programs and a briefing paper on the upcoming German elections for the Ambassador.

In addition to my projects, I represented the embassy at conferences and lectures of interest to the Economic and Political department, such as the United Nations Conference on Corruption. My supervisor also arranged meetings with the heads of the legal services, customs, agriculture, and public relations departments at the embassy. They described their work at the embassy and shared their stories about joining the State Department.

Living in Vienna was an added bonus, enabling me to explore the history and culture of the famous imperial city. I went to opera and waltz performances, toured where Franz Joseph once lived and reigned, and saw the work of Gustav Klimt and Egon Shilling. I also spent hours doing as the Viennese do: Drinking Melange in cafes, or watching the sun set over the city while drinking homemade wine in one of the numerous vineyards on the outskirts of town.

My summer internship was an invaluable experience that granted me an opportunity to meet many fascinating people, learn firsthand about American diplomacy abroad, and travel to a place I had only heard about before. — *Marie Schwieterman, Houston, Texas*

Internships International
1612 Oberlin Road
Raleigh, NC 27608
Tel.: (207) 443–3019/ (919) 832–1575
Fax: (207) 442–7942
Email: intintl@aol.com
www.rtpnet.org/~intintl/
Internships are available in the U.K., Ireland, France, Germany, Hungary, and other locations. All internships are unpaid; academic credit can be arranged.

U.S. State Department
2201 C Street NW
Washington, DC 20520
Tel.: (202) 647–4000
www.state.gov
The State Department's highly competitive internship program recruits students for internships in Washington, D.C. and foreign embassies. Interns get a taste of the work of a foreign service officer. Competitive candidates have strong foreign language skills, are full– or part–time juniors or seniors, or graduate students completing relevant studies, and come from a wide range of academic majors like business; public administration; social work; economics; information management; journalism; and the biological, physical, and engineering sciences. Intern duties and responsibilities vary according to post or assignment, from scientific and technical tasks to administrative projects and logistical support. Interns work a 40 hour week and serve for one semester or quarter during their academic year, or for at least 10 weeks during the summer. U.S. citizenship and good academic standing are required, along with the successful completion of a background investigation. The application process is lengthy: Summer interns must apply by November 1.

Types of Summer and Temporary Jobs in Europe

Agricultural Work

For those with the strength and endurance, agricultural work can almost always be found in Europe throughout the summer and into fall. Tasks include planting, shearing, and picking. Finding work in agriculture primarily means being in the right place at the right time. A farmer may advertise in a local pub, hostel, or market, but in general jobs aren't advertised. The quickest route to employment may be to approach a farmer directly. As a result, agricultural work is best sought from within the country.

Competition for agricultural work is fairly keen because it requires few advanced skills and attracts many workers from less–developed countries. The following organizations are involved in pan–European international agricultural placement. More specific agricultural employment information for some countries is given in the individual country chapters in Part II.

Agriventure
International Agricultural Exchange Association
1000 First Avenue S
Great Falls, MT 59401
Tel.: (406) 727 1999
Fax: (406) 727 1997
Email: usa@agriventure.com
www.agriventure.com
Agriventure places people ages 18 to 30 in jobs in agriculture, horticulture, and home management. Your Agriventure fee covers your job placement, airfare, room and board, insurance, and a two–year membership in the IAEA. In Europe, you can work in Austria, Belgium, Czech Republic, Denmark, Finland, France, Germany, Iceland, Ireland, Luxembourg, the Netherlands, Norway, Sweden, and Switzerland.

Future Farmers of America
National FFA Center
P.O. Box 68960
6060 FFA Drive
Indianapolis, IN 46268–0960
Tel.: (317) 802 6060
Fax: (317) 802–6061
Email: global@ffa.org
www.ffa.org
FFA coordinates the USDA/FAS Internship Program, in which students who

successfully pass the USDA employment selection process receive nine– to 12–month internships at a foreign U.S. Embassy. FFA also works with international organizations, such as the American Scandinavian Foundation, to help student secure jobs working on farms and other agricultural enterprises.

Au Pair Work

There are many positions available in most European countries for au pair work. Traditionally young women, au pairs live with families and help them with housework, child care, and other domestic tasks. For this, they receive room and board and perhaps a small salary. The primary goal of the au pair's stay is educational: the opportunity to become familiar with the customs and language of another country in an intimate setting is the au pair's true reward. Other benefits include the chance to build up a network of friends and future employment contacts, plus (with a bit of luck) the opportunity to travel with one's host family.

Some degree of competency in the language of the country you hope to live in is generally required for au pair work — you do need to be able to communicate with your host family. And many hiring agencies (and family employers) require a minimum commitment of two to three months, sometimes as much as a year. Program fees vary, so explore your options.

You can find an online directory of au pair agencies on the International Au Pair Association's website, (www.iapa.org). Susan Griffith and Sharon Legg's *The Au Pair and Nanny's Guide to Working Abroad* (2003, $17.95, 320 pages, available from Globe Pequot Press, P.O. Box 480, Guildford, CT 06437, (888) 249–7586, (203) 458–4500) is good general resource for someone interested in working as an au pair. It also includes lists of agencies sorted by country.

The chapters for individual nations in Part II of this book include many listings for au pair agencies that specialize in specific countries. The following placement agencies are active in several European countries.

Au Pair in Europe
P.O. Box 68056
Blakely Postal Outlet
Hamilton, Ontario, Canada L8M 3M7
Tel.: (905) 545 6305
Fax: (905) 544 4121
Email: aupair@princeent.com
www.princeent.com/aupair
Au Pair in Europe places students in Austria, Belgium, Denmark, England,

Finland, France, Germany, Greece, the Netherlands, Iceland, Italy, Norway, Spain, Sweden, and Switzerland. Positions last from six to nine months; the administration fee is $425.

Accord Cultural Exchange
750 La Playa
San Francisco, CA 94121
Tel.: (415) 386–6203

Fax: (415) 386–0240
Email: leftbank@hotmail.com
www.cognitext.com/accord/contact.htm
Accord places au pairs in Austria, France, Germany, Italy, and Spain. Au pairs are expected to work 30 hours per week for five to six hours per day, including two evenings of babysitting. Families are expected to provide room and board, plus a monthly salary of $250 to $400. Placement fees begin at $750.

Office and Clerical Work

Secretaries and typists with good office and language skills are needed for high–level appointments in many European countries. If you don't mind the insecurity of working as a temporary office worker, you can interview before you leave with an American temporary agency that has offices in the European city where you are interested in working. Manpower, for example, is the world's largest temporary agency and has offices throughout Europe and the United States. Check your local business or Yellow Pages for locations near you. Some large temporary agencies will allow you to take their aptitude tests in the U.S. and forward the results to their overseas branch.

In order to secure a clerical position, you must be fluent in the language of the employer's country. Some short–term contracts are available, but most are on a longer–term basis. You must have previous experience with secretarial work. In addition to working with a temporary agency, check out the websites listed in the individual country chapters in Part II for the best listings of clerical positions. Also, Chapter 7 lists temporary agencies that serve the international market.

 ## Cards with clout

The International Student Identity Card, International Teacher Identity Card, and International Youth Travel Card are available, respectively, to students, teachers, and anyone ages 12 through 25. Holders of these cards receive discounts up to 50 percent on commercial airfares, ground transportation, accommodations, museum admission, theater tickets, and so on. They also offer medical and accident insurance, a toll–free traveler's assistance service, and informational travel handbooks. The cards are sponsored by the International Student Travel Confederation, and you can obtain one from your university's study–abroad office, a travel agency that specializes in student travel, or the ISTC website at www.istc.org.

Recreational and Resort Work

There is a growing demand for sports instructors and teachers due to the increase in Club Med–type vacation centers. Resort work includes jobs as drivers, security personnel, food servers, and various other forms of low–skilled labor. Employers generally require language proficiency and relevant work experience. These jobs also require a written application, and employers often request letters of reference. You'll fine specific resort and hotel employment information, as well as a listing of major hotels and hotel chains, in the individual country chapters in Part II of this book.

The following organizations hire workers for resort and recreational positions:

Club Méditérranee
North America
c/o Human Resources Dept.
75 Valencia Avenue, 12th Floor
Coral Gables, Florida 33134
Fax: (305) 476–4100
email: resumes@clubmed.com
www.clubmedjobs.com
If you speak fluent French, are single, can work from May to October, and are over 21, this could be for you. Club Med hires workers in France, Greece, Israel, Italy, Morocco, Romania, Spain, Switzerland, Tunisia, Turkey, and elsewhere. Applications must be received by January 31. Club Med refers to their interviews as "auditions" — which should give you an idea of what they're looking for. Be forewarned that Club Med recruits in the U.S. primarily for North American positions, especially at the entry level.

Openwide International Ltd.
7 Westmoreland House
Cumberland Park
London NW10 6RE, U.K.
Tel.: [44] 20 8962 3409
Fax: [44] 20 8962 3440
www.openwideinternational.com
Openwide International is a booking agency that provides entertainers for hotels and cruise lines in Cyprus, Greece, Spain, and Turkey. The company regularly recruits singers, dancers, magicians, DJs, impressionists, and other performers. You must be able to work a minimum of four months. Knowledge of German, Spanish, or French is helpful but not required.

Thomson Holidays
Overseas Personnel Department
Greater London House

Hampstead Road
London NW1 7SD, U.K.
www.thomson–holidays.com
Thomson Holidays hires entertainers, children's activities leaders, and general staff for resorts throughout Europe. Opportunities are mostly for summer work (April to October), but limited winter resort opportunities may be available as well. You will need to be fluent in at least one European language.

Village Camps
14, rue de la Morâche
CH–1260 Nyon, Switzerland
Tel.: [41] 22 990 9400
Fax: [41] 22 990 9494
www.villagecamps.com
Village Camps operates co–ed European language and activity camps. The camps regularly recruit experienced camping professionals to lead programs, assist with staff training, manage facilities, and complete post–season clean-up. Applicants must be at least 27 years old. Village camps provides meals, accommodation, and accident/liability insurance in addition to a salary. Village Camps operates in Austria, England, France, and Switzerland.

YMCA International Camp Counselor Program
YMCA International Program Services
71 West 23rd Street, Suite 1904
New York, NY 10010
www.ymcaiccp.org
The YMCA's International Camp Counselor Program places volunteers between the ages of 21 and 29 as overseas summer camp counselors. Positions are strictly volunteer, with participants responsible for all travel and living expenses. Previous YMCA work experience is required.

For more information on opportunities at sea, you should consult *How to Get a Job with a Cruise Line*, by Mary Fallon (2001, $16.95, 336 pages, published by Ticket to Adventure, available from Planning/Communications, *see* Chapter 22); or *Working on a Cruise Ship*, by Sandra Bow (2003, $16.95, 224 pages, available from Globe Pequot Press, P.O. Box 480, Guildford, CT 06437, (888) 249–7586, (203) 458–4500).

Tourism, Hotels, and Restaurants

Throughout Europe, hotel and restaurant work is readily available for Americans. The pay is not the best, and if business becomes exceedingly hectic, they might expect you to work overtime and perform other duties without monetary compensation or time off.

Finding a job can often be as simple as locating a hotel or resort in a popular area that needs some extra help during high season. To find the hot vacation spots, turn to the country's national tourism office. It can often provide lists of hotels, resorts, restaurants, and other "tourist traps" — which to you are potential employers.

Shipping out for fun and profit

I just finished six months of working on a cruise ship and thought I might share a few things. The ship I was on started off in the Mediterranean, then headed to Southeast Asia and Australia. As you might imagine, cruise work is a great way to see the world! This can depend on your position on board, though. I worked in the ship's boutique. This made for eleven–hour days at sea but it also meant that my time was my own in port (the boutique was closed then). Other workers weren't so lucky (kitchen help, for example), and there always seemed to be something requiring their attention, whether we were at sea or not. The privileges you have on board may also vary by position. On my ship, staff members — ship officers, entertainment and fitness staff, and those of us in retail — could use the passenger pool and gym in our off hours. Crew members — stewards, waiters, and sailors — weren't allowed to be seen in public recreation areas after hours and could only use the crew facilities.

What did I like best about the job? Port time! What did I like the least? To be honest, being one of only 30 women on a ship with 270 men wasn't an experience I'd recommend to just anyone. I have a strong personality, but being so constantly the focus of so much attention got to be a bit much. For those willing to deal with both the up– and downsides of cruise work, though, a word of advice in parting: Both during the hiring process and on the job, be prepared and be patient. Oh — and going to Europe while you're waiting for an offer can work in your favor. Otherwise, those who are more immediately available might be hired before you. — *Kate Riley*

Simply write or call the tourism office of the country or countries you're interested in, requesting information on that country (or a region of the country) and the vacation areas within it. Then as information arrives, write to the establishments that interest you and hope for the best. Tourist offices for each country (in–country and in the United States, where applicable) are listed in the individual country chapters in Part II.

A few organizations specifically coordinate internships in the hospitality industry. CDS International and AIPT (described under "Work Exchange Organizations" beginning on page 107) offer particularly strong programs.

Youth hostels also hire summer and temporary workers. Many hostels will provide room and board in exchange for manual labor and other help.

American Youth Hostel Association
733 15th Street NW, Suite 840
Washington, DC 20005
Tel.: (202) 783 6161
Fax: (202) 783 6171
www.hiayh.org

The American Youth Hostel Association offers a list of hostels in Europe. Youth hostels also hire summer and temporary workers, often offering room and board in exchange for manual labor and other work. Many hostel websites list job opportunities.

Volunteer Opportunities

While it is sometimes difficult to obtain a work permit and find a job in Europe if you aren't an E.U. national, positions in work camps are relatively easy to obtain. Most offer work in agriculture, building construction and renovation, ecological and environmental work, forest clearing, and children's camps. Some work camps offer small wages in addition to free room and board, as well as evening activities like sports or language classes. Information about opportunities specific to a country appears in the individual country chapters in Part II.

work camps aren't the only option when it comes to volunteering in Europe, of course. Volunteer positions run the gamut from archaeology to teaching (and not just English) to — well, let your imagination wander. It's amazing how opportunities open up when you're willing to work for free. Good general sources on overseas volunteer opportunities include:

Alternatives to the Peace Corps by Joan Powell, 2001, $9.95. Food First Books, 309 60th Street, Oakland, CA 94618; www.foodfirst.org

Volunteer Vacations: Short–Term Adventures that Will Benefit You and Others by Bill McMillon. 2003. $17.95. Chicago Review Press, 814 N. Franklin Street, Chicago, IL 60610.

Organizations that recruit Americans volunteers for Europe include:

AFS Intercultural Programs
198 Madison Avenue, Eighth Floor
New York, NY 10016
Tel.: (212) 299–9000
www.afs.org

The AFS Educator Program provides opportunities for teachers to live and work in countries around the world. Short programs are available during American school holidays; semester and year–long programs are also available for people looking for a more in–depth experience. The program includes cultural lessons and events, family home stays, observation of local educational practices, and teaching in schools in the host country.

Council on International Educational Exchange (CIEE)
633 Third Avenue, 20th Floor
New York, NY 10017
Tel.: (800) 407 8839
www.ciee.org
CIEE manages over 800 international volunteer projects in 30 different countries. Projects are available in archeology, renovation, environmental projection, and social work. Program fees average $300, plus $40 mandatory insurance. Room and board is provided, but you are responsible for your own travel expenses. The Council's International Voluntary Service Department also recruits hundreds of volunteers per year for positions in work camps in several European nations. These camps bring together volunteers of from around the globe for tasks ranging from environmental conservation to castle restoration.

Global Volunteers
375 E. Little Canada Rd.
St. Paul, MN 55117
Tel.: 800–487–1074
www.globalvolunteers.org
Global Volunteers is a private, non-profit, non–sectarian organization that organizes "volunteer vacations," short–term volunteer assignments to host communities abroad. Projects last from two to three weeks, and you will be charged a tax–deductible program fee of about $2,200.

International Cultural Youth Exchange
ICYE European Association
P. de Ligne Straat 22
B–3001 Leuven, Belgium
Tel.: [32] 1 623 3762
Fax: [32] 1 623 3925
info@icye.be

www.icye.org
The ICYE Federation is an international, independent, nonprofit organization with 35 National Committees worldwide. Opportunities in Europe are offers in Austria, Belgium, Denmark, Finland, France, Germany, Iceland, Italy, Lithuania, Norway, Russia, Sweden, Switzerland, and the United Kingdom. The ICYE mission is to promote youth mobility and international understanding through long–term (from six to 12 months) voluntary service exchange programs.

International Partnership for Service–Learning
815 Second Avenue, Suite 315
New York, NY 10017
Tel.: (212) 986 0989
Fax: (212) 986 5039
Email: info@ipsl.org
www.ipsl.org
The International Partnership for Service–Learning is an incorporated nonprofit educational organization of colleges, universities, service agencies and related organizations that develops programs linking volunteer service and academic study for credit. Programs are available in France, the Czech Republic, England, and Scotland, among other locations.

The International Volunteer Program
210 Post Street
San Francisco, CA 94108
Tel.: (415) 477 3667
www.ivpsf.org
The International Volunteer Program places volunteers with nonprofit organizations in France and Great Britain. Projects are six weeks long during the summer. The $1,500 program fee includes a round–trip airline ticket and room and board.

International Volunteering Network
C/O Involvement Volunteers Association
P.O. Box 218
Port Melbourne, Victoria 3207, Australia
Tel.: [61] 3 9646 9392
Fax: [61] 3 9646 5504
Email: ivimel@iaccess.com.au

"WWOOF" your way across Europe

Need a break from big–city hassles and concrete jungles? WWOOFing might be just the ticket. World Wide Opportunities on Organic Farms (WWOOF) was founded in Britain in 1971 to expose city–dwellers to organic farming principles. WWOOFers perform a variety of tasks. Organic farming is more labor–intensive than conventional modern agriculture. Heavy machinery is rarely used, and there are no chemical pesticides. The latter means that volunteers may be asked to perform tasks never dreamed of in the nine–to–five workaday world, such as gathering ladybugs, praying mantises, or other garden predators for use as natural pesticides. The WWOOF network extends across Europe including Austria, Denmark, Finland, Germany, Italy, Slovenia, Switzerland, Sweden, and the U.K. Each WWOOF organization is independent, and you will need to contact specific WWOOF chapters to obtain a list of participating farms in that country. The fee for the list is generally about €18. Contact WWOOF, P.O. Box 2675, Lewes BN7 1RB, U.K.; www.wwoof.org.

www.volunteering.org.au
IVN offers volunteer opportunities in Denmark, England, Finland, Germany, Italy, Poland, Spain, and Turkey. Projects relate to sustainable environmental conservation or community–based social service and can run from two weeks to one year.

Service Civil International–USA
Route 2, Box 506
Crozet, VA 22932
Tel.: (804) 823–1826
www.sci–ivs.org
SCI manages work camps throughout Europe. Volunteers participate in conservation preservation, assist the elderly, or work with refugees. Most projects last from two to four weeks. Fees range from $50 to $100, and volunteers are responsible for their own travel expenses.

Volunteers for Peace
1034 Tiffany Road
Belmont, VT 05730–0202
Tel.: (802) 2592759
Fax: (802) 2592922
Email: vfp@vfp.org
www.vfp.org
VFP offers over 2,200 short–term voluntary service projects in 80 countries. Program fees range from $200 to $400 and cover the cost of the program and room and board; volunteers are responsible for their own transportation costs. Most work camps last from two to three weeks.

Chapter 10

Teaching English Abroad

Opportunities for non–certified teachers. Pros and cons of TEFL certification and programs to attain it. Names and addresses of language schools and placement services.

If you're a native English speaker and have a bachelor's degree, you probably qualify to teach English in Europe. The formation of the European Union and the fall of communism in Eastern Europe have made English language skills a hot commodity. The best opportunities are in countries that don't require students to learn English in school, such as Spain, Italy, Germany, Greece, and most of the Eastern European countries. This chapter focuses on teaching English abroad, a good option for people who are not certified teachers. See Chapter 8 for information about international careers for professional teachers.

Some schools will consider you qualified to teach if you are simply a native speaker of English. More credible organizations, however, will expect you to have earned a bachelor's degree, have some prior teaching experience, and be willing to sign a nine–month contract. Although it is possible to find work without a Teaching English as a Foreign Language (TEFL) certificate, this accreditation can make you more competitive in the job market. The pros and cons of TEFL certification are discussed later in this chapter.

Although you are expected to have a firm grasp of English grammar, native speakers are almost always hired to lead conversations rather than diagram sentences. You are likely to be placed in a total immersion classroom, one in which English is the only language used for instruction, and therefore your job search will not be hindered by weak foreign language skills. English teaching, especially if you are new to it, can be an exciting way to experience another culture. It can also be grueling work. Remember that most English–language classes sponsored by private companies are taught in the evenings and on weekends!

English teaching assignments vary from school to school and country to country. It is very important to thoroughly investigate the organization hiring you to teach English. Many fly–by–night operations hire teachers to work in unsatisfactory work conditions! If you are unfamiliar with an organization or you are being asked to pay up–front for placement, be sure to ask for references.

Useful Books

There are many useful books for people interested in teaching English abroad. Some are how–to manuals for job searchers; others offer useful bags of tricks for classroom teaching techniques.

More Than a Native Speaker: An Introduction for Volunteers Teaching Abroad, by Don Snow. TESOL, 700 South Washington Street, Suite 200, Alexandria, VA 22314, tel. (703) 836–0774, www.tesol.org. Ideas for English teaching techniques. $29.95, 321 pages, 1996.

Opportunities in Teaching English to Speakers of Other Languages, by Blyth Camenson. McGraw–Hill, www.books.mcgraw-hill.com. Overview of careers in teaching English as a foreign language. $11.95, 144 pages, 1995.

Teaching English Abroad, by Susan Griffith. Available from Globe Pequot Press, P.O. Box 480, Guildford, CT 06437, (888) 249–7586, (203) 458–4500). Probably the most comprehensive guide to teaching English abroad. $19.95, 544 pages, 2003. Published annually.

Teaching English Overseas: A Job Guide for Americans & Canadians, by Jeff Mohamed, English International Publications, www.english–international.com. Practical guide for North Americans about the TEFL job market, certifications, and programs. Includes information on over 450 schools. $19.95, 224 pages, 2000.

Work Abroad: The Complete Guide to Finding a Job Overseas. Clay Hubbs, editor. Transitions Abroad Publishing.Available from Planning/Communications — see the "Resource Center" beginning on page 472. Contains an extremely thorough section on finding work as an English teacher, even if you do not have TEFL certification. $15.95, 250 pages. 2003.

Freelance teaching?

An alternative to teaching in a language school is to hang out your proverbial shingle and market yourself as a freelance English teacher. You can often undercut the price of an established language school and pocket the change. Freelancing also gives you the flexibility to set your own hours and work load. Of course, your salary depends on you attracting and retaining students. Your clients will cancel and postpone lessons with an irritating frequency. Usually freelancing is not a good option if you plan to stay in a country for less than six months — it takes at least that long to network your way to building a stable base of students!

TEFL Certification

TEFL certification can significantly enhance your prospects for finding work, especially for inexperienced teachers. Most TEFL programs are month–long training institutes that include practice teaching sessions, observation, and job–placement assistance. Especially in Western Europe, a TEFL certificate helps pry open the door to a language school. TEFL–certified teachers also usually command higher salaries. TEFL certification is not required to find a job teaching English, and if you are planning to work for less than a year, the cost of the certificate may make it prohibitive. There are several programs that offer TEFL certification.

When selecting a TEFL program, it is important to do your homework. Some programs are better and more widely recognized than others. A few questions you should ask when evaluating programs include:

- ☑ Is the certificate the program issues widely recognized overseas?
- ☑ How long has the center been offering TEFL courses?
- ☑ What are the costs for certification? What is the refund policy?
- ☑ How many students are enrolled in the school?
- ☑ How long does it take to complete the program?
- ☑ What job–placement assistance is available?

Jeff Mohamed lists other questions and the appropriate answers in his highly informative *Teaching English Overseas* described on page 120.

TEFL versus TESOL?

The programs that train people to teach English abroad can sound like an acronym alphabet soup. In this book, we use the acronym TEFL, "teaching English as a foreign language," to refer to teacher training programs that award certificates upon completion. TESOL, "teaching English to speakers of other languages," is also used to designate these training programs. (TESOL is also the name of the professional association for teachers of English.) Here are some of the other terms you are likely to hear:

CELTA (Certificate in English Language Teaching to Adults) is a specific, brand name of a TEFL certificate course administered by the University of Cambridge Local Examinations Syndicate and Royal Society of Arts, based in England.

EFL (English as a foreign language) refers to English language programs in non–English–speaking countries.

ESL (English as a second language) refers to English–language programs in English–speaking countries where students learn English as a second language.

A useful way to learn about programs is through the *Directory of Professional Preparation Programs in TESOL in the U.S. and Canada.* It is published by TESOL, 700 South Washington Street, Suite 200, Alexandria, VA 22314; www.tesol.edu.

Certification Programs

Boston Language Institute
TEFL Programs
648 Beacon Street
Boston, MA 02215
Tel.: (877) 998–3500
Fax: (617) 262–3595
email: tefl@boslang.com
www.teflcertificate.com

Hamline TEFL Certificate Course
Hamline University
1536 Hewitt Avenue, MS 1750
St. Paul, MN 55104
Tel.: (651) 523–2900
www.hamline.edu/graduate/graded/sltl/tefl/index.html

Inlingua Teacher Service
1901 North Moore Street
Arlington, VA 22209
Tel.: (703) 527–0916
Fax: (703) 527–9866

Email: tefl@inlinguadc.com.
www.inlinguadc.com

RSA/Cambridge CELTA
(Certificate in English Language Teaching to Adults)
Embassy CES
330 Seventh Avenue
New York, NY 10001
Tel.: (212) 629–7300
Fax: (212) 736–7950
www.studygroupintl.com

University of Cambridge CELTA
Street Giles Language Teaching Center
One Hallidie Plaza, Third Floor
San Francisco, CA 94102
Tel.: (415) 788–3552
Fax: (415) 788–1923
www.stgiles–usa.org

Useful TEFL Websites

Dave's ESL Cafe
www.eslcafe.com
Dave's ESL Café describes itself as "the Internet's meeting place for ESL/EFL students and teachers from around the world." ESL Café maintains current, complete information on teaching abroad. It includes tips on selecting TEFL programs and job listings. It also maintains a chat room for people needing teaching tips. There is a section called "hint of the day" that features useful information for people teaching English. (Many English teachers find themselves also teaching American history and culture. For example, one day the "hint" was short biography of George Washington.)

English International
www.english–international.com
English International maintains current information on teaching English overseas. The site includes FAQs about teaching English abroad, tips for selecting a TEFL program, and an English grammar test that assesses your preparation to be an effective EFL teacher. It is maintained by Jeff Mohammed, author of *Teaching English Overseas.*

TEFL Jobs

www.tefl.net

TEFL Jobs is a comprehensive site for TEFL teachers. The job board lists nearly 40 positions, many of which are in Europe (there are more jobs listed in Asia). There is a section that features articles and essays about teaching English. The section "Lesson Plans" includes ideas for class activities. The site also has links to other websites for TEFL teachers.

Major Language School Chains

Berlitz International

400 Alexander Park
Princeton, NJ 08540–6306
Tel.: (609) 514–3400
Fax: (609) 514–3405
Email: Europe.careers@berlitz.com
www.berlitz.com
Berlitz is the granddaddy of private English–language instruction. The company has been in business for 125 years. Most Berlitz TEFL placements are in Spain, Italy, Germany, and France.

International House

106 Picadilly
London W1J 7NL, U.K.
Tel.: [44] 20 7518 6923
Fax: [44] 20 7518 6900
Email: worldrecruit@ihlondon.co.uk
www.ihworld.com
International House World Organisation is a network of more than 110 schools around the world, in over 30 countries. IH recruits teachers who are native speakers of English, and offers additional training.

Teacher Recruitment Programs

Working with a recruitment service can make finding a teaching job much easier. Some are nonprofit organizations that see their purpose as promoting cultural exchanges; others are for–profit organizations that schools hire for help finding teachers. Many of these organizations assist people who do not have TEFL certification and may even offer training. Recruitment services, including cultural exchange programs, often charge fees that range from a few hundred dollars to several thousand. Compare costs before selecting a particular service.

Bridges for Education

8912 Garlinghouse Road
Naples, NY 14512
Tel.: (716) 534–9344
Fax: (810) 761–9370
Email: mdodge@frontiernet.net
www.bridges4edu.org
BFE recruits volunteer teachers for summer camps in which children from Central Europe and the Newly Independent States learn conversational English. Teachers must have state certification or have successfully taught in a private school or college. Teaching assistants may include educated adults, student teachers and college students. There is an $850 placement fee; scholarships are available.

Central European Teaching Program

Beloit College
700 College Street
Beloit, WI 53511
Tel.: (608) 363 2619
Email: cetp@beloit.edu
www.beloit.edu/~cetp

The Central European Teaching Program is a nonprofit organization that places English teachers in public schools in Central and Eastern Europe. CETP sends 60 to 90 native English–speaking teachers each year to Hungary, Poland, Romania, Slovakia, and the Czech Republic. Conversation teachers are responsible for enhancing students' oral fluency through conversation practice, classroom drills, games, audio–visual instruction, and listening comprehension. CETP teachers also work closely with native teachers to emphasize important grammar concepts. Teachers are paid according to local standards and receive free accommodations. Teachers are not required to be certified; CETP provides teacher training.

Friends of World Teaching

P.O. Box 84480
San Diego, CA 92138–4480
Tel.: (800) 503–7436
Email: director@fowt.com
www.fowt.com
Friends of World Teaching maintains up–to–date lists of all American commu-

nity schools, international schools, church–related and industry–supported schools, private, and government schools where American and Canadian educators may seek employment. FOWT charges $20 for job listings in three countries.

Fulbright English Teaching Fellowship
Institute for International Education
809 United Nations Plaza
New York, NY 10017–3580
Tel.: (212) 883–8200
Fax: (212) 984–5452
www.iie.org
The Institute for International Education administers the Fulbright program. Not technically a recruiting services, IIE coordinates one–year fellowships in which new college graduates work in teaching assistantships in Austria, Belgium, France, Germany, Hungary, Luxembourg, Romania, and Turkey. The application process is competitive, and interested students should apply at least a year in advance.

InterExchange
161 Sixth Avenue
New York, NY 10013
Tel.: (212) 924–0446
Fax: (212) 924–0575
www.interexchange.org
InterExchange's Teaching English Abroad program places English teachers and tutors in Belgium, Spain, and Bulgaria. InterExchange requires you to be at least 18 years old, a U.S. citizen, and a native English speaker. Most positions require some knowledge of European languages.

Peace Corps
Attn.: Recruitment Office
1111 20th Street NW
Washington, D.C., 20526
Tel.: (800) 424 8580
www.peacecorp.gov
Since the end of the Cold War, the Peace Corps has been recruiting volunteers to work in the Czech Republic, Slovakia, and Poland as English teachers. The Peace Corps requires two years of service. Volunteers receive a salary comparable to local wages, mental and dental care, transportation to and from the country of service, 24 vacation days a year, deferral of student loans, and an adjustment allowance of $6,075 at the end of their service period.

Part II

Where the Jobs Are: A Country by Country Look

Cultural and historical summary of each country. The current economic climate. Getting around. Employment regulations for Americans. Short-term and temporary work. Internship programs. Volunteer opportunities. Major newspapers. Resources for further information, including websites, embassies, chambers of commerce, and world trade centers. Business directories. Listings of major employers.

Chapter 11

United Kingdom: England, Northern Ireland, Scotland, & Wales

Major employment centers: London, Birmingham, Aberdeen, Glasgow

Major business language: English

Language skill index: Pretty much the only language around

Currency: British pound

Telephone country code: 44

Time zone: Eastern Standard Time + 5 hours

Punctuality index: Protocol and formality in the U.K. are generally more important than in the U.S., although the Welsh and Scots may be more informal. Appointments and punctuality are generally expected.

Average daily temperature, high/low: January: 44°/35°; July: 73°/55° London

Average number of days with precipitation: January: 17 days; July: 12 days

Best bet for employment:

   For students: Apply to BUNAC and work in London

   Permanent jobs: Banking and finance in London

Chance of finding a job: Pretty good if you aren't picky

Useful tip: For the most part, the British are very keen on rules. Get ready to queue up, and never cut in line.

Britain is in northwestern Europe, surrounded by the Atlantic Ocean, English Channel, and the North Sea. Ireland and France are its nearest neighbors. Britain is about the size of Oregon. The northern part of U.K. and much of Wales and Scotland consist of highlands, while the rest of the country is characterized by a low, rolling landscape. Britain, or Great Britain, refers to England, Wales, and Scotland; the United Kingdom also includes Northern Ireland.

The British empire may have been vanquished, but the English language has conquered the world.

English is spoken throughout the United Kingdom, but Welsh is spoken in western parts of Wales by about 20 percent of the population, and Gaelic is spoken in some parts of Northern Ireland. The Church of England is Britain's established church, with a following among 20 percent of the population. Also significant are the Church of Wales, the Church of Scotland, the Church of Ireland, the Roman Catholic Church, and Methodist, Baptist, and Jewish institutions. Northern Ireland, two–thirds Protestant and one–third Catholic, suffers from severe sectarian unrest.

Britain served as one of the Roman Empire's farthest outposts until it was overrun by Norse and Germanic tribes. The Normans crossed the English Channel and conquered England in 1066. The English defeated the ruling house of Wales in 1283. England and Scotland were eventually peacefully united in 1603 when James VI of Scotland became England's James I. A long struggle between Parliament and the monarchy resulted in civil war, the declaration of a republic, a restoration, and a Bill of Rights. Parliamentary sovereignty was established by the early nineteenth century.

Britain established an extensive empire in the Americas, Africa, and Asia. Despite losing most of its North American possessions following the American Revolution, the British Empire stretched across the world. Britain provided a significant portion of the Allied efforts in both world wars with the British war effort extending beyond Europe into Africa, the Middle East, the Far East, and India. The empire began dissolving, generally peacefully, after World War II. The Commonwealth of Nations is an association of former British colonies.

Under Clement Atlee, Britain in the 1940s established an extensive social welfare system. By the 1970s, the country's visible economic stagnation led to popular disillusionment with the social welfare consensus and the election of a Conservative parliamentary majority in 1979. Prime Minister Margaret Thatcher and her successor, John Majors, emphasized private–sector economic growth and low taxation.

In 1997, the Labour Party shed its socialist mantel, swept national elections, and ousted the Conservative government. Prime Minister Tony Blair has, among other policies, backed referenda that gave Scotland and Wales greater degrees of self–government and London a mayor.

The on–again, off–again peace process with Northern Ireland has gained momentum since the 1997 elections. In June 1997, Dr. Mo Mowlam, Britain's Northern Ireland Secretary, promised to admit Sinn Fein, Ireland's oldest political party, to all party talks following a cease fire. This cleared the way for talks chaired by former United States Senator George Mitchell that led to the Good Friday agreement of April 10, 1998. This agreement allowed the people of Northern Ireland to decide their political future by majority vote and established a new Northern Irish parliament and high–level political links between the Republic of Ireland and Northern Ireland. Seventy–one percent of the voters on both sides of the Irish border approved the agreement. But subsequent tragedies, including the bombing at Omagh where 28 people were killed by a bomb planted by the radical Real Irish Republican Army (IRA), challenged both sides' commitment to a lasting peace. The Good Friday agreements reduced political tensions — only 20 people died due to sectarian violence in 2001 as opposed to 500 in the peak years of IRA activities. Yet the IRA's reluctance to decommission its weapons and an alleged discovery of an IRA spy ring at the heart of Northern Ireland's government keep peace from being fully realized.

The United Kingdom is one of the United States' closest allies, playing an active role in the U.S.–led war against terrorism following the September 11 attacks. British forces fought alongside U.S. troops in Afghanistan to remove the Taliban from power and disrupt the Al–Qaeda terrorist network. Tony Blair has been an unswerving supporter of the U.S. military action to force Saddam Hussein to destroy weapons of mass destruction.

Britain has suffered many setbacks during the last decade — a fire at Windsor Castle, the tragic death of Princess Diana, a distinct lack of success in international sport, a series of horrible train crashes, and two major epidemics that nearly destroyed the British beef industry (mad cow disease, followed by hoof–and–mouth disease). Yet despite a general cynicism among British youth, Britain remains the center of activity in Europe.

It is important to understand that the people of Scotland are Scots — not "Scottish" — and that the adjective for virtually everything else in Scotland is "Scottish." Also remember that although they are often combined for statistical purposes, the English and the Welsh are actually two separate cultures.

Business hours are generally from 9 a.m. to 5 p.m., Mondays through Fridays. Most shops are open on Saturdays from 9 a.m. to 5 p.m., except in rural areas, and on Sundays from 10 a.m. to 4 p.m. In country towns, some shops may observe an early closing day, usually Tuesday or Wednesday afternoon.

Current Economic Climate

Britain's economic mood is pessimistic. The stock market prices fell sharply in early 2003, and the pound sterling weakened. In addition to heightened fears over terrorism and a war in Iraq, there are concerns over industrial disputes, a possible housing market bubble, and worsening public finances. Even so, Britain's economic performance in 2002 was respectable, if not stellar. Britain is enjoying its lowest unemployment rates in 27 years (3.1 percent), with modest inflation (2.6 percent), and growth stronger than in other major European economies, notably Germany. The U.K. has initially decided to not participate in the European single currency, although this is a matter of much public debate.

Over the past two decades, the government has privatized most state-owned companies, including British Steel, British Airways, British Telecom, British Coal, British Aerospace, and British Gas, although in some cases the government retains a "golden share" in these companies. The Labour government has continued the privatization policy of its predecessor by encouraging "public–private partnerships" (partial privatization) in such areas as the National Air Traffic Control System. This has not been without controversy. The spate of horrible commuter train crashes in Britain have been blamed in part on sloppy oversight of a privatized rail system.

The United Kingdom's combined work force is 60 percent services, 25 percent manufacturing, and 5 percent agricultural. Major industries in England and Wales include steel, automobiles, shipbuilding, textiles, chemicals, financial and banking services, and machinery. Scotland's primary industries are machinery, automobiles, electronic products, and petroleum products. Northern Ireland's major industries are shipbuilding and textiles. As the 10th largest oil and gas producer in the world, the U.K. is an energy–rich country with significant reserves of oil and gas in the North Sea and the Irish Sea and large coal resources. U.S. oil and oil–service companies participate actively in the U.K's North Sea oil industry. Historically, manufacturing dominates the north of England as well as Scotland, while service industries have prospered in the wealthier southern part of the country, especially London. The U.S. and E.U. provide the vast majority of Britain's trade.

U.K.'s 10 Largest Companies

(2001, based on market capitalization)

1. BP
2. GlaxoSmithKline
3. Vodafone Group
4. HSBC Holdings
5. AstraZeneca
6. The Shell Transport and Trading Company
7. The Royal Bank of Scotland Group
8. Lloyds TSB Group
9. Unilever
10. Barclay's

Getting Around in Great Britain

Most people in Britain prefer to travel by car. Don't forget: the British drive on the left side of the road, with the steering wheel on the right side of the vehicle, like in Japan. Taxis are common in cities. London's subway system, the Underground or Tube, is among the most developed urban public transportation systems in the world. British Rail operates an extensive, but also rather expensive, rail network. The bus system is quite convenient and cheap, especially within cities. Buses and trains serve most major British cities, but public transportation in rural areas is not extensive. A three–hour train ride through the Channel Tunnel, or Chunnel, brings London passengers to Paris.

What's left of the British Empire

The 'Commonwealth' is an association former British colonies that maintain political and economic links with the U.K. In 1931, the Statute of Westminster established the British Commonwealth of Nations; 'British' was deleted after World War II. Most of the states granted independence, beginning with India in 1947, chose to be members of the Commonwealth. There are 13 former British colonies, including Bermuda, Gibraltar, and the Falkland Islands that elected to maintain their political links with London. They are known as United Kingdom Overseas Territories.

Members of the Commonwealth are: Antigua and Barbuda, Australia, Bahamas, Bangladesh, Barbados, Belize, Botswana, Brunei, Canada, Cyprus, Dominica, Gambia, Ghana, Grenada, Guyana, India, Jamaica, Kenya, Kiribati, Lesotho, Malawi, Malaysia, Maldives, Malta, Mauritius, Nauru, New Zealand, Pakistan, Papua New Guinea, St. Kitts and Nevis, St. Lucia, St. Vincent and the Grenadines, Seychelles, Sierra Leone, Singapore, Solomon Islands, Sri Lanka, Swaziland, Tanzania, Tonga, Trinidad and Tobago, Tuvalu, Uganda, United Kingdom, Vanuatu, Western Samoa, Zambia, Zimbabwe.

Employment Regulations and the Outlook for Americans

British immigration restrictions make it very difficult to obtain a work visa, although there are many special programs that will enable students and people seeking professional training to find work for short periods. U.S. citizens do not need a visa to enter Britain or to stay for fewer than six months. Those intending to work, however, must present a work permit from an employer in Britain when arriving in the country. British employers usually request work permits for foreign employees from the Department of Employment. The Immigration Office provides residence authorization. The Department of Employment will not issue work permits for unskilled and semiskilled workers. Nonetheless, unofficial jobs for non–E.U. nationals are still available.

Job Centres are located throughout the country and maintain bulletin boards on which jobs, especially agricultural work, are posted. Tourist work is readily found in London, Wales, Scotland, the Lake District, and along the southern coast of England. Hotels and restaurants, including fast–food chains, offer work at low wages. Jobs can also be found bartending in pubs.

On January 28, 2002, the British Home Office launched the Highly Skilled Migrant Programme (HSMP) as a new initiative to allow skilled individuals to request entry to work in the United Kingdom without a pre–arranged job. To be eligible, candidates must score 75 points in specific categories that demonstrate that they will be able to find work in the U.K. The criteria include:

☑ educational qualifications (advanced degrees = more points)

☑ work experience (a longer work history = more points)

☑ past earnings (the higher your most recent salary in the U.S. = more points)

☑ achievement in your chosen field (the better you are at your job = more points)

☑ the importance of your skill to U.K. employers (shortage of workers with your skill = more points)

Candidates must apply for the HSMP through the British Embassy. For more information about the HSMP, see www.workpermits.gov.uk.

If you are a student and an American citizen, you can bypass the usual employment restrictions by contacting BUNAC (British Universities North America Club). For a $250 fee, you can obtain a blue card that will permit you to work in Britain for up to six months. BUNAC has resources to help the student job searcher who arrives in London without a job or a place to stay. Most BUNACers work in casual jobs, such as waiting tables, clerical assignments, or retail jobs. Students, however, can make enough money to cover their living and travel expenses for their stay, making the program a good deal for those who qualify. If you plan to seek paid employment while studying at a British university, contact BUNAC for current information about your eligibility.

BUNAC
16 Bowling Green Lane
London EC1R 0QH, England
Tel.: [44] 020 7251–3472
Fax: [44] 020 7251–0215
Email: enquiries@bunac.org.uk
www.bunac.org

or

P.O. Box 430
Southbury, CT 06489, USA
Tel.: (203) 264–0901
Fax: (203) 264–0251

Short–term and Temporary Work

When it comes to finding short–term and temporary jobs, BUNAC has the market cornered. Thousands of Americans work each year in British pubs, offices, and restaurants courtesy of a BUNAC blue card. There are other organizations that can assist you with finding casual work, including positions as summer camp counselors.

Cultural Embrace
1304 Hollow Creek Drive, Suite B
Austin, TX 78704
Tel.: (512) 428–9089
www.culturalembrace.com

Cultural Embrace places young people in paid three– to six–month jobs with English pubs. Participants can expect to earn $195–320 per week, and many pubs provide free accommodations

One BUNACer's London experience

I arrived in London with practically no money, no job, no friends, no flat — nothing. Having nowhere to go, I did exactly what the BUNAC tells you *not* to do: I arrived at their door, luggage in hand. Serves me right for bucking their advice, too. They were closed. Although I had to wait a day to get started, the notice board at BUNAC had everything I needed. Apartment. Job. And through those, friends and money.

My first, tide–me–over type job was at the perfume counter at Harrod's. That job had its advantages, the main one being that Harrod's is like a big, really chic campus, with lots of socializing after hours. Plus, working there gave me time to interview elsewhere on my day off. The people I interviewed with were all wonderful, very receptive to hiring an American.

I ended up, through a little luck and a little planning, taking a job as a law clerk with one of the largest law firms in the world. Luck, I say, because you never know what kind of jobs you might find posted at BUNAC. Pub work. Sheep herding in Scotland. You just never know. Planning was involved, too, because just as with any job search, experience counts. My academic background is economics and, especially, knowing Spanish helped a lot.

Another important part of planning is to take decent clothes! It may sound obvious, but I was surprised at the number of people who apparently hadn't thought of this. No matter what kind of work you hope to find, you'll at least need one nice outfit for interviewing. Beyond that, take clothes that are specifically appropriate for the kind of job you want. This won't guarantee that you'll find exactly the job you had in mind, but if it does come along, you'll be ready. — *Karen Crook; Austin, Texas*

(usually an efficiency flat located over the pub.) Participants must be at least 18 years old, possess an U.S. passport, and be enrolled as full–time college students. Cultural Embrace charges a $700 program fee.

Globe Teach
Unit 52
116 Washington Street
Brighton, MA 02135
Tel.: (617) 787–4111
www.globeteach.net
GlobeTeach is an education recruitment service based in the U.S. dedicated to assisting qualified teachers and social workers from around the world obtain positions in U.K. schools. Globe Teach does not charge fees and can help arrange for your work visa.

Youth Hostel's Association
National Recruitment Department
(Hostel Staff)
Trevelyan House
Dimple Road, Matlock,
Derbyshire, DE4 3YH, U.K.
Tel.: [44] 01629 592600
Fax.: [44] 01629 592702

www.yha.org.uk
Each year, the YHA recruits wardens to run a number of small youth hostels in Cornwall, Dartmoor, the Brecon Beacons, the Peak and Lake Districts as well as other locations in England and Wales. Opportunities are also available to work in ground maintenance, marketing and professional services, and fundraising. You receive room and board as compensation for your work.

Internship Programs

Several internship programs offer students opportunities to obtain professional experience, frequently as part of a study–abroad program. Many of the programs focus on internship opportunities in London — as the seat of government, business, and theater in the U.K., it's a logical destination. Some programs will assist with internship opportunities in other locations, such as Arcadia University's Scottish Parliament Internship Program. See the resources in Chapter 9 for information about additional internship and work–exchange organizations.

Arcadia University London Internship Program
450 S. Easton Road
Glenside, PA 19038–3295
Tel.: (215) 572–2901
www.arcadia.edu/cea
Arcadia assists with internship placements in fields including the arts and philanthropic organizations, media and broadcasting companies, health–care establishments, government offices, and large corporate enterprises. Arcadia requires that you earn academic credit for the internship experience, and you must have completed at least three courses in your field of interest in order to qualify for an internship placement. Arcadia also manages an internship program with the Scottish Parliament.

Educational Programmes Abroad
Columbia Plaza, Suite 225
350 East Michigan Avenue
Kalamazoo, MI 49007
Tel.: (616) 382–0139
Fax: (616) 382–5222
Email: usoffice@epa–internships.org
www.studyabroad.com/epa/epa.html
EPA has managed international programs in the U.K. for over 25 years. The organization places student interns in assignments ranging from business and government to law and the arts. During the academic semester, students work three days per week in an internship and take two courses. During the summer, students work at an internship for 40 hours per week. All internships and programs are offered for academic credit transferable to the home institution. Graduated and graduate students are also eligible to participate in EPA's programs.

Hansard Scholar Programme
The Hansard Society
St. Philips, Building North
Sheffield Street
London WC2A 2EX, U.K.
Tel.: [44] 207 955 7478
Fax: [44] 207 955 7492
Email: hansard@hansard.lse.ac.uk
www.hansardsociety.org.uk/scholars.htm
The Hansard Scholars Programme arranges internships with either a Member of Parliament or a Lord, or another political organization. Students work three days a week, undertaking research and providing general support. Students must be able to receive academic credit for the internship experience. The program is accredited by the London School of Economics (LSE). In the past, Hansard Scholars have interned with such figures as Prime Minister Tony Blair (when he was just an MP), Gordon Brown (now Chancellor of the Exchequor), Ann Widdecombe (now shadow Secretary of State), and Lord Weatherill (former Speaker of the House of Commons).

Institute for Study Abroad, Butler University
1100 W. 42nd St. Suite 305
Indianapolis, Indiana 46208–3485
Tel.: (800) 858–0229
Fax: (317) 940–9704
www.ifsa–butler.org
ISA offers internships in conjunction with study–abroad programs in England, Ireland, and Scotland. There are good opportunities for students looking for internships in business, government, or the arts and media. ISA's programs require that participants receive academic credit for the internship. Participants interview with potential internship employers once they arrive in the U.K. and internship placements are not guaranteed.

Volunteer Opportunities

There is an active culture of volunteerism in the U.K. Many organizations have very long histories of recruiting volunteers to assist with conservation of the famous British countryside. Other organizations in the U.K. recruit volunteers to provide services to children and the elderly. See Chapter 9 for additional resources.

British Trust for Conservation Volunteers
36 St. Mary's Street, Wallingford
Oxfordshire OX10 0EU, U.K.
Tel.: [44] 1491 822600
Fax: [44] 1491 839646
www.btcv.org.uk
Britain's largest volunteer organization, BTCV, has managed sustainable development projects for 40 years. Conservation Holidays places volunteers in projects that preserve wildlife habitats. The number of participants is limited to four to 12 volunteers. Conservation Holidays cost from £320 to £1450 depending on destination and holiday duration.

Cathedral Camps
16 Glebe Avenue
Flitwick, Bedfordshire MK45 1HS, U.K.
Tel./Fax: [44] 1525 716237
Email: admin@cathedralcamps.org.uk
www.cathedralcamps.org.uk
Cathedral Camps conserves and restores cathedrals and other Christian buildings. Voluntary maintenance and conservation work is available from mid–July to early September each year for young people between the ages of 16 and 25. One–week camps cost £45.

Concordia International Voluntary Workcamps
Heversham House, 2nd floor
20–22 Boundary Road
Hove BN3 4ET, U.K.
Tel: (01273) 422218
Concordia (Youth Service volunteers) offers a variety of voluntary work opportunities. Volunteers receive room and board, but are expected to pay their own travel costs. Concordia charges a £70 program fee.

Council for British Archaeology
Bowes Morrell House
111 Walmgate
York YO1 9WA, U.K.
Tel.: [44] 1904 671417
Fax: [44] 1904 671384
Email: archaeology@csi.com
www.britarch.ac.uk
The CBA is an educational charity that campaigns for the better care and study of Britain's past. Council publishes CBA Briefing as a supplement to its magazine British Archaeology, in which it lists fieldwork opportunities. The work is seasonal and mainly voluntary, but occasionally is paid. Training excavations often charge a fee, which varies depending on the site.

Conservation Volunteers Northern Ireland
159 Ravenhill Road
Belfast BT6 0BP, Northern Ireland
Tel.: [44] 028 9064 5169
Fax: [44] 028 9064 4409

Email: cvni@btcv.org.uk
www.cvni.org
CVNI, the Northern Ireland branch of BTCV, has for 18 years recruited volunteers to clear ponds and footpaths, manage woodlands, rebuild dry stone walls, stop erosion, and the like. CVNI volunteers have planted more than 2.5 million trees in Northern Ireland. Volunteers participate in Conservation Holidays (see BTCV). Fees begin at £69.

The Monkey Sanctuary

Looe
Cornwall PL13 1NZ, U.K.
Tel./Fax: [44] 1503 262 532
Email: info@monkeysanctuary.org
www.ethicalworks.co.uk/monkeysanctuary
The Monkey Sanctuary is home to a colony of South American woolly monkeys and provides advice and support to primate rescue centers around the world. Although volunteers cannot handle the monkeys, they do help prepare food for the monkeys, run the sanctuary shop, build new enclosures to improve the monkey territory, and many other projects. Longer–term volunteers may help at the admission desk or assist visitors.

The National Trust

Volunteer's Office
33 Sheep Street
Cirencester
Gloucestershire GL7 1RQ, U.K.
Tel.: [44] 870 609 5383
www.nationaltrust.org.uk
The National Trust was founded in 1895 to act as a guardian for the English, Welch, and Northern Irish countryside. Each year 40,000 volunteers work on trust properties, completing projects ranging from practical countryside conservation, to interacting with the public, to behind–the–scenes professional, technical and administrative support. Non–E.U. volunteers are required to apply to the British Consulate for an entry–clearance in order to volunteer. The National Trust provides assistance with accommodations but no other renumeration.

The National Trust (Northern Ireland Region)

Northern Ireland Regional Office
Rowallane House, Saintfield
Ballynahinch
Co. Down BT24 7LH, Northern Ireland
Tel.: [44] 28 9751 0721
Fax: [44] 28 9751 1242
www.ntni.org.uk

The National Trust for Scotland (Thistle Camps)

5 Charlotte Square
Edinburgh EH2 4DU, Scotland
Tel.: [44] 131 243 9470
Fax: [44] 131 243 9444
www.ntseducation.org.uk

Queen Elizabeth's Foundation for Disabled People

Lulworth Court
Chalkwell Esplanade
Westcliff–on–Sea
Essex SS0 8JQ
Tel: [44] 1702 431725
Fax: [44] 1702 433615
Queen Elizabeth's is a registered charity that recruits volunteers to assist at a seaside holiday center to care for guests who are physically disabled. Board, lodging, and training is provided to volunteers who help staff with guests' personal care and outings to theaters, shops, pubs, and football games.

The Royal Horticultural Society

RHS Garden Wisley
Woking, Surrey GU23 6QB, U.K.
Tel.: [44] 1483 224234
Fax: [44] 1483 211750
www.rhs.org.uk
The RHS serves to encourage and improve the art, science, and practice of horticulture and offers volunteer student gardeners the opportunity to work alongside experts for periods of four weeks or more. Applicants must have completed a course of study in Vocational Horticulture. Volunteers are responsible for their own accommodations, but they will receive free lunch.

Royal Society for the Protection of Birds (RSPB)
The Lodge
Sandy
Bedfordshire SG19 2DL, U.K.
Tel.: [44] 1767 680551
www.rspb.org.uk
The RSPB is Europe's largest wildlife preservation charity, with more than a million members. Over 9,000 volunteers work each year on conservation projects that last from a few weeks to several months. Volunteer assignments range from conservation officer to fundraising letter–writer. RSPB maintains offices throughout the U.K., including Northern Ireland and Scotland.

Scottish Conservation Projects Trust
Balallan House, 24 Allen Park
Stirling FK8 2QG, Scotland
Tel.: [44] 1786 479697
Fax: [44] 1786 465359

The Scottish division of the British Trust for Conservation Volunteers recruits over 10,000 volunteers. The work is seasonal, available from March to November. A contribution to accommodation, food and insurance is required.

The Wildlife Trust West Wales
7 Market Street
Haverfordwest
Dyfed SA61 1NF, Wales
Tel.: [44] 1437 765 462
The Wildlife Trust West Wales has 66 reserves under its protection. Its conservation work extends the length and breadth of Dyfed and surrounding seas. It has responsibility to care for a variety of plants and animals, such as dolphins, puffins, badgers, seals, butterflies, and wildflowers. Volunteers serve as assistant wardens on Skomer Island, a National Nature Reserve off the Welsh coast.

Resources for Further Information

Newspapers in the United Kingdom

Aberdeen Press and Journal
Tel.: [44] 224 690222
Fax: [44] 224 663575
www.thisisnorthscotland.co.uk

Belfast Telegraph
Tel.: [44] 28 9026 4000
Fax: [44] 28 9055 4504
www.belfasttelegraph.co.uk

Daily Record
Tel.: [44] 141 309 3000
Fax: [44] 141 309 3340
www.record–mail.co.uk

Daily Telegraph
Tel.: [44] 20 7538 5000
Fax: [44] 20 7513 2506
www.telegraph.co.uk

The *Financial Times* of London
Tel.: [44] 20 7873 3000
Fax: [44] 20 7873 3194
www.ft.com

The *Guardian* (*Jobs & Money* section published on weekends)
Tel.: [44] 20 7239 9610
Fax: [44] 20 7833 4456
www.guardian.co.uk

The Independent
Tel.: [44] 20 7005 2000
Fax: [44] 20 7005 2435
www.independent.co.uk

The Times
Tel.: [44] 20 7782 5000
Fax: [44] 20 7782 5988
www.thetimes.co.uk

Tabloid culture in the U.K.

Every day, 12 million people in Britain read *The Sun*, infamous for its topless models on page three, its obsession with the private lives of the rich and famous, and its innovative way with the English language. Britain's most popular newspaper is just one of many tabloid titles that you can find at newsstands — *The Mirror, The Daily Mail,* and *The Star* also sustain a large British readership. The tabloids, known for their sensational headlines, have also come under fire for unethical journalistic practices. So, why do the normally restrained Brits enthusiastically consume these outrageous publications? There is no better place than a British tabloid to read the gossip, titillate with sexual innuendo, and get a good laugh at the expense of Britain's celebrities.

Useful Websites for Job Seekers

The Internet is a good place to begin your job search. Many British employers list job vacancies, especially those in technical fields, on the web. There are also many websites that provide useful information for job searchers researching the British job market. This list of sites is not comprehensive; Britain is second only to the United States in its number of websites. For a thorough collection of U.K. websites useful to job seekers, see the *International Job Finder: Where the Jobs are Worldwide*, described on page 7.

Businessfile.co.uk

www.businessfile.co.uk

The site lists over 70 jobs for executives earning at least £55,000 (approximately $80,000). You will find a link to a site listing jobs posted with *The Telegraph* (www.jobs.telegraph.co.uk).

Career Advisory Services

www.prospects.csu.man.ac.uk

The site features jobs for new college graduates and includes useful resources, like industry profiles, tips on choosing a graduate school, and a salary survey. Job seekers can register to receive job announcements via email.

Careers in Constructions

www.careersinconstruction.com

You can find jobs in all aspects of construction: contracting, project management, surveying, and structural engineering. Job seekers can register for email job alerts. The site also includes a resume database.

City Jobs

www.cityjobs.com

This site features 4,700 jobs in the niche sectors of banking and financial services, insurance, accounting, law, and technology.

Clickajob

www.clickajob.co.uk

The Clickajob search engine allows you to search 31 different job sites. The site claims that on average, tens of thousands of jobs are posted per day. You can post your resume for review by executive recruiters.

Doctor Job

www.doctorjob.com

The site targets jobs with over 350 companies to new college graduates. It includes resources for people who haven't yet decided what they want to do after graduation. The Moan Zone is a bulletin board where you can vent your job search frustrations.

Education Jobs U.K.
www.education–jobs.co.uk
This site was one of the first education job search sites on the Internet. It lists jobs in all aspects of education: teaching (primary to college); general (support staff, custodial, etc.), and other staff (nursing). The site does not require you to register in order to view jobs or submit your CV to employers.

Evergreen Resources
www.evergreen.org.uk
The site lists jobs in natural resources management, ecology, waste management, etc. You can search jobs by title, salary, or geographic location.

Fish4Jobs
www.fish4jobs.co.uk
Fish4Jobs lists 27,000 private sector jobs in the U.K. Job seekers can search the site by job title or location (city or zip code).

Health Professionals Worldwide
www.healthprofessionals.com
Health Professionals is a nursing recruitment company that concentrates on securing employment for specialist registered nurses. The site lists job vacancies, and you can complete an application online.

Hobson's U.K. Careers
www.get.hobsons.com
Hobson's lists 26,000 jobs for new college graduates. It also includes resources to make your job search more effective. The section "Job Descriptions" specifies the skills required for 120 types of jobs. "Career Guidance" includes tips about preparing for interviews and writing a CV. There is even an "Training" section with links to 850 interactive online courses.

Jobs Domain for U.K. IT Jobs
www.jobsdomain.co.uk
Jobs Domain lists thousands of IT jobs throughout the U.K. Although most of the employers are looking for British or E.U. citizens, there is a link to information for foreign workers.

Job Search U.K.
www.jobsearch.co.uk
The site lists 27,000 jobs throughout the U.K. Registration is free and it permits you to receive job announcements via email.

JobServe
www.engineering.jobserve.com
The site lists over 2,990 engineering and technical jobs. If you register, you can receive a daily email with all new jobs received by the site. Related sites include www.medical.jobserve.com and www.legal.jobserve.com.

Jobsite United Kingdom
www.jobsite.co.uk
Jobsite lists 19,515 jobs in private industry and education throughout the U.K. and Europe. Job seekers who register will receive email notification about new job listings.

Milkround Online
www.milkround.co.uk
Milkround, the British term for the process companies use to recruit college graduates, lists jobs in professions like accounting, law, education, and media. You must complete a free registration to use most of its services.

Monster Board U.K.
www.monster.co.uk
The site lists 17,000 jobs in the U.K. and 60,000 in the rest of Europe. You can search the jobs without registering, but you must set up a free account to apply for a job online, receive automatic email searchers, or post a resume. The site links to MonsterScotland.co.uk, which offers 2,100 jobs.

National Information Services and Systems
www.vacancies.ac.uk
The site lists 60 private industry and education jobs in the U.K., including faculty research and instruction, support staff, and administration. Twenty to 30 jobs are posted weekly.

Reed Graduates
www.reed.co.uk
You can search over 126,000 jobs in the U.K. and the rest of Europe. Registration is free and allows you to receive

email job announcements, or even have job alerts sent to your mobile phone.

SAT U.K. Recruitment Guide
www.recruit–online.co.uk
This site is a comprehensive database of recruitment consultants in the U.K. You can search by industry or by name of the consultancy.

Support 4 Learning
www.support4learning.org.uk
The site targets recent college graduates with practical information about preparing CVs, interviewing, and assessing online recruitment agencies. Follow the link "Working in the U.K." for a comprehensive set of links for potential expats seeking information on work visas.

TopJobs on the Net
www.topjobs.co.uk
TopJobs is a leading site for technical, management, and other professional jobs. The site includes a series of company profiles.

Total Jobs.com
www.totaljobs.com
Total Jobs lists 32,000 jobs in 28 different industries ranging from education to law to retail to travel and leisure. The site includes a career doctor to answer your job search questions, a directory of employers recruiting via TotalJobs.com, and a salary checker that can be searched by industry.

Embassies and Consular Offices

American embassies and consulates have commercial and/or economic sections that can provide you with business information and explain aspects of the local economy. Inquiries about business opportunities should be addressed either to "Commercial Officer" or "Commercial Section."

Representation of the United Kingdom in the United States

Embassy of Great Britain
3100 Massachusetts Avenue NW
Washington, DC 20008
Tel.: (202) 588–7800
Fax: (202) 588–7870
www.britainusa.org

British Consulates General
Atlanta, (404) 954–7700; Boston, (617) 245–4500; Chicago, (312) 970–3800; Dallas, (214) 521–4090; Houston, (713) 659–6270; Los Angeles, (310) 481–0031; Miami, (305) 374–1522; New York, (212) 745–0200; Orlando, (407) 426–7855; San Francisco, (415) 617–1300; Seattle, (206) 622–9255

Representation of the United States in the United Kingdom

American Embassy
24 Grosvenor Square
London W1A 1AE, U.K.
Tel.: [44] 020 7499 9000
Fax : [44] 020 7409 1637
www.usembassy.org.uk

American Consulate General — Northern Ireland
Queen's House, 14 Queen Street

Belfast BT1 6EQ, Northern Ireland
Tel.: [44] 28 9032 8239
Fax: [44] 28 9024 8482

American Consulate General — Scotland
3 Regent Terrace
Edinburgh EH7 5BW Scotland
Tel.: [44] 131 556 8315
Fax: [44] 131 557 6023

Chambers of Commerce

Chambers of commerce include member firms that are interested in international trade. These are appropriate companies to initially target in the job search.

American Chamber of Commerce U.K.
75 Brook Street
London W1K 4AD, U.K.
Tel.: [44] 207 4677400
Fax: [44] 207 4932394
Email: acc@amcham.co.uk
www.bacc.org

British–American Chamber of Commerce
52 Vanderbilt Avenue, 20th Floor
New York, NY 10017
Tel.: (212) 889–0680
Fax: (212) 661–4074
www.bacc.org

World Trade Centers in the United Kingdom

World trade centers usually include many foreign companies that conduct business in the host country.

Cardiff World Trade Center
Cardiff International Arena
Mary Ann Street
Cardiff CF1 2EQ, Wales
Tel.: [44] 1222 234 900
Fax : [44] 1222 234 901
Email:debbie@
worldtradecenter.btinternet.com
http://homer.cwtc.co.uk/cwtc

London World Trade Center Association
6 Harbour Exchange Square
London E14 9GE, U.K.
Tel.: [44] 20 79873456
Fax : [44] 20 79873498
Email: equiries@
www.worldtradecentrelondon.com

Other Informational Organizations

Foreign government missions in the United States, such as national tourist offices, can furnish visas and information on work permits and other important regulations. They may also offer economic and business information.

British Information Services
845 Third Avenue
New York, NY 10022–6691
Tel.: (212) 745–0277
Fax: (212) 745–0359
www.britain–info.org

British Tourist Authority
551 Fifth Avenue, Seventh Floor
New York, NY 10176–0799
Tel.: (212) 986–2266
Fax: (212) 986–1188
www.travelbritain.org

British Tourist Authority, U.K.
Thames Tower, Blacks Road
London W6 9EL, U.K.
www.visitbritain.com/uk

London Tourist Board
Glen House, Sixth Floor
Stag Place
London SW1E 5LT, U.K.
Tel.: [44] 20 79322000
Fax: [44] 20 79322022
www.londontown.com

Scottish Tourist Board
23 Ravelston Terrace
Edinburgh, Scotland
Tel.: [44] 1506 832 121
www.visitscotland.com

Wales Tourist Board
Veunwl Hjouaw
1 Fitzalan Road
Cardiff DF21UY, Wales

Tel.: [44] 12222 499909   info@tourism.wales.gov.uk
Fax: [44] 1222 485031   ww.i.visitwales.com

Business Directories

Although not always easy to find, business directories can prove invaluable in the international job search. Your best bet for locating these directories is to begin in the reference section of any public or university library. Most directories list company names, addresses, products, and phone numbers. Some directories include executive names and titles and financial information about the company. These sources provide you with the names of the people to contact for employment information as well as financial data, which can tell you how strong a company's position in a country may be.

Britain's Privately Owned Companies: The Top 10,000. Jordan's, 21 St. Thomas Street, Bristol, BS1 6JS, U.K.; www.jordans.co.uk. Describes and ranks 10,000 British companies according to various criteria. Five volumes with 2,000 companies each; £150 per volume; updated annually.

Britain's Top 3,000 Foreign–Owned Companies. Jordan's, 21 St. Thomas Street, Bristol, Avon BS1 6JS, U.K.; www.jordans.co.uk. Covers 3,000 major foreign–owned firms in England or Scotland. 425 pages in 2 volumes; £145 per volume; updated annually.

British Consultants Bureau Directory. British Consultants Bureau, 1 Westminster Palace Gardens, 1–7 Artillery Row, London SW1P 1RJ, U.K.; email: mail@bcbco.uk. Covers about 260 consulting firms in the U.K. engaged in worldwide practice in such specialties as engineering, architecture, and management. Available as a CD–ROM, £70

British Exports. Reed Business Information, Windsor Court, East Grinstead House, East Grinstead, West Sussex RH19 1XA, England; email: bnbshexports.mktg@reddinfo.co.uk. Lists 17,000 British exporters. 1,500 pages; £50, updated annually.

Directory of British Importers. Trade Research Publications, 2 Wycliffe Grove, Werrington, Peterborough PE 4 5DE, U.K. Lists 4,000 British importers and foreign suppliers. 850 pages; £150, updated in odd–numbered years.

Directory of Directors (United Kingdom corporations). Reed Business Information, Windsor Court, East Grinstead House, East Grinstead, West Sussex RH19 1XA, U.K.; email: gjackson@reedinfo.co.uk. Lists 50,000 directors of the top 15,000 public and private British corporations. 3,100 pages in two volumes; £275, updated annually.

Kelly's Industrial Directory. Kelly's Directories, Reed Business Information, Windsor Court, East Grinstead House, East Grinstead, West Sussex RH19 1XA, U.K.; email: kellys.mktg@reedinfo.co.uk; www.kellys.co.uk. Lists 74,000 British and foreign firms. 1,797 pages; £299 updated annually.

Key British Enterprises. Dun & Bradstreet, 50–100 Holmers Farm Way, High Wycombe, Buckinghamshire HP1 2 4UL, U.K. U.S. distributor Dun & Bradstreet, 3 Sylvan Way, Parsippany, NJ 07054. Describes 50,000 leading British firms. 4,737 in four volumes; £520 updated annually.

Kompass United Kingdom. Kompass Publishers, Windsor Court, East Grinstead House, East Grinstead, West Sussex RH19 1XA, U.K.; www.reedinfo.co.uk; www.kompass.com. U.S. distributor USID, 1100 Summer St., P.O. Box 3824, Stamford CT 06905–0824. Lists over 46,000 British manufacturing and service firms. Four volumes; updated annually.

London Directory of Industry and Commerce. Kemps Publishing, 11 The Swan Courtyard, Charles Edward Rd., Yardley GB B26 IBU, U.K. Lists industrial and commercial suppliers in London. 870 pages; £18, updated annually.

Scotland's Top 2,000 Companies. Jordan's, 21 St. Thomas Street, Bristol, BS1 6JS, U.K.; www.jordans.co.uk. Describes Scotland's leading public and private companies. 400 pages; £145, updated annually.

Who Owns Whom: United Kingdom and Ireland. Dun & Bradstreet, 50–100 Holmers Farm Way, High Wycombe, Buckinghamshire HP12 4UL, U.K.; email: customerhelp@dnb.com. U.S. distributor Dun & Bradstreet Information Services, 3 Sylvan Way, Parsippany, NJ 07054. Lists 53,000 British and Irish parent companies and their 176,000 domestic and foreign subsidiaries. £375, updated annually.

Leading Employers in the United Kingdom

The following companies are classified by business area: Banking and Finance; Industrial Manufacturing; Retailing and Wholesaling; Service Industries; and Technology. Company information includes firm name, address, phone and fax numbers, and specific business. In the case of American parent firms, your chances of securing employment abroad are substantially better if you contact the subsidiary company in Europe rather than the parent company in the United States.

The following list is subdivided into England, Northern Ireland, Scotland, and Wales. Each section lists American companies, followed by major European — mostly British — companies in each region. Keep in mind that the contact information for these companies can change pretty often. Before writing to any company, confirm the address and phone number by visiting its website.

American Companies in England

Banking and Finance

Bank of America National Trust and Savings Association
1 Alie Street
London E1 8DE, U.K.
Tel.: [44] 207 634 4000
Fax: [44] 207 634 4334
www.bankamerica.com
(Bank)

Chase Manhattan Bank
125 London Wall
London EC2Y 5AJ, U.K.
Tel.: [44] 207 777 2000
Fax: [44] 207 777 4743
www.chase.com
(Bank)

Citibank International
Oxford Street
London W1C 1JA, U.K.

Tel.: [44] 207 5081201
Fax: [44] 207 5081220
(Bank)

Merrill Lynch European Investment Trust
33 King William Street
London EC4R 9AS, U.K.
Tel.: [44] 207 743 3000
www.merrilllynch.com
(Securities)

Prudential
Laurence Pountney Hill
London EC4R 0HH, U.K.
Tel.: [44] 207 548 3835
Fax: [44] 207 548 3725
www.prudential.co.uk
(Insurance)

Industrial Manufacturing

Abbott Laboratories
Abbott House, Norden Road
Maidenhead, Berkshire SL6 4XE, U.K.
Tel.: [44] 162 877 3355
Fax: [44] 162 864 4305
(Medical research)

Amerada Hess
33 Grosvenor Place
London SW1X 7HY, U.K.
Tel.: [44] 207 823 2626
Fax: [44] 207 887 2199
(Petroleum products)

Armstrong World Industries
Fleck Way, Teesside Industrial Estate
Stockton–on–Tees,
Cleveland TS17 9JT, U.K.
Tel.: [44] 164 276 8666
Fax: [44] 164 275 0046
(Floor and ceiling coverings)

Baxter Healthcare
Caxton Way
Thetford, Norfolk IP24 3SE, U.K.
Tel.: [44] 1842 76 7000
Fax: [44] 1842 76 7099
(Medical supplies)

Black & Decker
210 Bath Road
Slough, Berkshire SL1 3YD, U.K.
Tel.: [44] 175 351 1234
Fax: [44] 175 355 1155

(Power tools)

Borden U.K.
Southampton, Hants S052 9ZB, U.K.
Tel.: [44] 23 80 732 131
Fax: [44] 23 80 738 656
(Resins and plastics)

Bristol–Myers Squibb International
141–149 Staines Road
Hounslow, Middlesex TW3 3JA, U.K.
Tel.: [44] 20 85 727 422
Fax: [44] 20 87 543 789
www.bms.com
(Pharmaceuticals)

Caterpillar
Peckleton Lane, Desford
Leicestershire, Leics LE9 9JT, U.K.
Tel.: [44] 145 582 6826
Fax: [44] 145 582 6900
www. caterpillar.com
(Earth–moving equipment)

Chevron Texaco
1 Westferry Circus, Canary Wharf
London E14 4HA, U.K.
Tel.: [44] 20 77 19 3000
Fax: [44] 20 77 19 5106
(Petroleum products)

Colgate–Palmolive
Middleton Road
Guildford Business Park
Guildford, Surrey GU2 8JZ, U.K.
Tel.: [44] 1 483 302 222
Fax: [44] 1 483 303 003
(Toiletries, cleaning products)

Conoco
Park House, 116 Park Street
London W1K 6NN, U.K.
Tel.: [44] 207 408 6000
Fax: [44] 207 408 6660
www. conoco.com
(Petroleum)

Esso Petroleum Co.
Ermyn Way
Leatherhead, Surrey KT22 8UX, U.K.
Tel.: [44] 137 222 2000
Fax: [44] 137 222 2556
(Petroleum products)

Exxon Mobil Chemical
P.O. Box 122, 4600 Parkway

Solent Business Park
Fareham P.O.15 7AP, U.K.
Tel.: [44] 148 988 4400
Fax: [44] 148 988 4463
www. exxon.com
(Petroleum products)

Ford Motor Co.
Basildon, Essex SS15 6EE, U.K.
Tel.: [44] 126 840 3000
www.ford.com
(Automobiles)

General Electric International Inc.
Basildon Service Centre
Crompton Close
Basildon, Essex SS14 3AY, U.K.
Tel.: [44] 126 828 7654
Fax: [44] 126 852 0274
(Electronic equipment)

Goodyear Great Britain
Stafford Road, Bushbury
Wolverhampton,
W. Midlands WV10 6DH, U.K.
Tel.: [44] 1 902 32 7000
Fax: [44] 1 902 32 7060
(Tires)

Honeywell Control Systems
Honeywell House
Arlington Business Park
Bracknell, Berkshire RG12 1EB, U.K.
Tel.: [44] 1344 656 000
Fax: [44] 1344 656 240
(Process control systems)

Ingersoll–Rand Co.
Swan Lake, Wigan
Lancs WN2 4EZ, U.K.
Tel.: [44] 194 225 7171
Fax: [44] 194 252 2747
(Compressors)

Kellogg Co. of Great Britain
The Kellogg Building, Talbot Road
Manchester, Lancs M16 0PU, U.K.
Tel.: [44] 161 869 2000
Fax: [44] 161 869 2100
(Food processing)

Kodak Polychrome Graphics
Howley Park Estate, Morley
Leeds, W. Yorkshire LS27 0QT, U.K.
Tel.: [44] 113 253 7711
Fax: [44] 113 283 0499

(Photographic supplies)

Eli Lilly Group
Kingsclere Road
Basingstoke, Hants RG21 6XA, U.K.
Tel.: [44] 1256 315 000
Fax: [44] 1256 315 170
(Pharmaceuticals)

Mars U.K.
Dundee Road
Slough, Berkshire SL1 4JX, U.K.
Tel.: [44] 1753 550 055
Fax: [44] 1753 550 111
(Confectionery)

Merck Sharp & Dohme Research Laboratories
Terlings Park, Eastwick Road
Harlow, Essex CM 20 2QR, U.K.
Tel.: [44] 127 944 0000
Fax: [44] 127 944 0390
(Scientific research centers and laboratories)

Mobil Oil Co.
Witan Gate House
500–600 Witan Gate
Milton Keynes, Bucks MK9 1ES, U.K.
Tel.: [44] 1908 853000
Tel.: [44] 1908 853999
(Petroleum products)

Monsanto U.K.
The Maris Centre
45 Hauxton Road, Trumpington
Cambridge, Cambs CB2 2LQ, U.K.
Tel.: [44] 1223 84 9200
Fax: [44] 1223 84 9414
(Chemicals and plastics)

Otis
187 Twyford Abbey Road
London NW10 7DG, U.K.
Tel.: [44] 208 955 3000
Fax: [44] 208 955 3001
(Elevators and escalators)

Phillips Petroleum Co. U.K.
Phillips Quadrant
35 Guildford Road
Woking, Surrey GU22 7QT, U.K.
Tel.: [44] 1483 75 6666
Fax: [44] 1483 75 2309
(Electronics)

Polaroid (UK)
Wheathampstead House
Codicote Road
Wheathampstead, Herts AL4 8SF, U.K.
Tel.: [44] 1582 63 2000
Fax: [44] 1582 63 2004
(Photographic equipment)

Procter & Gamble
Dunsbury Way, Leigh Park
Havant, Hants PO9 5DG, U.K.
Tel.: [44] 239 244 2000
Fax: [44] 239 245 1110
(Personal care products)

Quaker Oats
Southall, Middlesex UB2 4AG, U.K.
Tel.: [44] 208 574 2388
Fax: [44] 208 574 6615
(Processed foods)

Rockwell International
Unit 68 Sutton's Business Park
Sutton Park Avenue, Earley
Reading, Berks RG6 1AZ, U.K.
Tel.: [44] 118 926 1111
Fax: [44] 118 935 9018
(Industrial machinery)

Rohm & Haas (UK)
Lennig House, 2 Mason's Avenue
Croydon, Surrey CR9 3NB, U.K.
Tel.: [44] 2087 74 5300
Fax: [44] 2087 74 5301
(Industrial materials)

Retailing and Wholesaling

Jaguar Cars
Browns Lane, Allesley
Coventry, West Midlands CV5 9DR,
U.K.
Tel.: [44] 2476 402 121
Fax: [44] 2476 405 451
(Automobiles)

Timberland (U.K.)
72 New Bond Street
London W1S 1RR, U.K.
Tel.: [44] 207 495 2133
Fax: [44] 207 495 2137
(Apparel)

Service Industries

Acxiom (U.K.)
Counting House
53 Tooley Street
London SE1 2QN, U.K.
Tel.: [44] 207 526 5100
Fax: [44] 207 526 5200
www.acxiom.com
(Database management services)

AOL Time Warner (U.K.)
Interpark House
7 Down Street
London W1J 7DS, U.K.
Tel.: [44] 207 290 6000
Fax: [44] 207 290 6050
(Publishing and online services)

Leo Burnett
Leo Burnett Building
60 Sloane Avenue
London SW3 3XB, U.K.
Tel.: [44] 207 591 9111
Fax: [44] 207 591 9126
(Advertising)

D'Arcy
Warwick Buildings
Kensington Village Aven Moore Road
London SW14 8HQ, U.K.
Tel.: [44] 207 751 1800
Fax: [44] 207 838 5555
(Advertising)

Dun & Bradstreet
Holmers Farm Way, High Wycombe
Buckinghamshire HP12 4UL, U.K.
Tel.: [44] 149 442 2000
Fax: [44] 149 442 2260
(Financial service software and information)

Manpower
Finance Centre Manpower House
272 High St.
Slough, Berks SL1 1LJ, U.K.
Tel.: [44] 1753 573 111
Fax: [44] 1753 824 524
(Personnel recruitment, international)

McCann–Erickson Advertising
McCann–Erickson House
36 Howland Street
London W1A 1AT, U.K.

Tel.: [44] 207 837 3737
Fax: [44] 207 323 2883
(Advertising)

McGraw–Hill International (U.K.)
McGraw–Hill House
Shoppenhangers Road
Maidenhead, Berkshire SL6 2QL, U.K.
Tel.: [44] 1628 502 500
Fax: [44] 1628 770 224
(Publishing)

Ogilvy & Mather
10 Cabot Square, Canary Wharf
London E14 4QB, U.K.
Tel.: [44] 207 345 3000
Fax: [44] 207 345 9000
(Advertising)

Reader's Digest Association
11 Westferry Circus, Canary Wharf
London E14 4HE, U.K.
Tel.: [44] 207 715 8000
Fax: [44] 207 715 8181
(Publishing)

J. Walter Thompson
40 Berkeley Square
London W1J 5AG, U.K.
Tel.: [44] 207 499 4040
Fax: [44] 207 493 8432
(Market research and advertising)

Young & Rubicam
Greater London House
Hampstead Road
London NW1 7QP, U.K.
Tel.: [44] 207 387 9366
Fax: [44] 207 611 6570
(Advertising)

Technology

Amdahl (U.K.)
The Southmark Building
3 Barrington Road
Altrincham, Cheshire WA14 1HQ, U.K.
Tel.: [44] 161 927 7676
Tel.: [44] 161 941 4739
(Computer equipment)

Analog Devices
Station Avenue, Walton–on–Thames
Surrey KT12 1PF, U.K.
Tel.: [44] 193 226 6000
Fax: [44] 193 224 7401
(Semiconductors)

Hewlett–Packard
Cain Road, Bracknell
Berkshire RG12 1HN, U.K.
Tel.: [44] 1344 360 000
Fax: [44] 1344 363 344
(Printers and calculators)

IBM (U.K.)
Jackson House, Sibson Road
Sale, Cheshire M33 7DB, U.K.
Tel.: [44] 161 905 6000
Fax: [44] 161 969 6108
(Data processing equipment)

Motorola
Church Road, Lowfield Health
Crawley, W. Sussex RH11 0PQ, U.K.
Tel.: [44] 129 340 4343
Fax: [44] 1293 404 362
(Semiconductors and cell phones)

NCR
206 Marylebone Road
London NW1 6LY, U.K.
Tel.: [44] 207 723 7070
Fax: [44] 207 725 8224
(Data processing equipment)

Unisys
Baker's Court, Baker's Road
Uxbridge, Middlesex UB8 1RG, U.K.
Tel.: [44] 1895 237 137
Fax: [44] 1895 270 355
(Computer software and hardware)

Xerox Business Services
Bridge House, Oxford Road
Uxbridge, Middx UB8 1HS, U.K.
Tel.: [44] 1895251133
Fax: [44] 1895254095
(Office equipment)

European Companies in England

The following are major European firms that operate in the U.K. These selected European companies are not necessarily British. These companies will generally employ their own nationals before they hire Americans.

Banking and Finance

Barclay's
54 Lombard Street
London EC3P 3AH, U.K.
Tel.: [44] 207 699 5000
Tel.: [44] 207 699 2694
(Commercial bank)

Guardian Insurance
Royal Exchange
London EC3V 3LS, U.K.
Tel.: [44] 207 283 7101
Fax: [44] 207 621 2599
(Insurance)

Lloyds of London
1 Lime Street
London EC3M7HA, U.K.
Tel.: [44] 20 7327 1000
Fax: [44] 20 7327 5599
www.lloyds.com
(Insurance)

National Westminster Insurance Services
37 Broad Street
Bristol, Avon BS99 7NQ, U.K.
Tel.: [44] 117 926 3000
(Insurance and financial services)

Royal & Sun Alliance Insurance
Leadenhall Court
1 Leadenhall Street
London EC3V 1PP, U.K.
Tel.: [44] 207 337 5477
Fax: [44] 207 337 5233
(Insurance)

Standard Chartered Bank
1 Aldermanbury Square
London EC2V 7SB, U.K.
Tel.: [44] 207 280 7500
Fax: [44] 207 280 7156
(Banking and financial services)

Industrial Manufacturing

Laura Ashley
27 Bagleas Lane
Fulham, London SW6 2QA, U.K.
Tel.: [44] 207 880 5100
Fax: [44] 207 880 5200
(Clothing)

Associated British Foods
Weston Centre, Bowater House
68 Knightsbridge
London SW1X 7LQ, U.K.
Tel.: [44] 207 589 6363
Fax: [44] 207 584 8560
(Processed foods)

Bayer
Bayer House, Strawberry Hill
Newbury, Berkshire RG14 1JA, U.K.
Tel.: [44] 163 556 3000
Fax: [44] 163 556 3393
(Chemicals)

BICC
Quantum House, Maylands Avenue
Hemel Hempstead, Herts HP2 4SJ, U.K.
Tel.: [44] 144 221 0100
Fax: [44] 144 221 0158
(Transmission equipment)

Blue Circle Industries
84 Eccleston Square
London SW1V 1PX, U.K.
Tel.: [44] 207 828 3456
Fax: [44] 207 245 8195
(Building materials)

The Body Shop International
Watersmead Business Park
Littlehampton,
West Sussex BN17 6LS, U.K.
Tel.: [44] 1903 731 500
Fax: [44] 1903 726 250
(Personal care products)

British Aerospace (International)
Warwick House
Farnborough Aerospace Centre
Farnborough, Hants GU14 6YU, U.K.
Tel.: [44] 125 273 3232
Fax: [44] 125 238 3000
(Aircraft, defense equipment, and space systems)

BP (The British Petroleum Company)
Britannic House, 1 Finsbury Circus
London EC2M 7BA, U.K.
Tel.: [44] 207 496 4000
Fax: [44] 207 496 4630
(Petroleum products)

British Steel
Ashorne Hill Management Col
Leamington Spa,
Warks CV33 9QW, U.K.
Tel.: [44] 192 648 8029
Tel.: [44] 192 648 8024
(Iron and steel)

Cadbury Schweppes
25 Berkeley Square
London W1J 6HB, U.K.
Tel.: [44] 207 409 1313
Fax: [44] 207 830 5200
(Confectionery and beverages)

Castrol Industrial
Burmah Castrol House, Pipers Way
Swindon, Wiltshire SN3 1RE, U.K.
Tel.: [44] 1793 512 712
Fax: [44] 1793 491 442
(Holding companies)

Ciba Specialty Chemicals
Charter Way
Macclesfield, Cheshire SK10 2NX, U.K.
Tel.: [44] 1625 617 878
Fax: [44] 1625 888 701
(Chemicals)

Coats Viyella
Huthwaite Road
Sutton In Ashfield,
Notts NG17 2EJ, U.K.
Tel.: [44] 1623 44 5000
Fax: [44] 1623 44 5047
(Textiles, clothing, thread)

Electrolux
101 Oakley Road
Luton, Bedfordshire LU4 9QQ, U.K.
Tel.: [44] 1582 491 234
Fax: [44] 1582 490 214
(Electrical appliances)

GlaxoSmithKline
Glaxo Wellcome House
Berkeley Avenue
Greenford, Middx UB6 0NN, U.K.
Tel.: [44] 208 966 8000
Fax: [44] 207 408 0228
(Pharmaceuticals)

Glynwed Pipe Systems
Headland House
54 New Coventry Rd
Sheldon, Birmingham

W Midlands B26 3AZ, U.K.
Tel.: [44] 121 700 1000
Fax: [44] 121 700 1001
(Holding company)

Guinness
Park Royal Brewery
London NW10 7RR, U.K.
Tel.: [44] 208 965 7700
Fax: [44] 208 453 0222
(Brewing and distilling)

Hanson
1 Grosvenor Place
London SW1X 7JH, U.K.
Tel.: [44] 207 245 1245
Fax: [44] 207 235 3455
(Mining, chemicals)

Imperial Chemical Industries
Imperial Chemical House
9 Millbank
London SW1P 3JF, U.K.
Tel.: [44] 207 834 4444
Fax: [44] 207 834 2042
(Chemicals, pharmaceuticals, plastics)

Land Rover
International Headquarters
Warwick Technology Park
Warwick, Warks CV34 6RG, U.K.
Tel.: [44] 1926 482 000
Fax: [44] 1926 482 001
(Automobiles)

Lonrho Africa
Lancaster House, Mercury Court,
Tithebarn Street
Liverpool, Merseyside L2 2RG, U.K.
Tel.: [44] 151 243 5300
Fax: [44] 151 236 2190
(Holding company with interests in mining, agribusiness, hotels, and other land–related concerns)

Lucas Aerospace
Stafford Road, Wolverhampton
W Midlands WV10 7EH, U.K.
Tel.: [44] 1902 782 381
Fax: [44] 1902 782 720
(Aerospace and automotive components)

Nokia (U.K.)
Lancaster House, Lancaster Way
Ermine Business Park, Huntingdon

Cambridgeshire PE29 6YJ, U.K.
Tel.: [44] 1480 434 444
Fax: [44] 1480 435 111
(Telecommunications)

Peugeot Talbot Motor Co.
London Road
Coventry, W Midlands CV8 3DZ, U.K.
Tel.: [44] 247 688 6000
Fax: [44] 247 688 6001
(Automobile manufacturing)

Pilkington
Prescot Road, St. Helen's
Merseyside WA10 3TT, U.K.
Tel.: [44] 1744 69 2000
Fax: [44] 1744 69 2880
(Glass products)

Reckitt Benckiser
Delta 1200, Welton Road
Delta Business Park
Swindon, Wilts SN5 7XZ, U.K.
Tel.: [44] 1793 427 200
Fax: [44] 1793 511 572
(Household goods and
pharmaceuticals)

RMC Group
RMC House, Coldharbour Lane,
Thorpe
Egham, Surrey TW20 8TD, U.K.
Tel.: [44] 1932 568 833
Fax: [44] 1932 568 933
(Construction materials)

Rolls–Royce
65 Buckingham Gate
London SW1E 6AT, U.K.
Tel.: [44] 207 222 9020
Fax: [44] 207 227 9170
(Engines and aircraft equipment)

Shell International Petroleum Co.
Shell Centre
London SE1 7NA, U.K.
Tel.: [44] 20 7934 1234
Fax: [44] 20 7934 8060
(Oil products)

Simon Group
Simon House, 2 Eaton Gate
London SW1W 9BJ, U.K.
Tel.: [44] 207 730 0777
Fax: [44] 207 881 2200
(Port and engineering services)

Smith & Nephew
15 Adam Street
London WC2N 6LA, U.K.
Tel.: [44] 207 401 7646
Fax: [44] 207 930 3353
(Medical and health care products)

SmithKline Beecham
S B House, Great West Rd.
Brentford, Middlesex TW8 9EP, U.K.
Tel.: [44] 208 560 5151
(Pharmaceuticals)

Tate & Lyle
Sugar Quay, Lower Thames Street
London EC3R 6DQ, U.K.
Tel.: [44] 207 626 6525
Fax: [44] 207 623 5213
(Food processing)

T I Group
Lambourn Court
Abingdon Oxon OX14 1UH, U.K.
Tel.: [44] 1235 555 570
Fax: [44] 1235 705 570
(Specialized engineering products)

Unilever
PO Box 68, Unilever House, Blackfriars
London EC4P 4BQ, U.K.
Tel.: [44] 207 822 5252
Fax: [44] 207 822 5898
(Personal care products)

United Biscuits Holdings
Church Road, West Drayton
Middlesex UB7 7PR, U.K.
Tel.: [44] 1895 432 100
Fax: [44] 1895 448 848
(Food processing)

Vauxhall Motors
Griffin House, Osbourne Road
Luton, Bedfordshire LU1 3YT, U.K.
Tel.: [44] 1582 721 122
Fax: [44] 1582 427 400
(Motor vehicles)

Vodafone Group
The Courtyard, 2–4 London Road
Newbury, Berkshire, RG14 1JX, U.K.
Tel.: [44] 1635 33 251
Fax: [44] 1635 45 713
(Cellular phones)

Retailing and Wholesaling

Asda Group
Asda House, Southbank
Great Wilson Street
Leeds, W Yorks LS11 5AD, U.K.
Tel.: [44] 1132 435 435
Fax: [44] 1132 418 666
(Food, furnishings)

Boots Company
Nottingham NG90 1BS, U.K.
Tel.: [44] 1159 506 111
Fax: [44] 1159 592 727
(Pharmaceuticals)

Dixons Group
Maylands Avenue
Hemel Hempstead
Hertfordshire HP2 7TG, U.K.
Tel.: [44] 1442 353 000
Fax: [44] 1442 233 218
(Retailing outlets)

Gallaher
Members Hill, Brooklands Road
Weybridge, Surrey KT13 0QU, U.K.
Tel.: [44] 1932 859 777
Fax: [44] 1932 832 508
(Tobacco products and housewares)

Kingfisher
North West House
119 Marylebone Road
London NW1 5PX, U.K.
Tel.: [44] 207 724 7749
Fax: [44] 207 724 1160
(General merchandise retailing)

Littlewoods Retail
Sir John Moores Building
100 Old Hall Street
Liverpool, Merseyside L70 1AB, U.K.
Tel.: [44] 1512 352 222
(Mail order and chain stores)

Marks & Spencer
Michael House, 47–67 Baker Street
London W1U 8EP, U.K.
Tel.: [44] 207 935 4422
Fax: [44] 207 487 2679
(Clothing, food, household goods)

Wm Morrison Supermarkets
Hilmore House, Thornton Road
Bradford, West Yorkshire BD8 9AX,
U.K.
Tel.: [44] 1274 494 166
Fax: [44] 1274 494 831
(Supermarkets)

J. Sainsbury
33 Holborn
London EC1N 2HT, U.K.
Tel.: [44] 207 695 6000
Fax: [44] 207 695 7610
(Food products)

Selfridges Retail
400 Oxford Street, West End
London W1A 1AB, U.K.
Tel.: [44] 207 629 1234
Fax: [44] 207 495 8321
(Department stores)

W.H. Smith
Nation's House, 103 Wigmore Street
London W1U 1WH, U.K.
Tel.: [44] 20 7409 3222
Fax: [44] 20 7514 9633
www.whsmithplc.com
(Specialty retail)

Tesco
Tesco House, Delamare Road
Cheshunt, Hertfordshire EN8 9SL, U.K.
Tel.: [44] 1992 632 222
Fax: [44] 1992 630 794
(Food products)

Service Industries

Amec
Sandiway House, Hartford
Northwich, Cheshire, CW8 2YA, U.K.
Tel.: [44] 1606 883 885
Fax: [44] 1606 688 996
(Engineering and construction)

BAA
130 Wilton Road
London SW1V 1LQ, U.K.
Tel.: [44] 207 834 9449
Fax: [44] 207 932 6699
(Airport operations)

Bass Hotels & Resorts
Devonshire House, Mayfair Place
London W1J 8AJ, U.K.
Tel.: [44] 207 495 2500
Fax: [44] 207 495 2769

(Pub, hotel, and restaurant operation)

British Airways
PO Box 365 Harmondsworth
West Drayton, Middx UB7 0GB, U.K.
Tel.: [44] 8457 79 9977
(Airline)

British Railways Board
Whittle House, 14 Pentonville Road
London N1 9HF, U.K.
Tel.: [44] 207 904 5000
Fax: [44] 207 904 5040
(Rail transport)

British Telecommunications
BT Centre, 81 Newgate Street
London EC1A 7AJ, U.K.
Tel.: [44] 207 356 5000
Fax: [44] 207 356 5520
(Telecommunication services)

Costain Group
Costain House, Nicholsons Walk
Maidenhead, Berkshire, SL6 1LN, U.K.
Tel.: [44] 1628 842 575
Tel.: [44] 1628 842 554
(Engineering and construction)

Inchcape
33 Cavendish Square
London W1G 0PW, U.K.
Tel.: [44] 207 546 0022
Fax: [44] 207 546 0010
(International marketing and distribution)

Johnson Matthey
2–4 Cockspur Street, Trafalgar Square
London SW1Y 5BQ, U.K.
Tel.: [44] 207 269 8400
Fax: [44] 207 269 8433
(Materials technology)

John Laing
133 Page Street, Mill Hill
London NW7 2ER, U.K.
Tel.: [44] 208 959 3636
Fax: [44] 208 906 5297
(Engineering and construction)

John Mowlem & Co.
Fairway Court, Elland Road
Leeds, W Yorks LS11 8BU, U.K.
Tel.: [44] 113 283 0700
Fax: [44] 113 283 0701

(Engineering and construction)

The Peninsular & Oriental Steam Navigation Co.
Peninsular House, 79 Pall Mall
London SW1Y 5EJ, U.K.
Tel.: [44] 207 930 4343
Fax: [44] 207 925 0384
(Shipping, construction)

Reed Elsevier
25 Victoria Soad
London SW1H 0EX, U.K.
Tel.: [44] 207 222 8420
Fax: [[44] 207 227 5799
(Business publishing and information)

Reuters
85 Fleet Street
London EC4P 4AJ, U.K.
Tel.: [44] 207 250 1122
(News service and radio advertising management)

Severn Trent
2297 Coventry Road
Birmingham
West Midlands B26 3PU, U.K.
Tel.: [44] 1217 224 000
Fax: [44] 1217 224 800
(Water and waste treatment)

Shell International Trading & Shipping
Shellmax House, Strand
London WC2R 0ZA, U.K.
Tel.: [44] 20 7546 5000
Fax: [44] 20 7546 2786
(Shipping)

Tarmac
Millfields Road, Ettingshall
Wolverhampton
Midlands WV4 6JP, U.K.
Tel.: [44] 1902 382 511
Fax: [44] 1902 382 922
(Engineering and construction)

Transport Development Group
Windsor House, 50 Victoria Street
London, SW1H 0NR, U.K.
Tel.: [44] 207 222 7411
Fax: [44] 207 222 2806
(Storage, packing, and distribution)

United News & Media
Ludgate House
245 Blackfriars Road
London, SE1 9UY, U.K.
Tel.: [44] 207 921 5000
Fax: [44] 207 928 2719
(Publishing)

Whitbread
Chiswell Street
London, EC1Y 4SD, U.K.
Tel.: [44] 207 606 4455

Fax: [44] 207 615 1000

(Restaurants)

George Wimpey
Gates House, Turnpike Road
High Wycombe, Bucks HP12 3NR, U.K.
Tel.: [44] 1494 558 323
Fax: [44] 1494 885 663
(Engineering and construction services)

Northern Ireland

American Companies in Northern Ireland

Conoco
Airport Road West
Belfast, Co Antrim BT3 9EA
Northern Ireland
www.conoco.com
Tel.: [44] 28 904 54306
Fax: [44] 28 904 63999
(Petroleum products)

Grant Thornton
Water's Edge
Clarendon Dock
Belfast, Co Antrim BT1 3BH
Northern Ireland

Tel.: [44] 28 9031 5500
Fax: [44] 28 9031 4036
(Accounting consultancy)

Seagate Technology (Ireland)
1 Disc Drive
Springtown Industrial Estate
Londonderry
Co Londonderry BT48 0BF,
Northern Ireland
Tel.: [44] 28 7127 4000
Fax: [44] 28 7127 4207
www.seagate.com
(Computer software and hardware)

European Companies in Northern Ireland

Belfast Telegraph Newspapers
124 Royal Avenue
Belfast, Co Antrim BT1 1EB
Northern Ireland
Tel.: [44] 28 9026 4000
Tel.: [44] 28 9055 4502
(Publishing)

European Components Co.
770 Upper Newtownrds Road
Belfast BT16 0UL
Northern Ireland
Tel.: [44] 1232 480 595
Fax: [44] 1232 480 786
(Textiles)

**Harland & Wolff Shipbuilding &
Heavy Industries**
Queen's Island
Belfast, Co Antrim BT3 9DU
Northern Ireland
Tel.: [44] 28 9045 8456
Fax: [44] 28 9045 8515
(Shipping)

Ulster Bank
11–16 Donegall Square East
Belfast, Co Antrim BT1 5HD
Northern Ireland
Tel.: [44] 28 9027 6000
Fax: [44] 28 9027 5661
(Commercial bank)

American Companies in Scotland

Banking and Finance

American Express Europe
139 Prices Street
Edinburgh, Midlothian EH2 4BR
Scotland
Tel.: [44] 131 718 2500
Tel.: [44] 131 225 6116
www.americanexperess.com
(Traveler's financial services)

Chubb Insurance Company of Europe
163 West George Street
Glasgow G2 2GJ, Scotland
Tel.: [44] 141 221 5770
Fax: [44] 141 221 5217
www.chubb.com
(Insurance)

Industrial Manufacturing

Baker Oil Tools (U.K.)
Kirkhill Industrial Estates, Kirkhill Road
Aberdeen, Aberdeenshire AB21 0GQ
Scotland
Tel.: [44] 1224 223 500
Fax: [44] 1224 771 400
www.bakerhughes.com
(Oil field drilling)

Ethicon
P.O. Box 408, Bankhead Avenue
Edinburgh, Midlothian EH11 4HE
Scotland
Tel.: [44] 131 453 5555
Fax: [44] 131 453 6011
(Medical supplies)

Halliburton Manufacturing & Services
Kirkhill Industrial Estate
Howemoss Place, Dyce
Aberdeen, Aberdeenshire, AB21 0GS
 Scotland
Tel.: [44] 1224 795 000
Fax: [44] 1223 771 438
www.halliburton.com
(Energy construction)

Kodak
Scottish Business Centre
Pegasus House
375 West George Street
Glasgow G2 4NT Scotland
(Photographic chemicals and equipment)

Russell Corp. (U.K.)
1 Bain Square, Kirkton Campus
Livingston, W Lothian EH54 7BQ
Scotland
Tel.: [44] 1506502000
Fax: [44] 1506419494
(Athletic apparel)
Russell Corp.

National Semiconductor (U.K.)
Larkfield Industrial Estate
Greenock, Renfrewshire PA16 0EQ
Scotland
Tel.: [44] 1475 633733
Fax: [44] 1475 638515
www.nationa.com
(Semiconducters)

Service Industries

Drake Beam Morin
D B M House, 4 Wemyss Place
Edinburgh, Midlothian EH3 6DH
Scotland
Tel.: [44] 131 225 9333
Fax: [44] 131 225 9518
www.dbm.com
(Human resources management consulting)

ManpowerEdinburgh
38 George Street
Edinburgh EH2 2LE
Scotland
Tel.: [44] 131 226 5591
www.manpower.com
(Temporary services)

Technology

Compaq Computer Manufacturing
Erskine Ferry Road
Bishopton, Renfrewshire PA7 5PP
Scotland
Tel.: [44] 141 814 8000
Fax: [44] 141 812 7745
www.hp.com (Compaq is now owned by Hewlett–Packard)
(Business and personal computers)

European Companies In Scotland

Banking and Finance

Bank of Scotland
P.O. Box 5, The Mound
Edinburgh, Midlothian EH1 1YZ
Scotland
Tel.: [44] 131 442 7777
Fax: [44] 131 243 7082
(Bank)

The Royal Bank of Scotland
42 St. Andrew Square
Edinburgh, Midlothian EH2 2YE
Scotland
Tel.: [44] 131 556 8555
Fax: [44] 131 557 6565
(Bank)

Royal Bank Insurance Services
152 West Regent Street
Glasgow, Lanarkshire G2 2RQ
U.K.
Tel.: [44] 141 248 1212
Fax: [44] 141 248 6363
(Insurance)

Industrial Manufacturing

ABB Vetco Gray (U.K.)
Broadfold Road, Bridge of Don
Aberdeen, Aberdeenshire AB23 8EY
Scotland
Tel.: [44] 122 485 2000
Fax: [44] 122 485 2434
(Oil and gas machinery)

Alcan Packaging
321 Aikenhead Road
Glasgow, Lanarkshire G42 0PE
Scotland
Tel.: [44] 141 531 2800
Fax: [44] 141 531 2805
(Aluminum products)
Alcan Aluminium

Ciba Pigments
Hawkhead Road
Paisley, Renfrewshire PA2 7BG
Scotland
Tel.: [44] 141 887 1144
Fax: [44] 141 847 5199
(Chemicals and dyes)

Highland Distillers Operation
The Macallan Distrillery, Craigellachie
Aberlour, Banffshire AB38 9RX
Scotland
Tel.: [44] 1340 871 471
Fax: [44] 1340 871 212
(Whiskey distilling)

Scottish & Newcastle Breweries
50 East Fettes Avenue
Edinburgh, Midlothian EH4 1RR
Scotland
Tel.: [44] 131 523 2000
Fax: [44] 131 523 2315
(Alcoholic beverages)

TotalFinaElf
1 Claymore Drive, Bridge of Don
Aberdeen, Aberdeenshire AB23 8GB
Scotland
Tel.: [44] 122 429 7000
Fax: [44] 122 429 8999
(Petroleum)

Retailing and Wholesaling

John Menzies
Executive Suite, 108 Princes Street
Edinburgh Midlothian EH2 3AA
Scotland
Tel.: [44] 131 225 8555
Fax: [44] 131 225 1150
(Retail stores)

Russell Corp. (U.K.)
1 Bain Square, Kirkton Campus
Livingston West Lothian EH54 7BQ
Scotland
Tel.: [44] 150 650 2000
Fax: [44] 150 641 9494
(Furnishings)

Service Industries

Det Norske Veritas
Cromarty House
67–72 Recent Quay
Aberdeen, Aberdeenshire, AB11 5AR
Scotland
Tel.: [44] 122 433 5000
Tel.: [44] 122 459 3311
(Environmental services)

Todd & Duncan
Lochleven Mills
Kinross, Kinross Shire KY13 8DH
Scotland
Tel.: [44] 157 786 3521
Fax: [44] 157 786 4533
Fabric mills

Rohm & Haas (Scotland)
Wholeflats Road
Grangemouth, Stirlingshire FK3 9UY
United Kingdom
Tel.: [44] 1324 473 361
Fax: [44] 1324 474 303
(Industrial raw materials)

American Companies in Wales

GE Aircraft Engines
Caerphilly Road, Nantgarw
Cardiff, S Glamorgan CF15 7YJ
Wales
Tel.: [44] 144 384 1041
Fax: [44] 144 384 7287
(Aerospace technology)

Rockwell Automation
Units 13–14, Severn Farm Industrial Estate
Welshpool, Powys SY21 7DF
Wales
Tel.: [44] 1938 554 711
Fax: [44] 1938 552 823
www.rockwell.com
(Aerospace and defense products)

European Companies in Wales

Allied Steel & Wire
Cardiff, South Glamorgan CF24 5XQ
Wales
Tel.: [44] 29 2047 1333
Fax: [44] 29 2033 2001
(Steel manufacturing)

Det Norske Veritas
Cremona House, 2 Lon Ucha
Cardiff, South Glamorgan CF4 6HL
Wales
Tel.: [44] 836 74 1936
(Shipping; offshore platform services)

Pirelli General
Harriet Street

P.O. Box 1
Mid Glamorgan CF44 7EN
Wales
Tel.: [44] 685 87 0170
Fax: [44] 685 87 7071
(Tires)

Rowan Foods
6 Pit Hey Place
Skelmersdale WN8 9PS
Wales
Tel.: [44] 1695 726 228
Fax: [44] 1695 501 97
(Fruits and vegetables)

Major International Nonprofit Employers in the U. K.

Amnesty International
99–119 Rosebury Avenue
London EC1R 4RE, U.K.
Tel.: [44] 207 814 6200
Fax: [44] 207 833 1510
www.amnesty.org.uk

Friends of the Earth
26–28 Underwood Street
London N1 7JQ, U.K.
Tel.: [44] 207 490 1555
Fax: [44] 207 490 0881

www.foe.co.uk

International Youth Hostel Federation
Trevelyan House, Dimple Road
Matlock, Derbyshire, DE4 3YH, U.K.
Tel.: [44] 01629 592600
Fax.: [44] 01629 592702
www.yha.org.uk

Oxfam
274 Banbury Road
Oxford OX2 7DY, U.K.

Tel.: [44] 1865 312610
www.oxfam.org.uk

Royal Society for the Arts
8 John Adam Street
London WC2N 6EZ, U.K.
Tel.: [44] 207 930 5115
www.rsa.org.uk

The Salvation Army
101 Newington Causway
London SE1 6BN, U.K.
Tel.: [44] 20 7367 4500
Fax: [44] 20 7367 4728
www.salvationarmy.org.uk

International Schools in the United Kingdom

American Community School Heywood
Portsmouth Road
Cobham, Surrey KT11 1BL, U.K.
Tel.: [44] 1932 867 251
Fax: [44] 1932 869 795
Email: mkay@acs–england.co.uk
www.acs–england.co.uk
(U.S./International Baccalaureate curriculum: prekindergarten through grade 13)

The American School in London
One Waverley Place
London NW8 0NP, U.K.
Tel.: [44] 20 7449 1200
Fax: [44] 20 7449 1350
www.asl.org
(U.S. curriculum: kindergarten through grade 12)

TASIS England American School
Coldharbour Lane
Thorpe, Surrey TW20 8TE, U.K.
Tel.: [44] 1932 565 252
Fax: [44] 1932 564 644
www.tasis.com
(U.S. curriculum: prekindergarten through grade 12)

United World College of the Atlantic
Lynton House
Tavistock Square
London, WC1H 9LT
Tel.: [44] 20 7388 2066
Fax: [44] 20 7388 3166
Email: uwcio@uwc.org
www.uwc.org
(International Baccalaureate curriculum)

Chapter 12

Republic of Ireland

Major employment center: Dublin

Major business language: English

Language skill index: Plan to speak English; Gaelic is not used in the business place

Currency: Euro

Telephone country code: 353

Time zone: Eastern Standard Time + 5 hours

Punctuality index: The Irish are less strict about time than the English

Average daily temperature, high/low: January: 47°/35°; July: 67°/51° (Dublin)

Average number of days with precipitation: January: 18 days; July: 14 days

Best bet for employment:

    For students: Apply to the Council on International Educational Exchange's work abroad program

    Permanent jobs: High tech industry

Chance of finding a job: Opportunities are best in the high tech industry.

Useful tip: The Irish are more relaxed and talkative than either their U.S. or British counterparts. Local pubs are traditional places to meet and socialize. They are also one of Ireland's most famous exports.

Ireland, or Eire, approximately the size of West Virginia, is across the Irish Sea from Britain in northwestern Europe. The country covers about 83 percent of the island that bears its name and encompasses several low mountain ridges near the coasts, surrounding a low–lying interior. In the fourth century B.C., the Celts arrived and assimilated the local peoples, the Picts and the Erainn, to establish a Gaelic civilization. By the fifth century A.D., Gaelic culture had spread to Scotland and elsewhere and St. Patrick had largely converted the country to Christianity. Norse invaders were defeated in 1014. Gaelic is still spoken in the northwestern parts of the country, although virtually everyone speaks English as well.

Ireland has become Europe's Silicon Valley, the continent's center for high tech.

In the twelfth century, England received Ireland as a papal fief as Henry II began the English invasions. In 1801 Britain and Ireland became the United Kingdom of Great Britain and Ireland. A devastating famine and economic decline in the late nineteenth century eventually led to independence efforts. An unsuccessful rebellion in 1916 led to civil war until 1921, when the major part of Ireland received dominion status. Britain maintained Ulster as Northern Ireland. In 1949 the Irish Free State declared itself the Republic of Ireland and withdrew from the British Commonwealth.

Ireland has a parliamentary system of government. The prime minister is officially known in Gaelic as Taoiseach (pronounced tea shock). The president of Ireland is elected for seven years and is limited to two terms. The main political parties are Fianna Fáil, Somm Féin, and Fine Gael. Bernie Ahern was re–elected in June 2002 as prime minister; the current president is Mary MacAleese. Ireland is a member of the European Union and the United Nations and was an initial adopter of the Euro.

The ties between the U.S. and Ireland are deeply rooted in a shared ancestral heritage that began with mass emigration of Irish Catholics fleeing the potato famine of 1846–1848. This relationship, however, has now broadened and matured, given the substantial U.S. corporate involvement in the Irish economy. Investment by U.S. companies has been an important factor in the impressive economic growth that Ireland has experienced since 1996. Emigration has declined significantly with Ireland's economic boom. For the first time in its modern history, immigration to Ireland, especially of non–Europeans, is a growing phenomenon with political, economic, and social consequences. However, Irish citizens do continue the common practice of taking temporary residence overseas for work or study, mainly in the U.S., U.K., and elsewhere in Europe, before returning to establish careers in Ireland.

Ireland, which is over 95 percent Catholic, still struggles with such matters as divorce, the availability of contraception, and abortion. Divorce became legal only in 1997. Although abortion is illegal under the Irish constitution, officials estimate that 6,000 women travel to Britain to terminate a pregnancy each year.

Offices are usually open Monday through Friday from 9 a.m. to 5 p.m. Many shops remain open late on Thursdays or Fridays.

Current Economic Climate

Ireland, appropriately nicknamed the Celtic Tiger, has a small but highly open economy. Between 1993 and 1997, the economy grew by an unprecedented 40 percent. In 2001, Ireland's gross domstic product (GDP) grew by 6.6 percent, the largest percentage of any country in the world. Despite a slowing economy in 2002, Ireland is still experiencing low interest rates, low unemployment, high standards of living, and an explosion of new public sector spending.

The healthy state of the economy meant that Ireland could be as a founding member of the European single currency. It has a low unemployment rate (3.8 percent), although its inflation rate (4.5 percent) is more than twice that recommended by the E.U. The traditional focus of economic activity has shifted from agriculture to industry. Ireland has become the continent's own Silcon Valley, Europe's center for the high–technology sectors of manufacturing. Ireland is the second–largest exporter of software in the world behind the United States. Other major industries include fishing, pharmaceuticals, and financial services.

Ireland's literary history

The Irish are very proud of their literary tradition. Ireland has produced many important writers including Oscar Wilde, W.B. Yeats, George Bernard Shaw, Sean O'Casey, James Joyce, Samuel Beckett, and, more recently, Roddy Doyle. Ireland is so serious about its literary history that it does not tax writers.

Ireland's 10 Largest Companies

(2001, based on market capitalization)

1. Elan Corporation
2. Allied Irish Banks
3. Bank of Ireland
4. CRH
5. Irish Life & Permanent
6. Ryanair Holdings
7. Eircom
8. Jefferson Smurfit Group
9. Kerry Group
10. Anglo Irish Bank Corporation

Getting Around in Ireland

Since the rail network focuses primarily upon Dublin, buses serve as a convenient alternative in areas not covered by trains. Bus fares may be more expensive. Ferries provide passage across the English Channel and along the English and Irish coastline. Eurail and InterRail passes are accepted throughout Ireland, and pass holders are given various discounts on trains, ferries, and airplanes. Ireland's major airline, Aer Lingus, connects Dublin with London but is more expensive than several available ferry services. Ryan Air, a no–frills carrier, also connects Ireland and Britain.

Using the phone, fax, and Internet

Public phones in Ireland almost exclusively use phone cards, available from Telecom Éireann. In September 1998, seven–digit phone numbers were introduced throughout Ireland. A new prefix was placed between the area code and an existing five– or six–digit number. Directory assistance is "1190." Faxes can be sent from post offices. Email cafes are common in major cities like Dublin, Cork, and Galway.

Employment Regulations and Outlook for Americans

Unlike E.U. residents, U.S. citizens who wish to work must have a work permit from a prospective employer upon arriving in Ireland. A visa is not required for stays of less than 90 days.

If you are a student, you can bypass the usual employment restrictions by contacting the Council for International Educational Exchange (CIEE) about its Work & Travel Ireland Program. The Union of Students in Ireland Travel Service (USIT NOW), which cooperates with CIEE in administering the program, provides a resource center with job and housing listings, general information, and program advisors. See Chapter 9 for additional resources.

USIT NOW
19–21 Aston Quay
OConnell Bridge
Dublin 2, Ireland

Tel.: [353] 1 602 1600

Fax: [353] 1 679 2124

www.usit.ie

Short–Term and Temporary Work

A good bet for casual work in Ireland is to work as an au pair. There are also ample opportunities to work in pubs or hotels, especially in tourist centers such as Dublin, but these employers require you to apply in person. USIT (see above) can be most helpful with this work. See Chapter 9 for additional resources.

Job Options Bureau (Irish representative of the International Au Pair Association)

Tourist House

40/41 Grand Parade
Cork, Ireland
Tel.: [353] 21 427 5369
Fax: [353] 21 417 4829

Email: joboptionsbureau@eircom.ie   www.nanniesireland.com

Internship Programs

Several professional internship programs offer students opportunities to obtain professional experience. Some programs, such as the Arcadia University parliamentary internship program and Dublin Internships, also offer an opportunity for students to earn academic credit. See Chapter 9 for additional resources.

Arcadia University Dublin Parliamentary Internships
Arcadia University Center for Education Abroad
450 South Easton Road
Glenside, PA 19038–3295
Tel.: (215) 572–2901
www.arcadia.edu/cea/
Interns undertake research and support administrative activities under the direction of members of the Irish Parliament. Participants are also required to take three academic courses that cover Irish history, politics, and literature.

Dublin Internships
8 Orlagh Lawn
Scholarstown Road
Dublin 16, Ireland
Tel./Fax: [353] 1 494 5277
http://homepage.tinet.ie/
~dublinternships/di_home.html

Students from all academic majors are placed in appropriate internships. Positions are generally full–time and unpaid; students get credit through their home institutions.

Dublin Internship Program
Boston University International Programs
232 Bay State Road, 5th Floor
Boston, MA 02215
Tel.: (617) 353–9888
www.bu.edu/abroad/index.html
Internships are available in public administration, government, political science, business, arts, architecture, communications, marketing, and law. The program combines an internship with coursework on various aspects of Ireland's history and contemporary culture, including its art, economy, literature, media, and politics.

Volunteer Opportunities

Ireland has a strong tradition of volunteerism. Many international organizations manage work camps that recruit volunteers to help with conservation projects, peace and reconciliation conferences, and programs for the elderly. These programs usually involve volunteers from many countries and can be a unique way to experience living and working abroad. See Chapter 9 for additional volunteer opportunities.

An Oige (Irish Youth Hostel Association)
39 Mountjoy Square South
Dublin 1, Ireland
Tel.: [353] 1 830 4555
An Oige places people into voluntary work with hostels in exchange for room and board.

Conservation Volunteers Ireland
The Stewards House
Rathfarnham Castle

Dublin 14, Ireland
Tel.: [353] 1 495 2878
Fax: [353] 1 495 2879
Email: info@cvi.ie
www.cvi.ie
CVI offers environmental working holidays intended to protect Ireland's natural and cultural heritage. Most projects last less than two weeks. Program fees start at €40 including and room and board. You must join CVI in order to participate in projects.

Voluntary Service International
(SCI International Voluntary Service)
30 Mountjoy Square
Dublin 1, Ireland
Tel.: [353] 1 855 1011
Fax: [353] 1 855 1012
Email: vsi@iol.ie
www.iol.ie/~vsi/
VSI places groups of 10–20 volunteers
on service projects in Europe, including
Ireland. Volunteer assignments range
from conservation projects to assisting
the elderly to working with refugees.
Most projects last two to four weeks.
Fees range from $50 to $100, and vol-
unteers are responsible for their own
travel expenses.

Resources for Further Information

Newspapers in Ireland

Irish Independent
Tel.: [353] 1 705 5333
Fax: [353] 1 872 0304
www.independent.ie

The Irish Times
Tel.: (718) 392–7477 (U.S. subscriptions)
Fax: [353] 1 677 2130
www.ireland.com

Useful Websites for Job Seekers

The Internet is a good place to begin your job search. Most Irish employers
list vacancies, especially those in technical fields, on websites. There are also
many websites that provide useful information for researching the Irish job
market.

All Jobs in Ireland
www.jobs–in–ireland.com
Scans major Internet employment sites
and extracts over 3,000 positions daily.

All Jobz.cm
www.alljobz.com
Features job vacancies throughout Ireland in IT/eCommerce, finance, and
manfacturing.

BusinessWorld Ireland
www.businessworld.ie
A one–stop resource for information
about the Irish business market. The site
is intended for investors, but will be
equally valuable for job seekers who are
researching companies.

Ireland Hiring
www.irelandhiring.com
Non–members may browse job vacancies; members can design online CVs,
set up job search agents, and create online profiles accessible by headhunters.
Membership is free.

Irish Jobs
www.irishjobs.ie
Page for recruiters and job seekers to
contact each other. Features a large listing of jobs in Ireland, a resume posting
service, and regular column with tips on
the Irish job market. A good starting
place.

Jobs–Ireland
www.jobs–ireland.com
Features job advertisements from employers and recruitment agencies. Job
seekers can sign up for a Job Alert service that notifies you about new vacancies via email.

Recruit Ireland
www.recruitireland.com
Very large job bulletin board. The Career Centre offers job seekers particularly good information about
interviewing techniques, preparing a
CV, personal finance, living and working
in Ireland, and industry information.

StepStone
www.stepstone.ie

One of Europe's leading online recruitment sites.

Embassies and Consular Offices

American embassies and consulates have commercial and/or economic sections that can provide you with business information and explain aspects of the local economy. Inquiries about business opportunities should be addressed either to "Commercial Officer" or "Commercial Section."

Representation of Ireland in the United States

Embassy of Ireland
2234 Massachusetts Avenue NW
Washington, DC 20008
Tel.: (202) 4623939
Fax: (202) 2325993
www.irelandemb.org

Irish Consulates General:
Boston, (617) 267–9330; Chicago, (312) 337–1868; New York, (212) 319–2555; San Francisco, (415) 392–4214

Representation of the United States in Ireland

American Embassy
42 Elgin Road
Dublin 4, Ireland

Tel.: [353] 1 668 8777
Fax: [353] 1 668 9946
www.usembassy.ie

Chambers of Commerce

Chambers of commerce consist of member firms in both countries interested in international trade. These are appropriate companies to initially target in the job search.

Chamber of Commerce of Ireland
17 Merrion Square
Dublin 2, Ireland
Tel.: [353] 1 661 2888
Fax: [353] 1 661 2811
Email: info@chambersireland.ie
www.chambersireland.ie

Ireland Chamber of Commerce in the U.S.
556 Central Avenue
New Providence, NJ 07974
Tel.: (908) 2861300
Fax: (908) 2361200
www.iccusa.org

Cork Chamber of Commerce
Fitzgerald House
Summerhill North
Cork, Ireland
Tel.: [353] 21 450 9044
Fax: [353] 21 450 8568
Email: info@corkchamber.ie
www.corkchamber.ie

U.S. Chamber of Commerce in Ireland
6 Wilton Place
Dublin 2, Ireland
Tel.: [353] 1 661 6201
Fax: [353] 1 661 6217
Email: info@amcham.ie
www.amcham.ie

Other Informational Organizations

Foreign government missions in the United States, such as the Irish Tourist Board, can furnish visas and information on work permits and other important regulations. They may also offer economic and business information about the country.

Irish Tourist Board
345 Park Avenue
New York, NY 10154
Tel.: (212) 4180800
Fax: (212) 3719059
www.irelandvacations.com

Irish Tourist Board
Baggot Street Bridge
Baggot Street
Dublin 2, Ireland
Tel.: [353] 1 602 4000
Fax: [353] 1 602 4100
www.ireland.travel.ie

Business Directories

Although hard to find, business directories are valuable tools for the international job search. Most directories list company names, addresses, products, and phone numbers. Some include executive names and titles and company financial information. These sources provide you with the names of the people to contact for employment information as well as financial data, which can tell you how strong a company's position in a country may be.

American Business Directory. Published annually by the American Chamber of Commerce in Ireland, 20 St. Stephens Green, Dublin 2, Ireland; email: amcham@iol.ie. Lists the 350 members of the U.S. Chamber of Commerce in Ireland as well as U.S.–related business in Ireland. 160 pages, updated annually.

Ireland's Top Companies. Business and Finance Media Ltd., 50 Fitzwilliam Square W., Dublin 2, Ireland; email: belenos@tinet.id; www.businessand finance.ie. Lists top 1,000 firms in Ireland, based on turnover and market capitalization. Updated annually.

Irish Financial Services Directory. Kompass Ireland Publishers, Parnell Court, Granby Row, Dublin 1, Ireland; Email: info@kompass.ie; www.kompass.ie. Lists top 2,000 financial institutions in Ireland. Updated annually.

Overseas Companies in Ireland. Industrial Development Agency of Ireland, Wilton Park House, Wilton Place, Dublin 2, Ireland; U.S. distributor IDA Ireland, 345 Park Avenue, 17th Floor, New York, NY 10154. This free directory is updated continuously and printed on request. It covers 1,000 overseas manufacturers and international service companies with operations in Ireland. 100 pages.

Thom's Commercial Directory. Thom's Directories, 38 Merrion Square, Dublin 2, Ireland. Lists 93,000 manufacturers, industrial, commercial, and service companies, government agencies, banks, trade unions, and company executives. 1,151 pages, updated annually.

Who Owns Whom: United Kingdom and Ireland. Available annually from Dun & Bradstreet, 50–100 Holmers Farm Way, High Wycombe, Buckinghamshire HP12 4UL, U.K.; email: customerhelp.dnb.com. U.S. distributor Dun & Bradstreet Information Services, Three Sylvan Way, Parsippany, NJ 07054. Lists 53,000 British and Irish parent companies and 176,000 domestic and foreign subsidiaries. Published annually.

Leading Employers in Ireland

The following companies are classified by business area: Banking and Finance; Industrial Manufacturing; Retailing and Wholesaling; Service Industries; and Technology. Company information includes firm name, address, phone and fax numbers, and specific business. Your chances of securing employment abroad are substantially better if you contact the subsidiary company in Europe rather than the parent company in the U.S. Keep in mind that the contact information for companies listed in this section changes frequently. Before writing to any company, confirm its address.

American Companies in Ireland

Banking and Finance

AON
10–12 Lansdowne Road
Dublin 4, Ireland
Tel.: [353] 1 605 9300
Fax: [353] 1 660 1187
www.aon.com
(Insurance)

Bank of America
Russell Court
St. Stephens Green
Dublin 2, Ireland
Tel.: [353] 1 407 2100
Fax: [353] 1 407 2199
www.bankamerica.com
(Bank)

BDO Simpson Xavier
Beaux Lane House Mercer Street Lower
Dublin 2, Ireland
Tel.: [353] 1 4700000
Fax: [353] 1 4770000
www.bdo.com
(Accounting)

Citibank NA
1 North Wall Quay
Custom House Quay
Dublin 1, Ireland
Tel.: [353] 1622 2000
Fax: [353] 1622 2222
www.citibank.com
(Bank)

St. Paul International Insurance Co.
Block 1 Harcourt Centre
Harcourt Street
Dublin 2, Ireland
Tel.: [353] 1 609 5600
Fax: [353] 1 662 4945
www.stpaul.com
(Insurance)

Industrial Manufacturing

3M Ireland
3M House
Adelphi Centre
Dun Laoghaire
Dublin, Ireland
Tel.: [353] 1 280 3555
Fax: [353] 1 280 3509
www.3m.com.ie
(Adhesive products)

Bausch & Lomb Ireland
Contact Lens Plant Unit 424/425
Waterford Industrial Estates
Waterford, Ireland
Tel.: [353] 51 550 001
Fax: [353] 51 35 5639
www.bausch.com
(Contact lenses)

Becton Dickinson Insulin Syringe
Pottery Road Dun Laoghaire
Dublin, Ireland
Tel.: [353] 1 202 5222
Fax: [353] 1 285 4332
(Surgical equipment)

Borden
Unit 3 Pinewood Close Boghall Road,
Bray
Wicklow, Ireland

Tel.: [353] 285 2931
Fax: [353] 282 8057
(Food processing)

Braun Oral B Ireland
Dublin Road
Carlow, Ireland
Tel.: [353] 503 76400
Fax: [353] 503 76404
(Consumer appliances)

Colgate–Palmolive
3054 Lake Drive Citywest
Business Campus
Dublin 24, Ireland
Tel.: [353] 1 842 4711
Fax: [353] 1 403 9801
(Toiletries)

ConvaTec Ireland
Block 2, Unit 3, Two St. John's Court
Santry
Dublin 9, Ireland
www.bms.com
(Pharmaceuticals)

General Motors Distribution Ireland
Belgard Road, Tallaght
Dublin 24, Ireland
Tel.: [353] 1 514033
(Motor vehicles)

Grace Construction Products
Unit 200
Holly Road
Western Industrial Estate
Dublin 12, Ireland
Tel.: [353] 1 456 9600
Fax: [353] 1 456 9604
www.grace.com
(Chemicals)

The Kellogg Co. of Ireland
9 St John's Court Swords Road
Santry
Dublin 9, Ireland
Tel.: [353] 1 842 9100
Fax: [353] 1 842 9974
www.kellogg.com
(Breakfast cereals)

Rockwell Automation (Ireland)
Naas Road Industrial Park
Naas Road
Dublin 12, Ireland
Tel.: [353] 1 408 9600

Fax: [353] 1 456 5474
www.rockwell.com
(Electronic equipment)

Texaco (Ireland)
Texaco House Ballsbridge
Dublin 4, Ireland
Tel.: [353] 1 668 6822
Fax: [353] 1 668 4890
www.texaco.com
(Petroleum products)

Xerox
Ballycoolin Business Park
Blanchardstown
Dublin 15, Ireland
Tel.: [353] 1 608 6000
Fax: [353] 1 508 6521
www.xerox.com
(Copier equipment)

Retailing and Wholesaling

R.H. Macy & Co.
51 Wellington Road
Dublin 4, Ireland
(Department store)

Service Industries

Accenture
1 Harbourmaster Place IFSC
Dublin 1, Ireland
Tel.: [353] 1 646 2000
Fax: [353] 1 646 2020
(Management consulting)

Deloitte & Touche
Deloitte & Touch House 29
Earlsfort Terrace
Dublin 2, Ireland
Tel.: [353] 1 417 2200
Fax: [353] 1 417 2300
www.deloitte.com
(Accounting services)

Dun & Bradstreet
Office 606
27 Upper Fitzwilliam Street
Dublin 2, Ireland
Tel.: [353] 1 632 8662
Fax: [353] 1 632 8651
www.dnbcorp.com
(Business information)

Hewitt Associates
Iveagh Court
6 Harcourt Road
Dublin 2, Ireland
Tel.: [353] 1 418 9130
Fax: [353] 1 407 0310
www.hewitt.com
(Benefits consulting)

Kelly Temporary Services
21/22 Grafton Street
Dublin 2, Ireland
Tel.: [353] 1 679 3111
Fax: [353] 1 677 3048
www.kellyservices.com
(Temporary services)

Technology

Amdahl Ireland
Unit 100 Airside Business Park, Swords
Dublin, Ireland
Tel.: [353] 1 813 6000
Fax: [353] 1 813 6104
www.amdahl.com
(Computers)

Analog Devices BV
Raheen Business Park
Raheen, Limerick, Ireland
Tel.: [353] 61 22 9011
Fax: [353] 61 30 8448
(Semiconductors)

Apple Computer (Sales)
Hollyhill Industrial Estate
Hollyhill
Cork, Ireland
Tel.: [353] 21 428 4000
Fax: [353] 21 439 2220
www.apple.com
(Personal computers)

Cisco Systems Internetworking
Block P6 East Point Business Park
Clontarf
Dublin 3, Ireland
Tel.: [353] 1 819 2700
Fax: [353] 1 819 2701
www.cisco.com
(Computer networking systems)

Computer Associates
Embassy House Ballsbridge
Dublin 4, Ireland

Tel.: [353] 1 607 7300
Fax: [353] 1 607 7373
www.cai.com
(Computer consulting)

Hewlett–Packard Ireland
Park House 195 North Circular Road
Dublin 7, Ireland
Tel.: [353] 1 838 5433
Fax: [353] 1 838 5285
www.hp.com
(Computer hardware and software)

IBM Ireland
Oldbrook House 24–32 Pembroke Road
Ballsbridge
Dublin 4, Ireland
Tel.: [353] 1 815 4000
Fax: [353] 1 815 4040
www.ibm.com
(Information processing equipment)

Intel
Collinstown Industrial Park Leixlip
Kildare, Ireland
Tel.: [353] 1606 7000
Fax: [353] 1 606 8519
(Semiconductor manufacturer)

Lucent Technologies Europe
Blanchardstown Industrial Park
Blanchardstown
Dublin 15, Ireland
Tel.: [353] 1 886 4444
Fax: [353] 1 886 4400
www.lucent.com
(Communication systems)

Microsoft Ireland (European Operations Center)
Blackthorn Road
Sandyford Industrial Est.
Dublin 18, Ireland
Tel.: [353] 1 295 3826
Fax: [353] 1 295 3581
www.microsoft.com
(Computer software)

Motorola Ireland
Mahon Industrial Estate
Blackrock
Cork, Ireland
Tel.: [353] 21 435 7101
Fax: [353] 21 435 7635
www.mot.com

(Semiconductors, cell phones)

Oracle Corporation Ireland
Oracle House Herbert Street
Dublin 2, Ireland
Tel.: [353] 1803 1000
Fax: [353] 1 803 9400
(Database management software)

Sun Microsystems Ireland
Hamilton House
East Point Business Park
Dublin 3, Ireland
Tel.: [353] 1 819 9100
Fax: [353] 1 819 9200
www.sun.com
(Mainframe and microcomputers)

European Companies in Ireland

Banking and Finance

Allied Irish Banks
Ballsbridge
Dublin 4, Ireland
Tel.: [353] 1 660 0311
Fax: [353] 1 660 9137
(Bank)

Anglo Irish Bank Corporation
Stephen Court, 18–21
St. Stephen's Green
Dublin 2, Ireland
Tel.: [353] 1 616 2000
Fax: [353] 1 661 1852
www.angloirishbank.ie
(Bank)

Bank of Ireland
Lower Baggot Street
Dublin 2, Ireland
Tel.: [353] 1 661 5933
Fax: [353] 1 661 5671
www.bankofireland.ie
(Bank)

Ulster Bank
33 College Green
Dublin 2, Ireland
Tel.: [353] 1 677 7623
Fax: [353] 1 679 7941
(Bank)

Industrial Manufacturing

BP Chemicals
P.O. Box 8133
Dublin 13, Ireland
Tel.: [353] 1 407 3236
www.bp.com
(Industrial chemicals, polymers, and solvents)

Bula Resources (Holdings)
7 Priory Hall Stillorgan
Dublin, Ireland
Tel.: [353] 677 5222
Fax: [353] 677 5106
(Oil and gas exploration and development)

Cadbury Ireland
Malahide Road, Coolock
Dublin 5, Ireland
Tel.: [353] 1 848 0000
Fax: [353] 1 847 2905
(Confectionery)

CRH
Belgard Castle, Clondalkin
Dublin 22, Ireland
Tel.: [353] 1 404 1000
Fax: [353] 1 404 1007
www.crh.ie
(Cement producers)

Dragon Oil
60 Lower Baggot Street
Dublin 2, Ireland
Tel.: [353] 1 676 6693
Fax: [353] 1 661 8025
www.dragonoil.com
(Oil and gas exploration and production)

Elan Corporation
Lincoln House, Lincoln Place
Dublin 2, Ireland
Tel.: [353] 1 709 4000
Fax: [353] 1 662 4949
www.elan.com
(Drugs, cosmetics, and health care)

Fyffes
1 Beresford Street
Dublin 7, Ireland
Tel.: [353] 1 887 2700

www.flyffes.com
(Produce distribution)

Glanbia
Kilkenny, Ireland
Tel.: [353] 1 567 2200
www.glanbia.com
(Dairy products processing)

Guinness Ireland Group
St. James Gate
Dublin 8, Ireland
Tel.: [353] 1 453 6700
Fax: [353] 1 453 6938
www.guinness.com
(Beer)

Hibernia Foods
46 Merrion Square
Dublin 2, Ireland
Tel.: [353] 1 661 1030
Fax: [353] 1 661 1029
www.hiberniafoods.ie
(Frozen and convenience foods)

Irish Petroleum Company
Warrington House,
Mount Street Crescent
Dublin 2, Ireland
Tel.: [353] 1 660 7966
Fax: [353] 1 660 7952
(Petroleum products)

Irish Shell
Shell House
Beech Hill Clonskeagh
Dublin 4, Ireland
Tel.: [353] 1 202 8888
Fax: [353] 1 283 8318
(Petroleum products)

IWP International
19 Fitzwilliam Square
Dublin 2, Ireland
Tel.: [353] 1 661 1958
Fax: [353] 1 661 1957
www.iwp.ie
(Personal care products)

Jefferson Smurfit Group
Beech Hill Clonskeagh
Dublin 4, Ireland
Tel.: [353] 12027000
Fax: [353] 12694481
www.smurfit.ie
(Paper packaging products)

Kerry Group
Princes Street, Tralee
County Kerry, Ireland
Tel.: [353] 66 718 2000
Fax: [353] 66 718 2961
www.kerrygroup.com
(Food products)

Nestlé (Ireland)
3030 Lake Drive Citywest
Business Campus, Tallaght
Dublin 24, Ireland
Tel.: [353] 1 449 7777
Fax: [353] 1 449 7778
(Food products)

Trinity Biotech
IDA Business Park
Bray, Wicklow, Ireland
Tel.: [353] 1 276 9800
Fax: [353] 1 276 9888
www.trinitybiotech.com
(Diagnostic substances)

Unilever Best Foods
Whitehall Road Rathfarnham
Dublin 14, Ireland
Tel.: [353] 1 298 4344
Fax: [353] 1 298 4397
(Consumer products)

Waterford Wedgwood
12 Upper Hatch Street
Dublin 2, Ireland
Tel.: [353] 147 81855
Fax: [353] 147 84863
www.waterfordwedgwood.com
(Housewares and accessories)

Retailing and Wholesaling

Dunnes Stores
67 Upper Stephen Street
Dublin 8, Ireland
Tel.: [353] 1 475 1111
Fax: [353] 1 475 4405
www.dunnesstores.com
(Department stores)

Marks & Spencer (Ireland)
24/29 Mary Street
Dublin 1, Ireland
Tel.: [353] 1 872 8833
Fax: [353] 1 872 8995
(Department stores and shops)

Superquinn
Newcastle Road
Lucan Co., Dublin, Ireland
Tel.: [353] 1 630 2000
Fax: [353] 1 628 1443
www.superquinn.ie
(Grocery retailing)

Tesco Ireland
Gresham House, Marine Road
Dun Laoghaire, Ireland
Tel.: [353] 1 280 8441
Fax: [353] 1 280 0136
(Retailing outlets)

United Drug
United Drug House, Belgard Road,
Tallaght
Dublin 24, Ireland
Tel.: [353] 1 459 8877
Fax: [353] 1 459 6893
www.united–drug.ie
(Drugs and sundries)

Service Industries

Aer Lingus Group
Dublin Airport
Dublin, Ireland
Tel.: [353] 1 886 3705
Fax: [353] 1 886 3851
www.flyaerlingus.com
(Airline)

Bell Freight Transport Group Ltd.
Bell House
Dublin 2, Ireland
Tel.: [353] (1) 40 26 00
Fax: [353] 1 405 2696
(Transportation service)

CPL Resources
83 Merrion Square
Dublin 2, Ireland
Tel.: [353] 1 614 6000
Fax: [353] 1 614 6011
www.cpl.ie
(Staffing)

Gresham Hotel Group
23 Upper OConnell St.
Dublin 1, Ireland
Tel.: [353] 1 878 7966
Fax: [353] 878 6032
www.ryan–hotels.com

(Hotels)

Irish Continental Group
Alexandra Road
P.O. Box 19, Ferryport
Dublin 1, Ireland
Tel.: [353] 1 607 5628
Fax: [353] 1 855 2268
www.icg.ie
(Shipping; passenger ferries)

Irish Life & Permanent
Lower Abbey Street
Dublin 1, Ireland
Tel.: [353] 1 704 2000
Fax: [353] 704 1900
www.irishlifepermanent.ie
(Insurance)

McInerney Holdings
29 Kenilworth Square
Rathgar Dublin 6, Ireland
Tel.: [353] 1 496 2010
www.mcinerney.ie
(Building, structural work, contractors)

Reflex Group
19 Elgin Road, Ballsbridge
Dublin, Ireland
Tel.: [353] 1 660 0213
Fax: [353] 1 660 0366
(Fitness centers)

Ryanair Holdings
Dublin Airport
Dublin, Ireland
Tel.: [353] 1 812 1212
Fax: [353] 1 812 1213
www.ryanair.ie
(Airlines)

Technology

Datalex
Howth House, Harbour Road
Dublin, Ireland
Tel.: [353] 1 839 1787
Fax: [353] 1 839 1781
www.datalex.com
(Corporate, professional and financial software)

Eircom
Cumberland House Fenian Street
Dublin 2, Ireland
Tel.: [353]800501502

Fax: [353]17012943
www.eircom.ie
(Telecommunications)

Eurologic
Clonshaugh Industrial Estate,
Clonshaugh
Dublin 17, Ireland
Tel.: [353] 1 206 1300
Fax: [353] 1 2061299
www.eurologic.com
(Data storage devices)

Horizon Technology Group
14 Joyce Way, Park West Business Park,
Nangor Rd.
Dublin, Ireland
Tel.: [353] 1 620 4900
Fax: [353] 1 620 4902
www.horizon.ie

(Computer software and services)

IONA Technologies
The IONA Building
Shelbourne Road, Ballsbridge
Dublin 4, Ireland
Tel.: [353] 1 637 2000
Fax: [353] 1 637 2888
www.iona.com
(Computer software and services)

Rapid Technology Group
Pottery House, Pottery Road
Dun Laoghaire Co.
Dublin, Ireland
Tel.: [353] 1 235 0279
Fax: [353] 1 235 0361
www.screenkeys.com
(Telecommunications)

International Schools in Ireland

St. Andrew's College
Booterstown Avenue
Blackrock, Dublin, Ireland
Tel.: [353] 1 288 2785
Fax: [353] 1 283 1627
Email: information@st.andrew.ie
www.standrew.ie
(U.S./International Baccalaureate curriculum, grades 1 through 12)

Sutton Park School
St. Fintan's Road, Sutton
Dublin 13, Ireland
Tel: [353] 1 832 2940
Fax: [353] 1 832 5929
Email: info@suttonpark.ie
www.suttonpark.ie
(Kindergarten through grade 12)

Chapter 13

France

Major employment centers: Paris, Marseilles, Lyon, Toulouse

Major business language: French

Language skill index: Absolutely necessary. The French are particularly proud of their language and will generally not respond to inquiries initiated in English. If your French language skills are weak, you will find it difficult to find a job in France.

Currency: Euro

Telephone country code: 33

Time zone: Eastern Standard Time + 6 hours

Punctuality index: Somewhat lax. Paris is stricter

Average daily temperature, high/low: January: 42°/32°; July: 76°/55° (Paris)

Average number of days with precipitation: January: 15 days; July: 12 days

Best bet for employment:

  For students: Apply to an au pair agency

  Permanent jobs: Computer science + French could = Job

Chance of finding a job: Good for those with technical expertise and language skills

Useful tip: Don't look for a job in August; the whole country is on vacation.

The French Republic, larger than California but smaller than Texas, is in Western Europe. Shaped like a pentagon, France borders the Bay of Biscay to the west, Spain, Andorra, and the Mediterranean to the south, Italy, Switzerland, and Germany to the east, and the English Channel (La Manche), Belgium, and Luxembourg to the north. The Alps, the Vosges, and the Pyrenees mountains form France's eastern and southern borders. The rest of the country consists of river basins and a large central plateau.

Frequent strikes by public sector employees are common throughout France.

In addition to French, minorities speak German, Flemish, Italian, Breton, Basque, and Catalan. About 80 percent of the population are Roman Catholic, with significant Protestant and Jewish groups. France maintains an overseas province, French Guyana, in South America and several dependencies in the Caribbean and the Pacific, such as French Caledonia.

The Romans, under Julius Caesar, conquered Gaul in the first century B.C. and ruled the region until the Frankish invasions in the fifth century A.D. and Charlemagne's subsequent empire. The Carolingian, Valois, and Bourbon dynasties ruled France until the Revolution in 1789. France had established itself as a preeminent power, especially under ambitious rulers such as Louis XIV, the Sun King. After the Revolution, Napoleon Bonaparte eventually consolidated his power, replacing the republican government with the French Empire, which spread across the Continent. By 1815, France had been militarily defeated but remained one of Europe's major powers.

Two monarchies and two republics took turns ruling France until World War I, when the country suffered severe losses. The Third Republic finally collapsed in World War II in the face of German military power. The Nazi–installed Vichy regime survived until 1946, when a provisional government was installed. The Fourth Republic collapsed in 1958 in the midst of escalating tensions in French Algeria. Charles de Gaulle then wrote a new constitution, that created a powerful president, and was elected to that office to inaugurate the current Fifth Republic. France is a member of the European Union and the North Atlantic Treaty Organization, although French troops do not belong to NATO's central command structure.

In 1981, François Mitterrand was elected France's first Socialist president. In 1986, parliamentary elections gave the right–wing opposition, led by Jacques Chirac, a majority in the National Assembly. Mitterand was forced to work with the opposition, an unprecedented arrangement in French government that became known as cohabitation. In 1995, Chirac was elected president of France with 52 percent of the vote. He was re–elected as president in 1997, but his party lost support to a coalition of Socialists, Communists, and Greens that was led by Lionel Jospin, who became prime minister. Chirac was re–elected in a 2001 run–off election against far–right candidate Jean–Marie Le Pen. Although Chirac soundly defeated Le Pen, many French considered the campaign an embarrassment because of Le Pen's anti–immigration sentiments and racist ideas.

The perpetually prickly relationship between France and the U.S. has been especially contentious since the September 11 attacks. The French government has criticized U.S. foreign policy as being overly simplistic and argued that the U.S. has not adequately consulted with its European allies in its war on terrorism. These tensions culminated in mutual recriminations, complaints, and condemnations during the U.N.'s crisis of diplomacy over the war in Iraq. The depth of damage to the relationship of these erstwhile allies remains to be seen.

Weekday business hours in France vary by region and industry but almost always include a mid–day break from noon to 2:00 p.m. sometimes running as late as 3:30 or 4:00 p.m. in the south. Traditionally, stores close on Monday but are now usually open in the larger cities. Some stores are open on Sunday morning as well.

Current Economic Climate

The unemployment rate in France fell from 12.6 percent in June 1997 to 9 percent in January 2001, the lowest level since January 1984. This rate has remained stable through 2002. The government retains majority ownership of key railway, electricity, aircraft, and telecommunication firms, although it is now slowly selling off its holdings in France Telecom and Air France, among others. France remains the leading agricultural producer in Western Europe. The government has been reluctant to reduce its generous social welfare benefits or state bureaucracy and, instead, has chosen to raise taxes and reduce defense spending.

One of the most defining features of the French economy is union activity, strongest in the public sector where strikes are often a daily occurrence. The power of French unions to disrupt business distorts their size. Only about 15 percent of the French workforce is unionized — among the lowest rates in the E.U. — although France is one of the most industrialized nations in the world. The unions were key to reducing the work week to 35 hours, which has drawn criticism for lowering the competitiveness of French business.

Large numbers of immigrants from North Africa perform much of the unskilled labor in France. The E.U. and the U.S. are France's major trading partners, but the former African, Caribbean, and Pacific colonies are also important. The country's major industries include steel, machinery, chemicals, automobiles, metallurgy, aircraft, electronics, mining, textiles, food processing, and tourism.

France's 10 Largest Companies

(2001, based on market capitalization)

1. TotalFinaElf
2. Aventis
3. Vivendi Universal
4. France Telecom
5. AXA Société Anonyme

6. L'Oréal
7. Elf Aquitaine
8. Sanofi–Synthelabo
9. Carrefour
10. BNP Paribas

Getting Around in France

France enjoys one of the world's most extensive and efficient rail networks, the SNCF. It offers numerous discount specials for the frequent traveler, and Eurail passes are accepted. Seat reservations should be made in advance. Flying is expensive but fares are cheaper with discount packages that combine train travel with flights. Traveling by bus is cheap but slow.

Employment Regulations and Outlook for Americans

U.S. citizens normally do not need visas to stay less than 90 days. If you intend to work, you must present upon arrival a work permit obtained by your prospective employer from the French Ministry of Labor. A residence permit must also be arranged with the local Prefecture de Police or with the French Consulate. The government's concern about unemployment levels in France discourages further immigration, while stringent new rules regarding employment make it very difficult for foreigners to find a job. French laws are similarly strict regarding employment for international students studying at French universities.

Brush up on your penmanship!

In France, cover letters are traditionally handwritten because many employers still use handwriting analysis as a selection tool. This is especially common in fields such as public relations, marketing and sales, or for companies that do not recruit by email. Your handwritten cover letter must be perfect. You cannot cross out any words or use any correction fluid, a real challenge for those used to word processing! Typewritten letters are becoming more common, however, with the growth of email and the Internet.

The good news, however, is that there are ways for Americans, especially students and young professionals, to legally find work in France. Students can bypass the usual employment restrictions by contacting the Council for International Educational Exchange, IAESTE, or the Association for International Practical Training, described in the "Work Exchange" section of Chapter 9 beginning on page 107. The French Chamber of Commerce manages a Young Professional Program in France.

The national employment agency, Agence National pour l'Emploi (ANPE), maintains regional offices throughout France and offers a wide range of services. The ANPE maintains a partnership with the Office de Migration

Internationale and can assist the international job seeker, but it cannot arrange your work permit. The ANPE website lists over 100,000 job vacancies and is updated daily. One of the 32 regional Centres d'Information et de Documentation Jeunesse (CIDJ) could be useful for student workers looking for information on seasonal agricultural work and on regulations affecting foreign students. Students can obtain a free guide, *Employment in France for Students,* from the French Cultural Services, 972 Fifth Avenue, New York, NY 10021; phone, 212-439-1400, fax, 212-439-1455; www.info-france-usa.org/culture/education/index.html.

Unskilled work is fairly plentiful in France. Employers are very likely to hire foreign workers, especially in the tourist industry. Manual labor in hotels and restaurants in the south of France is readily found, but employers are often unscrupulous about paying the minimum wage to non–E.U. nationals. Tourist jobs are available in the Alps during the winter and on the Cote d'Azur in the summer. Americans may be able to find opportunities teaching English either at foreign language schools or to private individuals. Most universities also employ English speakers to work in their language labs. Agricultural work throughout the country can usually be found in the summer, picking various kinds of fruits. Grape–picking is usually plentiful, but the work is particularly unpleasant. Competition for all types of farm work is intense owing to the huge foreign labor pool.

ANPE
Espace Emploi International
48, Boulevard de la Bastille
F–75012 Paris, France
Tel.: [33] 1 53 02 25 50
www.anpe.fr

Centres d'Information et de Documentation Jeunesse (CIDJ)
101 Quai Branly
F–75740 Paris Cedex 15, France
Tel.: [33] 1 44 49 12 00
www.cidj.asso.fr

Short–term and Temporary Work

The best bet for casual work is as an au pair. In addition to the agencies described below, Au Pair in Europe and the Accord Cultural Exchange place au pair candidates in France. It is also possible to find casual work in the hospitality industry, but that requires very strong French language skills. CIEE's Work & Travel France program can assist people looking for these sorts of casual jobs. Chapter 9 provides details on these resources.

Butterfly et Papillon
5, Avenue de Geneve
F–74000 Annecy, France
Tel.: [33] 450 67 01 33
Fax: [33] 450 67 03 51
Email: aupair.france@wanadoo.fr
www.butterfly–papillon.com
The agency places au pairs between the ages of 18 and 25 in assignments that last from three to 18 months.

The French American Center
4, rue Saint Louis
F–34000 Montpellier, Languedoc, France
Tel.: [33] 4 67 92 30 66
www.frenchamericancenter.com/english/ExperienceFrance.asp
The Au Pair in France program serves the needs of French families in the Languedoc region in the south of France who need child–care assistance.

Studying to get to France

Ever since my first sojourn in France — a six–week stay in Paris the summer I was 17 — I've known I wanted to lead part of my life within the country's borders. Studying abroad in France during college was not a difficult decision to make. But deciding how to go about it was harder… should I go with a prearranged "study abroad" program, I wondered, and enjoy an easier option tailored to foreigners? Or should I strike out on my own, applying directly to the school of my choice? Ultimately, I decided on the latter option, spending a year as a directly enrolled student of the Institute for Political Studies of Paris (Sciences Po).

This was one of the best decisions I ever made. In my experience, successfully working abroad requires bucking the trend — finding a way to make yourself stand out from the many foreigners competing for the same position. My time at Sciences Po allowed me to develop a France–based network I probably would not enjoyed otherwise. The school's notoriety in France also set me a step ahead with French and France-based employers.

While searching for an apartment in the FUSAC, a well–known French–Anglo biweekly here in Paris, I stumbled across an ad from an American publishing house seeking an editorial intern for its Paris office. Not really thinking I would get the job, I decided to send in my CV anyway. Thanks, in part, to my diploma from Sciences Po, the company did offer me the internship, which eventually turned into an offer for a full–time editorial position.

If there's any advice I can offer to job–seekers in France, it's to keep your eyes and ears wide open. The best opportunities don't always come from traditional channels; often they come from random ads you see in the papers, or from your French friend's cousin's brother's hearing about a job. To learn about these opportunities, however, you have to be in the right place at the right time, which is usually off the beaten path. — *Jennifer Westerfield, Paris, France*

Internship Programs

Several professional internship programs offer students opportunities to obtain professional experience. Some programs, such as Internships International and Internships in Francophone Europe, also offer an opportunity to earn academic credit. See Chapter 9 for more summer job and internships resources. The French–American Chamber of Commerce, described on page 181, also offers programs.

Internships in Francophone Europe

26, rue Cmdt. Mouchotte J108

F–75014 Paris, France

Tel.: [33] 1 43 21 78 07

Fax: [33] 1 42 79 94 13
Email: ifeparis.worldnet.fr
www.ifeparis.org
IFE offers semester–long opportunities to current students and recent graduates interested in working for companies in French–speaking European countries. IFE places only 12 to 15 students per semester and works closely with American universities that grant academic credit for internships. Placements are available in parliament, NGOs, community service groups, museums, public relations offices, among others.

Volunteer Opportunities

There are many organizations that place volunteers for short– and long–term assignments in France. Service Civil International (SCI) manages work camps with projects ranging from environmental and ecological work, peace issues, Esperanto education, building renovation, and agriculture (see Chapter 9). The AFS Educator Program arranges short– and long–term exchanges for teachers. Other volunteer placements are available with archeological and restoration projects.

AFS Intercultural Programs
198 Madison Avenue, Eighth Floor
New York, NY 10016
Tel.: (212) 299–9000
www.afs.org
The AFS Educator Program provides opportunities for teachers to live and work in countries around the world. Short programs are available during American school holidays; semester and year–long programs are also available for people looking for a more in–depth experience. The program includes cultural lessons and events, family home stays, observation of local educational practices, and teaching in schools in the host country.

Concordia
Heversham House
20–22 Boundary Road
Hove, BN3 4ET, England
Tel.: [44] 1 273 4222 18
www.concordia–iye.org.uk
Concordia is a small nonprofit organization committed to community development and cultural exchange through international volunteering. The projects range from nature conservation, restoration, archaeology and construction to work with adults and children with special needs and teaching. Project fees are generally less than $100 and include room and board.

Resources for Further Information

Newspapers In France

International Herald Tribune (English)
Tel.: [33] 1 41 43 93 00
Fax: [33] 1 41 43 93 38
www.iht.com

Les Echos
Tel.: [33] 1 49 53 65 65
Fax: [33] 1 45 61 48 92
www.lesechos.fr

Le Figaro
Tel.: [33] 1 42 21 62 00
Fax: [33] 1 42 21 64 05
www.cadremploi.fr (Job vacancies only)
www.lefigaro.fr

Le Monde
Tel.: [33] 1 42 17 20 00
Fax: [33] 1 42 17 21 21
www.tout.lemonde.fr

La Tribune
Tel.: [33] 1 44 82 16 16

Fax: [33] 1 40 13 13 97
www.latribune.fr

Useful Websites for Job Seekers

The Internet is a good place to begin your job search. Many French employers list job vacancies, especially those in technical fields, on the web. There are also many websites that provide useful information for researching the French job market.

The Minitel

Be sure to check out the French Telecom subscriber services Minitel, an anachronistic but still popular computerized information system that operates via a screen that plugs into an ordinary telephone. With the screen, you can access a variety of databases listing job vacancies (as well as other information). The databases are available at all information centers and post offices. A list of Minitel services for the job searcher is available at www.minitel.com.fr.

An Anglophone's Resource on Paris
http://paris–anglo.com
Here is the place to start: housing, living, studying, working. This site offers abundant information for the American in Paris. The section on working in Paris features directories of employers in different industries. There are also articles on topics such as office culture and working for yourself.

Association Bernard Gregory
www.abg.asso.fr
The employment portal for young PhDs in science, engineering, humanities and social sciences. The information about searching for academic jobs in Europe is available in English, but all jobs are advertised in French.

Cadres Online
www.cadresonline.com
Features over 7,500 jobs in the high–tech, industrial, health, marketing, and finance industries. Most job listings include links to employer's websites for more information. This site is written in French.

JobPilot
www.jobpilot.fr

The database lists over 5,000 private sector jobs and offers a resume database and a directory of employers. Registration is free.

Jobsite France
www.gojobsite.fr
Features a database of private sector jobs, a searchable resume database, and an email notification system for new jobs. The site is written in French.

Job Universe
www.jobuniverse.fr
Features jobs in the high–tech industry and a salary survey. You can also register to receive job notification via email.

Government Information on Working in France
www.france.diplomatie.fr
The official website for the French Ministry of Foreign Affairs. In addition to getting the latest word on France's foreign policy, this is the source for the most current information on visas and immigration.

Invest in France
www.investinfrancena.org

This site targets potential investors, but the market research reports and general information about French business and industry will be useful for job seekers.

Manpower
www.manpower.com
Manpower is a recruitment agency. Its French site features private sector jobs in a searchable database.

Monster France
www.monster.fr
The database features over 7,500 private sector jobs. You must register to receive job alerts by email or to post your resume for available jobs.

Reseau European pour l'Emploi
www.reseau.org/emploi/index.htm
Includes job listings, places to submit your resume, and a list of online recruiters for France.

StepStone France
www.stepstone.fr
One of Europe's leading online recruitment sites. Features over 1,200 private sector and education jobs in France.

Embassies and Consular Offices

American embassies and consulates have commercial and/or economic sections that can provide business information and explain aspects of the local economy. Inquiries about business opportunities should be addressed either to "Commercial Officer" or "Commercial Section."

Representation of France in the United States

Embassy of France
4101 Reservoir Road NW
Washington, DC 20007
Tel.: (202) 944–6000
Fax: (202) 944–6166
www.info–france–usa.org

French Consulates General

Chicago, (312) 787–5359; Los Angeles (Westwood), (310) 235–3200; New York, (212) 606–3600; San Francisco (415) 397–4330

Representation of the United States in France

American Embassy
2 Avenue Gabriel
F–75382 Paris Cedex 08, France
Tel.: [33] 1 43 12 22 22
Fax: [33] 1 42 66 97 83
www.amb–usa.fr

American Consulate General — Marseilles
Place Varian Fry

F–13286 Marseilles Cedex 06, France
Tel.: [33] 4 91 54 92 00
Fax: [33] 4 91 55 09 47

American Consulate General — Strasbourg
15 Avenue D'Alsace
F–67082 Strasbourg Cedex France
Tel.: [33] 3 88 35 31 04
Fax: [33] 3 88 24 06 95

Chambers of Commerce

Chambers of commerce consist of member firms in both countries interested in international trade. These are appropriate companies to initially target in the job search.

Fruit–picking dates in France

Brittany: apples (mid–September to late October), cherries (mid–May to early July)

Languedoc: apples (mid–September to late October), strawberries (mid–May to late July), peaches (mid–June to mid–September)

Normandy: apples (mid–September to late October), cherries (mid–May to early July)

Paris region: peaches (mid–June to mid–September), pears (mid–July to mid–November), tomatoes (late August to early September)

American Chamber of Commerce in France
156 Boulevard Haussmann
F–75008 Paris, France
Tel.: [33] 1 56 43 45 67
Fax: [33] 1 56 43 45 60
amchamfrance@amchamfrance.org
www.amchamfrance.org

French–American Chamber of Commerce in the U.S.
1350 Avenue of the Americas
Sixth Floor
New York, NY 10019
Tel.: (212) 765–4460
Fax: (212) 765–4650
Email: info@faccnyc.org
www.faccnyc.org
Manages a Young Professional Program. Americans ages 18 to 35 can apply for internships that last as long as 18 months.

Chamber of Commerce and Industry of France
27, Avenue de Friedland
F–75382 Paris Cedex 08, France
Tel.: [33] 1 55 65 55 65
Fax: [33] 1 55 65 78 68
www.ccip.fr

Bordeaux Chamber of Commerce
12 Place de la Bourse
F–33076 Paris, France
Tel.: [33] 1 56 79 50 50
www.bordeaux.cci.fr

World Trade Centers in France

World trade centers usually include many foreign companies that conduct business in the country.

World Trade Center Bordeaux
2 Place de la Bourse
F–33076 Bordeaux, France
Tel.: [33] 5 56 79 50 22
Fax : [33] 5 56 79 44 38
Email: wtc@mailcity.com
www.aquitaineinternational.com

World Trade Center Grenoble
P.O. Box 1509
F–38025 Grenoble, Cedex 1, France

Tel.: [33] 4 76 28 28 43
Fax: [33] 4 76 28 28 35
Email: grex@grex.fr

World Trade Center Lille
58, rue de l'Hopital Militaire, BP 209
F–59029 Lille Cedex, France
Tel.: [33] 3 20 57 05 07
Fax: [33] 3 20 40 04 55
Email: p.leclercq@wtc–lille.org
www.wtc–lille.org

World Trade Center Lyon
16, rue de la Republique
F–69289 Lyon, France
Tel.: [33] 4 72 40 57 59
Fax: [33] 4 72 40 57 61
Email: wibaux@wtc–lyon.org
www.wtc–lyon.org

World Trade Center, Marseilles
Maison de l'International
2, rue Henri Barbusse
F–13241 Marseilles Cedex 01, France
Tel.: [33] 4 91 39 33 50
Fax : [33] 4 91 39 33 60
Email: info@wtc–marseille.com
www.wtc–marseille.com

World Trade Center Metz–Saarbr
Club WTC, Tour B
2, rue Augustin Fresnel Case 88248
F–57082 Metz Cedex 3, France
Tel.: [33] 38 77 58 500
Fax: [33] 38 77 58 529
Email: wtc–metz@moselle.cci.fr
www.moselle.cci.fr/wtc

World Trade Center Montpellier
Immeuble La Coupole
275, rue Leon Blum, BP 9531
F–34045 Montpellier, Cedex 01 France
Tel.: [33] 4 67 13 60 60

Fax : [33] 4 67 13 60 64
Email: wtc@mlrt.fr
www.tech–montpellier.com

World Trade Center Nantes
16 Quai Ernest Renaud, BP 90517
F–44105 Nantes Cedex 4, France
Tel.: [33] 2 40 44 60 55
Fax: [33] 2 40 44 63 80
Email: wtc@nantes.cci.fr
www.wtcnantes.com

World Trade Center Paris
Palais Des Congres
2, Place de la Porte Maillot, BP 18
F– 75853 Paris Cedex 17, France
Tel.: [33] 1 40 68 14 25
Fax: [33] 1 40 68 14 21
Email: wtcparis@ccip.fr
www.wtcparis.com

World Trade Center Strasbourg
Maison du Commerce International de
Strasbourg (MCIS)
4 Quai Kleber
F–67080 Strasbourg Cedex, France
Tel.: [33] 03 88 76 42 31
Fax : [33] 03 88 76 42 00
Email:wtc.eic@strasbourg.cci.fr
www.alsace–export.com

Other Informational Organizations

Foreign government missions in the United States, such as National Tourist Offices and embassies and consulates, can furnish visas and information on work permits and other important regulations. They may also offer economic and business information about the country.

Cultural Services of the French Embassy
972 Fifth Avenue
New York, NY 10021
Tel.: (212) 439–1400
Fax: (212) 439 1455
www.frenchculture.org

French Government Tourist Office
444 Madison Avenue
New York, NY 10022
Tel.: (212) 838–7800
Fax: (212) 838–7855
www.francetourism.com

French Institute/Alliance Francaise
22 East 60th Street
New York, NY 10022
Tel.: (212) 355–6100
Fax: (212) 935–4119
www.fiaf.org

Paris Tourism Office
127 Avenue de Champs–Éllysées
F–75008 Paris, France
Email: info@paris–touristoffice.com
www.paris–touristoffice.com

Business Directories

Although not always easy to find, business directories can prove invaluable in the international job search. Most directories list company names, addresses, products, and phone numbers. Some directories include executive names and titles and financial information about the company. These sources provide you with the names of the people to contact for employment information as well as financial data, which can tell you how strong a company's position in a country may be.

American Chamber of Commerce in France Membership Directory. American Chamber of Commerce in France, 156 Boulevard Haussmann, F–75008 Paris, France; email: membership@amchamfrance.org; www.amchamfranc.org. Lists American and French companies engaged in bilateral trade. 380 pages, $160, updated annually.

American Subsidiaries and Affiliates of French Firms. French Embassy Trade Office, 810 Seventh Avenue, 38th Floor, New York, NY 10019–5818; email: newyork@dree.org. Lists French firms and their American subsidiaries. 440 pages, $125, published every two years.

Annuaire France Telexport. Paris Chamber of Commerce and Industry, c/o Association Firmnet, 49 rue de Tocqueville, F–75813 Paris, France; email: telexport@ccip.fr; www.telexport.tm.fr. Covers 40,000 French companies involved in international trade. 1,900 pages, published annually in French, English, German, and Spanish.

Bottin Professions. Bottin SA, 5 rue Andre Boulle, F–75008 Paris Cedex 9, France; email: bettinwebmaster@bottin.fr; www.bottin.fr. Describes over 100,000 French firms with financial data. Published annually in French.

Directory of Corporations and Corporate Officers. DAFSA, 25 rue Leblanc, F–75010 Paris, France. 13,000 corporation board members and 1,200 companies listed on the French stock exchange. Published annually in two volumes.

ESSOR. Union Francaise d'Annuaires Professionnels, 13 Avenue Roger–Hennequin, F–78192 Trappes Cedex France; email: info@enor–contacts.tm.fr. Describes 30,000 exporting companies from all lines of business in France. 1,085 pages. This is a free directory, published annually in French, German, English, and Spanish.

L'Expansion–Le Classement Annuel des 1000 Premieres Enterprises Francaises. Groupe Expansion, 14 Boulevard Poissonniére, F–75008 Paris Cedex 9, France; www.lexpansion.fr. List of leading 1,000 French firms. Published annually in French.

France 30,000. Dun & Bradstreet France, 345 Avenue Georges Clemenceau, Tour Defense Bergere, F–92000 Nanterre Cedex 13, France. Describes 30,000 largest French firms. 2,000 pages, two volumes, published annually.

Kompass France. Kompass France, 66 Quai du Marechal Joffre, F–92415 Courbevoie Cedex France; email: infos@kompass–france.com; www.kompass.fr.

U.S. distributor Kompass USA, 121 Chalon Rd., New Providence, NJ 07974. Lists 150,000 French manufacturing and service companies. 6,900 pages, published annually in French.

Qui Represente Qui en France. Published annually in French by Kompass France, 66 Quai de Marechal Joffre, F–92145 Courbevoie Cedex France; email: infos@kompass–france.com; www.kompass.fr. U.S. distributor Kompass USA, 121 Chalon Rd., New Providence, NJ 07974. Lists French importers and distributors representing foreign firms in France. Published annually in French, German, English, and Spanish.

Working in Corsica

Corsica is a full province, or department, of France but has a distinctly Mediterranean character. Corsicans are much closer to Sardinians than they are to other French people. The island is mostly poor and underdeveloped, but it does provide opportunities in the tourist industry and in agriculture. Competition for most manual work comes from a very large number of Arab workers. Female workers often find the attention received from the single migrant Arab workers highly annoying.

The tourist industry centers around Ajaccio, Bastia, Bonifacio, and Propriano. Resorts are located throughout the coastal areas. Hotels, bars, and restaurants often advertise jobs in some of the mainland newspapers, especially in Nice and Marseilles. German speakers are especially sought due to the high levels of German tourists in Corsica.

Fruit–picking is available on the eastern coast from mid–November through December. The tropical fruits that grow on the island require hard work to pick. In addition, the midday heat mandates that work starts around dawn. The grape harvest occurs on the northern coast from September to early October. North African workers dominate the agricultural labor market in much of Corsica.

American Companies in France

Many American firms operate in France. The following companies are classified by business area: Banking and Finance; Industrial Manufacturing; Retailing and Wholesaling; Service Industries; and Technology. Company information includes firm name, address, phone and fax numbers, and specific business. Your chances of securing employment abroad are substantially better if you contact the subsidiary company in Europe rather than the parent company in the United States. Keep in mind that the contact information for companies listed in this section can change often. Confirm the company's address and phone number before writing to it.

Banking and Finance

American Express Bank
11, rue Scribe
F–75009 Paris, France
Tel.: [33] 1 47 14 50 00
Fax: [33] 1 42 68 17 17
(Bank)

AON France
45, rue Kléber
F– 92697 Levallois Perret, France
Tel.: [33] 1 58 75 75 75
Fax: [33] 1 58 75 77 77
www.aon.com
(Insurance)

Bank of America
43–47 Avenue de la Grande Armée
F–75016 Paris, 16, France
Tel.: [33] 1 45 02 68 00
Fax: [33] 1 45 01 77 89
www.bankamerica.com
(Bank)

Chase Manhattan Bank
42, rue Washington
F–75008 Paris, France
Tel.: [33] 1 53 77 10 00
Fax: [33] 1 53 77 10 50
(Bank)

Lehman Brothers
21, rue Balzac
F–75008 Paris, France
Tel.: [33] 1 53 89 30 00
Fax: [33] 1 53 89 31 30
www.lehman.com
(Financial services)

Industrial Manufacturing

3M France
Boulevard de l'Oise
F–95000 Cergy, France
Tel.: [33] 1 30 31 61 61
Fax: [33] 1 30 31 74 26
(Adhesives, coatings, sealants, etc.)

Baker Hughes Inteq France
Zone Induspal Avenue Barthélémy
Thimonnier
F–64140 Lons, France
Tel.: [33] 5 59 92 77 00
Fax: [33] 5 59 92 89 20

www.bakerhughes.com
(Oil field tools)

Bechtel International Corp
Centre Bassano
38, rue de Bassano
F–75008 Paris, France
Tel.: [33] 1 47 20 53 04
Fax: [33] 1 47 20 55 06
(Engineering construction)

Black & Decker France
34, Route d'Ecully
F–69570 Dardilly, France
Tel.: [33] 4 72 20 39 20
Fax: [33] 4 72 20 39 00
www.blackanddecker.com
(Handheld power tools)

Bridgestone Firestone France
Parc Médicis
47, allée des Pépinières
94260 Fresne, France
Tel.: [33]1 46 15 56 00
Fax: [33] 1 46 15 56 39
www.bridgestone–eu.com
(Tires and tubes)

Colgate–Palmolive
55, Boulevard de la Mission–Marchand
F–92400 Courbevoie Cedex, France
Tel.: [33] 1 47 68 60 00
Fax: [33] 1 47 68 68 13
www.colgate.fr
(Household, personal care products)

Dow Corning France
Immeuble Brittania
20, Boulevard Eùgène Deruelle
F–69003 Lyon, France
Tel.: [33] 4 72 84 13 60
 Fax: [33] 4 72 84 13 79
(Silicone & lubricants)

Dow France
22, Avenue des Nations
F–93420 Villepinte, France
Tel.: [33] 1 49 90 72 72
Fax: [33] 1 49 90 73 73
(Chemicals and pharmaceuticals)

Du Pont Pharma
137, rue de l'Université
F–75007 Paris 07, France
Tel.: [33] 1 45 50 65 50
Fax: [33] 1 47 53 09 65

(Chemical and electronic products)

Eastman Chemical
65, rue de Bercy
F–75012 Paris 12, France
Tel.: [33] 1 44 67 88 88
Fax: [33] 1 44 67 88 99
www.eastman.com
(Chemicals)

Esso SAF
2, rue des Martinets
F–92500 Rueil Malmaison, France
Tel.: [33] 1 47 10 60 00
Fax: [33] 1 47 10 66 03
(Petroleum products)

Goodyear France
8, rue Lionel Terray
F–92500 Rueil Malmaison, France
Tel.: [33] 1 47 16 23 00
Fax: [33] 1 47 16 23 12
(Rubber products)

Graco Puericulture
Paris Nord 2
53, Avenue Bois de la Pie
F–93290 Tremblay en France, France
Tel.: [33] 1 49 90 95 95
Fax: [33] 1 49 90 95 96
(Infant products)

Halliburton
Tour Litwin 10, rue Jean Jaurès
F–92800 Puteaux, France
Tel.: [33] 1 55 92 95 60
Fax: [33] 1 55 91 95 70
www.halliburton.com
(Oil field construction)

International Paper
Parc Ariane 5–7, Boulevard des Chênes
F–78280 Guyancourt, France
Tel.: [33] 1 39 30 34 00
Fax: [33] 1 39 30 35 28
(Paper products)

Johnson and Johnson Consumer
Route de Retortat
F–51120 Sezanne, France
Tel.: [33] 3 26 42 53 00
Fax: [33] 3 26 81 30 50
(Household products)

Kodak–Pathé
26, rue Villiot

F–75012 Paris 12, France
Tel.: [33] 1 40 01 30 00
Fax: [33] 1 40 01 37 57
(Photographic equipment and optical lenses)

Laboratoire GlaxoSmithKline
100, Route de Versailles
F–78150 Marly Le Roi, France
Tel.: [33] 1 39 17 80 00
Fax: [33] 1 39 17 88 99
(Pharmaceuticals)

Eli Lilly
13–17, rue Pagès
F–92150 Suresnes Cedex, France
Tel.: [33] 1 49 11 34 34
Fax: [33] 1 46 02 27 67
(Pharmaceuticals)

Merck S.A.
201, rue Carnot
F–94120 Fontenay Sous Bois, France
Tel.: [33] 1 43 94 54 00
(Pharmaceuticals)

Monsanto
Immeuble Elysses La Défense
1, Avenue Jacques Monod
F–69500 Bron, France
Tel.: [33] 4 72 14 40 40
Fax: [33] 4 72 14 41 41
www.monsanto.com
(Life sciences products)

Procter & Gamble France
96 Avenue Charles de Gaulle
F–92200 Neuilly–sur–Seine, France
Tel.: [33] 1 40 88 55 11
Fax: [33] 1 40 88 58 58
(Household products)

Retailing and Wholesaling

Foot Locker France
20, rue de l'Arc de Triomphe
F–75017 Paris 17, France
Tel.: [33] 1 55 37 17 37
Fax: [33] 1 55 37 17 38
(Shoes and sneakers)

Toys R Us
La Remise
2, rue Thomas Edison
F–91090 Lisses, France
Tel.: [33] 1 60 76 83 00

Fax: [33] 1 60 86 24 48
(Toy retailer)

Service Industries

Accenture
55 Avenue George V
F–75008 Paris, France
Tel.: [33] 1 53 23 55 55
Fax: [33] 1 53 23 53 23
(Management consulting)

Bain et Compagnie
21 Boulevard de la Madeleine
F–75001 Paris 01, France
Tel.: [33] 1 44 55 75 75
Fax: [33] 1 44 55 76 00
www.bain.com
(Management consulting)

Baker & McKenzie
32 Avenue Kleber
F–75116 Paris, France
Tel.: [33] 1 44 17 53 00
Fax: [33] 1 44 17 45 75
www.bakerinfo.com
(Law firm)

Burson–Marsteller Paris
6, rue Escudier
F–92100 Boulogne Billancourt, France
Tel.: [33] 1 41 86 76 76
Fax: [33] 1 41 86 76 00
www.bm.com
(Public relations)

Century 21 France
rue des Cévennes, Bâtiment 3
F–91017 Lisses, France
Tel.: [33] 1 69 11 12 21
Fax: [33] 1 60 86 90 07
www.century21.com
(Real estate)

Euro Disney
Service du Recruitement–Casting
Disneyland Paris
F–77700 Chessy, France
Tel.: [33] 1 60 26 66 66
www.eurodisney.com
(Theme parks, recreational services)

Hyatt Regency Paris, Madeleine Hotel
24 Boulevard Malesherbes
F–75008 Paris, France

Tel.: [33] 1 55 27 1234
Fax: [33] 1 55 27 1235
www.hyatt.com
(Hotels)

A.T. Kearney Executive Search
7–10, Place D'Iéna
F–75116 Paris 16, France
Tel.: [33] 1 56 62 55 55
Fax: [33] 1 56 62 55 56
www.atkearney.com
(Executive search)

Marriott Courtyard Neuilly
58 Boulevard Victor Hugo
F–92200 Neuilly, France
Tel.: [33] 1 55 636 465
(Hotels)

Ogilvy & Mather International
40, Avenue George V
F–75008 Paris 08, France
Tel.: [33] 1 53 23 30 00
Fax: [33] 1 53 23 30 30
(Advertising and public relations)

Saatchi & Saatchi Advertising
30 Boulevard Vital–Bouhot
F–92200 Neuilly–sur–Seine, France
Tel.: [33] 1 40 88 40 00
Fax: [33] 1 40 88 40 88
(Advertising)

Warner Music France
29, Avenue Mac Mahon
F–75017 Paris 17, France
Tel.: [33] 1 56 60 40 00
Fax: [33] 1 56 60 40 50
(Music distributor)

Young et Rubicam France
57 Avenue Morizet
F–92100 Boulogne Billancourt, France
Tel.: [33] 1 46 84 33 33
Fax: [33] 1 46 84 32 72
(Advertising)

Technology

ADP Europe
148, rue Anatole France
F–92300 Levallois Perret, France
Tel.: [33] 1 55 63 50 00
Fax: [33] 1 55 63 50 79
www.fr.adp.com
(Data processing services)

Business Objects
157–159, rue Anatole France
F–92300 Levallois–Perret, France
Phone: [33] 1 41 25 21 21
Fax: [33] 1 41 25 31 00
www.businessobjects.com
(Computer software and services)

Cisco Systems Europe
rue Camille Desmoulins
F–92130 Issy Les Moulineaux, France
Tel.: [33] 1 58 04 60 00
Fax: [33] 1 58 04 61 00
www.cisco.com
(Computer networking systems)

Computer Associates
14 Avenue Françoise Arago
F–92003 Nanterre, France
Tel.: [33] 1 40 97 50 50
Fax: [33] 1 40 97 51 51
www.cai.com
(Computer consulting)

Dell Computer
1, Rond Point Benjamin Franklin
F–34000 Montepellier, France
Tel.: [33] 4 99 75 40 00
Fax: [33] 4 99 75 40 01
www.dell.com
(Computers)

IBM France
2, Avenue Gambetts
Tour Descartes La Défense
F–92400 Courbevoire, France
Tel.: [33] 1 49 05 70 00
Fax: [33] 1 49 05 62 93
(Information systems)

LSI Logic
Immeuble Europa
53 bis, Avenue de l'Europe
F–78140 Velizzy–Villacoublay, France

Tel.: [33] 1 34 63 13 13
Fax: [33] 1 34 63 13 26
www.lsilogic.com
(Semiconducters)

Microsoft Europe
Zac de Courtaboeuf
18, Avenue du Québec
F–91957 Villebon sur Yvette, France
Tel.: [33] 8 25 82 78 29
Fax: [33] 1 64 46 06 60
www.microsoft.com/France
(Computer)

Motorola Semiconducteurs
18, rue Grangedame Rose
F–78140 Velizy Villacoublay, France
Tel.: [33] 1 34 63 59 00
Fax: [33] 1 34 63 59 01
www.mot.com
(Semiconductors)

Sun Microsystems France
13, Avenue Morane Saulnier
F–78140 Velizy Villacoublay, France
Tel.: [33] 1 34 03 00 00
Fax: [33] 1 34 03 00 01
www.sun.com
(Computers)

Texas Instruments France
8–10, Avenue Morane Saulnier
F–78140 Velizy Villacoublay, France
Tel.: [33] 1 30 70 10 01
Fax: [33] 1 30 70 10 54
(Electronic equipment)

Yahoo! France
11 bis, rue Torricelli
F–75017 Paris 17, France
Tel.: [33] 1 70 91 20 00
Fax: [33] 1 70 91 20 01
www.yahoo–inc.com
(Internet media provider)

European Companies in France

The following are major non–American firms operating in the country. These selected companies either can be French or based in another European country. Such companies will generally hire their own nationals first but may employ Americans.

Banking and Finance

AXA S.A.
25 Avenue Matignon
F–75008 Paris La Defense, France
Tel.: [33] 1 40 75 57 0
Fax: [33] 1 40 75 46 96
www.axa.com
(Insurance)

Assurances Général de France (AGF)
87, rue de Richelieu
F–75113 Paris Cedex 02, France
Tel.: [33] 1 44 86 20 00
Fax: [33] 1 44 86 29 60
www.agf.fr
(Insurance)

BNP Paribas
16 Boulevard des Italiens
F–75009 Paris Cedex 09, France
Tel.: [33] 1 40 14 45 46
Fax: [33] 1 40 14 69 73
www.bnpparibas.com
(Bank)

Compagnie Financiér Edmond de Rothschild
47, rue du Saint–Honoré
F–75008 Paris, France
Tel.: [33] 1 40 17 25 25
Fax: [33] 1 40 17 24 02
(Bank)

Crédit Commercial de France
103, Avenue des Champs–Élysées
F–75008 Paris, France
Tel.: [33] 1 40 70 70 40
Fax: [33] 1 40 70 70 09
(Bank)

Credit Lyonnais
19 Boulevard des Italiens
F–75002 Paris, France
Tel.: [33] 1 49 53 15 15
Fax: [33] 1 49 53 13 52
www.creditlyonnais.com
(Bank)

Deutsche Bank
3, Avenue de Friedland
F–75008 Paris, France
Tel.: [33] 1 44 95 64 00
Fax: [33] 1 53 75 07 01
(Bank)

Groupe Arnault S.A.
30 Avenue Hoche
F–75008 Paris, France
Tel.: [33] 1 44 13 22 22
Fax: [33] 1 44 13 22 87
(Financial Services)

Lazard LLC
121 Boulevard Haussmann
F–75382 Paris Cedex 08, France
Tel.: [33] 1 44 13 01 11
Fax: [33] 1 44 13 01 00
www.lazard.com
(Financial services)

Union des Assurances Fédérales (UAF)
27 Avenue Claude Vellefaux
F–75499 Paris Cedex 10, France
[33] 1 40 03 10 00
[33] 1 42 49 35 35
www.uafdirect.fr
(Insurance)

Union Financière de France Banque
32 Avenue d'Iéna
F–75116 Paris, France
[33] 1 47 69 65 17
[33] 1 47 20 09 20
www.uffbanque.fr
(Asset management)

Industrial Manufacturing

Alcatel
54, rue la Boétie
F–75008 Paris, France
Tel.: [33] 1 40 76 10 10
Fax: [33] 1 40 76 14 00
www.alcatel.com
(Telecommunications equipment)

Airbus
1, Rond Point Maurice Bellonte
F–31707 Blagnac Cedex, France
Tel.: [33] 5 61 93 33 87
Fax: [33] 5 61 93 49 55
www.airbus.com
(Aerospace)

Arianespace
Boulevard de l'Europe
F–91006 Évry–Courcouronnes, France
Tel.: [33] 1 60 87 60 00
Fax: [33] 1 60 87 62 47

www.arianespace.com
(Aerospace)

**Assistance Aeronautique et
Aerospatiale (AAA)**
18, Boulevard Voltaire
F–75011 Paris 11, France
Tel.: [33] 1 48 06 85 85
Fax: [33] 1 48 06 32 19
(Aerospace equipment)

ATOFINA
4–8, Cours Michelet
La Défense 10
F–92091 Paris La Défense, France
Tel.: [33] 1 49 00 80 80
Fax: [33] 1 49 00 83 96
www.atofina.com
(Chemicals)

Aventis S.A.
1, Avenue de l'Europe
F–67300 Schiltigheim, France
Tel.: [33] 3 88 99 11 00
Fax: [33] 3 88 99 11 01
www.aventis.com
(Pharmaceuticals)

Beghin–Say
14 Boulevard du Général Leclerc
F–92572 Neuilly–sur–Seine Cedex,
France
Tel.: [33] 1 41 43 14 00
Fax: [33] 1 41 43 14 46
www.beghin–say.com
(Sugar)

Bic S.A.
14, rue Jeanne d'Asnieres
F–92611 Clichy Cedex, France
Tel.: [33] 1 45 19 52 00
Fax: [33] 1 45 19 52 99
www.bic.fr
(Writing instruments)

Dassault Aviation
9, Rond–Point des Champs–Elysées
Marcel Dassault
F–75008 Paris, France
Tel.: [33] 1 53 76 93 00
Fax: [33] 1 53 76 93 20
www.dassault–aviation.fr
(Aerospace, defense)

Electricité de France
22–30, Avenue de Wagram

F–75382 Paris Cedex 08, France
Tel.: [33] 1 40 42 54 30
Fax: [33] 1 40 42 79 40
www.edf.fr
(Electricity production)

**Elf Aquitaine Exploration
Production**
Route de Bayonne
F–64170 LACQ, France
Tel.: [33] 5 59 92 22 22
Fax: [33] 5 59 92 23 03
(Oil & gas exploration)

Fromageries Bel
4, rue d'Anjou
F–75008 Paris, France
Tel.: [33] 1 40 07 72 50
Fax: [33] 1 40 07 72 01
www.fromageries–bel.fr
(Dairy products)

Groupe Bourbon
19, rue du Jura
F–39170 St. Lupicin, France
Tel.: [33] 3 84 41 40 50
Fax: [33] 3 84 41 40 92
www.groupe–bourbon.com
(Food products)

Groupe Danone
7, rue de Téhéran
F–75008 Paris, France
Tel.: [33] 1 44 35 20 20
Fax: [33] 1 42 25 67 16
www.danonegroup.com
(Dairy products)

L'Air Liquide
75 Quai d'Orsay
F–75321 Paris Cedex 07, France
Tel.: [33] 1 40 62 55 55
Fax: [33] 1 40 62 54 65
www.airliquide.com
(Chemicals)

Laboratoires Arkopharma
BP 28
F–06510 Carros, France
Tel.: [33] 4 93 29 11 28
Fax: [33] 4 93 29 11 62
www.arkopharma.com
(Pharmaceuticals)

Laurent–Perrier
32 Avenue de Champagne

F–51150 Tours–sur–Marne, France
[33] 3 26 58 91 22
[33] 3 26 58 77 29
www.laurent–perrier.fr
(Beverages)

Legrand
128 Avenue du Maréchal de Lattre
de Tassignay
F–87045 Limoges Cedex, France
Tel.: [33] 5 55 06 87 87
Fax: [33] 5 55 06 88 88
www.legrandelectric.com
(Electrical equipment)

Leroy–Somer Electric Motors
Boulevard Marcellin Leroy
F–16000 Angoule France
Tel.: [33] 5 45 64 45 64
Fax: [33] 5 45 64 45 04
(Machinery)

L'Oréal
41, rue Martre
F–92117 Clichy, France
Tel.: [33] 1 47 56 70 00
Fax: [33] 1 47 56 80 02
www.loreal.com
(Cosmetics and toiletries)

**Compagnie Général des
Etablissements Michelin**
12, cours Sablon
F–63000 Clermont–Ferrand, France
Tel.: [33] 4 73 98 59 00
Fax: [33] 4 73 98 59 04
www.michelin.com
(Tires and rubber products)

Pechiney
7, place du Chancelier Adenauer
F–75116 Paris, France
Tel.: [33] 1 56 28 20 00
Fax: [33] 1 56 28 33 38
www.pechiney.com
(Aluminum and packaging products)

Pernod Ricard
142, Boulevard Haussmann
F–75008 Paris, France
Tel.: [33] 1 40 76 77 78
Fax: [33] 1 42 25 95 66
www.pernod–ricard.fr
(Alcoholic beverages)

PSA Peugeot Citroen
75, Avenue de la Grande–Armée
F–75116 Paris, France
Tel.: [33] 1 40 66 55 11
Fax: [33] 1 40 66 54 14
www.psa–peugeot–citroen.com
(Auto manufacturers)

Rémy Cointreau
152, Avenue des Champs–Elysées
F–75008 Paris, France
Tel.: [33] 1 44 13 44 13
Fax: [33] 1 45 62 82 52
www.remy–cointreau.com
(Alcoholic beverages)

Renault
13–15 Quai le Gallo
F–92100 Boulogne–Billancourt Cedex,
France
Tel.: [33] 1 41 04 04 04
Fax: [33] 1 41 04 51 49
www.renault.com
(Automobiles)

**SAGEM (Société d'Applications
Générales d'Electricité et de
Mecanique)**
Le Ponant de Paris
27, rue Leblanc
F–75512 Paris Cedex 15, France
Tel.: [33] 1 40 70 63 63
Fax: [33] 1 47 20 39 46
www.sagem.com
(Communications and electronic equip-
ment)

Schneider Electric
43–45 Boulevard Franklin–Roosevelt
F–92500 Rueil–Malmaison, France
Tel.: [33] 1 41 29 70 00
Fax: [33] 1 41 29 71 00
www.schneider–electric.com
(Electric equipment generation)

Skis Rossignol S.A.
B.P. 329
F–38509 Voiron Cedex, France
Tel.: [33] 4 76 66 65 65
Fax.: [33] 4 76 05 90 85
www.skirosingnol.com
(Sporting goods)

Technip–Coflexip
Tour Technip, 170 Place Henri Régnault

La Défense 6
F–92973 Paris La Défense Cedex,
France
Tel.: [33] 1 47 78 21 21
Fax: [33] 1 47 78 33 40
www.technip–coflexip.com
(Engineering and construction)

TotalFinaElf
2, Place de la Coupole
La Défense 6
F–92400 Courbevoie, France
Tel.: [33] 1 47 44 45 46
Fax: [33] 1 47 44 78 78
www.totalfinaelf.com
(Oil and gas exploration)

Transgene
11, rue de Molsheim
F–67082 Strasbourg Cedex, France
Tel.: [33] 3 88 27 91 00
Fax: [33] 3 88 27 91 11
www.transgene.fr
(Biotechnology)

Retailing and Wholesaling

Auchan Group
200, rue de la Recherche
F–59650 Villeneuve d'Ascq Cedex,
France
Tel.: [33] 3 28 37 67 00
Fax: [33] 3 20 67 55 20
www.auchan.com
(Supermarkets, restaurants)

Carrefour
6, Avenue Raymond Poincaré
B.P. 419.16
F–75771 Paris, France
Tel.: [33] 1 53 70 19 00
Fax: [33] 1 53 70 86 16
www.carrefour.com
(Retail grocery)

Cartier
51, rue François Premier
F–75008 Paris, France
Tel.: [33] 1 40 74 60 60
Fax: [33] 1 45 63 05 65
www.cartier.com
(Luxury consumer products)

Chanel
135, Avenue Charles de Gaulle

F–92521 Neuilly–sur–Seine Cedex,
France
Tel.: [33] 1 46 43 40 00
Fax: [33] 1 47 47 60 34
www.chanel.com
(Luxury consumer products)

Christian Dior
30, Avenue Montaigne
F–75008 Paris, France
Tel.: [33] 1 44 13 24 98
Fax: [33] 1 44 13 27 86
www.dior.com
(Luxury consumer products)

Galeries Lafayette
40, Boulevard Haussmann
F–75009 Paris 09, France
Tel.: [33] 1 42 82 34 56
Fax: [33] 1 42 82 83 84
(Department stores)

Groupe André
28, Avenue de Flandre
F–75019 Paris, Cedex 19, France
Tel.: [33] 1 44 72 30 01
Fax: [33] 1 40 05 09 37
(Apparel retail)

Hermès International
24, Faubourg Saint–Honoré
F–75008 Paris, France
Tel.: [33] 1 40 17 49 20
Fax: [33] 1 40 17 49 21
www.hermes.com
(Luxury consumer products)

LVMH Moët Hennessy Louis Vuitton
30 Avenue Hoche
F–75008 Paris, France
Tel.: [33] 1 44 13 22 22
Fax: [33] 1 44 13 21 19
www.lvmh.com
(Luxury consumer products)

Marne et Champagne
22, rue Maurice Cerveaux
F–138–51 205 Epernay, Cedex, France
Tel.: [33] 3 26 78 50 50
Fax: [33] 3 26 78 50 99
www.marne–champagne.com
(Wineries)

Naf Naf
6/10 Boulevard Foch

F–93807 Épinay–sur–Seine Cedex,
France
Tel.: [33] 1 48 13 88 88
Fax: [33] 1 48 13 88 50
www.nafnaf–sa.com
(Apparel)

Pinault–Printemps–Redoute
18, Place Henri–Bergson
F–75381 Paris Cedex 08, France
Tel.: [33] 1 44 90 61 00
Fax: [33] 1 44 90 62 80
www.pprgroup.com
(Department stores)

Service Industries

Accor
2, rue de la Mare–Neuve
F–91021 Évry Cedex, France
Tel.: [33] 1 69 36 80 80
Fax: [33] 1 69 36 79 00
www.accor.com
(Hotels and restaurants)

Air France
45, rue de Paris
F–95747 Roissy, France
Tel.: [33] 1 41 56 78 00
Fax: [33] 1 41 56 56 00
www.airfrance.com
(Airline)

Cap Gemini Ernst & Young
6–8, rue Duret
F–75116 Paris 16, France
Tel.: [33] 1 53 64 44 44
Fax: [33]1 53 64 44 45
www.cgey.com
(Management consulting)

Cegedim Group
110–116, rue d'Aguesseau
F–92103 Boulogne–Billancourt Cedex,
France
Tel.: [33] 1 49 09 22 00
Fax: [33] 1 46 03 45 95
www.cegedim.fr
(Marketing and public relations services)

Club Med
11, rue de Cambrai
F–75957 Paris Cedex 19, France
Tel.: [33] 1 53 35 35 53
Fax: [33] 1 53 35 36 16

www.clubmed.com
(Tourism)

Expand
89, rue Escudier
F–92100 Boulogne–Billancourt Cedex,
France
Tel.: [33] 1 47 12 40 40
Fax: [33] 1 47 12 40 94
www.expand.fr
(Television production, programming
and distribution)

Groupe Flo
157, Avenue Charles de Gaulle
F–92200 Neuilly–sur–Seine, France
Tel.: [33] 1 41 92 30 00
Fax: [33] 1 41 92 30 19
(Restaurants)

Hachette Filipacchi Medias
149–151, rue Anatole France
F–92300 Levallois–Perret, France
Tel.: [33] 1 41 34 60 00
Fax: [33] 1 41 34 77 77
www.hachette–filipacchi.com
(Publishing)

Havas Advertising
84, rue de Villiers
F–92683 Levallois Perret, France
Tel.: [33] 1 41 34 30 00
Fax: [33] 1 41 34 12 48
www.havas–advertising.fr
(Communications and travel)

Michelin
46 Avenue de Breteuil
F–75007 Paris, France
Tel.: [33] 1 45 66 12 34
Fax: [33] 1 45 66 11 63
(Publishing)

Publicis
133, Avenue des Champs–Elysées
F–75008 Paris, France
Tel.: [33] 1 44 43 73 00
Fax: [33] 1 44 43 75 25
www.publicis.fr
(Communication)

**SNCF (Société Nationale des
Chemins de Fer Français)**
34, rue du Commandant René
Mouchotte
F–75014 Paris 14, France

Tel.: [33] 1 53 25 60 00
Fax: [33] 1 53 25 64 45
www.sncf.com
(Railway transport)

Synergie
11, Avenue du Colonel Bonnet
F–75016 Paris, France
Tel.: [33] 1 44 14 90 20
Fax: [33] 1 45 25 97 10
www.synergie.fr
(Staffing, outsourcing and other human resources)

Valtech
Grande Arche de La Défense
F–92044 Paris La Defense France
Tel.: [33] 1 41 88 23 00
Fax: [33] 1 41 88 23 01
www.valtech.com
(Information technology consulting services)

Vivendi Universal
42 Avenue de Friedland
F–75380 Paris Cedex 08, France
Tel.: [33] 1 71 71 10 00
Fax: [33] 1 71 71 11 79
www.vivendiuniversal.com
(Media)

Technology

AEDIAN
3 rue Moncey
F–75009 Paris, France
Tel.: [33] 1 53 32 30 00
Fax: [33] 1 56 35 33 95
www.aedian.com
(Computer software)

Société Alten
40, Avenue André Morizet
F–92513 Boulogne–Billancourt Cedex, France
Tel.: [33] 1 46 08 70 00
Fax: [33] 1 46 08 70 01
www.alten.fr
(Information technology consulting)

Altran Technologies
251 Boulevard Péreire
F–75017 Paris, France

Tel.: [33] 1 44 09 64 00
Fax: [33] 1 44 09–64 89
www.altran.net
(Technical and scientific consulting)

ARES
3–9 Avenue de Norvège
B.P. 390
F–91959 Courtaboeuf 1 Cedex, France
Tel.: [33] 1 69 86 60 00
Fax: [33] 1 69 28 19 18
www.ares.fr
(Computer software and services)

Business Objects
157–159 rue Anatole France
F–92309 Levallois–Perret, France
Tel.: [33] 1 41 25 21 21
Fax; [33] 1 41 25 31 00
www.businessobjects.com

CS Communication & Systèmes
88, rue Brillat Savarin
F–75013 Paris, France
Tel.: [33] 1 40 78 75 00
Fax: [33] 1 40 78 75 50
www.c–s.fr
(Information systems)

France Telecom Group
6, Place d'Alleray
F–75505 Paris Cedex 15, France
Tel.: [33] 1 44 44 22 22
Fax: [33] 1 44 44 95 95
www.francetelecom.fr
(Telecommunications)

Lectra
16–18, rue Chalgrin
F–75016 Paris, France
Tel.: [33] 1 53 64 42 00
Fax: [33] 1 53 64 43 00
www.lectra.com
(CAD/CAM Software)

Webraska Mobile Technologies
22, rue Guynemer
F–78600 Maisons–Laffitte, France
Tel.: [33] 1 39 12 88 00
Fax: [33] 1 39 12 88 88
www.webraska.com
(Wireless communications services)

International Nonprofit Employer in France

UNESCO (United Nations Educational, Scientific, and Cultural Organization)
7 Place de Fontenoy Tresor

F–75007 Paris, France
Tel.: [33] 1 45 68 10 00
www.unesco.org

International Schools in France

American School of Paris
41, rue Pasteur
F–92216 Saint–Cloud, France
Tel.: [33] 1 41 12 82 82
Fax: [33] 1 46 02 23 90
Email: headmaster@asparis.org
www.asparis.org
(U.S./International Baccalaureate curriculum, prekindergarten through grade 12)

The International School of Monaco
12 Quai Antoine 1er
F–98000 Monte Carlo, Monaco
Tel.: [33] 93 25 68 20
Fax: [33] 93 25 68 30
Email: intlschl@monaco.mc
www.ismonaco.org
(Curriculum in English and French)

International School of Paris
6, rue Beethoven
F–75016 Paris, France
Tel.: [33] 1 42 24 09 54
Fax: [33] 1 45 27 15 93
Email: info@isparis.edu
www.isparis.edu

(U.S./U.K./International Baccalaureate curriculum, prekindergarten through grade 12)

Marymount School
72 Boulevard de la Saussaye
F–92200 Neuilly–sur–Seine, France
Tel.: [33] 1 46 24 10 51
Fax: [33] 1 46 37 07 50
Email: school@ecole–marymount.fr
www.ecole–marymount.fr
(U.S. curriculum, prekindergarten through grade 8)

Mougins School
615 Avenue Dr. Maurice Donat
Font de l'Orme
BP 401 Cedex
F–06250, Mougins, France
Tel: [33] 4 93 90 15 47
Fax: [33] 4 93 75 31 40
Email: information@mougins–school.com
www.mougins–school.com
(U.K. curriculum, prekindergarten through grade 12)

Chapter 14

Italy

Major employment centers: Rome, Milan, Naples, Turin
Major business language: Italian
Language skill index: Really should know it
Currency: Euro
Telephone country code: 39
Time zone: Eastern Standard Time + 6 hours
Punctuality index: Punctuality means being twenty minutes late
Average daily temperature, high/low: January: 54°/39°; July, 88°/64° (Rome)
Average number of days with precipitation: January: 11 days; July: 1 day
Best bet for employment:
　For students: Au pair
　Permanent jobs: Specialized skills and assignment from an American company
Chance of finding a job: Not so good, thanks to relatively high unemployment rates
Useful tip: It pays to be fashion conscious! The Italians spend more per capita on clothes than any other nationality in Europe, and Italians feel that detailed care of how you look reflects how you work. If you are up–to–date in fashion, your work skills will likely be considered current as well.

Italy stretches into the Mediterranean Sea from south–central Europe. The country is about the size of Arizona, and it borders France, Switzerland, Austria, and the former Yugoslavia to the north. The Adriatic Sea separates Italy from the Balkan peninsula to the east. North Africa is across the Mediterranean to the south. Sardinia and Sicily form the western edge of the Tyrrhenian Sea. The Apennine Mountains traverse the length of the peninsula, and the Alps form the northern borders.

Italy's Prime Minister is the country's richest man and its most powerful businessman, controlling about 90 percent of the nation's broadcast TV.

The Western Roman Empire lasted until the fifth century A.D. The northern Italian city–states developed into flourishing cultural and commercial centers in the late Middle Ages and during the Renaissance. France, Austria, and Spain continuously fought over territory and influence in Italy, thereby contributing to the country's political fragmentation. By the mid–nineteenth century, the House of Savoy had become a significant European power, and in 1861 Victor Emmanuel II of Sardinia was proclaimed King of Italy. The country fought with the Allies in World War I, but Benito Mussolini's Fascists assumed power in 1922, allying with the Nazis in Germany. Following World War II, Italy changed sides to the Allies and became a republic in 1946. Italy was a founding member of both the European Union and the North Atlantic Treaty Organization.

Italy, with nearly fifty governments in the post–World War II era, has a reputation for having a revolving political door. The governments have consisted, for the most part, of various reincarnations of the same five political parties: the Christian Democrats, Socialists, Republicans, Social Democrats, and the Liberals. In 1996, the Olive Tree coalition, a center–left coalition, was elected to office. Led by the economist Romano Prodi, who is a former president of the European Commission, the governing coalition included communists for the first time in Italian history. Under Prodi, Italy ushered in a period of fiscal austerity in order to guarantee the country's entry into the European Monetary Union (EMU) in 1998.

In May 2001, colorful television empresario Silvio Berlusconi, the richest man in Italy, was re–elected prime minister. He was first elected prime minister in 1993 as head of Forza Italia, the party he founded and named for the popular cheer associated with the Italian football league, but resigned seven months later. In 1996, he lost the election to Prodi. Berlosconi's re–election presents Italy with an exceptional situation: Its prime minister owns the three largest private television networks and controls three large public networks, which effectively gives him control over 90 percent of broadcast television. Although he may be Italy's most powerful businessman, he is also a man in a lot of legal trouble. Berlosconi currently is facing bribery and corruption charges dating back to the 1980s and is fighting to stay out of jail.

Many businesses close daily from 1 p.m. to 3 p.m. Banking hours are Mondays through Fridays from 9 a.m. to 1 p.m. and from 2:30 p.m. to 4 p.m.

Current Economic Climate

Although Italy has the fifth–largest economy in the world, it is currently experiencing moderate economic trouble. Italy's national unemployment rate is approximately 9 percent nationwide, but nearly 19 percent in Southern Italy. The country experienced a severe economic crisis in 1992–93 that resulted in a succession of governments attempting extreme measures, such as the privatization of the country's large public sector. Italy has pursued a tight fiscal policy for the past decade to meet the requirements of the E.M.U. and has benefitted from lower interest and inflation rates. Italy's economic performance has lagged behind that of its E.U. partners, and the current government is enacting short–term reforms aimed at improving competitiveness and long–term growth. Italy's economic challenges are to stimulate employment, promote wage flexibility, hold down the growth in pensions, and tackle the informal economy.

Speaking the language

In most parts of Italy you will need to speak the native tongue to get a job. Next to Americans, Italians are the least likely nationality to speak a second language. Don't expect Italians to respond to inquiries in English.

Despite privatization efforts, many of Italy's large conglomerates are still owned by the state and considered fairly well–run. These giant corporations usually own interests in numerous industries throughout the country. This became a political issue after Fiat, the sixth–largest car maker in the world, announced that it would lay off 8,100 workers in an effort to stem a financial meltdown. Prime Minister Berloscuni contemplated a bailout of Fiat, even claiming at one point that he could better run the company than its current management. His efforts to meddle in the affairs of the troubled company have been halted and restructuring plans have been implemented, but the future of the car–maker is hardly secure.

Italy's labor force is 58 percent government and services, 32 percent industrial, and 10 percent agricultural. Its major industries include tourism, machinery, iron and steel, chemicals, food processing, textiles, motor vehicles, clothing, footwear, and ceramics. Italy's closest trade ties are with the other countries of the European Union, with whom it conducts nearly half of its total trade. Italy's largest E.U. trade partners are Germany (16.1 percent), France (11.7 percent), and the United Kingdom (5.9 percent).

Italy's 10 Largest Companies

(2001, based on market capitalization)

1. Telecom Italia Societa per Azioni
2. Telecom Italia Mobile (T.I.M.)

3. Ente Nazionale Idrocarburi (ENI)
4. ENEL Societe per Azioni
5. Assicurazioni Generali
6. UniCredito Italiano
7. IntesaBCI
8. San Paolo IMI
9. Fiat
10. Ing. C. Olivetti & C.

Getting Around in Italy

Italy's modern railway system still offers relatively inexpensive fares. Eurail and InterRail passes are accepted on all railways. In some mountainous regions, buses are sometimes faster than trains. Buses also serve as a better alternative transportation within cities. Since the Italian highway system, the autostrade, is well–kept and expressways are readily available, renting a car can be a good option. Tolls, however, can be expensive. And some cities, such as Florence, prohibit private vehicles from key parts of their urban center. Air travel within Italy is expensive, making it less–attractive. Traveling is congested in August, a vacation period in most parts of the country.

Employment Regulations and Outlook for Americans

Italy's high unemployment rate continues to limit job opportunities for foreigners, regardless of whether the work is professional or unskilled. U.S. citizens do not need visas for stays of fewer than 90 days, but you must obtain one if staying longer. The Ministry of Home Affairs must grant a prospective employee a residence permit for employment. A work permit from an employer must be obtained prior to arrival. Employers must also provide a statement explaining that no Italians in the area can perform the job. Visitors should register with the local police headquarters, the *questura*, within three days of arrival. The police headquarters also provides residence permits.

The best job opportunities for Americans are generally for senior executives of multinational firms. Some companies may give short–term assignments in Italy. The best opportunities for students are with summer camps or au pair agencies. As members of the European Union, British citizens enjoy an advantage for English teaching jobs because employers do not have to provide work permits. North Africans perform much of the agricultural work in Italy, decreasing your chances for jobs on farms. Tourist work in hotels and restaurants is generally difficult to find because of the plentiful supply of local labor. It is possible to be self–employed, for example as a translator, language teacher, or consultant.

Short–term and Temporary Work

The best bet for temporary and casual work in Italy is as an au pair. See Chapter 9 for additional resources for au pair and casual work including Au

Pair in Europe and the Accord Cultural Exchange which place au pairs candidates in Italy.

Au Pair International
via S. Stefano 32
I–40125 Bologna, Italy
Tel.: [39] 051 26 7575
Fax: [39] 051 23 6594
Email: info@au–pair–international
www.au–pair–international.com
Au Pair International places au pairs for assignments throughout Italy, ranging from a month to a year.

ACLE Summer Camps
via Roma 54
I–18038 San Remo, Italy
Tel./ Fax: [39] 01 84 50 60 70

Email: info@acle.org
www.acle.org
The Associazione de Culturale Linguistica Educational, a nonprofit group organized by the Italian Ministry of Culture, runs summer camps that provide English–language immersion experiences for Italian children. ACLE recruits 150 English–speaking counselors to work in 50 summer camps located throughout Italy. The camps teach English through creative methods such as games, songs, and drama. Summer positions are paid.

Internship Programs

Several internship programs offer students opportunities to obtain professional experience. Some programs, such as that run by IES in Milan, also offer an opportunity to earn academic credit. See Chapter 9 for additional resources.

Global Experiences
P.O. Box 396
Arnold, MD 21012
www.globalexperiences.com
Global Experiences offers internships in Italy in public relations, marketing, information technology, graphic design, architecture, hospitality, fashion design, social work, government, and law. Internships are unpaid and require a high proficiency in Italian. Global Experiences offers some special programs that combine intensive Italian language courses with practical work experiences.

IES (Institute for International Education of Students)

33 North LaSalle Street, 15th floor

Chicago, IL 60602

Tel.: (800) 995 2300

www.IESabroad.org/milan/milan.html

IES offers a variety of internships in Milan, such as assignments with fashion designers, photographers, and international companies. Internships feature a strong academic component.

Volunteer Opportunities

Many of the volunteer opportunities in Italy involve work on conservation issues, social service, or international understanding. Additional resources appear in Chapter 9.

Associazione Culturale Linguistica Educational
via Roma, 54
I–18038 San Remo, Italy
Tel.: [39] 01 845 06070
www.acle.org
ACLE offers restoration projects in historic sites in Italy. The projects are phys-

ically demanding and include tasks such as landscaping, painting, and maintenance. Volunteers receive free accommodation on site.

Heritage Conservation Network
1557 North Street
Boulder, CO 80304
Tel.: (303) 444 0128

www.heritageconservation.net
Heritage Conservation Network organizes hands–on building conservation
workshops at sites around the world.
Participants work with and learn from
experts in the field of heritage conservation. They also join an international network of people working to conserve
historic structures and sites. The project
in Italy is at the Cappella Dell
Immacolatella, a small chapel on a farm
in Sicily. The program fee is $875,
which does not include transportation to
the site.

Resources for Further Information

Newspapers in Italy

Corriere della Sera
Tel.: [39] 02 63 39
Fax: [39] 22 9009 668
www.rcs.it/corriere

Il Giornale d'Italia
Tel.: [39] 668 33 663

Il Giornale di Napoli
Tel.: [39] 81 24 58 111
Fax: [39] 81 24 51 104

La Repubblica
Tel.: [39] 649 821
Fax: [39] 649 8229 23
www.repubblica.it

La Stampa
Tel.: [39] 1165 6811
Fax: [39] 1165 53 06
www.lastampa.it

Useful Websites for Job Seekers

The Internet is a good place to begin your job search. Many websites provide useful information for job searchers researching the Italian job market.
There are also several that list job vacancies, especially in technical industries.

American Chamber of Commerce in Italy Job Search
www.amcham.it/English/cercolavoro.asp
Features job vacancies with companies
that are members of the chamber. Site
also includes a database in which job
seekers can register. You can't post your
resume, but you can provide a brief
summary of your qualifications.

La Bacheca
www.bacheca.com
General job listing database. Written in
Italian.

Job–Net
www.job–net.it
Features over 125 jobs and an email
notification service.

JobOnline Italy
www.jobonline.it
Features a database of over 34,000 private sector jobs. Includes information
about employment sectors in Italy. You

can register to receive an email newsletter with job search information.

Jobsite Italy
www.gojobsite.it
Features a database of 1,300 private
sector jobs in 35 industries. Site includes
a searchable resume database and an
email notification system for new jobs.
Written in Italian.

Italy JobPilot
www.jobpilot.it
The database includes over 1,300 private sector jobs, a resume database,
and a directory of employers. Free registration.

Lavoro Online
www.lavoro.org
Features a wide range of job listings and
a resume database. Written in Italian.

Manpower Italy
www.manpower.it

Manpower is a recruitment agency. Its Italian site features a database of private sector jobs.

StepStone Italy
www.stepstone.it
One of Europe's leading online recruitment sites. Features over 4,700 private sector and education jobs in Italy.

Talent Manager

www.talentmanager.it

Dedicated to mid–level professional positions in Italy and Europe. You can search by position or by company, create a search agent, or post a resume. Viewable in Italian or English.

Embassies and Consular Offices

American embassies and consulates have commercial and/or economic sections that can provide you with business information and explain aspects of the local economy. Inquiries about business opportunities should be addressed either to "Commercial Officer" or "Commercial Section."

Representation of Italy in the United States

Embassy of Italy
3000 Whitehaven Street NW
Washington, DC 20008
Tel.: (202) 612–4400
Fax: (202) 518–2154
www.italyemb.org

Italian Consulates General

Chicago, (312) 467–1550; Los Angeles, (310) 820–0622; New York, (212) 737–9100

Representation of the United States in Italy

American Embassy
via Veneto 119/A
I–00187 Rome, Italy
Tel.: [39] 06 4674 1
Fax: [39] 06 4882 672
www.usembassy.it

**American Consulate General —
Florence**
Lungarno Amerigo Vespucci 38
I–50123 Florence, Italy
Tel.: [39] 05 52 39 8276
Fax: [39] 05 52 84 088

**American Consulate General —
Milan**
via Principe Amedeo 2/10
I–20121 Milan, Italy
Tel.: [39] 02 290 351
Fax: [39] 02 2900 1165

**American Consulate General —
Naples**
Piazza Della Republica 2
I–80122 Naples, Italy
Tel.: [39] 081 5838 111
Fax: [39] 081 7611 869

Chambers of Commerce

Chambers of commerce consist of member firms in both countries interested in international trade. These are appropriate companies to initially target in the job search.

**American Chamber of
Commerce in Italy**
via Cantù 1
I–20123 Milan, Italy
Tel.: [39] 02 869 06 61

Fax: [39] 02 805 77 37

Email: amcham@amcham.it

www.amcham.it

Italy–America Chamber of Commerce
730 Fifth Avenue, Suite 600
New York, NY 10019
Tel.: (212) 4590044
Fax: (212) 4590090
Email: info.newyork@italchambers.net
www.italchambers.net/newyork

Chamber of Commerce of Bologna
Piazza Affari
Piazza Costituzione 8
I–40128 Bologna, Italy
Tel.: [39] 05 16 09 31 11

Fax: [39] 05 16 09 34 51
www.bo.camcom.it

Milan Chamber of Commerce
via Meravigli 9/B11
I–20123 Milan, Italy
Tel.: [39] 02 85 15 1
Fax: [39] 02 85 15 42 32

Rome Chamber of Commerce
Piazza Sullustio 21
I–00187 Rome, Italy
Tel.: [39] 06 470 41
Fax: [39] 06 474 4741

World Trade Centers In Italy

World trade centers usually include many foreign companies that operate in the country.

World Trade Center Genoa
via De Marini 1
I–16149 Genoa, Italy
Tel.: [39] 010 235 91
Fax: [39] 010 645 6802
Email: info@wtc.genova.it

World Trade Center Milan
via Tamburini 13
I–20123 Milano, Italy
Tel.: [39] 02 48 56 161
Fax: [39] 02 48 56 260

Other Informational Organizations

Foreign government missions in the U.S., such as national tourist offices, can furnish visas and information on work permits and other important regulations. They may also offer economic and business information about Italy.

Italian Cultural Institute
686 Park Avenue
New York, NY 10021
Tel.: (212) 879–4242
www.italcultny.org/new_main.htm

Italian Government Travel Office
630 Fifth Avenue, Suite 1565
Rockefeller Center
New York, NY 10111
Tel.: (212) 245–5618
Fax: (212) 586–9249
www.italiantourism.com

Business Directories

Although not always easy to find, business directories can prove invaluable in the international job search. Your best bet for locating these directories is to begin in the reference section of any public or university library. Most directories list company names, addresses, products, and telephone numbers. Some directories include executive names and titles and financial information about the company. These sources provide you with the names of the people to contact for employment information as well as financial data, which can tell you how strong a company's position in a country may be.

Guide to the Italian Clothing Industry. GESTO s.r.l., via Mercato 28, I–20121 Milan, Italy; email: gesto@gestoit.com; www.modainitaly.it. Over 5,000 apparel manufacturers, 1,000 suppliers of fabrics and machinery, and 3,500 trade names. 461 pages, €62 updated annually.

Italian–American Business Directory. American Chamber of Commerce in Italy, via Cesare Cantu 1, I–20123 Milan, Italy; email: amcham@amcham.it; www.amcham.it. Describes 40,000 Italian and American firms engaged in bilateral trade. $150, 400 pages, updated annually.

Italian General Directory. Guida Monaci s.p.a., via Vitorchiano 107/109, I–00189 Rome, Italy; email: guidamonaci@italybygm.it; www.italyby gm.it. Lists 100,000 industrial and commercial firms; 100,000 prominent Italians; the national government; and about 50,000 provincial and local government, educational, and cultural institutions. 2,790 pages, updated annually.

Kompass Italia. Kompass Italia, via A. Filippa 16, I–10130 Turin, Italy; email: kompass@kompassitalie.com; www.kompass.com. Includes 55,000 manufacturing and service companies. 6,000 pages, updated annually.

United States–Italy Trade Directory. Italy–America Chamber of Commerce, 730 Fifth Avenue, Suite 600, New York, NY 10019; email: info@newyork @italchambers.net; www.italchambers.net/newyork. Lists 4,000 American firms with Italian business interests. $150, 400 pages, updated biennially.

Leading Employers in Italy

The following companies are classified by business area: Banking and Finance; Industrial Manufacturing; Retailing and Wholesaling; Service Industries; and Technology. Company information includes firm name, address, phone and fax numbers, and specific business. Your chances of securing employment abroad are substantially better if you contact the subsidiary company in Europe rather than the parent company in the U.S. Keep in mind that the contact information for companies listed in this section can change rapidly. It is a good idea before submitting correspondence to any company to double–check the address and phone number.

American Companies In Italy

Banking And Finance

AON Italia
via Andrea Ponti 10
I–20143 Milan, Italy
Tel.: [39] 02 818 021
Fax: [39] 02 818 028 00
www.aon.com
(Insurance)

JPMorgan Chase Bank
via Catena 4
I–20121 Milan, Italy
Tel.: [39] 02 88 951
Fax: [39] 02 88 952 218
(Bank)

Industrial Manufacturing

3M Italia
via S. Bovio 3
I–20090 Segrate (MI), Italy
Tel.: [39] 02 7035 1
Fax: [39] 02 7035 3090
(Adhesives, copying equipment)

Abbott
S.S. Pontina 148 Km. 52
I–04010 Aprilia, Italy
Tel.: [39] 06 92 89 21
(Pharmaceuticals)

Albadoro
Corso Asti 18
I–12050 Guarene d'Alba CN, Italy
Tel.: [39] 0173 622111
Fax: [39] 0173 33783
(Packaged foods)

Bridgestone Firestone Italia
via delle Margherita 40 ZI
I–70026 Modugno (BA), Italy
Tel.: [39] 080 506 3111
Fax: [39] 080 506 3333
(Tires)

Bristol–Myers Squibb
via del Murillo Km 2,800
I–04010 Sermoneta (LT), Italy
Tel.: [39] 07733101
Fax: [39] 07733101
(Pharmaceuticals and chemicals)

Chiquita Italia
via Tempio del Cielo 3
I–00144 Rome, Italy
Tel.: [39] 06 52 08 31
Fax: [39] 06 52 95 499
(Fruit and fruit products)

Coca–Cola Bevande Italia
Viale Monza 338
I–20100 Milan, Italy
Tel.: [39] 02270771
(Soft drinks)

Colgate–Palmolive
Via Giorgione 59/63
I–00147 Rome, Italy
Tel.: [39] 06 549061
Fax: [39] 06 54906351
(Soap, toiletries, cosmetics)

Dolma
via Dante 40
I–27011 Belgioioso, Italy
Tel.: [39] 0382 9791
Fax: [39] 0382 970493
(Pet foods)

Dow Italia
via Patroculo 21

I–20151 Milan, Italy
Tel.: [39] 02 48 221
Fax: [39] 02 48 224 383
(Chemicals and plastics)

Exxon Chemical Films
Strada per Pandi 4
I–72100 Brindisi, Italy
Tel.: [39] 08315091
Fax: [39] 0831509315
(Chemicals)

Ford Italiana
Via Andrea Argoli 54
I–00143 Rome, Italy
Tel.: [39] 06518551
Fax: [39] 0651962349
(Automobiles)

Goodyear Dunlop Tires Italia
Piazza G Marconi 25
I–00144, Rome, Italy
Tel.: [39] 06 543 901
Fax: [39] 06 543 902 31
(Tires)

W.R. Grace Italiana
via Trento 7
I–20017 Rho, Italy
Tel.: [39] 02 935371
Fax: [39] 02 93537572
(Chemicals and pharmaceuticals)

Ingersoll–Rand Italiana
Strada Provinciale Cassanese 108
I–20060 Vignate, Italy
Tel.: [39] 02 95 0561
Fax: [39] 02 95 60 315
(Industrial equipment and machinery)

International Paper Italia
via Ornago 55
I–20040 Bellusco, Italy
Tel.: [39] 039 627451
Fax: [39] 039 6022366
(Paper products)

Johnson Wax
Piazzale Burke 3
I–20020 Arese, Italy
Tel.: [39] 02 93371
Fax: [39] 02 9337 407
(Household cleaning products)

Kodak
viale Matteotti 62

I–20092 Cinisello Balsamo, Italy
Tel.: [39] 02 660281
Fax: [39] 02 6601 0168
(Photographic equipment)

Kraft Foods Italia
via Nizzoli 3
I–20147 Milan, Italy
Tel.: [39] 02 41 351
Fax: [39] 02 41 35 4500
(Food processing)

Levi Strauss Italia
Corso Como 15
I–20154 Milan, Italy
Tel.: [39] 02 29 0231
Fax: [39] 02 29 00 3681
(Clothing)

Eli Lilly Italia
via Gramsci 731733
I–50019 Sesto Fiorentino, Italy
Tel.: [39] 055 42571
Fax: [39] 055 4257 707
www.lilly.com
(Pharmaceuticals)

Litton Precision Products
Viale Testi 126
I–20092 Cinisello Balsamo, Italy
Tel.: [39] 022479161
Fax: [39] 022440669
(Measurement equipment)

Mattel
via Vittorio Veneto 119
I–28040 Oleggio Castello (NO), Italy
Tel.: [39] 03 22 23 13 11
Fax: [39] 03 22 45 842
(Toys and games)

Merck Sharp e Dohme (Italia)
via Fabbroni 6
I–00191 Rome, Italy
Tel.: [39] 06 36 1911
Fax: [39] 06 3332555
(Pharmaceuticals)

Pfizer Italiana
via Valbondone 113
I–00188 Rome, Italy
Tel.: [39] 06 33 1821
Fax: [39] 06 33 62 6019
(Chemicals and pharmaceuticals)

Pharmacia and Upjohn
via Robert Koch 1/2
I–20152 Milan, Italy
Tel.: [39] 02 48 381
Fax: [39] 02 48 38 2734
(Pharmaceuticals)

Procter & Gamble Italia
viale Cesare Pavese 385
I–00144 Rome, Italy
Tel.: [39] 06 500901
Fax: [39] 06 50972930
(Cleaning products)

Reebok Italia
via Bartolomeo Colleoni 1
I–20041 Agrate Brianza, Italy
Tel.:[39]03960181
Fax:[39]0396018400
www.reebok.com
(Athletic shoes)

Xerox
via Antolisei 6
I–00173 Roma, Italy
Tel.: [39] 06729941
Fax: [39] 72994402
(Office machines)

Retailing And Wholesaling

Tiffany & Co. Milan at Faraone
via Montenapoleone 7A
I–20121 Milan, Italy
Tel.: [39] 02 7601 3656
www.tiffany.com
(Jewelry)

Timberland Europe
Centro Direzionale Colleoni
Palazzo Orione
viale Colleoni
I–20041 Agrate Brianza, Italy
(Footwear and apparel)

Service Industries

Accenture
Largo Donegani 2
I–20121 Milan, Italy
Tel.: [39] 02 29 0381
Fax: [39] 02 65 98076
(Management consulting)

Associated Press
Piazza Grazioli 5

I–00186 Rome, Italy
Tel.: [39] 06 6798382
Fax: [39] 066790103
www.ap.com
(News gathering agency)

DHL International
Strada 5 Milanofiori Palazzo u/3
I–20089 Rozzano, Italy
Tel.: [39] 02 57 57 21
Fax: [39] 02 89 20 80 99
(Air cargo services)

Kelly Services Italia
via Dante 7
I–20123 Milan, Italy
Tel.: [39] 02 880731
Fax: [39] 02 88073370
www.kellyservices.com
(Temporary services)

Spencer Stuart & Associates
via Visconti di Modrone 12
I–20122 Milan, Italy
Tel.: [39] 02 771251
Fax: [39] 02 782452
www.spencerstuart.com
(Executive recruitment)

Towers Perrin Forrest & Crosby
via Pontaccio 10
I–20121 Milan, Italy
Tel.: [39] 02 863 921
Fax: [39] 02 809 754
www.towers.com
(Benefits consulting)

Warner Bros. Italia
via Varese 16/B
I–00185 Rome, Italy
Tel.: [39] 06 448891
Fax: [39] 06 4440177

Technology

Apple Computer
Viale San Marco 35
I–41049 Sassuolo, Italy

Tel.: [39] 0536808713
Fax: [39] 0536807980
(Computers)

Hewlett–Packard Italiana
via G. di Vittorio 9
I–20063 Cernusco Sul Naviglio (MI),
Italy
Tel.: [39] 02 92121
Fax: [39] 02 92122033
(Printers, computers)

IBM Italia
Località Tregaresso
I–20090 Segrate, Italy
Tel.: [39] 02 59621
Fax: [39] 02 5962 5937
(Data processing equipment)

Microsoft Italy
Centro Direzionale San Felice
via Rivoltana 13m
I–20090 Segrate (Milan), Italy
Tel.: [39] 02 703921
Fax: [39] 02 703 92020
www.microsoft.com
(Computer software)

Motorola
via Muzio Attendolo 13
I–20141 Milan, Italy
Tel.: [39] 02522071
Fax: [39] 02 52207290
(Electronic equipment)

Sun Microsystems Italia
via Fulvio Testi 327
I–20126 Milan, Italy
Tel.: [39] 01 641511
www.sun.com
(Mainframes and microcomputers)

Unisys Italia
via B Crespi 57
I–20159 Milan, Italy
Tel.: [39] 02 69851
Fax: [39] 02 69 85588
(Software and electronic equipment)

European Companies in Italy

The following are major non–American firms operating in the country. These selected companies either can be Italian or based in another European country. While these companies will generally hire their own nationals first, they may also employ Americans.

Banking and Finance

Alleanza Assicurazioni
Viale Luigi Sturzo, 35
I–20154 Milan, Italy
Tel.: [39] 02 62 961
Fax: [39] 02 653 718
www.alleanzaassicurazioni.it
(Insurance)

Allianz Subalpina
via Alfieri, 22
I–10121 Turin, Italy
Tel.: [39] 011 51 61111
Fax: [39] 011 51 61255
www.allianzsubalpina.it
(Insurance)

Assicurazioni Generali
Piazza Duca degli Abruzzi, 2
I–34132 Trieste, Italy
Tel.: [39] 040 6711
Fax: [39] 040 67 1600
www.generali.com
(Insurance and reinsurance)
(Commercial bank)

Banca Nazionale del Lavoro
via Vittorio Veneto, 119
I–00187 Rome, Italy
Tel.: [39] 06 47 02 1
Fax: [39] 06 47 02 7336
www.bnl.it
(Bank)

**Banca Popolare Commercio e
Industria (BPCI)**
via Moscova, 33
I–20121 Milan, Italy
Tel.: [39] 02 6275 1
Fax: [39] 02 6599 072
www.bpci.it
(Bank)

Bastogi
via Tamburini, 13
I–20123 Milan, Italy
Tel.: [39] 02 4856 161
Fax: [39] 02 4632 08
www.bastogionline.it
(Financial services)

IntesaBCI
Piazza Paolo Ferrari, 10
I–20121 Milan, Italy
Tel.: [39] 02 8844 1
Fax: [39] 02 8844 3638
www.bancaintesa.it
(Bank)

Sanpaolo IMI
Piazza San Carlo 156
I–10121 Turin, Italy
Tel.: [39] 011 55 51
Fax: [39] 011 55 2989
www.sanpaolo.it
(Bank)

UniCredito Italiano
Piazza Cordusio 2
I–20121 Milan, Italy
Tel.: [39] 02 8862 1
Fax: [39] 02 8862 8503
www.credit.it
(Bank)

Industrial Manufacturing

Automobili Lamborghini Holding
via Modena 12
I–40019 Sant Agata Bolognese, Italy
Tel.: [39] 051 68 17 611
Fax: [39] 051 68 17 737
www.lamborghini.com
(Auto manufacturers)

Bassetti
via Legnano, 24
I–20027 Rescaldina, Milan, Italy
Tel.: [39] 0331 44 8111
Fax: [39] 0331 44 8500
www.bassetti.it
(Textile manufacturing)

Benetton Group
Villa Minelli
I–31050 Ponzano Veneto, Treviso, Italy
Tel.: [39] 04 22 513 111
Fax: [39] 04 22 969 501
www.benetton.com
(Apparel)

Bulgari
Lungotevere Marzio 11
I–00186 Rome, Italy
Tel.: [39] 06 688 10477
Fax: [39] 06 688 10401
www.bulgari.it
(Consumer luxury goods)

Caffaro
via Friuli, 55
I–20031 Cesano Maderno, Milan, Italy
Tel.: [39] 0362 514 1
Fax: [39] 0362 514 889 (454)
www.caffarochem.com/caffaro/ENG
/index_english.htm
(Chemicals)

Camfin
via Sempione, 230
I–20016 Pero, Milan, Italy
Tel.: [39] 02 3537 41
Fax: [39] 02 35374305
www.gruppocamfin.it
(Oil and gas refining and marketing)

Danieli & C. Officine Meccaniche
via Nazione, 41
I–33042 Buttrio, Italy
Tel.: [39] 04 3259 81
Fax: [39] 04 3259 8289
www.danieli.it
(Industrial machinery)

Davide Campari–Milano
Via Filippo Turati 27
I–20121 Milan, Italy
Tel.: [39] 026 2251
Fax: [39] 026 225312
www.campari.com
(Distillers)

DeLonghi
via L. Seitz 47
I–31050 Treviso, Italy
Tel.: [39] 04 22 4131
Fax: [39] 04 22 413647
www.delonghi.com
(Appliances)

Diesel
via dell Industria 7
I–36060 Molvena, Vicenza, Italy
Tel.: [39] 0424 477 555
Fax: [39] 0424 411 955
www.diesel.com
(Apparel)

Dolce & Gabbana
via Santa Cecilia, 7
I–20122 Milan, Italy
Tel.: [39] 02 77 42 71
Fax: [39] 02 76 02 06 00
www.dolcegabbana.it

(Apparel)

Ducati Motor Holding
via Cavalieri Ducati, 3
I–40132 Bologna, Italy
Tel.: [39] 051 641 3111
Fax: [39] 051 641 3223
www.ducati.com
(Motorcycles)

ENEL
Viale Regina Margherita, 137
I–00198 Rome, Italy
Tel.: [39] 06 8509 1
Fax: [39] 06 8585 7097
www.enel.it
(Electricity)

Ente Nazionale Idrocarburi (ENI)
Piazzale Enrico Mattei 1
I–00144 Rome, Italy
Tel.: [39] 65 982 1
Fax: [39] 65 982 2631
www.eni.it
(Oil and gas)

ERG Petroli
Torre WTC, Via Demarini, 1
I–16149 Genoa, Italy
Tel.: [39] 10 24011
Fax: [39] 10 2401533
www.erg.it
(Oil refining)

Ericsson
via Anagnina, 203, C.P. 4197
I–00040 Rome, Italy
Tel.: [39] 06 725 81
Fax: [39] 06 726 708 38
www.ericsson.it
(Telecommunications equipment)

Ferrari
via Abetone Inferiore, 4
I–41053 Maranello, Modena, Italy
Tel.: [39] 0536 949 111
Fax: [39] 0536 949 714
www.ferrari.it
(Auto manufacturers)

Fiat
250 Via Nizza
I–10126 Turin, Italy
Tel.: [39] 011 686 1111
Fax: [39] 011 686 3798
www.fiatgroup.com

(Automobiles and commercial vehicles)

Fila Holding
Viale Cesare Battisti, 26
I–13900 Biella, Italy
Tel.: [39] 01 535 061
Fax: [39] 01 535 06481
www.fila.com
(Apparel)

Gianni Versace
via Manzoni 38
I–20121 Milan, Italy
Tel.: [39] 02 760 931
Fax: [39] 02 760 04122
www.versace.it
(Consumer luxury goods)

Giorgio Armani
Via Borgonuovo 11
I–20121 Milan, Italy
Tel.: [39] 02 723 18 1
Fax: [39] 02 723 18 455
www.giorgioarmani.com
(Consumer luxury goods)

Giovanni Crespi
Viale Pasubio, 38
I–20025 Legnano, Milan, Italy
Tel.: [39] 03 3144 6111
Fax: [39] 03 3159 7078
www.crespi.it
(Chemicals)

Martini & Rossi
Corso Vittorio Emanuele II 42
I–10123 Turin, Italy
Tel.: [39] 011 810 81
Fax: [39] 011 810 8200
www.martini.com
(Wineries)

Olivetti
Via Jevis 77
I–10015 Ivrea, Torino, Italy
Tel.: [39] 0125 52 00
Fax: [39] 0125 52 2524
www.olivetti.it
(Information technology, office products)

Pirelli
Viale Sarca, 222
I–20126 Milan, Italy
Tel.: [39] 02 6442 4688
Fax: [39] 02 6442 4686

www.pirelli.com
(Tires and cables)

SNIA
via Borgonuovo, 14
I–20121 Milan, Italy
Tel.: [39] 02 63321
Fax: [39] 02 633 2311
www.snia.it
(Medical products)

Service Industries

Alitalia Linee Aeree Italiane
Viale A. Marchetti 111
I–00148 Rome, Italy
Tel.: [39] 06 6562 2151
Fax: [39] 06 6562 4733
www.alitalia.it
(Airlines)

Italgas
41 via XX Settembre
I–10121 Turin, Italy
Tel.: [39] 011 239 41
Fax: [39] 011 239 4795
www.italgas.it
(Natural gas)

Compagnia Italiana dei Jolly Hotels
via Bellini, 6
I–36078 Valdagno, Italy
Tel.: [39] 0445 410 000
Fax: [39] 0445 411 472
www.jollyhotels.it
(Hotels)

Technology

Telecom Italia
Corso d'Italia 41
I–00198 Rome, Italy
Tel.: [39] 06 368 81
Fax: [39] 06 368 83388
www.telecomitalia.it
(Telecommunications)

Tiscali
Viale Trento, 39
I–09123 Caligari, Italy
Tel.: [39] 070 460 11
Fax: [39] 070 460 1400
www.tiscali.it
(Internet and online service provider)

Major International Nonprofit Organizations In Italy

Food and Agriculture Organization of the U.N.
via delle Terme di Caracalla
I–00100 Rome, Italy
Tel.: [39] 06 5705 1
Fax: [39] 06 5705 3152
Email: FAO–HQ@fao.org

www.fao.org

Italo–Latin American Institute
Piazza Guglielmo Marconi 26
I–00144 Rome, Italy
Tel.: [39] 06 59 09 1
Fax: [39] 06 59 14 92 3

International Schools In Italy

American International School of Florence
via del Carota 23/25
I–50012 Bagno a Ripoli
Florence, Italy
Tel.: [39] 055/6461007
Fax: [39] 055/644226
Email: admin.aisf@interbusiness.it
www.aisfitaly.org
(U.S./International Baccalaureate curriculum, prekindergarten through grade 12)

American International School in Genoa
via Quarto 13/C
I–16148 Genoa, Italy
Tel.: [39] 010 386528
Fax: [39] 010 398700
Email: aisgenoa@libero.it
http://space.tin.it/internet/elrosser
(U.S curriculum, prekindergarten through grade 8)

American Overseas School of Rome
via Cassia 811
I–00189 Rome, Italy
Tel.: [39] 06 33 4381
Fax: [39] 06 3326 2608
Email: aosr@aosr.org
www.aosr.org
(U.S./International Baccalaureate curriculum, prekindergarten through grade 13)

American School of Milan
Villagio Mirasole
I–20090 Noverasco di Opera
Milan, Italy
Tel.: [39] 02 53 00 00 1
Fax: [39] 02 57 60 62 74
Email: directorasm@planet.it
www.asmilan.org

(U.S./International Baccalaureate curriculum, prekindergarten through grade 13)

International School of Milan
via Caccialepori 22
I–20148 Milan, Italy
Tel.: [39] 02 487 08076
Fax:(+39) 02 487 03644
Email: ismhigh@ismac.it
www.ismac.it
(U.K./International Baccalaureate curriculum, prekindergarten through grade 13)

International School of Naples
Viale della Liberazione 1
I–80125 Bagnoli, Naples, Italy
Tel.: [39] 08 17 21 20 37
Fax: [39] 081 570 0248
Email: info@intschoolnaples.it
www.intschoolnaples.it
(U.S. curriculum, prekindergarten through grade 12)

International School of Trieste
via Conconello 16 (Opicina)
I–34016 Trieste, Italy
Tel.: [39] 04 02 11 452
Fax: [39] 04 02 13 122
Email: info@istrieste.org
www.geocities.com/athens/oracle/1329
(U.S. curriculum, prekindergarten through grade 8)

International School of Turin (ACAT)
Vicolo Tiziano 10
I–10024 Moncalieri, Turin, Italy
Tel.: [39] 11 645 967
Fax: [39] 11 643 298
Email: acatist@hotmail.com
www.saa.unito.it/ist

Help us keep you current with free updates

We realize that companies move, go out of business, or start anew. We know that websites come and go. Many of the companies and websites listed in *How to Get a Job in Europe* could undergo change in the coming months and years.

You are the key to keeping this book current. If you would be so kind as to alert us of any changes to the job sources described in this book, we will post those changes on our free online Update Sheet at http://jobfindersonline.com.

When you find that a website described here no longer exists, has a new URL, has changed the job resources it offers — or if you have found any new European job resources you think we should add — send us an email that tells us the name of the job resource, its URL, and the page of this book on which the job source appears. Please tell us what has changed. We will confirm your information and post it online. Similarly, please tell us about any changes in print resources or company information so we can post the changes online.

Send your email with changes to:
europe_update@planningcommunications.com

To see the free Update Sheet which you can print from your web browser, visit http://jobfindersonline.com — the links to the free Update Sheet will be obvious on our home page.

(U.S./Italian/International Baccalaureate curriculum, prekindergarten through grade 12)

Marymount International School
via di Villa Lauchli 180
I–00191 Rome, Italy

Tel.: [39] 06 362 9101
Fax: [39] 06 363 01738
Email: marymount@pronet.it
www.marymountrome.com
(U.S./International Baccalaureate curriculum, prekindergarten through grade 13)

Chapter 15

Germany

Major employment centers: Frankfurt, Munich, Hamburg, Berlin

Major business language: German

Language skill index: English is spoken by younger people, and it is possible to get by in informal situations with English. German proficiency, however, is usually required in business.

Currency: Euro

Telephone country code: 49

Time zone: Eastern Standard Time + 6 hours

Punctuality index: Germans are very formal and punctuality is absolutely required

Average daily temperature, high/low: January: 35°/26°; July, 74°/55° (Munich)

Average number of days with precipitation: January: 11 days; July: 19 days

Best bet for employment:

For students: Apply to work abroad programs through CDS International or the Council on International Educational Exchange

Permanent jobs: Information technology

Chance of finding a job: Not bad using the above options, but expect stiff competition due to high unemployment.

Useful tip: German workers enjoy 42 paid holidays per year, the most in the world.

Located in north–central Europe, Germany borders Denmark and the Baltic Sea to the north; the Netherlands, Belgium, Luxembourg, and France to the west; Switzerland and Austria to the south; and the former Czechoslovakia and Poland to the east. Germany is larger than New Mexico but smaller than California. Northern and central Germany are generally flat, while the west is hilly and the south is mountainous.

Even after 13 years of unification, some East Germans view liberation as West German occupation.

Charlemagne conquered most of the Germanic tribes occupying the territories of present–day Germany, which became the German Empire following his death. Germany eventually dissolved into numerous principalities, with religious conflicts between Catholics and Protestants exacerbating the process during the Reformation. Following the Napoleonic period, Prussia and Hapsburg Austria contended for control of Germany. Under the guidance of the Chancellor Otto von Bismarck, the Prussians eventually outmaneuvered the Austrians and the French. The second German Empire was proclaimed in 1871.

Following its defeat in World War I, Germany lost its overseas colonies and large tracts of its European lands. The Republic of Germany was proclaimed in 1919, embodying the most liberal principles of the time. The Weimar Republic suffered from economic turmoil, an undemocratic political culture, and onerous sanctions imposed by the Treaty of Versailles. The worldwide depression shattered the republic and led to the appointment of Adolf Hitler as chancellor in 1933. By 1938, Hitler had established a Nazi totalitarian state, violated the Versailles Treaty, and occupied Austria and much of Czechoslovakia. In 1939 Germany invaded Poland, and World War II began.

Following Germany's defeat in 1945, the U.S., the U.S.S.R., Britain, and France divided the country into occupation zones. Berlin, fully within the Soviet sector, was similarly divided. Germany lost large portions of land in the east to Poland and the Soviet Union. The Federal Republic was created in 1949 in the American, British, and French zones. In response, the Soviets imposed a blockade upon West Berlin. West Germany became fully independent in 1955.

The German Democratic Republic was declared in 1949 and proclaimed independent in 1954. West Germany joined the European Community and the North Atlantic Treaty Organization, while East Germany joined the Warsaw Pact Organization and Comecon. Both German states entered the United Nations in 1973. West Germany's major parties included the Christian Democrats, the Social Democrats, the Free Democrats, and the Greens. The communist Socialist Unity party dominated East Germany until the collapse of the Eastern European regimes in late 1989.

Two of the most enduring symbols of the end of the cold war — the opening of the Berlin Wall on November 9, 1989, and the unification of the two Germanys on October 3, 1990 — were sudden and largely unexpected. For forty years, the two German states had existed side–by–side, looking back on the same historical traditions but taking diametrically opposite paths. The West was democratic, federalist, and oriented to a market economy, while the East was socialist, centralist, and operated on a planned economy. Unification, although long desired, was not easy. It has both benefited and strained the German economy, and it has pushed Germany into the forefront as the European Union's most powerful nation. Although now united in name as a country, Germany is not yet united in spirit. Even 13 years after unification, some *Ossis* (East Germans) still view the East German reunification with *der Vaterland* as more a West German occupation than a liberation. East Germany, which once enjoyed the highest standard of living of the Eastern European countries, has faced economic turmoil and mild prejudice from *Wessis* counterparts since The Change. The unemployment rate in the Eastern states is still higher than in the Western states. The government decided in June 1991 to move Germany's capital from Bonn to Berlin, and the Bundestag resumed sitting in Berlin's Reichstag building in September 1999.

Gerhard Schroeder, a Social Democrat, was elected Prime Minister in October 1998. Schroeder's government entered into a coalition with the Greens. In a stinging humiliation, Helmut Kohl and his Christian Democrats (CDU), who had been in power for 16 years, won only 35 percent of the national vote. In 1999, Kohl, the Prime Minister who led Germany's reunification, became embroiled in a serious scandal as financial irregularities during his administration came to light, including more than $1 million in secret campaign contributions. Refusing to disclose the source of funds paid to him and with his reputation in shambles, Kohl was forced to resign as honorary chairman of the CDU. In 2001, he agreed to pay a fine in exchange for an end to the criminal investigation of his role in the campaign contributions scandal.

Schroeder's re–election in September 2002 strained Germany's normally good relations with the U.S. In an extremely tight election against conservative challenger Edmund Stoiber, Schroeder sought to swing German voters — 80 percent of whom told opinion polls that they wanted Germany to have no part in an attack on Iraq — by announcing his opposition to a possible U.S.–led war against Saddam Hussein. The U.S. administration was also infuriated by alleged comments from the former German Justice Minister Herta Daeubler–Gmelin, who likened George Bush to Adolf Hitler. Although she denied making the remarks, Schroeder did apologize to the U.S. and subsequently left Dauebler–Gmelin out of his coalition government. Bush publicly rebuffed Schroeder after his re–election, but both leaders are making efforts to thaw their recently frosty relations.

Post offices in Germany are usually open from 8 a.m. to 6 p.m. weekdays, and from 8 a.m. to noon on Saturdays. Banks are open weekdays from 9 a.m. to 4 p.m., with a break from noon to 2 p.m. Normal weekday business hours are from 8:30 am to 6 p.m. Some retail businesses remain open until 8 p.m. Don't plan on conducting much business in August, the major vacation month in Germany.

Current Economic Climate

Germany possesses the world's third most technologically powerful economy after the United States and Japan, yet it struggles under the burden of generous social benefits. Structural rigidities — like a high rate of social contributions on wages — have made unemployment a long–term, not just cyclical, problem, while Germany's aging population has pushed social security outlays to exceed contributions from workers. Unemployment hovers at about 9.7 percent, although it fluctuates widely in different regions of Germany. The rate is 7.8 percent in the former West Germany and a staggering 17.6 percent in the East. The integration and upgrading of the Eastern German economy remains a costly, long–term problem, with annual transfers from the West amounting to roughly $100 billion. Despite these issues and the general economic slowdown of its trading partners, economists predict Germany will see moderate growth during the next two years.

In a highly controversial move, the German government launched an employment program that allows computer experts from other countries to work there. The idea, based on the U.S. Green Card permit, is designed to attract foreign technical expertise to support the country's information technology industry. The German Information Technology Association estimates that 25 percent of IT vacancies in Germany remain unfilled. To cope with this problem, Germany will issue work visas valid for five years to up to 20,000 information technology experts. Applicants must have a university qualification or the promise of a salary of at least €50,000 a year. This is the first time Germany has formally opened its doors to economic immigrants since it invited guest workers from Turkey and southern Europe to help rebuild its economy after World War II.

About 60 percent of the work force is industrial, 30 percent services, and 10 percent agricultural. The major industries in Germany are among the world's largest and most technologically advanced producers of iron, steel, coal, cement, chemicals, machinery, vehicles, machine tools, electronics, food and beverages, shipbuilding, and textiles. Most German trade is conducted with the E.U., and Germany consistently ranks as the world's first– or second–largest exporter.

Germany's 10 Largest Companies

(2001, based on market capitalization)

1. Mannesmann (acquired by Vodafone)
2. Allianz
3. Deutsche Telekom
4. Muenchener Rückversicherungs–Gesellschaff Aktiengesellschaft
5. DaimlerChrysler
6. Siemens
7. Systeme Anwendungen Produkte (SAP)
8. Deutsche Bank Aktiengesellschaft
9. E.ON
10. Hoechst Aktiengesellschaft

Getting Around in Germany

Eurail and InterRail passes are accepted in Germany. The national railway network, GermanRail, also offers various discounts. The Deutsche Bundesbahn (DB), the railroad system in the west, is one of Europe's fastest networks. Since the reunification of East and West, Germany has experienced some difficulty linking up the former East Germany's rail system, the Reichsbahn, with its Western counterpart. Commuter trains are rather slow. The KD German Rhine steamers provide transportation services along the Rhine, Moselle, and Main rivers. Buses are also available. Lufthansa is one of Europe's busiest airlines and offers connections to various parts of Eastern Europe.

The German Lebenslauf

Your American–style resume may need to be tweaked to appeal to the German employer.

Your *lebenslauf* (resume) should begin with your personal information *(Persönliche–Daten):* name, address, telephone, date and place of birth, citizenship, and marital status, including any children. You should next list your qualifications in this precise order:

◆ Your educational history *(Schulausbildung);*

◆ Your professional or vocational training *(Berufliche Ausbildung),* including any courses or seminars you have taken;

◆ Your practical training or internship history *(Praktikum);*

◆ Your employment history *(Berufstätigkeit).*

Be sure to list any foreign languages you know and how well you know them. State whether you have a drivers license *(Fuhrerschein)* and if you do, what class. List your interests and hobbies *(Interesse)* if they relate to the job you are applying for. Finally, date and sign your resume, and attach your photo with a paperclip to the upper right–hand corner.

Employment Regulations and Outlook for Americans

Americans do not need a visa for stays of fewer than 90 days in Germany. Work permits, which are required to obtain employment in Germany, may be applied for at the employment office after entering the country. Local embassies and consulates can provide applications for visas and residence permits, which are required for anyone seeking employment. German employers tend to emphasize academic performance and expect detailed academic records from applicants. In order to hire a foreign worker, however, a Germany company will have to prove that no one from Germany or the European Union exists to fulfill that job. Thanks to the new green card regulations, IT jobs are most likely to meet this requirement.

There are ways for Americans, especially students and young profession-als, to legally find work in Germany. Students can bypass the usual employ-ment restrictions by contacting the Council for International Educational Exchange (CIEE) to obtain a work visa that will permit American students to work in Germany for up to four months. IAESTE can assist students majoring in science, engineering, or architecture with obtaining work visas necessary to employed as an intern. IAESTE's parent organization, the Association for In-ternational Practical Training, manages the Americans Abroad program that can help young professionals (U.S. citizens ages 18 to 35) obtain a profes-sional internship of up to 18 months in Germany. CDS International can also assist students and young professionals with arranging work visas for short–term jobs and internships in Germany. Chapter 9 provides contact informa-tion for these organizations.

Most unskilled labor in Germany is performed by more than 1 million for-eign workers, *gastarbeiter*, limiting employment opportunities for Americans seeking temporary work. The German Central Placement Office, *Zentralstelle fur Arbeitsvermittlung* (ZAV), may review a foreign job applicant's chances for employment in Germany. American citizens, as non–E.U. nationals, must demonstrate some special skill to be received favorably and get listed in ZAV's bulletins to employers. The Federal Employment Institute operates an exten-sive chain of employment offices throughout the country. These employment offices, the *Arbeitsamter*, maintain a virtual legal monopoly on job placement, although some private employment agencies have recently begun operating. The *Bundesanstadt* also sets up temporary employment offices, *Service–Vermittlung*, when necessary.

Federal Employment Institute
Bundesanstalt fur Arbeit
Regenburgerstrasse 104
D–9023 Nurnberg, Germany
Tel.: [49] 922 179 0
www.arbeitsamt.de

Zentralstelle fur Arbeitsvermittlung
Villemombler STR 76
D–53123 Bonn, Germany
Tel.: [49] 228 713 0
Fax: [49] 228 713 1036
www.arbeitsamt.de/zav

Unregulated jobs in the black market, known as *schwarzarbeit*, can be found in bars and hotels. These jobs usually pay in cash without tax withhold-ing but offer no legal protections. The best places to find tourist work are in Munich, Berlin, the southern Bavarian Alps, coastal areas, and forest areas in the southwestern part of the country.

Short–term and Temporary Work

There are plenty of opportunities for work as an au pair. In addition to the agencies described below, see Chapter 9 for details on Au Pair in Europe and the Accord Cultural Exchange which place au pair candidates in Germany.

Au Pair in Deutschland
Baunscheidtstrasse 11
D–53113 Bonn, Germany
Tel.: [49] 228 95730 0
Fax: [49] 228 9573 10

Email: gijk@gijk.de
www.gijk.de
Managed by Gesellschaft für Internationale Jugendkontakte, the Ger-man subsidiary of the American Insti-

tute for Foreign Study (AIFS). Au pair placements are for one year.

Au Pair Network International
Augustastrasse 1
53173 Bonn, Germany
Tel.: [49] 228 956 950
www.step–in.de

STEP IN (Student Travel Education Programmes International) manages exchanges intended to promote the study of German language and culture. Among its various other programs, STEP IN places au pairs between the ages of 18 and 27.

Internship Programs

Several professional internship programs offer students opportunities to obtain professional experience. CDS International offers several internship programs in Germany. Some programs, such as that run by IES, also offer an opportunity to earn academic credit. See Chapter 9 for details.

IES (Institute for International Education of Students)
33 North LaSalle Street, 15th floor
Chicago, IL 60602
Tel.: (800) 995 2300
www.IESabroad.org

IES offers a variety of internships in Berlin and Freiburg in fields including business, the arts, education, politics, and nonprofit management. Internships feature a strong academic component.

Volunteer Opportunities

Several organizations maintain work camps in Germany. Service Civil International (SCI) operates over 40 such camps, attracting participants from throughout Europe and beyond. Several of SCI's work camps revolve around peace, anti–fascist/anti–racist, and Third World Solidarity themes. The Council on International Educational Exchange (CIEE) coordinates work camps with local German agencies. See Chapter 9 for details.

IBG (Internationale Begegnung in Gemeinschaftsdiensten)

Schlosserstrasse 28

70180 Stuttgart, Germany

Tel.: [49] 711 649 11 28

Fax: [49] 711 640 98 67

www.workcamps.com

IBG organizes work camps in Germany and Switzerland. The work camps are voluntary services lasting two to four weeks. There are usually 10 to 20 volunteers from about six different countries taking part in one camp. Volunteers are expected to work about 30 hours a week. The work undertaken at camps is intended to serve the local community or benefit the environment.

NIG (Norddeutsche Jugend im Internationalen Gemeinschaftsdient)
Am Gerberbruch 13a
D–18055 Rostock, Germany
Tel.: [49] 381 492 2914
Fax: [49] 381 490 0930
Email: nig@campline.de
www.campline.de

NIG is a German organization committed to the idea of international understanding among the world's youth. The organization facilitates camps that complete projects in environmental conservation, the preservation of historical monuments, and social services. Projects last from two to three weeks, and most participants are between 18 and 30 years old.

Resources for Further Information

Newspapers in Germany

Berliner Morgenpost (daily)
Tel.: [49] 30 25 910
Fax: [49] 30 25 913 244
Email: berliner–morgenpost@de

Bild (daily)
Tel.: [49] 40 347 00
Fax: [49] 40 347 22 134
www.bild.de

Die Welt
Tel.: [49] 30 259 10
Fax: [49] 30 251 6071
www.welt.de

Frankfurter Allgemeine (daily, except Sunday)
Tel.: [49] 69 75 91 0

Fax: [49] 69 75 91 2172
www.faz.de

Handelsblatt (business news, daily)
Tel.: [49] 211 88 70
Fax: [49] 211 88 71400
Email: handelsblatt@vhb.de
www.handelsblatt.com

Rheinische Post (daily)
Tel.: [49] 211 50 50
Fax: [49] 211 50 47 562
www.rp–online.de

Süddeutche Zeitung (daily)
Tel.: [49] 89 218 30
Fax: [49] 89 218 3787
Email: szinfo@sueddutsche.de
www.sueddeutsche.de

Mixing work and play

Working in Germany for the summer provided wonderful insight into the cultural differences between workplaces in different countries. The most notable difference between the American and German workplace is the pace. My German co–workers placed a strong emphasis on quality–of–life issues. As a result, people worked fewer hours, received more vacation time, and the work atmosphere was much more relaxed. I did not get the same rushed Go! Go! feeling that I got when I worked in Austin the previous summer. The department in which I worked spontaneously got together several times during the summer to do things after work. On several occasions, we relaxed in one of Munich's many beautiful beer gardens. Once, the department planned a four–hour bike tour of the entire city. We all left work early, biking from one end to the other, stopping in the middle for ice cream. The tour conveniently ended in a beer garden, where we had dinner. — *Nipul Bharani, Houston, Texas*

Useful Websites for Job Seekers

The Internet is a good place to begin your job search. Many German employers list job vacancies, especially those in technical fields, on the web. There are also many websites that provide useful information for job seekers researching the German job market.

Arbeitsmarkt Online
www.mamas.de
The searchable database has 7,000 private sector jobs in Germany. You can also register for emailed job announcements. The new feature, JOBTelevision, permits you to post a short video advertising yourself to potential employers.

Breitbach
www.breitbach.com
A German executive search firm, Breitbach's website features the positions for which it is currently recruiting. Most are in information technology and sales. Viewable in German and English.

CareerGardens
www.career–service.de
Recruitment site for university graduates and young professionals. Features jobs in IT, engineering, finance, sales and marketing, and consulting.

Germany JobPilot
www.jobpilot.de
Includes over 300 private sector jobs, a resume database, and a directory of employers. Registration is free. Also includes resources for career coaching and a forum with articles by experts on different industries.

Forum–Job online
www.forum–jobline.de
Permits new graduates to post their resumes for review by employers and offers information about recruiting fairs. Written in German.

Job Office
www.job–office.de
Job Office features a resume database, searchable job listings, and company information. Written in German with some instructions in English.

JobsOnline
www.jobonline.de

The site includes a database with over 3,500 jobs, a resume database, and information about major companies in Germany. Written in German.

Jobsite Germany
www.gojobsite.de
Features a database of private sector jobs, a searchable resume database, and an email notification system for new jobs. Written in German.

Job Universe.de
www.jobuniverse.de
Features over 1,700 IT jobs throughout Germany plus a resume database and an email job notification service.

JobWare International
www.jobware.de
Features over 5,700 jobs for technical and high–level personnel, plus general information including alerts about employment scams.

Karriere Führer
www.karrierefuehrer.de
Karriere Führer is a magazine; its comprehensive website includes information about major employment sectors, special recruiting events, and general employment trends. Written in German.

Manpower Germany
www.manpower.de
Manpower is a recruitment agency. Its German site features private sector jobs in a searchable database.

StepStone Germany
www.stepstone.de
One of Europe's leading online recruitment sites. Features over 9,000 private sector and education jobs in Germany.

Zeit Robot
www.jobs.zeit.de
Employment section of the German newspaper, *Die Zeit*. Features over 150,000 jobs in a variety of industries.

Embassies and Consular Offices

American embassies and consulates have commercial and/or economic sections that can provide you with business information and explain aspects of the local economy. Inquiries about business opportunities should be addressed either to "Commercial Officer" or "Commercial Section."

Representation of Germany in the United States

Embassy of the Federal Republic of Germany
4645 Reservoir Road NW
Washington, DC 20007–1998
Tel.: (202) 298–4000
Fax: (202) 471–5530

www.germany–info.org

German Consulates General:
Chicago, (312) 580–1199; Los Angeles, (213) 930–2703; New York, (212) 610–9700

Representation of the United States in Germany

American Embassy
Neustädtische Kirchstrasse 4–5
D–10117 Berlin, Germany
Tel.: [49] 30 8305 0
www.usembassy.de

Embassy of the United States Berlin, Consular Section
Clayallee 170
D–14195 Berlin, Germany
Tel.: [49] 30 832 9233
Fax: [49] 30 8305 1215

American Consulate General — Düsseldorf
Willi–Becker–Allee 10
D–40227 Düsseldorf
Federal Republic of Germany
Tel.: [49] 02 11 788 8927
Fax: [49] 02 11 788 8938

American Consulate General — Frankfurt
Siesmayerstrasse 21

D–60323 Frankfurt am Main, Germany
Tel.: [49] 69 7535 0
Fax: [49] 69 7535 2277

American Consulate General — Hamburg
Alsterufer 27/28
D–20354 Hamburg, Germany
Tel.: [49] 40 411 71 00
Fax: [49] 40 41 32 79 33

American Consulate General — Leipzig
Wilhelm Seyfferth Strasse 4
D–04107 Leipzig, Germany
Tel.: [49] 341 213 840

American Consulate General — Munich
Köeniginstrasse 5
D–80539 Munich, Germany
Tel.: [49] 89 2888 0
Fax: [49] 89 280 9998

Chambers of Commerce

Chambers of commerce consist of member firms in both countries interested in international trade. These are appropriate companies to initially target in the job search.

American Chamber of Commerce in Germany

12 Rossmarkt, Postfach 100162

D–60311 Frankfurt, Germany

Tel.: [49] 69 929 1040

Fax: [49] 69 929 10411

Email: amcham@amcham.de

www.amcham.de

Association of German Chambers of Industry and Commerce
One Farragut Square Street NW
Sixth Floor
Washington, DC 20006
Tel.: (202) 347–0247
Fax: (202) 347–3685

German–American Chamber of Commerce
40 West 57th Street, 31st Floor

New York, NY 10019

Tel.: (212) 974–8830

Fax: (212) 974–8867

Email: info@gaccny.com

www.gaccny.com

German–American Chamber of Commerce
456 California, #506
San Francisco, CA 94104
Tel.: (415) 392–2262
Fax: (415) 392–1314
www.gaccwest.org

World Trade Centers in Germany

World trade centers usually include many foreign companies that conduct business in Germany.

World Trade Center Bremen
Birkenstrasse 15
D–28195 Bremen, Germany
Tel.: [49] 421 174 660
Fax : [49] 421 174 6622
Email: bbi@wtc–bremen.com
www.wtc–bremen.de

World Trade Center Hamburg
Van–der–Smissen–Strasse 3
D–22767 Hamburg, Germany
Tel.: [49] 40 37 502 319
Fax : [49] 40 37 480 599
Email: wtc–hamburg@
dialup.nacamar.de

World Trade Center Hannover
EXPO Plaza 11
D–30539 Hannover, Germany
Tel.: [49] 511 302 900
Fax : [49] 511 302 9020
Email: service@wtc–hannover.de
www.wtc–hannover.de

World Trade Center Leipzig
Walter–Koehn–Strasse 1c
D–04356 Leipzig, Germany
Tel.: [49] 341 528 5101
Fax : [49] 341 528 5110
Email: wtc@wtc–leipzig.de
www.wtc–leipzig.de

World Trade Center Rostock
Parkstrasse 53
D–18119 Rostock, Germany
Tel.: [49] 3 815 1395
Fax : [49] 3 815 2255
Email: tprostock@t–online.de
www.wtca.org/wtc/rostock.html

World Trade Center Ruhr Valley
Sparkassenstrasse 1
D–45879 Gelsenkirchen, Germany
Tel.: [49] 209 17971 0
Fax : [49] 209 17971 59
Email: wtciv@wtc.gelsen–net.de

Other Informational Organizations

Foreign government missions in the United States, such as national tourist offices, can furnish information on work permits and other important regulations. They may also offer economic and business information about the country. The German Academic Exchange Service coordinates educational exchanges with Germany.

German Academic Exchange Service (DAAD)
871 United Nations Plaza
New York, NY 10022
Tel.: (212) 758–3223
Fax: (212) 755–5780
Email: daadny@daad.org
www.daad.org

German National Tourist Office
122 East 42nd Street, 52nd Floor
New York, NY 10168
Tel.: (212) 661–7200
Fax: (212) 661–7174
Email: gntonyc@d–z–t.com
www.germany–tourism.de; www.visits–to–germany.com

Business Directories

Although not always easy to find, business directories can prove invaluable in the international job search. Your best bet for locating these directories is to begin in the reference section of any public or university library. Most directories list company names, addresses, products, and phone numbers. Some directories include executive names and titles and financial information about the company. These sources provide you with the names of people to contact for employment information as well as financial data, which can tell you how strong a company's position in a country may be.

American Chamber of Commerce in Germany Membership Directory and Yearbook. American Chamber of Commerce in Germany, Luisenstrasse 44, D–10117 Berlin 30, Germany; email: intern@amcham.de; www.amcham.de. Lists 2,300 American and German business and approximately 1,600 American subsidiaries interested in bilateral trade. 300 pages, $200, published annually.

Banken–Jahrbuch. Hoppenstedt Produktinformationen, Havelstrasse 9, D–64295 Darmstadt, Germany; email: info@hoppenstedt–fastx.de; www.hoppenstedt.com. Directory of 1,200 German banks. €364, published annually in German.

BDI: Germany Supplies. Verlag W. Sachon GmbH, Schloss Mindelburg, D–87714 Mindelheim, Germany; email: info@sachon.de; www.sachon.de. Lists German export manufacturers. 3,500 pages, $135, published annually in English, German, French, and Spanish.

Companies in the New Federal States (East Germany). Hoppenstedt Produktinformationen, Havelstrasse 9, D–64295 Darmstadt, Germany; email: info@hoppenstedt–fastx.de; www.hoppenstedt.com. Lists 20,000 companies in the former German Democratic Republic. €270, published annually.

Directory of German Motor Industry Manufacturers. Federation of the German Motor Industry (VDA), Westendstrasse 61, Postfach 70563,

Fair jobs in Germany

You may be able to find work at various trade, wine, and beer fairs held in Germany. These jobs primarily involve manual labor setting up tents and rides. Oktoberfest is a popular annual event in Bavaria — especially near Munich. It usually starts the last Saturday in September and lasts two weeks. Local brewers usually need manual workers as early as three months in advance.

Trade Fairs: Frankfurt (March, August), Hanover (April)

Wine Fairs: Mainz (August), Neustadt (September – October), Rudesheim (August), Wiesbaden (August – October)

Beer Fairs: Munich (September – October), Stuttgart (September – October)

D–60079 Frankfurt, Germany. Lists 500 major car manufacturers and associated businesses. 310 pages, updated infrequently.

Directory of Major German Companies. Hoppenstedt Produktinformationen, Havelstrasse 9, D–64295 Darmstadt, Germany; email: info@hoppenstedt–fastx.de; www.hoppenstedt.com. Covers 25,000 enterprises with annual revenues in excess of €15 million, or that have at least 150 employees. €455. published annually in German.

Directory of Medium–Sized German Companies. Hoppenstedt Produktinformationen, Havelstrasse 9, D–64295 Darmstadt, Germany; email: info@hoppenstedt–fastx.de; www.hoppenstedt.com. Includes information on over 55,000 firms with 20–150 employees. €335, 2,500 pages, published annually.

Firmen Information Bank. AZ Direct Marketing Bertelsmann GmbH, Carl Bertelsmann Strasse 161, D–33311 Guetersloh, Germany; www.bedirect.de. Lists 150,000 German companies. Available as a CD–ROM.

German–American Chamber of Commerce Membership Directory. Published by the German–American Chamber of Commerce in the U.S., 40 West 57th Street, New York, NY 10019–4092; email: gaccny@info.com. Lists the 2,000 Chamber members in the U.S. and Germany. $80, 159 pages, published annually in English and German.

Germany's Top 500. Frankfurter Algemeine Zeitung Institut, Postfach 200163, D–60605 Frankfurt, Germany; email: german.business@fazinstitut.de; www.german–business–info.com. Top 500 companies in Germany, top 50 banks, and top 50 insurance companies. 690 pages, published annually.

Kompass Deutschland. Kompass Deutschland Verlags und Vertriebsgellschaft, GmbH, Jechtinger Strasse 13, D–79111 Freiburg, Germany; email: info@kompass–deutschland.de; www.kompass.com. U.S. distributor Kompass USA, 1255 Routhe 70, Suite 25S, Lakewood, NJ 08701. Covers over 40,000 leading German manufacturers, distributors, and service companies. €42, 8,000 pages, published annually in German, English, French, and Spanish.

Wer Gehort zu Wem (Who Belongs to Whom?) Commerzbank, Zentraler Stab Kommunikation, Informations–Zentrum, D–60261 Frankfurt am Main, Germany; email: info@commerzbank.com. Lists 11,000 German companies and their domestic and foreign shareholders. 1,234 pages, updated every three years.

American Companies in Germany

The following companies are classified by business area: Banking and Finance; Industrial Manufacturing; Retailing and Wholesaling; Service Industries; and Technology. Company information includes the firm's name, address, telephone and fax numbers, and specific business. Your chances of securing employment abroad are substantially better if you contact the subsidiary company in Europe rather than the parent company in the United

States. Because the contact information for companies can change pretty often, confirm a company's address and phone number before writing to it.

Banking and Finance

Bank of America (NTCSA)
Grüneburgveg 15
D–60322 Frankfurt, Germany
Tel.: [49] 69 71 00 10
Fax: [49] 69 71 00 1261
(Bank)

The Bank of New York
Niedenau 61–63
D–60235 Frankfurt/Main 17, Germany
Tel.: [49] 69 971 510
Fax: [49] 69 721 798
www.bankofny.com
(Bank)

Chase Bank
Ulmenstrasse 30
D–60325 Frankfurt, Germany
Tel.: [49] 69 71 580
Fax.: [49] 69 715 82 209
www.chase.com
(Bank)

Chubb Insurance Co. of Europe
Martin–Luther Platz 28
D–40212 Düsseldorf, Germany
Tel.: [49] 211 8773 0
Fax: [49] 211 8773 333
www.chubb.com
(Insurance)

Morgan Stanley Bank
Junghofstrasse 13–15
D–60311 Frankfurt, Germany
Tel.: [49] 69 216 60
Fax: [49] 69 20 99
(Bank)

Industrial Manufacturing

Alcoa Deutschland
Robert–Bosch–Strasse 6
D– 68519 Viernheim, Germany
Tel.: [49] 620470050
Fax: [49] 6204700570
(Metal products)

Avon Cosmetics
Am Hart 2
D–85375 Neufahrn, Germany
Tel.: [49] 8165 720

Fax: [49] 8165 721 226
(Cosmetics and jewelry)

Black & Decker
Black–&–Decker–Strasse 40
D–65510 Idstein, Germany
Tel.: [49] 6126 21 0
Fax: [49] 6126 21 2799
(Power tools)

Bristol–Myers Squibb
Sapporobogen 6–8
D–80809 Munich, Germany
Tel.: [49] 89 12 14 20
Fax: [49] 89 12 14 23 92
(Chemicals and pharmaceuticals)

Coca–Cola
Max–Keith–Strasse 66
D–45136 Essen 1, Germany
Tel.: [49] 201 821 01
Fax: [49] 201 821 15 10
(Beverages)

Deutsche Goodyear
Xantenerstrasse 105
D–50733 Cologne, Germany
Tel.: [49] 221 97 66 61
Fax: [49] 221 97 66 65 85
(Tires and rubber products)

Dow Corning
Rheingaustrasse 34
D–65201 Wiesbaden, Germany
Tel.: [49] 611 23 71
Fax: [49] 611 23 76 20
(Chemicals and plastics)

Ford–Werke
Henry Ford Strasse 1
D–50735 Cologne, Germany
Tel.: [49] 221 90 0
Fax: [49] 221 901 26 41
(Automobiles and parts)

Gillette Deutschland
Oberlandstrasse 75
D–12099 Berlin, Germany
Tel.: [49] 30 756 40
Fax: [49] 30 756 425 36
(Toiletries)

Grace Darex
Erlengang 31
D–22844 Norderstedt, Germany
Tel.: [49] 40 52601–100
Fax: [49] 40 52601–190
(Plastics)

Halliburton
Bruchkampweg 7
D–29227 Celle, Germany
Tel.: [49] 5141 9990
Fax: [49] 5141 999168
www.halliburton.com
(Oil field construction)

Johnson & Johnson
Kaiserswerther Strasse 270
D–40474 Düsseldorf, Germany
Tel.: [49] 211 430 50
Fax: [49] 211 430 5352
(Personal care products)

Kellogg (Deutschland)
Auf der Muggenberg 30
D–28217 Bremen, Germany
Tel.: [49] 421 39 99 0
Fax: [49] 421 39 10 67
(Food products)

Kodak
Breitwiesenstrasse 27
D–70565 Stuttgart, Germany
Tel.: [49] 711 783 00
Fax: [49] 711 783 0140
www.kodak.com
(Photographic equipment)

Kraft
Langemarckstrasse 4–20
D–28199 Bremen, Germany
Tel.: [49] 42 15 99 01
Fax: [49] 42 15 99 36 75
www.kraft.com
(Food products)

Mattel
An der Trift 75
D–63303 Dreiech, Germany
Tel.: [49] 6103 89 10
Fax: [49] 6103 89 1300
www.mattel.com
(Toys)

Pepsi–Cola
Martin Behaim Strasse 12
D–63263 Neu Isenburg, Germany

Tel.: [49] 6102 74 90
Fax: [49] 6102 74 9200
(Beverages)

Procter & Gamble
Sulzbacherstrasse 40–50
D–65824 Schwalbach, Germany
Tel.: [49] 6196 89 01
Fax: [49] 6196 89 4929
(Household products)

Wrigley
Albrecht–Dürer Strasse 2
D–82008 Unterhaching, Germany
Tel.: [49] 8966 51 00
Fax: [49] 8966 51 0309
(Chewing gum)

Retailing and Wholesaling

Foot Locker Germany
Hapstrasse 63
D–69117 Heidelberg, Germany
Tel.: [49] 6221 21344
(Shoes and sneakers)

Lands' End
In der Langwiese
D–66693 Mettlach, Germany
Tel.: [49] 6864 971 0
Fax: [49] 6864 921 111
www.landsend.com
(Apparel mail order catalog)

Tiffany & Co. Munich
Residenzstrasse 11
D–80333 Munich, Germany
Tel.: [49] 89 29 00430
www.tiffany.com
(Jewelry)

F.W. Woolworth & Co.
Lyonerstrasse 52
D–60528 Frankfurt, Germany
Tel.: [49] 69 660 11
Fax: [49] 69 660 23 99
(General merchandise)

Service Industries

Accenture
Otto–Volger–Strasse 15
D–65843 Sulzbach, Germany
Tel.: [49] 61965760
Fax: [49] 6196576710
(Management consulting)

Associated Press
Moselstrasse 27
D–60329 Frankfurt/Main, Germany
Tel.: [49] 69 272300
Fax: [49] 69 25 1289
www.ap.com
(News gathering agency)

BBDO Düsseldorf
Königsallee 92
D–40212 Düsseldorf, Germany
Tel.: [49] 211 137 90
Fax: [49] 211 137 96 21
(Advertising)

Booz Allen & Hamilton International
Königsallee 106
D–40215 Düsseldorf, Germany
Tel.: [49] 211 38 900
Fax: [49] 211 37 10 02
(Management consulting)

Burson–Marsteller
Untermainkai 20
D–60329 Frankfurt/Main, Germany
Tel.: [49] 69 23 8090
Fax: [49] 69 23 80914
www.bm.com
(Public relations)

Diebold Deutschland
Frankfurter Strasse 27
D–65760 Eschborn, Germany
Tel.: [49] 6196 90 30
Fax: [49] 6196 903456
(Consulting and public relations)

Dun & Bradstreet
Hahnstrasse 31–35
D–60528 Frankfurt, Germany
Tel.: [49] 69 660 90
Fax: [49] 69 6609 2175
(Commercial information services)

Grand Hyatt Berlin Hotel
Marlene–Dietrich Platz 2
D–10785 Berlin, Germany
Tel.: [49] 30 2553 1234
Fax: [49] 30 2553 1235
www.hyatt.com
(Hotel)

Korn/Ferry International
Altköinstrasse 8
D–61462 Köenigstein, Germany
Tel.: [49] 617429050

Fax: [49] 61742905129
(Executive search)

McCann–Erickson Hamburg
Grosser Hasenpfad 44
D–60598 Frankfurt/Main, Germany
Tel.: [49] 69605070
Fax: [49] 6960507666
(Advertising)

McKinsey & Company, Inc.
Königsallee 60c
D–40212 Düsseldorf, Germany
Tel.: [49] 211 136 40
Fax: [49] 211 136 4700
www.mckinsey.com
(Management consulting)

Saatchi & Saatchi Compton
Wiesenau 38–40
D–60323 Frankfurt, Germany
Tel.: [49] 69 71 420
Fax: [49] 69 714 22 84
(Advertising)

Wiley VCH Verlag
Pappelallee 3
D–69469 Weinheim, Germany
Tel.: [49] 6201 6060
Fax: [49] 6201 606328
www.wiley.com
(Publishing)

Young & Rubicam
Kleyerstrasse 25
D–60326 Frankfurt am Main, Germany
Tel.: [49] 69 75 06 01
Fax: [49] 69 75 06 14 30
(Advertising)

Technology

3Com Germany
Max–Planck–Strasse 3
D–85609 Aschheim, Germany
Tel.: [49] 8925 00 00
Fax: [49] 8925 00 0111
www.3com.com
(Computer networks)

Amdahl Deutschland
Balanstrasse 55
D–81541 Munich, Germany
Tel.: [49] 8949 05 80
Fax: [49] 8949 05 8222
(Computers)

Cisco Systems
Lilienthalstrasse 9
D–85399 Hallbergmoos, Germany
Tel.: [49] 811 55430
Fax: [49] 811 554310
www.cisco.com
(Computer networking systems)

Dell Computer
Monzastrasse 4
D–63225 Langen, Germany
Tel.: [49] 61037667000
Fax: [49] 61037668000
www.dell.com
(Computers)

Hewlett–Packard
Herrenberger Strasse 140
D–71034 Böblingen, Germany
Tel.: [49] 7031140
Fax: [49] 7031142999
(Data processing equipment)

IBM Deutschland GmbH
Ernst Reuterplatz 2
D–10587 Berlin, Germany
Tel.: [49] 30 31 150
Fax: [49] 30 31 15 1447
(Data processing equipment)

Intel Semiconductor
Dornacher Strasse 1
D–85633 Feldkirchen, Germany
Tel.: [49] 89 99143 0
Fax: [49] 89 9 043948

www.intel.com
(Semiconductors)

Lucent Technologies Network Systems
Josef–Wirmer–Strasse 6
D–53123 Bonn, Germany
Tel.: [49] 2282430
Fax: [49] 2282430
www.lucent.com
(Communications networks)

Motorola Computer Group
Schatzbogen 7
D–81829 Munich, Germany
Tel.: [49] 89921030
Fax: [49] 89 92 10 3101
(Semiconductors and cell phones)

NCR
Ulmerstrasse 160
D–86156 Augsburg, Germany
Tel.: [49] 8214050
Fax: [49] 821405462
www.ncr.com
(Data processing equipment)

Texas Instruments Deutschland
Haggertystrasse 1
D–85350 Freising, Germany
Tel.: [49] 8161 80 0
Fax: [49] 8161 84 516
www.ti.com
(Electronic equipment)

European Companies in Germany

The following are major non–American firms operating in the country. These selected companies can be either German or based in another European country. Such companies will generally hire their own nationals first but may employ Americans.

Banking and Finance

Allianz
Königinstrasse 28
D–80802 Munich, Germany
Tel.: [49] 89 38 000
www.allianz.com
(Insurance)

AXA Konzern
Gereonsdriesch 9–11

D–50670 Cologne, Germany
Tel.: [49] 221 148 101
Fax: [49] 221 1482 1704
www.axa.de
(Insurance)

Bankgesellschaft Berlin
Alexanderplatz 2, P.F. 110801
D–10178 Berlin, Germany
Tel.: [49] 30 245 500
Fax: [49] 30 245 509

www.bankgesellschaft.de
(Bank)

Bayerische Landesbank Girozentrale
Brienner Strasse 18
D–80333 Munich, Germany
Tel.: [49] 89 2171 01
Fax: [49] 89 2171 23579
www.blb.de
(Financial services)

Commerzbank
Kaiserplatz
D–60261 Frankfurt, Germany
Tel.: [49] 69 136 20
Fax: [49] 69 28 53 89
www.commerzbank.com
(Commercial and investment banking)

Deutsche Bank
Taunusanlage 12
D–60262 Frankfurt, Germany
Tel.: [49] 69 910 00
Fax: [49] 69 910 34227
www.deutsche–bank.de
(Bank)

Dresdner Bank
Jürgen–Ponto–Platz 1
D–60301 Frankfurt, Germany
Tel.: [49] 692 630
Fax: [49] 692 63 4831
www.dresdner–bank.de
(Bank)

**Muenchener Rückversicherungs–
Gesellschaff Aktiengesellschaft
(MUVGn)**
Koenigstrasse 107
D–80802 Munich, Germany
Tel.: [49] 89 38 91 0
Fax: [49] 89 39 90 56
www.munichre.com
(Insurance)

**Westdeutsche Landesbank
Girozentrale**
Herzogstrasse 15
D–40217 Düsseldorf, Germany
Tel.: [49] 211 826 01
Fax: [49] 211 826 6119
www.westlb.com
(Bank)

Industrial Manufacturing

Adidas–Salomon
Adi–Dassler Strasse 1–2
D–91074 Herzogenaurach, Germany
Tel.: [49] 9132 84 0
Fax: [49] 9132 84 2241
www.adidas.com
(Athletic shoes and clothing)

ADVA Optical Networking
Fraunhoferstrasse 11
D–82152 Martinsried/Munich, Germany
Tel.: [49] 89 89 06 65 0
Fax: [49] 89 89 06 65 199
www.advaoptical.com
(Telecommunications)

Alcatel SEL
Lorenzstrasse 10
D–70435 Stuttgart, Germany
Tel.: [49] 711 821 446 86
Fax: [49] 711 821 460 55
www.alcatel.de
(Electronics)

Asclepion–Meditec
Goeschwitzer Strasse 51 – 52
D–07745 Jena, Germany
Tel.: [49] 3641 2200
Fax: [49] 3641 220112
www.asclepion.com
(Medical equipment)

Audi
Finanzanalytik und Publizität I/FF–12
D–85045 Ingolstadt, Germany
Tel.: [49] 841 89 40300
Fax: [49] 841 89 30900
www.audi.com
(Automobiles)

BASF
Carl–Bosch–Strasse 38
D–67056 Ludwigshafen, Germany
Tel.: [49] 621 60 0
Fax: [49] 621 60 42525
www.basf.de
(Chemicals)

Bayer
Werk Leverkusen
D–51368 Leverkusen, Germany
Tel.: [49] 214 30 58992
Fax: [49] 214 307 1985

www.bayer–ag.de
(Chemicals and plastics)

Bayerische Motoren Werke (BMW)
Petuelring 130
D–80788 Munich, Germany
Tel.: [49] 89 382 0
Fax: [49] 89 382 244 18
www.bmw.com
(Automobiles and parts)

Robert Bosch
Robert–Bosch–Platz 1
D–70839 Gerlingen–Schillerhöhe,
Germany
Tel.: [49] 711 811 0
Fax: [49] 711 811 6630
www.bosch.com
(Automotive equipment)

Celanese
Frankfurter Strasse 111
D–61476 Kronberg in Taunus
Germany
Tel.: [49] 69 305 4888
Fax: [49] 69 315 605
www.celanese.com
(Chemicals, plastics, fibers)

CyBio
Goeschwirtzer Strasse 40
D–07745 Jena, Germany
Tel.: [49] 3641 651 400
www.cybio–ag.de
(Health products)

DaimlerChrysler
Epplestrasse 225
D–70546 Stuttgart, Germany
Tel.: [49] 711 170
Fax: [49] 711 17 94075
www.daimlerchrylser.com
(Automobiles)

E.ON
E.ON Platz 1
D–40479 Düsseldorf, Germany
Tel.: [49] 2 11 45 79 0
www.eon.com
(Electricity)

Henkel
Henkelstrasse 67
D–40191 Düsseldorf, Germany
Tel.: [49] 211 797 3533
Fax: [49] 211 798 4040

www.henkel.com
(Chemicals)

HOCHTIEF
Opernplatz 2
D–45128 Essen, Germany
Tel.: [49] 201 824 0
Fax: [49] 201 824 2777
www.hochtief.de
(Construction materials, civil engineering)

Hoechst
Brueningstrasse 50
D–65926 Frankfurt, Germany
Tel.: [49] 69 30 50
www.hoechst.com
(Chemicals, pharmaceuticals, cosmetics)

Phillip Holzmann
Taunusanlage 1
D–60229 Frankfurt, Germany
Tel.: [49] 69 2 62 1
Fax: [49] 69 2 62 433
www.phillip–holzmann.de
(Construction and civil engineering)

Klöckner–Werke
Klöcknerstrasse 29
D–47057 Duisburg, Germany
Tel.: [49] 203 3 96 32 96
Fax: [49] 203 3 96 34 56
www.kloecknerwerke.de
(Packaging)

Linde
Abraham–Lincoln–Strasse 21
D–65189 Wiesbaden, Germany
Tel.: [49] 611 770 0
Fax: [49] 611 770 269
www.linde.com
(Engineering, industrial gases)

MAN
Ungererstrasse 69
D–80805 Munich, Germany
Tel.: [49] 89 3 60 98 0
Fax: [49] 89 3 60 98 2 50
www.man.de
(Machinery and construction)

Mannesmann Röhren–werke
Wiesenstrasse 35
D–45473 Mülheim a.d. Ruhr, Germany
Tel.: [49] 208 458 01
Fax: [49] 208 458 1999

www.mannesmann.de
(Industrial machinery)

Merck
Frankfurter Strasse 250
D–64293 Darmstadt, Germany
Tel.: [49] 6151 72 0
Fax: [49] 6151 72 2000
www.merck.de
(Pharmaceuticals)

Porsche
Porscheplatz 1
D–70435 Stuttgart, Germany
Tel.: [49] 711 911 0
Fax: [49] 711 911 5777
www.porsche.com
(Automobiles and parts)

Puma Rudolf Dassler Sport
Würzburgerstrasse 13
D–91074 Herzogenaurach, Germany
Tel.: [49] 9132 81 0
Fax: [49] 9132 81 22 46
www.puma.com
(Sports shoes and equipment)

Schering
Muellerstrasse 178
D–13353 Berlin, Germany
Tel.: [49] 30 468 1111
Fax: [49] 30 468 15305
www.schering.de
(Pharmaceuticals)

Siemens
Wittelsbacherplatz 2
D–80333 Munich, Germany
Tel.: [49] 89 636 3300
Fax: [49] 89 636 342 42
www.siemens.de
(Electronics)

ThyssenKrupp
August–Thyssen Strasse 1
D–40221 Düsseldorf, Germany
Tel.: [49] 211 824 0
Fax: [49] 211 824 36000
www.thyssenkrupp.com
(Steel products)

Villeroy & Boch
Saaruferstrasse
D–66688 Mettlach, Germany
Tel.: [49] 6864 81 0
www.villeroyboch.com

(Tiles and tableware)

Volkswagen
Brieffach 1848–2
D–38436 Wolfsburg, Germany
Tel.: [49] 53 61 90
Fax: [49] 53 61 92 82 82
www.vokswagen.de
(Automobiles)

Wella
Berliner Allee 65
D–64274 Darmstadt, Germany
Tel.: [49] 6151 34 0
Fax: [49] 6151 34 27 48
www.wella.de
(Personal care products)

Retailing and Wholesaling

AVA Allgemeine Handelsgesellschaft Der Verbrauche
Fuggerstrasse 11
D–33689 Bielefeld, Germany
Tel.: [49] 52 05 94 01
Fax: [49] 52 05 94 1029
www.ava.de
(Department stores)

Escada
Margaretha–Ley–Ring 1
D–85609 Aschheim/Munich, Germany
Tel.: [49] 899 9440
Fax: [49] 899 9441 5000
www.escada.com
(Apparel)

Etienne Aigner
Marbachstrasse 9
D–81369 Munich, Germany
Tel.: [49] 89 7 69 93 0
Fax: [49] 89 7 60 77 85
www.aignermunich.com
(Apparel)

Hugo Boss
Dieselstrasse 12
D–72555 Metzingen, Germany
Tel.: [49] 7123 940
Fax: [49] 7123 94 2014
www.hugo–boss.de
(Apparel)

Karstadt Quelle
Theodor–Althoff–Strasse 2
D–45133 Essen, Germany

Tel.: [49] 20 17271
Fax: [49] 20 1727 5216
www.karstadtquelle.com
(Department stores)

Tengelmann
Wissollstrasse 5–43
D–45478 Mülheim an der Ruhr,
Germany
Tel.: [49] 208 5806 7601
Fax: [49] 208 5806 7605
www.tengelmann.de
(Grocery stores)

Service Industries

AGIV
Woehlerstrasse 10
D–60323 Frankfurt, Germany
Tel.: [49] 69 170 80 0
Fax: [49] 69 170 80 8
www.agiv.com
(Property development)

Bertelsmann AG
Carl–Bertelsmann–Strasse 270
D–33311 Gütersloh, Germany
Tel.: [49] 52 41 80 24 38
Fax: [49] 52 41 80 66 13
www.bertelsmann.de
(Media, publishing)

Cap Gemini Ernst & Young
Karl–Hammerschmidt–Strasse 32
D–85609 Ascheim, Germany
Tel.: [49] 8994000
Fax: [49] 8994001111
(Management consulting)

Deutsche Lufthansa
Von Gablenz Strasse 2–6
D–50679 Cologne, Germany
Tel.: [49] 221 8260
www.lufthansa–financials.de
(Airline)

Hapag–Lloyd
Ballindamm 25
D–20095 Hamburg, Germany
Tel.: [49] 40 3001 0
Fax: [49] 40 33 64 32
www.hapag–lloyd.de
(Shipping)

Stinnes
Stinnes–Platz 1
D–45472 Mülheim am der Ruhr,
Germany
Tel.: [49] 208 494 0
Fax: [49] 208 494 7228
www.stinnes.de
(Transportation)

Technology

Biodata Information Technology
Burg Lichtenfels
D–35104 Lichtenfels, Germany
Tel.: [49] 64 54 91 20–0
www.biodata.com
(Computer hardware)

Debitel
Schelmenwasenstrasse 37–39
D–70567 Stuttgart, Germany
Tel.: [49] 711 721 7000
Fax: [49] 711 721 7490
www.debitel.de
(Telecommunications)

Deutsche Telekom
Friedrich–Ebert–Allee 140
D–53113 Bonn, Germany
Tel.: [49] 228 181 0
Fax: [49] 228 181 8872
www.telekom.de
(Telecommunications)

**Sap AG Systeme Anwendungen
Produkte in der Datenverarbeitung**
Neurottstrasse 16
D–69190 Walldorf, Germany
Tel.: [49] 6227 74 7474
Fax: [49] 6227 75 7575
www.sap.com
(Software)

SER Solutions
Innovationspark Rahms
D–53577 Neustadt/Wied,Germany
Tel.: [49] 2683 984 0
Fax: [49] 2683 984 222
www.ser.de
(Software)

T–Online International
Waldstrasse 3
D–64331 Weiterstadt, Germany
Tel.: [49] 61 51 6 80 0
Fax: [49] 61 51 6 80 6 80
www.t–online.de

(Internet and online service providers)

Vodafone
Mannesmannufer 3

D–40213 Düsseldorf, Germany
Tel.: [49] 211 820 18 85
www.vodafone.com
(Telecommunications)

International Nonprofit Organizations in Germany

Goethe Institute
Sonnenstrasse 25
D–80331 Munich, Germany
Tel.: [49] 89 5519030
Fax: [49] 89 551903 35

International Association for Religious Freedom
Dreieichstrasse 59
D–6000 Frankfurt 70, Germany
Tel.: [49] 69 62 87 72
www.iarf–religiousfreedom.net

International Schools in Germany

Berlin International School
Lentzeallee 8–10
D–14195 Berlin, Germany
Tel.: [49] 30 82007790
Fax: [49] 30 82007799
Email: office@berlin–international–school.de
www.berlin–international–school.de
(U.S./International Baccalaureate curriculum, kindergarten through grade 12)

Bonn International School
Friesdorfer Strasse 57
D– 53175 Bonn 2, Germany
Tel.: [49] 228 308 540
Fax: [49] 228 308 5420
Email: admin@bis.bonn.org
www.bis.bonn.org
(U.S./International Baccalaureate curriculum, grades six through 12)

The Frankfurt International School
An der Waldlust 15
D–61440 Oberursel 1, Germany
Tel.: [49] 6171 2020
Fax: [49] 6171 202384
Email: petra_rischke@fis.edu
www.fis.edu
(U.S./U.K./International Baccalaureate curriculum, prekindergarten through grade 12)

International School of Düsseldorf
Niederrheinstrafle 338
D–40489 Düsseldorf, Germany
Tel.: [49] 211 9406–799
Fax: [49] 211 408 0774

Email: info@isdedu.de
www.isdedu.de
(U.S./International Baccalaureate curriculum, prekindergarten through grade 113)

International School Hamburg
Holmbrook 20
D–22605 Hamburg, Germany
Tel.: [49] 40 883 0010
Fax: [49] 40 881 1405
Email: info@international–school–hamburg.de
www.international–school–hamburg.de
(U.S./U.K./International Baccalaureate curriculum, prekindergarten through grade 12)

John F. Kennedy School
Teltower Damm 87–93
D–14167 Berlin, Germany
Tel: [49] 30 6321 5701
Fax:[49] 30 6321 6377
Email: school/ad@jfks.de
www.jfks.de
(U.S./German Arbitur curriculum, kindergarten through grade 13)

Munich International School
Schloss Buchhof
D–82319 Starnberg/Percha, Germany
Tel.: [49] 8151 366 120
Fax: [49] 8151 366 129
Email: admissions@mis–munich.de
www.mis–munich.de
(U.S./U.K./International Baccalaureate curriculum, kindergarten through grade 12)

Chapter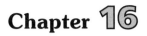

Spain

Major employment centers: Madrid, Barcelona, Valencia

Major business language: Spanish

Language skill index: Spanish is it. Even poor Spanish is better than none.

Currency: Euro

Telephone country code: 34

Time zone: Eastern Standard Time + 6 hours

Punctuality index: Spaniards are a bit laid back.

Average daily temperature, high/low: January: 47°/33°; July: 87°/62° (Madrid)

Average number of days with precipitation: January: 8 days; July: 4 days

Best bet for employment:

> **For students:** Au pair for a Spanish family
>
> **Permanent jobs:** Finance and manufacturing

Chance of finding a job: Unemployment is sufficiently high at present to make finding work difficult. Casual work is a good option.

Useful tip: The workday in Spain usually begins at 9 a.m., stops from 1 p.m. to 4 p.m. for lunch, and then ends at 8 p.m. Most Spaniards eat dinner relatively late, usually after 9 p.m.

The Kingdom of Spain occupies about 85 percent of the Iberian Peninsula in southwestern Europe. Spain, approximately twice the size of Wyoming, borders Portugal to the west, the Bay of Biscay to the north, France, Andorra, and the Mediterranean to the east, and Africa lies across the Strait of Gibraltar to the south. The Pyrenees Mountains form the border with France in the northeast. Most of the country consists of a high plateau interrupted by mountain ranges. The southern region, however, is a flat plain with a much warmer climate. The Balearic Islands are located off the Mediterranean coast, and the Canary Islands are slightly west of Western Africa. Spain also controls two small enclaves on the northern coast of Morocco: Ceuta and Melilla.

Thanks to the huge number of retirees living there, Spain's Andalusia region has often been compared to Florida.

Spanish, or Castellano, is the official language, but Catalan, Basque, and Galician are also spoken in the autonomous areas. Approximately 17 percent of the population is Catalan, 8 percent Galician, and 2 percent Basque. The remaining 73 percent is classified as Spanish. The vast majority of the population is Roman Catholic.

Spain, originally inhabited by Celts, Basques, and Iberians, was conquered by the Romans in 206 B.C. The Visigoths ruled the region from A.D. 412 to 711, when Muslim armies invaded from Africa. The Christian states of Aragon and Castile were united in 1469 and defeated the Muslims in 1492. Roman Catholicism became the official religion, and Muslims and Jews were heavily persecuted.

In the early sixteenth century, Spain conquered Mexico and Peru, establishing an extensive empire in the Americas. The ruling dynasty, the Spanish Hapsburgs, also established control over the Netherlands and parts of Italy and Germany. Although Spain then ranked as the most powerful state in the world, its power began to decline in the late sixteenth century. In 1588 Spain's "Invincible Armada" was defeated by the English, and Spain never regained its major–power status. By the late nineteenth century, the American empire had been lost through revolutions. The United States acquired several Spanish possessions in 1898, as a result of the Spanish–American War.

Spain remained neutral in both world wars. In 1931 strong anti–monarchial sentiments led to the declaration of a republic under socialist guidance. The Popular Front, composed of socialists, communists, and anarchists won a large majority in the 1936 election. Army officers led by Francisco Franco then revolted against the government, initiating a bloody civil war. By 1939, Franco's forces, aided by Fascist Italy and Nazi Germany, had defeated the government Loyalists, aided by France, the Soviet Union, and the Abraham Lincoln Brigade from the United States. Franco became Caudillo, head of state and government, as well as the right–wing Falange Party. In 1947 Spain again became a monarchy — this time a constitutional monarchy, with Franco continuing as head of government, but not head of state. Prince Juan Carlos was designated to become king of Spain when Franco's government ended.

Franco died in 1975; Juan Carlos became king, and still reigns today. In free elections in 1977, the Democratic Center won power and granted autonomy to the Catalonian and Basque regions. Economic instability and political violence led to the victory of prime minister Felipe Gonzalez Marquez and the Spanish Socialist Workers Party in 1982. Spain entered the European Community in 1986. In 1992, Spain drew world interest by hosting the World Exposition in Seville and the Olympic Games in Barcelona.

José Maria Aznar of the Popular Party (PP) was elected president in 1996. Aznar moved to decentralize powers to the regions and liberalize the economy with a program of privatizations, labor market reform, and measures to increase competition in markets such as telecommunications. During Aznar's first term, Spain fully integrated into European institutions, qualifying for the European Monetary Union. Spain participated, along with the United States and other NATO allies, in military operations in the former Yugoslavia. Aznar and the PP won re-electon in March 2000.

The government of Spain is involved in a long-running campaign against Basque Fatherland and Liberty (ETA), a terrorist organization founded in 1959 and dedicated to promoting Basque independence. ETA's targets are primarily Spanish security forces, military personnel, and Spanish government officials. Official sources attribute over 800 deaths to ETA terrorism since its campaign of violence began. In November 1999, ETA ended a cease-fire it had declared in September 1998 and has since been blamed for the deaths of some 30 Spanish citizens and officials. ETA remains a serious threat but, even as it has vowed a renewed campaign of violence, it is important to keep perspective. The overall level of terrorist activity is considerably less than in the recent past, and the trend appears to be downward.

Most businesses are closed on weekends, except for Saturday morning. Banks are open from 9 a.m. to 2 p.m., Mondays through Fridays, and 9 a.m. to 1 p.m. on Saturdays. Businesses generally close from 1 p.m. to 4 p.m. and reopen from 4 p.m. to 8 p.m. Banks are notoriously slow and usually closed on Saturdays from June to September. Post offices are open from 9 a.m. to 2 p.m.; some reopen from 4 p.m. to 7 p.m.

Using the language

A knowledge of Spanish is usually necessary to find employment in Spain. Although some young people will likely know English, most Spaniards will not expect to be approached in English. Spanish as spoken in Spain differs in accent from the versions spoken in various parts of Latin America. Even if you know Spanish, it will take you a little time to adapt to the local dialects. But Spanish isn't the only language you'll hear when working in Spain. Catalan is spoken by about two-thirds of the people in Catalonia and the Balearic Islands and half of those in the Valencia region. Galician, which resembles Spanish and Portuguese, is spoken in the northwest. Basque is spoken by a minority in the Pais Vasco and Navarro.

Current Economic Climate

Spain's gross national product has grown at the fastest rate in Europe, nearly two percent annually. Unfortunately, the Spanish economy also suffers from some of Europe's highest unemployment. The Spanish government's official unemployment figure, based on the number of people registered for unemployment benefits, is above 13 percent. Spain's inflation rate, though still high, has lowered along with the national deficit. The underground economy accounts for about 15 to 20 percent of the total economic activity. In recent years, the government has invested a percentage of its GDP to improve and expand Spain's public transportation and to create a more attractive environment for businesses. Although the Spanish government successfully met the criteria for the common currency, the adjustment to the monetary and other economic policies of an integrated Europe — and reducing the high level of unemployment — poses difficult challenges to Spain.

The country's per capita income has grown steadily in recent years as has the price of products. Spain's major industries include textiles and apparel (including footwear), food and beverages, metals and metal manufactures, chemicals, shipbuilding, automobiles, machine tools, and tourism. About 50 percent of the workforce is employed in the service industries, 35 percent in manufacturing, and 15 percent in agriculture. Spanish trade primarily occurs within the E.U., although the United States is an important trade partner.

Spain's tourist industry continues to grow at a rapid pace. More than 50 million tourists visit Spain each year, creating jobs for about 10 percent of the nation's labor force. Southern Spain, primarily the region of Andalusia, has long been compared to Florida because of its large number of European retirees.

Spain's 10 Largest Companies

(2001, based on market capitalization)

1. Telefonica
2. Banco Santander Central Hispanoamerican
3. Banco Bilbao Vizcaya Argentaria
4. Amadeus Global Travel
5. Repsol–YPF
6. Endesa
7. Iberdrola
8. Inditex
9. Gas Natural SDG
10. Banco Popular España

Getting Around in Spain

There are plenty of bus routes serviced by dozens of independent companies, and the bus network is more extensive than the train system. Bus fares are generally comparable to train fares but may run a little higher for long–distance trips. Passenger boats and ferries are available for traveling from the mainland to nearby islands or across the Strait of Gibraltar and the Mediterranean to Africa. Flying by Spain's national airline, Iberia, is sometimes a better choice than traveling by boat because it's quicker and sometimes cheaper.

Spain's highway system consists of the national highways, often mere two–lane roads, and the *Autopistas*, multilane expressways. The expressways are found only near major cities and almost always are congested. A twenty–mile commute into Madrid, for instance, can take almost two hours. Relief is

Catalan in Catalunya

I manage a university's MBA program. I was hired because I was a native English speaker (and hopefully because I have other skills) to work in a international setting. Over 60 percent of our students come from outside Spain, so the university needed someone who could speak and write English fluently. However, I am also expected to use Castellano (and we do NOT call it Spanish here!) as we have a two sections, an English section and Spanish section in the first year.

What I did not expect, but should have, was how often my coworkers would use Catalan among themselves. Since Catalan is the language that you first use when you meet a person, it makes sense that it is the language that you use for all of your workplace conversations — unless there is a need to use Castellano (i.e. there is a non–Catalan parlante). Well, everyone was so excited that I could speak a bit of Catalan (I can only talk about things that happened today, not yesterday or tomorrow) that they all began speaking Catalan to me because they all wanted to see me become a fluent Catalan speaker. It is a gift not only to have one native tongue, but two.

A little history may be in order. After 40 years of linguistic repression under Franco (Catalan was not allowed to be taught in schools or spoken on the streets — under the guise of "One Spain One Language"), Catalan has surged forth these last 25 years as the language of politics, news, and the official language spoken in the schools here in Catluyna, often to the detriment of knowledge of Spanish. Foreigners often find it more difficult to learn Castellano here in Barcelona, because the language of the street, television and radio is overwhelmingly Catalan. Also, within families, many speak Catalan at home, as was my experience. My husband's family speaks Catalan among themselves and Castellano with me (although now I understand about 80 percent of spoken Catalan).

So if you visit Barcelona know how to say *Bon dia* (hello), *Moltes gracies* (Thanks a lot) and *Estic tipa* (I'm full). — *Betsey Tufano; Barcelona, Spain*

at hand, though; the government is spending lavishly to improve the country's overburdened transportation system.

Employment Regulations and Outlook for Americans

Current employment opportunities in Spain are limited due to the country's high unemployment rate. Visas aren't required for U.S. citizens staying fewer than three months. If you intend to live in Spain, you will need to acquire a Residence Entry Visa (*visado espacial*) from the nearest Spanish consulate–general. To be hired legally, you will need a work permit or work visa from the Spanish consulate in America, a contract of employment from your employer stating that they are willing to hire you for a certain amount of time and a license from INEM (Spain's employment office). Spanish employers must demonstrate that no Spanish citizen is available for the job before hiring a foreign national. Because Spanish labor authorities are particularly diligent, illegal employment in Spain has been highly discouraged, even in the tourist industry.

Americans often have difficulty competing with U.K. citizens for teaching jobs, since British workers do not require a work permit in Spain. Agricultural work in Spain is virtually unavailable. Entrepreneurial ventures, especially those English or catering to the tourist industry, often present the best opportunities for Americans who want to work in Spain.

Eat a good meal!

Meals are a very important part of Spanish culture. Lunches frequently last two hours and are then followed by another hour of coffee and conversation. This is often where business deals are conducted. Many Spaniards consider the American practice of working through lunch odd and unproductive.

Short–term and Temporary Work

There are many agencies that specialize in au pair placements in Spain. In addition to the agencies listed below, see Chapter 9 for information about Accord Cultural Exchange and other resources.

GIC
Pintor Sorolla 29
E–46901 Monte Vedat–Valencia, Spain
Tel./Fax: [34] 96 156 5837
Email: gic@eresmas.net
www.villaardilla.com/gic/

Most of GIC's au pair placements last between three and six months. Au pairs can expect to earn about €48 per week, in addition to room and aboard. Program fees begin at €180 plus €24 for a mandatory child–care course.

Instituto Hemingway de España
Bailen 5, 2dcha
E–48003 Bilbao, Spain
[34] 944 167 901
www.institutohemingway.com
Instituto Hemingway places au pairs with families throughout Spain. The Instituto also coordinates volunteer and internship programs in Spain.

Planet Au Pair
Calle Los Centelles 45–6–11
E46006–Valencia, Spain

Tel.: [34] 96 320 6491

Email: info@planetaupair.com

www.planetaupair.com

Planet Au Pair is a Spanish agency that places people for assignments ranging from three to 12 months. Au pairs participate in cultural and educational activities designed to teach them about Spanish life, and they assist with child care and teaching the children English. Au pairs can expect to earn between €65 and €95 per week.

Relaciones Culturales Internacionales
Callez Ferraz no. 82
E–28008 Madrid, Spain
Tel.: [34] 91 541 71 03
Fax: [34] 91 559 11 81
RCI is a nonprofit organization that specializes in international exchanges. The organization hires au pairs and language assistants who work as private tutors for Spanish families. Placements last from three months to one year. Applicants have an option to also enroll in Spanish language classes.

Internship Programs

Spain is a popular destination for student interns, but the high unemployment rate among young people makes it a notoriously difficult place to find placements. Organizations that can help you find internship opportunities in Spain include AIESEC and IAESTE (see Chapter 9), as well as the below.

Adelante Spain
P.O. Box 323
Surfside, CA 90743
Tel.: (562) 235–5266
www.adelantespain.com
Adelante Spain offers very flexible internship assignments. You can work from one to six months, you can participate in academic or nonacademic in-

ternships, positions may or may not be paid. You can expect to work four hours a day in a Spanish–owned company or a larger, international company with offices in Spain. Placements are available in Madrid and Bilbao. Fees are $1,750 for a one–month program, and $2,995 for a three–month program. Fees include your housing.

Volunteer Opportunities

The most common volunteer opportunities in Spain involve humanitarian and environmental projects. In addition to the programs listed below, the Council on International Educational Exchange, Global Volunteers, the International Volunteering Network, Service Civil International, and Volunteers for Peace manage work camps in Spain. (See Chapter 9 for details.)

BEST Language Services
Volunteer in Madrid Program
Calle Solano 11, 3–C
Pozuelo de Alarcón
E–28223 Madrid, Spain
Tel.: [34] 92 518 7110
www.inglespain.com
Combines language study with volunteer internships at humanitarian organizations in Madrid. Participants should have an intermediate level of Spanish

and be available for two– to three–month assignments.

Deya Archaeological Museum and Research Center
Deya, Mallorca
Balleares, Spain
Tel./Fax: [34] 71 63 90 01
Recruits volunteers for archaeological excavations in Mallorca.

Instituto de Juventud
Jose Ortega y Gasset 71

E–28006 Madrid, Spain

Tel.: [34] 91 347 7700

www.mtas.es/injuve/english/english.htm

INJUVE is a government organization that promotes cultural youth exchanges. It runs work camps throughout Spain for 20,000 volunteers each year.

Resources for Further Information

Newspapers in Spain

ABC

Tel.: [34] 91 33 99 000

Fax: [34] 91 32 03 620

www.abc.es

Majorca Daily Bulletin (English)

Tel.: [34] 9717 88409

Fax: [34] 9717 19706

www.majorcadailybulletin.es

El Mundo (daily)

Tel.: [34] 91 586 48 00

El Pais (daily)

Tel.: [34] 91 337 82 00

Fax: [34] 91 3048 766

www.elpais.es

Useful Websites for Job Searchers

The Internet is a good place to begin your job search. Many websites provide useful information for job searchers researching the Spanish job market; there are also several that list job vacancies.

Bolsa de Trabajo en España

www.trabajo.org

Features over 1,000 private sector jobs. The database permits you to search by industry and location. Written in Spanish.

Expansion & Empleo

www.expansionyempleo.com

Spanish–language site that features over 1,600 private sector jobs. Database can be searched by industry and location, and you can also post your CV.

Expatriot Cafe

www.expatriatecafe.com

Dedicated to helping people find jobs teaching English in Spain. Includes very good tips about the practical aspects of finding teaching jobs and links to bulletin boards that advertise vacancies. Also features success stories.

InfoJobs

www.infojobs.net

Features over 13,000 jobs throughout Spain. Database can be searched by industry or geographic location. Written in Spanish.

Job Universe Spain

www.idg.es/jobuniverse/

Features IT jobs throughout Spain, a resume database, and an email notification service. Candidates can apply for jobs online. Written in Spanish.

Jobsite Spain

www.gojobsite.es

Features a database of private sector jobs, a searchable resume database, and an email notification system for new jobs. Written in Spanish.

El Pais — exoge

www.excoge.com

Includes over 100 job vacancies throughout Spain. Also includes rental and ownership real estate listings. Written in Spanish.

Si, Spain

www.SiSpain.org

A good first stop for general information about Spain. Includes links to major Spanish media outlets and other useful sites with information on topics ranging from medicine to real estate to law.

Spain JobPilot

www.jobpilot.es

Features a database with over 300 private sector jobs, a resume database, and a directory of employers. Free registration. The site also includes resources for career coaching and a forum with articles by experts on different industries.

TESOL Spain
www.tesol–spain.org
Features a lot of information helpful for prospective English teachers, including job vacancies and a place to post your CV. You can also find information about TESOL conferences in Spain. The directory of TESOL Spain board members may be helpful for networking.

Trabajos.com
www.trabajos.com
Spanish–language site features over 3,300 private sector jobs throughout Spain. You must complete a free registration to submit your resume online to prospective employers.

Embassies and Consular Offices

American embassies and consulates have commercial and/or economic sections that can provide you with business information and explain aspects of the local economy. Inquiries about business opportunities should be addressed either to "Commercial Officer" or "Commercial Section."

Representation of Spain in the United States

Embassy of Spain
2375 Pennsylvania Avenue NW
Washington, DC 20037
Tel.: (202) 452–0100
Fax: (202) 833–5670
www.spainemb.org

Consulates General of Spain:

Chicago, (312) 782–4588; Houston, (713) 783–6200; Los Angeles, (323) 938–0158; New York, (212) 355–4080.

Representation of the United States in Spain

American Embassy
Serrano 75
E–28006 Madrid, Spain
Tel.: [34] 91 587 2200
Fax: [34] 91 587 2303
www.embusa.es

American Consulate General — Barcelona
Paseo Reina Elisenda de Montcada 23–25
E–08034 Barcelona, Spain
Tel.: [34] 93 280 2227
Fax: [34] 93 205 5206

American Consulate General — Las Palmas
Edificio ARCA
Calle Los Martinez Escobar, 3, Oficina 7
E–35007 Las Palmas, Spain

Tel.: [34] 928 222 552
Fax: [34] 928 225 863

American Consulate General — Seville
Paseo de las Delicias, 7
E–41012 Seville, Spain
Tel.: [34] 954 231 885
Fax: [34] 954 232 040

American Consulate General — Valencia
Dr. Romagosa, 1, 2–J
E–46002 Valencia, Spain
Tel.: [34] 96 351 6973
Fax: [34] 96 352 9565

Chambers of Commerce

Chambers of commerce consist of member firms in both countries interested in international trade. These are appropriate companies to initially target in the job search.

American Chamber of Commerce in Spain — Barcelona
Tuset 8
E–08006 Barcelona, Spain
Tel.: [34] 34 93 415 9963
Fax: [34] 34 93 415 1198

Spain Chamber of Commerce
Avenida Diagonal 452–454
E–08006 Barcelona, Spain
Tel.: [34] 93 416 9300

Fax: [34] 93 416 9301
Email: amchamspain@retemail.es

Spain–U.S. Chamber of Commerce
350 Fifth Avenue, Suite 2029
New York, NY 10118
Tel.: (212) 967–2170
Fax: (212) 564–1415
Email: info@spainuscc.org
www.spainuscc.org

World Trade Centers in Spain

World trade centers usually include many foreign companies that conduct business in Spain.

World Trade Center Barcelona
Moll de Barcelona s/n
Edifici Est 2a planta
E–08039 Barcelona, Spain
Tel.: [34] 93 508 8000
Fax: [34] 93 508 8010
Email: Lrovira@wtcbarcelona.es
www.wtcbarcelona.com

World Trade Center Madrid
Paseo de la Habana, 26
Third Floor, Suite No. 4
E–28036 Madrid, Spain
Tel.: [34] 91 411 6145
Fax: [34] 91 562 4004
Email: wtcmadrid@retemail.es

World Trade Center Seville
Centro de Empresas Pabelló de Italia
Issac Newton s/n
Isla de la Cartuja
E–41092 Seville, Spain
Tel.: [34] 95 446 7199
Fax: [34] 95 446 0332
Email: servicios@wtc.es
www.wtc.es

World Trade Center Valencia
c/o Paseo de la Habana
No. 26, Third Floor, Suite 4
E–28036 Madrid, Spain
Tel.: [34] 91 411 6145
Fax: [34] 91 562 4004

Other Informational Organization

Foreign government missions in the United States, such as national tourist offices, can furnish information on work permits and other important regulations. They may also offer economic and business information about the country.

Tourist Office of Spain
666 Fifth Avenue, 35th Floor
New York, NY 10103
Tel.: (212) 265–8822

Fax: (212) 265–8864
Email: fdbksp@eclipse.here–i.com
www.okspain.org

Business Directories

Although not always easy to find, business directories can prove invaluable in the international job search. Your best bet for locating these directories is to begin in the reference section of any public or university library. Most directories list company names, addresses, products, and phone numbers. Some directories include executive names and titles and financial information about the company. These sources provide you with the names of the people to contact for employment information as well as financial data, which can tell you how strong a company's position in a country may be.

American Chamber of Commerce in Spain Membership Directory. American Chamber of Commerce in Spain, Tuset 8., E–08006 Barcelona, Spain; email: amchamspain@reternail.es. Lists 1,500 American and Spanish firms engaged in bilateral trade. $150, 162 pages, updated annually.

Anuario Financiero y de Sociedades Anonimas de Espana. Editorial SOPEC, Villanueva 24–30, E–28001 Madrid, Spain. Describes publicly held companies, including financial information. 2,000 pages, updated annually.

Anuario de Sociedades, Consejeros y Directivos. DICODI, Calle Doctor Castelo 10, E–28009 Madrid, Spain. Covers over 50,000 of Spain's largest companies, including listings of 160,000 top executives. 4,000 pages, updated annually.

Dun's 15,000 Largest Companies Spain. Dun and Bradstreet Corporation, Three Sylvan Way, Parsippany, New Jersey, 07054–3896; email: dnbmdd@dnb.com. Directory of industrial, trading, banking, insurance, and service companies in Spain. Published annually.

Guia de Exportadores de la Comunidad de Madrid. Madrid Chamber of Commerce, Calle Huertas 13, E–28012 Madrid, Spain; www.camaraunadaid.es. Directory contains information on 3,500 Madrid firms active in exporting. 750 pages, updated biennially.

Kompass España. Published annually by Ibericom, Manuel Gonzalez Longoria 7, E–28010 Madrid, Spain. Describes 24,000 manufacturing and service companies. $339, two volumes, published annually in English, French, German, Italian, and Spanish.

Spain's 30,000 Top Companies. Dun and Bradstreet Corporation, Three Sylvan Way, Parsippany, New Jersey, 07054; email: dnbmdd@dnb.com. Lists companies with annual sales of at least $500,000. $385, 1,500 pages, updated annually.

The 2,000 Top Spanish Companies. Fomento de la Produccion, Casanova 57, E–08011 Barcelona, Spain. 2,000 leading companies in Spain. $15, 300 pages, updated annually.

Who Sells Foreign Products in Spain? Prointer–Ediciones Alfonso Luengo, Puerta del Sol 11, Madrid, Spain. Lists Spanish importers and distributors. 1,300 pages, updated biennially.

Who's Who in Spain. email: whoswhogc@attglobal.net; www.whoswho–sutter.com. U.S. distributor EBSCO Industries Inc., P.O. Box 1943, Birmingham, AL 35201. Includes statistical information on about 3,300 companies, institutions, and organizations. $260, 1,220 pages, updated every 16 months.

Youth Policy and Youth Work in Spain. International Youth Exchange and Visitors Service, Hochkreuzalle 20, D–53175 Bonn, Germany. Organizations for children and youth in Spain. 75 pages, updated semi–regularly.

American Companies in Spain

The following companies are classified by business area: Banking and Finance; Industrial Manufacturing; Retailing and Wholesaling; Service Industries; and Technology. Company information includes the firm's name, address, phone and fax numbers, and specific business. Your chances of securing employment abroad are substantially better if you contact the subsidiary company in Europe rather than the parent company in the United States. Keep in mind that the contact information for companies can change frequently. Confirm a company's address and phone number before you write to it.

Banking and Finance

Bank of America
Paseo de la Castellana, 35
E–28046 Madrid, Spain
Tel.: [34] 91 396 5000
Fax: [34] 91 396 5123
www.bankamerica.com
(Bank)

Chase Manhattan Bank España
Paseo de la Castellana 51, planta 5
E–28046 Madrid, Sapin
Tel.: [34] 91 349 2800
Fax: [34] 91 319 7323
(Bank)

Seguros Genesis
Paseo de las Doce Estrellas 4, Piso 4
Campo de las Naciones
E–28042 Madrid, Spain
Tel.: [34] 91 000 0000
Fax: [34] 91 721 0704
(Insurance)

Industrial Manufacturing

3M España
Provenza, 388, 4ª Planta
E–08025 Barcelona, Spain
Tel.: [34] 93 208 1230
Fax: [34] 93 48 4572
(Adhesive products)

Bechtel International Group
Serrano 51, 2 Ocha
E–28006 Madrid, Spain
Tel.: [34] 91 431 4900
Fax: [34] 91 576 3975
www.bechtel.com
(General engineering contractors)

Black & Decker Spain
Parque de Negocios Mas Blau,
1 Oficina, 6
E–08020 Barcelona, Spain
Tel.: [34] 93 479 7413
Fax: [34] 93 479 7419
www.blackanddecker.com
(Power tools)

Braun España
Enrique Granados 46–48
Esplugues De Llobregat
E–08950 Barcelona, Spain
Tel.: [34] 93 401 9300
Fax: [34] 93 372 9105
(Domestic appliances)

Bridgestone–Firestone Hispania
Fuerteventura, 9 Pgno Ind Norte
San Sebastian de los Reyes
E–28700 Madrid, Spain
Tel.: [34] 91 623 3013
Fax.: [34] 91 623 3044
(Tires and accessories)

Colgate–Palmolive
General Aranaz, 88
E–28027 Madrid, Spain
Tel.: [34] 91 393 9600

Fax: [34] 91 393 9698
(Toiletries)

Eastman Chemical España
Ctra. Nal. 6 KM 23
E–28230 Las Rozas – Madrid, Spain
Tel.: [34] 91 626 7268
Fax: [34] 91 626 7340
www.eastman.com
(Chemicals)

Ford España
Paseo de la Castellana 135
E–28046 Madrid, Spain
Tel.: [34] 91 336 9100
Fax: [34] 91 336 9473
(Cars)

Kodak
Carretera de la Coruna Km 23
Las Rozas de Madrid
E–28230 Madrid, Spain
Tel.: [34] 91 626 7273
Fax: [34] 91 626 7378
(Photographic equipment)

Mattel España
Aribau, 200 21
E–08036 Barcelona, Spain
Tel.: [34] 93 306 7900
Fax.:[34] 93 201 5204
(Toys)

Merck Sharp & Dohme España
Josefa Valcá 38
E–28027 Madrid, Spain
Tel.: [34] 91 321 0600
Fax: [34] 91 321 0700
(Pharmaceuticals)

Procter & Gamble España
Avenido del Parteron 16–18
E–28042 Madrid, Spain
Tel.: [34] 91 722 2100
Fax: [34] 91 722 2226
(Soaps, pharmaceuticals)

Xerox España
Ribera del Loira 16–18
E–28042 Madrid, Spain
Tel.: [34] 91 520 3333
Fax: [34] 91 520 3321
(Office equipment)

Retail and Wholesale

Foot Locker Spain
Gan Vma 6
E–48001 Bilbao, Spain
Tel.: [34] 94 423 9170
(Shoes)

Service Industries

Accenture
Plaza de Pablo Picasso
E–28020 Madrid, Spain
Tel.: [34] 91 596 6000
Fax: [34] 91 596 6695
(Management consulting)

Bassat Ogilvy & Mather
Avda. Josep Tarradellas 123
E–08029 Barcelona, Spain
Tel.: [34] 93 495 5555
Fax: [34] 93 495 5500
(Advertising)

Century 21 Iberia
Heroes de Toledo 46
E–41006 Seville, Spain
Tel.: [34] 95 493 2921
www.century21.com
(Real estate)

Hyatt Regency La Manga Resourt
Los Belones
E–30385 Cartagena, Murcia, Spain
Tel.: [34] 96 833 1234
Fax: [34] 96 833 1235
www.hyatt.com
(Hotels, resorts)

A.T. Kearney
Paseo de la Castellana 31–1
E–28046 Madrid, Spain
Tel.: [34] 91 000 0000
Fax: [34] 91 310 2292
www.atkearney.com
(Executive search)

TMP Worldwide Spain
Velazquez, 29 3 Izda
E–28001 Madrid, Spain
Tel.: [34] 91 435 3555
Fax: [34] 91 789 8601
(Recruitment advertising)

Technology

Computer Associates
Carabaela La Nina 12
E–08017 Barcelona, Spain
Tel.: [34] 93 227 8100
Fax: [34] 93 227 8101
(Computer systems consulting)

Hewlett–Packard España
Carretera de la Cruña N-Vi, Km 16.500
Las Rosas de Madrid
E–28230 Madrid, Spain
Tel.: [34] 91 631 1600
Fax: [34] 91 631 1830
(Computers and printers)

IBM España
Santa Hortensia 26–28
E–28002 Madrid, Spain
Tel.: [34] 91 397 6000

Fax: [34] 91 519 3987
www.ibm.com
(Data processing equipment)

**Lucent Technologies
Microelectrónicas**
Pol. Indl. Tres Cantos, s/n. Zona Oeste
E–28760 Tres Cantos, Madrid, Spain
Tel.: [34] 91 807 1700
Fax: [34] 91 807 1699
www.lucent.com
(Communications systems and software, networking systems)

Unisys España
Avenida del Partenon 4
Campo de las Naciones
E–28042 Madrid, Spain
Tel.: [34] 91 721 1212
Fax.: [34] 917 211 288
(Data processing systems)

European Companies in Spain

The following are major non–American firms operating in the country. These selected companies can be either Spanish or based in another European country. These companies will generally hire their own nationals first but may employ Americans.

Banking and Finance

Banco Bilbao Vizcaya
Gran Vía #1
E–48001 Bilbao, Vizcaya, Spain
Tel.: [34] 94 487 5555
Fax: [34] 94 487 6161
www.bbv.es
(Bank)

Banco España de Credito (BANESTO)
Avenida Gran Vía Hortaleza, 3
E–28043 Madrid, Spain
Tel.: [34] 91 338 3100
Fax: [34] 91 3384 925
(Bank)

Banco Popular España
Velazquez· 34
E–28001 Madrid, Spain
Tel.: [34] 91 520 7000
Fax: [34] 91 577 9208
www.bancopopular.es
(Bank)

Banco de Santander
C/ Princesa, 31
E–28008 Madrid, Spain
Tel.: [34] 915 41 2627
Fax: [34] 915 41 1940
(Bank)

Industrial Manufacturing

BP Oil España
Avenida de Bruselas, 36
Parque Empresarial Arroyo de la Vega
Alcobendas
E–28108 Madrid, Spain
Tel.: [34] 90 210 7001
Fax: [34] 90 210 7002
(Petroleum products)

Compañia España De Petroleos (CEPSA)
Avenida del Partenon 12
E–28042 Madrid, Spain
Tel.: [34] 91 337 6770
Fax: [34] 91 333 7662
(Chemicals and petroleum)

Dragados y Construcciones
Avenida Tenerí 4 6
E–28700 Madrid, Spain
Tel.: [34] 91 583 3000
Fax: [34] 91 742 7753
(Construction and engineering)

Endesa
Principe de Vergara 187
E–28002 Madrid, Spain
Tel.: [34] 91 213 1000
Fax: [34] 91 563 8181
www.endesa.es
(Electric power companies)

Gas Natural SDG
Avenida Portal de l'Angel 20
E–08002 Barcelona, Spain
Tel.: [34] 93 402 5100
Fax: [34] 93 402 5870
www.gasnatural.com
(Natural gas company)

Iberdrola
Cardenal Gardoqui 8
E–48008 Bilbao, Vizcaya, Spain
Tel.: [34] 94 415 1411
Fax: [34] 94 415 4579
www.iberdrola.es
(Electric power companies)

Inditex
Avenida de la Diputacion s/n
E–15142 Arteixo A Coruna, Spain
Tel.: [34] 98 118 5400
www.inditex.com
(Textile manfucturing)

Renault España
Avenida de Burgos, 89
E–28050 Madrid, Spain
Tel.: [34] 91 374 2200
Fax.: [34] 91 754 0456
(Automobiles and parts)

Repsol–YPF
Paseo de la Castellana 278
E–28046 Madrid, Spain
Tel.: [34] 91 348 8100
Fax: [34] 91 348 2821
www.repsol–ypf.com
(Petroleum products)

Siemens
Orense, 2
E–28020 Madrid, Spain
Tel.: [34] 91 514 8000
Fax: [34] 91 514 8013
(Telephones and electronic equipment)

Unión Eléctrica–Fenosa
Avenida de San Luis, 77
E–28033 Madrid, Spain
Tel.: [34] 91 567 6000
Fax: [34] 91 567 6329
www.uef.es
(Electricity supply)

Retail and Wholesale

El Corte Inglés
Hermosilla 112–3A Planta
E–28009 Madrid, Spain
Tel.: [34] 91 402 8112
Fax: [34] 91 402 5821
www.elcorteingles.es
(Department store)

Service Industries

Amadeus Global Travel Distribution
Salvador de Madariaga 1
E–28027 Madrid, Spain
Tel.: [34] 91 582 0100
Fax: [34] 91 582 0188
www.amadeus.com
(Travel agency)

Ibéria Líneas Aéreas d' España
Velazquez 130
E–28006 Madrid, Spain
Tel.: [34] 91 587 8787
Fax: [34] 91 587 7469
www.iberia.com
(National airline)

Technology

Telefonica
Gran Vía 28 3a Planta
E–28013 Madrid, Spain
Tel.: [34] 92 584 4713
Fax: [34] 91 531 9347
www.telfonica.com
(Telecommunications)

International Schools in Spain

American School of Barcelona
Balmes 7
Esplugas de Llobregat
E–08950 Barcelona, Spain
Tel.: [34] 93 371 4016
Fax: [34] 93 473 4787
Email: info@a–s–b.com
www.a–s–b.com
(U.S., Spanish curriculum,
prekindergarten through grade 12)

American School of Bilbao
Soparda Bidea 10
E–48640 Berango, Vizcaya, Spain
Tel.: [34] 94 668 0860/61
Fax: [34] 94 668 0452
Email: asb@asb.sarenet.es
www.sarenet.es/asb
(U.S. curriculum, prekindergarten
through grade 10)

American School of Madrid
Apartado 80
E– 28080 Madrid, Spain
Tel.: [34] 91 740 1900
Fax: [34] 91 357 2678
Email: jobs@amerschmad.org
www.amerschmad.org
(U.S., Spanish curriculum,
prekindergarten through grade 12)

International College Spain
C/Vereda Norte, #3, La Moraleja
E–28109 Aclobendas Madrid, Spain
Tel: [34] 91 650 2398
Fax: [34] 91 650 1035
Email: ics@icsmadrid.org
www.icsmadrid.com
(U.S., U.K., International Baccalaureate
curriculum, prekindergarten through
grade 12)

Portugal

Major employment centers: Lisbon, Porto

Major business language: Portuguese

Language skill index: French and Spanish can help those whose Portuguese is lacking, but your best bet is a solid knowledge of Portuguese.

Currency: Euro

Telephone country code: 351

Time zone: Eastern Standard Time + 6 hours on the mainland, + 5 hours in Madeira

Punctuality index: Much like Spaniards, the Portuguese are a laid–back folk.

Average daily temperature, high/low: January: 59°/47°; July: 78°/63° (Lisbon)

Average number of days with precipitation: January: 13 days; July: 5 days

Best bet for employment:

    For students: Resort jobs in the Algarve

    Permanent jobs: Venture capitalism with your own money

Chance of finding a job: None too promising without loads of tenacity and pluck

Useful tip: Prefer a nonsmoking work environment? Portugal is not the place for you, as the Portuguese have one of the highest smoking rates in the European Union, second only to Greece.

The Portuguese Republic, approximately the size of Indiana, occupies 15 percent of the Iberian Peninsula. Spain borders Portugal to the north and east, the Atlantic Ocean to the west, and Africa to the south across a stretch of ocean. Southern Portugal, the Algarve, attracts tourists to its warm, Mediterranean climate. The northern part of the country is mountainous, while the southern region consists of rolling plains. The Azores Islands are located about 900 miles west of the Portuguese coast; and the Madeira Islands are about 530 miles southwest of Portugal. Portuguese is the national language. Most Portuguese speakers can understand, but probably not speak, Spanish. In the Algarve tourist areas, many people speak French or English. The vast majority of people are ethnically homogeneous, but there is a sizable African minority. About 97 percent of the population is Roman Catholic.

Portugal's gross national product and low per-capita income make it one of Europe's smallest and poorest economies.

Until it achieved independence under King John I in the twelfth century, Portugal was one of Spain's linguistically distinct regions. Prince Henry the Navigator coordinated Portugal's extensive voyages of exploration in the late fifteenth century. By the mid–sixteenth century, Portugal had acquired possessions in South America, Africa, Eastern Asia, and India. In 1581, Spain invaded the country and held it until 1640, when Portugal regained its independence. Portugal lost much of its empire during the occupation, although it retained Brazil until 1822 and its African colonies until 1974. Napoleon invaded in 1807, forcing the king temporarily to move his court to Brazil. A parliamentary republic was proclaimed in 1910.

Portugal fought with the Allies in World War I. A military coup in 1926 initiated the authoritarian reign of Antonio Oliveira Salazar. Portugal remained neutral in World War II but later joined the North Atlantic Treaty Organization. Following Salazar's death in 1970, his successor, Marcello Caetano, continued the policy of opposition to independence movements in the African colonies. A left–wing military coup in 1974 ended the Caetano regime and granted independence to Angola and Mozambique. Communist Party pressure in 1975 lead to extensive nationalization until a counter–coup in November stopped the trend. The country has gone through nearly 20 governments since then.

Portugal secured a measure of stability when it entered the E.U. in 1986 and became a full member of the European Monetary System in 1992. E.U. membership boosted Portugal's development and modernization, yet the 1990s were fraught with recession and high unemployment.

In December 2001, voters gave a decisive victory to the center–right Social Democratic party (PSD) in municipal elections, forcing the resignation of Portugal's Socialist Prime Minister. National elections, which took place two years ahead of schedule in March 2002, returned the PSD to national office. The new prime minister, Jose Manuel Durao Barroso, formed an alliance with the conservative Popular Party (CDS/PP), giving the ruling coalition an absolute majority in the parliament. The new government is committed to public–sector austerity and business incentives to promote growth, trade, and productivity.

Weekday business hours are from 9 a.m. to 1 p.m., followed by a mid–day break, then from 3 p.m. to 7 p.m. Many businesses are open on Saturday morning but usually not on Sunday. On weekdays, banks are open 8:30 a.m. to 11:45 a.m. and then again from 1 p.m. to 2:45 p.m. Post offices are open from 8:30 a.m. to 6:30 p.m., Mondays through Fridays, and from 9 a.m. to noon on Saturdays. In the smaller towns, post offices close for lunch and are never open on Saturdays.

Using the language

Portuguese, French, and Spanish speakers can usually understand one another, although they rarely speak the other language. Knowledge of Spanish or French will certainly help you to communicate in Portugal, but you should speak and understand Portuguese if you hope to gain employment.

Current Economic Climate

Portugal's gross national product and low per–capita income make it one of Europe's smallest and poorest economies. The nation has managed to keep its inflation rate at a comfortable 2.9 percent and is enjoying a period of economic expansion, largely due to investment in infrastructure and increased privatization. Portugal has benefitted considerably from its entry into the E.U. through much–needed funding to improve the country's infrastructure. The current unemployment rate has fallen to 4.7 percent. Improving education and reducing the growing deficit are critical for continued economic growth.

Major industries include textiles and footwear; wood pulp, paper, and cork; metalworking; oil refining; chemicals; fish canning; wine; and tourism. Manufacturing claims 34 percent of the workforce, agriculture 22 percent, and services 44 percent. The E.U. and United States are Portugal's major trading partners. The country looks set to benefit from low labor costs, a young population, and strong trading links with South America and Africa.

Portugal's 10 Largest Companies

(2001, based on market capitalization)

1. Portugal Telecom
2. Banco Comercial Portugues
3. EDP–Electricidade de Portugal
4. Modelo Continente SGPS
5. Brisa–Auto Estradas de Portugal
6. Banco Espirito Santo
7. CIMPOR–Cimentos de Portugal
8. BPI

9. Banco Totta & Acores

10. Telecel–Comunicacoes Pessoais (acquired by Vodafone)

Getting Around in Portugal

Traveling by train in Portugal is slow, but express trains are available from Lisbon to Porto and from Lisbon to Algarve. The rail system generally runs until midnight. Buses are faster and more comfortable when traveling inter–city, but fares are more expensive than rail. Eurail and InterRail passes are accepted throughout the country.

Employment Regulations and Outlook for Americans

U.S. citizens do not need a visa for stays in Portugal of less than 90 days. In order to work in Portugal, however, a work permit (obtained by one's employer from the Ministry of Labor) and a visa (from the Portuguese Consulate) must be presented upon arrival. Work prospects are generally limited, except as English–language teachers. Portugal enacted a new immigration law in July 2002 that establishes limits on the entry of non–E.U. foreigners based on economic criteria and favors the entry of skilled foreigners. Americans who are teaching can apply for appropriate work permits after they arrive in Portugal at the Serviço de Estrangeiros e Fronteiras, Avenida António Augusto Aguiar 20, Lisbon, Portugal, tel.: [351] 21 315 9681.

Short–term and Temporary Work

There are many opportunities to teach at private language schools (see Chapter 10 for more information). The organization listed below trains teachers and places them in jobs in Portugal. As in Spain, your chances of working as an English language teacher improve with TEFL certificaton.

Via Lingua
Encounter English
Avenida Fernao de Magalhaes, 604
P–4300 Porto, Portugal
Tel.: [351] 4202 217 02 101
www.vialingua.org
Via Lingua is one of the world's largest TEFL certificate course providers. Via Lingua aims to produce well–trained teachers who will have the necessary skills and confidence to take up a teaching position anywhere in the world; to raise the standards of English language teaching worldwide; and to increase international understanding through education. The school offers a four–week, 120–hour intensive course, with ten hours of observed teaching practice in order to prepare candidates for the practicalities of the classroom. Upon successful completion of the course, graduates receive lifelong job placement assistance.

Internship Programs

AIESEC and IAESTE offer students an opportunity to obtain professional experience in a technical or business field. See Chapter 9 for details on these and other resources.

Volunteer Opportunities

Several organizations maintain work camps in Portugal. Volunteers for Peace attracts participants from throughout Europe and beyond to its 29 work camps. Several of VFP's work camps center on peace, restoration, arts, and community service projects. See Chapter 9 for additional resources. Other organizations address women's studies and intercultural groups.

Institute of Cultural Affairs (ICA)
Volunteer Service Programme
P.O. Box 171
Manchester, M15 5BE U.K.
Tel.: [44] 161 232 8444
Email: ica–www@ica–uk.org.uk
www.ica-uk.org.uk
ICA offers short courses for the orientation, training and preparation of volunteers, and a small number of placements each year, with local development organizations worldwide, on projects that emphasize community participation and self–help initiatives. The project in Portugal is with Teatro Re-gional de Serra de Montemuro, a small touring community theatre company, looking for volunteers to support their touring work and their annual festival.

Instituto Portugues da Juventude (IPJ)
Avenida da Liberdade 194 R/C
P–1200 Lisbon, Portugal
Tel. [351] 1 352 2699
Fax: [351] 1 314 3688
IJP is a government agency that arranges conservation projects for youth volunteers.

Resources for Further Information

Newspapers in Portugal

Anglo–Portuguese News (English)
Tel.: [351] 2 44 31 15

Diario de Noticias
Tel.: [351] 21 31 87 500
Fax: [351] 21 31 87 516
www.dn.pt

Expresso
Tel.: [351] 21 31 14 00

Fax: [351] 21 35 43 858

www.expresso.pt

Jornal de Noticias

Tel.: [351] 22 2096 100

Fax: [351] 22 20 06 330

www.jnoticias.pt

Useful Websites for Job Seekers

The Internet is a good place to begin your job search. Although Portuguese employers are just beginning use the Internet in earnest to list jobs, the following are websites that provides useful information for job searchers researching the job market.

e–jobs

www.e–jobs.pt

Features a database of private sector jobs, a resume database, and emailed job alerts. The site, written in Portuguese, also includes tips on writing an effective CV.

Manpower Portugal
www.manpower.pt
Manpower is a recruitment agency. Its Portuguese site features a database of private sector jobs.

Portuguese info/jobs
www.portugal–info.net

Offers a lot of information for people planning to relocate to Portugal, including tips on real estate, Portuguese culture, business and commerce, and current events. It has a small and unimpressive list of job vacancies.

Portugal Live
www.portugal–live.com

Targets tourists, but the information on the history, culture, and geography in Portugal will help job seekers.

StepStone Portugal
www.stepstone.pt
One of Europe's leading online recruitment sites. Features over 2,000 private sector and education jobs in Portugal.

Embassies and Consular Offices

American embassies and consulates have commercial and/or economic sections that can provide you with business information and explain aspects of the local economy. Inquiries about business opportunities should be addressed either to "Commercial Officer" or "Commercial Section."

Representation of Portugal in the United States

Embassy of Portugal
2125 Kalorama Road NW
Washington, DC 20008
Tel.: (202) 328–8610
Fax: (202) 463–3726

Consulates General of Portugal:
Boston (617) 536–8740; San Francisco, (415) 346–3400; New York, (212) 246–4580

Representation of the United States in Portugal

American Embassy
Avenida das Forças Armadas
P–1600–081 Lisbon, Portugal
Tel.: [351] 21 727 3300
Fax: [351] 21 727 9109
www.american–embassy.pt

American Consulate — Sao Miguel
Apartado 209, 9502
Ponta Delgada, Sao Miguel
Azores, Portugal
Tel.: [351] 296 282 216
Fax: [351] 296 28 72 16

Chambers of Commerce

Chambers of commerce consist of member firms in both countries interested in international trade. These are appropriate companies to initially target in the job search.

American Chamber of Commerce in Portugal
Rua D. Estefânia 155–5º E
P–1000–154 Lisbon, Portugal
Tel.: [351] 21 357 25 61
Fax: [351] 21 357 25 80

Portugal Chamber of Commerce and Industry
Rua das Postes de Santo Antao 89
P–2080 Lisbon, Portugal

Portugal–U.S. Chamber of Commerce
590 Fifth Avenue
New York, NY 10036
Tel.: (212) 354–4627
Fax: (212) 575 4737
Email: anaosori@ix.netcom.com
www.portugal–us.com

World Trade Center in Portugal

World trade centers usually include many foreign companies that conduct business in the country.

World Trade Center Lisbon
Avenida do Brasil, 1–9
P–1700 Lisbon, Portugal
Tel.: [351] 21 792 3700

Fax: [351] 21 792 3701
Email: administracao@centro–
escritorios.com

Other Informational Organizations

Foreign government missions in the United States, such as national tourist offices, can furnish visas and information on work permits and other important regulations. They may also offer economic and business information about Portugal.

Portuguese National Tourist Office
590 Fifth Avenue, Fourth Floor
New York, NY 10036–4704
Tel.: (212) 354–4403

Fax: (212) 764 6137
Email: toursim@portugal.org
www.portugal.org

Business Directories

Although not always easy to find, business directories can prove invaluable in the international job search. Your best bet for locating these directories is to begin in the reference section of any public or university library. Most directories list company names, addresses, products, and phone numbers. Some directories include executive names and titles and financial information about the company. These sources provide you with the names of the people to contact for employment information as well as financial data, which can tell you how strong a company's position in a country may be.

American Chamber of Commerce in Portugal Membership Directory. American Chamber of Commerce in Portugal, Rua de Estefània 155, P–1000 Lisbon, Portugal. List of members of the chamber. Published biennially.

Dun's 15,000 Largest Companies Portugal. Dun & Bradstreet, Three Sylvan Way, Parsippany, NJ 07054–3896; email: dnbmbbc@dnb.com. Directory of industrial, trading, banking, insurance, and service companies in Portugal. Published annually.

Export Directory of Portugal. Interpropo Lda., Rua Coronel Bento Roma 28, P–1700–122 Lisbon, Portugal; email: exp.dir.portugal@clix.pt. Includes 4,500 manufacturers engaged in export from continental Portugal, Madeira, and the Azores. 750 pages, published annually.

Kompass Portugal. Interpropo Lda., Rua Coronel Bento Roma 28, P–1700–122 Lisbon, Portugal; email: portugal@kompass.pt. Leading companies and exporters in Portugal. 1,350 pages, published annually.

American Companies in Portugal

The following companies are classified by business area: Banking and Finance; Industrial Manufacturing; Retailing and Wholesaling; Service Industries; and Technology. Company information includes firm name, address, phone and fax number, and specific business. Your chances of securing employment abroad are substantially better if you contact the subsidiary company in Europe rather than the parent company in the United States. Keep in mind that the contact information for these companies change frequently. Before writing to a company, confirm its address and phone number.

Banking and Finance

BankBoston Latino American
Avenida Eng. Duarte Pacheco
Edifício Amoreiras, Torre 2–3° Sala 4
P–1070–102 Lisbon, Portugal
Tel.: [351] 213832312
Fax: [351] 213832313
(Bank)

JPMorgan Chase
Rua Barata Salgueiro 30
P–1250–046 Lisbon, Portugal
Tel.: [351] 213515400
Fax: [351] 213526302
www.chase.com
(Bank)

Citibank Portugal
Rua Barata Salgueiro 30, 4th floor
E–1269–056 Lisbon, Portugal
Tel.: [351] 213116300
Fax: [351] 213116399
www.citibank.com
(Bank)

Marsh & McLennan
Avenida Fontes Pereira de Melo, 51 – 1°
Edifí Monumental
P–1050–000 Lisbon, Portugal
Tel.: [351] 213113700
Fax: [351] 213113701
www.marshmac.com
(Insurance)

Industrial Manufacturing

3M de Portugal Ltd.
Rua Conde de Redondo 98
P–1169–009 Lisbon, Portugal
Tel.: [351] 213134500
Fax: [351] 213134680
(Office equipment)

Avon–Cosméticos
Avenida Fontes Pereira De Melo 14–5
P–1069–008 Lisbon, Portugal
Tel.: [351] 213165100
Fax: [351] 213165120
(Cosmetics)

Bristol–Myers Farmaceutica Portuguesa
Edifí Fernando Magalhães 85
Estrada Paço D'Arcos
P–2780–672 Paço D'Arcos, Portugal
Tel.: [351] 214407000
Fax: [351] 214407090
www.bms.com
(Pharmaceuticals)

Colgate–Palmolive
Rua Mário Castelhano, 1
P–2745–000 Quelez, Portugal
Tel.: [351] 214363371
Fax: [351] 214358222
(Cleaning products and toiletries)

Eli Lilly Farma–Produtos Farmaceuticos
Rua Dr. Antonio Loureiro Borges 4, Piso 3
Arquiparque–Miraflores
P–1495–131 Algés Portugal
Tel.: [351] 214126000
Fax: [351] 214109944
www.lilly.com
(Pharmaceuticals)

Esso Portuguesa
Rua Filipe Folque 2–3
P–1069–022 Lisbon, Portugal
Tel.: [351] 213500700
Fax: [351] 213538366
(Petroleum products)

Johnson & Johnson
Rua Mário Castelhano, 40

Queluz de Baixo
P–2745–000 Queluz, Portugal
Tel.: [351] 214355071
Fax: [351] 214360448
(Medical equipment)

Merck Sharp & Dohme
Edifí Vasco da Gama – 19
Quinta da Fonte Porto Salvo
P–2780–730 Paço D'Arcos, Portugal
Tel.: [34] 214465700
Fax: [34] 214465880
(Pharmaceuticals)

Rockwell Automation
Taguspark Edif. Inovação II, No. 314
P–2784–521 Porto Salvo, Portugal
Tel.: [351] 214225500
Fax: [351] 214225528
www.rockwell.com
(Aerospace products)

Xerox (Portugal) Equipamentos de Escritorio
Rua Cidade de Córdova n. 2 e 2E
P–2720–100 Amadora, Portugal
Tel.: [351] 214709000
Fax: [351] 214709001
www.xerox.com
(Electronic equipment)

Service Industries

Accenture
Amoreiras, Torre 1–16
P–1070–101 Lisbon, Portugal
Tel.: [351 213803500
Fax: [351] 213713500
(Management consulting)

AMS Management Systems
Rua Tomás da Fonseca
Torres de Lisboa
Torre G12
P–1600–209 Lisbon, Portugal
Tel.: [351] 217219000
Fax: [351] 217219100
www.amsinc.com
(Management consulting)

Deloitte & Touche–Auditores e Consultores
Avenida Eng. Duarte Pacheco 1–21
P–1070–100 Lisbon, Portugal
Tel.: [351] 213895000

Fax: [351] 213824891
(Accounting)

Editora McGraw–Hill de Portugal
Rua Barata Salgueiro, n° 51 – A
P–1250–043 Lisbon, Portugal
Tel.: [351] 213553180
Fax: [351] 213553189
(Publishing)

A.J. Gonçalves de Moraes
Rua Nova Alfândega 18
P–4050–000 Porto, Portugal
Tel.: [351] 223323741
Fax: [351] 223323217
(Warehousing and transport)

Manpower Portuguesa
Praça José Fontana, 9 – C
P–1050–129 Lisbon, Portugal
Tel.: [351] 213134000
Fax: [351] 213134070
www.manpower.com
(Temporary labor)

McCann–Erickson/Hora Publicidada
Edifício McCann
Rua José da Costa Pedreira, Lote 12
P–1750–000 Lisbon, Portugal
Tel.: [351] 217576823
Fax: [351] 217572133
(Advertising)

PriceWaterhouseCoopers
Avenida da Liberdade, 245 – 8°
P–1269–034 Lisbon, Portugal
Tel.: [351] 213197000
Fax: [351] 213197148
www.pwcglobal.com
(Accounting)Technology

Technology

Companhia IBM Portuguesa
Praça de Alvalade, 7
P–1700–036 Lisbon, Portugal
Tel.: [351] 217915000
Fax: [351] 217915140
(Data processing equipment)

Hewlett–Packard Portugal
Edifício Park
Rua da Paz, 66-Parcela E55
P–4000 Porto, Portugal
Tel.: [351] 22 606 4191
Fax: [351] 00 600 5895

www.hp.com
(Printers and computers)

Motorola Portugal Comunicações
Avenida Jose Gomes Ferreira 9–9/A 2,
Sala 22
P–1495–000 Algé Portugal
Tel.: [351] 214121415
Fax: [351] 214121414
www.mot.com
(Semiconductors and cell phones)

Texas Instruments Samsung Electrónica
Rua Eng Frederico Uirich 2650

P–4470–000 Maia, Portugal
Tel.: [351] 229431500
Fax: [351] 229431501
(Electronic components)

Unisys Portugal– Sistemas de Informação
Edifício Monumental–Avenida
Praia da Vitória 71–A, 7°
P–1069–002 Lisbon, Portugal
Tel.: [351] 213127500
Fax: [351] 213150490
www.unisys.com
(Data processing equipment)

European Companies in Portugal

The following are major non–American firms operating in Portugal. They can be Portuguese or based in another European country. These companies generally hire their own nationals first but may employ Americans.

Banking and Finance

Banco Comercial Portugues
Praça D. João I, 28
P–4000–295 Porto, Portugal
Tel.: [351] 21 321 1000
Fax: [351] 21 321 1759
www.bcp.pt
(Commercial bank)

Banco Espirito Santo & Commercial de Lisboa
Avenida da Liberdade 195
P–1250–000 Lisbon, Portugal
Tel.: [351] 213 59 7000
Fax: [351] 213 59 7309
(Bank)

Banco de Portugal
Rua Do Comércia 148
P–1100–150 Lisbon, Portugal
Tel.: [351] 213 21 5300
Fax: [351] 213 46 4843
(Central Bank)

Banco Totta & Acores
Rua do Aurea, 88
P–1100–063 Lisbon, Portugal
Tel.: [351] 21 321 1500
Fax: [351] 21 321 1694
www.bta.pt
(Commercial banks)

BPI–SGPS
Rua Tenente Valadim, 284
P–4100–476 Porto, Portugal
Tel.: [351] 22 607 3100
Fax: [351] 22 600 2954
www.bpi.pt
(Commercial banks)

Industrial Manufacturing

BP Portugesa
Rua de Castilho, 165
P–1070–050 Lisbon, Portugal
Tel.: [351] 21 389 1000
Fax: [351] 21 389 1600
(Petroleum products)

Brisa–Auto Estradas de Portugal
Quinta da Torre da Aguilha
P–2785–599 São Domingos de Rana, Portugal
Tel.: [351] 21 444 85 00
Fax: [351] 21 444 91 93
www.brisa.pt
(Construction)

Central de Cervejas
Rua Manuel Madeira
P–3020–303 Coimbra, Portugal
Tel.: [351] 23 982 7061 (/5)
Fax: [351] 23 949 2097
(Brewery)

CIMPOR–Cimentos de Portugal
Rua Alexandre Herculano 35
P–1250–009 Lisbon, Portugal
Tel.: [351] 21 311 81 00
Fax: [351] 21 356 13 81
www.cimpor.pt
(Cement producers)

Corticeira Amorim Industria
Rua de Meladas, 260
P–4536–902 Mozelos VFR, Portugal
Tel.: [351] 22 747 5300
Fax: [351] 22 747 5304
(Cork products)

EDP–Electricidade de Portugal
Avenida José Malhoa, Lote A13
P–1070–155 Lisbon, Portugal
Tel.: [351] 21 726 3013
Fax: [351] 21 726 5029
www.edp.pt
(Electric power companies)

Nestlé Portugal SGPS
Rua Alexandre Herculano, 8–8/A
P–2795–010 Linda–A–Velha, Portugal
Tel.: [351] 21 414 8870
Fax: [351] 21 414 3744
(Food products)

Philips Portuguesa
Rua Dr. Antonio Loureiro Borges, 5
Arquiparque – Miraflores
P–2796–975 Linda–A–Velha, Portugal
Tel.: [351] 21 416 3333
Fax: [351] 21 416 3366
(Household appliances)

Retailing and Wholesaling

Jeronimo Martins Distribuidor Produtos de Consumo
Rua Tierno Galvan, Torre 3
9 Piso, S. 903
P–1009–008 00B Lisbon, Portugal
Tel.: [351] 21 381 8400
Fax: [351] 21 385 3239
(Retailing outlets)

Modelo Continente SGPS
Rua Joã Mendonça 505
P–4460–000 Senhora da Hora, Portugal
Tel.: [351] 22 953 2678

Fax: [351] 22 953 2676
www.modelocontinente.pt
(Grocery retailers)

Service Industries

Estoril–Sol
Praça José Teodoro dos Santos
P–2765–237 Estoril, Portugal
Tel.: [351] 21 466 7700
Fax: [351] 21 466 7966
(Resorts)

Lisnave Estaleiros Navais de Lisboa
Rocha Conde de Obidos
P–1300–000 Lisbon, Portugal
Tel.: [351] 21 275 4121
Fax: [351] 21 276 4670
(River transport)

Mota & Companhia
Rua Rêgo Lameiro, 38
P–4300–000 Porto, Portugal
Tel.: [351] 22 519 0300
Fax: [351] 22 519 0303
(Public work and civil construction)

Transportes Aéreos Portugueses
Aeroporto de Lisboa
P–1704–801 Lisbon, Portugal
Tel.: [351] 21 841 5000
Fax: [351] 21 841 5772
(International airline)

Technology

Portugal Telecom
Avenida Fontes Pereira de Melo, 40
P–1069–300 Lisbon, Portugal
Tel.: [351] 21 500 2000
Fax: [351] 21 356 2624
www.telecom.pt
(Telecommunications)

Vodafone Telecel, Comunicações Pessoais
Rua Tomas da Fonseca, Torre A–14
P–1649–032 Lisbon, Portugal
Tel.: [351] 21 091 5252
Fax: [351] 21 091 5480
www.vodafone.pt
(Wireless telecommunications provider)

International Schools in Portugal

American International School — Lisbon

Rua António dos Reis 95 Linhó
P–2710–301, Sintra, Portugal
Tel: [351] 21 923 9800
Fax: [351] 21 923 9899
Email: tesc0893@mail.telepac.pt
www.ecis.org/aislisbon/index.html
(U.S. curriculum, prekindergarten through grade 12)

St. Julian's School (English Section)

Quinta Nova
P–2777 Carcavelos, Portugal
Tel.: [351] 21 458 5300
Fax: [351] 21 458 5313
Email: mail@stjulians.com
www.stjulians.com
(U.K., International Baccalaureate curriculum, prekindergarten through grade 12)

Chapter 17

Scandinavia: Denmark, Finland, Norway, & Sweden

Denmark

Major employment center: Copenhagen

Major business language: Danish

Language skill index: Most Danes speak English, and if you are looking for a job in a tourist spot, it may not be necessary to learn Danish. Many Danes also speak German, so knowledge of German may help in a pinch.

Currency: Krone

Telephone country code: 45

Time zone: Eastern Standard Time + 6 hours

Punctuality index: Danes find punctuality very important.

Average daily temperature, high/low: January, 36°/29°; July, 72°/55° (Copenhagen)

Average number of days with precipitation: January, 15 days; July, 13 days

Best bet for employment:

   For students: Apply to the American–Scandinavian Foundation

   Permanent jobs: Information technology

Chance of finding a job: Just so–so; you really need a special skill

Useful tip: The Danes are considered to be self-contained (some people call them introverted). Although there is a lively nightlife in Copenhagen, most Danes prefer the idea of *hygge*, or socializing in small gatherings. If invited to someone's home for dinner, be sure to thank your host for a cozy evening.

The smallest of the Scandinavian countries, Denmark is about half the size of Maine. Made up of the Jutland Peninsula and more than 500 islands (of which only 100 are inhabited), Denmark stretches north from Germany, separating the North Sea on the west from the Baltic Sea on the east. Excluding Denmark's territories of the Færce Islands and Greenland, the country covers over 16,000 square miles. While in Denmark, you are never more than 35 miles from the sea. Denmark is so flat that Danes claim you can see from one end of the country to the other while standing on a carton of beer. Denmark is separated by narrow waters from Norway on the northwest and Sweden on the northeast. Its capital, Copenhagen, is located on the largest Baltic Island, Zealand. Almost 85 percent of the population is urban; the four largest cities are Copenhagen, Alborg, Odense, and Arhus.

> **Denmark is so flat that Danes claim you can see from one end of the country to the other while standing on a carton of beer.**

The Viking raids on western Europe and England in the early Middle Ages were largely carried out by Danes. Until the seventeenth century, the Kingdom of Denmark was a major power in northern Europe. Denmark lost Norway to Sweden in 1815, after supporting Napoleon. Denmark remained neutral in World War I and was occupied by the Nazis in World War II. Iceland declared its independence in 1944, and in 1945 Denmark was liberated by British troops. Denmark joined the United Nations in 1945 and NATO in 1949.

The Kingdom of Denmark is one of the world's oldest monarchies. Queen Margrethe II was crowned in 1972 after the Danish constitution was amended to allow female succession. Legislative power rest with the *Folketing*, Denmark's parliament, which is made up of 179 elected members who serve four–year terms. The prime minister is appointed by the Queen. The nation's major political parties are the Social Democrats, the Conservative People's Party, the Socialist People's Party, and the Liberal Party.

Denmark has been hesitant to support expansion of the E.U. In fact, when the Maastricht Treaty came up for ratification in 1992, Danish voters rejected it by a margin of 51 percent to 49 percent. The Danes only voted to accept it in 1993 when they were granted four exemptions—from common defense, the common currency, E.U. citizenship, and certain aspects of legal cooperation, including law enforcement. Danish support for the E.U. remains lukewarm: Many Danes fear the loss of local control to a European bureaucracy dominated by stronger countries. This issue was at the forefront of the September 2000 referendum on Denmark's adoption of the euro. More than 53 percent of Danes voted against the measure and so Denmark has retained the kroner as its currency.

As in all Scandinavian countries, the cost of living in Denmark is higher than in the United States and much higher than in the Mediterranean countries. Scandinavia is known for its extensive welfare system and good record on civil rights; Denmark, for example, grants formal legal status to gay couples. The number of working–age Danes, however, living mostly on government welfare programs is very high, more than 800,000 people or 23 percent of the working–age population. Although this number has been reduced in recent years, taxes remain extremely high in order to support the government's social programs.

July and August are bad months for conducting business in Denmark: Because the Danes love summer, it is difficult and considered inconsiderate to try to conduct heavy business in these months. Weekday business hours are generally from 9 a.m. to 4 p.m. Most stores are open until 5:30 p.m. on weekdays and until 2 p.m. on Saturdays.

Current Economic Climate

High–tech agriculture, up–to–date small–scale and corporate industry, extensive government welfare measures, comfortable living standards, and high dependence on foreign trade characterize Denmark's thoroughly modern market economy. Denmark has one of the highest per capita GNPs in the world and maintains a very high standard of living. The unemployment rate, now at 5.2 percent, is at its lowest in 25 years. The inflation rate, now at 2.2 percent, is one of the lowest of any E.U. country. Denmark's extremely high taxes have enabled it to enjoy one of the most advanced systems of government–provided welfare and social services in the world. Denmark chose not to join the other 11 E.U. members that launched the euro on January 1, 1999.

Denmark's labor force is 65 percent services, 28 percent industry, and 6 percent agricultural. Denmark is the world's leading exporter of canned meat. Although the fishing industry employs only about one–half of one percent of the workforce, Denmark leads the E.U. in terms of fish catches. Other important exports include butter, cheese, beer, furniture, electronics, silverware, and porcelain. Denmark's major trading partners include Germany, Sweden, the U.K., and the United States.

Denmark's 10 Largest Companies

(2001, based on market capitalization)

1. Novo Nordisk
2. Danske Bank
3. Dampskibsselskabet af 1912
4. Dampskibsselskabet Svendborg
5. TDC
6. H. Lundbeck
7. Vestas Wind Systems
8. Carlsberg
9. International Service System
10. Group 4 Falck

Getting Around in Denmark

The Danish State Railway (DSB) provides extensive train services in and around Denmark, and the major routes have high–speed IC3 trains. Private and government–owned ferry lines serve passengers traveling in the Great Belt (the channel between the mainland and surrounding islands). Ferries with rails carry trains across the water. Regional buses serve smaller towns not reached by trains. Eurail and InterRail passes are accepted on all DSB trains in Denmark, and holders may ride the state–run ferries for free. A web of bike paths link the country, so cycling is a practical way to get around Denmark, both within towns and also from town to town.

Employment Regulations and Outlook for Americans

U.S. citizens do not need visas for stays in Denmark of fewer than 90 days, but this 90–day period begins as soon as you enter any Scandinavian country. Immigration is not encouraged, and work permits are only granted to foreigners who possess special training or skills not readily available in Denmark, although the rules are less restrictive if you have special ties to Denmark. You must submit proof that you have a job offer, for example in the form of a contract or letter of intent containing the nature of the job and the agreed–upon salary. A work permit is valid only for the specific job for which it is issued. The best opportunities for Americans seeking to work in Denmark are for college students. Danish immigration is very strict, but the work exchange programs sponsored by the American–Scandinavian Foundation can help students secure a job and legal permission to accept it.

Short–term and Temporary Work

The best bet for casual work in Denmark, as in all of Scandinavia, is as an au pair. In addition to the agency below, Au Pair in Europe makes placements in Denmark. See Chapter 9 for more resources.

Exis
Rebslagergade 3
DK–6400 Sønderborg, Denmark
Tel.: [45] 74 42 97 49
Fax: [45] 74 42 97 47
Email: info@exis.dk
www.exis.dk
Exis places au pairs in Denmark, Norway, and Iceland. Exis offers three au pair programs: regular au pairs work about 30 hours per week with a weekly salary of 550 kroner; an Au Pair Plus works about 35 hours and earns 600 kroner a week; and a Mother's Helper works about 40 hours and earns from 600–700 kroner per week.

Internship Programs

There are opportunities for students to gain professional experience, usually in technical fields. The American–Scandinavian Foundation offers the best opportunities; IAESTE, and AIESEC also coordinate programs. Chapter 9 proffers details and contact information for these and other organizations that offer internships in Scandinavia and the rest of Europe.

American–Scandinavian Foundation
58 Park Avenue
New York, NY 10016
Tel.: (212) 879–9779
email: trainscan@amscan.org
www.amscan.org
This foundation organizes trainee programs for college juniors majoring in a technical field. To be eligible, you must be at least 21 years old, a U.S. citizen or permanent resident, a college junior or senior, maintain a minimum 2.5 GPA, and have relevant work experience. Most of the overseas assignments last no more than 18 months, and the program emphasizes engineering opportunities in Denmark and Finland. The foundation can also assist you with arranging a work permit if you have found your own internship.

Volunteer Opportunities

Denmark offers many voluntary service opportunities in international student work camps. Through the Council on International Educational Exchange, students can do volunteer work protecting the environment or sending supplies to developing countries. The International Volunteering Network and Volunteers for Peace also offer environmental and community service projects, while WOOFF offers the opportunity to work on an organic farm. See Chapter 9 for details.

MS/Mellemfolkeligt Samvirke
(Danish Association for International Cooperation)
Borgergade 14
D–1300 Copenhagen, Denmark
Tel.: [45] 7731 0000
Fax: [45] 7731 0101
Email: info@msdan.dk

www.ms.dk

MS is a Danish organization that combines development assistance with political activism and grassroots organization. MS manages summer work camps in Denmark and Greenland.

Resources for Further Information

Newspapers in Denmark

Berlingske Tidende
Tel.: [45] 33 75 75 75
Fax: [45] 33 75 20 20
www.berlingske.dk

Børsen
Tel.: [45] 33 12 24 45
www.borsen.dk

Ekstra Bladet
Tel.: [45] 33 11 13 13
Fax: [45] 33 14 10 00

www.ekstrabladet.dk

Information
Tel.: [45] 33 69 60 00
Fax: [45] 33 69 61 10
www.information.dk

Politiken
Tel.: [45] 33 11 85 11
Fax: [45] 33 15 41 17
www.politiken.dk

Useful Websites for Job Seekers

The Internet is a good place to begin your job search. Many Scandinavian employers list job vacancies, especially those in technical fields, on the web.

There are also many websites that provide useful information for job seekers researching the Danish job market.

Akademikernes Job Bank
www.jobbank.dk
Features 370 private sector jobs, a resume database, and a directory of employers. Written in Danish.

Jobsoger
www.jobfinder.dk
Features 200 job opportunities in information technology. Written in Danish.

Job Match Denmark
www.jobmatch.dk
Matches job seekers and employers. Site features 750 active jobs in a variety of industries. Candidates can post resumes in a searchable database.

Job Index
www.jobindex.dk
Lists 7,000 jobs and features a resume database and an email notification service. Written in Danish.

Manpower Denmark
www.manpower.dk
Manpower is a recruitment agency. Its Danish site features a database of private sector jobs.

StepStone Denmark
www.stepstone.dk
One of Europe's leading online recruitment sites. Features over 1,500 private sector and education jobs in Denmark.

Embassies and Consular Offices

American embassies and consulates have commercial and/or economic sections that can provide you with business information and explain aspects of the local economy. Inquiries about business opportunities should be addressed either to "Commercial Officer" or "Commercial Section."

Representation of Denmark in the United States

Embassy of the Kingdom of Denmark
3200 Whitehaven Street NW
Washington, DC 20008
Tel.: (202) 234–4300
Fax: (202) 328–1470
Email: wasamb@um.dk

www.denmarkemb.org

Danish Consulates General:
Minneapolis, (612) 338–7283; Houston, (713) 622–9018; Detroit, (313) 875–9856; St. Louis, (3140 603–2470.

Representation of the United States in Denmark

American Embassy
Dag Hammarskjölds Allé 24
DK–2100 Copenhagen, Denmark

Tel.: [45] 35 55 31 44
Fax: [45] 35 43 02 23
www.usembassy.dk

Chambers of Commerce

Chambers of commerce consist of member firms in both countries interested in international trade. These are appropriate companies to initially target in the job search.

American Chamber of Commerce in Denmark

Christians Brygge 28

DK–1559 Copenhagen, Denmark
Tel.: [45] 33 93 29 32
Fax: [45] 33 13 05 17

Email: landman@amchan.dk
www.amcham.dk

Danish–American Chamber of Commerce
885 Second Avenue, 18th Floor
New York, NY 10017
Tel.: (212) 980–6240
Fax: (212) 754–1904

Email: daccny@aol.com

Danish Chamber of Commerce
Boersen
DK–1217 Copenhagen, Denmark
Tel.: [45] 33 95 05 00
Fax: [45] 33 32 52 16
Email: commerce@commerce.dk
www.commerce.dk

World Trade Center in Denmark

World trade centers usually include many foreign companies that conduct business in Denmark.

World Trade Center Copenhagen
Bygstubben 13–2950
Vedbaek, Denmark

Tel.: [45] 39 17 98 00
Fax : [45] 31 20 55 21

Other Informational Organizations

Foreign government missions in the United States, such as tourist and trade offices, can furnish visas and information on work permits and other important regulations. They may also offer economic and business information about Denmark.

Danish Foreign Trade Council
Udenrigsministeriet
Asiatisk Plads 2
DK–1448 Hellerup, Denmark
Tel.: [45] 33 92 00 00
Fax: [45] 32 54 05 33
www.eksportraadet.dk/

Denmark–America Foundation
Fiolstræde 24, 3
DK–1171 Copenhagen K, Denmark
Tel.: [45] 33 12 82 23
www.daf–fulb.dk

Scandinavian Tourist Board
655 Third Avenue, 18th Floor
New York, NY 10017
Tel.: (212) 885–9700
Fax: (212) 885–9710
www.goscandinavia.com

Youth Information Copenhagen
Radhusstraede 13
DK–1466 Copenhagen K, Denmark
Tel.: [45] 33 73 06 20
Fax: [45] 33 73 06 49
www.useit.dk

Business Directories

Although not always easy to find, business directories can prove invaluable in the international job search. Your best bet for locating these directories is to begin in the reference section of any public or university library. Most directories list company names, addresses, products, and phone numbers. Some include executive names, titles and financial information, which can tell you how strong a company's position in a country may be.

Export Directory of Denmark. Kraks Forlag, Virumgardsvej 21, DK–2830 Virum, Denmark; email: krak@krak.dk; www.krak.dk. Lists 5,500 export, service, transport, software, and research firms. Also includes a business guide with information about Denmark, Greenland, and the Færce Islands. 1,000 pages or CD–ROM; published annually in English, French, German, and Spanish.

Greens–Handbogen om Dansk Erhvervsliv (Danish Company Yearbook). Greens Erhvervsinformation, Falkoner Aller 1,4, DK-2000 Frederiksberg, Denmark; email: greens@greens.dk; www.greens.dk. Covers 5,000 of Denmark's largest companies, with financial information and names and titles of key personnel. 4,500 pages in four volumes; published annually.

Kommunal Handbogen (Danish business and government). Mostrups Forlag Telia Infomedia, 2 Farvergade, DK-1017 Copenhagen, Denmark; email: mostrup@mostrup.dk; www.mostrup.dk. Contains government departments, institutes, universities, associations, and Danish and foreign manufacturers and distributors that sell to the Danish government. 684 kroner; 1,600 pages, published annually.

Kompass Scandinavia. Published annually by Bureau van Dijksn, Avenue Louise 250, Box 14, B-1050 Brussels, Belgium. Available in the U.S. from the Bureau van Dijk Electronic Publishing, 90 Park Avenue, Suite 1600, New York, NY 10016. Lists over 65,000 Scandinavian companies and their products and services. Published semiannually in English, Danish, Swedish, Norwegian, and Finnish.

Kraks Vejviser (Business and Industry, Denmark). Kraks Forlag, 21 Virumgardsvej, DK-2830 Virum, Denmark; email: krak@krak.dk; www.krak.dk. Volume 1 lists 60,000 Danish companies by business type, then geography. Volume 2 lists the same firms alphabetically, with addresses and phone numbers. 8,150 pages in five volumes.

Trade Directory for Denmark. Udenrigshandelens Informationsbureau, Holsteinsgade 19, DK–2100 Copenhagen, Denmark. Manufacturers, exporters, importers, service firms, and other businesses operating in Denmark, the Færce Islands, Iceland, and Greenland. 1,200 pages, published annually.

American Companies in Denmark

The following companies are classified by business area: Banking and Finance; Industrial Manufacturing; Retailing and Wholesaling; Service Industries; and Technology. The information includes firm name, address, phone and fax number, and specific line of business. Your chances of securing employment abroad are substantially better if you contact the subsidiary company in Europe rather than the parent company in the United States. Because the contact information for companies can change frequently, be sure to confirm a company's address and phone number before contacting it.

Banking and Finance

BDO ScanRevision Aktieselskab
Kristineberg 3
DK–2100 Copenhagen K, Denmark
Tel.: [45] 39 15 52 00
Fax: [45] 39 15 52 01

(Accounting firm)

Citibank
Dagmarhus
H.C. Andersen's Boulevard 12
DK–1553/V Copenhagen, Denmark
Tel.: [45] 33 63 83 83

Fax: [45] 33 63 83 33
(Bank)

Industrial Manufacturing

Bristol–Myers Squibb Danmark
Jaegersborgvej 64–66
DK–2800 Lyngby, Denmark
Tel.: [45] 45 93 05 06
Fax: [45] 45 45 93 32 50
(Pharmaceuticals)

Coca–Cola Danmark
Fabriksparken 7–9
DK–2600 Glostrup, Denmark
Tel.: [45] 43 43 17 17
Fax: [45] 43 43 41 17
(Beverages)

Colgate–Palmolive
Smedeland 9
DK–2600 Glostrup, Denmark
Tel.: [45] 43 20 92 00
Fax: [45] 43 20 93 93
(Soap and cosmetics)

Dow AgroSciences Danmark
Sorgenfrivej 15
DK–2800 Lyngby, Denmark
Tel.: [45] 45 28 08 00
Fax: [45] 45 28 08 01
(Chemicals)

Goodyear Dunlop Tires Danmark
Universitetsvej 2
DK–4000 Roskilde, Denmark
Tel.: [45] 43 20 81 88
Fax: [45] 43 45 68 14
(Rubber products)

Hydro Texaco
Standvejen 70
DK–2900 Hellerup, Denmark
Tel.: [45] 39 47 81 00
Fax: [45] 39 47 81 10
(Petroleum)

Kraft Foods Danmark
Smedeland 36
DK–2500 Glostrup, Denmark
Tel.: [45] 43 96 96 22
Fax: [45] 43 96 01 02
(Food products)

Mobil Oil Danmark
Kongevejen 150B

DK–3460 Birkerød, Denmark
Tel.: [45] 45 99 02 00
Fax: [45] 45 99 02 99
(Petroleum products)

Scan–Globe
25 Ulvevej
DK–4622 Havdrup, Denmark
Tel.: [45] 46 18 54 00
Fax: [45] 46 18 52 70
(World globes)

3M
Fabriksparken 15
DK–2600 Glostrup, Denmark
Tel.: [45] 43 48 01 00
Fax: [45] 43 96 85 96
(Adhesive and imaging tapes)

Xerox
Borupvang 5
DK–2750 Ballerup, Denmark
Tel.: [45] 88 17 88 17
Fax: [45] 88 17 88 88
(Copier equipment)

Retailing and Wholesaling

Ikon Office Solutions
Vallensbækvej 44
DK–2625 Vallensbæk, Denmark
Tel.: [45] 70 10 67 68
Fax: [45] 43 66 69 69
(Office machines and equipment)

Service Industries

Accenture Denmark Holdings
Lautrupsgade 7
DK–2100 Copenhagen, Denmark
Tel.: [45] 33 42 20 00
Fax: [45] 33 42 71 00
(Management consulting)

Associated Press
Sankt Annæ Plads 7
DK–1250 Copenhagen, Denmark
Tel.: [45] 33 11 15 04
Fax: [45] 33 32 36 60
www.ap.com
(News gathering agency)

McDonald's Denmark
Falkoner Alle 20
DK–2000 Frederiksberg, Denmark
Tel.: [45] 33 26 60 00

Fax: [45] 33 26 60 60
(Food Service)

Ogilvy Danmark
Aldersrogade 8
DK–2100 Copenhagen Ø, Denmark
Tel.: [45] 39178888
Fax: [45] 39 17 88 89
(Advertising agency)

PriceWaterhouseCoopers
Strandvejen 44/ Tuborg Blvd. 1
DK–2900 Hellerup, Denmark
Tel.: [45] 39 45 39 45
Fax: [45] 39 45 39 87
(Accounting)

Wunderman
Enhjørnings Bastion
Langebrogade 6 V
DK–1411 Copenhagen, Denmark
Tel.: [45] 32 88 77 77
Fax: [45] 32 88 77 88
www.wcj.com
(Advertising and marketing)

Technology

Analog Devices
Smedeholm 10
DK–2730 Herlev, Copenhagen,
Denmark
Tel.: [45]44 84 58 00
Fax: [45]44 84 03 22
(Electrical components)

Computer Associates Scandinavia
Kongevejen 195 B
DK–2840 Holte, Denmark
Tel.: [45] 45 47 41 41
Fax: [45] 45 47 41 10
(Computer consultants)

Hewlett–Packard
Kongevejen 2
DK–3460 Birkerød, Denmark
Tel.: [45] 45 99 10 00
Fax: [45] 45 99 10 01
(Computers and printers)

IBM Danmark
Nymøllevej 91
DK–2800 Kgs. Lyngby, Denmark
Tel.: [45] 45 23 30 00
Fax: [45] 45 93 24 20
(Data processing equipment)

Motorola
Sydvestvej 15
DK–2600 Glostrup, Denmark
Tel.: [45] 43488000
Fax: [45] 43488001
(Semiconductors and cell phones)

NCR Danmark
Svanevej 14
DK–2400 Copenhagen NV, Denmark
Tel.: [45] 70 23 91 00
Fax: [45] 70 23 91 70
(Software packages)

Oracle Danmark
Lautrupbjerg 2–6
DK–2750 Ballerup, Denmark
Tel.: [45] 44 80 80 80
Fax: [45] 44 80 80 90
(Software)

Unisys
Lejrvej 17, Kirke Væø
DK–3500 Værløse, Denmark
Tel.: [45] 44 38 38 38
Fax: [45] 44 47 11 00
(Computer network systems)

European Companies in Denmark

The following companies are major non–American firms that operate in Denmark. They may be either Danish or based in another European country. They generally hire their own nationals first but may employ Americans.

Banking and Finance

Danske Bank
2–12 Holmens Kanal
DK–1092/K Copenhagen, Denmark

Tel.: [45] 33 44 00 00
Fax: [45] 39 18 58 73
www.danskebank.com
(Commercial bank)

The East Asiatic Company
Asia House, Indiakaj 1
DK–2100 Copenhagen, Denmark
Tel.: [45] 35 25 43 00
Fax: [45] 35 25 43 13
(Bank)

Sparekassen Faaborg
Torvet 6
DK–5600 Faaborg, Denmark
Tel.: [45] 63 61 18 00
Fax: [45] 63 61 18 08
(Savings bank)

Industrial Manufacturing

Aarhus Oliefabrik
M.P. Bruuns Gade 27, P.O. Box 50
DK–8100 Aarhus C, Denmark
Tel.: [45] 87 30 60 00
Fax: [45] 87 30 60 12
www.aarhus.com
(Food products)

Arla Foods
Skanderborgvej 277
DK–8260 Viby J, Denmark
Tel.: [45] 89 38 10 00
Fax: [45] 86 18 16 91
www.arlafoods.com
(Food products)

Bang & Olufsen
Peter Bangs Vej 15
DK–7600 Struer, Denmark
Tel.: [45] 96 84 11 22
Fax: [45] 97 85 18 88
www.bang–olufsen.com
(Audio & video home products)

Carlsberg
Valby Langgade 1
DK–2500 Valby, Denmark
Tel.: [45] 33 27 27 27
Fax: [45] 33 17 48 50
www.carlsberg.com
(Brewery)

Dampskibsselskabet af 1912
Esplanaden 50
DK–1098 Copenhagen K, Denmark
Tel.: [45] 33 63 33 63
Fax: [45] 33 63 41 08
(Shipping)

Danisco
Langebrogade 1
DK–1001 Copenhagen K, Denmark
Tel.: [45] 32 66 20 00
Fax: [45] 32 66 21 75
www.danisco.com
(Food products)

FLS Industries
Vigerslev Allé 77
DK–2500 Valby, Denmark
Tel.: [45] 36 18 18 00
Fax: [45] 36 30 44 41
www.flsindustries.dk
(Cement)

J. Lauritzen Holding
Sankt Annae Plads 28
DK–1291 Copenhagen K, Denmark
Tel.: [45] 33 96 80 00
Fax: [45] 33 96 80 01
(Ship broker)

Lego Company
LEGO Center
DK–7190 Billund, Denmark
Tel.: [45] 79 50 60 70
Fax: [45] 75 35 33 60
www.lego.com
(Toys)

H. Lundbeck
9 Ottiliavej
DK–2500 Copenhagen, Denmark
Tel.: [45] 36 30 13 11
Fax: [45] 36 30 19 40
www.lundbeck.com
(Pharmaceuticals)

Novo Nordisk
Novo Allé
DK–2880 Bagsvaerd, Denmark
Tel.: [45] 44 44 88 88
Fax: [45] 44 49 05 55
www.novonordisk.com
(Pharmaceuticals and industrial enzymes)

Philips Danmark
Frederikskaj 6
DK–1780 Copenhagen S, Denmark
Tel.: [45] 33 29 33 33
Fax: [45] 33 29 39 44
(Electronic equipment)

Unilever Danmark
Stationsparken 25
DK–2600 Glostrup, Denmark
Tel.: [45] 43 28 41 00
Fax: [45] 43 44 45 35
(Tea, snacks)

Vestas Wind Systems
Smed Sorensens Vej 5
DK–6950 Ringkobing, Denmark
Tel.: [45] 96 75 25 75
Fax: [45] 96 75 24 36
www.vestas.com
(Machinery equipment)

Retailing and Wholesaling

IKEA International
Ny Strandvej 21
DK–3050 Humlebaek, Denmark
Tel.: [45] 49 15 50 00
Fax: [45] 49 15 50 01
www.ikea.com
(Furniture retailing)

Service Industries

Cap Gemini Danmark
Ømegårdsvej 16
DK–2820 Gentofte, Denmark
Tel.: [45] 70 11 22 00
Fax: [45] 70 11 22 01
(Management consulting)

Group 4 Falck
Polititorvet
DK–1780 Copenhagen V, Denmark
Tel.: [45] 70 13 43 43
Fax: [45] 33 91 00 26
www.group4falck.com
(Security products and services)

Integrated Service System
Bredgade 30
DK–1260 Copenhagen, Denmark
Tel.: [45] 38 17 00 00
Fax: [45] 38 17 00 11
www.ISS–group.com
(Cleaning service)

Sophus Berendsen
Klausdalsbrovej 1

DK–2860 Søborg, Denmark
Tel.: [45] 39 53 85 00
Fax: [45] 39 53 85 85
www.berendsen.com
(Pest control & tropical plants)

Technology

Digiquant
Universitetsvej 2
DK–4000 Roskilde, Denmark
Tel.: [45] 70 12 25 00
Fax: [45] 70 12 25 01
www.digiquant.com
(Internet services & software)

Navision
Frydenlunds Allé 6
DK–2950 Vedbæk, Denmark
Tel.: [45] 65 50 00
Fax: [45] 65 50 01
www.navision.com
(Internet services)

NetDoktor Group
Bredgade 41
DK–1260 Copenhagen K, Denmark
Tel.: [45] 33 17 92 50
Fax: [45] 33 17 92 59
www.netdoktor.com
(Online health care information)

Olicom
Nybrovej 110
DK–2800 Lyngby, Denmark
Tel.: [45] 45 27 00 00
Fax: [45] 45 27 01 01
www.olicom.dk
(Software)

TDC
Norregade 21
DK–0900 Copenhagen C, Denmark
Tel.: [45] 33 43 77 77
Fax: [45] 33 43 76 19
www.teledanmark.com
(Telecommunications)

International School in Denmark

Copenhagen International School
Hellerupvej 22–26
DK–2900 Hellerup, Denmark
Tel.: [45] 39 46 33 00
Fax: [45] 39 61 22 30

Email: cis@cisdk.dk
www.cis–edu.dk
(International Baccalaureate curriculum, kindergarten through grade 12)

Finland

Major employment center: Helsinki

Major business languages: Finnish, Swedish

Language skill index: Unlike other Scandinavian languages, Finnish is not an Indo–European language and many people find they can't pick it up easily. English is widely spoken in the business community.

Currency: Euro

Telephone country code: 358, 90

Time zone: Eastern Standard Time + 7 hours

Punctuality index: Appointments are necessary, punctuality a must

Average daily temperature, high/low: January, 27°/17°; July, 71°/57° (Helsinki)

Average number of days with precipitation: January, 15 days; July, 8 days

Best bet for employment:

    For students: American–Scandinavian Foundation

    Permanent jobs: Forestry and paper

Chance of finding a job: Good opportunities for summer jobs. Fewer opportunities for permanent jobs.

Useful tip: Finland is the least corrupt country in which to do business, according to the annual corruption perceptions index compiled by Transparency International.

The Republic of Finland extends 700 miles north from the Gulf of Norway and into the Arctic Circle for more than 200 miles. Finland's neighbors include the northern tip of Norway to the north, Sweden to the west, and Russia along the entire eastern border. Covering over 130,000 square miles, Finland is three times the size of Ohio or almost the size of Montana. Southern and central Finland have over 200,000 glacially carved lakes and are mostly flat with low hills. Northern Finland is sparsely populated and mountainous. The Finns are racially mixed, most being either of East Baltic stock (living mainly in eastern Finland) or of Nordic stock (in the west and south, especially on the coast and in Ahvenanmaa). A small number of Lapps live in northern Finland. Other ethnic groups include about 2,800 Russian speakers, 2,500 English speakers, 2,200 German speakers, 5,500 Gypsies, and 1,000 Jews.

More than half the world's ice breakers are built in Finland.

In the seventh century, the Finns came from the Ural area and took the country from the Lapps. After repelling Finnish raiding parties, Sweden conquered the country in 1157. By 1809 the whole of Finland had been overtaken by the Russian Empire. Finland declared its independence in 1917 and became a republic in 1919. In 1939 the Soviet Union attacked, and the Finns ceded 16,000 square miles to them. During World War II, Finland joined Germany against the Soviet Union in an effort to reclaim their territory but were defeated and forced to cede even more land to the Soviets. The Finns signed a 20–year treaty of mutual aid and friendship with the Soviets in 1948 and again in 1970. Finland joined the E.U. in 1995. On March 1, 2000, Finland adopted a new constitution.

Finns are known for their stubborn independence. One reason for this is probably the cultural and language differences between Finland and its closest neighbors, Sweden and Russia. Although Finns have a unique language, it does not totally isolate them, as most also speak English, Swedish, or German. Finland plays an important part in the group of five Nordic countries. The Finns are much affected through television and consumer goods by American culture. Finland is ranked sixth in the latest United Nations survey of quality of life. And if the implementation of equal rights for women is included as a factor that enhances the state of a nation, Finland rises to fifth position in the world. (Finland was the first country in Europe to grant women the right to vote.) For the past two years, Finland was ranked by Transparency International the least corrupt country in the world.

Stores close early: between 4 and 5 p.m., Mondays through Fridays, and around 1 p.m. on Saturdays. This is especially true in the countryside. Since winters are long and dark, Finns abandon the cities in the summer for the picturesque countryside to bask in the midnight sun. July, August, and early September are, therefore, bad months for business trips or heavy business.

Current Economic Climate

Finland has a highly industrialized, largely free–market economy, with per capita output roughly that of the U.K., France, Germany, and Italy. Its key economic sector is manufacturing — principally in the wood, metals, engineering, telecommunications, and electronics industries. Trade accounts for over one–third of the Finnish GDP.

Unemployment in Finland currently stands at about 9 percent, reduced from highs of over 16 percent in the early 1990s. Inflation hovers at about 3 percent. The economy experienced a modest decline in 2001, largely brought on by weaknesses in the technology sector. Nokia, Finland's largest company, was largely cited as the cause of this economic hiccup. The company is now so large that fluctuations in production can strongly distort the image of the overall development of the economy. Finland was one of the 11 countries that joined the euro monetary system on January 1, 1999, and integration with Western Europe is certain to dominate the Finnish economic picture over the next few years. Finland has the dubious distinction of having the highest tax rates in the world — 95 percent of the price of a bottle of vodka, for example, goes to the government.

Finland's labor force is divided as follows: 9 percent agriculture and forestry, 21 percent manufacturing and construction, and 60 percent service sector (communications, commerce, administration).The wood–processing industry has traditionally played an important part in the Finnish economy. Finland is the world's second–largest exporter of paper and cardboard. The metal and engineering industry is the nation's most important employer and also contributes a major part of exports. Over half of the world's ice breakers are built in Finland. Finland is known internationally for its architecture and design.

Finland's 10 Largest Companies

(2001, based on market capitalization)

1. Nokia Corporation
2. Stora Enso
3. UPM–Kymmene Corporation
4. Sampo
5. Sonera
6. Fortum
7. Tietoenator
8. Elisa Communications Corporation
9. Kone
10. Sanoma–WSOY

Getting Around in Finland

Finnair offers economical flights within and across Finland's borders. Finnish railways are not only efficient, they are among the least expensive in

Europe. Express trains are available but advance reservations may be necessary. Eurail passes are valid throughout the country, although buses serve as a more leisurely means of transportation and cost about the same as trains. Express buses are also available at an extra charge. Ferries and steamers provide transportation along the coastline.

Employment Regulations and Outlook for Americans

Americans need a passport but not a visa to visit Finland for short stays. Visas are required for stays of over three months, and the count begins as soon as you enter any Scandinavian country. Those wanting to stay longer should check with the Finnish embassy. A firm offer of employment is required before applying for a work permit. Contact the Embassy of Finland for more information. Embassy personnel advise that it can be very difficult for Americans to find work in Finland. It is possible, in exceptional circumstances, for a foreigner who finds a job in Finland after arriving in the country to apply for a work permit, but you probably should not count on this tactic. As in other Scandinavian countries, the best opportunities are for students who intern through the American–Scandinavian Foundation.

Short–term and Temporary Work

The best bet for casual jobs in Finland, as in all of Scandinavia, is as an au pair. Au Pair in Europe, described in Chapter 9, places nannies in Finland.

Internship Programs

In addition to the agency listed below, there are opportunities for students to gain professional experience, usually in technical fields. The American–Scandianavian Foundation offers the best opportunities, but IAESTE, AIESEC and International Cooperative Education have programs in Finland, and ASF recruits English teachers for Finland. See Chapter 9 for details.

American–Scandinavian Foundation
58 Park Avenue
New York, NY 10016
Tel.: (212) 879–9779
email: trainscan@amscan.org
www.amscan.org
This foundation organizes trainee programs for college juniors majoring in a technical field. To be eligible, you must be at least 21 years old, a U.S. citizen or permanent resident, a college junior or senior, maintain a minimum 2.5 GPA, and have relevant work experience. Most of the overseas assignments last no more than 18 months, and the program emphasizes engineering opportunities in Denmark and Finland. The foundation also manages the "Teach English in Finland" program, which places young American adults as a foreign language instructors in Finnish kindergartens, schools, colleges, and private and public institutions and universities. The foundation can also assist you with arranging a work permit if you have found your own internship.

Center for International Mobility (CIMO)
P.O. Box 343
FIN–00531 Helsinki, Finland
Tel.: [358] 1080 6767
Fax: [358] 9 7747 7064
Email: cimoinfo@cimo.fi
http://finland.cimo.fi/
Training opportunities in Finland are available for both full–time students who have completed at least two years of college and students who have re-

cently graduated. The training is directly related to the student's particular field of study. Previous work experience in the field is desirable but not always a requirement. The training period normally takes place during the summer (June, July, August), but it is also possible during the winter. The minimum training period is one month, maximum 18 months. The shorter periods may be extended to up to 18 months. Placements are available in agriculture, hospitality, teaching, business, and technology.

Volunteer Opportunities

The Council on International Educational Exchange coordinates several volunteer projects in Finland. Service Civil International and Volunteers for Peace are the coordinating bodies for work camps in Finland. WWOOF recruits volunteers to work on organic farms. See Chapter 9 for details about these organizations and the opportunities they offer.

Interning with the American–Scandinavian Foundation

I was offered a summer internship through the American–Scandinavian Foundation's exchange program. The position was an engineering internship at Abo Akademi, a Swedish university in Turku, which is a small city about two hours west of Helsinki. Beyond that and a two–sentence job description, I knew very little about what to expect. But what an opportunity! Working in Finland, of all places, seemed like a novel idea, a chance to explore totally new territory. By the end of the summer I had discovered with some amazement that Nokia cell phones, Fiskars scissors, the Linux operating system, and even a techno song popular in the U.S., *Darudes Sandstorm*, all originated in Finland.

To me, the most interesting aspect of the Finnish culture is its dual love for advanced technology and for the simple things in life. On the one hand, just about everyone carries at least one cell phone; I knew one person who had three, each for a different purpose. Electronic banking seemed to be even more popular there than it is here in the U.S. On the other hand, their summer vacations frequently involve retreating to family cabins or cottages in the woods. I even joined my coworkers on a one–day excursion to the forest, where we hiked, had a picnic, and participated in team activities. Also, one must not forget the national pastime: the sauna (actually a Finnish word). I heard enthusiastic stories about the pleasure of sitting in a steam–filled wooden sauna — nude, of course — and then plunging into a nearby lake to cool off. One of my coworkers even showed me a picture of his friends floating in a hole in the ice over a frozen lake!

The experience has left me with a very large collection of photographs, a unique entry for my resume, and many unforgettable memories. —*Danielle Dunn, Houston, Texas*

Resources for Further Information

Newspapers in Finland

Aamulehti
Tel.: [358] 3 266 6111
Fax: [358] 3 266 259
www.aamulehti.fi

Helsingin Sanomat
Sanoma Corp.
Tel.: [358] 9 1221
Fax: [358] 9 122 656
www.helsinginsanomat.fi

Kauppalehti (The Commercial Daily)
Tel.: [358] 950 781

www.kauppalehti.fi

Tekniikka & Talous (Trade journal targeting engineering and business)
Tel.: [358] 914 8801
Fax: [358] 968 56612
www.tekniikatalous.fi

Turun Sanomat/Turun Sanomat Extra
Tel.: [358] 2 2693 311
Fax: [358] 2 2693 274
www.turunsanomat.fi

In addition to the newspapers, you might want to subscribe to *The Spirit of Finland*, a quarterly newsletter that provides industrial and economic news from Finland. It is available free from the Finland Promotion Board, P.O. Box 324, FIN–00131 Helsinki, Finland.

Useful Websites for Job Seekers

The Internet is a good place to begin your job search. Many Scandinavian employers list job vacancies, especially those in technical fields, on the World Wide Web. There are also many websites that provide useful information for job searchers researching the Finnish job market.

Academic Career Services
www.aarresaari.net
Free job and resume board for new college graduates. Most of the job advertisements are in Finnish, but the English language section has useful tips for finding work in Finland.

Jobline
www.jobline.fi
Lists job vacancies in Finland and the rest of Europe. It includes a resume database and an email notification service. This site is owned by Monster.com. Written in Danish.

Manpower Finland
www.manpower.fi
Manpower is a recruitment agency. Its Finnish site features a database of private sector jobs.

Rekry.com
www.rekry.com
Features 400 jobs in a variety of industries. Written in Finnish.

StepStone Finland
www.stepstone.fi
One of Europe's leading online recruitment sites. Features about 100 private sector and education jobs in Finland.

Uranus
www.uranusfin.com
This Finnish recruitment site lists almost 700 job openings in Finland and the rest of Europe. The site includes very good job search tips for non–Europeans and can be viewed in English.

Uratie
www.uratie.net
Features a limited number of jobs in Finland. It includes a resume database that requires a pretty good command of Finnish to navigate.

Virtual Finland
http://virtual.finland.fi
A good resource for current information on Finland produced by the Finnish Ministry of Foreign Affairs.

Interviewing tip

A trademark of Finnish culture is a capacity for silence and reflection. In an interview, you can expect that your Finnish employer will be especially formal and straightforward. He or she may not automatically react verbally to your comments. Your potential employer is not being distant, but instead typically Finnish, and will appreciate your being equally straightforward. Other tips: Finns avoid small talk, try not to interrupt each other, and tend to distrust those who talk too much.

Embassies and Consular Offices

American embassies and consulates have commercial and/or economic sections that can provide you with business information and explain aspects of the local economy. Inquiries about business opportunities should be addressed either to "Commercial Officer" or "Commercial Section."

Representation of Finland in the United States

Embassy of Finland
3301 Massachusetts Avenue
Washington, DC 20008
Tel.: (202) 298 5800
Fax: (202) 298 6030
Email: info@finland.org

www.finland.org

Consulates General of Finland:
Los Angeles, (310) 203–9903; New York, (212) 750–4400

Representation of the United States in Finland

American Embassy
Itäinen Puistotie 14B
FIN–00140 Helsinki, Finland

Tel.: [358] 9 171 931
Fax: [358] 9 174 681
www.usembassy.fi

Chambers of Commerce

Chambers of commerce consist of member firms in both countries interested in international trade. These are appropriate companies to initially target in the job search.

Central Chamber of Commerce of Finland
P.O. Box 1000
FIN–00101 Helsinki, Finland
Tel.: [358] 9 696969
Fax: [358] 9 650303
www.keskuskauppakamari.fi

Finnish–American Chamber of Commerce
866 U.N. Plaza, Suite 249

New York, NY 10017
Tel.: (212) 821–0225
Fax: (212) 750–4417
www.finlandtrade.com

Finnish American Chamber of Commerce — West Coast
1900 Avenue of the Stars, Suite 1025
Los Angeles, CA 90067
Tel.: (310) 203–9903
www.finlandtrade.com

World Trade Center in Finland

The world trade center is likely to include many foreign companies that conduct business in Finland.

World Trade Center Helsinki
Aleksanterinkatu 17
P.O. Box 800
FIN–00100 Helsinki, Finland

Tel.: [358] 9 6969 2020
Fax: [358] 9 6969 2027
Email: sirpa.rissa–anttilainen@wtc.fi
www.wtc.fi

Other Informational Organizations

Foreign government missions in the United States, such as tourist boards, can furnish visas and information on work permits and other important regulations. They may also offer economic and business information about Finland.

Finnish Tourist Board
P.O. Box 4649
New York, NY 10163
Tel.: (212) 885–9700
Fax: (212) 885–9710

Finnish Tourist Board
P.O. Box 625

Töölönkatu 11
FIN–00101 Helsinki, Finland
Tel.: [358] 9 417 6911
Fax: [358] 9 4176 9399
Email: mek@mek.fi
www.mek.fi

Business Directories

Although not always easy to find, business directories can prove invaluable in the international job search. Your best bet for locating these directories is to begin in the reference section of any public or university library. Most directories list company names, addresses, products, and phone numbers. Some directories include executive names and titles and financial information about the company. These sources provide you with the names of the people to contact for employment information as well as financial data, which can tell you how strong a company's position in a country may be.

Directory of Finnish Exporters. Finnish Foreign Trade Association, Arkadiankatu 2, P.O. Box 908, FIN–00100 Helsinki, Finland; email: info@ finpro.fi; www.trade–finland.com. Lists approximately 1,700 Finnish exporters. Free, 240 pages, published annually in English.

Kompass Finland. Kompass Finland Oy, Kuparitie 2, FIN–00440 Helsinki, Finland; email: kompass@kompassfinland.fi; www.kompass.com. U.S. distributor Croner Publications, 34 Jericho Turnpike, Jericho, NY 11753. Lists over 14,500 Finnish companies and their products and services. 1,500 pages, updated annually.

Sininen Kirja: Suomen Talouselaman Hakemisto. Helsinki Media, Blue Book, Hoylaamotie 1D, P.O. Box 100, FIN–00400 Helsinki, Finland; email: bluebook@helsinkimedia.fi; http://bluebook.helsinkimedia.fi. Includes manufacturers, service companies, chambers of commerce, and trade associations. 1,800 pages, published annually in Finnish.

Taseet ja Taustat (Finnish banks and limited companies). Helsinki Media, Blue Book, Hoylaamotie 1D, P.O. Box 100, FIN–00400 Helsinki, Finland; email: bluebook@helsinkimedia.fi; http://bluebook.helsinkimedia.fi. Lists 5,000 banks, insurance companies, and industrial firms. 780 pages, published annually.

American Companies in Finland

The following companies are classified by business area: Banking and Finance; Industrial Manufacturing; Retailing and Wholesaling; Service Industries; and Technology. Company information includes firm name, address, phone and fax numbers, and specific business. Your chances of securing employment abroad are substantially better if you contact the subsidiary company in Europe rather than the parent company in the United States. Keep in mind that the contact information for these companies can change pretty often. Before writing, be sure to confirm the address and phone number.

Banking and Finance

AON Finland
Oulunkylän tori 1
FIN–00640 Helsinki, Finland
Tel.: [358] 201266200
Fax: [358] 201266201
www.aon.com
(Insurance)

Chase Manhattan Bank
P.O. Box 50
Kaivokatu 10A
FIN–00100 Helsinki, Finland
www.chase.com
(Bank)

Citibank
Aleksanterinkatu 48A
FIN–00101 Helsinki, Finland
Tel.: [358] 9348871
Fax: [358] 934887388
www.citibank.com
(Bank)

Industrial Manufacturing

Bristol–Myers Squibb (Finland)
Metsänreidonkuja 8, Spektri–Trio
FIN–02130 Espoo, Finland
Tel.: [358] 925121230
Fax: [358] 925121240
(Pharmaceuticals)

Dow Suomi
Et Esplanadi 22 C

FIN–00130 Helsinki, Finland
Tel.: [358] 9 58 45 53 00
Fax: [358] 9 58 45 53 30
(Chemicals)

Esso
Kuunkehrä 6
FIN–02210 Espoo, Finland
Tel.: [358] 1055711
Fax: [358] 98030004
(Petroleum and petroleum products)

Ford
Malminkaari 9 B
FIN–00700 Helsinki, Finland
Tel.: [358] 9 35 17 00
Fax: [358] 9 3 74 30 81
(Motor vehicles)

Hoover
Lautamiehent 3
FIN–02770 Espoo, Finland
Tel.: [358] 94393000
Fax: [358] 943930030
(Household cleaning products)

Kodak
Mäkelänkau 91
FIN–00610 Helsinki, Finland
Tel.: [358] 9 58 40 71
Fax: [358] 9 58 40 78 90
(Photographic equipment)

Procter & Gamble Finland
Lars Sonckin kaari 10
FIN–02600 Espoo, Finland

Tel.: [358] 9 61 33 99
Fax: [358] 9 61 33 97 50
(Chemicals and household products)

Service Industries

KPMG Wideri
Mannerheimintie 20 B
FIN–00100 Helsinki, Finland
Tel.: [358] 9 69 39 31
Fax: [358] 9 69 39 33 99
www.kpmg.com
(Accounting services)

PriceWaterhouseCoopers Ltd.
Itämerentori A–rappu
FIN–00100 Helsinki, Finland
Tel.: [358] 9 2 28 00
Fax: [358] 9 17 41 02
www.pwcglobal.com
(Accounting services)

Radisson SAS Royal Hotel Helsinki
Runebergink 2
FIN–00100 Helsinki, Finland
Tel.: [358] 9 69 58 60 00
Fax: [358] 9 69 58 71 00
www.radisson.com
(Hotels)

Technology

Cisco Systems Finland
Jaakonkatu 2
FIN–01620 Vantaa, Finland
Tel.: [358] 9 87 80 61
Fax: [358] 9 87 80 63 00
www.cisco.com
(Computer networking systems)

Computer Associates Finland
Itälahdenkatu 15–17
FIN–00210 Helsinki, Finland
Tel.: [358] 9 34 84 84
Fax: [358] 9 34 84 85 85
(Computer consultants)

Hewlett–Packard
Keilaranta 1
FIN–02150 Espoo, Finland
Tel.: [358] 205350
Fax: [358] 205352020
(Printers and computers)

IBM
Laajalahdent 23
FIN–00330 Helsinki, Finland
Tel.: [359] 9 45 91
Fax: [359] 9 459 44 42
(Data processing equipment)

Major Blue Company
Nuijamiestent 3C
FIN–00400 Helsinki, Finland
Tel.: [358] 2050020
Fax: [358] 2050020
www.jdedwards.com
(Computer software)

Microsoft
Keilaranta 7
FIN–02150 Espoo, Finland
Tel.: [358] 9525501
Fax: [358] 98788778
www.microsoft.com
(Computer software)

Novell Finland
Lars Sonckin kaari 14
FIN–02600 Espoo, Finland
Tel.: [358] 9 50 29 51
Fax: [358] 9 50 29 53 00
www.novell.com
(Electronic data processing)

Unisys
Niittykatu 8
FIN–02200 Espoo, Finland
Tel.: [358] 9 4 52 81
Fax: [358] 9 4 52 84 00
(Computer networking software)

European Companies in Finland

The following major non–American firms operating in Finland. They can be either Finnish or based in another European country. They generally hire their own nationals first, but may employ Americans.

Banking and Finance

Alandsbanken
Nygatan 2
FIN–22101 Mariehamn, Finland
Tel.: [358] 204 29 011
www.alandsbanken.fi
(Bank)

Merita Asset Management
Fabianink 29 B
FIN–00100 Helsinki, Finland
Tel.: [358] 9 16 51
Fax: [358] 9 16 54 38 18
(Bank)

OKOBANK (Osuuspankkien Keskuspankki)
Teollisuuskatu 1b
FIN–00101 Helsinki, Finland
Tel.: [358] 9 4041
www.okobank.fi
(Commercial bank)

Pohjola–Yhtiöt Pääkonttori
Lapinmaentie 1
FIN–00013 Helsinki, Finland
Tel.: [358] 10 559 11
www.pohjola.fi
(Insurance)

Sampo
Yliopistonkatu 27, Sampo–Leonia
FIN–20075 Turku, Finland
Tel.: [358] 10 515 10
Fax: [358] 10 514 1811
www.sampo–leonia.fi
(Financial services)

Industrial Manufacturing

Ahlström Corp.
Eteläesplanadi 14
FIN–00101 Helsinki, Finland
Tel.: [358] 10 8880
Fax: [358] 10 888 4709
www.ahlstrom.com
(Paper manufacturing)

BP Finland Chemicals
Laversint 86
FIN–06830 Kulloonkylä Finland
Tel.: [358] 208 35 26 68
Fax: [358] 208 35 26 69
(Petrochemicals)

Fiskars
Mannerheimintie 14A
FIN–00101 Helsinki, Finland
Tel.: [358] 9 618 861
Fax: [358] 9 604 053
www.fiskars.fi
(Scissors)

Fortum
Keilaniemi
FIN–00048 Espoo, Finland
Tel.: [358] 10 451 1
Fax: [358] 10 45 24447
www.fortum.com
(Energy production and distribution)

Instrumentarium Corporation
Kuortaneenkatu 2, P.O. Box 100
FIN–00031 Helsinki, Finland
Tel.: [358] 10 394 11
Fax: [358] 9 146 4172
www.instrumentarium.fi
(Medical equipment and instrumentation)

Kemira
Porkkalankatu 3
FIN–00101 Helsinki, Finland
Tel.: [358] 10 8611
Fax: [358] 10 862 1119
www.kemira.com
(Chemicals)

Kone
Munkkiniemen Puistotie 25, P.O. Box 8
FIN–00331 Helsinki, Finland
Tel.: [358] 204 751
Fax: [358] 204 75 4496
www.kone.com
(Elevators)

Metsä Tissue Corporation
Italahdenkatu 15–17
FIN–00210 Helsinki, Finland
Tel.: [358] 1046 16
www.metsatissue.com
(Paper products)

Metso
Fabianinkatu 9 A, PO Box 1220
FIN–00101 Helsinki, Finland
Tel.: [358] 20 484 100
Fax: [358] 20 484 101
www.metsocorporation.com
(Fiber and paper machinery)

Orion Corporation Ltd.
Orionintie 1
FIN–02200 Espoo, Finland
Tel.: [358] 10 4291
Fax: [358] 10 429 2801
www.orion.fi
(Pharmaceuticals)

Outokumpu
Riihitontuntie 7 B, P.O. Box 140
FIN–02201 Espoo, Finland
Tel.: [358] 9 4211
Fax: [358] 9 421 3888
www.outokumpu.com
(Steel, metals)

Rautaruukki
Fredrikinkatu 51–53
FIN–00101 Helsinki, Finland
Tel.: [358] 9 41 7711
www.rautaruukki.com
(Steel)

Stora Enso
Kanavaranta 1
FIN–00101 Helsinki, Finland
Tel.: [358] 2046 131
Fax: [358] 2046 21471
www.storaenso.com
(Paper products)

Tamfelt
P.O. Box 427
FIN–33101 Tampere, Finland
Tel.: [358] 3 363 9111
Fax: [358] 3 356 0120
www.tamfelt.fi
(Textiles)

UPM–Kymmene Corporation
Etelä 2, P.O. Box 380
FIN–00101 Helsinki, Finland
Tel.: [358] 204 15 111
Fax: [358] 204 15 110
www.upm–kymmene.com
(Paper products)

Valmet Chemical Pulping
Teollisuusk 1
FIN–28100 Pori, Finland
Tel.: [358] 20 48 21 76
Fax: [358] 20 48 21 79
(Paper and cardboard manufacturing)

Retailing and Wholesaling

Kesko
Satamakatu 3
FIN–00016 Helsinki, Finland
Tel.: [358] 10 5311
Fax: [358] 9 657 465
www.kesko.fi
(Consumer goods, builder supplies)

Service Industries

Finnair
Tietotie 11A
FIN–01053 Finnair, Finland
Tel.: [358] 9 818 81
Fax: [358] 9 818 4092
www.finnair.com
(Airline)

Sanoma–WSOY
Erottajankatu 11A
FIN–00101 Helsinki, Finland
Tel.: [358] 105 1999
www.sanomawsoy.fi
(Publishing)

YIT Yntyma
Panuntie 11
FIN–00621 Helsinki, Finland
Tel.: [358] 20 433 111
www.yit.fi
(Building & construction services)

Technology

Elisa Communications Corporation
Korkeavuorenkatu 35–37
FIN–00131 Helsinki, Finland
Tel.: [358] 102 6000
Fax: [358] 102 625723
www.elisa.fi
(Telecommunications)

Nokia Corporation
Keilalahdentie 4
FIN–00045 Espoo, Finland
Tel.: [358] 7180 08 000
Fax: [358] 7180 38226
www.nokia.com
(Telecommunications equipment)

Sonera
Teollisuusk 15
FIN–00510 Helsinki, Finland

Tel.: [358] 20 4 01

Fax: [358] 20 4 06 00 25

www.sonera.com

(Telecommunications equipment)

Tietoenator
Kutojantie 10
FIN–02630 Espoo, Finland
Tel.: [358] 9 862 6000
www.tietoenator.com
(IT services)

International School in Finland

International School of Helsinki
Selkämerenkatu 11
FIN–00180 Helsinki, Finland
Tel.: [358] 9 686 61 60
Fax: [358] 9 685 66 99

Email: mainoffice@ish.edu.hel.fi
www.ish.edu.hel.fi
(International Baccalaureate curriculum,
kindergarten through grade 12)

Norway

Major employment centers: Oslo, Bergen

Major business language: Norwegian

Language skill index: More important with older people than with younger; more important in long–term and professional positions than for short–term work.

Currency: Kroner

Telephone country code: 47

Time zone: Eastern Standard Time + 6 hours

Punctuality index: This is a very punctual place.

Average daily temperature, high/low: January, 30°/20°; July, 73°/56° (Oslo)

Average number of days with precipitation: January, 18 days; July, 16 days

Best bet for employment:

> **For students:** An internship through the American–Scandinavian Foundation
>
> **Permanent jobs:** Merchant marine, fishing, and oil and gas industries

Chance of finding a job: Summer jobs, maybe. Others are hard to get.

Useful tip: There are two Norwegian languages, Bokmal and Nynorsk. Bokmal is used by the majority of the population and is the major language for business. Nynorsk is more common in areas with strong dialects and with the older generation. Although many Norwegians speak English, you'll be expected to demonstrate a good command of the Norwegian language in the workplace.

The Kingdom of Norway is located on the western part of the Scandinavian peninsula. Geographically, it extends northward from the North Sea for more than 1,000 miles along the Norwegian Sea into the Arctic Circle, farther north than any other European land. Sweden, Finland, and Russia all share borders with Norway on the east and the northeast. With an area of over 125,000 square miles, Norway is slightly larger than New Mexico.

Norway has very little vegetation; more than 70 percent of its land is covered by mountains, glaciers, and rivers, and is uninhabitable. Its numerous and deep fjords give Norway over 12,000 miles of oceanfront. Tens of thousands of islands off the coast form a sheltered coastal shipping channel. Norway also has sovereignty over five islands, the largest being Spitsbergen, in the Arctic Ocean. Norway north of Bodø experiences the midnight sun for a few weeks on either side of the summer solstice (June 21).

Norway's many deep fjords give it 12,000 miles of oceanfront.

The majority of the population lives in villages and on small, isolated farmsteads, with about two–thirds of the population concentrated in the valleys of the southeast and close to the coast in southern Norway. The population is extremely sparse in northern Norway and inland. Norway's overall population density is the lowest in Europe, excluding Iceland.

Norse Vikings raided England and the northwestern coast of Europe repeatedly from the eighth to the eleventh centuries. More than just pillagers, the Vikings explored Iceland, Greenland, and North America. This time period and its myths are chronicled in the Icelandic Sagas. In 872 A.D. the first ruler of a united Norway, Harold the Fairhaired, came to power.

Norway was part of the Danish kingdom for almost 500 years until Sweden won control in 1814. The country became officially independent in 1905, with a Danish prince on the Norwegian throne. Norway was committed to neutrality in World War I. The country was occupied by the Germans for five years during World War II. Abandoning its neutrality, Norway joined the NATO alliance in 1949. However, Norway did have good relations with its neighbor, the Soviet Union.

After a referendum in 1972, which divided the country, Norway decided not to join the European Common Market. In 1994, Norway once again rejected closer ties to other European nations when voters turned down a referendum to join the E.U. The current prime minister, Kjell Magne Bondevik, came to power in 2001 when his party, the Christian Democrats, replaced Labor and formed a coalition with the Conservatives, Liberals, and right–populist Progress Party.

Norse people speak Norwegian, a language similar to Icelandic and Swedish. Although they speak different languages, Scandinavians can often understand one another since the languages (except Finnish) are all descended from the language of the Vikings.

Banks are open from 8:15 a.m. to 3:30 p.m., Mondays through Fridays, and until 5 p.m. on Thursdays. From mid–May to August, all banks close at 3 p.m., except on Thursdays, when they close at 4 p.m. Stores are open from 9 a.m. to 4 p.m., weekdays, and until 7 p.m. on Thursdays and to 2 p.m. on Saturdays. Bad times for business trips include Easter and July and August.

Current Economic Climate

Norway has one of the highest standards of living in the world, but it is also extremely expensive, even compared with the rest of Scandinavia. The per capita income is one of the world's highest. Despite low unemployment (3.4 percent) and inflation rates (3.7 percent), the Norwegian economy has begun to slow from its impressive growth in the 1990s.

The country is richly endowed with natural resources — petroleum, hydropower, fish, forests, and minerals — and is highly dependent on its oil production and international oil prices. Only Saudi Arabia exports more oil than Norway. The Norwegian economy is, not surprisingly, responsive to levels of investment in the oil and gas sector. The government maintains a Petroleum Fund, a rough equivalent to America's Social Security Trust Fund, although it derives revenues from taxes on offshore oil and gas producers rather than from payroll taxes.

Although there are concerns about the long–term future developments in the non–oil sector, all sectors of the economy are currently operating at near capacity levels. The extensive welfare system helps propel public sector expenditures to more than 50 percent of GDP. A major shipping nation, Norway depends on international trade and largely exports raw materials and semi–processed goods.

The Norwegian labor force is composed of 7 percent agriculture workers, 47 percent industrial workers, 18 percent service workers, and 26 percent government employees. Only 3 to 4 percent of the country's surface area is cultivable; therefore, most grain is imported. The majority of the country's forests are owned privately and feed the large timber, furniture, and paper industries. Shipbuilding and shipping are the mainstays of the economy, and the abundant hydroelectric power provides the basis for a number of industries ranging from aluminum to steel. Norway's chief trading partners are the E.U., the Nordic countries, the United States, and Japan. Exports account for almost 40 percent of Norway's GNP.

Norway's 10 Largest Companies

(2001, based on market capitalization)

1. Den Norske Stats Oljeselskap
2. Norsk Hydro
3. Telenor
4. Orkla
5. DNB Holding

6. Tomra Systems
7. Storebrand
8. Norske Skogindustrier
9. Gjensidige Nor Sparebanken
10. Frontline

Getting Around in Norway

Norway's five railroad lines provide service from the capital city of Oslo to Bergen, Trodheim, and Bodø. Eurail and InterRail passes are valid on all trains in Norway. Buses also provide extensive service, though bus fares are rather expensive. The numerous airlines in Scandinavia also have flights with reasonable fares and discount for those traveling extensively within the Scandinavian countries. Norway's main domestic airlines — SAS, Braathens and Widerø Norsk Air — fly to almost 50 airports scattered across the country. Norway is a big country and distances are great, which means air travel should be considered, even by budget travelers. Ferries are available everywhere along the coasts. Hydrofoils and car ferries are other options in traveling across the water.

Employment Regulations and Outlook for Americans

A ban has been in effect since 1975 on the issuance of first–time work permits to foreign nationals in Norway. The ban was put in place to improve conditions for foreigners already living in Norway and to develop a program for their educational, housing, and social needs. Although Norway's strict immigration policies are beginning to liberalize as the country's population ages, visas and work permits are granted only if the foreigner demonstrates a specific need to work in Norway (such as family reunification, cultural exchange, study, or research) or fills a specific labor need unavailable in the domestic workforce.

You must file the application for a work permit in your home country before you enter Norway. An offer of employment is required to apply for a work permit. Workers on offshore drilling rigs, students studying at Norwegian schools who desire part–time or summer work, and summer job seekers during the period May 15 to September 30 are exempt from this ban and may apply for a work permit after they have arrived in Norway. Special exemptions may be made for people with special skills (such as musicians or scientists), trainees, au pairs, and youth exchanges.

Summer jobs are gaining popularity among Norwegian youth, so it is increasingly difficult to find summer employment. Your chances of obtaining a job are greater both before and after the period between June 15 and July 15, when the influx of job–seeking Norwegian youths into the labor market is at its peak. Hotels can be a good bet for lucrative work.

Short–term and Temporary Work

There best opportunities in Norway are in agriculture or as an au pair. In addition to the organizations listed below, Au Pair in Europe, described in Chapter 9, recruits for positions in Norway.

Atlantis Youth Exchange
Kirkegata 32
N–0153 Olso, Norway
Tel.: [47] 22 47 71 70
Email: post@atlantis–u.no
www.atlantis–u.no
The Working Guest program places people ages 18 to 30 with Norwegian families on farms. The program is intended as a cultural exchange program — participants are expected to take part in all aspects of the family's regular activities. In exchange, participants are expected to help with tasks connected to the farming business. Atlantis also manages an au pair program in Norway.

Exis
Rebslagergade 3
DK–6400 Sønderborg, Denmark
Tel.: [45] 74 42 97 49
Fax: [45] 74 42 97 47
Email: info@exis.dk
www.exis.dk
Exis places au pairs in Denmark, Norway, and Iceland. Exis offers three au pair programs: regular au pairs work about 30 hours per week; an Au Pair Plus works about 35 hours for higher wages; and a Mother's Helper works about 40 hours per week for higher wages.

Internship Programs

There are opportunities for students to gain professional experience, usually in technical fields. The American–Scandinavian Foundation and IAESTE coordinate the most extensive programs; AIESEC also places trainees in internships in Norway. See Chapter 9 for details.

Volunteer Opportunities

The Year Abroad Program sponsored by the International Christian Youth Exchange places students in volunteer projects in Norway. Participants work on various projects, including work in health care, construction, education, and conservation. Service Civil International and Volunteers for Peace coordinate service projects and work camps in Norway. They and other sources of volunteer opportunities are described in Chapter 9.

Resources for Further Information

Newspapers in Norway

Adresseavisen
Tel.: [47] 72 50 00 00
Fax: [47] 72 580 623
www.adressa.no

Aftenposten
Tel.: [47] 22 86 30 00
Fax: [47] 22 863 817
www.aftenposten.no

Bergens Tidende
Tel.: [47] 55 21 45 00
Fax: [47] 55 32 49 44
www.bergens–tidende.no

Dagens Naeringsliv
Tel.: [47] 22 00 10 00
Fax: [47] 22 00 11 10
www.dn.no

Useful Websites for Job Seekers

The Internet is a good place to begin your job search. Many Scandinavian employers list job vacancies, especially those in technical fields, on the web. There are also many websites that provide useful information for job searchers researching the Norwegian job market.

Companies in Norway
www.randburg.com/no/index.html
The site targets investors interested in Norwegian companies, but the information will be helpful for job seekers.

deltidsjobb.no
www.deltidsjobb.no
Features over 120 positions, a resume database, and an email notification service. Written in Norwegian.

FINN Jobb
www.finn.no/finn/job
Lists 2,700 jobs. Written in Norwegian.

jobb direkte
www.jobbdirekte.no
Features about 500 positions throughout Norway, a resume database, and an email notification service. Written in Norwegian.

Jobbguiden
www.jobbguiden.no
Features about 300 positions throughout the country. Written in Norwegian.

jobbnett
www.jobbnett.no

Includes about 300 positions throughout Norway and a resume posting service. Written in Norwegian.

jobbnord
www.jobbnord.com
Features a limited number of positions and an email job notification service. Written in Norwegian.

jobbtilbud.no
www.jobbtilbud.no
Features nearly 8,100 vacancies, a resume database, and a directory of major employers in Norway. Written in Norwegian.

Manpower Norway
www.manpower.no
Manpower is a recruitment agency. Its Norwegian site features a database of private sector jobs.

StepStone
www.stepstone.no
One of Europe's leading online recruitment sites. Features private sector and education jobs in Norway.

Embassies and Consular Offices

American embassies and consulates have commercial and/or economic sections that can provide you with business information and explain aspects of the local economy. Inquiries about business opportunities should be addressed either to "Commercial Officer" or "Commercial Section."

Representation of Norway in the United States

Embassy of Norway
2720 34th Street NW
Washington, DC 20008
Tel.: (202) 333–6000
Fax: (202) 337–0870
www.norway.org

Norwegian Consulates General:

New York, (212) 421–7333; Houston, (713) 521–2900; Miami, (305) 358–4386; Minneapolis, (612) 332–3338; San Francisco, (415) 986–0766

Representation of the United States in Norway

American Embassy
Drammensveien 18
N–0244 Oslo 2, Norway

Tel.: [47] 22 44 85 50
Fax: [47] 22 44 33 63
www.usa.no

Chambers of Commerce

Chambers of commerce consist of member firms in both countries interested in international trade. These are appropriate companies to initially target in the job search.

American Chamber of Commerce in Norway
P.O. Box 2604 Solli
N–0203 Oslo, Norway
Tel.: [47] 22 546 040
Fax: [47] 22 546 720
Email: amchamno@online.no
www.am–cham.com

New York, NY 10022
Tel.: (212) 421–1653
Fax: (212) 838–0374
www.norway.org

Norwegian Trade & Technology Office
20 California Street, 6th Floor
San Francisco, CA 94111
Tel.: (415) 986–0770
Fax: (415) 986–6025
www.ntc–usa.org
–and–
821 Marquette Avenue
Minneapolis, MN 55402–2961
Tel.: (612) 332 3338
Fax: (612) 332 1386

Association of Norwegian Chambers of Commerce
P.O. Box 2900
N–0230 Oslo, Norway
Tel.: [47] 22 541 755
Fax: [47] 22 561 700
www.chamber.no

Norwegian–American Chamber of Commerce
800 Third Avenue

World Trade Center in Norway

This world trade center usually includes many foreign companies that conduct business in Norway.

World Trade Center Oslo
P.O. Box 334
N–1379 Nesbru, Norway

Tel.: [47] 66 85 8700
Fax : [47] 66 85 8709
Email: arnt.sundli@sundli–gruppen.no

Other Informational Organizations

Foreign government missions in the United States, such as tourist offices, can furnish visas and information on work permits and other regulations. They may also offer economic and business information about Norway.

Norwegian Information Service in the U.S.
825 Third Avenue, 38th Floor
New York, NY 10022
Tel.: (212) 421–7333
Fax: (212) 754–0583

Email: cg.newyork@mfa.no
www.norway.org

Norwegian Tourist Board
655 Third Avenue, Suite 1810
New York, NY 10017

Tel.: (212) 885–9700
Fax: (212) 885–9710
www.visitnorway.com

Norwegian Trade Council
800 Third Avenue, 23rd floor

New York, NY 10022
Tel.: (212) 421 9210
Fax: (212) 838 0374
Email: new.york@ntc.no
www.ntc.no

Business Directories

Although not always easy to find, business directories can prove invaluable in the international job search. Your best bet for locating these directories is to begin in the reference section of any public or university library. Most directories list company names, addresses, products, and phone numbers. Some directories include executive names and titles and financial information about the company. These sources provide you with the names of the people to contact for employment information as well as financial data, which can tell you how strong a company's position in a country may be.

Kompass Norge. Kompass Norge, Postboks 647, N–4003 Stavanger, Norway; email: firmapost@kompass.no. Lists 17,000 service, distributing, and manufacturing companies. 2,875 pages, published annually.

Largest Companies in Norway. Okonomisk Literatur, Langkaia 1, Havnelageret, Postboks 457, N–0511 Oslo, Norway; email: post@ekolit.no; www.largestcompanies.com. Lists 10,000 of the largest companies in Norway. 800 pages, published annually.

Norwegian American Chamber of Commerce Membership Directory. Norwegian American Chamber of Commerce, 800 Third Avenue, New York, NY 10022. Contains 1,000 American and Norwegian companies involved in trade and investment in the two countries. 200 pages, published biennially.

Norwegian Directory of Commerce. S.M. Bryde, Lorenveien 68, Postboks 6377, N–0604 Oslo, Norway. Includes information on over 200,000 industrial, trade and service companies. 4,000 pages in two volumes, published annually.

American Companies in Norway

The following companies are classified by business area: Banking and Finance; Industrial Manufacturing; Retailing and Wholesaling; Service Industries; and Technology. Company information includes firm name, address, phone and fax numbers, and specific business. Your chances of achieving employment abroad are substantially better if you contact the subsidiary company in Europe rather than the parent company in the United States. Keep in mind that the contact information for these companies changes pretty often. Before writing to one, be sure to confirm its address and phone number.

Banking and Finance

Citibank
Tordenskioldsgaten 8/10
N–0160 Oslo, Norway
Tel.: [47] 22 00 96 00
Fax: [47] 22 00 96 22
(Commercial bank)

JPMorgan Europe
Fridtjof Nansens P/2, 5th Floor
N–0160 Oslo, Norway
Tel.: [47] 22 94 19 19
Fax: [47] 22 42 58 61
(Bank)

Industrial Manufacturing

Amerada Hess Norge
Langkaia 1
N–0150 Oslo, Norway
Tel.: [47] 22 94 00
Fax: [47] 22 42 63 27
(Oil and natural gas)

Baker Hughes Norge
Ekofiskveien 1
N–4056 Tananger, Norway
Tel.: [47] 51 71 75 00
Fax: [47] 51 71 75 01
www.bakerhughes.com
(Oil tools)

Colgate–Palmolive Norge
Vollsv 13B
N–1325 Lysaker, Norway
Tel.: [47] 67 59 00 25
Fax: [47] 67 59 18 64
(Hygiene products)

Esso Norge (ExxonMobil)
Drammensveien 149
N–0212 Oslo, Norway
Tel.: [47] 22 66 30 30
Fax: [47] 22 66 37 77
(Petroleum refining and marine lubricants)

Halliburton
Eldfiskveien 1
N–4065 Stavanger, Norway
Tel.: [47] 51 83 70 00
Fax: [47] 51 83 83 83
(Oil and gas exploration)

Kraft Foods
Johan Throne Holsts plass 1
N–0502 Oslo, Norway
Tel.: [47] 22 04 40 22
Fax: [47] 22 37 96 48
(Confections)

Eli Lilly Norge
Grensev 99
N–0663 Oslo, Norway
Tel.: [47] 22 88 18 00
Fax: [47] 22 88 18 50
www.lilly.com
(Pharmaceuticals)

Norske Conoco
Tangen 7
N–4070 Randaberg, Norway
Tel.: [47] 51 41 60 00
Fax: [47] 51 41 05 55
(Oil and gas exploration)

3M Norge
Hvamveien 6
N–2026 Skjetten, Norway
Tel.: [47] 06 3 84
Fax: [47] 63 84 17 88
(Surgical dressings, tapes)

Wrigley Scandinavia
Ryensvingen 15
N–0680 Oslo, Norway
Tel.: [47] 22 08 32 10
Fax: [47] 22 08 32 20
(Chewing gum)

Service Industries

Boston Consulting Group
Karl Johans Gate 45
N–0162 Oslo, Norway
Tel.: [47] 23 10 20 00
Fax: [47] 23 10 20 99
www.bcg.com
(Management consulting)

Burson–Marsteller
Sjølyst Plass 4
N–0278 Oslo, Norway
Tel.: [47] 23 16 45 00
Fax: [47] 23 16 45 01
www.bm.com
(Advertising)

Deloitte & Touche Advokater
Karenlyst Alle 20

N–0278 Oslo, Norway
Tel.: [47] 23 27 96 00
Fax: [47] 23 27 96 01
(Financial advisors, consultants)

Korn/Ferry International
Munkedamsvn. 45
N–0250 Oslo, Norway
Tel.: [47] 22 82 39 00
Fax: [47] 22 82 39 01
www.kornferry.com
(Executive search)

Technology

Computer Associates Norway
Fornebuv. 7/9
N–1366 Lysaker, Norway
Tel.: [47] 67 52 40 00
Fax: [47] 67 52 40 01
www.cai.com
(Computer systems consulting)

Dell Computer
Lysaker 8
Lysaker Torg 8
N–1325 Lysaker, Norway

Tel.: [47] 67 11 68 00
Fax: [47] 67 11 68 65
www.dell.com
(Computers)

**Electronic Data
Systems (EDS) Norway**
Stenersg. 1 E
N–0050 Oslo, Norway
Tel.: [47] 22 93 83 00
Fax: [47] 22 93 83 01
(Computer consultants)

IBM Norway
Rosenholmv. 25
N–1411 Kolbotn, Norway
Tel.: [47] 66 99 80 00
Fax: [47] 66 99 82 42
(Office equipment)

Motorola Norway
Tevlingvn.23
N–1086 Oslo, Norway
Tel.: [47] 23 28 80 00
Fax: [47] 23 28 80 01
www.mot.com
(Cell phones and semiconductors)

European Companies in Norway

These major non–American firms conduct business in Norway. They can be either Norwegian or based in another European country. They generally hire their own nationals first but may also employ Americans.

Banking and Finance

DNB Holding
Stranden 21
N–0021 Oslo, Norway
Tel.: [47] 22 48 10 50
www.DnB.no
(Bank)

Gjensidige NOR
Kirkegaten 18
N–0107 Oslo, Norway
Tel.: [47] 22 31 90 50
www.nor.no
(Bank)

Storebrand
Filipstad Brygge 1
N–0114 Oslo, Norway
Tel.: [47] 22 31 50 50
www.storebrand.no

(Insurance)

Industrial Manufacturing

Bergesen
Drammensveien 106
N–0204 Oslo, Norway
Tel.: [47] 22 12 05 05
www.bergesen.no
(Shipping)

**Den norske stats oljeselskap
(Statoil)**
Forusbeen 50
N–4035 Stavanger, Norway
Tel.: [47] 51 99 00 00
Fax: [47] 51 99 00 50
www.statoil.com
(Oil & gas exploration)

Elkem
Hoffsveien 65 B, Majorstuen
N–0303 Oslo, Norway
Tel.: [47] 22 45 01 00
www.elkem.com
(Metals)

Frontline
Brygggegten 3
N–0250 Oslo, Norway
Tel.: [47] 22 01 75 00
Fax: [47] 22 01 75 10
(Shipping)

Kvaerner
Prof. Kohts vei 15
N–1325 Lysaker, Norway
Tel.: [47] 67 51 30 00
Fax: [47] 67 51 31 00
www.kvaerner.com
(Construction, shipbuilding)

Norsk Hydro
Bygdøy allé 2
N–0240 Oslo 2, Norway
Tel.: [47] 22 53 81 00
Fax: [47] 22 53 27 25
www.hydro.com
(Aluminum, energy, & chemicals)

Norske Skogindustrier
Oksenoyveien 80
N–1366 Lysaker, Norway
Tel.: [47] 67 59 90 00
Fax: [47] 67 59 91 81
www.norske–skog.com
(Paper products)

Opticom
Stoperigata 2
N–0124 Oslo, Norway
Tel.: [47] 23 01 12 40
www.opticomasa.com
(Optics)

Orkla
N–0213 Skoyen, Norway
Tel.: [47] 22 54 40 00
www.orkla.com
(Detergents, cosmetics, and frozen foods)

Petroleum Geo–Services
Strandveien 4
N–1366 Lysaker, Norway
Tel.: [47] 67 52 66 00

Fax: [47] 67 53 68 83
www.pgs.com
(Petroleum services)

Smedvig
Finnestadveien 28, P.O. Box 110
N–4001 Stavanger, Norway
Tel.: [47] 51 50 99 00
Fax: [47] 51 50 96 88
www.smedvig.no
(Off–shore drilling)

Tomra Systems
Drengsrudhagen 2
N–1371 Asker, Norway
Tel.: [47] 66 79 91 00
Fax: [47] 66 79 91 11
www.tomra.com
(Automated beverage systems)

Service Industries

NCL Holding
Grensen 3, PO Box 1885 Vika
N–0124 Oslo, Norway
Tel.: [47] 22 944 120
Fax: [47] 22 830 014
www.ncl.com
(Cruise ships)

Schibsted
Apotekergaten 10
N–0107 Oslo, Norway
Tel.: [47] 23 10 66 00
Fax: [47] 23 10 66 01
ww.schibsted.no
(Publishing)

Star Shipping
Fortunen 1
N–5809 Bergen, Norway
Tel.: [47] 55 23 96 00
Fax: [47] 55 23 25 30
(Shipping company)

StepStone
Calmeyersgate 8
N–0183 Oslo, Norway
Tel.: [47] 22 03 3333
www.stepstone.com
(Online recruitment)

Technology

EDB Business Partner
Ruseløkkveien 6

N–0251 Oslo, Norway
Tel.: [47] 23 32 45 00
Fax: [47] 22 83 25 28
www.edb.com
(Computer systems and consulting)

Merkantildata
Brynsalleen 2–4
N–0605 Oslo, Norway
Tel.: [47] 22 09 50 00
www.merkantildata.com
(Computer software and consulting)

Opera Software
Waldemar Thranes gate 98

N–0175 Oslo, Norway
Tel.: [47] 24 16 40 00
Fax: [47] 24 16 40 01
www.opera.com
(Software)

Telenor
Snarøyveien 30
N–1331 Fornebu, Norway
Tel.: [47] 810 77 000
Fax: [47] 22 20 79 97
www.telenor.com
(Telecommunications)

International Schools in Norway

International School of Bergen
Vilhelm Bjerknesvei 15 Landäs
N–5081 Bergen, Norway
Tel.: [47] 55 30 63 30
Fax: [47] 55 30 63 31
Email: murison@isb.gs.hl.no
www.isb.gs.hl.no

International School of Stavanger
Treskeveien 3
N–4043 Hafrsfjord, Norway
Tel.: [47] 51 55 43 00
Fax: [47] 51 55 43 01
Email: intschol@iss.stavanger.rl.no
www.iss.stavanger.rl.no

Sweden

Major employment center: Stockholm
Major business language: Swedish
Language skill index: Many business people are fluent in English. You will likely fare much better, though, by speaking Swedish rather than expecting others to accommodate you.
Currency: Krona
Telephone country code: 46
Time zone: Eastern Standard Time + 6 hours
Punctuality index: The Swedes are always punctual.
Average daily temperature, high/low: January, 31°/23°; July, 70°/55° (Stockholm)
Average number of days with precipitation: January, 12 days; July, 12 days
Best bet for employment:
  For students: An internship through the American–Scandinavian Foundation
  Permanent jobs: You'll need to speak some Swedish and possess a special skill
Chance of finding a job: Summer jobs: possible. Others: very difficult
Useful tip: Swedes are known for their long life expectancy. Life expectancy at birth is 74 for men, 80 for women.

The Kingdom of Sweden is located on the eastern section of the Scandinavian peninsula. The Kjólen Mountains form the Norwegian border on the west. To the east, Finland lies across the Gulf of Bothnia, and Russia is across the Baltic Sea. Denmark is across the Kattegat to the south. Poland and Germany also lie to the south across the Baltic Sea. The north contains numerous lakes, while the rest of the country consists of forest lands and plains.

Sweden, the third–largest nation in Western Europe after France and Spain, is twice the size of Britain but doesn't have many more citizens than London. Sweden is about the size of California. About 95 percent of the population belong to the established Lutheran Church. Rural Swedes speak dialects that other Swedes have a hard time understanding. Otherwise, Sweden is extremely homogeneous.

Known for progressive attitudes, some Swedes are downright puritanical when it comes to alcohol. Liquor stores are open inconvenient hours, and drunk drivers are severely punished.

The Swedes have lived in their country for over 5,000 years, longer than any other people in Europe. Gothic tribes from Sweden invaded the Roman Empire, and later Swedes entered Russia. In the eleventh century, Sweden was converted to Christianity. The Riksdag, Sweden's parliament, was first called in 1435. The Danish kings ruled Sweden from 1397 until a rebellion led by Gustavus I in 1523.

By the seventeenth century, Sweden had become a major European power, controlling various Baltic provinces and playing an important role in the Thirty Years War. In 1721 Russia, Poland, and Denmark forced Sweden to relinquish most of its Baltic empire, including Finland. Norway was acquired in the Napoleonic Wars and held until 1905.

Sweden maintained a policy of neutrality in both world wars. Today, Sweden belongs to no military alliance but is a member of the European Free Trade Association. In 1995, Sweden joined the E.U., a move that some argued went against Sweden's historic policy of neutrality (Sweden had not joined the E.U. during the Cold War because it was incompatible with neutrality). Others viewed the move as a natural extension of the economic cooperation with the rest of Europe that had been developing since the early 1970s. In response to this controversy, Sweden reserved the right to opt out of any future E.U. defense alliance.

In polls taken a few years after the referendum, many Swedes indicated that they were unhappy with Sweden's membership in the E.U. After Sweden successfully hosted its first presidency of the E.U. in the first half of 2001, however, many people developed a more positive attitude toward their membership. Swedes are even becoming more supportive to membership of E.M.U according to recent polls: Prime Minister Göran Persson has announced that there could be a referendum on Sweden's adoption of the euro in 2003.

Sweden's extensive social welfare state has become a model for other developed countries. However, the Social Democrats, the architects of the system, warn that the cradle–to–grave welfare system is about to end.

Swedes appreciate visitors who have an understanding of the differences between the Scandinavian countries. Although they possess many progressive attitudes, some Swedes are practically puritanical when it comes to alcohol. Liquor is only available from government stores that are open inconvenient hours, and drunk drivers are severely punished.

Most young Swedes speak English, and if you are looking for a job in a tourist spot, it may not be necessary to learn Swedish. Many business people are fluent in English and one other language. In the Swedish alphabet, the vowels å, ä, and ö go at the end. Also, "v" and "w" are alphabetized as the same letter; for example, "van" comes after "wait" and before "was." Similarly, the letter "c" is alphabetized with the "ks." Although Scandinavians speak different languages, they can often understand one another since, with the exception of Finnish, all Scandinavian languages are descended from the language of the Vikings.

Banks, post offices, and most businesses are usually open weekdays from 9 a.m. to 5 p.m. or 6 p.m., and until the afternoon on Saturdays.

Current Economic Climate

Aided by peace and neutrality during the whole twentieth century, Sweden has achieved an enviable standard of living under a mixed system of high–tech capitalism and extensive welfare benefits. It is also one of the most socialized countries in the world. Sweden joined the E.U. in 1995, but decided not to join the EMU at its outset in January 1999. Unemployment is currently at about 4.2 percent. The Swedish tax rates are among the highest in the world.

Approximately 24 percent of the workforce is involved in manufacturing, 5 percent in agriculture, and 63 percent in the service sector, although nearly 35 percent of service employees work for the government. More than 40 percent of Sweden's industrial production is exported. Major industries include machinery, automobiles, steel products, wood products, and agriculture. Sweden's primary trading partners are Norway, Germany, Denmark, and Finland.

Sweden's 10 Largest Companies

(2001, based on market capitalization)

1. Telefonaktiebolaget LM Ericsson
2. Nordea
3. H & M Hennes & Mauritz
4. Telia
5. Svenska Handelsbanken
6. Investor
7. Skandia

8. Aktiebolaget Volvo
9. Securitas
10. Skandinaviska Enskilda Banken

Getting Around in Sweden

Sweden's rail network extends to all the south and most of the north, but fares are expensive. It is usually better to take the bus when traveling off the beaten track. Eurail and InterRail passes are valid on all trains but not buses. Ferries are also available for traveling in the gulf. The numerous Scandinavian airlines offer discounts for those traveling extensively in the Scandinavian region.

Employment Regulations and Outlook for Americans

Finding employment in Sweden is difficult. Strict labor regulations are compounded by the fact that Sweden is, after all, a small country: there simply aren't that many jobs to go around. The country enjoys a high standard of living, but employment opportunities for foreigners are especially limited. Swedish workers are well–educated and highly skilled, further limiting demand for foreign workers. American citizens intending to work in Sweden must possess a work permit upon arrival.

There are strict limits on the number of foreigners allowed to work in Sweden. Students, however, are allowed to work in the summer, provided they have obtained their work permits before entering the country. Even so, given the difficulty of locating employment, most seasonal work will very likely be arranged on the black market. Tourist work may be found on the western coast, although even hotel work can be difficult to find. Malmö, across from Denmark, has the largest number of restaurants in the country and four youth hostels. Some agricultural work may be found in the southern counties as well. Stockholm and Göteberg both have port facilities that might on occasion require additional manual workers.

Short–term and Temporary Work

The best bet for casual work in Sweden, as in all of Scandinavia, is as an au pair. In addition to the agency below, Au Pair in Europe places nannies in Sweden. It is described in Chapter 9 as are additional resources.

Au Pair Center
Nedre Långvinkelsgatan 36
SE–252 34 Helsingborg, Sweden
Tel.: [46] 42 12 60 45
Fax: [46] 42 12 60 25
Email: sweden@aupaircenter.com

www.aupaircenter.com

The Au Pair Center places young people with families in Sweden and Poland. Au pairs are expected to work for 30 hours per week.

Internship Programs

There are opportunities for students to gain professional experience, usually in technical fields. The American–Scandinavian Foundation and IAESTE coordinate the most extensive programs. AIESEC also places student trainees in Sweden. See Chapter 9 for details and more resources.

Volunteer Opportunities

There are many organizations that coordinate work camps in Sweden. International Cultural Youth Exchange, Service Civil International and Volunteers for Peace partner with local organizations to organize work camps and other service exchange programs. See Chapter 9 for details.

Resources for Further Information

Newspapers in Sweden

Arbetetarbladet
Tel.: [46] 26 15 93 00
Fax: [46] 26 18 52 70
www.arbetarbladet.se

Dagens Industri
Tel.: [46] 8 736 50 00
Fax: [46] 8 736 58 64
www.di.se

Dagens Nyheter
Tel.: [46] 8 738 10 00

Fax: [46] 8 738 21 90
www.dn.se

Götesberg–Posten
Tel.: [46] 31 62 40 00
Fax: [46] 31 80 27 69
www.gp.se

Sydsvenska Dagbladet
Tel.: [46] 40 28 12 00
Fax: [46] 40 93 54 76
www.sydsvenskan.se

Useful Websites for Job Seekers

The Internet is a good place to begin your job search. Many Scandinavian employers list job vacancies, especially those in technical fields, on the web. There are also many websites that provide useful information for job searchers researching the Swedish job market.

**Arbetsformedlingen
(Swedish employment service)**
www.ams.se
Features a database of private sector jobs. Written in Swedish.

CSjobb
http://csjobb.idg.se/
Features information technology jobs and a resume bank.

Jobfinder.se
www.jobfinder.se
Includes a database of private sector jobs and a resume bank. It also includes job search information relevant for new college graduates. Written in Swedish.

Manpower Sweden
www.manpower.se
Manpower is a recruitment agency. Its Swedish site features a database of private sector jobs.

Mercuri–Urval
www.mercuri–urval.com
Mercuri–Urval is also a recruitment agency. The Swedish site, which can be viewed in English, features some professional private sector jobs.

StepStone Sweden
www.stepstone.se
One of Europe's leading online recruitment sites. Features over 800 private sector and education jobs in Sweden.

Embassies and Consular Offices

American embassies and consulates have commercial and/or economic sections that can provide you with business information and explain aspects of the local economy. Inquiries about business opportunities should be addressed either to "Commercial Officer" or "Commercial Section."

Representation of Sweden in the United States

Embassy of Sweden
1501 M Street NW, Suite 900
Washington DC 20005
Tel.: (202) 467–2600
Fax: (202) 467–2699
www.swedish–embassy.org/

Consulates General of Sweden:

Chicago, (312) 781–6262; Los Angeles, (310) 445–4008; New York, (212) 583–2550; Boston, (617) 451–3456; Atlanta, (678) 686–1006

Representation of the United States in Sweden

American Embassy
Dag Hammarskjölds Väg 31
SE–115 89 Stockholm, Sweden

Tel.: [46] 8 783 5300
Fax: [46] 8 661 1964
www.usis.usemb.se

Chambers of Commerce

Chambers of commerce consist of member firms in both countries that are interested in international trade. These are appropriate companies to initially target in the job search.

American Chamber of Commerce in Sweden
P.O. Box 16050
SE–103 Stockholm, Sweden
Tel.: [46] 8 5061 2610
Fax: [46] 8 5061 2910
Email: mara@gsh.se

Swedish–American Chamber of Commerce
599 Lexington Avenue, 13th Floor
New York, NY 10022
Tel.: (212) 838–5530
Fax: (212) 755–7953
www.saccny.org

Stockholm Chamber of Commerce
P.O. Box 16050
SE–10321 Stockholm, Sweden
Tel.: [46] 8 555 10000
Fax: [46] 8 566 31600
Email: stock@chamber.se
www.chamber.se

Swedish–American Chamber of Commerce of the Western U.S.
564 Market Street, Suite 305
San Francisco, CA 94104
Tel.: (415) 781 4188
Fax: (415) 781 4189
Email: saccsf@ix.netcom.com
www.sacc–usa.org/sanfrans

World Trade Center in Sweden

The world trade center in Stockholm includes many foreign companies that conduct business in Sweden.

Scandinavian World Trade Center
Klarabergsviadukten 70

P.O. Box 70354
SE–107 24 Stockholm, Sweden

Tel.: [46] 8 700 45 00
Fax: [46] 8 700 4571

Email: info@wtc.se
www.wtc.se

Other Informational Organizations

Foreign government missions in the United States, such as national tourist offices, can furnish visas and information on work permits and other important regulations. They may also offer economic and business information about the country.

Swedish Information Service
P.O. Box 7542
SE–103 93 Stockholm, Sweden
Tel.: [46] 8 789 2400
Fax: [46] 8 789 2450
Email: info@stoinfo.se
www.stockholmtown.com

Swedish National Tourist Office
P.O. Box 4649
New York, NY 10163–4649
Tel.: (212) 855–9700
Fax: (212) 855–9710
www.goscandinavia.com

Business Directories

Although not always easy to find, business directories can prove invaluable in the international job search. Your best bet for locating these directories is to begin in the reference section of any public or university library. Most directories list company names, addresses, products, and phone numbers. Some directories include executive names and titles and financial information about the company. These sources provide you with the names of the people to contact for employment information as well as financial data that can tell you how strong a company's position in a country may be.

Kompass Sweden. Kompass Sverige, Torsgatan 21, SE–11390 Stockholm, Sweden. Over 12,000 service, distributing, and manufacturing companies, including wholesalers, manufacturers, importers/exporters, and distributors. Two volumes, published annually in English, French, German, Spanish, and Swedish.

Sweden's Largest Companies. Ekonomisk Litteratur, P.O. Box 14113, SE–16714 Bromma, Sweden; email: info@ekolitt.se; www.ekolitt.se. Distributed in the United States by Nesgan Inc., 1200 Westlake Avenue N., Suite 512, Seattle, WA 98109. Includes 10,000 firms in Sweden. 1,000 pages, published annually.

Swedish–American Chamber of Commerce Membership Directory. Swedish–American Chamber of Commerce, 599 Lexington Avenue, New York, NY 10022; email: business.services@saccny.org. 1,800 United States and 200 Swedish companies involved in commercial trade between the two countries. 300 pages, published annually.

Swedish Export Directory. Swedish Trade Council, Box 5513, SE–11485 Stockholm, Sweden; email: info@swedishtrade.se; www.sed.swedishtrade.se. Approximately 2,500 Swedish manufacturers and exporters involved in international trade. 720 pages, published annually.

Swedish Technical Directory. Forlags AG Fournir, Tideliusgatan 42–44; SE–11869 Stockholm, Sweden. Lists major technical companies and products. 624 pages, published triennially.

Western Sweden Chamber of Commerce List of Members. Western Sweden Chamber of Commerce, P.O. Box 5253, SE–40225 Gothenburg, Sweden. Lists over 2,300 members involved with foreign trade. 220 pages, updated biennially (spring of even years).

American Companies in Sweden

The following companies are classified by business area: Banking; Industrial Manufacturing; Retailing and Wholesaling; Service Industries; and Technology. Company information includes firm name, address, phone number, and specific business. Your chances of securing employment abroad are substantially better if you contact the subsidiary company in Europe rather than the parent company in the U.S. Contact information changes frequently; confirm a company's address and phone number before you contact it.

Banking

Citibank International
Norrlandsgatan 15 9c
SE–111 43 Stockholm, Sweden
Tel.: [46] 8 723 34 00
Fax: [46] 8 611 48 43
(Bank)

Industrial Manufacturing

Abbott Scandinavia
Gårdsv 8, 5 tr
SE–169 70 Solna, Sweden
Tel.: 46 8 546 567 00
Fax: 46 8 546 569 00
(Pharmaceuticals)

Bristol–Myers Squibb
Gustavslundsvägen 145
SE–167 15 Bromma, Sweden
Tel.: [46] 8 704 71 00
Fax: [46] 8 704 89 60
(Pharmaceutical products)

Grace
Berg Alle 1
SE–254 52 Helsingborg, Sweden
Tel.: [46] 42 16 78 00
Fax: [46] 42 16 78 05
www.grace.com
(Chemicals)

Johnson & Johnson
Staffans Vag 2
SE–192 78 Sollentuna, Sweden
Tel.: [46] 8 626 22 00
Fax: [46] 8 754 58 50
(Hospital products)

Kodak Nordic Jakobsberg
Kanalv 10 A
SE–194 61 Upplands Väsby, Sweden
Tel.: [46] 8 555 635 00
Fax: [46] 8 555 637 30
(Photographic equipment)

Pfizer
Nytorpsv 36
SE–183 53 Täby, Sweden
Tel.: [46] 8 519 062 00
Fax: [46] 8 519 062 12
(Pharmaceuticals)

3M Svenska
Bollstanäsv 3, Rotsunda
SE–192 78 Sollentuna, Sweden
Tel.: [46] 40 8 92 21 00
Fax: [46] 40 8 754 55 37
(Textiles, chemicals, machinery)

Service Industries

Bain & Company Nordic Inc USA Sverigefiliale
Regeringsg 38
SE–111 56 Stockholm, Sweden
Tel.: [46] 8 412 54 00
Fax: [46] 8 412 54 10
(Management consulting)

Baker & McKenzie Advokatbyra
Eriksbergsgatan 46
P.O. Box 26163
SE–100 41 Stockholm, Sweden
Tel.: [46] 8 676 7700
Fax: [46] 8 248 920
www.bakerinfo.com
(Law firm)

Deloitte & Touche Väst
Arenav 55
SE–121 77 Johanneshov, Sweden
Tel.: [46] 8 725 36 00
Fax: [46] 8 600 36 00
(Accounting)

Watson Wyatt & Co.
Norr Mälarstrand 6
SE–112 20 Stockholm, Sweden
Tel.: [46] 8 555 517 50
Fax: [46] 8 555 517 51
www.watsonwyatt.com
(Benefits consulting)

Technology

Electronic Data Systems (EDS)
Solna strandv 96
SE–171 85 Solna, Sweden
Tel.: [46] 8 619 10 00
Fax: [46] 8 619 18 00
(Systems consulting)

Hewlett–Packard Sverige
Skalholtsgaten 9
SE–164 40 Kista, Sweden
Tel.: [46] 8 444 20 00
Fax: [46] 8 444 26 66
(Printers)

IBM Svenska
Oddegatan 5
SE–164 40 Kista, Sweden
Tel.: [46] 8 793 10 00
Fax: [46] 8 793 49 48
(Data processing equipment)

Microsoft Sweden
Finlandsgatan 30
SE–164 74 Kista, Sweden
Tel.: [46] 8 752 56 00
Fax: [46] 8 750 51 58
www.microsoft.com
(Computers)

Motorola
Dalvägen 2
SE–169 56 Solna, Sweden
Tel.: [46] 8 734 88 00
Fax: [46] 8 27 67 17
(Semiconductors and cell phones)

Rational Software Scandinavia
Skalholtsgatan 10
SE–164 40 Kista, Sweden
Tel.: [46] 8 566 282 00
Fax: [46] 8 566 282 10
(Software consultants)

Sun Microsystems
Esbogatan 14
SE–164 74 Kista, Sweden
Tel.: [46] 8 631 10 00
Fax: [46] 8 631 10 05
(Minicomputers and mainframes)

Unisys
Armégatan 40
SE–171 71 Solna, Sweden
Tel.: [46] 8 470 15 00
Fax: [46] 8 470 15 35
(Computer data systems)

European Companies in Sweden

The following major non–American firms conduct business in Sweden. They companies can be either Swedish or based in another European country. They generally hire their own nationals first but may employ Americans.

Banking and Finance

Investor
Arsenalsgatan 8c, Box 16174
SE–111 47 Stockholm, Sweden
Tel.: [46] 8 614 20 00
Fax: [46] 8 614 215 50
www.investorab.com
(Financial services)

Nordea
Hamngatan 10
SE–105 71 Stockholm, Sweden
Tel.: [46] 8 614 7000
Fax: [46] 8 105 069
www.meritanordbanken.com
(Bank)

Securitas
Lindhagensplan 70, Box 12307
SE–102 28 Stockholm, Sweden
Tel.: [46] 8 657 74 00
Fax: [46] 8 657 70 72
www.securitasgroup.com
(Securities)

Skandia
Sveävagen44
SE–11134 Stockholm, Sweden
Tel.: [46] 8 788 10 00
Fax: [46] 8 788 30 80
www.skandia.se
(Insurance)

Skandinaviska Enskilda Banken
Kungsträdgrårdsgatan 8
SE–106 40 Stockholm, Sweden
Tel.: [46] 8 763 80 00
http://swp2.vv.sebank.se/cgi–bin/pts3/
pow/default.asp
(Bank)

Svenska Handelsbanken
Kungsträdgrårdsgatan 2
SE–106 70 Stockholm, Sweden
Tel.: [46] 8 701 10 00
Fax: [46] 8 701 23 45
www.handelsbanken.se
(Bank)

Industrial Manufacturing

ABB Automation Technology Products
Ingenjör Bååths g T1
SE–721 77 Västerås, Sweden
Tel.: [46] 21 32 93 00
Fax: [46] 21 12 41 03
(Electric motors)

AGA
Rissneleden 14
SE–174 53 Sundbyberg, Sweden
Tel.: [46] 8 706 95 00
Fax: [46] 8 628 23 15

(Industrial gases and measuring instruments)

Amersham Biosciences
SE–751 84 Uppsala, Sweden
Tel.: [46] 18 612 19 00
Fax: [46] 18 612 19 20
www.amershambiosciences.com
(Biotechnology research)

Atlas Copco Controls
SE–105 23 Stockholm, Sweden
Tel.: [46] 8 743 80 00
Fax: [46] 8 644 90 45
www.atlascopco_group.com
(Electric motors)

Biora
Medeon Science Park
SE–205 12 Malmö, Sweden
Tel.: [46] 40 32 13 33
Fax: [46] 40 32 13 55
www.biora.se
(Medical instruments and supplies)

Electrolux
St. Göransgatan 143
SE–105 45 Stockholm, Sweden
Tel.: [46] 8 738 64 00
Fax: [46] 8 656 44 78
www.electrolux.com
(Household appliances)

Esselte
Box 1371
SE–171 27 Solna, Sweden
Tel.: [46] 8 545 219 00
Fax: [46] 8 705 16 72
www.esselte.com
(Office supplies)

Lundin Petroleum
Hovslagargatan 5
SE–111 48 Stockholm, Sweden
Tel.: [46] 8 440 5450
Fax: [46] 8 440 5459
www.lundin–petroleum.com
(Oil and gas exploration and production)

Pergo
Strandridaregatan 8, PO Box 1010
SE–231 25 Trelleborg, Sweden
Tel.: [46] 410 363 100
Fax: [46] 410 155 60
www.pergo.com

(Flooring)

Perstorp
SE–284 80 Perstorp, Sweden
Tel.: [46] 435 380 00
Fax: [46] 435 381 00
www.perstorp.se
(Chemicals)

Saab
SE–461 89 Trollhättan, Sweden
Tel.: [46] 520 850 00
Fax: [46] 520 815 38
www.saab.com
(Automobiles and parts)

Sandvik
Storgatan 2
SE–811 81 Sandviken, Sweden
Tel.: [46] 26 26 00 00
Fax: [46] 26 26 10 22
www.sandvik.com
(Tools)

Stora Enso
Klarabergsviadukten 70
World Trade Center
SE–111 64 Stockholm, Sweden
Tel.: [46] 8 613 66 00
Fax: [46] 8 10 60 20
www.storaenso.com
(Paper products)

Svenska Cellulosa Aktiebolaget
Box 7827
SE–103 97 Stockholm, Sweden
Tel.: [46] 8 788 51 00
Fax: [46] 8 660 74 30
www.sca.com
(Paper and electrical products)

TeliaSonera
Mårbackagatan 11
SE–123 86 Farsta, Sweden
Tel.: [46] 8 713 1000
Fax: [46] 8 713 3333
www.telia.se
(Telecommunications)

Volvo
SE–405 08 Göthenburg, Sweden
Tel.: [46] 31 59 66 00
Fax: [46] 31 54 57 72
www.volvo.com
(Automobiles and farm machinery)

Retailing and Wholesaling

Axel Johnson
Villagaten 6
P.O. Box 26008
SE–100 41 Stockholm, Sweden
Tel.: [46] 8 701 61 00
Fax: [46] 8 21 3026
www.axel–johnson.se
(Supermarkets and department stores)

H & M Hennes & Mauritz
Norrlandsgatan 15, Box 1421
SE–111 84 Stockholm, Sweden
Tel.: [46] 8 796 55 00
Fax: [46] 8 20 99 19
www.hm.com
(Apparel retail store)

IKEA International
Box 640
SE–25 106 Helsingborg, Sweden
Tel.: [46] 42 267 100
Fax: [46] 42 132 805
www.ikea.com
(Furniture)

Service Industries

Cap Gemini Ernst & Young
Gustavslundsv 131
SE–167 51 Bromma, Sweden
Tel.: [46] 8 704 50 00
Fax: [46] 8 704 55 55
(Management consulting)

Scandic Hotel
P.O. Box 6197
SE–102 33 Stockholm, Sweden
Tel.: [46] 8 517 350 00
Fax: [46] 8 517 352 80
www.scandic–hotels.com
(Hotels and restaurants)

Scandinavian Airlines System (SAS)
Frösundavik Allé 1, Solna
SE–195 87 Stockholm, Sweden
Tel.: [46] 8 797 00 00
Fax: [46] 8 797 12 10
(Airline for Denmark, Norway, and Sweden)

Skanska
Klarabergsviadukten 90
SE–111 91 Stockholm, Sweden

Tel.: [46] 8 753 88 00
Fax: [46] 8 755 12 56
www.skanska.com
(Construction services)

Technology

Synergenix Interactive
Strandväg 96, Plan 6
SE- 171 54 Stockholm, Sweden
Tel.: [46] 8 764 9196
www.synergenix.se
(Computer games)

Telefonaktiebolaget LM Ericsson
Telefonvägen 30

SE–126 25 Stockholm, Sweden
Tel.: [46] 8 719 0000
Fax: [46] 8 18 40 85
www.ericsson.com
(Telecommunications)

Telelogic
Kungsgatan 6
SE–203 12 Malmö, Sweden
Tel.: [46] 40 650 00 00
Fax: [46] 40 650 65 55
www.telelogic.com
(Development tools, operating systems
and utility software)

International School in Sweden

International School of Stockholm
Johannesgatan 18
SE–111 38 Stockholm, Sweden
Tel.: [46] 8 412 4000

Fax: [46] 8 412 4001
Email: admin@intsch.se
www.intsch.se

Chapter 18

Benelux Countries: Belgium, Luxembourg, & the Netherlands

Belgium

Major employment centers: Brussels, Antwerp

Major business languages: Flemish (a dialect of Dutch), German, French

Language skill index: Expect to speak French when applying for positions with the E.U. If applying for non–governmental jobs, you will find that English is more widely used in business in the north, Flanders, than French. In the southern part of the country, Wallonia, French is clearly the language of preference. Many young Belgians speak English, and most people speak more than one language.

Currency: Euro

Telephone country code: 32

Time zone: Eastern Standard Time + 6 hours

Punctuality index: Very important

Average daily temperature, high/low: January: 40°/34°; July: 72°/56° (Brussels)

Average number of days with precipitation: January: 14 days; July: 14 days

Best bet for employment:

For students: Apply to IAESTE

Permanent jobs: International organization and public policy work associated with the European Union in Brussels

Chance of finding a job: Not too good outside of public policy

Useful tip: Members of the opposite sex and women kiss each other on alternate cheeks three times as a greeting.

The Kingdom of Belgium lies in Western Europe just south of the Netherlands, north of France, and west of Germany. The North Sea comprises 40 miles of Belgium's west coast. Belgium is about the size of Maryland. The Ardennes region in the southeast consists of forests while the rest of the country is mostly flat.

Belgium is linguistically divided between Flanders to the north and Wallonia to the south. Walloons speak French while the people in Flanders speak Flemish, a dialect of Dutch. Brussels, Belgium's capital, is officially bilingual. About 55 percent of the population is Flemish and almost 33 percent is Walloon. A small German-speaking population also lives in the far eastern portion of the country. Over 85 percent of the population belong to the Roman Catholic Church.

Headquarters for the E.U. and NATO, Belgium houses huge numbers of foreign diplomats.

The Belgae, a Celtic people, were the country's first inhabitants. Julius Caesar conquered the region, which was subsequently ruled by the Franks, the Spanish and Austrian Hapsburgs, and the French. After the Napoleonic Wars, Belgium became part of the Netherlands. In 1830, the country became an independent monarchy. Belgium attempted to remain neutral in both world wars but was overrun by the Germans each time. King Leopold III, who surrendered to Germany in 1940, was forced to abdicate in favor of his son, King Baudouin, in 1951. King Albert II succeeded King Baudouin in 1993.

The federal government is a constitutional and hereditary monarchy. The Christian Democrats, Socialists, and Liberals dominate politics, although support for the Greens is increasing. In August 1980, the Belgian Parliament passed a devolution bill and amended the Constitution, establishing a Flemish legislative assembly and government in Flanders, a francophone community legislative council in Wallonia, and a Walloon regional legislative assembly and government. Subsequent constitutional reform established similar regional and community councils for the German cantons in 1983, and for Brussels in 1989.

Headquarters for the European Union (E.U.) and the North Atlantic Treaty Organization (NATO), Belgium is characterized by strong internationalism — a huge number of foreign diplomats have made Brussells their home.

Weekday business hours are generally from 8:30 a.m. to 6 p.m. Retail shops are also open on the weekend.

Current Economic Climate

Belgium is densely populated and located at the heart of one of the world's most highly industrialized regions. In the 1880s, it was the first country on the European continent to undergo the industrial revolution, and has placed an emphasis on developing an excellent transportation infrastructure of ports, canals, railways, and highways to integrate its industry with its neighbors. Belgium was one of the founding members of the European Community and strongly supports deepening the powers of the E.C. to integrate European economies.

Belgium ranks seventh in per capita GDP worldwide. With few natural resources, Belgium imports substantial quantities of raw materials and exports a large volume of manufactured goods, making its economy unusually dependent on the state of world markets. Exports account for roughly two–thirds of Belgium's GNP. Belgium exports twice as much per capita as Germany and five times as much as Japan. Germany, France, and the Netherlands are Belgium's primary trading partners. Belgium's trade advantages are derived from its central geographic location, and a highly skilled, multilingual, and productive work force.

In 2001, the per capita income was $22,578. For 2002, the federal government presented a budget that was almost balanced (0.2 percent of GDP deficit). GDP growth remains moderate at 2.2 percent. Unemployment currently hovers around 6.8 percent. Belgium became a charter member of the European Monetary Union in January 1999.

The workforce is 60 percent services, 28 percent industrial, and 2 percent agricultural. Major industries include engineering and metal products, motor vehicle assembly, processed food and beverages, chemicals, basic metals, textiles, glass, petroleum, and coal.

Belgium's 10 Largest Companies

(2001, based on market capitalization)

1. Fortis
2. Dexia
3. Tractebel
4. Eletrabel
5. KBC Bankverzekeringsholding
6. Interbrew
7. Groupe Bruxelles Lambert
8. Almanij
9. UCB
10. Solvay Societe Anonyme

Getting around in Belgium

Eurail and InterRail passes are valid on intercity buses and trains throughout Belgium. The Belgian railroad network, known for its reliability and extensive service, offers special discounts for exclusive traveling within the Benelux countries or within Belgian borders. Train travel in Belgium is relatively inexpensive.

Employment Regulations and Outlook for Americans

American citizens don't need a visa to visit Belgium for less than 90 days. However, a residence permit is required for longer stays. As in most E.U. countries, a work permit must be presented upon arrival if you intend to work. Your prospective employer must apply for the work permit, and before a permit is granted, the employer must prove that no Belgian or European Union citizen is able to do the job. Foreign workers are normally granted a Permit B, which is only valid for one employer and must be renewed each year. A foreigner may apply for a Permit A after a certain number of years, which allows you to work for any employer in Belgium, not just the original one. If you wish to be self-employed, you will need to apply for a Professional Card. The application process can take up to a year, and the permit must be renewed annually.

The visa restrictions to work as an au pair are similarly strict. The au pair must have a basic knowledge of one of the three national languages (French, Dutch, or German) and must enroll in language courses. The school at which the au pair is enrolled will provide a certificate of enrollment every three months. Au pairs may not have obtained previously any kind of work permit and can only begin work in July, August, and September.

The upshot for an American seeking to work in Belgium? Expect to find that employers will find it difficult to hire foreign workers. If you are a student, work with an organization that places temporary workers and interns. If you are looking for a permanent job, plan to demonstrate your high-demand skills and give yourself lots of time.

Short-term and Temporary Work

Like most of Europe, a good bet for casual work is as an au pair. There are a few opportunities to work as an English teacher. In addition to the agencies listed below, Au Pair in Europe and InterExchange can assist with placements. Both are described in Chapter 9.

Euro Business Languages
Leuvensesteenweg 325
B-1932 Zavantem, Belgium
Tel.: [32] 2 720 15 10
Fax: [32] 2 720 25 80
Email: infos@eurobl.net
Euro Business Languages is a private language school that sometimes hires TEFL-certified teachers.

Stufam
Vierwindenlaan 7
B-1780 Wemmel, Belgium
Tel.: [32] 2 460 33 95
Fax: [32] 2 460 00 71
Stufam is an au pair agency that specializes in placements that last from two to nine months.

Internship Programs

The best bet for students interested in obtaining practical experience in Belgium is to work with established organizations such as IAESTE, AIESEC, or the International Cooperative Education. One-year Fulbright English Teaching Fellowships are also available in Belgium. Chapters 9 and 10 provide additional details.

Education Programs Abroad
Columbia Plaza, Suite 225
350 East Michigan Avenue
Kalamazoo, MI 49007
Tel.: (616) 382–0139
Education Programs Abroad offers semester and summer internships with the European Parliament. Students work at least three days a week in an internship and take two related courses. During the summer, students work in the internship full time (no course work). All internships and programs are available for academic credit. Business internships are also available; proficiency in French is required for business internships.

Internships with the European Union

For students interested in international affairs, an internship with the European Union is the perfect gateway to for an up–close–and–personal view of policymaking in action. The best opportunities for U.S. citizens are with the delegation of the European Commission in Washington, D.C. These unpaid internships are intended to provide college and university students and recent graduates with the opportunity to acquire considerable knowledge of the European Union, its institutions, activities, laws, statistics and relations with the U.S. A working knowledge of French is useful but not essential. Internships are offered in the spring (October 15 application deadline), summer (February 15 application deadline), and fall (June 15 application deadline). For more information, contact:

European Union
Internship Coordinator
Press and Public Affairs Section
Delegation of the European Commission to the United States
2300 M Street NW, Third Floor
Washington, DC 20037
Tel.: (202) 862–9500
Fax: (202) 429–1766
http://www.eurunion.org/delegati/ppa/interns.htm

There are also a limited number of internships with the E.U. in Brussels, although they are mostly limited to students from member countries. Interns can work with the European Commission, the European Economic and Social Committee, the European Parliament, the European Central Bank, or the Office for Harmonization in the Internal Market. Interns must be under the age of 30. Application information can be obtained from the delegation for the European Commission in the U.S. (see above.)

Volunteer Opportunities

Numerous organizations offer an array of voluntary service opportunities in Belgium, including the Council on International Educational Exchange, the International Christian Youth Exchange, the International Cultural Youth Exchange, Service Civil International, and Volunteers for Peace. Get details on these and other organizations that offer volunteer opportunities in Chapter 9.

Archeolo–J
23 Avenue Paul Terlinden
B–1330 Rixensart, Belgium
Tel.: [32] 2 673 25 82
Fax: [32] 2 673 40 85
Email: arceolo–J@skynet.be
www.skene.be

Recognized by the Ministries for the Walloon Area and the French Community, Archeolo–J promotes archeological preservation. Volunteers excavate Roman villas, perform topographical surveys, and restore archeological artifacts. Fee for all ages start at €235.

Resources for Further Information

Newspapers in Belgium

The Bulletin (English)
Tel.: [32] 2 373 99 09
Fax: [32] 2 374 15 31
www.ackroyd.be

Het Laatste Nieuws **(Flemish)**
Tel.: [32] 2 454 24 02
Fax: [32] 2 454 28 31
www.hln.be

Het Nieuwsblad **(Flemish)**
Tel.: [32] 2 467 22 11
Fax: [32] 2 466 76 21
www.nieuwsblade.be

Het Volk
Tel.: [32] 2 467 22 11
Fax: [32] 2 463 04 38
www.hetvolk.be

Le Soir **(French)**
Tel.: [32] 2 225 54 32
Fax: [32] 2 225 59 14
www.lesoir.com

De Standaard
Tel.: [32] 2 467 26 78
Fax: [32] 2 466 99 84
www.standaard.be

Useful Websites for Job Seekers

The Internet is a good place to begin your job search. Many Belgium employers list job vacancies, especially those in technical fields, on the web. There are also many websites that provide useful information for job searchers researching the Belgium job market.

Belgium JobPilot
www.jobpilot.be
Includes over 800 private–sector jobs, a resume database, and a directory of employers. Free registration. Viewable in both Dutch and French.

Careers in Belgium
www.jobs–careers.be
Features over 5,100 jobs in Belgium. You can create a CV Lite (a short online version of your resume) for employers to view and you can register to receive job announcements by email.

Interim Partnerships
www.interimpartnership.be
Features listings from several Belgian recruitment agencies for full–time and temporary positions. You may register online as a candidate and view actual job vacancies.

Manpower Belgium
www.manpower.be
Manpower is a recruitment agency. Its Belgian site features a database of private–sector jobs.

Monster Belgium
www.monster.be
Lists over 1,900 jobs in Belgium and profiles of 140 major Belgian employers. You may post your resume to the online database and register to receive email job notifications. Viewable in French, Dutch, and English.

Randstad
www.be.randstad.com
Randstad is one of Europe's leading temporary employment agencies, assisting employers in industries ranging from automotive to retail to health care to hospitality. The Belgian site includes

links to Randstad's other European offices.

References.be
www.references.be
Lists mostly engineering and IT jobs. The searchable database provides profiles of the companies listing job vacancies. Written in French.

Talent on Line
www.vacature.com
Lists job vacancies in management, sales, IT, clerical, human resources, and engineering. Written in Dutch.

Search & Selection
www.searchselection.com
Primarily a site for jobs in Belgium, the Netherlands, and Luxembourg, this site also includes postings throughout Europe. It features about 80 jobs in Belgium.

StepStone Belgium
www.stepstone.be
One of Europe's leading online recruitment sites. Features over 4,400 private sector and education jobs in Belgium. Viewable in English, French, Dutch, and German.

Embassies, Consular Offices, and Missions

American embassies and consulates have commercial and/or economic sections that can provide you with business information and explain aspects of the local economy. Inquiries about business opportunities should be addressed either to "Commercial Officer" or "Commercial Section," followed by the appropriate street address.

Representation of Belgium in the United States

Embassy of Belgium
3330 Garfield Street NW
Washington, DC 20008
Tel.: (202) 333–6900
Fax: (202) 333–5457
www.diplobel.us

Consulates General of Belgium:

Chicago, (312) 263–6624; Los Angeles, (323) 857–1244; New York, (212) 586–5110

Representation of the United States in Belgium

American Embassy
27 Boulevard du Régent
B–1000 Brussels, Belgium

Tel.: [32] 2 508 2111
Fax: [32] 2 511 2725
www.usinfo.be

Chambers of Commerce

Chambers of commerce consist of member firms in both countries interested in international trade. These are appropriate companies to initially target in the job search.

American Chamber of Commerce in Belgium
50 Avenue des Arts, Boite 5
B–1000 Brussels, Belgium
Tel.: [32] 2 513 6770
Fax: [32] 2 513 3590
Email: gch@post1.amcham.be
www.amcham.be

Belgian–American Chamber of Commerce in the U.S.
575 Madison Avenue, 24th Floor
New York, NY 10022
Tel.: (212) 319–7080
Fax: (212) 319–7086
Email: bacc@ix.netcom.com
www.belcham.org

World Trade Centers in Belgium

World trade centers, such as these, usually include many foreign companies that conduct business in Belgium.

**The World Trade Center
Association of Antwerp**
Regus Center, Koningin Astridplein 5
B–2018 Antwerp, Belguim
Tel.: [32] 3 206 18 50
Fax : [32] 3 206 18 80
Email: info@wtcantwerp.be
www.wtcantwerp.be

**World Trade Center
Association of Brussels**
30 Boulevard du Roi Albert II 30
P.O. Box 5
B–1000 Brussels, Belgium
Tel.: [32] 2 203 04 00
Fax : [32] 2 203 04 05
Email: wtc.brussels@pophost.eunet.be
www.brussels.wtc.be

Other Informational Organizations

Foreign government missions in the U.S., such as tourist and trade offices, can furnish visas and information on work permits and other regulations. They may also offer economic and business information about the country.

Belgian National Tourist Office
780 Third Avenue, Suite 1501
New York, NY 10017
Tel.: (212) 758–8130

Fax: (212) 355 7675
Email: info@visitbelgium.com
www.visitbelgium.com

Business Directories

Although not always easy to find, business directories can prove invaluable in the international job search. Your best bet for locating these directories is to begin in the reference section of any public or university library. Most directories list company names, addresses, products, and phone numbers. Some directories include executive names and titles and financial information about the company. These sources provide you with the names of the people to contact for employment information as well as financial data, which can tell you how strong a company's position in a country may be.

ABC Belge Pour le Commerce et l'Industrie. ABC Belge Pour le Commerce et l'Industrie, Doornveld 11 B28, B–1731 Asse, Belgium; email: info@abc-belgium.com; www.abc–d.be. Covers over 28,000 manufacturers, traders, and business–service providers in Belgium. 3,500 pages, published annually in French and Dutch.

Belgian Export Register. Federation des Chambres de Commerce Belgas a l'Etranger, 8 rue des Sols, B–1000 Brussels, Belgium. Lists leading exporters and organizations aiding exporters. 400 pages, published biennially.

Dun's 15,000 Largest Companies–Belgium. Dun & Bradstreet Information Services, Dun & Bradstreet Company, Three Sylvan Way, Parsippany, NJ 07054–3896; email: dnbmdd@dnd.com. Covers 15,000 industrial, trading, banking, insurance, and service companies in Belgium. Published annually.

Kompass Belgium. Editus Belgium, 256 Avenue Moliere, B–1060 Brussels, Belgium; email: editus@kompass.be; www.kompass.com. Available in the United States from IPC Business Press, 205 East 42nd Street, New York, NY 10017. Lists 24,000 manufacturers, distributors, and service companies. $335; 3,500 pages; published annually in French and Dutch.

American Companies in Belgium

The following companies are classified by business area: Banking and Finance; Industrial Manufacturing; Retailing and Wholesaling; Service Industries; and Technology. Company information includes firm name, address, phone and fax numbers, and type of business. Your chances of securing employment abroad are substantially better if you contact the subsidiary company in Europe rather than the parent company in the United States. Contact information for companies can change frequently. So be sure to confirm its address and phone number before writing to a company.

Banking and Finance

Bank of America
Uitbreidingstraat 180, PB 6
B–2600 Antwerp, Belgium
Tel.: [32] 3 280 4211
Fax: [32] 3 239 6109
(Bank)

CIGNA Life Insurance
Avenue de Cortenbergh 52
B–1000 Brussels, Belgium
Tel.: [32] 2 740 27 50
Fax: [32] 2 740 27 80
(Insurance)

Citibank
263 Boulevard Général Jacques
B–1050 Brussels, Belgium
Tel.: [32] 26265111
Fax: [32] 26265584
(Bank)

Diners Club Benelux
Boulevard de la Plaine 11
B–1050 Brussels, Belgium
Tel.: [32] 2 206 95 11
Fax: [32] 2 206 99 99
(Credit card finance)

Industrial Manufacturing

Baxter
80 Boulevard Renèe Branquart
B–7860 Lessines, Belgium
Tel.: [32] 68 27 22 11
Fax: [32] 68 33 53 91

(Pharmaceuticals)

Black & Decker Belgium
Weihock 1
B–1930 Brussels, Belgium
Tel.: [32] 2 719 07 11
Fax: [32] 2 721 40 45
www.blackanddecker.com
(Power tools)

Caterpillar
Avenue des Etats–Unis 1
B–6041 Gosselies, Belgium
Tel.: [32] 71 25 21 11
Fax: [32] 71 25 29 56
(Earth moving machinery)

Coca–Cola Enterprises Belgium
Bergensesteenweg 1424
B–1070 Brussels, Belgium
Tel.: [32] 2 529 15 00
Fax: [32] 2 559 21 38
(Soft drinks)

Crown Cork Co. (Belgium)
Merksemsteenweg 148
B–2100 Deurne, Belgium
Tel.: [32] 3 360 48 11
Fax: [32] 3 325 82 20
(Packaging and closures)

Dow Corning Europe
Parc Industriel Zone C
B–7180 Seneffe, Belgium
Tel.: [32] 2 64 88 80 00
Fax: [32] 2 64 88 84 01
(Silicon products)

DuPont (Belgium)
Hoge 98
B–8500 Kortrijk, Belgium
Tel.: [32] 56 20 32 09
Fax: [32] 56 22 80 29
(Chemicals)

Duracell Batteries
Nijverheidslaan 7
B–3220 Aarschot, Belgium
Tel.: [32] 16 55 20 11
Fax: [32] 16 55 20 10
(Electrical components)

Esso
Polderdijkweg 3, Haven 447
B–2030 Antwerp, Belgium
Tel.: [32] 3 543 31 11
Fax: [32] 3 543 34 95
(Petroleum products)

Ethyl
Zoning Industriel Zone C
B–7181 Feluy, Belgium
Tel.: [32] 67 87 52 11
Fax: [32] 67 87 52 35
www.ethyl.com
(Chemicals and petroleum products)

Ford Motor Co.
Groenenborgerlaan 16
B–2610 Wilrijk, Belgium
Tel.: [32] 3 821 20 00
Fax: [32] 3 821 20 09
www.ford.com
(Motor vehicles)

Hallmark Cards Belgium
Botermelkbaan 14
B–2900 Schoten, Belgium
Tel.: [32] 3 685 11 30
Fax: [32] 3 685 10 88
(Greeting cards)

Honeywell Europe
1 Avenue du Bourget
B–1140 Brussels, Belgium
Tel.: [32] 2 728 27 11
Fax: [32] 2 728 24 68
(Process control equipment)

Kimberly–Clark
Adolf Stocletlaan 3
B–2570 Duffel, Belgium
Tel.: [32] 15 30 06 11
Fax: [32] 15 31 39 34

(Paper products)

Kraft Foods Belgium
Brusselsesteenweg 450
B–1500 Halle, Belgium
Tel.: [32] 2 362 31 11
Fax: [32] 2 362 38 40
(Prepared foods)

Levi Strauss & Co. Europe
Avenue Arnaud Fraiteur 15–23
B–1050 Brussels, Belgium
Tel.: [32] 2 641 60 11
Fax: [32] 2 640 29 97
(Apparel)

Master Foods
Kleine Kloosterstraat 8
B–1932 Sint–Stevens–Woluwe, Belgium
Tel.: [32] 2 712 72 22
Fax: [32] 2 721 49 32
(Confectionery)

Monsanto Europe
270–272 Avenue de Terveuren
B–1150 Brussels, Belgium
Tel.: [32] 2 776 41 11
Fax: [32] 2 776 40 40
(Chemicals)

Owens–Corning Composite
Route de Maestricht
B–4651 Battice, Belgium
Tel.: [32] 87 69 22 11
Fax: [32] 87 67 57 51
(Fiber products)

Pfizer
102, rue Leon Theodor
B–1090 Brussels, Belgium
Tel.: [32] 2 421 15 11
Fax: [32] 2 421 17 98
(Pharmaceuticals and chemicals)

Pharmacia
Rijksweg 12
B–2870 Puurs, Belgium
Tel.: [32] 3 890 92 11
Fax: [32] 3 889 65 32
(Pharmaceuticals)

Unilever BestFoods Belgium
Humaniteitslaan 292
B–1190 Brussels, Belgium
Tel.: [32] 2 333 66 66
Fax: [32] 2 333 63 33

(Prepared foods)

Procter & Gamble Belgium
Temselaan 100
B–1853 Strombeek–Bever, Belgium
Tel.: [32] 2 456 21 11
Fax: [32] 2 456 45 70
(Cleaning and personal products)

Société Europe des Carburants (SECA)
Mechelsesteenweg 520
B–1800 Vilvoorde, Belgium
Tel.: [32] 2 254 15 11
Fax: [32] 2 254 16 71
(Diesel and fuel oils)

Texaco Belgium
25 Avenue Arnaud Fraiteur
B–1050 Brussels, Belgium
Tel.: [32] 2 639 91 11
Fax: [32] 2 639 99 11
(Petroleum products)

Tyco Electronics Raychem
Diestsesteenweg 692
B–3010 Kessel–Lo, Belgium
Tel.: [32] 16 35 10 11
Fax: [32] 16 35 16 96
(Plastics)

Service Industries

Aramark/Belgium
Rue Maurice Charlent 53
B–1160 Brussels, Belgium
Tel.: [32] 2 663 49 40
Fax: [32] 2 663 49 60
(Managed food service)

Baker & McKenzie
40 Boulevard du Regent–Regentlaan, 5th Floor
B–1000 Brussels, Belgium
Tel.: [32] 2 506 3611
Fax: [32] 2 522 6280
www.bakerinfo.com
(Law firm)

Edelman PR Worldwide
20, rue des Deux Eglises
B–1000 Brussels, Belgium
Tel.: [32] 2 227 61 70
Fax: [32] 2 227 61 89
www.edelman.com
(Public relations)

A.T. Kearney
46 Avenue des Arts
B–1000 Brussels, Belgium
Tel.: [32] 2 504 48 11
Fax: [32] 2 511 01 03
(Executive search)

Korn/Ferry Carré Orban
523 Avenue Louise, Boite 25
B–1050 Brussels, Belgium
Tel.: [32] 2 640 32 40
Fax: [32] 2 640 83 82
(Executive search)

McKinsey & Co.
480 Avenue Louise, Boite 22
B–1050 Brussels, Belgium
Tel.: [32] 2 645 42 11
Fax: [32] 2 646 45 48
(Management consulting)

Ogilvy & Mather
13 Boulevard de l'Impératrice
B–1000 Brussels, Belgium
Tel.: [32] 2 545 65 00
Fax: [32] 2 545 65 01
(Advertising)

Radisson SAS Hotel Brussels
Wolvengracht 47
B–1000 Brussels, Belgium
Tel.: [32] 2 219 28 28
Fax: [32] 2 219 62 62
(Hotels)

Watson Wyatt & Co.
52 Avenue Herrmann–Debroux, Boite 3
B–1160 Brussels, Belgium
Tel.: [32] 2 678 15 11
Fax: [32] 2 678 36 01
www.watsonwyatt.com
(Benefits consultants)

Technology

Belgacom Mobile (Airtouch Communications)
Rue du Progrès 55
B–1210 Brussels, Belgium
Tel.: [32] 2 205 40 00
Fax: [32] 2 205 40 40
(Wireless communications)

Cisco Systems Brussels
Marcel Thirylaan 77

B–1200 Brussels, Belgium
Tel.: [32] 2 778 42 00
Fax: [32] 2 778 43 00
www.cisco.com
(Computer networking systems)

Hewlett–Packard Belgium
Rue de L'aeronef 1
B–1140 Brussells, Belgium
Tel.: [32] 2 778 31 11

Fax: [32] 2 763 06 13
(Printers and calculators)

Unisys Belgium
20 Avenue du Bourget
B–1130 Brussels, Belgium
Tel.: [32] 2 728 07 11
Fax: [32] 2 726 68 10
(Computer hardware and software)

European Companies in Belgium

The following are selected major non–American firms operating in Belgium. These selected companies can be Belgian or based in another European country. Such companies will generally hire their own nationals first but may employ Americans.

Banking and Finance

Almanij
Snydershuis, Keizerstraat 8
B–2000 Antwerp, Belgium
Tel.: [32] 32 3 202 87 00
Fax: [32] 32 3 202 87 05
www.almanij.com
(Financial services)

Banque Nationale de la Belgique
14, Boulevard de Berlaimont
B–1000 Brussels, Belgium
Tel.: [32] 2 221 21 11
www.banquenationale.be
(Central bank)

Dexia
Square de Meeûs 1
B–1000 Brussels, Belgium
Tel.: [32] 2 213 57 00
Fax: [32] 2 213 57 01
www.dexia.com
(Financial services)

Euronext Brussels
Place de la Bourse
B–1000 Brussels, Belgium
Tel.: [32] 02 509 1211
Fax: [32] 02 509 1212
www.bxs.be
(Financial services)

Fortis
Rue Royale 20
B–1000 Brussels, Belgium

Tel.: [32] 2 510 52 11
Fax: [32] 2 510 56 26
www.fortis.com
(Banking & insurance)

KBC Bankverzekeringsholding
Havenlaan 2
B–1080 Brussels, Belgium
Tel.: [32] 2 429 5594
Fax: [32] 2 429 4416
www.kbc.be
(Banking and financial services)

Industrial Manufacturing

AGFA–Gevaert
Septestraat 27
B–2640 Mortsel, Belgium
Tel.: [32] 3 444 2111
Fax: [32] 3 446 0094
www.agfa.com
(Chemical and electronic imaging systems)

Belgonucleaire
Avenue Ariane 4
B–1200 Brussels, Belgium
Tel.: [32] 2 774 0511
Fax: [32] 2 774 0547
www.belgonucleaire.be
(Alternative energy sources)

Cockerill Sambre
187, Chaussé de la Hulpe
B–1170 Brussels, Belgium
Tel.: [32] 2 679 9327

Fax: [32] 4 236 7378
www.cockrill–sambre.com
(Iron and steel)

Electrabel
8, Boulevard du Régent
B–1000 Brussels, Belgium
Tel.: [32] 2 518 6111
Fax: [32] 2 518 6400
www.electrabel.be
(Electric utilities)

Interbrew
Vaartstraat 94
B–3000 Leuven, Belgium
Tel.: [32] 16 24 71 11
Fax: [32] 16 24 74 07
www.interbrew.com
(Brewery)

Mobistar
149, rue Colonel Bourg
B–1140 Brussels, Belgium
Tel.: [32] 2 745 71 11
Fax: [32] 2 745 70 00
www.mobistar.be
(Telecommunications)

Nouvelles Verreries de Momignies
20, rue Mandenne
B–6590 Momignies, Belgium
Tel.: [32] 60–51 02 11
Fax: [32] 60 51 16 75
www.nvminc.com
(Consumer products)

Solvay Societe Anonyme
Rue du Prince Albert 33
B–1050 Brussels, Belgium
Tel.: [32] 2 509 6111
Fax: [32] 2 509 6624
www.solvay.com
(Chemicals)

Tractebel
1, place du Trône
B–1000 Brussels, Belgium
Tel.: [32] 2 510 71 11
Fax: [32] 2 510 73 88
www.tractebel.com
(Utilities)

UCB
Allé de la Recherche 60
B–1070 Brussels, Belgium
Tel.: [32] 2 559 99 99

Fax: [32] 2 559 95 71
www.ucb–group.com
(Pharmaceuticals)

Umicore
Broekstraat 31 rue du Marais
B–1000 Brussels, Belgium
Tel.: [32] 2 227 71 11
Fax: [32] 2 227 79 00
www.um.be/umhome.htm
(Mining & minerals)

Retailing and Wholesaling

C&A
Senneberg, Jean Monnetlaan
Vilvoorde, Belgium
Tel.: [32] 22 57 68 64
Fax: [32] 22 57 65 12
www.c–and–a.com
(Department stores)

Carrefour
Avenue des Olympiades 20
B–1140 Brussels, Belgium
(Supermarkets, hypermarts)

Service Industries

Belgacom
27, Boulevard du Roi Albert II
B–1030 Brussels, Belgium
Tel.: [32] 2 202 41 11
Fax: [32] 2 203 65 93
www.belgacom.be
(Telecommunications)

GIB
Avenue des Olympiades 20
B–1140 Brussels, Belgium
Tel.: [32] 2 729 21 11
Fax: [32] 2 729 18 18
www.gib.be
(Restaurants)

Roularta Media Group
Meiboomlaan 33
B–8800 Roeselare, Belgium
Tel.: [32] 051 266 111
Fax: [32] 051 266 866
www.roularta.be
(Publishing)

SN Brussels Airlines
Sabena House Brussels National Airport, Zaventem

B–1930 Brussels, Belgium
Tel.: [32] 2 723 3111
Fax: [32] 2 723 8496
www.brussels–airlines.com
(Airline)

Virgin Express Holdings
Brussles Airport, Building 116
B–1820 Melsbroek, Belgium
Tel.: [32] 2 752 05 11
Fax: [32] 2 752 05 06
www.virgin–express.com
(Airlines)

B–8500 Kortrijk, Belgium
Tel.: [32] 56 262 611
Fax: [32] 56 262 262
www.barco.com
(Computer hardware)

Reef
35 rue de Stassart
B–1050 Brussels, Belgium
Tel.: [32] 02 510 83 83
Fax: [32] 02 510 83 33
www.reef.com
(Internet software)

Technology

Barco
President Kennedy Park 35

Major International Nonprofit Employer in Belgium
Amnesty International
9, rue Berckmans
B–1060 Brussels, Belgium

Tel.: [32] 2 538 81 77
Fax: [32] 2 537 37 29

International Schools in Belgium
The Antwerp International School
Veltwijcklaan 180
B–2180 Ekeren, Belgium
Tel.: [32] 3 543 93 00
Fax: [32] 3 541 82 01
Email: ais@ais–antwerp.be
www.ais–antwerp.be
(Kindergarten through grade 12)

The International School of Brussels
Kattenberg–Boitsfort 19
B–1170 Brussels, Belgium
Tel.: [32] 2 661 42 11
Fax: [32] 2 661 42 00

Email: admissions@isb.be
www.isb.be
(Kindergarten through grade 12)

St. John's International School
146 Drève Richelle
B–1410 Waterloo, Belgium
Tel.: [32] 2 352 06 10
Fax: [32] 2 352 06 20/30
Email: admissions@stjohns.be
www.stjohns.be
(U.S., International Baccalaureate
curriculum, kindergarten through
grade 12)

Luxembourg

Major employment center: Luxembourg City

Major business languages: French, German

Language skill index: Many Luxembourg citizens speak English. Both German and French are used in the press, in politics, and in daily life. French is most common in government and schools, though Luxembourgish (similar to German) is the language you'll hear most frequently on the street.

Currency: Euro

Telephone country code: 352

Time zone: Eastern Standard Time + 6 hours

Punctuality index: Punctuality is expected.

Average daily temperature, high/low: January: 36°/29°; July 71°/55°

Average number of days with precipitation: January: 14 days; July: 13 days

Best bet for employment:

   For students: Apply to IAESTE

   Permanent jobs: Banking and insurance

Chance of finding a job: Depends on your skill and experience in international trade.

Useful tip: Like the Belgians, the people of Luxembourg like to kiss as a greeting; however, they only kiss twice and don't kiss just anyone.

The Grand Duchy of Luxembourg sits between Belgium on its west, Germany on the east, and France to the south. Luxembourg's 370,000 residents live on just 1,000 square miles of land. The nation's only major city is its capital, Luxembourg City, with a population of just 86,000 people.

Luxembourg was founded circa 963 and ruled by the House of Luxembourg, beginning in 1060. Between the fifteenth and the eighteenth centuries, Spain, Burgundy, France, and Austria ruled the heavily fortified city. In 1815, it was declared a Grand Duchy of the Netherlands. This small country was invaded by Germany in both world wars. The Grand Duchy's neutrality was abandoned in 1948, when customs borders between Belgium and the Netherlands were removed, creating Benelux.

Luxembourg is a high–density nation, squeezing 370,000 people onto just 1,000 square miles of land.

The present sovereign, Grand Duke Henri, succeeded his father, Grand Duke Jean, in October 2000. Grand Duke Jean abdicated in December 1999, after a 35–year reign. The prime minister, Jean–Claude Juncker, is head of the government. Luxembourg's legislative body is the Chamber of Deputies, consisting of 60 members elected every five years. The major parties in the Chamber of Deputies are the Christian Socialists, the Workers–Socialist Party, and the Democratic Party. Despite a large influx of foreign workers, the social and political systems are quite stable, in part because most of the foreign residents are Roman Catholics or Western Europeans.

Normal weekday banking hours are from 9:30 a.m. to 5 p.m. Shops often stay open until 6 p.m. on weekdays and until noon on Saturdays. Most stores close for lunch from noon to 2 p.m.

Current Economic Climate

Luxembourg is an affluent nation with a highly developed industrial sector. Luxembourg reports some of the lowest unemployment in Europe, currently at about 2.5 percent. Luxembourg's labor force is concentrated in industry and commerce (42 percent) and in service industries such as hotels (45 percent). Less than 1 percent of the labor force works in the agriculture sector. The primary industries in Luxembourg are banking, iron and steel, food processing, chemicals, metal products, engineering, tires, glass, and aluminum. Most trade is conducted with the Netherlands and Belgium, as well as the E.U. and the United States. The economy depends on foreign workers (mostly from other E.U. countries) for 30 percent of its labor force. Although Luxembourg has suffered from the global economic slump, the country has maintained a fairly robust growth rate of 4 percent. Luxembourg joined with other E.U. members to launch the Euro in January 1999.

Luxembourg's 10 Largest Companies

(2001, based on market capitalization)

1. RTL Group
2. Kredietbank Luxembourgeoise
3. Arbed
4. Millicom International Cellular
5. Thiel Logistik
6. Espirito Santo Financial Group
7. Stolt–Nielsen Sociedad Anonima
8. Stolt Offshore
9. Quilmes Industrial
10. SBS Broadcasting

Getting Around in Luxembourg

Eurail and InterRail passes are accepted throughout Luxembourg. Trains and buses provide adequate transportation for traveling over Luxembourg's 2,600 square kilometers.

Employment Regulations and Outlook for Americans

The Centre d'Information pour Jeunes (see Other Informational Organizations, below, for contact information) distributes a free visitor's guide, *Focus on Luxembourg*, that includes a section on working in Luxembourg. Jobs are limited, but the casual job hunter may have luck at hotels. The Luxembourg Embassy will send you a list of hotels upon request. Luxembourg is a good place for a polyglot to work, and fluency in English may be an advantage.

As with other E.U. countries, Luxembourg requires a work permit — presented upon arrival — in order to work legally. Permits can be arranged through the company or organization you plan to work for. All Luxembourg work permit applications are processed by a single civil servant who works part–time. This is a strong indication that Luxembourg does not plan to accommodate a large number of immigrants.

Short–term and Temporary Work

In addition to hospitality jobs, a good bet for casual work in Luxembourg is as an au pair. Additional resources are described in Chapter 9.

Europair
14, rue de Luxembourg
8077 Bertrange, Luxembourg

Tel.: [352] 31 93 14
Au pair placement agency in Benelux countries.

Internship Programs

Luxembourg is a small country, and internship opportunities are limited. The best bet for students to obtain practical experience in Luxembourg is to work with established organizations such as IAESTE, which is described in

Chapter 9. The Fulbright Commission also offers an English–language teaching fellowship program that is described in Chapter 10.

Resources for Further Information

Newspapers in Luxembourg

Luxemburger Wort (German/French)
Tel.: [352] 49 93 1
Fax: [352] 49 93 394
www.wort.lu

Luxembourg News (English)
Tel.: [352] 46 11 22 310
Fax [352] 467 00 56
www.news.lu

Useful Websites for Job Seekers

The Internet is a good place to begin your job search. Some Luxembourg employers list job vacancies, especially those in technical fields, on the web. There are also many websites that provide useful information for job searchers researching the Luxembourg job market. Because Luxembourg is so small, few recruitment websites will feature very many jobs. Be sure to also use websites that serve all of Europe.

***Luxembourg News* Online**
www.news.lu
This online magazine is not necessarily for job seekers, but the information about current events in Luxembourg will be helpful for anyone planning to relocate.

Manpower Luxembourg
www.manpower.lu

Manpower is a recruitment agency. Its Luxembourg site features a database of private sector jobs.

StepStone Luxembourg
www.stepstone.lu
One of Europe's leading online recruitment sites. Features about 30 private sector and education jobs in Luxembourg.

Embassies and Consular Offices

American embassies and consulates have commercial and/or economic sections that can provide you with business information and explain aspects of the local economy. Inquiries about business opportunities should be addressed either to "Commercial Officer" or "Commercial Section."

Representation of Luxembourg in the United States

Embassy of the Grand Duchy of Luxembourg
2200 Massachusetts Avenue NW
Washington, DC 20008
Tel.: (202) 265–4171

Fax: (202) 328–8270

www.luxembourg–usa.org

Representation of the United States in Luxembourg

American Embassy
22 Boulevard Emmanuel–Servais
L–2535 Luxembourg City, Luxembourg

Tel.: [352] 46 0123
Fax: [352] 46 1401
www.amembassy.lu

Chambers of Commerce

Chambers of commerce consist of member firms in both countries interested in international trade. These are appropriate companies to initially target in the job search.

American Chamber of Commerce in Luxembourg

7, rue Alcide de Gasperi

L–2981 Luxembourg City, Luxembourg

Tel./Fax: [352] 43 17 56

Email: contact@amcham.lu

www.amcham.lu

Luxembourg American Chamber of Commerce

825 Third Avenue, 36th Floor
New York, NY 10022
Tel.: (212) 888 6701
Fax: (212) 888 1162
Email: info@luxembourgbusiness.org
www.luxembourgbusiness.com

World Trade Center in Luxembourg

A world trade center such as this one usually includes many foreign companies that conduct business in Luxembourg.

World Trade Center Luxembourg
6–10 Place de la Gare, First Floor
L–1616 Luxembourg, Luxembourg

Tel.: [352] 40 86 54
Fax: [352] 40 86 08
Email: rorelux@pt.lu

Other Informational Organizations

Foreign government missions in the United States, such as tourist and trade offices, can furnish visas and information on work permits and other important regulations. They may also offer economic and business information about the country.

Centre d'Information Jeunes (CIJ)
Youth Information Center
26 Place de la Gare, Geleria Kons
L–1616 Luxembourg City, Luxembourg
Tel.: [352] 478 6477
Fax: [352] 26 48 31 89
Email: youth–europe@snj.lu
www.jugend.lu

Luxembourg Accueil Information
Information Service for the Grand
Duchy of Luxembourg
10 Bisserwee
L–1238 Luxembourg–Grund
Luxembourg
Tel.: [352] 4 17 17

Luxembourg Board of Economic Development
17 Beekman Place
New York, NY 10022
Tel.: (212) 888–6664
Fax: (212) 888–6116
Email: info@luxembourgnyc.org

Luxembourg National Tourist Office
P.O. Box 1001
L–1010 Luxembourg, Luxembourg
Tel.: [352] 42 82 82 10
Fax: [352] 42 82 82 38
Email: info@ont.lu
www.ont.lu

Business Directories

Although not always easy to find, business directories can prove invaluable in the international job search. Your best bet for locating these directories is to begin in the reference section of any public or university library. Most directories list company names, addresses, products, and phone numbers. Some directories include executive names and titles and financial information about the company. These sources provide you with the names of the people to contact for employment information as well as financial data, which can tell you how strong a company's position in a country may be.

ABC Luxembourgeois pour le Commerce et l'Industrie. ABC pour le Commerce et l'Industrie, Doornveld 11 B28, B–1731 Asse, Belgium; email: abc–belgium.com; www.abc–d.lu. Lists 2,500 manufacturing, importing, and service firms in Luxembourg. 325 pages; published annually in French and German.

L'Industrie Luxenbourgeoise. Federation des Industries Luxembourgeois, 7 rue Alcide de Gaspari, P.O. Box 1304, L–1013, Luxembourg City, Luxembourg. Lists approximately 320 leading industrial companies. 170 pages; published annually in English, French, and German.

Inter Region. Editus Luxembourg, 28 rue Michel Rodange, L–2348 Luxembourg City, Luxembourg; email: phone@editus.lu. Covers 15,000 top companies in the Saar–Lor–Lux area (southern Belgium, Saarland, Trier, Luxembourg, and Lorraine). 764 pages; published annually in English, French, and German.

Kompass Luxembourg. Editus Luxembourg, 28 rue Michel Rodange, L–2348 Luxembourg City, Luxembourg; email: phone@editus.lu. Information on the top 2,100 service companies, distributors, and manufacturers in Luxembourg. 800 pages; published annually in English, German, and Spanish.

American Companies in Luxembourg

The following companies are classified by business area: Banking and Finance, Industrial Manufacturing, Retailing and Wholesaling, Service Industries, and Technology. Company information includes firm name, address, phone and fax number, and specific business. Your chances of securing employment abroad are substantially better if you contact the subsidiary company in Europe rather than the parent company in the United States. Keep in mind that the contact information for companies may change frequently. It's savvy to confirm a company's address and phone number before writing to it.

Banking and Finance

BDO Compagnie Fiduciaire
5 Boulevard de la Foire
L–1528 Luxembourg City, Luxembourg
Tel.: [352] 45 123–1
Fax: [352] 45 123–201
www.bdo.com
(Accounting)

Citibank (Luxembourg)
58 Blvd Grande Duchesse Charlotte
L–1330 Luxembourg City, Luxembourg
Tel.: [352] 45 14 14–1
Fax: [352] 45 14 14 75
(Commercial bank)

Fidelity Investments Luxembourg
Kanasallis House

Place de l'Etolie
L–1021 Luxembourg City, Luxembourg
Tel.: [352] 25 04 04–1
Fax: [352] 25 03 40
www.fidelity.com
(Financial services)

JP Morgan Bank
5, rue Plaetis
L–2338 Luxembourg City, Luxembourg
Tel.: [352] 46 26 85–1
Fax: [352] 46 26 85–880
(Commercial bank)

Industrial Manufacturing

DuPont Engineering Products
rue Général Patton, contern
L–2984 Luxembourg City, Luxembourg
Tel.: [352] 36 66 1000
Fax: [352] 36 66 5006
(Chemical products)

GE FANUC Automation
Zone Industrielle
Ecternach
L–6468 Luxembourg City, Luxembourg
Tel.: [352] 72 79 79–1
Fax: [352] 72 79 79–214
(Electrical products)

Goodyear
Avenue Gordon Smith
L–7750 Colmar–Berg, Luxembourg
Tel.: [352] 302 81 99
(Tires and inner tubes)

Retailing and Wholesaling

Foot Locker Luxembourg
43 Avenue de la Gare

L–1611 Luxembourg City, Luxembourg
Tel.: [352] 491214
(Shoes and sneakers)

Service Industries

Accenture
46 Avenue J.F. Kennedy
L–1855 Luxembourg City, Luxembourg
Tel.: [352] 264 23–1
Fax: [352] 264 23–233
(Management consulting)

Kelly Services Luxembourg
7 – 11 Route d'Esch
L–1470 Luxembourg City, Luxembourg
Tel.: [352] 46 62 66
Fax: [352] 46 62 67
www.kellyservices.com
(Temporary services)

PriceWaterhouseCoopers
400 Route d'Esch
L–1014 Luxembourg City, Luxembourg
Tel.: [352] 49 48 48–1
Fax: [352] 49 48–2900
www.pwcglobal.com
(Accounting and auditing)

Technology

IBM Belgium
Ceinture Um Schlass 1
B–5880 Hesperange, Luxembourg
Tel.: [352] 36 03 85–1
Fax: [352] 36 04 16
(Digital equipment processing)

European Companies in Luxembourg

Several major non–American firms operate in Luxembourg. They can be either domestic or based in another European country. Such companies will generally hire their own nationals first but may employ Americans.

Banking and Finance

Banque & Caisse d'Epargne de l'Etat
1 Place de Metz
L– 2954 Luxembourg City,
Luxembourg
Tel.: [352] 40 15–1

Fax: [352] 40 15–2099
(Bank)

Banque General du Luxembourg (B.G.L.)
50 Avenue John F. Kennedy
L–2951 Luxembourg City, Luxembourg

Tel.: [352] 42 42–1
Fax: [352] 42 42–2579
(Commercial bank)

The Cronos Group
16 Allé Marconi, Boite Postale 260
L–2120 Luxembourg City, Luxembourg
Tel.: [352] 453 145
Fax: [352] 453 147
www.cronos.com
(Financial services)

Espirito Santo Financial Group
37 Rue Notre–Dame
Luxembourg City, Luxembourg
Tel.: [352] 476 8101
www.esfg.com
(Financial services, banks)

Kredietbank Luxembourgeoise
43 Boulevard Royal
L–2955 Luxembourg City, Luxembourg
Tel.: [352] 47 97 1
www.kbl.lu
(Bank)

Industrial Manufacturing

Arbed
19, Avenue de la Liberte
L–2930 Luxembourg City, Luxembourg
Tel.: [352] 4792 2360
www.arbed.com
(Iron and steel)

Millicom International Cellular
75 Route de Longwy
L–8080 Bertrange, Luxembourg
Tel.: [352] 27 759 101
Fax: [325] 27 759 359
www.millicom.com
(Telecommunications)

Quilmes Industrial
84 Grand–Rue
L–1660 Luxembourg City, Luxembourg
Tel.: [352] 473 884
Fax: [352] 226 056
www.quinsa.com
(Breweries and soft drinks)

SES Global
Chateau de Betzdorf

L–6815 Betzdorf, Luxembourg
Tel.: [352] 710 725 1
Fax: [352] 710 725 227
www.ses–global.com/index.htm
(Satellite systems)

Thiel Logistik
5 Ave. de Laengten
L–6776 Grevenmacher, Luxembourg
Tel.: [352] 719 690 1000
Fax: [352] 719 690 1198
www.thiel–logistik.com
(Logistics)

Service Industries

RTL Group
45 Boulevard Pierre Frieden
L–2850 Kirchberg, Luxembourg
Tel.: [352] 421 421
Fax: [352] 421 42 2760
www.rtlgroup.com
(Radio & TV broadcast)

SBS Broadcasting
8–10 rue Mathias Hardt
L–1717 Luxembourg City, Luxembourg
Tel.: [352] 40 78 78
Fax: [352] 40 78 04
www.sbsbroadcasting.com
(Radio & TV broadcast)

Technology

Europe Online Networks
Media Center
11, Rue Pierre Werner
L–6832 Betzdorf, Luxembourg
Tel.: [352] 719 785
Fax: [352] 719 787
www.europeonline.com
(Internet and online services)

Gemplus International
Aerogolf Center, 1 Hohenhof
L–2633 Senningerberg, Luxembourg
Tel.: [352] 2634 6100
Fax: [352] 2634 6161
www.gemplus.com
(Computer software)

International School in Luxembourg

American International
School of Luxembourg

36 Boulevard Pierre DuPont
L–1430 Luxembourg City, Luxembourg

Tel.: [352] 260 440
Fax: [352] 260 44704
Email: admin@islux.lu
www.islux.lu

Help us keep you current with free updates

We realize that companies move, go out of business, or start anew. We know that websites come and go. Many of the companies and websites listed in *How to Get a Job in Europe* could undergo change in the coming months and years.

You are the key to keeping this book current. If you would be so kind as to alert us of any changes to the job sources described in this book, we will post those changes on our free online Update Sheet at http://jobfindersonline.com.

When you find that a website described here no longer exists, has a new URL, has changed the job resources it offers — or if you have found any new European job resources you think we should add — send us an email that tells us the name of the job resource, its URL, and the page of this book on which the job source appears. Please tell us what has changed. We will confirm your information and post it online. Similarly, please tell us about any changes in print resources or company information so we can post the changes online.

Send your email with changes to:
europe_update@planningcommunications.com

To see the free Update Sheet which you can print from your web browser, visit http://jobfindersonline.com — the links to the free Update Sheet will be obvious on our home page.

The Netherlands

Major employment centers: Amsterdam, The Hague, Rotterdam

Major business language: Dutch

Language skill index: English is spoken by most, although Dutch is appreciated.

Currency: Euro

Telephone country code: 31

Time zone: Eastern Standard Time + 6 hours

Punctuality index: Appointments and punctuality are expected.

Average daily temperature, high/low: January: 40°/34°; July: 69°/59° (The Hague)

Average number of days with precipitation: January: 19 days; July: 13 days

Best bet for employment:

    For students: Apply to IAESTE

    Permanent jobs: International trade and business

Chance of finding a job: Good, but it takes persistence

Useful tip: Although the name Holland is used interchangeably with the Netherlands, technically "Holland" refers to two western coastal provinces, North and South Holland. Today, Dutch people use either word to indicate their home country.

The Kingdom of the Netherlands lies in northwestern Europe on the North Sea. The country, about half the size of Maine, is one of the smallest and most densely populated European nations. It is often called Holland after a historic region now a part of the modern nation. Most of the Netherlands consists of flat plains, with an average elevation of just 37 feet above sea level. Much of the country is below sea level, protected by an extensive series of dikes.

The Dutch speak their own language and are largely ethnically homogeneous. In terms of religious affiliations, Dutch society is divided between Roman Catholics, over 40 percent of the population, and Protestants belonging to the Dutch Reformed Church, about 20 percent. Cleavages in the Netherlands have historically occurred around the religious difference.

> **Even with tolerant policies on prostitution and drugs, the Netherlands is an extremely orderly society.**

Celtic and Germanic tribes inhabited the area when Julius Caesar arrived in 55 B.C. The Franks, Burgundy, and the Spanish Hapsburgs ruled the low countries. William the Silent, Prince of Orange, led the Union of Utrecht in 1579 and demanded independence from Spain in 1581. In the seventeenth century, the United Dutch Republic achieved economic, military, and artistic prominence in Europe. Napoleon invaded in 1795, creating the Batavian Republic. Following the Napoleonic Wars, the Netherlands became an independent kingdom, uniting Holland and Belgium. In 1830 Belgium seceded; Luxembourg did the same shortly afterward.

The Netherlands remained neutral in World War I but was invaded by Germany in World War II. The colonial empire faded in 1949, when independence was granted to Indonesia, following a protracted war. Large numbers of people have fled to the Netherlands following the independence of former colonies.

The Netherlands maintains a parliamentary democracy under a constitutional monarchy, headed by Queen Beatrix who assumed the throne in 1980. The country's political scene, usually characterized by coalition governments pursuing policies of compromise, was rocked by scandal that made for a tumultuous 2002. After a report by the Netherland's Institute for War Documentation was released that harshly criticized the Dutch government for its failure to prevent the 1995 Srebenica massacre, Prime Minister Wim Kok's coalition government resigned en masse in April 2002. During the Bosnian war, the Dutch military had been in charge of peacekeeping operations in the region when Serb forces attacked and slaughtered at least 7,500 men and boys, an attack considered the worst European atrocity since World War II. The NIWD's report said that the Dutch troops were hindered by an inadequate mandate from the Dutch government and the U.N. and had been sent on an impossible mission.

The coalition government subsequently elected in May 2002 included the conservative Christian Democrats (CDA), the liberal VVD, and the right–wing Pim Fortuyn List (LPF), but it collapsed in October after only 100 days in office. The controversial LPF, founded by the anti–immigrant and openly gay former TV analyst Pim Fortuyn, was thought to mirror other European right–wing parties like that headed by Jean–Marie Le Pen in France. The LPF saw its public support increase when Fortuyn was assassinated 15 days before the national elections. Yet the party never governed effectively and the coalition government's collapse was blamed on infighting in the LPF. In January 2003 elections, Dutch voters roundly rejected the LPF and returned their support to the country's two mainstream parties, the CDA and the Labor Party.

The Dutch are well known for their extensive social welfare system. Medical care and a basic income are considered rights for all citizens. There are strong laws against age, race, religious, or sex discrimination. The Dutch are also well known for their liberal social attitudes. The national health insurance will even pay for a gender reassignment surgery. Yet even with their famously tolerant policies on prostitution and drugs, the Netherlands is an extremely orderly society.

Typical business hours are from 9 a.m. to 5 p.m. Mondays through Fridays. On Friday evenings, many retail shops stay open until 9 p.m.

Current Economic Climate

Despite its size, the Netherlands' economy is strong. The unemployment rate is approximately 2.9 percent. The country's major industries include agro–industries, metal and engineering products, electrical machinery and equipment, chemicals, petroleum, construction, microelectronics, and fishing with the high–tech industry creating most of the new jobs. The Netherlands has a highly developed horticultural industry, and agriculture, especially dairy farming, plays an especially important role in the economy. The Dutch rank third worldwide in the value of its agricultural exports, behind only the United States and France. The Rotterdam harbor, which handles the most shipping tonnage in the world, significantly contributes to the strength of the Dutch economy. The Netherlands' trading partners are the E.U., especially Germany and Belgium, and the United States. The Dutch were among the first members of the E.U., and adopted the euro as their currency in early 1999.

The Netherlands' 10 Largest Companies

(2001, based on market capitalization)

1. Royal Dutch/Shell Group
2. ING Groep
3. Unilever
4. AEGON
5. Koninklijke Philips Electronics
6. ABN AMRO Holding
7. Koninklijke Ahold
8. Fortis (NL)
9. European Aeronautic Defence and Space Co.
10. Heineken

Getting Around in the Netherlands

The railway system in Holland is very efficient and covers all parts of the country. With a *strippenkaart,* you can have access to trams, buses, subways, and other public transportation. Eurail and InterRail passes are valid on all trains.

The Netherlands?

When referring to the Netherlands, you should always use the definite article "the." The only time you simply use "Netherlands" is with addresses. Otherwise, you describe a person as being from *the Netherlands,* or that you would like to find a job in *the Netherlands.* The capital of the Netherlands is The Hague. Unlike the definite article that appears before the name of the country, the Netherlands' capital always takes a capitalized "The" before The Hague.

Employment Regulations and Outlook for Americans:

As in most E.U. countries, obtaining employment in the Netherlands as a foreigner is very difficult. An application for a residence permit for the purpose of employment should be filed with the Consulate–General well in advance. Your employer should apply for an employment permit at the Ministry of Social Affairs and Labor at least 30 days before you will start work. Employers will be expected to demonstrate that they attempted to find qualified applicants in the Netherlands and the E.U. The shortage of Dutch applicants with some types of IT and telecom skills now means that work permit applications can sometimes be made for these positions without the employer showing details of the recruitment search. You should be aware that a working knowledge of Dutch is essential to successfully landing a job in the Netherlands.

Even if you are not planning to look for a job right away, you will need to report to the local police, *Section Vreemdelingenpolitie,* within eight days of your arrival if you plan to stay in the country for more than three months. You will be required to show proof of (1) sufficient means to finance your stay, (2) adequate housing, and (3) health insurance covering all medical/hospital costs.

Most of the jobs that you would find quickly in Holland are in low–skill, menial positions that the Dutch themselves disdain. The minimum wage is fairly high, but you may forfeit such benefits by working illegally. Temporary work may be found through employment agencies, although their ability to locate work for non–E.U. nationals will be limited. Work is always more difficult to find during August, the student vacation month. Agricultural work, for example, is popular with local youth. Employers expect you to have medical insurance.

Short–term and Temporary Work

Au pair work is plentiful in the Netherlands. In addition to the agencies below, Au Pair in Europe and InterExchange recruit nannies to work in the Netherlands. Both are described in Chapter 9.

Activity International
P.O. Box 7097
NL–9701 JB Groningen, Netherlands
Tel.: [31] 50 313 0666
Fax: [31] 50 313 1633
Email: aupair@noord.bart.nl
www.activity.aupair.nl
Activity International has been facilitating au pair placements in the Netherlands since 1988.

Juno Au Pairs
Weide 37
NL–3121 XV Schiedam, Netherlands
Tel.: [31] 10 4715 431
Fax: [31] 10 4717 662
Email: juno@worldonline.nl
www.junoaupairs.com

Juno Au Pairs was established by the Chamber of Commerce in Rotterdam to facilitate au pair placements in the Netherlands. Juno's application process is quite stringent. They require an application form, a resume, a "Dear Family" letter written by the applicant, two letters of reference, a current photograph, and a medical certification.

Travel Active
P.O. Box 107
NL–5800 Venray, Netherlands
Tel.: [31] 478 551900
Email: info@travelactive.nl
www.travelactive.nl
Travel Active is a Dutch company that runs an au pair placement service in the Netherlands.

Internship Programs

The best bet for students interested in obtaining practical experience in the Netherlands is to work with established organizations, such as AIESEC or IAESTE, which are described in Chapter 9.

Volunteer Opportunities

The volunteer opportunities in the Netherlands are quite varied. In addition to the organizations described below, Volunteers for Peace, Service Civil International, and the Bretheren Volunteer Service coordinate projects that address environmental, social, and political issues. They are detailed in Chapter 9. The world headquarters of Greenpeace International, described on page 353, is in the Netherlands.

Lisle Intercultural Programs
900 County Road, #269
Leander, TX 78641
Tel.: (800) 477–1538
Fax: (512) 259–0392
Email: lisle@io.com
www.lisle.utoledo.edu/
Lisle's purpose is to broaden global awareness and appreciation of other cultures through programs that bring together people of diverse religious, cultural, sexual, political, and racial backgrounds to interact and reflectively

consider their experience. The program in the Netherlands is intended to provide participants a chance to learn about how a densely populated country like Holland copes with immigration and integration issues, and how the Dutch methods compare to those in other countries. The program fee is $1,500 for three weeks, inclusive of room, board and in–country travel. Airfare to Europe is not included.

NJBG (Nederlandse Jeugdbond voor Geschiedenis)
Prins Willem Alexanderhof 5
NL–2595 BE The Hague, Netherlands
Tel.: [31] 70 347 6598
Fax: [31] 70 335 2536
Email: info@njbg.nl
www.njbg.nl
The Dutch Youth Association for History (NJBG) coordinates archaeological work camps throughout the Netherlands. NJBG also sponsors theme excursions, in which participants may live like the group they are studying.

Universal Esperanto–Asocio
Nieuwe Binneweg 176
NL–3015 BJ Rotterdam, Netherlands
Tel.: [31] 10 436 1044
Fax: [31] 10 436 1751
Email: uea@inter.nl.net
www.uea.org
UEA works not only to promote Esperanto, a fabricated international language, but also to stimulate discussion of the world language problem and to call attention to the necessity of equality among languages. Volunteers are required to speak Esperanto fluently.

Resources for Further Information

Newspapers in the Netherlands

Algemeen Dagblad
Tel.: [31] 10 40 67 211
Fax: [31] 10 40 66 969
www.ad.nl

De Volkskrant
Tel.: [31] 20 562 9222

Fax: [31] 20 562 289
www.volskrant.nl

NRC Handelsblad
Tel.: [31] 10 406 6111
Fax: [31] 10 406 6967
www.nrc.nl

Useful Websites for Job Seekers

The Internet is a good place to begin your job search. Many Dutch employers list job vacancies, especially those in technical fields, on the web. There are also many websites that provide useful information for job searchers researching the Dutch job market.

Arbeids Bureau
www.werk.net
Maintained by the national employment office, the Center for Work and Income. The searchable database includes all of the jobs currently posted with the center. (These jobs can also be viewed on the Teletext page of Belgian TV stations.) The "Working in the Netherlands" page offers useful tips for foreigners seeking a job in the Netherlands.

Banenbeurs
www.banenbeurs.nl
Site features over 300 jobs for IT professionals. In addition to job vacancies, the site offers some useful tips about how to begin looking for work, including how to write a CV.

CareerNet
www.careernet.nl
Features positions in finance, IT, and marketing and sales. You can create a personal profile potential employers can view online. Written in Dutch.

Carp
www.carp.nl
Includes a database of jobs, an online career interest inventory, and links to career coaches who can provide job search assistance. Written in Dutch.

Click Work
www.clickwork.nl
Includes nearly 600 job vacancies in the Netherlands. You may search jobs by specific criteria, industry, or specific em-

ployer. To access other search capabilities, you must register. Written in Dutch.

Executives Only
www.executivesonly.nl
Lists only management positions with a salary over €54,000. You may also post your CV for review by executive recruiters. Written in Dutch.

Flexhunter
www.flexhunter.nl
The search engine on this site permits you to sort jobs by industry, type of work, and geography. Also features several links to other job–searching sites in the Netherlands. Written in Dutch.

Hufkens Human Resources
www.hufkens.nl
Hufkens is an executive search firm that specializes in job vacancies in the southern part of the Netherlands. The site also includes links to other Dutch job listings. The site, which can be viewed in English, warns job seekers that because Dutch employers expect to interview candidates many times, it is almost impossible to find work in the Netherlands without living there.

Intermediair
www.intermediair.nl
The job listings may be searched by industry or geographic location. The site includes sections with tips for student job seekers, vocational interest tests, and instructions for preparing a CV. Written in Dutch.

Jobbing Mall
www.jobbingmall.nl
Jobbing Mall lists over 3,800 vacancies. It also features a resume database. Written in Dutch.

JobNet
www.jobnet.nl
Lists jobs in the private sector in the Netherlands. The site targets job seekers according to the amount of work experience they have: young professional, professional, manager, or executive.

JobZone
www.jobzone.nl
Lists hundreds of jobs in categories ranging from IT to au pair. Written in Dutch.

Jobnews
www.jobnews.nl
Features over 1,000 private sector jobs in the Netherlands as well as a resume bank. Includes a special section for students with tips on job searching and a salary index. Written in Dutch.

Manpower Netherlands
www.manpower.nl
Manpower is a recruitment agency. Its Dutch site features 700 private sector jobs.

Medweb
www.medweb.nl
Offers information about the health care industry in the Netherlands, as well as job vacancies. About 200 jobs are posted on the site, and you may submit your resume to a CV bank. Written in Dutch.

Netherlands JobPilot
www.jobpilot.nl
Includes private–sector jobs, a resume database, and a directory of employers. Free registration.

StepStone Netherlands
www.stepstone.nl
One of Europe's leading online recruitment sites, it features over 2,900 private sector and education jobs in the Netherlands.

Vacant.nl
www.vacant.nl
Lists a huge number of jobs in industries including IT, finance, and nonprofit management. You can post your resume here. Written in Dutch.

Van Zoelen Recruitment
www.vz–recruitment.nl
Van Zoelen is an executive search firm. Its site lists some jobs, provides a place for candidates to register, and provides a useful set of links to other Dutch job posting sites. It even includes an online art gallery.

Embassies and Consular Offices

American embassies and consulates have commercial and/or economic sections that can provide you with business information and explain aspects of the local economy. Inquiries about business opportunities should be addressed either to "Commercial Officer" or "Commercial Section."

Representation of the Netherlands in the United States

Royal Netherlands Embassy
4200 Linnean Avenue NW
Washington, DC 20008
Tel.: (202) 244–5300
Fax: (202) 362 3430
www.netherlands–embassy.org

Netherlands Consulates General:

Chicago, (312) 856–0110; Houston, (713) 622–8000; Los Angeles, (310) 268–1598; Miami, (305) 789–6605 ; New York, (212) 246–1429

Representation of the United States in the Netherlands

American Embassy
Lange Voorhout 102
NL–2514 EJ The Hague, Netherlands
Tel.: [31] 70 310 9209
Fax: [31] 70 361 4688
www.usemb.nl

**American Consulate
General — Amsterdam**
Museumplein 19
NL–1071 DJ Amsterdam, Netherlands
Tel.: [31] 20 575 5309
Fax: [31] 20 575 5310

Chambers of Commerce

Chambers of commerce consist of member firms in both countries interested in international trade. These are appropriate companies to initially target in the job search.

**American Chamber of
Commerce in the Netherlands**
Van Karnebeeklaan 14
NL–2585 The Hague, Netherlands
Tel.: [31] 70 365 9808
Fax: [31] 70 364 6992
Email: office@amcham.nl
www.amcham.nl

**Netherlands Chamber
of Commerce in the U.S.**
One Rockefeller Plaza, Suite 1420
New York, NY 10020
Tel.: (212) 265–6460
Fax: (212) 265–6402
www.netherlands.org

World Trade Centers in the Netherlands

These world trade centers usually include many foreign companies that conduct business in the Netherlands.

World Trade Center Amsterdam
Strawinskylaan 1
NL–1007 XW Amsterdam, Netherlands
Tel.: [31] 20 575 9111
Fax: [31] 20 662 7255
Email: aarts@wtc–amsterdam.nl
www.wtcamsterdam.com

World Trade Center Eindhoven
Bogert 1
P.O. Box 2085
NL–5600 CB Eindhoven, Netherlands
Tel : [31] 40 265 36 53
Fax : [31] 40 244 90 41
Email: wtce@iae.nl
www.wtce.nl

World Trade Center Rotterdam
Beursplein 37
P.O. Box 30055
NL–3001 DB Rotterdam, Netherlands

Tel.: [31] 10 405 4444
Fax: [31] 10 405 5016
Email: info@wtcro.nl
www.wtcrotterdam.nl

Other Informational Organizations

Foreign government missions in the United States, such as tourist offices, can furnish visas and information on work permits and other important regulations. They may also offer economic and business information about the Netherlands.

Netherlands Board of Tourism
355 Lexington Avenue, 19th Floor
New York, NY 10017

Tel.: (212) 370–7367

www.goholland.com

Business Directories

Although not always easy to find, business directories can prove invaluable in the international job search. Your best bet for locating these directories is to begin in the reference section of any public or university library. Most directories list company names, addresses, products, and phone numbers. Some directories include executive names and titles and financial information about the company. These sources provide you with the names of the people to contact for employment information as well as financial data, which can tell you how strong a company's position in a country may be.

Dun's 20,000 Netherlands. Dun & Bradstreet Company, 3 Sylvan Way, Parsippany, NJ 07054–3896; email: dnbmdd@dnb.com. Covers 20,000 industrial, trading, transportation, banking, insurance, and service companies in the Netherlands. 450 pages; published annually in Dutch.

Holland Exports. ABC voor Handel en Industrie, Koningin Wilhelminalaan 16, P.O. Box 190, NL–2000 AD Haarlem, Netherlands; email: info@abc–d.nl; www.hollandexports.com. Lists over 8,300 exporters and manufacturers in the Netherlands. Published annually; online version available.

Kompass Nederland. Kompass Nederland, Perkinsbaan 12E, NL–3439 ND Nieuwegein, Netherlands; email: info@kompass.nl; www.kompass.nl. Distributed in the United States by Croner Publications, 34 Jericho Turnpike, Jericho, NY 11753. Lists 3,000 service companies, distributors, and manufacturers. €245; 3,100 pages; published annually.

Netherlands–American Trade Directory. American Chamber of Commerce in the Netherlands, Burg. Van Karnebeeklaan 14, NL–2585 BB The Hague, Netherlands; email: office@amcham.nl, info@amcham.nl. Includes data on 5,000 Dutch and American businesses trading and investing in the two countries. $140; published biennially.

American Companies in the Netherlands

The following companies are classified by business area: Banking and Finance; Industrial Manufacturing; Retailing and Wholesaling; Service Industries; and Technology. Company information includes firm name, address, phone and fax number, and specific business. Your chances of securing employment abroad are substantially better if you contact the subsidiary company in Europe rather than the parent company in the U.S. Keep in mind that the contact information for companies can change quite often. Be sure to confirm a company's address and phone number before writing to it.

Banking and Finance

Bank of America
Herengracht 459–469
NL–1017 BP Amsterdam, Netherlands
Tel.: [31] 20 557 1888
Fax: [31] 20 557 1700
www.bankamerica.com
(Bank)

Citibank
Hoogoorddreef 54/B Europlaza
1101 BE Amsterdam Zuidoost,
Netherlands
Tel.: [31] 20 651 42 11
Fax: [31] 20 651 42 34
(Bank)

Zwolsche Algemeene
Buizerdlaan 12
NL–3435 SB Nieuwegein, Netherlands
Tel.: [31] 30 607 7911
Fax: [31] 30 603 9347
www.thehartford.com
(Financial services)

Industrial Manufacturing

Air Products Nederland
Noordkade 100
NL–2741 GA Waddinxveen,
Netherlands
Tel.: [31] 182 6214 21
Fax: [31] 182 6160 72
(Chemicals and industrial gases)

ALCOA Chemie Nederland
Theemsweg 30
NL–3197 KM Botlek Rotterdam,
Netherlands
Tel.: [31] 181 27 01 00
Fax: [31] 181 21 78 53
(Aluminum products)

Bristol–Myers
Vijzelmolenlaan 9
NL–3447 GX Woerden, Netherlands
Tel.: [31] 348 574 222

Fax: [31] 348 423 084
(Pharmaceuticals)

Cargill
Coenhavenweg 2
NL–1013 BL Amsterdam, Netherlands
Tel.: [31] 20 580 19 11
Fax: [31] 20 682 01 93
(Agricultural products)

Carrier
Rijnkijk 141
NL–2394 AG Hazerswoude,
Netherlands
Tel.: [31] 71 341 7111
Fax: [31] 71 341 4192
www.carrier.com
(Air conditioning systems)

Exxon Chemical Holland
Botlekweg 121/HAVENNR–406
NL–3197 KA Botlek Rotterdam,
Netherlands
Tel.: [31] 10 487 59 11
Fax: [31] 10 487 4461
(Chemical products)

Ford Nederland
Amsteldijk 217
NL–1079 LK Amsterdam, Netherlands
Tel.: [31] 20 504 45 04
Fax: [31] 20 504 45 43
(Motor vehicles and parts)

Hallmark Nederland
Rietbaan 48
NL–2908 LP Capelle Aan Den IJssel,
Netherlands
Tel.: [31] 10 459 65 66
Fax: [31] 10 458 3685
(Greeting cards)

Mars
Taylorweg 5
NL–5466 AE Veghel, Netherlands
Tel.: [31] 413 38 33 33
Fax: [31] 413 35 16 70
(Confectionery)

Merck Sharp & Dohme
Waarderweg 39
NL–2031 BN Haarlem, Netherlands
Tel.: [31] 23 515 3153
Fax: [31] 23 514 8000
(Pharmaceuticals)

Pfizer
Rivium Westlaan 142
2909 LD Capelle Aan Den Ijssel
Netherlands
Tel.: [31] 10 406 42 00
Fax: [31] 10 406 4299
(Pharmaceuticals)

Polaroid Nederland
Bijster 15
NL–4817 HZ Breda, Netherlands
Tel.: [31] 76 531 5050
Fax: [31] 76 531 5055
(Photographic materials)

Texaco Nederland
Weena–Zuid 166
NL–3012 NC Rotterdam, Netherlands
Tel.: [31] 10 403 34 00
Fax: [31] 10 403 35 86
(Petroleum)

Service Industries

AT&T Communications Services Netherlands
Laarderhoogteweg 25
NL–1101 EB Amsterdam, Netherlands
Tel.: [31] 20 570 2100
Fax: [31] 20 664 8990
(Telecommunications)

A.C. Nielsen Nederland
Diemerhof 2
NL–1112 XL Diemen, Netherlands
Tel.: [31] 20 398 87 77
Fax: [31] 20 690 31 75
(Market research)

Radisson SAS Hotel Amsterdam
Rusland 17
NL–1012 CK Amsterdam, Netherlands
Tel.: [31] 20 623 1231
Fax: [31] 20 520 8200
www.radisson.com
(Hotels)

Technology

Amdahl Nederland
Weg der Verenigde naties 1
NL–KT Utrecht, Netherlands
Tel.: [31] 30 290 6222
Fax: [31] 30 296 1744
www.amdahl.com
(Computers)

Applied Materials Europe
Schipholweg 293
N–1171 PK Badhoevedorp,
Netherlands
Tel.: [31] 20 449 6111
Fax: [31] 20 449 6199
www.appliedmaterials.com
(Manufacturing systems for the semi-conductor industry)

Computer Associates Products Nederland
Wattbaan 27
NL–3439 ML Nieuwegein, Netherlands
Tel.:[31] 30 604 8345
Fax: [31] 30 604 7357
www.cai.com
(Computer systems consulting)

Dell Computer
Kabelweg 37
NL–1014 BP Amsterdam, Netherlands
Tel.: [31] 20 674 4857
Fax: [31] 20 674 4775
www.dell.com
(Computers)

Hewlett–Packard Nederland
Startbaan 16
NL–1187 XR Amstelveen, Netherlands
Tel.: [31] 20 547 69 11
Fax: [31] 20 547 77 55
(Printers and calculators)

IBM Nederland
Johan Huizingalaan 765
NL–1066 VH Amsterdam, Netherlands
Tel.: [31] 20 513 51 51
Fax: [31] 20 504 06 13
(Data processing equipment)

Lycos Europe
Richard Holkade 36
NL–2033 PZ Haarlem, The Netherlands
Tel.: [31] 23 750 1111

Fax: [31] 23 553 0390
www.lycos.com
(Internet provider)

Sun Microsystems
Computerweg 1
3821 AA Amersfoort
NL–3821 AA Amersfoort, Netherlands
Tel.: [31] 33 450 1234
Fax: [31] 33 455 3058

www.sun.com
(Mainframes and microcomputers)

Unisys Nederland
Tupolevlaan 1
NL–1101 BA Amsterdam Zuidoost,
Netherlands
Tel.: [31] 20 526 2626
Fax: [31] 20 697 7755
(Computer hardware and software)

European Companies in the Netherlands

The following are several major non–American firms operating in the country. These selected companies can be either domestic or other based in another European country. Such companies will generally hire their own nationals first but may employ Americans.

Banking and Finance

ABN–AMRO Bank
Foppingadreef 22
NL–1102 BS Amsterdam, Netherlands
Tel.: [31] 20 628 9393
Fax: [31] 20 629 9111
www.abnamro.nl
(Bank)

AEGON
AEGONplein 50
NL–2501 The Hague, Netherlands
Tel.: [31] 70 344 3210
Fax: [31] 70 344 8445
www.aegon.com
(Insurance)

Eureko
Entrada 501
NL–1096 EH Amsterdam, Netherlands
Tel.: [31] 20 660 7654
Fax: [31] 20 660 7655
www.eureko.net
(Insurance)

Euronext
Beursplein 5
NL–1012 JW Amsterdam, Netherlands
Tel.: [31] 20 550 4444
Fax: [31] 20 550 4644
www.euronext.com
(Stock exchange)

Fortis (NL)
Archimedeslaan 6
NL–3584 BA Utrecht, Netherlands

Tel.: [31] 30 257 65 76
Fax: [31] 30 257 78 35
www.fortis.com
(Insurance)

ING
Strawinskylaan 2631
NL–1077 ZZ Amsterdam, Netherlands
Tel.: [31] 20 541 54 11
Fax: [31] 20 541 54 44
www.ing.com
(Insurance and savings bank)

Marsh
Marten Meesweg 50
NL–3068 AV Rotterdam, Netherlands
Tel.: [31] 10 406 09 22
Fax: [31] 10 420 68 06
(Insurance)

Rabobank Nederland
Croeselaan 18
NL–3521 CB Utrecht, Netherlands
Tel.: [31] 30 216 00 00
Fax: [31] 30 216 26 72
www.rabobank.nl
(Cooperative bank)

Industrial Manufacturing

Acordis
Westervoortsedijk 73, 6827 AV
P.O. Box 9600
NL–6800 TC Arnhem, Netherlands
Phone: [31] 26 366 4444
Fax: [31] 26 366 4692
www.acordis.com

(Plastics and fibers)

Akzo Nobel
Velperweg 76
NL–6824 BM Arnhem, Netherlands
Tel.: [31] 26 366 4433
Fax: [31] 26 366 3250
www.akzonobel.com
(Chemical products)

Anker
Larikslaan 8
NL–3833 AM Leusden, Netherlands
Tel.: [31] 33 4341 400
Fax: [31] 33 4341 401
www.anker–systems.com
(Electronic business equipment)

Crucell
Archimedesweg 4
NL–2333 CN Leiden, Netherlands
Tel.: [31] 71 524 8701
Fax: [31] 71 524 8702
www.crucell.com
(Biotechnology research)

CSM
Nienoord 13
NL–1112 XE Diemen, Netherlands
Tel.: [31] 20 590 6911
Fax: [31] 20 695 1942
www.csm.nl
(Food, sugar and confectionery)

DSM
Het Overloon 1
NL–6411 TE Heerlen, Netherlands
Tel.: [31] 45 578 81 11
Fax: [31] 45 571 37 41
www.dsm.com
(Chemicals)

European Aeronautic Defence and Space Co.
Beechavenue 130–132
NL–1119 PR Schiphol–Rijk
Netherlands
Tel.: [31] 20 655 48 00
www.eads.net
(Aerospace)

Fokker Services
Aviolandalaan 31
NL–4631 RP Hoogerheide, Netherlands
Tel.: [31] 164 61 80 00
Fax: [31] 164 61 40 73

(Aircraft and aerospace equipment)

Head
Blaak 16
NL–3011 TA Rotterdam, Netherlands
Tel.: [31] 10 214 1923
Fax: [31] 10 401 6462
www.head.com
(Sporting equipment)

Heineken
Tweede Weteringplantsoen 21
NL–1017 ZD Amsterdam, Netherlands
Tel.: [31] 20 523 92 39
Fax: [31] 20 626 35 03
www.heinekencorp.nl
(Brewery)

Hunter Douglas
2 Piekstraat
NL–3071 EL Rotterdam, Netherlands
Tel.: [31] 10 486 9911
Fax: [31] 10 485 0355
www.hunterdouglas.com
(Window coverings)

Jomed
Sehlstedsgatan 1
NL–25439 Helsingborg, Netherlands
www.jomed.com
(Medical instruments and supplies)

Koninklijke Philips Electronics
The Rembrandt Tower, Amstelplein 1
NL–1096 HA Amsterdam, Netherlands
Tel.: [31] 20 59 77 777
Fax: [31] 20 59 77 070
www.philips.com
(Electrical products and systems)

Maxxium Worldwide
J.J. Viottastraat 46–48
NL–1071 JT Amsterdam, Netherlands
Tel.: [31] 20 574 0000
Fax: [31] 20 574 0009
www.maxxium.com
(Distillers)

Pharming Group
Archimedesweg 4
NL–2333 CN Leiden, Netherlands
Tel.: [31] 71 524 74 00
Fax: [31] 71 521 65 07
www.pharming.com
(Biotechnology research)

Royal Dutch Petroleum Co.
Carel van Bylandtlaan 30
NL–2596 HR The Hague, Netherlands
Tel.: [31] 70 377 9111
Fax: [31] 70 377 3115
www.shell.com
(Petroleum products)

Royal Grolsch
Brouwerijstraat 1
NL–7523 XC Enschede, Netherlands
Tel.: [31] 53 483 3333
Fax: [31] 53 483 3100
www.grolsch.com
(Brewery)

Unilever Nederland
Weena 455
NL–3013 AL Rotterdam, Netherlands
Tel.: [31] 10 217 4000
Fax: [31] 10 217 4798
www.unilever.com
(Food processing and consumer products)

Retailing and Wholesaling

Gucci Group
Rembrandt Tower, 1 Amstelplein
NL–1096 HA Amsterdam, Netherlands
Tel.: [31] 20 462 1700
Fax: [31] 20 465 3569
www.gucci.com
(Luxury goods)

Hagemeyer
Rijksweg 69
NL–1411 GE Naarden, Netherlands
Tel.: [31] 35 695 76 11
Fax: [31] 35 694 43 96
www.hagemeyer.nl
(Electronics & consumer products retailer)

Koninklijke Ahold
Albert Heijnweg 1
NL–1507 EH Zaandam, Netherlands
Tel.: [31] 75 659 9111
www.ahold.com
(Food retailing)

Koninklijke Vendex KBB
De Klencke 6
NL–10083 HH Amsterdam,
Netherlands

Tel.: [31] 20 549 0500
Fax: [31] 20 646 1954
www.vendexkbb.com
(Department stores)

Service Industries

Ballast Nedam
Ringwade 1
NL–3430 BH Nieuwegein, Netherlands
Tel.: [31] 30 284 3333
www.ballast–nedam.nl
(Civil, electrical, and mechanical engineering)

Cap Gemini Ernst & Young Netherlands
Daltonlaan 300
NL–3584 BK Utrecht, Netherlands
Tel.: [31] 30 689 8989
Fax: [31] 30 689 9999
(Management consulting)

Elsevier
Van de Sande Bakhuyzenstraat 4
NL–1061 AG Amsterdam, Netherlands
Tel.: [31] 20 515 9111
Fax: [31] 20 683 2617
www.reed–elsevier.com
(Publishing)

KLM Royal Dutch Airlines
Amsterdamweg 55
NL–1182 GP Amstelveen, Netherlands
Tel.: [31] 20 649 9123
Fax: [31] 20 648 8069
www.klm.nl
(Airline)

KPMG International
Burgemeester Rijnderslaan 20
NL–1185 MC Amstelveen, Netherlands
Tel.: [31] 20 656 7890
Fax: [31] 20 656 7700
www.kpmg.com
(Accounting)

Nederlandse Spoorwegen
Laan van Puntenburg 100
NL– 3511 ER Utrecht, Netherlands
Tel.: [31] 30 235 9111
Fax: [31] 30 233 2458
(Rail transport)

Randstad Holding
Diemermere 25

NL–1112 TC Diemen, Netherlands
Tel.: [31] 20 569 5911
Fax: [31] 20 569 5520
www.randstad.com
(Temporary staffing)

United Pan–Europe Communications
Boeing Avenue 53
1119 PE Schiphol–Rijk
P.O. Box 74763
NL–1070 BT Amsterdam, Netherlands
Tel.: [31] 20 778 9840
Fax: [31] 20 778 8419
www.upccorp.com
(Cable TV & satellite systems

Technology

ASM International
Jan van Eycklaan 10
NL–3723 BC Bilthoven, Netherlands
Tel.: [31] 30 229 8411
Fax: [31] 30 228 7469
www.asm.com
(Semiconductor equipment, materials)

Baan Company
Apeldoornsestraat 131
NL–3780 BA Voorthuizen, Netherlands
Tel.: [31] 342 428 888
Fax: [31] 342 428 822
www.baan.com

(Computer software and services)

Equant
21–23 Gatwickstraat, Sloterdijk
NL–1043 GL Amsterdam, Netherlands
Tel.: [31] 20 581 8383
Fax: [31] 20 688 0388
www.equant.com
(Internet and online service providers)

Getronics
Donauweg 10
NL–1043 AJ Amsterdam, Netherlands
Tel.: [31] 20 586 14 12
Fax: [31] 20 586 15 68
www.getronics.com
(Information technology consulting)

KPN Mobile
Maanplein 5
NL–2516 The Hague, Netherlands
Tel.: [31] 70 332 3426
Fax: [31] 70 332 4485
www.kpn–mobile.com
(Wireless communications)

Libertel–Vodafone
Avenue Ceramique 300
NL–6221 KX Maastricht, Netherlands
Tel.: [31] 43 355 7338
www.vodafone.nl
(Wireless communications)

Major International Nonprofit Employer in the Netherlands

Greenpeace International
Keizersgracht 176
NL–1016 DW Amsterdam, Netherlands

Tel.: [31] 20 523 6222
Fax: [31] 20 523 6200
www.greenpeace.org

International Schools in the Netherlands

The American School of The Hague
Rijksstraatweg 200
NL–2241 BX Wassenaar, Netherlands
Tel.: [31] 70 512 1060
Fax: [31] 70 512 1070
Email: bgerritz@ash.nl
www.ash.nl

ANFORTH International School
Ferdinand Bolstraat 1
NL–6445 EE Brunssum, Netherlands
Tel.: [31] 45 527 82 20
Fax: [31] 45 527 82 33

Email: Ais.Directorate@
eu.odedodea.edu
www.afnorthschool.com
(Kindergarten through grade 12)

The British School in the Netherlands
Rosenburgherlaan 2 Voorschoten
NL–2252 BA The Hague, Netherlands
Tel.: [31] 71 560 2250
Fax: [31] 71 560 2290
Email: info@britishschool.nl
www.britishschool.nl

International School of Amsterdam
Sportslaan 45
NL–1185 TB Amstelveen, Netherlands
Tel.: [31] 20 347 11 11
Fax: [31] 20 347 12 22

Email: info@is.nl

www.isa.nl

(International Baccalaureate curriculum,
kindergarten through grade 12)

Chapter

Switzerland, Austria, & Liechtenstein

Switzerland

Major employment centers: Zurich, Basel, Geneva, Bern

Major business languages: German, French, Italian

Language skill index: Count on knowing German or French to gain employment, although most business professionals also speak English. Even if you know German, you may find that the Swiss dialect takes some getting used to.

Currency: Swiss franc

Telephone country code: 41

Time zone: Eastern Standard Time + 6 hours

Punctuality index: In a country famous for its clocks, you'd better be on time.

Average daily temperature, high/low: January: 39°/29°; July: 77/58 (Geneva)

Average number of days with precipitation: January: 11 days; July: 12 days

Best bet for employment:

    For students: Apply to IAESTE for a technical internship.

    Permanent jobs: Banking and finance

Chance of finding a job: Low unemployment and strict immigration laws will limit your prospects

Useful tip: Business customs will vary in the different regions of the country. The Swiss Germans tend to get straight to business when convening a meeting. The French and Italian Swiss will be more laid back and may spend time exchanging small talk about history, culture, or travel before addressing business.

Larger than Massachusetts but smaller than Maine, Switzerland is a geographically compact country. It's in the center of Europe, bordering France to the west, Germany to the north, Liechtenstein and Austria to the east, and Italy to the south. The Swiss Alps cover about a fourth of the country. Large lakes form parts of the borders with France and Germany.

About 65 percent of the resident population, which includes a large number of noncitizens, is German in ethnicity. About 18 percent of the population is French, 10 percent Italian, and 1 percent Ramansch. Language use tends to follow ethnicity; German, French, and Italian are all official languages. Many Swiss speak three languages, occasionally including English. The particular German dialect spoken in Switzerland, *Scheizerdeutsch*, is generally incomprehensible to other German speakers unfamiliar with this variation. Depending upon what part of the country you are in, begin your conversations in German, French, or Italian. Some people in western Switzerland speak only French.

> Switzerland has overcome its lack of natural resources by basing its economic development on inventiveness, frugality, and perseverance.

The former Roman province of Helvetia, now Switzerland, is organized along a federal system, with substantial powers reserved for the 23 regional units, the cantons. In 1291, three cantons formed a defensive union that others later joined to form the present country. The Swiss Confederation (Switzerland's official name) achieved its independence from the Holy Roman Empire in 1648. France occupied the country from 1798 to 1815, renaming it the Helvetic Republic. The Catholic cantons seceded in 1847 but re–entered with the establishment of a federal constitution in 1848. The Swiss population is currently evenly divided between Roman Catholics and Protestants.

The Swiss policy of strict neutrality and nationalistic independence prevents membership in the European Union, the United Nations, or NATO. Switzerland is, though, a member of the European Free Trade Association. The country has experienced extraordinary stability, with most major parties participating in the coalition government that is headed by a sort of collective executive presidency. Despite a policy of neutrality, Switzerland maintains a 400,000–person army and spends approximately two percent of its GNP on defense to maintain a relatively high level of preparedness.

Revelations in 1995 that implicated Swiss bankers in hiding Nazi plunder during World War II have challenged Switzerland's official claims of neutrality. After a careful investigation and an audit of Swiss bank accounts, conducted by a committee led by former Federal Reserve Board Chairman Paul Volcker, the Swiss published lists of 5,559 dormant accounts, many belonging to Holocaust victims. In 1998, legal action prompted the banks to offer a $1.25 billion settlement.

In recent years, Switzerland has seen a gradual shift in its normally conservative political landscape. The rightist Swiss People's Party (SVP), traditionally the junior partner in the four–party coalition government, more than doubled its voting share from 11 percent in 1987 to 22.5 percent in 1999, overtaking its three coalition partners. This shift has put a strain on the "magic formula," the power–brokering agreement of the four coalition parties. Since 1959, the seven-seat cabinet comprises two Free Democrats, two Christian Democrats, two Social Democrats, and one SVP. Most observers believe that if the SVP sustains its voting share in the 2003 federal elections, the magic formula will have to yield to accord the SVP a second seat on the cabinet.

Standard business hours in Switzerland are from 8 a.m. to 6:30 p.m., with a break from noon to 2 p.m., Mondays through Fridays. Post offices in the larger cities are open weekdays from 7:30 a.m. to 6:30 p.m., with some services available until 10:30 p.m. or 11 p.m. and on Saturday morning in some locations. Vacation time is in July and August.

Current Economic Climate

Switzerland has overcome its lack of natural resources by basing its economic development on inventiveness, frugality, and perseverance. More than one–fourth of the country's territory is unusable; fully one–half is either forested or non–arable grassland, and, except for potential waterpower, no energy or mineral resources are available for profitable exploitation. Nevertheless, Switzerland is one of the most highly industrialized countries in the world, consistently ranked as one of the world's richest countries. Trade has been the key to prosperity in Switzerland. The country depends on export markets to generate income and on imports for raw materials and the range of goods and services in the country.

The Swiss are not pursuing membership in the European Union, but they have sought to conform their economic practices with those of the E.U. in order to enhance their international competitiveness. Switzerland's unemployment rate is about 2.6 percent; inflation is approximately 1.2 percent. The country has a mixed economy with an emphasis on private ownership. Telecommunications were privatized in 1998; the only industries still nationalized outright are the postal service and federal railway. Switzerland is still considered a safe haven for investors because it has maintained a degree of bank secrecy, despite the government's modification of some laws to discourage laundering proceeds from illegal drug trafficking.

Economic prosperity benefits from a well–educated workforce and highly technical industries. Major industries include machinery, chemicals, watches, textiles, and precision instruments. The labor force is 50 percent services, 40 percent commerce and industrial, and 10 percent agricultural. Most trade occurs with members of the European Union and with the United States.

Switzerland's 10 Largest Companies

(2001, based on market capitalization)

1. Novartis
2. Nestlé
3. Roche Holding

4. UBS
5. Credit Suisse Group
6. Zurich Financial Services
7. Swisscom
8. Serono
9. Compagnie Financiere Richemont
10. ABB Limited

Getting Around in Switzerland

The Swiss railway system is an excellent network, that includes both private and government–owned lines. Trains are clean, reliable, and frequent. Fares, however, are expensive and Eurail and InterRail passes are accepted only on government rail lines. Though less expensive than trains, buses do not accept Eurail or InterRail passes and tend to be slower. Steamers along the lakes will accept Eurail and InterRail passes.

Employment Regulations and Outlook for Americans

U.S. citizens don't need a visa for stays in Switzerland of less than 90 days, but no foreigner is allowed to stay in the country for longer than six months. The Swiss issue an Assurance of Residence Permit, which is both a work and residence permit. It is difficult to obtain and must be presented upon arrival. Your Swiss employer must apply for the Assurance of Residence Permit for you. Employment for foreigners in Switzerland is extremely difficult; preference in hiring is by law given to E.U. nationals. This combined with the country's almost nonexistent unemployment rate and well–trained workforce means that few foreigners meet the specialized requirements specified by Swiss employment regulations.

Temporary workers from Spain, Portugal, and other less–developed European countries constitute most of the unskilled workforce. Some tourist work in hotels and restaurants may be found but usually requires long hours. Agricultural work in Switzerland is also known to require long hours. An agreement between the United States and Switzerland permits 150 American trainees to work in Switzerland each year. The work exchange program is managed by AIPT which is described in Chapter 9.

Resume tips

The Swiss generally use two resumes: an English and a German version. The English version is the one to send to international companies, and it should resemble the standard resume described in Chapter 5. The German version should reflect the particular requirements of the German *lebenslauf* described in Chapter 15.

Short–term and Temporary Work

Switzerland has ample opportunities for au pair work. In addition to the agency below, Au Pair in Europe recruits for positions in Switzerland. Village Camps also recruits staff for Swiss camps. For details on these an other resources, *see* Chapter 9.

Pro Filia
Beckenhoftsrasse 16
CH–8035 Zurich, Switzerland
Tel./Fax: [41] 1 361 53 31
Email: info@profilia.ch

www.profilia.ch
Pro Filia places au pairs with families in French and German–speaking Switzerland. Au pairs must be available for 12 to 18 month placements.

Internship Programs

Students seeking practical experience in Switzerland have several options. In addition to the agencies listed below, AIPT, IAESTE, AIESEC, and International Cooperative Education offer internships that last from a few months to more than a year. They are described in Chapter 9.

Agroimpuls
Laurstrasse 10
CH–5201 Brugg AG1, Switzerland
Tel.: [41] 56 462 51 44
Fax: [41] 56 442 22 12
www.agroimpuls.ch
Agroimpuls is a program of the Swiss Farmers Union and places foreign trainees in Switzerland. Trainees must possess a relevant degree or have three years of experience in the fields of agriculture, horticulture, or rural home economics. Trainees live and work with host families, who pay placement fees. Applicants must be between 18 and 30 years old, although exceptions can be made.

CDS International
871 United Nations Plaza, 15th Floor
New York, NY 10017–1814
Tel.: (212) 497–3500
Email: info@cdsintl.org
www.cdsintl.org
CDS International is a nonprofit organization committed to international practical training opportunities for young professionals, students, and educators. The Swiss program provides opportunities for recent U.S. graduates in culinary arts or hospitality management. All 18–month placements at four– to five–star hotels and high–end restaurants are paid. You should apply at least three months prior to your desired start date and must be between 21 and 30.

United Nations International Computing Center

Internship Scheme

Palais des Nations

CH–1211 Geneva 10, Switzerland

Email: personnel@unicc.org

www.unicc.org

UNICC offers a limited number of six–month internships. To be eligible, you must be a full–time college student majoring in computer science and from a U.N. member country.

Volunteer Opportunities

Service Civil International and Volunteers for Peace recruit volunteers for social, environmental, and peace projects that last from a few weeks to several months. They are described in Chapter 9. In addition, a number of smaller organizations also recruit volunteers to serve in Switzerland.

Gruppo Volontari della Svizzera Italiana
CP 12
CH–6517 Arbedo, Switzerland
Tel.: [41] 79 354 0161
www.gvsi.org
GVSI is a Christian organization that organizes work camps of people who can speak one of Switzerland's official languages. Most projects focus on environmental issues, community improvement, or disaster relief.

ICYE Federation Schweiz
Postfach 473
CH–3000 Bern 14, Switzerland
Tel.: [41] 313 717 780
Fax: [41] 313 714 078

Email: icye@datacomm.ch
www.icye.ch
The ICYE Federation is an international, independent, nonprofit organization with 35 National Committees in Africa, Asia–Pacific, Europe, Latin America and North America. ICYE's mission is to promote youth mobility and international understanding through long–term (from six to 12 months) voluntary service exchange programs. The projects in Switzerland are located in either the German– or the French–speaking part of the country and include working with children, the elderly or the disabled. There are also projects with NGOs and cultural centers.

Resources for Further Information

Newspapers in Switzerland

Basler Zeitung
Tel.: [41] 61 639 1111
Fax: [41] 61 639 1582
www.baz.ch

Berner Zeitung
Tel.: [41] 31 330 3111
Fax: [41] 31 331 6087
www.bernerzeitung.ch

Blick
Tel.: [41] 1 259 6483
Fax: [41] 1 262 2976
www.blick.ch

Corriere del Ticino
Tel.: [41] 91 960 3351
Fax: [41] 91 968 2977

Le Matin
Tel.: [41] 21 349 4949

Fax: [41] 21 349 4929
www.lematin.ch

Neue Zürcher Zeitung
Tel.: [41] 1 258 1111
Fax: [41] 1 252 1329
www.nzz.ch

Tages Anzeiger
Tel.: [49] 1 248 4111
Fax: [49] 1 248 5061
www.tamedia.ch

24 Heures
Tel.: [41] 21 349 4949
Fax: [41] 21 349 4929

Die Weltwoche
Tel.: [41] 1 448 7311
Fax: [41] 1 448 7766
www.weltwoche.ch

Useful Websites for Job Seekers

The Internet is a good place to begin your job search. Many Swiss employers list job vacancies, especially those in technical fields, on the web. There are also many websites that provide useful information for job searchers researching the Swiss job market.

Academic Job Exchange Board
www.telejob.ethz.ch

Features jobs for young academics in Switzerland and the rest of Europe. Jobs are available with both academic institutions and private industry. Candidates may also register to receive job announcements via email.

emploi.ch
www.emploi.ch
This site, which can be viewed in French, Italian, and German, lists hundreds of jobs in industries ranging from IT to hospitality to social work.

Jobclick Switzerland
www.jobclick.ch
Jobclick lists over 1,400 private–sector jobs in Switzerland, searchable by industry or geographic location. Written in French and German.

Manpower Switzerland
www.manpower.ch
Manpower is a recruitment agency. Its Swiss site features a database of private sector jobs.

Math–jobs Switzerland
www.math–jobs.ch
This site has all math jobs, all the time. You can find jobs in education, banking, IT, and others. The job ads are written in English, French, and German, but the navigation tools are all in English.

NEXUS
www.nexus.ch
This German–language site includes nearly 300 IT jobs in Switzerland. Candidates may register, post a resume online, and receive emailed job announcements.

StellenAnzeiger Joboter
www.stellenanzeiger.ch

The German–language site lists over 3,000 jobs. It includes an alphabetical directory of Swiss companies and tips and tricks for conducting a successful job search.

StepStone Switzerland
www.swisswebjobs.ch
One of Europe's leading online recruitment sites. Features over 400 private sector and education jobs in Switzerland, and can be viewed in French or German.

Swiss Search Engine
www.search.ch
This multi–lingual search engine provides links for information on topics ranging from government to travel and tourism to business and the economy. It includes links to a few employment sites and to Swiss newspapers and magazines.

Switzerland JobPilot
www.jobpilot.ch
This database includes over 2,400 private sector jobs, a resume database, and a directory of employers. Free registration. Written in German, French, and Italian.

TopJobs
www.topjobs.ch
TopJobs lists hundreds of positions throughout Switzerland. It also includes a searchable database of key Swiss employers and an email job notification service. TopJobs includes a small but useful section listing companies that target new college graduates.

Embassies and Consular Offices

American embassies and consulates have commercial and/or economic sections that can provide business information and explain aspects of the local economy. Inquiries about business opportunities should be addressed either to "Commercial Officer" or "Commercial Section."

Representation of Switzerland in the United States
Embassy of Switzerland
2900 Cathedral Avenue NW
Washington, DC 20008

Tel.: (202) 745–7900
Fax: (202) 387–2564
www.swissemb.org

Consulates General of Switzerland:
Atlanta, (404) 870–2000; Chicago, (312) 915–0061; Houston, (713) 650–0000; Los Angeles, (310) 575–1145; New York, (212) 599–5700; San Francisco, (415) 788–2272

Representation of the United States in Switzerland

American Embassy
Jubiläumsstrasse 93
CH–3001 Bern, Switzerland
Tel.: [41] 31 357 7011
Fax: [41] 31 357 7344
www.usembassy.ch

U.S. Consular Agency, Geneva
America Center of Geneva
7, rue Versonnex
CH–1207 Geneva, Switzerland
Tel.: [41] 22 840 5160
Fax: [41] 22 840 5162

U.S. Consular Agency, Zurich
Dufourstrasse 101, Third Floor
Zurich, Switzerland
Tel.: [41] 1 422 25 66
Fax: [41] 1 383 98 14

Chambers of Commerce

Chambers of commerce consist of member firms in both countries interested in international trade. These are appropriate companies to initially target in the job search.

Basel Chamber of Commerce
P.O. Box 1548
CH–Basel, Switzerland
Tel.: [41] 61 272 1888
Fax: [41] 61 272 6228
www.hkbb.ch

Chambre de Commerce et Industrie de Geneva
4 Boulevard de Theatre
CH–1211 Geneva, Switzerland
Tel.: [41] 22 819 9111
Fax: [41] 22 819–9100

Swiss–American Chamber of Commerce
Talacker 41
CH–8001 Zurich, Switzerland

Tel.: [41] 1 211 2454
Fax: [41] 1 211 9572
Email: info@amcham.ch
www.amcham.ch

Swiss–American Chamber of Commerce
608 Fifth Avenue, Suite 309
New York, NY 10020
Tel.: (212) 246–7789
Fax: (212) 246–1366

Swiss Business Federation
Hegibachstrasse 47
CH–8032 Zurich, Switzerland
Tel.: [41] 1 421 3535
Fax: [41] 1 421 3434
www.economiesuisse.ch

World Trade Centers in Switzerland

World trade centers usually include many foreign companies that conduct business in Switzerland.

World Trade Center Basel
Picassoplatz
Lautengartenstrasse 6
CH–4052 Basel, Switzerland
Tel.: [41] 61 225 4450
Fax : [41] 61 225 4410
Email: wtcbasel@trinat.ch
www.messebasel.ch/e/index.htm

World Trade Center Geneva
Route de Pre–Bois 29
CH–1215 Geneva 15, Switzerland
Tel.: [41] 22 929 5656
Fax : [41] 22 791 0885
Email: info@wtc–geneva.ch
www.wtc–geneva.ch

World Trade Center Lugano
One World Trade Center
C.P. 317
CH–6982 Lugano–Agno, Switzerland
Tel.: [41] 91 610 21 11
Fax: [41] 91 610 21 01
Email: info@wtclugano.ch
www.wtclugano.ch

World Trade Center Zurich
Leutschenbachstrasse 95
CH–8050 Zurich, Switzerland
Tel.: [41] 1 309 1111
Fax : [41] 1 309 1122
Email: trade@wtc–zu.ch
www.wtc–zurich.ch

Other Informational Organization

Foreign government missions in the United States, such as tourist offices, can furnish visas and information on work permits and other important regulations. They may also offer economic and business information about Switzerland.

Swiss National Tourist Office
608 Fifth Avenue
New York, NY 10020
Tel.: (212) 757–5944

Fax: (212) 262–6116

www.myswitzerland.com

Business Directories

Although not always easy to find, business directories can prove invaluable in the international job search. Your best bet for locating these directories is to begin in the reference section of any public or university library. Most directories list company names, addresses, products, and phone numbers. Some directories include executive names and titles and financial information about the company. These sources provide you with the names of the people to contact for employment information as well as financial data, which can tell you how strong a company's position in a country may be.

Dun & Bradstreet Swiss Company Information. Dun & Bradstreet AG, Schoenegstrasse 5, CH–8026 Zurich, Switzerland. Lists 180,000 businesses in Switzerland and Liechtenstein. Updated monthly; available in English, German, Italian, and French.

Kompass Schweiz/Liechtenstein. Kompass Schweiz Verlag AG, 14 ln Grosswiesen, CH–8044 Zurich–Gockhausen, Switzerland. U.S. distributor Croner Publications, 34 Jericho Turnpike, Jericho, NY 11753. Lists 50,000 manufacturers, distributors, and service companies in Switzerland and Liechtenstein. 4,400 pages, 240 Swiss francs; updated annually.

List of Professional & Trade Associations in Switzerland. Office Federal de l'Industrie, P.O. Box 2170, CH–3001 Bern, Switzerland. Lists 1,120 active professional associations in Switzerland. 50 pages; 12 Swiss francs; updated infrequently.

Swiss–American Chamber of Commerce Yearbook. Swiss–American Chamber of Commerce, Talacker 41, CH–8001 Zurich, Switzerland; email: info@amcham.che. Lists Swiss and American firms engaged in bilateral trade. 500 pages; $130; updated annually.

Swiss Export Directory. Swiss Office for Trade Promotion, Stampfenbach-strasse 85, CH–8035 Zurich, Switzerland; www.osec.ch. Includes 10,000 Swiss firms engaged in export. 1,400 pages; $35; updated biennially.

Swiss Watch Directory. Indicateur Suisse, Route de la Glane 31, CH–1700, Fribourg, Switzerland. Lists Swiss retailers, associations, and manufacturers' guilds. 900 pages; $52; updated annually.

Verzeichnis der Verwaltungsrate. (Corporate Directors, Switzerland.) Orell Fussli Verlag AG, Dietzingerstrasse 3, CH–8036 Zurich, Switzerland; email: info@ofv.ch; www.profl.ch. Lists chairmen and directors of Swiss companies, including the 100 most influential people in the Swiss economy. 1,600 pages; updated annually.

American Companies in Switzerland

The following companies are classified by business area: Banking and Finance; Industrial Manufacturing; Retailing and Wholesaling; Service Industries; and Technology. Company information includes the firm's name, address, phone and fax number, and specific business. Your chances of securing employment abroad are substantially better if you contact the subsidiary company in Europe rather than the parent company in the U.S. Keep in mind that the contact information for companies listed can change quite often. Be savvy: confirm a company's address and phone number before contacting it.

Banking and Finance

Bank of America
40, rue du Marché
CH–1204 Geneva, Switzerland
Tel.: [41] 223186938
Fax: [41] 223186939
www.bankamerica.com
(Bank)

Citibank Switzerland
Bahnhofstrasse 63
Postfach 3760
CH–8021 Zurich, Switzerland
Tel.: [41] 1 205 71 71
Fax: [41] 1 205 75 59
(Bank)

Bank Morgan Stanley
Bahnhofstrasse 92
CH–8001 Zurich, Switzerland
Tel.: [41] 1 220 91 11
Fax: [41] 1 220 98 00
(Bank)

Industrial Manufacturing

Bridgestone Firestone Schweiz
Limmatpark

CH–8957 Spreitenbach, Switzerland
Tel.: [41] 56 418 71 11
Fax: [41] 56 401 34 68
(Tires and tubes)

Bristol–Myers
Neuhofstrasse 6
CH–6340 Baar, Switzerland
Tel.: [41] 41 767 73 50
Fax: [41] 41 767 73 05
(Pharmaceuticals)

Cargill International
14, Chemin de Normandie
CH–1206 Geneva 12, Switzerland
Tel.: [41] 22 703 22 11
Fax: [41] 22 703 25 55
(Import–export)

DuPont de Nemours International
2 Chemin du Pavillon
CH–1218 Le Grand–Saconnex, Switzerland
Tel.: [41] 22 717 40 00
Fax: [41] 22 717 40 01
(Chemical products)

General Motors Suisse
Stelzenstrasse 4

CH–8152 Glattbrugg, Switzerland
Tel.: [41] 1 828 28 26
Fax: [41] 1 828 21 55
www.gm.com
(Automobiles)

Goodyear Dunlop Tires Suisse
Industriestrasse 21
CH–8604 Hegnau, Switzerland
Tel.: [41] 1 947 85 00
Fax: [41] 1 947 86 80
(Chemical products)

Honeywell
Honeywell–Platz 1
CH–8157 Dielsdorf, Switzerland
Tel.: [41] 1 855 24 24
Fax: [41] 1 855 24 25
(Process control equipment)

Johnson Control Systems SA
38 Chemin du Grand Puit
CH–1217 Meyrin, Switzerland
Tel.: [41] 22 783 10 50
Fax: [41] 22 783 10 51
www.johnsoncontrols.com
(Control systems)

Eli Lilly (Suisse)
P.O. Box 590
16 Chemin de Coquelicots
CH–1214 Vernier/ Geneva, Switzerland
Tel.: [41] 22 306 0333
Fax: [41] 22 306 0470
www.lilly.com
(Pharmaceuticals)

NCR Schweiz
Hertistrasse 25
CH–8301 Glattzentrum b.Wallisellen,
Switzerland
Tel.: [41] 1 832 11 11
Fax: [41] 1 830 74 95
(Office equipment)

Pfizer
Flüelastrasse 7
CH–8048 Zurich, Switzerland
Tel.: [41] 1 495 71 11
Fax: [41] 1 495 72 80
(Medical, chemical, botanical products)

3M Schweiz
Eggstrasse 93
CH–8803 Rüschlikon, Switzerland
Tel.: [41] 1 724 90 90

Fax: [41] 1 724 94 50
(Adhesives, tapes, and packaging)

Xerox
Lindenstrasse 25
CH–8302 Kioten, Switzerland
Tel.: [41] 1 43 305 12 12
Fax: [41] 1 43 305 14 72
(Copier equipment)

Retailing and Wholesaling

The Sharper Image
Lowenstrasse 32
CH–80001 Zurich, Switzerland
Tel.: [41] 1 211 0147
www.sharperimage.com
(Specialty retailer)

Tiffany & Company Zurich
Bahnhofstrasse 24
CH–8022 Zurich 1, Switzerland
Tel.: [41] 1 211 1010
www.tiffany.com
(Jewelry retail)

Service Industries

Accenture
Fraumünsterstrasse 16
CH–8001 Zürich, Switzerland
Tel.: [41] 1 219 98 89
Fax: [41] 1 219 88 89
(Management consulting)

**AMS Management Systems
(Switzerland)**
St.Martinsplatz 8
CH–7000 Chur, Switzerland
Tel.: [41] 81 257 06 92
Fax: [41] 81 257 06 91
www.amsinc.com
(Systems consulting)

**Baker & McKenzie
/ Etienne & Associe**
6, rue Bellot
CH–1206 Geneva, Switzerland
Tel.: [41] 22 346 7608
Fax: [41] 22 347 0284
www.bakerinfo.com
(Law firm)

Kelly Services (Suisse)
20, avenue Edouard–Dubois
CH–2006 Neuchâtel, Switzerland

Tel.: [41] 32 732 11 00
Fax: [41] 32 732 11 30
www.kellyservices.com
(Temporary placements)

Korn/Ferry International
Limmatpark
CH–8957 Spreitenbach, Switzerland
Tel.: [41] 56 418 11 11
Fax: [41] 56 401 65 07
www.kornferry.com
(Executive search)

PriceWaterhouseCoopers
St. Jakobs Strasse 25
CH–4002 Basel, Switzerland
Tel.: [41] 61 270 51 11
Fax: [41] 61 270 55 88
(Auditors)

Warner Bros.
Baslerstrasse 52
CH–8048 Zurich, Switzerland
Tel.: [41] 1 495 77 77
Fax: [41] 1 495 77 95
(Media)

Technology

Dell Computer
29, route de l'Aéroport
CH–1215 Geneva 15, Switzerland
Tel.: [41] 22 799 01 01
Fax: [41] 22 799 01 90
www.dell.com
(Computers)

Hewlett–Packard Schweiz
In der Luberzen 29
CH–8902 Urdorf/Zurich, Switzerland
Tel: [41] 844 711 111
Fax: [41] 844 711 112
(Printers and calculators)

IBM (Schweiz)
21 Quai Bandliweg
CH–8048 Zurich, Switzerland
Tel.: [41] 1 58 333 44 55
Fax: [41] 1 58 333 40 40
(Data processing equipment)

Microsoft Switzerland
Alte Winterthurerstrasse 14A
CH–8304 Wallisellen, Switzerland
Tel.: [41] 1 839 6111
Fax: [41] 1 831 0869
(Computers)

European Companies in Switzerland

The following are major non–American firms operating in the country. These selected companies can be either Swiss or based in another European country. Such companies will generally hire their own nationals first but may employ Americans.

Banking and Finance

Crédit Suisse Group
Paradeplatz 8, P.O. Box 1
CH–8070 Zurich, Switzerland
Tel.: [41] 1 212 1616
Fax: [41] 1 333 2587
www.credit–suisse.com
(Bank)

Swiss Life Insurance and Pension Company
General Guisan–Quai 40
CH–8022 Zurich, Switzerland
Tel.: [41] 1 284 3311
Fax: [41] 1 281 2080
www.swisslife.com
(Life Insurance)

Swiss National Bank
Borsenstrasse 15
CH–8022 Zurich, Switzerland
Tel.: [41] 1 631 3111
Fax: [41] 1 631 3911
www.snb.ch/e/homepage.html
(Banking)

Swiss Reinsurance Company
Mythenquai 50/60
CH–8022 Zurich, Switzerland
Tel.: [41] 1 43 285 21 21
Fax: [41] 1 43 285 54 93
www.swissre.com

(Reinsurance)

UBS
Bahnhofstrasse 45
CH–8098 Zurich, Switzerland
Tel.: [41] 1 234 4100
Fax: [41] 1 234 3415
www.ubs.com
(Bank)

Winterthur Swiss Insurance Company
General–Guisan–Strasse 40
CH–8401 Winterthur, Zurich,
Switzerland
Tel.: [49] 52 261 1111
Fax: [49] 52 213 6620
www.winterthur.com
(Insurance)

Zurich Financial Services
Mythenquai 2
CH–8022 Zurich, Switzerland
Tel.: [41] 1 625 2525
Fax: [41] 1 625 3555
www.zurich.com
(Insurance)

Industrial Manufacturing

ABB Ltd.
Affolternstrasse 44
CH–8050 Zurich, Switzerland
Tel.: [41] 43 317 7111
Fax: [41] 43 317 7958
www.abb.com
(Power automation technology products)

Actelion Ltd.
Gewerbestrasse 16
CH–4123 Allschwil, Baselland,
Switzerland
Tel.: [41] 61 487 45 45
Fax: [41] 61 487 45 00
www.actelion.com
(Medical research)

Chocoladefabriken Lindt & Sprüngli
Seestrasse 204
CH–8802 Kilchberg, Zurich, Switzerland
Tel.: [41] 1 716 22 33
Fax: [41] 1 715 39 85
www.lindt.com
(Candy)

Ciba Speciality Chemicals
Klybeckstrasse 141
CH–4002 Basel, Switzerland
Tel.: [41] 61 636 1111
Fax: [41[61 636 1212
www.cibasc.com
(Chemicals)

Clariant
Rothausstrasse 61
CH–4132 Muttenz, Basel, Switzerland
Tel.: [41] 61 469 5111
Fax: [41] 61 469 5999
www.clariant.com
(Chemicals)

Compagnie Financiere Richemont
8 Boulevard James–Fuzy
CH–61201, Geneva, Switzerland
Tel.: [44] (0) 207 838 8581
Fax: [44] (0) 207 838 8333
www.richemont.com
(Luxury goods)

Crypto
P.O. Box 460
CH–6301 Zug, Switzerland
Tel.: [41] 41 749 77 22
Fax: [41] 41 741 22 72
www.crypto.ch
(Security software and services)

Georg Fischer
Amsler–Laffon–Strasse 9
CH–8201 Schaffhausen, Switzerland
Tel.: [41] 52 631 1111
Fax: [41] 52 631 2837
www.georgfischer.com
(Automotive products, manufacturing technology, piping systems)

Lonza Group
Munchensteinerstrasse 38
CH–4002 Basel, Switzerland
Tel.: [41] 1 316 81 11
www.lonzagroup.com
(Chemicals)

Mercer International
Geisshubelstrasse 15
CH–8045 Zurich, Switzerland
Tel.: [41] 1 201 7710
Fax: [41] 1 201 7717
www.mercerinternational.com
(Paper and paper products)

Montres Rolex
Rue Francois–Dussaud 3
CH–1211 Geneva 24, Switzerland
Tel.: [41] 22 308 2200
Fax: [41] 22 300 2255
www.rolex.com
(Watches)

Nestlé
Avenue Nestlé 55
CH–1800 Vevey, Vaud, Switzerland
Tel.: [41] 21 924 21 11
Fax: [41] 21 924 18 85
www.nestle.com
(Foods and confections)

Novartis
Lichstrasse 35
CH–4056 Basel, Switzerland
Tel.: [41] 61 324 1111
Fax: [41] 61 324 8001
www.novartis.com
(Pharmaceuticals)

Roche Group
Grenzacherstrasse 124
CH–4070 Basel, Switzerland
Tel.: [41] 61 688 1111
Fax: [41] 61 691 9391
www.roche.com
(Pharmaceuticals)

Schindler Holding Ltd.
Seestrasse 55
CH–6052 Hergiswil, Nidwalden,
Switzerland
Tel.: [41] 41 632 85 50
Fax: [41] 41 445 31 34
www.schindler.com
(Escalators and elevators)

Serono
Chemin des Mines 15 bis
CH–1211 Geneva 20, Switzerland
Tel.: [41] 22 739 3000
Fax: [41] 22 731 2179
www.serono.com
(Pharmaceuticals)

Siemens Building Technologies
Bellerivestrasse 36
CH–8034 Zurich, Switzerland
Tel.: [41] 1 385 22 11
Fax: [41] 1 385 25 25
www2.sibt.com

(Building automation, security systems)

Sulzer
CH–8401 Winterthur, Zurich,
Switzerland
Tel.: [41] 52 262 11 22
Fax: [41] 52 262 01 01
www.sulzer.com
(Mechanical and process engineering)

The Swatch Group
Seevorstadt 6
CH–2501 Biel, Bern, Switzerland
Tel.: [41] 32 343 68 11
Fax: [41] 32 343 69 11
www.swatchgroup.com
(Watches)

Syngenta
Schwarzwaldalle 215
CH–4058 Basel, Switzerland
Tel.: [41] 61 697 1111
www.syngenta.com
(Chemicals)

Retailing and Wholesaling

Bally Management Ltd.
Via Industria 1
CH–6987 Caslano, Ticino, Switzerland
Tel.: [41] 91 612 9111
Fax: [41] 91 612 9112
www.bally.com
(Apparel)

COOP
Postfach 2550
Thiersteinerallee 12
CH–4002 Basel, Switzerland
Tel.: [41] 61 336 6666
Fax: [41] 61 336 6040
www.coop.ch
(Food and consumer goods retailer)

Federation of Migros Cooperatives
Limmatstrasse 152
CH–8005 Zurich, Switzerland
Tel.: [41] 1 277 2111
Fax: [41] 1 277 2525
www.migros.ch
(Grocery retailer)

Jelmoli Grands Magasins
St. Annagasse 18
CH–8001 Zurich 1, Switzerland
Tel.: [41] 220 44 11

www.huginonline.ch/JEL
(Department store)

Service Industries

Adecco
Hertistrasse 23
CH–8304 Wallisellen, Zurich,
Switzerland
Tel.: [41] 1 878 88 88
Fax: [41] 1 878 87 87
www.adecco.com
(Staffing)

Cap Gemini Ernst & Young
Leutschenbachstrasse 95
CH–8050 Zurich, Switzerland
Tel.: [41] 1 560 24 00
Fax: [41] 1 560 25 00
(Management consulting)

Danzas Group
Peter Merian–Strasse 88
CH–4002 Basel, Switzerland
Tel.: [41] 61 274 74 74
Fax: [41] 61 274 74 75
www.danzas.com
(Logistics and transportation services)

Kuoni Travel Holding
Neue Hard 7
CH–8010 Zurich, Switzerland
Tel.: [41] 1 277 45 29
Fax: [41] 1 271 40 31
www.kuoni.com
(Travel agency)

Mövenpick Holding
Zuerichstrasse 106
CH–8134 Adliswil, Zurich, Switzerland
Tel.: [41] 71 712 22 22
Fax: [41] 71 712 22 38
www.movenpick.ch
(Restaurants)

Panalpina
Viaduktstrasse 42
CH–4002 Basel, Switzerland
Tel.: [41] 61 226 11 11
Fax: [41] 61 226 11 01
www.panalpina.com
(Logistics)

PubliGroupe Ltd.
12 Avenue des Toises
CH–1002 Lausanne, Switzerland
Tel.: [41] 21 317 71 11
Fax: [41] 21 317 75 55
www.publigroupe.com
(Advertising)

Technology

Carrier 1 International
Militarstrasse 36
CH–8004 Zurich, Switzerland
Tel.: [41] 1 297 2600
Fax: [41] 1 297 2633
www.carrier1.com
(Telecommunications)

Logitech International
Moulin du Choc
CH–1122 Romanel–sur–Morges, Vaud,
Switzerland
Tel.: [41] 21 863 51 11
Fax: [41] 21 863 53 11
www.logitech.com
(Computer hardware)

Micronas Semiconductor Holding
Technopark, Technoparkstrasse 1
CH–8005 Zurich, Switzerland
Tel.: [41] 1 445 3960
Fax: [41] 1 445 3961
www.micronas.com
(Semiconductors)

Swisscom
Alte Tiefenaustrasse 6
CH–3050 Bern, Switzerland
Tel.: [41] 31 342 11 11
Fax: [41] 31 342 25 49
www.swisscom.ch
(Telecommunications)

Swisslog Holding
Webereiweg 3
CH–5033 Buchs, Switzerland
Tel.: [41] 62 837 95 37
Fax: [41] 62 837 95 10
www.swisslog.com
(IT consulting services)

Major International Nonprofit Employers in Switzerland

Federation Internationale de Football Association
FIFA House, Hitzigweg 11
P.O. Box 85
CH–8030 Zurich, Switzerland
Tel.: [41] 1 384 9595
Fax: [41] 1 384 9696
www.fifa.com

Fédération Internationale de L'Automobile
2 Chemin de Blandonnet
CH–1215 Geneva 15, Switzerland
Tel.: [41] 22 54 44 00
Fax: [41] 22 544 44 50
www.fia.com

International Committee of the Red Cross
19 Avenue de la Paix
CH–1202 Geneva, Switzerland
Tel.: [41] 22 734 6001
Fax: [41] 22 733 20 57
www.icrc.org

International Olympic Committee
Chateau de Vidy, Case Postale 356
CH–1007 Lausanne, Switzerland
Tel.: [41] 21 621 6111
Fax: [41] 21 621 6216
www.olympic.org

World Health Organization
20 Avenue Appia
CH–1211 Geneva 27, Switzerland
Tel.: [41] 22 791 2111
Fax: [41] 22 791 3111
www.who.int

World Organization of the Scout Movement
P.O. Box 241
CH–1211 Geneva 4, Switzerland
Tel.: [41] 22 705 1010
Fax: [41] 22 705 1020
www.scout.org

World Trade Organization
Centre William Rappard
154, rue de Lausanne
CH– 1211 Geneva 21, Switzerland
Tel.: [41] 22 739 5111
Fax: [41] 22 739 5458
www.wto.org

International Schools in Switzerland

American International School of Zurich
Nidelbadstrasse 49
CH–8802 Kilchberg, Switzerland
Tel.: [41] 1 715 27 95
Fax: [41] 1 715 26 94
Email: aisz@aisz.ch
www.zis.ch
(U.S. curriculum, grades 7 through 13)

Collège du Léman International School
74 Route de Sauverny
CH–1290 Versoix/Geneva, Switzerland
Tel.: [41] 22 755 5555
Fax: [41] 22 775 5559
Email: info@cdl.ch
www.cdl.ch
(U.S., U.K., Swiss, French curriculum, kindergarten through grade 13)

International School of Basel
Burggartenstr 1
P.O. Box 316
CH–4103 Bottmingen, Switzerland
Tel.: [41] 61 426 9626
Fax: [41] 61 426 9625
Email: info@isbasel.ch
www.isbasel.ch
(U.S., U.K. curriculum, pre–kindergarten through grade 12)

Austria

Major employment center: Vienna

Major business language: German

Language skill index: Crucial for gaining employment. Local employment offices, for example, will ignore inquiries in any other language.

Currency: Euro

Telephone country code: 43

Time zone: Eastern Standard Time + 6 hours

Punctuality index: Austrians are very punctual

Average daily temperature, high/low: January: 34°/26°; July: 75°/59° (Vienna)

Average number of days with precipitation: January: 11 days; July: 15 days

Best bet for employment:

For students: Hospitality jobs or au pair positions

Permanent jobs: Finance and banking

Chance of finding a job: Good

Useful tip: Austrians are proud of their national heritage and are reputed to be friendlier than their northern neighbors, the Germans. Do not commit the faux pas of referring to an Austrian as a German.

About the size of Maine, Austria is located in Central Europe. Switzerland and Liechtenstein border it to the west, Germany and the former Czechoslovakia to the north, Hungary to the east, and Italy and the former Yugoslavia to the south. Almost the entire country is blanketed by the Alps, except for the area around Vienna, which rests in the Danube basin. Ninety–five percent of the population speaks German; a large Slovene minority lives in the eastern portion of the country.

The areas comprising Austria were originally settled by Celtic tribes, who were conquered by the Romans. Eventually, the area became part of Charlemagne's empire. In 1271, the House of Hapsburg gained possession of the Austrian territories, founding a state that would encompass much of Central and Eastern Europe. In the nineteenth century, Vienna became Europe's clear cultural focus, especially in music. A dual Austro–Hungarian monarchy dominated vast areas of Europe until World War I. The empire collapsed in defeat and a republic was declared in 1918. A dictatorship followed and Hitler's Germany easily occupied the country in 1938. Following World War II, the Soviets occupied the eastern portion of the republic until 1955, when Parliament declared Austria to be permanently neutral.

Foreign workers, mostly from Eastern Europe, bolster Austria's economy.

Austria is a federal republic with nine states. The Social Democrats (SPÖ) and the conservative Peoples Party (ÖVP) have alternated or shared power for over 40 years, providing political consensus and stability. Austria drew an international outcry in 1986 when former U.N. Secretary General Kurt Waldheim was elected president, despite revelations that suggested he may have collaborated in war crimes during his tenure in the German army. The controversy resulted in the country's temporary internal isolation. Austria was again embroiled in political controversy in 2000 when a coalition government was formed that included the far–right Freedom Party, which gained popularity for its mixture of populism and anti–establishment themes. Even the resignation of the Freedom Party's leader, Joerg Haider, known for his pro–Nazi statements, failed to stem international criticism. The party was soundly defeated in November 2002 elections, receiving only 10 percent of the vote, down from 27 percent in 1999. Despite this, Haider may be asked to help form a coalition government with the Conservatives in 2003.

Normal banking hours in Austria are 7:45 a.m. to 4 p.m., with a break from 12:30 p.m. to 2:15 p.m., Mondays through Fridays. In Vienna, banks are open from 8 a.m. to 3 p.m., Mondays through Fridays, except for Thursdays, when they are open until 5:30 p.m. Post offices in the larger cities are usually open 24 hours.

Current Economic Climate

Austria's gross national product and per capita income rank it as one of Europe's wealthiest countries. Its economy is closely tied to other European

Union economies, especially Germany. Unemployment stands at 4.3 percent and inflation hovers at 2 percent. In January 1995, Austria became a member of the European Union.

Austria has a strong labor movement: The Austrian Trade Union Federation (OGB) has a total membership of 1.5 million, almost half the country's wage and salary earners. Since 1945, the OGB has pursued a moderate, consensus–oriented wage policy, cooperating with industry, agriculture, and the government on a broad range of social and economic issues in what is known as Austria's "social partnership." The government's calls for budget consolidation, social reform, and improvements in the business climate have been opposed by the OGB, which suggests that Austria's peaceful social climate could become more confrontational.

A large number of foreign workers, mostly from Eastern Europe, bolster Austria's economy. Austria's principal products include construction, machinery, vehicles and parts, food, chemicals, lumber and wood processing, paper and paperboard, communications equipment, and tourism. Most trade occurs with E.U. and EFTA members, although Eastern Europe is also important. The labor force is 60 percent industrial and commercial, 28 percent services, and 12 percent agricultural.

Austria's 10 Largest Companies
(2001, based on market capitalization)

1. Telekom Austria
2. Osterreichische Elektrizitatswirtschafts
3. Erste Bank der Osterreichischen Spar–kass
4. OMV Aktiengesellschaft
5. Austria Tabakwerke
6. EVN Aktiengesellschaft
7. Wiener Staedtische Allg. Versicherung
8. Wienerberger
9. Generali Holding Vienna
10. Voest–Alpine Stahl

Getting Around in Austria

The Austrian Federal Railways system offers a variety of choices in traveling — trains, boats, buses, and cable cars. It also provides rental car services, with 52 locations in various cities. Eurail passes are valid for both trains and steamboats (along the Danube River). The bus, tram, and rail systems are all efficient but tend to be rather expensive.

Employment Regulations and Outlook for Americans

U.S. citizens don't need a visa for stays of fewer than 90 days, but will need one in order to live in Austria for three to six months. A simmering political culture hostile to immigrants has made some companies wary of hiring non–

E.U. nationals. Yet for all the political posturing, there has not yet been any formal change to immigration law or procedure. Work permits are distributed by the State Employment Office, and an employer must declare that an Austrian cannot fill the position. Some knowledge of German is necessary for seasonal work, which may be sought in advance by writing to local employment offices, but you must write in German.

Work in the tourist industry, primarily in hotels and restaurants in ski areas, can be found, especially in the Tyrol. You should remember that most of these jobs are probably illegal and will pay comparatively low wages. Some employers, such as bars and clubs in tourist areas, actually prefer to hire foreigners with appropriate language skills. As in other countries of Europe, there are opportunities to work as an au pair.

Short–term and Temporary Work

There are many opportunities for casual work: See Chapter 9 for information about Accord Cultural Exchange, Au Pair in Europe, and Village Camps. In addition, the Austrian–American Educational Commission, described in Chapter 10, places Americans into English–teaching jobs.

Auslands–Sozialdienst

Johannesgasse 16/1

A–1010 Vienna, Austria

Tel.: [43] 1 512 7941

Fax: [43] 1 513 94 60

Email: aupair–asd@kath–jugend.at

www.volunteer.at/aupair

A well–established agency that places foreign students as au pairs in Austria. Although most placements last six to 12 months, some three–month summer positions are available.

ESDC (English Summer Day Camps) Austria

Paul Schmückplatz 18

A–7100 Neusiedl am See, Austria

An English–speaking summer day camp with locations throughout Austria and Germany. Austrian children ages 6 through 12 attend one–week camps with the goal of learning or improving their English. Counselors are recruited for programs that begin in June. Counselors are paid and receive free room and board.

Internship Programs

The best bet for students to obtain practical experience in Austria is to work with established programs such as AIESEC and IAESTE, described in Chapter 9. Teaching fellowships are available through the Fulbright program administered by the Institute for International Education, detailed in Chapter 10.

Volunteer Opportunities

Most Austrian work camps are run by Service Civil International or Volunteers for Peace. Camps are organized around such themes as agriculture, gardening, cultural concerns, gay issues, and women's issues. Familiarity with German is recommended for all programs. In addition, WWOOF offers volunteer opportunities on organic farms in Austria. See Chapter 9 for information on these and other resources.

International Cultural Youth Exchange
ICYE Federation Austria
Liechtensteinstrasse 20/9
D–1090 Wien, Austria
Tel.: [43] 1 315 76 36
Fax: [43] 1 315 76 37
Email: grenzenlos@chello.at
www.icye.org
The ICYE Federation is an international, independent, nonprofit organization with 35 National Committees in Africa, Asia–Pacific, Europe, Latin America and North America. ICYE's mission is to promote youth mobility and international understanding through long–term (from six to 12 months) voluntary service exchange programs. Placements in Austria include child–care centers, youth centers, working with the disabled, the elderly, ethnic minorities, and with environmental groups.

Resources for Further Information

Newspapers in Austria

Kleine Zeitung
Tel.: [43] 316 87 50
Fax: [43] 316 875 014
www.kleinezeitung.at

Kurier
Tel.: [43] 1 52 100 0
Fax: [43] 1 52 100 2263

Die Presse
Tel.: [43] 1 5 14 14 0
Fax: [43] 1 5 14 14 400
www.diepresse.at

Salzburger Nachrichten
Tel.: [43] 662 83 730
Fax: [43] 662 83 3799

www.salzburg.com

Der Standard
Tel.: [43] 1 531 70
Fax: [43] 1 531 70131
www.derstandard.at

Tiroler Tageszeitung
Tel.: [43] 512 53 540
Fax: [43] 512 575 924
www.tirol.com/tt

Wiener Zeitung
Tel.: [43] 1 797 890
Fax: [43] 1 797 89443
www.wienerzeitung.at

Useful Websites for Job Seekers

The Internet is a good place to begin your job search. Many Austrian employers list job vacancies, especially those in technical fields, on the web. There are also many websites that provide useful information for job searchers researching the Austrian job market.

AMS
www.ams.or.at
German–language site featuring over 12,000 private sector jobs, a resume bank, and an email job notification service.

Austria JobPilot
www.jobpilot.at
Hundreds of private sector jobs, a resume database, and a directory of employers. Free registration. Written in German.

Jenewein
www.jenewein.at
An executive search firm specializing in services for professionals ages 25 through 50. The firm recruits mostly for positions in Austria, although the site offers some jobs in Eastern Europe.

Job Direct
www.job–direct.co.at/job–direct
This German–language site lists about 100 private sector jobs. Candidates can apply for positions online.

Job News
www.jobnews.at
Lists about 1,000 jobs in Austria. Candidates can register to be notified about jobs via email. The site also includes information about career coaching services in Austria.

Job Universe
www.jobuniverse.at
Features jobs in the high–tech industry. You can register to receive job notification via email. The site can be searched in English and German.

Manpower Austria
www.manpower.at

Manpower is a recruitment agency. Its Austrian site features a database of private sector jobs.

StepStone Austria
One of Europe's leading online recruitment sites. Features over 700 private sector and education jobs in Austria, and can be viewed in German.

Zentrum fur Berufsplanning
www.zbp–mc.at
This website for the Center for Career Planning provides job listings and services for recent college graduates (defined as having less than five years work experience).

Embassies and Consular Offices

American embassies and consulates have commercial and/or economic sections that can provide you with business information and explain aspects of the local economy. Inquiries about business opportunities should be addressed either to "Commercial Officer" or "Commercial Section."

Representation of Austria in the United States

Embassy of Austria
3524 International Court NW
Washington, DC 20008–3027
Tel.: (202) 895–6700
Fax: (202) 895–6750
www.austria.org

Austrian Consulates General:

Chicago, (312) 222–1515; Los Angeles, (310) 444–9320; New York, (212) 737–6400

Representation of the United States in Austria

American Embassy
Boltzmanngasse 16
A–1090 Vienna, Austria

Tel.: [43] 1 313339–0
Fax: [43] 1 310 06 82
www.usembassy.at

Chambers of Commerce

Chambers of commerce consist of member firms in both countries interested in international trade. These are appropriate companies to initially target in the job search.

American Chamber of Commerce in Austria
Porzellangasse 35
A–1090 Vienna, Austria
Tel.: [43] 1 319 5751
Fax: [43] 1 319 5151
Email: office@amcham.or.at
www.amcham.or.at

Federal Economic Chamber of Commerce
Widner Hauptstrasse 63
A–1045 Vienna, Austria
Tel.: [43] 1 50105 4503
Fax: [43] 1 50206 255

Tyrolean Chamber of Commerce
Meinhardstrasse 14

A–6021 Innsbruck, Austria
Tel.: [43] 512 5310 1293
Fax: [43] 512 5310 1275
Email: aw@tirol.wk.or.at
www.tirol.wk.or.at

U.S.–Austrian Chamber of Commerce
165 West 46th Street, Suite 1112
New York, NY 10036
Tel.: (212) 819–0117
Fax: (212) 819–0117
www.usatchamber.com

World Trade Centers in Austria

These world trade centers usually house many foreign companies that conduct business in Austria.

World Trade Center Salzburg
c/o World Trade Center Development
Novotel Salzburg City
Franz Josef Strasse 26
A–5020 Salzburg, Austria
Tel.: [43] 1 7007 36000
Fax: [43] 1 7007 36027
Email: office@world–trade–center.at

World Trade Center Vienna
A–1300 Vienna, Austria
Tel.: [43] 1 7007 36000
Fax: [43] 1 7007 36027
Email: office@world–trade–center.at
www.conference.at

Other Informational Organizations

Foreign government missions in the United States, such as tourist offices can furnish visas and information on work permits and other important regulations. They may also offer economic and business information about Austria.

Austrian Cultural Forum
11 East 52nd Street
New York, NY 10022
Tel.: (212) 319–5300
Email: desk@acfny.org
www.acfny.org

Austrian National Tourist Office
P.O. Box 1142
New York, NY 10108–1142
Tel.: (212) 944–6880
Fax: (212) 730–4568
Email: info@oewnyc.com
www.austria–tourism.at/us

Austrian Trade Commission
11601 Wilshire Blvd., Suite 2420
Los Angeles, CA 90025
Tel.: (310) 477–9988
Fax: (310) 477–1643
Email: losangeles@wko.at
www.austriantradeus.org

Austrian Trade Commission
150 East 52nd Street, 32nd Floor
New York, NY 10022
Tel.: (212) 421–5250
Fax: (212) 751–4675
Email: newyork@wko.at
www.austriantradeus.org

Business Directories

Although not always easy to find, business directories can prove invaluable in the international job search. Your best bet for locating these directories is to begin in the reference section of any public or university library. Most directories list company names, addresses, products, and phone numbers. Some directories include executive names and titles and financial information about the company. These sources provide you with the names of the people to contact for employment information as well as financial data, which can tell you how strong a company's position in a country may be.

American Chamber of Commerce in Austria List of Members. American Chamber of Commerce in Austria, Porzellangasse 35, A–1090 Vienna, Austria; email: office@amcham.or.at; www.amcham.or.at/amcham/members. Distributed in the United States by the United States Chamber of Commerce, International Division Publications, 1615 H Street NW, Washington, DC 20062–2000. Lists Austrian and American firms engaged in bilateral trade. 70 pages; published biennially.

Austrian Commercial Directory. Jupiter Verlagsgesellschaft, Robertgasse 2, A–1020 Vienna, Austria. Lists 120,000 manufacturing, trade, industrial, and service firms. 5,300 pages; published annually.

Finanz–Compass Osterreich. Compass–Verlag, Matznergasse 17 32, A–1141 Vienna, Austria; email: office@compass.at; www.compnet.at. Lists banks, insurance companies, and other public companies. 1,200 pages; published annually in German.

Grosse und Mittelstandische Unternehmen in Osterreich (Major and Medium–Sized Companies in Austria). Hoppenstedt Produktinformationen, Havelstrasse 9, D–64295 Darmstadt, Germany; email: info@hoppenstedt–fastx.de; www.hoppenstedt.com. Lists 14,000 leading industrial and service companies with a minimum of 70 employees. €275, published annually.

Made in Austria. Jupiter Verlagsgesellschaft, Robertgasse 2, A–1020 Vienna, Austria. U.S. distributor Croner Publications, 34 Jericho Turnpike, Jericho, NY 11753. Lists 2,500 major Austrian firms engaged in export and distribution. 320 pages; $75; published annually in English, German, and French.

U.S. List of American Firms, Subsidiaries, Affiliates, and Licencees. American Chamber of Commerce in Austria, Porzellangasse 35, A–1090 Vienna, Austria; email: office@amcham.or.at; www.amcham.or.at/. Covers 400 subsidiaries of American companies in Austria. 80 pages; $50; published biennially.

Wer Liefert Was? Wer Liefert Was? Normannenweg 16–20, D–20537 Hamburg, Germany; email: info@wlw.de; www.wlw.de. A CD–ROM that lists 100,000 German, 12,000 Austrian, and 13,000 Swiss manufacturers.

American Companies in Austria

The following companies are classified by business area: Banking and Finance; Industrial Manufacturing; Retailing and Wholesaling; Service Industries; and Technology. Company information includes firm name, address, phone and fax number, and specific business. Your chances of securing employment abroad are substantially better if you contact the subsidiary company in Europe rather than the parent company in the U.S. Keep in mind that the contact information for companies listed in this section can change frequently. Before writing to any company, confirm its address and phone number.

Banking and Finance

American Express Bank Ltd.
Käerntnerstrasse 21–23
A–1010 Vienna, Austria
Tel.: [43] 1 515 11 550
Fax: [43] 1 515 11 555
(Banking and financial services)

AON Jauch & Hübener
Blechturmgasse 9–11
A–1050 Vienna, Austria
Tel.: [43] 1 545 16 86 0
Fax: [43] 1 545 168 644
www.aon.com
(Insurance)

BDO Auxilia Treuhand
Herrengasse 2–4
A–1130 Vienna, Austria
Tel.: [43] 1 878 79–0
www.bdo.com
(Accounting)

Citibank International
Lothringerstrasse 7
A–1010 Vienna, Austria
Tel.: [43] 1 717 17–0
Fax: [43] 1 717 92 06
(Commercial bank)

Industrial Manufacturing

Bristol–Myers
Columbusgasse 4
A–1100 Vienna, Austria
Tel.: [43] 1 601 43
Fax: [43] 1 601 4329
(Pharmaceuticals)

Coca–Cola Amatil Österreich
Triester Str. 217
A–1230 Vienna, Austria
Tel: [43] 1 661 71–0
Fax: [43] 1 661 719
(Beverages)

Colgate–Palmolive
Argentinierstrasse 22/1
A–1040 Vienna, Austria
Tel.: [43] 1 505 89 51–0
Fax: [43] 1 505 89 516
(Household and personal care products)

Conoco Austria Mineralöl
Sarnergasse 27
A–5020 Salzburg, Austria
Tel.: [43] 662 82 74 80–0
Fax: [43] 662 87 78 80 18
(Petroleum products)

Ford Motor Co. (Austria)
Fürbergstrasse 51
A–5020 Salzburg, Austria
Tel.: [43] 662 6581–0
Fax: [43] 662 611328
(Automobiles and parts)

Honeywell Austria
Handelskai 388
A–1020 Vienna, Austria
Tel.: [43] 1 72 780–0
Fax: [43] 1 72 78 08
(Process control equipment)

Master Foods Austria
Eisenstädterstrasse 80
A–7091 Breitenbrunn Neusiedler,
Austria
Tel.: [43] 682 601–0
Fax: [43] 6282 601 611
(Chocolate bars, rice)

Mead Coated Board Europe Kartonvertriebs
Alserbachstrasse 14–16
A–1090 Vienna, Austria
Tel.: [43] 1 310 05 120
Fax: [43] 1 310499–0
www.mead.com
(Paper products)

Nalco Chemical
Scheydgasse 34–36
A–1210 Vienna, Austria
Tel.: [43] 1 270 26 35–0
Fax: [43] 1 270 2699
www.nalco.com
(Chemicals)

NCR Österreich
Storcheng 1
A–1150 Vienna, Austria
Tel.: [43] 1 891 11–0
Fax: [43] 1 891 11 20 10
(Office equipment and software)

Pfizer Corp. Austria
Mondsceingasse 16
A–0170 Vienna, Austria
Tel.: [43] 1 521 15
Fax: [43] 1 526 913
www.pfizer.com
(Medical research)

Procter & Gamble
Mariahilferstrasse 77–79
A–1060 Vienna, Austria
Tel.: [43] 1 58 85 7–0
Fax: [43] 1 58 70071
(Consumer products)

3M Österreich Gesellschaft
Brunnerfeldstrasse 63
A–2380 Perchtoldsdorf, Austria
Tel.: [43] 1 866 86–0
Fax: [43] 1 86 68 62 42
(Office equipment and supplies)

Xerox Austria
Handelskai 94–96
A–1200 Vienna, Austria
Tel.: [43] 1 240 50–0
Fax: [43] 1 24 05 0310
(Copier equipment)

Service Industries

Accenture
Schottenring 16
A–1010 Vienna, Austria
Tel.: [43] 1 205 02 0
Fax: [43] 1 205 021
(Management consulting)

Deloitte & Touche Danubia Treuhand GmbH
Friedrichstrasse 10
A–1010 Vienna, Austria
Tel.: [43] 1 588 54–0
Fax: [43] 1 588 543 099
(Financial services)

Arthur D. Little International
Palais Todesco
Kärntner Strasse 51
A–1015 Vienna, Austria
Tel.: [43] 1 515 41–0
Fax: [43] 1 515 41/23
www.adlittle.com
(Management consulting)

A.C. Nielsen Co.
Moeringgasse 20–22
A–1150 Vienna, Austria
Tel.: [43] 1 981 10–0
Fax: [43] 1 981 1077
(Marketing research)

Spencer Stuart & Associates
Marc–Aurel Strasse 4/14
1010 Vienna, Austria
Tel.: [43] 1 368 87 00
Fax: [43] 1 368 8777
www.spencerstuart.com
(Executive recruitment)

Warner Bros.
Ziegler Gasse 10
A–1070 Vienna, Austria
Tel.: [43] 1 523 86 26
Fax: [43] 1 523 94 62
(Motion picture distribution)

Technology

Apple Computer
Ungargasse 59
A–1030 Vienna, Austria
Tel.: [43] 1 71 1820
Fax: [43] 1 711 3255
(Computers)

Cisco Systems
Handelskai 94–96
A–1200 Vienna, Austria
Tel.: [43] 1 240 30–6000
Fax: [43] 1 240 306 300
www.cisco.com
(Computer networking systems)

Hewlett–Packard
Lieblgasse 1
A–1220 Vienna, Austria
Tel.: [43] 1 250 00 0
Fax [43] 1 22 250 006 444
(Printers and calculators)

Symbol Technologies Austria
Prinz–Eugen Strasse 70, Suite 3,
2. Haus, 5. Stock
A–1040 Vienna, Austria
Tel.: [43] 1 505 5794–0
Fax: [43] 1 505 3962
www.symbol.com
(Bar code systems)

European Companies in Austria

The following are non–American firms operating in Austria. These selected companies can be either Austrian or based in another European country. These firms generally hire their own nationals first but may employ Americans.

Banking and Finance

Bank Austria
Vordere Zollamtsstrasse 13
A–1030 Vienna, Austria
Tel.: [43] 1 711 91
Fax: [43] 1 711 916155
(Bank)

Die Erste der Oesterrichischen Spar–kassen
Graben 21
A–1010 Vienna, Austria
Tel.: [43] 5 0100 11286
Fax: [43] 5 0100 13112
www.erstebank.at
(Bank)

Generali Holding Vienna
Landskrongasse 1–3
A–1011 Vienna, Austria
Tel.: [43] 1 534 01 0
Fax: [43] 1 534 01 1226
www.generali–holding.at
(Insurance)

Industrial Manufacturing

Böhler–Uddeholm
Modecenterstrasse 14/A/3
A–1030 Vienna, Austria
Tel.: [43] 1 798 6901 707
Fax: [43] 1 798 6901 713
www.bohler–uddeholm.com
(Steel production)

BBAG Österreich Brau–Beteiligungs
35 Poschacherstrasse
A–4020 Linz, Austria
Tel.: [43] 732 69 51 2566
Fax: [43] 732 69 51 2568
www.bbag.com
(Brewers)

EVN Aktiengesellschaft
EVN Platz
A–2344 Maria Enzerdorf am Gebirge, Austria
Tel.: [43] 2236 200 0
Fax: [43] 2236 200 2030
www.evn.at
(Energy production and distribution)

Glock
P.O. Box 9
A–2232 Deutsch–Wagram, Austria
Tel.: [43] 2247 90300 0
Fax: [43] 2247 90300 312
www.glock.com
(Guns, sporting equipment)

Miba Aktiengesellschaft
Dr.–Mittervauer, Strasse 3
A–4663 Laakirchen, Austria
Tel.: [43] 7613 2541 0
Fax: [43] 7613 2541 2172
www.miba–at.com
(Autoparts)

OMV
Otto–Wagnerplatz 5
A–10091 Vienna, Austria
Tel.: [43] 1 404 40 0
Fax: [43] 1 404 40 91
www.omv.com
(Oil & chemicals)

Red Bull
Brunn 115
A–5330 Fuschl am See, Austria
Tel.: [43] 662 6582 0
Fax: [43] 662 6582 31
www.redbull.at
(Soft drinks)

Semperit
Modecenterstrasse 22
A–1031 Vienna, Austria
Tel.: [43] 1 79 777 300
www.semperit.at
(Rubber products)

Wienerberger Baustoffindustrie
Wienerbergerstrasse 11
Wienerberger City, Vienna Twin Tower
A–1100 Vienna, Austria
Tel.: [43] 1 601 92 0

Fax: [43] 1 601 92 466
www.wienerberger.com
(Building materials)

Voest–Alpine
Voest–Alpine Strasse 1
A–4020 Linz, Austria
Tel.: [43] 732 65 85 0
www.voestalpine.com
(Steel products)

Wolford
Wolfordstrasse 1
A–6901 Bregenz, Austria
Tel.: [43] 5574 690 0
Fax: [43] 5574 690 1545
www.wolford.com
(Apparel)

Retailing and Wholesaling

Julius Meinl
Jasormigottstrasse 6
A–1010 Vienna, Austria
Tel.: [43] 1 533 96 11
www.meinl.com
(Food retailing)

Service Industries

Allgemeine Baugesellschaft–A. Porr
Absberggasse 47

A–1103 Vienna, Austria
Tel.: [43] 50 626 0
www.porr.at
(Construction & civil engineering)

**Osterreichische
Elektrizitatswirtschafts**
Am Hof 6a
CH–1010 Vienna, Austria
Tel.: [43] 1 531 13 0
www.verbund.at
(Electricity)

Technology

Telekom Austria
Schwarzenbergerplatz 3
CH–1010 Vienna, Austria
Tel.: [43] 1 590 5910
Fax: [43] 1 718 2100
www.telekom.at
(Telecommunications)

TOPCALL International
A–1230 Talpagasse 1 Vienna, Austria
Tel.: [43] 1 86353 0
Fax: [43] 1 86353 21
www.topcall.com
(Computer software and services)

International Schools in Austria

American International School
Salmanndorferstrasse 47
A–1190 Vienna, Austria
Tel.: [43] 1 401 32 0
Fax: [43] 1 401 32 5
Email: info@ais.at
www.ais.at
(U.S., Austrian, International Baccalaureate, curriculum, prekindergarten through grade 12)

Vienna International School
Strasse der Menschenrechte 1
A–1220 Vienna, Austria
Tel.: [43] 1 203 55 95
Fax: [43] 1 203 03 66
Email: info@vis.ac.at
www.vis.ac.at
(International Baccalaureate, curriculum, prekindergarten through grade 13)

Liechtenstein

Major employment centers: Vaduz, Schaan

Major business language: German

Language skill index: Knowledge of German is important, although there are times when English may suffice. Allemanic is the local German dialect.

Currency: Swiss franc

Telephone country code: 41

Time zone: Eastern Standard Time + 6 hours

Punctuality index: As in Switzerland and Austria, be on time.

Best bet for employment:

For students: Hospitality or work as an au pair

Permanent jobs: Banking and finance

Chance of getting a job: Not bad for those with high–level business skills. But remember, this is a small country.

Useful tip: Foreign workers comprise over one–third of Liechtenstein's total population of 28,600.

The principality of Liechtenstein covers only 62 square miles, making it less than one–twentieth the size of Rhode Island, America's smallest state. Liechtenstein is nestled in the Alps, between Switzerland to the west and Austria to the east. The Alps actually cover about two–thirds of the country; the remainder is occupied by the Rhine Valley. Relations with Austria and Switzerland are cozy, not only in terms of geography but in other ways as well. Although Liechtenstein gained sovereignty in the nineteenth century, Austria administered its ports until 1920. Switzerland continues to administer its postal system, as it has since 1921, and the two countries are also joined by monetary and telecommunications unions.

> **Liechtenstein is a very prosperous country, known for its wines, postage stamps, dentures, and status as a tax haven.**

Liechtenstein as we know it was established in 1712, when the house of Liechtenstein forged a union between the lordships of Vaduz and Schellenberg, both of which had been fiefdoms of the Holy Roman Empire. The line of succession of Liechtenstein's hereditary constitutional monarchy has remained unbroken ever since. The present head of state is Prince Hans Adam II, who has held his position since November 1989. The Liechtenstein government is a collegiate body and consists of the head of government and four governmental councilors. The head of government as well as the ministers are appointed by the Prince following the proposals of the Parliament. Only men and women born in Liechtenstein and eligible to be elected to parliament may be elected to the government. The current head of government is Otmar Hasler.

Liechtenstein joined the U.N. in 1990 and the European Economic Area in 1995. Liechtenstein currently has no plans to seek full E.U. membership.

Liechtensteiners enjoy a literacy rate of 100 percent. Population growth is fairly steady, at a rate of less than one percent per year. Religious preference in Liechtenstein leans overwhelmingly Roman Catholic, at close to 90 percent of the population. Liechtenstein has no military — it was disbanded in 1868.

Current Economic Climate

Liechtenstein is a very prosperous country, known for its wines, postage stamps, dentures, and status as a tax haven. In 1998, the country had, by its standards, a high level of unemployment: 2 percent, or a mere 482 people.

Since the signing of the Customs Treaty in 1924, Liechtenstein and Switzerland have represented one mutual economic area. The borders between those states are open, Liechtenstein uses the Swiss franc as its national currency, and Swiss customs officers secure its border with Austria.

Liechtenstein is known for its very low business taxes — a maximum rate of 18 percent — which has induced over 73,000 holding or so–called letter box companies to establish nominal offices in Liechtenstein, providing over 30 percent of the state revenues. Legislation passed in 2000 attempted to strengthen regulatory oversight of illicit funds transfers that had become rampant in a country known for its lax banking laws.

The country was heavily agrarian well into the twentieth century. From the 1930s to 1960s Liechtenstein's farm population declined from 60 percent to just 8 percent of the population. At present, a mere 4 percent of the labor force is engaged in agriculture, with the vast majority of workers involved in industry and service occupations. Its primary industries include precision instruments, chemicals, and ceramics.

Employment Regulations and Outlook for Americans

U.S. citizens don't need a visa for tourist visits of less than 90 days, but a combination work and residence permit is required for foreign workers. Your employer should make arrangements for this permit. Although the paperwork required for working in Liechtenstein is similar to that required by Switzerland, the actual work regulations are not identical. Consequently, even though it can be very difficult for foreigners to secure permission to work in Switzerland, fully one–third of Liechtenstein's residents are foreign workers.

Students interested in working in Liechtenstein should contact organizations that are active in Switzerland, such as IAESTE. Few organizations keep separate offices in Liechtenstein, but the Swiss offices may be able to help.

Volunteer Opportunities

Several United States–based organizations coordinate work camps throughout Europe. Opportunities for volunteer work in Liechtenstein are relatively slim, due to the country's tiny size. Contacting one of the major coordinators such as Service Civil International or Volunteers for Peace, described in Chapter 9, is probably your best bet.

Resources for Further Information

Useful Websites for Job Seekers

The Internet is a good place to begin your job search. There are websites that provide useful information for job searchers researching the Liechtenstein job market. Because Liechtenstein is such a small country there are few websites devoted exclusively to job–hunting in Liechtenstein. You should also use websites that serve all of Europe.

Liechtenstein News
www.news.li
Includes general information on business and information in Liechtenstein and features a small job–posting board.

Liechtenstein Online
www.lol.li
The site for an online magazine that offers financial/economic information. It is not specifically a job–search site, but the

information is useful for researching the employment market.

StepStone Liechtenstein
www.stepstone.li
One of Europe's leading online recruitment sites. Features private sector and education jobs with a few jobs in Liechtenstein posted.

Embassies and Consular Offices

American embassies and consulates have commercial and/or economic sections that can provide you with business information and explain aspects of the local economy. Inquiries about business opportunities should be addressed either to "Commercial Officer" or "Commercial Section."

Representation of Liechtenstein in the United States

Embassy of the Principality of Liechtenstein

633 Third Avenue, 27th Floor   Tel.: (212) 599–0220
New York, NY 10017   Fax: (212) 599–0064

Representation of the United States in Liechtenstein

There is no U.S. embassy or consulate in Liechtenstein. U.S. citizens should contact the U.S. embassy in Switzerland shown on page 363.

Business Directories

Although not always easy to find, business directories can prove invaluable in the international job search. Most directories list company names, addresses, products, and phone numbers. Some directories include executive names and titles and financial information about the company. These sources provide you with the names of the people to contact for employment information as well as financial data, which can tell you how strong a company's position in a country may be.

Dun & Bradstreet Swiss Company Information. Dun & Bradstreet AG, Schoenegstrasse 5, CH–8026 Zurich, Switzerland. Lists 180,000 businesses in Switzerland and Liechtenstein. Updated monthly; available in English, German, Italian, and French.

Kompass Schweiz/Liechtenstein. Kompass Schweiz Verlag AG, 14 ln Grosswiesen, CH–8044 Zurich–Gockhausen, Switzerland. U.S. distributor Croner Publications, 34 Jericho Turnpike, Jericho, NY 11753. Lists 50,000 manufacturers, distributors, and service companies in Switzerland and Liechtenstein. 4,400 pages, 240 Swiss francs; updated annually.

Who's Who in Switzerland and the Principality of Liechtenstein. Orelli Fussli, Dietzingerstrasse 3, CH–8036 Zurich, Switzerland; email: info@orelli–fuessli–verlag.ch. Lists 2,500 influential business, government, and other leaders in Switzerland and Liechtenstein.

Major Companies in Liechtenstein

Small country, few companies; there's not much more to be said. Company information below includes firm name, address, phone and fax number, and specific business. In the case of American parent firms, your chances of securing employment abroad are substantially better if you contact the subsidiary company in Europe rather than the parent company in the United States. Keep in mind that the contact information for these companies can change often. Before sending correspondence to a company, be sure to confirm its address and phone number.

Allianz Suisse
Heiligkreuz 52
FL–9490 Vaduz, Liechtenstein
Tel.: [423] 237 2700
Fax: [423] 237 2790
www.allianz–suisse.li
(Insurance)

Bank von Ernst
Egertastrasse 10
FL–9490 Vaduz,Liechtenstein
[423] 265 53 53
[423] 265 53 63
www.bve.li
(Bank)

BNP Paribas
Landstrasse 40
FL–9495 Triesen, Liechtenstein
Tel.: [423] 239 8888
Fax: [423] 239 8889
www.bnpparibas.li
(Bank)

Inform
Landstrasse 182
FL–9495 Triesen, Liechtenstein
Tel.: [423] 399 3250
Fax: [423] 399 3251
www.ics.li
(Computer software)

LGT Group
Herrengasse 12
FL–9490 Vaduz, Liechtenstein

Tel.: [41] 423 235 1532
Fax: [41] 423 235 1656
www.lgt.com
(Private bank)

Hilti
Feldkircher Strasse 100
FL–9490 Vaduz, Liechtenstein
Tel.: [423] 233 2575
Fax: [423] 233 2510
(Power tools)

Liechtensteinische Landesbank
FL–9490 Vaduz, Liechtenstein
Tel.: [41] 75 236 88 11
Fax: [41] 75 236 88 22
www.llb.li
(Bank)

**Revikon Kontroll &
Beratungsaktiengesellschaft**
Aeulstresse 60
FL–9490 Vaduz, Liechtenstein
Tel.: [423] 236 0546
Fax: [423] 236 0506
(Trust company)

Volksbank
Heiligkreuz 42
FL–9490 Vaduz, Liechtenstein
[423] 237 6930
[423] 237 6948
www.volksbank.li
(Bank)

Chapter 20

Central Europe: Czech Republic, Slovakia, Hungary, Poland, & Romania

Czech Republic/Slovakia

Czech Republic

Major employment center: Prague

Major business language: Czech

Language skill index: French and German can be useful alternatives to Czech, although an increasing number of people also speak English.

Currency: Koruna

Telephone country code: 420

Time zone: Eastern Standard Time + 6 hours

Punctuality index: Punctuality is expected. Schedule appointments in advance.

Average daily temperature, high/low: January: 34°/25°; July: 74°/58° (Prague)

Average number of days with precipitation: January: 20 days; July: 14 days

Best bet for employment:

For students: Teaching English

Permanent jobs: Business and manufacturing

Chance of finding a job: Continually improving along with liberalization.

Useful tip: In both the Czech Republic and Slovakia, you may find that people allow you less personal space than you are accustomed to. You should, however, resist the urge to back away if you feel like someone is standing too close to you in conversation. It might be taken as an insult.

Slovakia

Major employment centers: Bratislava, Kosice

Major business languages: Slovak, Hungarian

Language skill index: German is the most useful non–Slavic language to know. Pride in language is an aspect of Slovak nationalism, so it is useful to know some Slovak.

Currency: New koruna

Telephone: country code: 421

Time zone: Eastern Standard Time + 6 hours

Punctuality index: Punctuality is expected. Schedule appointments in advance.

Best bet for employment:

For students: Teaching English

Permanent jobs: New business development

Chance of finding a job: Improving, but options are still limited.

Useful tip: Business cards are *de rigeur* in both the Czech Republic and Slovakia. You will make a good impression by having yours printed in English on one side and either Czech or Slovak on the other as appropriate.

Slavic tribes settled in the region now known as the Czech Republic and Slovakia during the fifth century. Bohemia and Slovakia were both part of the Great Moravian Empire during the ninth century. Slovakia eventually came under Magyar domination. Bohemia and Moravia were ruled by a Czech dynasty and became units of the Holy Roman Empire. The kings of Bohemia transformed medieval Prague into Europe's cultural center. Bohemia and Moravia became Hapsburg possessions in 1526 and, along with Slovakia, remained part of Austria–Hungary until 1918.

> **Economic reforms were harder on the Slovak region in the east than on the Czech region in the west, creating discontent.**

Czech and Slovak nationalists proclaimed the Republic of Czechoslovakia at the Treaty of Versailles following World War I. Under President Masaryk, the country maintained Central Europe's only functioning democracy until 1938, when Adolf Hitler instigated tensions among the German minority in the Sudetenland in Bohemia. At Munich, Britain and France agreed to Hitler's annexation of the Sudetenland in order to prevent war. In 1939 the Nazis occupied Bohemia and Moravia as protectorates, ousted President Benes, and established a puppet Slovak republic. Soviet troops liberated Prague in 1945, and Benes again became president. The 1946 elections resulted in a Communist Party prime minister. In 1948 the communists seized complete power in a Soviet–supported coup.

Stalin's death led to a liberalization period, culminating in the Prague Spring of 1968, in which conservatives were replaced by reformers led by Alexander Dubcek. The forces of five Warsaw Pact countries invaded Czechoslovakia in August 1968, forcing Dubcek's resignation in 1969. A human rights group, Charter 77, signed a petition demanding observance of the Helsinki Accords, instigating another crackdown in 1977. The Communist regime finally collapsed in surprisingly rapid fashion in late 1989, leading to what is known as the Velvet Revolution.

Around the time of the Revolution, the country's name was changed to the Czech and Slovak Federative Republic. Although the name change represented a symbolic gesture to Slovakia, the country was still referred to as Czechoslovakia. After the fall of communism, nationalist movements emerged, and some Slovaks began a movement to form their own state. Economic reforms were harder on the Slovak region in the east than the Czech region in the west, creating discontent. On August 26, 1992, the central government agreed to split into two independent states, the Czech Republic and Slovakia.

The Czech Republic is a democratic, unitary state that appears to have had little difficulty eradicating the vestiges of the communist Czechoslovak regime. Former dissident playwright Vaclav Havel was elected president by the Czech Parliament in 1993. His finished his third and final term as president in February 2003, symbolizing the end of the Czech Republic's post–Cold War transition. The Czech parliament has begun the complex process of selecting Havel's successor. In 1999, the Czech Republic joined NATO, and in 2002, it was approved for membership in the E.U., beginning in 2004.

Ex–boxer Vladimír Meciar, head of the nationalist Movement for a Democratic Slovakia (HZDS), came to power in the 1992 Slovakian elections. He had a reputation for exercising semi–authoritarian rule and was criticized by human rights organizations and other European leaders for passing anti–democratic laws. Meciar's controversial reign came to an end when Mikulas Dzurinda, head of the right–leaning Slovak Democratic Coalition (SDK), was elected prime minister in a divisive 1998 election. He was re–elected in 2002, forming a government with three other centrist–right parties: the Hungarian Coalition Party (SMK), the Christian Democrats (KDH), and the Alliance of New Citizens (ANO.) The main priorities of the new coalition are gaining NATO and E.U. invitations, fighting corruption, attracting foreign investment, and reforming social services such as the health care system.

Slovak is the only official language, exacerbating ethnic tensions with the large Hungarian minority that cannot use their native language in public transactions.

Business hours are generally from 8:30 a.m. to 5 p.m. in the Czech Republic, and from 8 a.m. to 5 p.m. in Slovakia, Mondays through Fridays. Very few retail businesses are open on weekends in Slovakia.

Current Economic Climate

The Czech Republic is highly industrialized compared to other former Eastern Bloc countries. The country has a well–educated population and a well–developed infrastructure, but many of its industrial plants and equipment date from communist days and are obsolete. The country's strategic location in Europe, low–cost structure, and skilled work force has attracted strong inflows of foreign direct investment. This investment is rapidly modernizing the Czech Republic's industrial base and increasing productivity. The principal industries are motor vehicles, machine–building, iron and steel production, metal–working, chemicals, electronics, transportation equipment, textiles, glass, brewing, china, ceramics, and pharmaceuticals. The primary agricultural products are dairy products, hops, and grapes that make for successful brewing and wine–making industries. The Czech Republic's largest trading partners are Germany, Slovakia, Russia, and Austria. Most trade is in manufactured goods, machinery, and transportation equipment.

The best indication of the relative strength of the Czech economy is its approval to enter the E.U. in 2004. Inflation is approximately 2.5 percent, its lowest rate since 1999. Unemployment, however, lingers at roughly 9.8 percent, and growth in the GDP is slowing, in part a result of the devastating floods in August 2002. An important reason for the relative strength of the Czech economy is that the post–Communist government moved quickly to privatize industry and agriculture and to encourage foreign investment in the economy. The Prague stock market began trading in June 1993.

Less developed and affluent than the Czech Republic, Slovakia has had more difficulty making the transition to a liberal market economy, partly because of the reluctance of national leaders and partly because living standards are not high. Since 1998, the government has taken important steps toward reforming the economy using measures that have been widely endorsed by the international community, principally the E.U. The real GDP growth in 2002 was nearly 4 percent, and it is expected to keep a similar pace in 2003. Despite these gains, unemployment remains a serious problem. In December 2002, unemployment soared to 17.5 percent. This rate, however, varies greatly by region: Unemployment is as low as 5 percent in Bratislava, and as high as 25 percent in the eastern parts of the country. Slovakia's key industries are metal and metal products; food and beverages; energy production; chemicals and man–made fibers; machinery, paper and printing; ceramics; transport vehicles; textiles; and rubber products. Its major trading partners are Germany, the Czech Republic, Austria, Russia, and Italy.

Czech Republic's 10 Largest Companies

(2001, based on market capitalization)

1. Cesky Telecom
2. CEZCes Energeticke Zav
3. Ceska Sporitelna
4. Komercni Banka
5. Philip Morris CR
6. Ceske Radiokomunikace Akciova Spolecnos
7. Unipetrol
8. Ceska Pojistovna
9. Prazska Energetika
10. Jihomoravska Energetika

Slovak Republic's 9 Largest Companies

(2001, based on market capitalization)

1. Slovnaft
2. Vychodoslovenske Zeleziarne Holding
3. Vseobecna Uverova Banka
4. Slovenska Poistovna
5. Slovakofarma
6. Zavod Slovenskeho Narodneho Povstania
7. Zeleziarne Podbrezova
8. Slovenske Energeticke Strojarne
9. Plastika a.s. Nitra

Getting Around in the Czech Republic and Slovakia

The national rail systems are inexpensive and fairly efficient. However, some train services in the Czech Republic have been canceled due to lack of passengers, making some of the more remote parts of the country harder to reach. In the Czech Republic buses are often easier and faster than the train; in Slovakia, by contrast, buses are more expensive and often serve fewer routes on weekends.

Employment Regulations and Outlook for Americans

American visitors don't need a visa for stays of less than 30 days. To work in the Czech Republic, you have to apply for a work visa and permission for a long–term stay at a consulate or the embassy in the U.S. For the visa application, you will need a work contract or letter from your employer and a detailed job description. Your employer will need to apply for the work permit at the local employment office (your visa for a long–term stay will not be approved before the employment office guarantees the work permit.) Foreigners are expected to register with the Police Office for Foreigners after arriving.

The process in Slovakia is similarly cumbersome. All foreign nationals must obtain a work and/or residence permit to live and work in Slovakia. These should be obtained prior to arrival, although in reality, this is more a recommendation than a requirement, and work permits are often obtained after arriving in Slovakia but before starting work. The work permit and residence permit must be obtained separately; however, a work permit is invalid without a residence permit. Within three days of their arrival, people who intend to stay and work in the country for one month or more should notify the Foreign Police of their address in Slovakia and their intended length of stay.

It is somewhat easier to obtain a work visa to teach in the Czech Republic or Slovakia. Your school will need to make arrangements at the local employment office. The work permit is valid only for the teaching position at the school for which it was issued; if you have more than one teaching position with different schools, you must have a work permit for each job. The work permit is issued for one year. To get an extension, you must apply at the local employment office at least six weeks before your permit's expiration date.

Short–term and Temporary Work

Opening the Czech and Slovak economies to the West has created a huge demand for English teachers, particularly for business people, resulting in a booming industry. Bridges for Education and the Central European Teaching Program recruit Americans to teach English, both of which are described in Chapter 10). The organizations below place teachers in camps and public schools.

Czech Academic Information Agency
Senovázné Námesti 26
CZ–11121 Prague, Czech Republic
[42] 2 24 22 9698
Email: aia@dzs.cz
www.dzs.cz/aia/lektori.htm
Helps prospective English teachers find posts, mainly in state schools but also in private institutes.

English for Everybody
Spanielova 1292
CZ–16 300 Prague 6, Czech Republic
Tel./Fax: [420] 1 301 9784
Email: EFE@itc–training.com
A large agency that recruits teachers for private language instruction.

Panorama International
Trida Svobody 31

CZ–77200 Olomouc, Czech Republic
Tel.: [420] 68 551 8301
Fax: [420] 68 523 4008
Email: panoramaila@panoramaila.cz
www.panoramaila.cz

A small but expanding language agency in Moravia. Teachers earn approximately 14,000 koruna per month, plus an accommodation allowance.

Internship Programs

The best bet for students to obtain practical experience in the Czech Republic and Slovakia is to work with established programs such as AIESEC and IAESTE. See Chapter 9 for details.

Teaching English in Central Europe

In the years since the collapse of communism, opportunities to teach English in the former Eastern Bloc countries have expanded as quickly as Western investment. Teaching English is the single easiest job for an American to obtain in the Czech Republic, Slovakia, and other Central European countries. For more information and a list of resources, see Chapter 10, Teaching English Abroad, in Part I.

Volunteer Opportunities

The Council on International Educational Exchange places American students in summer volunteer positions in the Czech Republic and Slovakia. Workcamp opportunities are also available through Volunteers for Peace. The International Partnership for Service Learning offers programs that link volunteerism with academic study. See Chapter 9 for details and additional resources. Other opportunities include:

Brontosaurus Movement
Brontosaurus Council
Michalova 4
628 00 Brno, Czech Republic
Tel.: [420] 5 44215585
Email: hnuti@brontosaurus.cz
www.brontosaurus.cz
The Brontosaurus Movement places volunteers in 30 to 40 work camps that focus on environmental projects. The aim of the organization is to educatee people about a sustainable way of life. You must be younger than 26 in order to participate in the programs.

Concordia
Heversham House
20–22 Boundary Road
Hove, BN3 4ET, England
Tel.: [44] 1 273 4222 18

www.concordia–iye.org.uk
Concordia is a small nonprofit organization committed to community development and cultural exchange through international volunteering. The projects range from nature conservation, restoration, archaeology and construction to projects that are more socially based including work with adults and children with special needs and teaching. Project fees are generally less than $100 and include room and board.

Foundation for a Civil Society
Masaryk Fellowship Program
P.O. Box 2235
New York, NY 10021
Tel.: (212) 717–9778
Fax: (212) 717–5255
www.fcsny.org

Fax: (212) 717–5255
www.fcsny.org
The mission of FCS is to foster free and pluralistic societies in emerging democracies in Europe. FCS originally sought to assist the Czech Republic's and Slovakia's transition to democracy, and now it aims to transfer lessons from that experience to other newly independent states, such as those in the Balkans. Most FCS projects are subcontracted to NGOs in Central and Eastern Europe.

INEX
Senovázunénámeustí 24

CZ–116 47 Prague 1, Czech Republic
Tel.: [420] 2 24 10 25 27
Fax: [420] 24 10 23 90
Email: inex.czn.cz
http://webhost.cz/inex/
INEX, the Association of Volunteers, organizes about 30 work camps throughout the Czech Republic. Most camps last two to three weeks, and the language of the camp is usually English. Projects include working with the disabled, assisting on nature reserves or organic farms, helping with cultural festivals, and participating in archaeological restoration.

Resources for Further Information

Newspapers in the Czech Republic and Slovakia

Hospodarske Noviny
Tel.: [420] 233 07 11
Fax: [420] 233 07 2307
www.ihned.cz

Hospodarske Noviny
Tel.: [421] 752 9629 37
Fax: [421] 750 633 608
www.hnx.sk

Prague Post
Tel.: [420] 296 33 4400
Fax: [420] 296 33 4450
www.praguepost.cz

The Slovak Spectator **(English)**
Tel.: [421] 759 23 3300
Fax: [421] 759 23 3319
www.slovakspectator.sk

Useful Websites for Job Searchers

The Internet is a good place to begin your job search. A growing number of employers in Central Europe list jobs on the web, and there are websites that provide useful information about the Czech and Slovak job markets.

Czech Info Center
www.muselik.com
The business directory, which can be searched by industry, provides full contact information for the listed companies. There is also a place for job seekers to post a job–wanted ad. In English.

Czech JobPilot
www.jobpilot.cz
The database includes over 350 private sector jobs, a resume database, and a directory of employers. Registration is free. In Czech.

CV Online
www.cvonline.cz

The database can be searched by the following job categories: IT/high tech, sales and marketing, banking and finance, and jobs for new graduates. You can also post your resume online. Can be searched in both Czech and English.

Czech Republic
www.czech.cz
This English–language site provides a good overview of living, working, and traveling in the Czech Republic, including information about visa regulations for foreign job seekers and a database of Czech companies.

Job Master
www.jobmaster.cz

Lists 1,800 private sector jobs. The ads are written in Czech or in English, depending on the expected language skills of the applicants, with the jobs for English language speakers in green.

Jobs in the Czech Republic
www.jobs.cz
Lists over 4,500 jobs with a special sections for high school and college students and for foreign job seekers. The navigation tools are written in English, but the jobs are listed in Czech.

Prague Business Journal
www.pbj.cz
Another site with good information about current business and economic issues in the Czech Republic. It has a small section with information about job listings and executive search firms.

Embassies and Consular Offices

American embassies and consulates have commercial and/or economic sections that can provide you with business information and explain aspects of the local economy. Inquiries about business opportunities should be addressed either to "Commercial Officer" or "Commercial Section."

Representation of the Czech Republic in the United States

Embassy of the Czech Republic
3900 Spring of Freedom Street NW
Washington, DC 20008

Tel.: (202) 363–9100
Fax: (202) 966–8540
www.mzv.cz/washington/

Representation of the United States in the Czech Republic

American Embassy
Triziste 15
CZ–118 01 Prague 1, Czech Republic

Tel.: [420] 257 530 663
Fax: [420] 257 534 028
www.usembassy.cz

Representation of Slovakia in the United States

Embassy of the Slovak Republic
3523 International Court, NW
Washington, DC 20008

Tel.: (202) 237–1054
Fax: (202) 237–6438
www.slovakembassy–us.org/

Representation of the United States in Slovakia

American Embassy
P.O. Box 309
814 99 Bratislava, Slovakia

Tel.: [421] 2 5443 3338
Fax: [421] 2 5443 0096
www.usis.sk

Chambers of Commerce

Chambers of commerce consist of member firms in both countries interested in international trade. These are appropriate companies to initially target in the job search.

American Chamber of Commerce in the Czech Republic
Stupartska 7
CZ–110 00 Prague, Czech Republic

Tel.: [420] 2 24826551
Fax: [420] 2 24826082
Email: amcham@amcham.cz
www.amcham.cz

American Chamber of Commerce of Slovakia
Hotel Danube
Rybne nam 1
81 338 Bratislava, Slovakia
Tel.: [421] 7 59340508
Fax: [421] 7 59340556
Email: director@amcham.sk
www.amcham.sk

Czech Chamber of Commerce and Industry
Argentinska 38
CZ–170 05 Prague 7, Czech Republic
Tel.: [420] 2 667994939
Fax: [420] 2 875438
www.hosp–komora.cz

Czech–U.S. Business Council
1615 H Street NW
Washington, DC 20062
Tel.: (202) 463 5473
Fax: (202) 463–3114
Email: eurasia@uschamber.com
www.uschamber.com/intl/abate/index.html

Slovak Chamber of Commerce and Industry
Gorkeho 9
816 03 Bratislava, Slovakia
Tel.: [421] 7 5443 3272
Fax: [421] 7 5443 0754
www.scci.sk

Peace Corps: The toughest job you'll ever love

Since the end of the Cold War, the Peace Corps has placed volunteers in assignments throughout Central and Eastern Europe, including the Czech Republic, Slovakia, and Poland. Peace Corps volunteers find themselves in many different jobs: teaching children the basics of math, science, and English; working with a community to protect the local environment; conducting public health education programs. The Peace Corps requires two years of service. Volunteers receive a salary comparable to local wages, mental and dental care, transportation to and from the country of service, 24 vacation days a year, deferral of student loans, and an adjustment allowance of $6,075 at the end of their service period. Although the Peace Corps interviewing and application process is rigorous and competitive, volunteers will tell you that the best reason to join is that you will make a real difference in the lives of real people. Applications may be obtained from the Peace Corps at:

Peace Corps; Recruitment Office; 1111 20th Street, NW; Washington, D.C., 20526; Tel.: (800) 424 8580; www.peacecorps.gov

World Trade Centers in the Czech Republic and Slovakia

World trade centers usually include many foreign companies that conduct business in the host country.

World Trade Center Bratislava
Viedenska cesta 7
852 51 Bratislava, Slovakia
Tel.: [421] 7 672 72026,
Fax: [421] 7 624 11665

Email: incheba@incheba.sk
www.incheba.sk

World Trade Center Brno
Vystaviste 1
CZ–648 50 Brno, Czech Republic

Tel.: [420] 5 4115 2670
Fax: [420] 5 4115 2929
Email: wtc@bvv.cz
www.bvv.cz/wtc
World Trade Center Prague
Seifertova 22

Prague 3 –Zizkov
CZ–130 00 Prague, Czech Republic
Tel.: [42] 02 240 96481
Fax: [42] 02 2409227
Email: wtcpr@hkcr.cz
www.komora.cz

Other Informational Organization

Foreign government missions in the United States, such as tourist offices, can furnish visas and information on work permits and other regulations. They may also offer economic and business information about the country.

Tatra, Travel Bureau
212 East 51st Street
New York, NY 10022

Tel.: (212) 486 0533

Fax: (212) 486–1456

Business Directories

Although not always easy to find, business directories can prove invaluable in the international job search. Your best bet for locating these directories is to begin in the reference section of any public or university library. Most directories list company names, addresses, products, and telephone numbers. Some directories include executive names and titles and financial information about the company. These sources provide you with the names of the people to contact for employment information as well as financial data, which can tell you how strong a company's position in a country may be.

Major and Medium–Sized Companies in the Czech Republic. Hoppenstedt Produktinformationen GmbH, Havelstrasse 9, D–64295 Darmstadt, Germany; email: info@hoppenstedt–fastx.de; www.hoppbonn.hu. CD–ROM listing 18,000 companies in the Czech Republic. €195; updated annually.

Major Companies of Slovakia. I.S.M.C. Information Systems and Marketing Contacts, Nam. Slobody 9, P.B. 47, 81499 Bratislava, Slovakia; email: ismc@ismc.sk. Lists the most important companies in the Slovak Republic. 600 pages, Kcs 164, updated annually.

Major Firms in the Czech Republic. I.S.M.C. Information Systems and Marketing Contacts, Nam. Slobody 9, P.B. 47, 81499 Bratislava, Slovakia; email: ismc@ismc.sk. Lists significant business in the Czech Republic. 600 pages, $164, updated annually.

MZM World Business. MZM Publications Publishing Promotion, P.O. Box 464, PL–81705 Sopot 5, Poland; email: mzmpublications@wp.pl. Lists companies in 33 post–socialist countries involved in international trade. 860 pages; $154; updated infrequently.

American Companies in the Czech Republic and Slovakia

The following companies are classified by business area: Banking and Finance, Industrial Manufacturing, Retail and Wholesaling, Service Industries, and Technology. Company information includes firm name, address, telephone number, and specific business. Your chances of achieving employment abroad are substantially better if you contact the subsidiary company in Europe rather than the parent company in the United States. Keep in mind that the contact information for these companies can change frequently. Confirm a company's address and phone number before writing to it.

Banking and Finance

Citibank
Evropska 178
CZ– 166 50 Prague, Czech Republic
Tel.: [420] 233 061 111
Fax: [420] 233 061 613
www.citibank.com
(Bank)

Citibank
Viedenska cesta 5
851 01 Bratislava, Slovakia
Tel.: [421] 268278111
Fax: [421] 268278499
www.citibank.com
(Bank)

Industrial Manufacturing

Avon Cosmetics
Na Maninach 7
CZ–170 00 Prague 1, Czech Republic
Tel.: [420] 2 96 396 363
Fax: [420] 2 57 089 333
www.avon.com
(Cosmetics)

GE FANUC Automation
U Studanky 3
CZ–170 00 Prague 7, Czech Republic
Tel.: [420] 233 372 501
Fax: [420] 233 370 821
www.ge.com
(Electronic equipment)

Eli Lilly
Sedlarska 5
811 01 Bratislava, Slovakia
Tel.: [421] 2 59224111
Fax: [421] 2 59224119
www.lilly.com
(Pharmaceuticals)

Service Industries

Accenture Central Europe
Jiraskovo nam. 6
CZ–120 00 Prague 1, Czech Republic
Tel.: [420] 221 984 545
Fax: [420] 221 984 646
(Management consulting)

Baker & McKenzie
Celakovskeho sady 4
CZ–120 00 Prague 2, Czech Republic
Tel.: [420] 2 2422 7330
Fax: [420] 2 2422 2124
www.bakerinfo.com
(Law firm)

Donath–Burson–Marsteller
Vaclavske Namesti 21
CZ–110 11 Prague 1, Czech Republic
Tel.: [420] 224 211 220
Fax: [420] 224 211 620
www.bm.com
(Public relations and public affairs consulting)

Arthur D. Little International
Konviktska 24
CZ–110 00 Prague 1, Czech Republic
Tel.: [420] 224 231 963
Fax: [420] 224 231 829
www.adlittle.com
(Management consulting)

Radisson SAS Hotels Praha
Stepanska ulica 40
CZ–110 00 Prague, Czech Republic
Tel.: [420] 2 242 353 90
Fax: [420] 2 242 353 90
(Hotels)

White & Case
Michalski 7
811 01 Bratislava, Slovakia
Tel.: [421] 531 4126
Fax: [421] 531 3989
www.whitecase.com
(Law firm)

Technology

Cisco Systems (Czech Republic)
V Celnici 10
CZ–117 21 Prague 1, Czech Republic
Tel.: [420] 221 435 111
Fax: [420] 222 244 488
www.cisco.com
(Computer networking systems)

Dell Computer Czech Republic
Sokolovska 84–86
CZ 186 00 Prague 8, Czech Republic
Tel.: [420] 222 832 711
Fax: [420] 222 832 714
www.dell.com
(Computers)

Sybase Slovenski
Rozalska 1
841 03 Bratislava, Slovakia
Tel.: [421] 2 64782282
Fax: [421] 2 64782284
www.sybase.com
(Computer software)

European Companies in the Czech Republic and Slovakia

The following are non–American firms operating in the countries. These selected companies are mostly Czech or Slovak. Such companies will generally hire their own nationals first, but may employ Americans.

Banking and Finance

Ceska Pojistovna
Na Pankraci 121
CZ–140 00 Prague 4, Czech Republic
Tel.: [420] 2 6131 9111
www.cpoj.cz
(Insurance)

Ceska Sporitelna
Olbrachtova 1929/62
CZ–140 00 Prague 4, Czech Republic
Tel.: [420] 261 071 111
Fax: [420] 261 073 006
www.csas.cz
(Bank)

Komercni Banka
Na Prikope 33
CZ–114 07 Prague 1, Czech Republic
Tel.: [420] 2 22 43 21 11
www.koba.cz
(Bank)

Slovenska Poistovna
Dostojevskeho rad 4
815 74 Bratislava, Slovakia
Tel.: [421] 2 529 208 48
Fax: [421] 2 529 277 30
www.allianzsp.sk
(Insurance)

Vseobecna Uverova Banka
Mlynske Nivy 1
829 90 Bratislava, Slovakia
Tel.: [421] 7 5055 1111
Fax: [421] 25556 6650
www.vub.sk
(Commercial banking)

Zivnostenska Banka
Na Prikope 858/20
CZ–113 80 Prague 1, Czech Republic
Tel.: [420] 2 2412 1111
www.zivnobanka.cz
(Banks)

Industrial Manufacturing

Aliachem
Semtin 103
CZ–532 17 Prague, Czech Republic
Tel.: [420] 46 682 1111
www.aliachem.com
(Chemicals)

CEZ – Ces Energeticke Zav
Jungmannova 29/35
CZ–111 48 Prague 1, Czech Republic
Tel.: [420] 2 7113 1111
www.cez.cz
(Electricity)

Skanska CZ
Kubanska nam. 11/1391
CZ–100 05 Prague 10, Czech Republic
Tel.: [420] 267 095 111
[420] 267 310 644
www.skanska.cz
(Civil engineering)

Jihomoravska Energetika
Lidicka 36
CZ–659 44 Brno, Czech Republic
Tel.: [420] 545 141 111
Fax: [420] 545 143 067
www.jme.cz
(Electricity)

Metrostav
Kozeluzska 2246
CZ–180 00 Prague 8, Czech Republic
Tel.: [420] 2 667 09 179
www.metrostav.cz
(Civil engineering)

Nafta
Naftarska 965
908 45 Gbely, Slovakia
Tel.: [421] 34 662 1500
Fax: [421] 34 662 1249
www.nafta–stroj.sk
(Oil and gas exploration)

Nova Hut
Vratimovska 689
CZ–707 02 Ostrava–Kuncice
Czech Republic
Tel.: [421] 59 568 11 11
www.novahut.cz
(Steel)

**Plzensky Prazdroj, a. s.,
Pivovar Radegast**
CZ–739 51 Nosovice, Czech Republic
Tel.: [420] 558 602 111
Fax: [420] 558 641 414
www.radegast.cz
(Brewery)

Pliva–Lachema
Karasek 1/1767
CZ–621 33 Brno, Czech Republic
Tel.: [420] 5 41 127 111
www.lachema.cz
(Pharmaceuticals)

Prazska Energetika
Na Hroude 1492/4
CZ–100 05 Prague 10, Czech Republic
Tel.: [420] 2 6705 1111
www.pre.cz
(Electric power)

Prazske Pivovary
Nadrazni 84
CZ–150 54 Prague 5, Czech Republic

Tel.: [420] 2 571 91 111
www.staropramen.cz
(Brewery)

Prazska Teplarenska
Partyzanska 7
CZ–170 00 Prague 7, Czech Republic
Tel.: [420] 266 751 111
Fax: [420] 220 875 835
www.ptas.cz
(Electricity)

Setuza
Zukova 100
CZ–401 29 Usti nad Labem
Czech Republic
Tel.: [420] 475 291 111
 Fax: [420] 475 293 999
www.setuza.cz
(Personal hygiene products)

Severomoravska Energetika
28 rijna 152
CZ–709 02 Ostrava – Marianske Hory,
Czech Republic
Tel.: [420] 596 671 111
Fax: [420] 596 612 388
www.sme.cz
(Electric power)

Sklarny Kavalier
Sklarska 359
CZ–285 96 Sazava, Czech Republic
Tel.: [420] 327 550 111
Fax: [420] 327 321 426
(Glassware)

Slovakofarma
Nitrianska 100
920 27 Hlohovec, Slovakia
Tel.: [421] 33736 1111
Fax: [421] 33730 0890
www.slovakofarma.sk
(Pharmaceuticals)

Slovnaft
Vlcie Hrdlo
824 12 Bratislava, Slovakia
Tel.: [421] 2585 91111
Fax: [421] 245 243750
www.slovnaft.sk
(Oil refining)

Spolana
ul. Prace 657
CZ–277 11 Neratovice, Czech Republic

Tel.: [420] 315661111
Fax: [420] 315 682 821
www.spolana.cz
(Chemicals)

Unipetrol
Trojská 13
CZ–182 21 Prague, Czech Republic
Tel.: [420] 2 840 12 111
Fax: [420] 2 846 81 516
www.unipetrol.cz
(Oil refining)

Vahostav
Hlinska 40
CZ–011 18 Zilina, Slovakia
Tel.: [421] 415171111
Fax: [421] 41 7632841
www.vahostav.sk
(Construction)

Vychodoslovenske Zeleziarne Holding
04 454 Kosice, Slovakia
Tel.: [421] 95 6732121
www.vsz.sk
(Iron products)

Zavod Slovenskeho Narodneho Povstania
Priemyselna 12
965 63 Ziar Nad Hronom, Slovakia
Tel.: [421] 45 672 2201 9
www.zsnp.sk
(Aluminum products)

Zeleziarne Podbrezova
Kolkaren 35
976 81 Podbrezova, Slovakia
Tel.: [421] 486451111
Fax: [421] 486453032
www.zelpo.sk
(Metal products)

Service Industries

Ceske Radiokomunikace
U Nakladoveho nadrazi 3144/4
CZ–130 00 Prague 3, Czech Republic
Tel.: [420] 267 005 111
Fax: [420] 271 774 885
www.cra.cz
(Radio broadcasting)

Technology

Cesky Telecom
Olsanská 5
CZ–130 34 Prague 3, Czech Republic
Tel.: [42] 84 114 114
jobs@ct.cz
www.telecom.cz
(Telecommunications)

Podnik Vypocetni Techniky
Zizkova 1
CZ–371 18 Ceske Budejovice,
Czech Republic
Tel.: [420] 387747111
Fax: [420] 386359928
www.pvt.cz
(Information technology)

International Schools in the Czech Republic and Slovakia

British International School
J Valastana Dolinské 1
84102 Bratislava, Slovakia
Tel.: [421] 2 64 366 992
Fax: [421] 2 64 364 784
Email: bis@computel.sk
www.bis.sk

International School of Prague
Nebusick· 700
CZ–164 00, Prague, 6, Czech Republic
Tel.: [420] 2 203 84215
Fax: [420] 2 203 84555
Email: blimova@isp.cz
www.isp.cz

Hungary

Major employment center: Budapest

Major business language: Hungarian

Language skill index: The national language is Magyar (Hungarian). Some Hungarians also speak German, but English is becoming more common. Many Hungarians over the age of 30 also speak Russian, although most prefer not to use it.

Currency: Forint

Telephone country code: 36

Time zone: Eastern Standard Time + 6 hours

Punctuality index: Promptness is expected.

Average daily temperature, high/low: January: 35°/26°; July: 82°/61° (Budapest)

Average number of days with precipitation: January: 11 days; July: 12 days

Best bet for employment:

    For students: Teaching English

    Permanent jobs: Finance

Chance of finding a job: Things are looking up.

Useful tip: Hungarians place the surname before the given name. Keep this in mind when reading business cards and correspondence.

Located in eastern Central Europe, Hungary borders Austria to the west, the Czech Republic and Slovakia to the north, Ukraine and Romania to the east, and the former Yugoslavia to the south. About the size of Indiana, Hungary is crossed by the Danube River. The western part of the country consists of a plain, the Alfold, while the north and west are hilly. Hungary's population is 92 percent Magyar, 4 percent Romany, 2 percent German, 1 percent Slovak. Magyar is the official language. The population is 67 percent Roman Catholic and 25 percent Protestant.

Hungary has emerged from a decade of hardship with one of the strongest economies among the former Eastern Bloc nations.

The present area of Hungary formed parts of the outer provinces of the Roman Empire. Magyars invaded the region in the ninth century, overwhelming the original Germanic and Slavic inhabitants. By the fourteenth century, Hungarian dominions stretched throughout Central Europe. The Ottoman Turks began invading Hungary in 1389. In 1526 western and northern Hungary accepted Hapsburg domination to avoid Turkish rule. Eastern Hungary, including Transylvania, became independent. Louis Kossuth led a nationalist revolt in 1848, which eventually led to the formation of a joint Austro–Hungarian monarchy in 1867. Austria–Hungary dissolved after its defeat in World War I and Hungary lost over 68 percent of its territory and become a republic. Following a chaotic communist uprising and a subsequent Romanian invasion, Nicholas Horthy became Regent in a renewed monarchy in 1920.

Hungary joined the German invasion of the USSR in 1941 but was defeated by 1944. In 1945 a republic was again proclaimed, but the Communist Party seized control of Hungary in 1948 and inaugurated a harshly repressive regime. In 1956, a Soviet invasion crushed the liberal movement led by Imre Nagy. Nearly 200,000 Hungarians fled the country. Nagy was executed. Janos Kadar became the premier and attempted a policy of reconciliation. In 1989 Kadar's successor, Karoly Grosz, allowed free parliamentary elections in which the opposition easily won. In October 1989, radical amendments were made to the constitution, and the Hungarian Peoples Republic became the democratic Republic of Hungary.

The first free parliamentary election was held in May 1990. It was a plebiscite of sorts on the communist past. The revitalized and reformed communists performed poorly despite having more than the usual advantages of an "incumbent" party. Populist, center–right, and liberal parties fared best. Prime Minister Jozsef Antall formed a center–right coalition government that commanded a 60 percent majority in the parliament. Peter Boross succeeded as Prime Minister after Antall died in December 1993. The Antall/Boross coalition governments achieved a reasonably well–functioning parliamentary democracy and laid the foundation for a free market economy.

In May 1994, the socialists (MSZP) came back to win a plurality of votes and 54 percent of the seats after an election campaign focused largely on economic issues and the substantial decline in living standards since 1990. The MSZP continued economic reforms and privatization, adopting a painful but necessary policy of fiscal austerity (the "Bokros plan") in 1995. The government pursued a foreign policy of integration with Euro–Atlantic institutions and reconciliation with neighboring countries. Despite an invitation to join NATO and an improving economy, the MSZP was not re–elected. Voters, dissatisfied with the pace of economic recovery, rising crime, and cases of government corruption, elected center–right parties into power following national elections in May 1998.

This government, headed by 35–year–old Prime Minister Viktor Orban, promised to stimulate faster growth, curb inflation, and lower taxes. The Orban administration also pledged continuity in foreign policy, and continued to pursue Euro–Atlantic integration as its first priority, but was a more vocal advocate of minority rights for ethnic Hungarians abroad than the previous government. In April 2002, the country voted to return the MSZP–Free Democrat coalition back into power in one of the closest elections of the post–Communist era. The new government, led by Prime Minister Peter Medgyessy, now holds a very slim majority in Parliament. Yet, after a decade of economic transition and hardship, Hungary has emerged with one of the strongest economies among the former Eastern Bloc countries. Hungary joined NATO in 1999 and will be formally admitted into the E.U. in 2004.

Weekday business hours are from 8 a.m. to 4:30 p.m., except on Thursdays, when most businesses are open until 8 p.m. Commercial banks are open weekdays from 8 a.m to 3 p.m. and until 1 p.m. on Fridays. Most businesses are open on Saturday mornings and closed on Sundays.

Current Economic Climate

Hungary's painful economic restructuring may finally be paying off. Hungarian living standards plummeted during the first half of the 1990s, particularly difficult for a population shielded for more than 40 years by a communist government. Unemployment, officially zero percent under communism, rose as high as 14 percent in 1994. Inflation topped out at 35 percent, and the forint lost half its value between 1992 and 1996. Signs are, however, that the Hungarian economy is strengthening and may reach a level comparable to its Western neighbors. Unemployment has dropped to 6.5 percent and inflation, still a concern, hangs at just over 10 percent. Hungary's central bank has made reducing inflation a priority so that the country may be qualify for the euro by 2006.

In recent years, many Western companies have established a Central European base by expanding operations or establishing research facilities in Hungary. Companies are attracted to Hungary's skilled, educated labor force, which is competitively priced when compared with Western European pay scales.

Major industries include: steel, chemicals, textiles, pharmaceuticals, machinery, and electronic equipment. Approximately 48 percent of the workforce is engaged in manufacturing, 27 percent in services, and 20 percent in agriculture. Its major trade partners are the E.U. nations, with Austria, Italy, and Germany having particularly extensive economic and trading relationships with Hungarian enterprises. Austria, especially, has capitalized on its traditionally close ties to pursue investment opportunities in Hungary.

Hungary's 10 Largest Companies

(2001, based on market capitalization)

1. Magyar Tavkozlesi Vallalat
2. Hungarian Oil & Gas
3. Orszagos Takarek es Kereskedelmi Bank
4. Richter Gedeon Vegyeszeti Gyár
5. Egis Gyógyszergyár Reszvnytarsas
6. Tiszai Vegyi Kombinát
7. BorsodChem
8. Budapesti Elektromos Muvek
9. Eszak–Dunantuli Aramszolgaltato
10. Antenna Hungaria Magyar Mûsórszóro és Rádiöhírközlési

Getting Around in Hungary

The rail system is clean and reliable but notoriously slow, although express trains are available in major cities. Eurail and InterRail passes are accepted throughout Hungary. The bus system is expensive but more crowded than the trains. As with most transportation services in Hungary, buses primarily serve Budapest and branch out from there. The national airline, Malev, is rather expensive. Hydrofoil transportation on the Danube is a convenient but very expensive way to travel between Vienna and Budapest.

Employment Regulations and Outlook for Americans

Visas are not required for U.S. citizens for stays of three months or less. A Hungarian company must submit a workforce demand application form to the Labor Office before it can even apply for a work permit for a foreigner. Only after the Labor Office has established that, indeed, there are no Hungarian nationals for the job will it then accept the work permit application. Non–Hungarian companies, however, can avoid this process if the number of foreigners with valid work permits does not exceed 2 percent of the registered labor force. Foreign nationals are required to report their address to immigration authorities within 30 days of their arrival in Hungary.

Short–term and Temporary Work

The best bet for temporary work in Central Europe is to teach English. The Central European Teaching Program and Bridges for Education are two organizations that recruit teachers. See Chapter 10 for contact and other information about organizations that place English teachers in camps and schools. It is also possible to find teaching jobs on your own.

Internship Programs

For the best opportunities for students to obtain practical experience in Hungary, work with established programs such as AIESEC, IAESTE, or Internships International, which are described in Chapter 9.

Volunteer Opportunities

The Council on International Educational Exchange places volunteers in international work camps in Hungary. Projects include restoration and environmental conservation. The Hungarian Association of Organic Growers assists volunteers with finding temporary assignments on organic farms. See Chapter 9 for information about these and other resources.

Resources for Further Information

Newspapers in Hungary

Budapest Business Journal
Tel.: [36] 1 374 33 44
Fax: [36] 1 374 3345
www.bbj.hu

HVG
Tel.: [36] 1 35 55 411
Fax: [36] 1 35 55 693
www.hvg.hu

Figyelö
Tel.: [36] 1 437 1414
Fax: [36] 1 437 1420
www.figyelo.hu

Népszabadság
Tel.: [36] 1 43 64 444
Fax: [36] 1 43 64 604
www.nepszabadsag.hu

Useful Websites for Job Seekers

The Internet is a good place to begin your job search. Although Hungarian employers are just beginning to use the Internet to list job vacancies, there are websites that provide useful information about the job market.

CV Online Hungary
www.cvonline.hu
Lists IT/high tech, sales and marketing, banking and finance, industry and production, media, and administration jobs, and jobs for new graduates. It also features an online resume bank. Searchable in Hungarian and English.

JobLine
www.jobline.hu
Lists over 450 private sector jobs in Hungary. You can search the jobs without registering. If you register (free), you can build and submit your CV online, and receive email job notifications. Searchable in English and Hungarian.

Hungary JobPilot
www.jobpilot.hu
Includes private sector jobs, a resume database, and a directory of employers. Registration is free. In Hungarian.

Job Universe
www.jobuniverse.hu
Lists IT jobs throughout Hungary and offers a resume database and email notification. Candidates can apply for jobs online. In Hungarian.

Manpower Hungary
www.manpower.hu
Manpower is a recruitment agency. Its Hungarian site features a database of private sector jobs.

Embassies and Consular Offices

American embassies and consulates have commercial and/or economic sections that can provide you with business information and explain aspects of the local economy. Inquiries about business opportunities should be addressed either to "Commercial Officer" or "Commercial Section."

Representation of Hungary in the United States

Embassy of the Republic of Hungary
3910 Shoemaker Street NW
Washington, DC 20008
Tel.: (202) 966–7726

Fax: (202) 686–6412

Email: office@huembwas.org

www.hungaryemb.org

Representation of the United States in Hungary

American Embassy
Szabadság tér 12
H–1054 Budapest, Hungary
Tel.: [36] 1 475 4703/4924

Fax: [36] 1 475 4764

Email: acs.budapest@state.gov

www.usis.hu

Chambers of Commerce

Chambers of commerce consist of member firms in both countries interested in international trade. These are appropriate companies to initially target in the job search.

American Chamber of Commerce in Hungary
Deak Ferenc Utca 10
H–1052 Budapest, Hungary
Tel.: [36] 1 2669880
Fax: [36] 1 2669888
Email: info@amcham.hu
www.amcham.hu

Budapest Chamber of Commerce
Kristina Krt 99
H–1016 Budapest, Hungary
Tel.: [36] 1 488 2111
Fax: [36] 1 488 2119
www.bkik.hu

Hungarian–American Chamber of Commerce
205 Deanza Blvd.
San Mateo, CA 94402–3989

Tel.: (650) 573–7351

Hungarian Chamber of Commerce
Kossuth Lajos ter. 6–8
H–1055 Budapest, Hungary
Tel.: [36] 1 4745141
Fax: [36] 1 4745149
Email: intdept@mkik.hu
www.mkik.hu

Hungarian–U.S. Business Council
11615 H Street NW
Washington, DC 20062
Tel.: (202) 463–5473
Fax: (202) 463–3114
Email: eurasia@uschamber.com
www.uschamber.com/intl/abate.index.html

World Trade Center in Hungary

This world trade center houses foreign firms that conduct business in Hungary.

World Trade Center Budapest
Kecskemeti utca 14
H–1053 Budapest, Hungary
Tel.: [36] 1 338 2416

Fax: [36] 1 318 3731
Email: jvasvari@dbassoc.hu
www.dbassoc.hu

Other Informational Organizations

Foreign government missions in the United States, such as tourist offices, can furnish visas and information on work permits and other important regulations. They may also offer economic and business information about Hungary.

Hungarian National Tourist Board
150 East 58th Street, 33rd Floor
New York, NY 10155–2958
Tel.: (212) 355 0240
Fax: (212) 207 4103
Email: info@gotohungary.com
www.gotohungary.com

Ministry of Economy and Transport
Honvéd u. 13–15
H–1055 Budapest, Hungary
Tel.: [36] 1 374 2700
Fax: [36] 1 374–2925
Email: webmaster@gkm.hu
www.gm.hu

Business Directories

Although not always easy to find, business directories can prove invaluable in the international job search. Your best bet for locating these directories is to begin in the reference section of any public or university library. Most directories list company names, addresses, products, and telephone numbers. Some directories include executive names and titles and financial information about the company. These sources provide you with the names of the people to contact for employment information as well as financial data, which can tell you how strong a company's position in a country may be.

Industry Almanac–Hungary. CompAlmanach Kft., Vahot u 6, H–1119 Budapest, Hungary. Lists over 14,000 companies in Hungary. 2,400 pages; published regularly in Hungarian and German.

Major and Medium–Sized Companies in Hungary. Hoppenstedt Produktinformationen GmbH, Havelstrasse 9, D–64295 Darmstadt, Germany; email: info@hoppenstedt–fastx.de; www.hoppbonn.hu. CD–ROM listing 19,000 companies in Hungary. €194, updated annually.

MZM World Business Directory. MZM Publications Publishing Promotion, P.O. Box 465, PL–81–705 Sopot 5, Poland. Lists companies in 33 post–socialist countries involved in international trade. 860 pages; $154; updated infrequently.

American Companies in Hungary

The following companies are classified by business area: Banking and Finance, Industrial Manufacturing, Retailing and Wholesaling, Service Industries, and Technology. Company information includes firm name, address, telephone number, and specific business. Your chances of achieving employment are substantially better if you contact the subsidiary company in Europe rather than the parent company in the United States. Keep in mind that the contact information for companies can change frequently. Confirm a company's address and phone number before writing to it.

Banking and Finance

AON Hungary Ltd.
Hermina út 17
H–1146 Budapest, Hungary
Tel.: [36] 1 471 98 00
Fax: [36] 1 471 98 07
www.aon.com
(Insurance)

Citibank
Citibank Tower
Bank Center
Szabadsag ter 7
H–1051 Budapest, Hungary
Tel.: [36] 1 374 50 00
Fax: [36] 1 374 51 00
www.citibank.com
(Bank)

CS First Boston
Credit Suisse Asset Management
Rokoczi UT7072
H–1072 Budapest, Hungary
Tel.: [36] 1 413 29 50
Fax: [36] 1 413 29 60
(Investment bank)

Industrial Manufacturing

Avon Cosmetics Hungary
Haraszti u. 3
H–2100 Gödöllõ Hungary
Tel.: [36] 28 53 00 00
Fax: [36] 28 41 84 50
www.avon.com
(Cosmetics)

Johnson Control Systems
Fertö u I/D
H–1107 Budapest, Hungary
Tel.: [36] 1 263 30 33
Fax: [36] 1 263 13 17
www.johnsoncontrols.com
(Control systems)

Johnson & Johnson
Tó Park
H–2045 Törökblánint, Hungary
Tel.: [36]23510919
Fax: [36] 23510929
(Personal care products)

Levi Strauss Trading
Rákóczi út 42

H–1072 Budapest, Hungary
Tel.: [36] 1 327 7600
Fax: [36] 1 267 9937
www.levistrauss.com
(Apparel)

Service Industries

Hyatt Regency Budapest
Roosevelt Ter. 2
H–1051 Budapest V, Hungary
Tel.: [36] 1 266 1234
Fax: [36] 1 266 9101
www.hyatt.com
(Hotel)

KPMG Hungaria
XIII Váci út 99
H–1139 Budapest, Hungary
Tel.: [36] 1 270 71 00
Fax: [36] 1 270 71 01
www.kpmg.com
(Accounting)

Spencer Stuart & Associates
Riado U. 12
H–1026 Budapest, Hungary
Tel.: [36] 1 200 08 50
Fax: [36] 1 394 10 97
www.spencerstuart.com
(Executive search)

Weil, Gotshal & Manges
Bank Center
Granite Tower
H–1944 Budapest, Hungary
Tel.: [36] 1 302 9200
Fax: [36] 1 302 9110
www.weil.com
(Law firm)

Technology

IBM Hungary
Neumann János u. 1.
H–1117 Budapest, Hungary
Tel.: [36] 1 382 55 00
Fax: [36] 1 382 55 01
www.ibm.com
(Data processing equipment)

Microsoft Hungary
Graphisoft Park 3
H–1031 Budapest, Hungary
Tel.: [36] 1 437 28 00

Fax: [36] 1 437 28 99
www.microsoft.com

(Computer software)

European Companies in Hungary

The following are major non–American firms operating in the country. These selected companies are mostly Hungarian. Such companies will generally hire their own nationals but may employ Americans.

Banking and Finance

Inter–Euró Bank
Szabadság Tér 15
H–1054 Budapest, Hungary
Tel.: [36] 1 373 60 00
Fax: [36] 1 269 25 26
www.ieb.hu
(Retail bank)

Novotrade Investment Company
Szent István Korut. 18
H–1137 Budapest, Hungary
Tel.: [36] 1 452 17 00
Fax: [36] 1 452 17 01
(Financial services)

Industrial Manufacturing

Biorex
8201 Veszprém Szabadságpuszta
POB 348
Budapest, Hungary
Tel.: [36] 88 545 203
Fax: [36] 88 545 201
www.biorex.hu
(Pharmaceuticals)

BorsodChem
Bólyai tér 1.
H–3702 Kazincbarcika, Hungary
Tel.: [36] 48 51 02 11
Fax: [36] 48 51 12 11
www.borsodchem.hu
(Paints and resins)

Brau Union Hungária Sörgyárak
Vándor Sándor utca 1.
H–9400 Sopron, Hungary
Tel.: [36] 99 51 61 00
Fax: [36] 99 51 61 11
www.brau.hu
(Brewery)

Budapesti Elektromos Mûvek
Váci út 72–74.

H–1132 Budapest, Hungary
Tel.: [36] 1 238 38 38
Fax: [36] 1 238 38 48
www.elmu.hu
(Electric power)

Egis Gyógyszergyár Reszvnytarsas
Keresztúri út 30–38
H–1106 Budapest, Hungary
Tel.: [36] 1 265 55 55
Fax: [36] 1 265 55 29
www.egis.hu
(Pharmaceuticals)

Észak–Dúnantuli Áramszolgáltató
Kandó Kálmán u. 13
H–9027 GyôrHungary
Tel.: [36] 96 52 10 00
Fax: [36] 96 52 18 88
www.edasz.hu
(Electric power)

MOL Magyar Olaj–és Gázipan
Október Huszonharmadika u.18
H–1117 Budapest, Hungary
Tel.: [36] 1 209 0000
Fax: [36] 1 464 1335
www.mol.hu
(Oil and gas exploration)

Pannonflax Reszvenytarsasag
Kando Kalman u. 1.
H–9027 Gyor, Hungary
Tel.: [36] 96 507 700
www.pannon–flax.hu
(Textiles)

Richter Gedeon Vegyeszeti Gyár
Gyömrôi út 19–21.
H–1103 Budapest, Hungary
Tel.: [36] 1 43140 00
Fax: [36] 1 260 48 91
www.richter.hu
(Pharmaceuticals)

Service Industries

Antenna Hungaria Magyar Mûsórszóro és Rádióhírközlési
Petzvál József u. 31–33.
H–1119 Budapest, Hungary
Tel.: [36] 1 203 60 60
Fax: [36] 1 464 25 25
www.ahrt.hu
(Radio and television broadcasting)

Danubius Beta Hotels
Tárógató út 2–4
H–1021 Budapest, Hungary
Tel.: [36] 1 200 40 60
Fax: [36] 1 200 39 31
www.danubiusgroup.com
(Hotels)

Eravis Szálloda és Vendéglátó
Bartók Béla út 152
H–1113 Budapest, Hungary
Tel.: [36] 1 204 11 11
Fax: [36] 1 204 11 11
www.eravishotels.hu
(Hotels and restaurants)

Matá Magyar Távközlési
Krisztina korut 55
H–1013 Budapest, Hungary
Tel.: [36] 1 457 40 00
Fax: [36] 1 458 71 05
www.matav.hu
(Telecommunications)

Technology

Graphisoft
Graphisoft Park 1
H–1031 Budapest, Hungary
Tel.: [36] 437 3000
Fax: [36] 437 3099
www.graphisoft.com
(CAD/CAM software)

Synergon Informatika
Baross u. 91–95.
H–1047 Budapest, Hungary
Tel.: [36] 1 399 55 00
Fax: [36] 1 399 55 99
www.synergon.hu
(Information technology)

Tiszai Vegyi Kombinát
Gyári út 1
H–3581 Tiszaújváros, Hungary
Tel.: [36] 49 32 22 22
Fax: [36] 49 32 13 22
www.tvk.hu
(Chemicals)

International School in Hungary

American International School of Budapest
P.O. Box 53
H–1525 Budapest, Hungary
Tel.: [36] 26 556 000
Fax: [36] 26 556 003
www.aisb.hu
(International Baccalaureate curriculum, kindergarten through grade 12)

Poland

Major employment centers: Warsaw, Krakow, Lodz

Major business language: Polish

Language skill index: If you can't manage Polish, German, or Russian, you can find many people who speak at least some English.

Currency: Zloty

Telephone country code: 48

Time zone: Eastern Standard Time + 6 hours

Punctuality index: Be punctual.

Average daily temperature, high/low: January: 30°/21°; July: 75°/56° (Warsaw)

Average number of days with precipitation: January: 13 days; July: 10 days

Best bet for employment:

    For students: Teaching English

    Permanent jobs: Business

Chance of finding a job: Pretty good.

Useful tip: Most business customs in Poland are similar to those in other parts of Europe. Charming customs, such as kissing a woman's hand on meeting and bringing an odd number of flowers to dinner, however, still persist.

Poland is in the northern part of Central Europe, bordering the Baltic Sea to the north, Germany to the west, the former Czechoslovakia to the south, and Belarus and the Ukraine to the east. The country is about the size of New Mexico. Most of Poland consists of lowlands. Following World War II, Poland lost almost 70,000 square miles of its eastern territories to the USSR but gained about 40,000 square miles from Germany, thus moving the country westward. Over 98 percent of the population is Polish, with some German, Ukrainian, and Belorussian minorities. Over 95 percent of the population is Roman Catholic.

The Catholic Church has extensive influence over social policy, heavily lobbying for a law that made abortion illegal.

Polish history begins in the eleventh century with a Slavic kingdom centered around Bohemia, Moravia, and Saxony. In 1410 the Teutonic Knights became Polish vassals. Poland was a great power in the fifteenth century, when its borders reached deep into Russia and extended from the Baltic to the Black Seas. By 1772, however, the elective monarchy produced weak governments that succumbed to foreign invaders. Austria, Prussia, and Russia completely partitioned Poland by 1795. Napoleon created a brief Grand Duchy of Warsaw, which was soon reabsorbed by Russia.

Following World War I, Poland again emerged as an independent state under Marshal Josef Pilsudski in 1918. In 1926, Pilsudski began ruling as a dictator. Poland signed a non–aggression pact with Germany in 1934, but the Nazis invaded in 1939, following the German–Soviet Nonaggression Pact. Poland was again partitioned. The legal Polish government in exile was opposed by the Soviets who recognized the communist–dominated Provisional Government, which eventually established itself in Warsaw. Poland's borders shifted in 1945.

Poland established a Stalinist model of government until 1956, when riots forced a liberalization. Wladyslaw Gomulka in 1956 and Edward Gierek in 1970 both attempted reforms but failed to stabilize the economy. The Polish people were the first to challenge the hegemony of communist rule in the Eastern Bloc and started the trend toward democratization in the region. In 1981, the first independent trade union in a communist country, Solidarity, led by Lech Walesa, succeeded in exacting concessions from the government; however, General Wojciech Jaruzelski then imposed martial law and banned Solidarity. The U.S. imposed economic sanctions until 1987, when the Polish government enacted a sweeping amnesty for all political prisoners.

Solidarity was re–legalized in 1989. Its sweeping victory in June of that year caused the communist government to fall apart, and Tadeusz Mazowiecki, head of a Solidarity–led coalition, became the first non–communist prime minister in Eastern Europe since World War II. Lech Walesa was elected president in 1990. Political instability, lowered living standards, and soaring unemployment made the successive centrist governments that led post–communist Poland very unpopular among those hit hardest by economic austerity measures, including pensioners, industrial workers, and low-ranking civil servants.

In the 1995 presidential elections, the Solidarity movement fragmented into a large number of factions and Walesa was defeated by Aleksander Kwasniewski, a former communist who was head of the Democratic Left Alliance (SLD). A new Solidarity–based coalition, Solidarity Electoral Action (AWS), returned to power in 1997 and established a center–right coalition with the Freedom Union (UW). In September 2001, the SLD again won the parliamentary election and formed a coalition with the Polish Peasants' Party (PSL). Leszek Miller is the current prime minister. Poland was approved for membership in the E.U. beginning in 2004.

The line in Poland between church and state has always been a thin one. The Church openly supported Solidarity throughout the years in which it was banned and considered the fall of communism also a victory for Catholics. The Catholic Church has extensive influence over social policy. In 1993, the Catholic Church heavily lobbied parliament, which ultimately passed a law that made abortion, legal since 1956, a crime.

Normal business hours are from 8 a.m. to 4 p.m., Mondays through Fridays. Banking hours are from 8 a.m. to 6 p.m., Mondays through Fridays. The postal system is extremely unreliable. Most of the population speaks Polish, but English is increasingly common. It is also common to hear German and Russian spoken.

Poland's 10 Largest Companies

(2001, based on market capitalization)

1. Telekomunikacja Polska
2. Bank Pekao
3. Polski Koncern Naftowy ORLEN Spolka Akcy
4. Bank Handlowy w Warszawie
5. KGHM Polska Miedz
6. Bank Slaski Spolka Akcyjna w Katowicach
7. Agora
8. BRE Bank
9. Bank Przemyslowo–Handlowy
10. Powszechny Bank Kredytowy

Current Economic Climate

The Polish economy grew rapidly during the mid–1990s but has slowed considerably in recent years. The GDP grew 4 percent in 2000 but only 1 percent in 2002, boosting unemployment to almost 18 percent. Tight monetary policy and slow growth helped temper inflation, down to 1.3 percent, but the slowing economy drove the budget deficit up to an estimated 5.2 percent of GDP in 2002. Until Poland can reign in its budget deficit, prospects remain slim for joining the European Monetary Union, which is a priority for the Polish government.

The country's major industries include machine building, iron and steel, coal mining, chemicals, shipbuilding, food processing, glass, beverages, and textiles. Approximately 25 percent of the workforce is involved in the manufacturing sector, 11 percent in services, and 30 percent in agriculture. Central Europe and Russia provide most of Poland's trade, but extensive commerce also takes place with the E.U. and the United States.

Getting Around in Poland

Traveling by rail is inexpensive, and trains stop at almost every town. In general, Polish trains are slow, crowded, and uncomfortable, but express trains are sometimes available. Neither Eurail nor InterRail is accepted in Poland. Buses are even slower and more crowded than the trains, although fares are comparable. The national airline, LOT, serves most Polish cities and offers relatively economical flights within the country.

Employment Regulations and Outlook for Americans

U.S. passport holders may enter and remain in Poland for up to 90 days without a visa. To work, you'll need a visa with a right–to–work or a temporary residence card, plus a permit for employment or other gainful work with the employer. Your employer must file an application for a work permit, showing well–reasoned grounds for employing a foreign individual. Only the head of Polish diplomatic agency or consulate in your home country can issue your first visa with the right–to–work card, which is valid for up to 12 months. Applications for residence permits also should be made prior to arrival. Employment without prior authorization is strictly prohibited.

Short–term and Temporary Work

The best employment opportunities are with Poland's thriving English language schools. The Central European Teaching Program and Bridges for Education both recruit and place English teachers. They are described in Chapter 10.

English School of Communication Skills
ul.sw.Agnieszki 2/Ip
P–31–068 Krakow, Poland
Tel.: [48] 12 422 85 83

This is one of many private language schools in Poland. Teachers are not required to be TEFL–certified, but you must complete the school's training program before beginning work.

Internship Programs

The best bet for students wanting to obtain practical experience in Poland is to work with established programs such as AIESEC or IAESTE, described in Chapter 9.

Volunteer Opportunities

Many organizations coordinate work camps in Poland. Volunteer work may involve archaeology, peace issues, and forest or other ecological work. Contact Volunteers for Peace, the Council on International Educational Exchange, Global Volunteers, the International Volunteering Network, or Service Civil International to learn about opportunities, described in Chapter 9.

Resources for Further Information

Newspaper in Poland

Gazette Wyborcza
Tel.: [48] 22 8412 936

Fax: [48] 22 8416 920
www.gazeta.pl

Useful Websites for Job Searchers

The Internet is a good place to begin your job search. Although Polish employers are just beginning to use the Internet to list job vacancies, there are websites that provide useful information about the job market.

CV Online
www.cvonline.pl
Lists IT/high tech, sales and marketing, banking and finance jobs, plus jobs for new graduates. Features an online resume bank. Searchable in Polish and English.

JobAid
www.jobaid.pl
Posts jobs in a variety of industries. You can register to receive job announcements by email. In Polish.

Jobs in Poland
www.jobs.pl
Includes a special section for high school and college students and for foreign job seekers. In Polish.

Poland.pl
www.poland.pl
Offers comprehensive information on living and working in Poland. Topics include local government, telecommunications, sports and recreation.

Poland JobPilot
www.jobpilot.pl
Includes hundreds of private sector jobs, a resume bank, and a directory of employers. Registration is free. In Polish.

TopJobs
www.topjobs.pl
Features hundreds of jobs in Poland, searchable by industry or by company name. In Polish and English.

Embassies and Consular Offices

American embassies and consulates have commercial and/or economic sections that can provide you with business information and explain aspects of the local economy. Inquiries about business opportunities should be addressed either to "Commercial Officer" or "Commercial Section."

Representation of Poland in the United States

Embassy of Poland
2640 16th Street NW
Washington, DC 20009
Tel.: (202) 234–3800

Fax: (202) 328–6271
Email: information@ioip.com
www.polandembassy.org

Consulates General of Poland:
Los Angeles, (310) 442–8500; Chicago,
(312) 337–8166; New York, (212) 686–
1541.

Representation of the United States in Poland

American Embassy
Aleje Ujazdowskie 29/31
PL–00 540 Warsaw, Poland
Tel.: [48] 22 628 3041
Fax: [48] 22 625 6731
www.usaemb.pl

American Consulate General
Ulica Stolarska 9
PL–31 043 Krakow, Poland
Tel.: [48] 12 424 5100
Fax: [48] 12 424 5103

Chambers of Commerce

Chambers of commerce consist of member firms in both countries interested in international trade. These are appropriate companies to initially target in the job search.

American Chamber of Commerce in Poland
Warsaw Financial Center l
ul. Emilii Plater 53
PL–00 113 Warsaw, Poland
Tel.: [48] 22 622 55 25
Email: office@amcham.com.pl
www.amcham.com.pl

Polish Chamber of Commerce
ulica Trebacka 4
PL–00 916 Warsaw, Poland

Tel.: [48] 22 826 0143
Fax: [48] 22 828 4199

Polish–U.S. Business Council
1615 H Street NW
Washington, DC 20062–2000
Tel.: (202) 463–5473
Fax: (202) 463–3114
Email: eurasia@uschamber.com/intl/
abate/index.html
www.uschamber.com/intl/abate/in-
dex.html

World Trade Centers in Poland

These world trade centers typically house many foreign companies that conduct business in Poland.

World Trade Center Gdynia
Waszyngtona 34/36, Room 301
PL–81 342 Gdynia, Poland
Tel.: [48] 58 620 5714
Fax: [48] 58 620 1302
Email: wtc@wtcgdynia.com.pl
www.wtcgdynia.com.pl

World Trade Center Poznan
ul. Bukowska 12
PL–60 810 Poznan, Poland
Tel.: [48] 61 866 1050
Fax: [48] 61 866 6134

Email: wtc–poznan@wtc–
poznan.com.pl
www.wtc–poznan.com.pl

World Trade Center Warsaw
The Palace of Culture and Science
1 Plac Defilad (PKiN)
PL–00 901 Warsaw, Poland
Tel.: [48] 22 656 7711
Fax: [48] 22 656 7133
Email: wtcwaw@polbox.pl

Other Informational Organizations

Foreign government missions in the United States, such as tourist offices, can furnish visas and information on work permits and other important regulations, as well as economic and business information about the country.

Polish National Tourist Office
275 Madison Ave, Suite 1711
New York, NY 10016
Tel.: (212) 338–9412

Fax: (212) 338–9283
Email: pnto–nyc@polandtour.org
www.polandtour.org

Business Directories

Although not always easy to find, business directories can prove invaluable in the international job search. Your best bet for locating these directories is to begin in the reference section of any public or university library. Most directories list company names, addresses, products, and telephone numbers. Some directories include executive names and titles and financial information about the company. These sources provide you with the names of the people to contact for employment information as well as financial data, which can tell you how strong a company's position in a country may be.

Business Foundation Book: General Trade Index and Business Guide–Poland. Business Foundation Co., Krucza 38/42, PL–00512, Warsaw, Poland. Includes data on 3,500 Polish businesses and firms interested in trade with the West. 1,050 pages; updated annually.

Major Companies in Poland. Hoppenstedt Produktinfomationen GmbH, Havelstrasse 9, D–64295 Darmstadt, Germany; email:info@hoppenstedt–fastx.de; www.hbc.pl. CD ROM only. Includes 25,000 companies in Poland. €249, updated annually.

MZM World Business. MZM Publications Publishing Promotion, P.O. Box 464, PL–81705 Sopot 5, Poland; email: mzmpublications@wp.pl. Lists companies in 33 post–socialist countries involved in international trade. 860 pages; $154; updated infrequently.

American Companies in Poland

Company information includes firm name, address, telephone, and fax number, and specific business. Your chances of securing employment abroad are substantially better if you contact the subsidiary company in Europe rather than the parent company in the United States. Keep in mind that the contact information for companies can change frequently. Confirm a firm's address and phone number before writing to it.

Banking and Finance

JPMorgan Chase Bank
ul. Emilii Plater 53
PL–0 113 Warsaw, Poland
Tel.: [48] 22 520 5100
Fax: [48] 22 520 5120
www.chase.com
(Bank)

Industrial Manufacturing

Coca–Cola Amatil Ltd.
ul. Annopol 20
PL–03 236 Warsaw, Poland

Tel.: [48] 22 519 5100
Fax: [48] 22 519 5555
www.coca–cola.com
(Soft drinks)

Johnson Controls
ul. Szyszkowa 20
PL–02 285 Warsaw, Poland
Tel.: [48] 22 668 0000
Fax: [48] 22 668 0001
www.johnsoncontrols.com
(Control systems)

Kimberly–Clark Poland
ul. Domaniewska 41
PL–02 672 Warsaw, Poland
Tel.: [48] 22 606 1104
Fax: [48] 22 606 1105
www.kimberly–clark.com
(Tissue, paper products)

Timex Polska
ul. Goplanska 2b
PL–02 954 Warsaw, Poland
Tel.: [48] 22 651 6860
Fax: [48] 22 651 6512
(Watches)

Service Industries

Accenture
ul. Sienna 39
PL–00 121 Warsaw, Poland
Tel.: [48] 22 528 8000
Fax: [48] 22 528 8000
www.ac.com
(Management consulting)

Deloitte & Touche
ul. Fredry 6
PL–00 097 Warsaw, Poland
Tel.: [48] 22 511 0811
Fax: [48] 22 511 0813

www.dtti.com
(Accounting)

Heidrick & Struggles
ul. Emilii Plater 53/XXIp.
PL–00 113 Warsaw, Poland
Tel.: [48] 22 520 5140
Fax: [48] 22 520 5140
www.h–s.com
(Staff recruitment services)

Hewitt Associates
ul. Wspolna 47/49
PL–00 684 Warsaw, Poland
Tel.: [48] 22 696 5220
Fax: [48] 22 696 5221
(Benefits consulting)

PriceWaterhouseCoopers
ul. Nowogrodzka 68
PL–02 014 Warsaw, Poland
Tel.: [48] 22 523 4000
Fax: [48] 22 523 4040
(Accounting)

Technology

Apple Computer Poland
ul. Mangalia 4
PL–02 758 Warsaw, Poland
Tel.: [48] 22 651 6155
Fax: [48] 22 642 7008
www.apple.com
(Computers)

Hewlett–Packard
University Business Center II
ul. Szturmowa 2A
PL–02 678 Warsaw, Poland
Tel.: [48] 22 565 7700
Fax: [48] 22 565 7600
www.hp.com
(Computers and peripherals)

European Companies in Poland

The following are major non–American firms operating in the country. These selected companies are not necessarily Polish. Such companies will generally hire their own nationals but may employ Americans.

Banking and Finance

Bank Handlowy w Warszawie
ul. Chalubinskiego 8
PL–00 950 Warsaw, Poland

Tel.: [48] 22 690 3000
Fax: [48] 22 830 0113
www.handlowy.com.pl
(Retail and investment banking)

Bank Pekao
ul. Grzybowska 53/57
PL–00 950 Warsaw, Poland
Tel.: [48] 22 656 00 00
Fax: [48] 22 656 00 04
www.pekao.com.pl
(Retail banking)

Bank Przemyslowo–Handlowy
Aleja Pokoju 1
PL–31 548 Krakow, Poland
Tel.: [48] 12 618 68 88
Fax: [48] 12 618 63 43
www.bph.pl
(Retail banking)

BRE Bank
ul. Senatorska 18
PL–00 950 Warsaw, Poland
Tel.: [48] 22 829 00 00
Fax: [48] 22 829 00 33
www.brebank.com.pl
(Commercial banking)

Powszechny Bank Kredytowy
ul. Towarowa 25 A
PL–00 958 Warsaw, Poland
Tel.: [48] 22 531 80 00
Fax: [48] 22 531 80 42
www.pbk.pl
(Commercial banking)

Industrial Manufacturing

Agros Holding
ul. Chalubinskiego 8
PL–00 613 Warsaw, Poland
Tel.: [48] 22 830 1702
Fax: [48] 22 830 1753
www.agros.com.pl
(Food products)

Frantschach Swiecie
ul. Bydgoska 1
PL–86 100 Swiecie, Poland
Tel.: [48] 52 33 10 111
Fax: [48] 52 33 21 910
(Packaging materials)

KGHM Polska Miedz
ul. Marii Sklodowskiej–Curie 48
PL–59 301 Lubin, Poland
Tel.: [48] 76 847 8800
Fax: [48] 76 847 8500
(Mining)

Polski Koncern Naftowy ORLEN
ul. Chemików 7
PL–09 411 Plock, Poland
Tel.: [48] 24 365 00 00
Fax: [48] 24 365 40 40
www.orlen.pl
(Oil and gas refining and marketing)

Wolczanka
ul. Wolczanska 243
PL–93 035 Lodz, Poland
Tel.: [48] 42 681 86 90
Fax: [48] 41 681 39 90
www.wolczanka.com.pl
(Apparel)

Service Industries

Agora
ul. Bobrowiecka 1
PL–00 732 Warsaw, Poland
Tel.: [48] 22 555 4202
Fax: [48] 22 555 4850
www.agros.pl
(Publishing)

Technology

Computerland
Al. Jerozolimskie 180
PL–02 486 Warsaw, Poland
Tel.: [48] 22 571 1000
Fax: [48] 22 571 1001
www.computerland.pl
(IT services)

Netia Holdings
UL. Poleczki 13
PL–02 822 Warsaw, Poland
Tel.: [48] 22 330 2000
Fax: [48] 22 330 2323
www.netia.pl
(Telecommunications)

Optimus
ul. Nawojowska 118
PL–33 300 Nowy Sacz, Poland
Tel.: [48] 18 44 40 500
Fax: [48] 18 44 37 185
(Computer equipment)

Polska Telefonia Cyfrowa
Jerozolimskie 181
PL–02 222 Warsaw, Poland
Tel.: [48] 22 699 60 00

Fax: [48] 22 699 61 09
www.eragsm.pl
(Wireless communications services)

Prokom Software
ul. Polczynska 31
PL–01 377 Warsaw, Poland
Tel.: [48] 22533 9610
Fax: [48] 22533 9611
www.prokom.pl

(Information technology)

Telekomunikacja Polska
3 Swietokrzyska
PL–00 945 Warsaw, Poland
Tel.: [48] 22 657 1111
Fax: [48] 22 826 5653
www.tpsa.pl
(Telecommunications)

International Schools in Poland

The American School of Warsaw
Bielawa, ul. Warszawska 202
PL–05 520, Konstancin–Jeziorna,
Poland
Email: admissions@asw.waw.pl
www.asw.waw.pl
(U.S. curriculum, prekindergarten
through grade 12)

The British School, Warsaw
ul. Orkana 14
PL–02 656 Warsaw, Poland
Tel./Fax: [48] 22 843 4453
Fax: [48] 22 843 7365
Email: british@thebritishschool.pl

www.britishschool.waw.ids.pl
(U.K., International Baccalaureate curriculum)

**St. Paul's British International
School**
Zielona 14 Piaseczno
PL–05 500 Warsaw, Poland
Tel.: [48] 22 756 7797
Fax: [48] 22 756 2609
Email: jod@arts.gla.ac.uk
http://stpaulswarsaw.tripod.com/
main2.htm
www.stpbis.com.pl

Romania

Major employment center: Bucharest

Major business languages: Romanian, English, French, German

Language skill index: You pretty much need to use one of the business languages. English and French are the first foreign languages taught in schools. Romanian is closer to classical Latin than it is to other Romance languages, and speakers of Italian, Spanish, and French may be able understand written Romanian.

Currency: Lei

Telephone country code: 40

Time zone: Eastern Standard Time + 7 hours

Punctuality index: Very punctual.

Average daily temperature, high/low: January: 33°/20°; July: 86°/61° (Bucharest)

Average number of days with precipitation: January: 12 days; July: 12 days

Best bet for employment:

    For students: Technical work through IAESTE or teaching English

    Permanent jobs: Teaching English

Chance of finding a job: Not very good

Useful tip: Many Romanians have a fascination with the French and French culture. Most locals use the French *merci* to say thank you.

Romania, located in the northern section of the Balkan Peninsula, is bordered by the Black Sea on the east, Ukraine and Moldova to the north, Hungary to the west, the former Yugoslavia to the southwest, and Bulgaria to the south. The Carpathian mountain range runs across the northern part of the country, and the Transylvanian Alps run through the central regions. Previously part of the Ottoman Empire, Romania became an independent kingdom in 1881.

Romania's 1.5 million Gypsies constitute the largest Gypsy community on earth.

Romania was an ally of Nazi Germany in World War II, and in 1945 succumbed to pressure by the Soviet Union to allow a communist–led coalition to form a government. The Communist Party led the government until December 1989, when demonstrations against President Nikolai Ceausescu's plan of forced urbanization led to violence and the overthrow of the government. The coup lasted eight days and resulted in 1,033 deaths. (Original estimates immediately after the coup listed as many as 64,000 people dead.) Ceausescu and his wife, Elena, were tried by an anonymous court and executed by firing squad.

The National Salvation Front, led by Ion Iliescu, replaced Ceausescu's regime in 1990 with 85 percent of the popular vote. In 1992, a new constitution was ratified, and the Democratic National Salvation Front won elections in September of that year. Iliescu was re–elected president in October 1992. His quasi–communist policies, however, were the source of widespread discontent, and he was unable to secure a third term as president. In November 1996, Emil Constantinescu, head of the Democratic Convention in Romania, was elected president. He was replaced in November 2000 by Iliescu, who this time won with a landslide victory. Iliescu emphasized throughout the campaign that membership in the European Union was a priority, and his government has implemented economic reforms, privatization, and restructuring. Romania joined NATO in 2002 and hopes to become a full member of the E.U. no later than 2010.

Romania has made great progress in consolidating its democratic institutions. The press is free and outspoken, independent radio networks have proliferated, and a private television network now operates nationwide. The reorganized security services have a much reduced role in civil society, but still maintain sole control over the secret police files of the former Communist regime.

Romania has a population of 23.2 million, a tenth of whom live in the capital city of Bucharest. The population is 89 percent Romanian. There are small minority communities of Germans and Hungarians in Romania, as well as roughly 1.5 million Gypsies, the largest Gypsy community in the world. Romania is the only country with a Romance language that does not have a Roman Catholic background — 70 percent of Romanians belong to the Romanian Orthodox Church.

Business hours are from 8 a.m. to 4 p.m., although private business and banks keep longer hours. All retail shops and markets are closed on Sundays.

Current Economic Climate

Romania is a country of considerable potential: rich agricultural lands; diverse energy sources (coal, oil, natural gas, hydro, and nuclear); a substantial, if aging, industrial base encompassing almost the full range of manufacturing activities; an intelligent, well–trained work force; and opportunities for expanded development in tourism on the Black Sea and in the mountains. Yet, the various government economic reforms initiated periodically throughout the 1990s have had little lasting effect. Although privatization has met with some success in the services sector, the large industrial enterprises remain primarily in the hands of the state due to stiff resistance from Romania's powerful labor unions and from the enterprises themselves. The new government embarked upon an ambitious new privatization program in early 2001 that targets 62 enterprises, including larger banking and steel concerns.

Declining domestic demand and public sector austerity combined with external factors to push the Romanian economy into recession in 1997–1998 as real GDP declined approximately 7 percent each year. While the economy contracted a another 3.2 percent in 1999, government policy initiatives stabilized the situation during the second half of the year, laying the foundation for a rebound, led by surging exports, in 2000. The inflation rate has improved, 21 percent in 2002, down from 50 percent in 1999. It is projected to decline to 14 percent in 2003 and 9 percent in 2004. Unemployment stands at 10 percent. The GDP grew at approximately 4.5 percent in 2002. Living standards remain very low, and political infighting threatens to stall economic reforms. Yet Romania's economic prospects are bright enough that the country expects to be ready to enter the E.U. by 2010, perhaps earlier.

Half of the nation's GDP comes from the industrial sector, including chemical production, metallurgy, machinery, and petroleum refinement. The agricultural sector is an important contributor to economic growth. Romania is a major producer of wheat, corn, sunflower seeds, potatoes, and sugar beets. Romania's principal trade partners include the E.U. and Russia.

Foreign investment has been slow to take off. After 12 years, Romania has been successful at attracting only $11 billion in foreign investment, a trend that seems unlikely to change in the near future. Some of the issues that prevent foreign investment include a changing legal framework, concerns about political corruption, and a lack of know–how in terms of making projects viable. However, there are still several large companies operating in Romania, including Shell, Coca–Cola, and Colgate–Palmolive. McDonald's already has five restaurants in Bucharest, the first of which broke all Eastern European sales records.

Getting Around in Romania

Train travel in Romania requires hours of waiting in line for tickets. Express trains charge a little more but are worth the extra expense. Buses offer extensive service and are recommended where trains are not available. Fares are cheap, but buses are often uncomfortable, overcrowded, and unreliable.

Employment Regulations for Americans

U.S. citizens do not need a visa for tourist or business travel to this country for a stay in Romania up to 90 days, although a valid U.S. passport is required. Obtaining a work visa in Romania is, unlike other European countries, fairly straightforward. Your employer is required to obtain approval to hire you from the Ministry of Labor, obtain the employment visa, and request the work visa.

Short–term and Temporary Work

The best bet for temporary work in Central Europe is to teach English. There are many opportunities to teach in private language schools; both Bridges for Education and the Central European Teaching Program recruit Americans. See Chapter 10 for information and resources.

Internship Programs

The best opportunities for students to obtain practical experience in Romania is to work with established programs such as AIESEC or IAESTE which are described in detail in Chapter 9.

Volunteer Opportunities

Organizations that operate work camps in Romania include Global Volunteers, Service Civil International, and Volunteers for Peace which are described in Chapter 9. Other organizations that offer volunteer opportunities in Romania are involved with providing services and care for children in orphanages.

Children on the Edge
Watersmad, Littlehampton
West Sussex, England
BN17 6LS
Tel.: [44] 1903 850906
Fax: [44] 1903 859296
www.cote.org.uk
Anita Roddick of "The Body Shop" founded Children On The Edge in 1990 by to help alleviate the suffering within Romania's orphanages. Volunteers typically participate in the Summer Playscheme in Romania. Volunteers from all over the world usually stay for two weeks at a summer play camp for children and young adults living within institutions in the Iasi district of Romania. Volunteers are expected to pay their own expenses.

Project Concern International
3550 Afton Road
San Diego, CA 92123
Tel.: (858) 279–9690
Fax: (858) 694–0294
Email: postmaster@projectconcern.org
www.projectconcern.org
PCI develops partnerships between Romanian and American hospitals, universities, and medical and social service professionals. Highly skilled volunteers from the U.S. provide technical assistance and support to their Romanian counterparts at the local and national level. All partnerships result from a comprehensive needs assessment and involve a collaborative effort. Volunteers may support their travel and living expenses, but PCI has funds available for anyone who wishes to participate.

Newspapers in Romania

Adevarul
Tel.: [40] 1 22 42 832
Fax: [40] 1 22 43 612
www.adevarul.kappa.ro

Libertatea
Tel.: [40] 120 30 804

Fax: [40] 20 30 830
Email: ralin@liberatea.ro

Romania Libera
Tel.: [40] 1 20 28100
Fax: [40] 1 223 2071
www.romanialibera.ro

Useful Websites for Job Searchers

The Internet is a good place to begin your job search. Although few Romanian employers list jobs on the Internet, there are websites that provide useful information about the job market.

IT Generator
www.itgenerator.com
Lists only a few jobs for IT specialists, a likely indication that there are not many jobs in general in Romania. Register to receive job notifications by email, build a CV online, and apply electronically.

Romanian Jobs Database
www.jobsearch.ro

Lists about 65 jobs in Romania and the Czech Republic. You can post your resume to the online database. Written in both English and Romanian.

Embassies and Consular Offices

American embassies and consulates have commercial and/or economic sections that can provide you with business information and explain aspects of the local economy. Inquiries about business opportunities should be addressed either to "Commercial Officer" or "Commercial Section."

Representation of Romania in the United States
Embassy of Romania
1607 23rd Street NW
Washington, DC 20008

Tel.: (202) 332–4846
Fax: (202) 232–4748
www.roembus.org

Representation of the United States in Romania
American Embassy
Strada Tudor Arghezi 7–9
Bucharest, Romania

Tel.: [40] 210 4042
Fax: [40] 210 0395
www.usembassy.ro

Chambers of Commerce

Chambers of commerce consist of member firms in both countries interested in international trade. These are appropriate companies to initially target in the job search.

American Chamber of Commerce in Romania
Eminescu nr 105–107, Ap. 1
Bucharest, Romania

Tel.: [40] 1 211 7515
Fax: [40] 1 210 4964
Email: amcham@amcham.ro
www.amcham.ro

Chamber of Commerce of Romania
2 Octavian Goga Boulevard
R–79502 Bucharest, Romania

Tel.: [40] 1 322 9535 39
Fax: [40] 1 322 9542
www.ccir.ro

World Trade Center in Romania

The world trade center usually includes many foreign companies that engage in business in Romania.

World Trade Center Bucharest
Piata Montreal no. 10, Sector 1
R–71234 Bucharest Romania
Tel : [40] 1 224 1272,

Fax : [40] 1 224 2770

Email: wtcb@wtcb.ro

www.wtcb.ro

Other Informational Organization

Foreign government missions in the United States, such as economic councils, can offer business information about the country.

American–Romanian Business Council
423 S. Laureltree Dr., Suite B
Anaheim, CA 92808

Tel.: (714) 998–2614

Fax: (714) 637–9443
http://amrocham.org

Business Directory

Although not always easy to find, business directories can prove invaluable in the international job search. Your best bet for locating these directories is to begin in the reference section of any public or university library. Most directories list company names, addresses, products, and telephone numbers. Some directories include executive names and titles and financial information about the company. These sources provide you with the names of the people to contact for employment information as well as financial data, which can tell you how strong a company's position in a country may be.

MZM World Business. MZM Publications Publishing Promotion, P.O. Box 464, PL–81705 Sopot 5, Poland; Email: mzmpublications@wp.pl. Lists companies in 33 post–socialist countries involved in international trade. 860 pages; $154; updated infrequently.

American Companies in Romania

There are many more companies operating in Romania than are listed here, but business information about these operations can be difficult to find. The following companies are classified by business area: Banking and Finance; Industrial Manufacturing; Service Industries; and Technology. Company information in this section includes firm name, address, telephone and fax number, and specific business. Your chances of securing employment abroad are substantially better if you contact the subsidiary company in Europe rather than the parent company in the U.S. Keep in mind that this information changes frequently. Confirm the firm's address and phone number before writing to it.

Banking and Finance

AON Worldwide KaRo–Servicci de Asigurari
Strada Henri Coanda 15
Bucharest 1, Romania
Tel.: [40] 21 212 58 16
Fax: [40] 21 315 57 58
www.aon.com
(Insurance)

Citibank
Bulevardul Iancu de Hunedoara 8
Bucharest 1, Romania
Tel.: [40] 21 210 18 50
Fax: [40] 21 210 18 54
www.citibank.com
(Banking and financial services)

J & H Marsh & McLennan Romania
Strada Alexandru Constantinescu
46–48 ap. 2
Bucharest, Romania
Tel.: [40] 21 223 23 70
Fax: [40] 21 223 23 92
www.marshmac.com
(Insurance)

Industrial Manufacturing

Best Foods Romania
Strada Eroului 169
Chiajna, Romania
Tel.: [40] 21 221 01 66
Fax: [40] 21 312 83 13
www.bestfoods.com
(Prepared commercial food)

Eli Lilly (Suisse)
Strada Costache Negri 1–5 bl.
Centru Opera et. 7

Bucharest, Romania
Tel.: [40] 21 410 09 10
Fax: [40] 21 410 41 30
www.lilly.com
(Pharmaceuticals)

Pharmacia & Upjohn
Luterana St. 2/4
Bucharest Sector 1, Romania
www.pnu.com
(Pharmaceuticals)

Service Industries

PriceWaterhouseCoopers
Strada Costache Negri 1–5
Bucharest, Romania
Tel.: [40] 21 202 85 00
Fax: [40] 21 202 86 00
(Management consulting)

Technology

IBM Romania Ltd.
World Trade Center Entr. D, 3rd Floor
2 Expozitiei Boulevard
R–78334 Bucharest 1, Romania
Tel.: [40] 21 224 15 44
Fax: [40] 21 224 39 22
www.ibm.bom
(Data processing equipment)

Motorola Romania
Calea Victoriei 15 bl. Bucharest
Financial Plaza, Intr. E et. 4
Bucharest, Romania
Tel.: [40] 21 310 42 52
Fax: [40] 21 310 42 53
www.mot.com
(Cell phones, semiconductors)

European Companies in Romania

The following are major non–American firms operating in the country, mostly Romanian. Such companies will generally hire their own nationals first but may employ Americans.

Banking and Finance

Banca Commerciala Romana
Bulevardul Regina Elisabeta 5
Bucharest, Romania
Tel.: [40] 21312 61 85
Fax: [40] 21312 00 56

Banc Post
Bulevardul Libertatii 18 bl. 104
Bucarest, Romania
Tel.: [40] 21 336 11 24
Fax: [40] 21 336 07 72
www.bancpost.ro

(Bank)

Banca Romana Pentru Dezvoltare
Strada Doamnei 4
R–70016 Bucharest, Romania
Tel.: [40] 21 313 32 00
Fax: [40] 21 315 96 00
(Commercial bank)

Industrial Manufacturing

BASF
Calea Victoriei
155 bl. D1 sc. 7–8 et. 5–6
R–71102 Bucharest, Romania
Tel.: [40] 21 313 46 11
Fax: [40] 21 310 07 62
(Plastics and resins)

Oltchim
Strada Uzinei 1
R–1000 Ramnicu Valcea, Romania
Tel.: [40] 250 73 61 02
Fax: [40] 250 73 61 88
www.oltchim.ro
(Chemicals)

Petrolexportimport
Bulevardul Unirii, Nr: 72
Bucharest, Romania
Tel.: [40] 21 320 14 44
Fax: [40] 21 320 84 56
www.petex.ro
(Petroleum products)

Politub
Strada Romana 17 A
R–4400 Bistrita, Romania
Tel.: [40] 263 23 48 43
Fax: [40] 263 23 42 48
(Pipeline manufacturing)

RER Ecologic Service
Strada Tudor Vladimirescu 79
R–3700 Oradea, Romani
Tel.: [40] 259 43 30 44
Fax: 40] 259 43 16 21
(Waste management)

Shell Romania
Bulevardul Carol I, Nr: 64
R–70334 Bucharest, Romania
Tel.: [40] 21 312 78 06
Fax: [40] 21 312 78 28
(Petroleum products)

Tehnoforestexport
4, Piata Rosetti
R–79936 Bucharest, Romania
Tel.: [40] 21 312 53 95
Fax: [40] 21 312 44 40
www.tehnof.rdsnet.ro
(Paper products)

Universal Tractor
5 Strada Turnului
R–2200 Brasov, Romania
Tel.: [40] 268 42 24 61
Fax: [40] 268 42 63 51
www.univtr.ro
(Agricultural machines)

Unilever
291 Bulevardul Republicii
R–2000 Prahova, Romania
Tel.: [40] 244 40 16 00
Fax: [40] 244 19 82 70
www.unileversce.ro
(Cleaning products)

Technology

Electronum
Bulevardul Ficusului 8
Bucharest, Romania
Tel.: [40] 21 232 64 00
Fax: [40] 21 232 64 09
(Electronic equipment)

Ewir Est West Informatique Roumanie
Strada Constantin Radulescu
Motru 13 bl. Executive Center
et. 5 ap. 53
Bucharest, Romania
Tel.: [40] 21 330 07 56
Fax: [40] 21 330 10 69
(Software)

Mobifon
3 Strada Nerva Traian
R–74228 Bucarest, Romania
Tel.: [40] 21 302 10 00
Fax: [40] 21 302 11 11
www.connex.ro
(Telecommunications)

Romtelecom
Calea Victoriei 13 bl. Bucharest
Financial Plazza – Intrarea E
Bucarest, Romania

Tel.: [40] 21 400 43 13
Fax: [40] 21 400 43 40
(Telecommunications)

Siemens Tehnica Medicala
Strada Popa Soare 39

R–73105 Bucharest, Romania
Tel.: [40] 21 321 00 32
Fax: [400 21 320 66 60
(Electronics)

International Schools in Romania

American International School of Bucharest
Sos. Pipera–Tunari 196
Bucharest, Romania
Tel.: [40] 21 2044 4300
Fax: [40] 21 204 4306
www.aisb.ro

International School of Bucharest
428 Mihai Bravu Street
Sector 3
Bucharest, Romania
Tel.: [40] 1 327 5433
Fax: [40] 1 327 5058
Email: isbucharest@yahoo.com
www.isb.ro

Chapter

Greece, Turkey, Cyprus, & Malta

Greece

Major employment centers: Athens, Thessaloniki

Major business language: Greek

Language skill index: English is spoken by most business people. Meetings will frequently be conducted in English if a non–Greek speaker is present. As in most countries, though, not knowing the host language will limit your employment opportunities.

Currency: Euro

Telephone country code: 30

Time zone: Eastern Standard Time + 7 hours

Punctuality index: Greeks are fairly flexible about time, but don't push your luck.

Average daily temperature, high/low: January: 54°/42°; July: 90°/72° (Athens)

Average number of days with precipitation: January: 12 days; July: 2 days

Best bet for employment:

    For students: Working at resorts

    Permanent jobs: Tourism

Chance of finding a job: Not too good, thanks to a soft economy.

Useful tip: Be aware of nonverbal communication in Greece: A nod of the head means no, and a slight tilt to the side means yes.

The Hellenic Republic, about the size of New York State, is located on the southern end of the Balkan Peninsula in southeastern Europe, bordering the former Yugoslavia, Albania, and Bulgaria to the north, Turkey and the Aegean Sea to the east, the Ionian Sea to the west, and the Mediterranean to the south. Most of the country is mountainous, with the highest point, Mt. Olympus, rising to 9,570 feet. Fewer than 170 of Greece's more than 2,000 islands are inhabited. The larger islands include Crete and the Ionian, Cyclades, and Sporades groups. About 97 percent of the population is affiliated with the Greek Orthodox Church.

Growing concerns about construction deadlines, cost overruns, and heightened international scrutiny of security surround the Olympic Games in Athens set for 2004.

Greece, especially the area around Athens, reached its apex in the fourth century B.C. but eventually became a Roman province, part of the Byzantine Empire, and an outpost of the Ottoman Empire. Turkish rule lasted until 1827, ending after a bloody war of independence. Greece maintained a monarchy until 1923, when a republic was declared under military rule. The monarchy was restored in 1941 but collapsed during the Axis invasion. Italians, Germans, and Bulgarians occupied the country in World War II until its liberation in 1944. Communist guerrillas conducted a civil war against the government from 1947–49 but were defeated with extensive U.S. assistance. A military regime seized power in 1967 and declared a republic in 1973. The next year, the military regime resigned, following a failed attempt to capture Cyprus.

The Panhellenic Socialist Movement (PASOK) won the 1981 election. Andreou Papandreou became Greece's first socialist prime minister and a regular player in Greek politics for the next fifteen years. In 1988, Papandreou had a widely publicized affair with a flight attendant (whom he later married), and the government collapsed after PASOK became embroiled in a serious financial scandal. In 1989, a conservative and communist government took over and implemented a *katharsis*, a campaign of purification, to investigate Papandreou and his ministers. The government ruled that they should stand trial for embezzlement, telephone tapping, and illegal grain sales. Papandreou's government was marked by cronyism: his wife served as his chief of staff, his son was deputy foreign minister, and his personal physician was appointed minister of health.

Constantine Mitsotakis of the New Democracy Party (NDP) took over as premier in 1990, but the NDP lost its parliamentary majority in 1993. In general elections held that October, Papandreou, now cleared of all charges, and PASOK captured a majority of seats. Papandreou resigned in 1996 after a protracted illness, and Costas Simitis, an experienced economist and lawyer, was elected prime minister. He successfully implemented economic reforms, including an overhaul of the country's taxation system. Simitis and PASOK were re–elected in April 2000, although by a thin margin. Greece adopted the euro in January 2001.

Greece's foreign policy is dominated by its extremely sensitive relationship with Turkey, its Muslim neighbor. The two NATO allies have repeatedly come close to war. In 1974, the Greek army attempted to assassinate the Cyprus leader, Archbiship Makarios. Makarios escaped, and the governing Greek junta replaced him with the extremist Nikos Samson. This prompted mainland Turkey to occupy North Cyprus in support of the island's 20 percent Turkish minority. This continued occupation remains one of the most contentious issues in Greek politics.

As the Olympic Games slated for Athens on August 13 to 29, 2004 approach, concerns are growing about construction deadlines, cost overruns, and heightened international scrutiny of security. Prime Minister Simitis has appointed Yianna Angelopoulou–Daskalaki, who led the Greek bid to host the Olympics, as coordinator of the Athens Olympic Organizing Committee.

Normal weekday business hours are from 9 a.m. to 6 p.m., with an afternoon break from 2 p.m. to 5 p.m. Government offices may be open to the public only from 11 a.m. to 1 p.m.

Current Economic Climate

Greece, having surmounted considerable obstacles, became the twelfth member of the European Monetary Union on January 1, 2001. The country has demonstrated steady progress in rehabilitating an economy burdened by a large public sector, persistently high inflation, reform–resistant labor unions, and massive public indebtedness. Although the standard of living in Greece is roughly 30 percent lower than that of other countries in the European Union, it is substantially higher than its neighboring countries. Greece's annual growth rate averages a respectable 3.7 percent. Unemployment hovers at about 9.6 percent — a decline from previous years, but still high enough to prompt the Greek government to pledge to create 86,500 new jobs in 2003. Unemployment has hit young people the hardest: 28 percent of Greeks between 15 and 24 are unemployed, more than anywhere else in Europe. The inflation rate is approximately 3.9 percent. The Greek government is concerned about its very large underground economy, estimated at over 30 percent of total economic activity.

The labor force is officially 43 percent service, 29 percent industrial, and 28 percent agricultural. Major industrial products include textiles, chemicals, and processed foods. The economy is sustained by a massive tourism sector — roughly 12 million tourists visited Greece in 2001 with net revenues exceeding 5 billion euros. Greece's food industry is expanding rapidly to support new markets in neighboring countries. High–tech equipment production, especially for telecommunications, is also a fast–growing sector. Greece, historically a sea–faring nation, has a large shipping and shipbuilding industry. The E.U. and the United States are Greece's predominant trading partners. Greece also trades significantly with the Middle East.

Both improving relations with Turkey and the 2004 Olympic Games are bright spots in Greece's overall economic health. Athens inaugurated a new, $1.9 billion international airport in late March 2001 in an effort to both become a regional air travel hub as well as support a thriving tourism sector, which could be further enhanced by the Olympics.

Greece's 10 Largest Companies

(2001, based on market capitalization)

1. Hellenic Telecommunications Organization
2. National Bank of Greece
3. EFG Eurobank Ergasias
4. Alpha Credit Bank
5. Cosmote Mobile Telecommunications
6. Commercial Bank of Greece
7. Panafon Hellenic Telecom Company
8. Coca–Cola HBC
9. Hellenic Petroleum
10. Bank of Piraeus

Getting Around in Greece

The bus service, KTEK, is generally fast and extensive, whereas the train system, OSE, is slower and less convenient than other European networks. Ferry and train services offer reasonable rates. The national airline, Olympic Airways, connects many of the Greek islands at fairly reasonable prices and is often heavily booked.

Employment on the Greek Islands and Tourism

Over 12 million tourists visit Greece annually, providing jobs in the tourist industry, which is centered on the Greek Aegean Sea islands. Pubs and hotels often seek individuals with language skills to serve tourists. Ferries, which provide much of the transportation between islands, also offer job opportunities. The best islands for tourist work include Rhodes, Corfu, Ios, Augina, Mykonos, and Paros. Boating and yacht companies generally like to hire English speakers to accommodate tourists. Americans may also find work in Glyfada, south of Athens, which plays host to a U.S. military base. Many bars around the base, as well as in Athens, have English names and cater to the American crowd.

Using the language

Most employment in the tourist industry does not necessarily require a knowledge of Greek. Employment in other sectors of the economy, however, necessitates Greek language skills. Foreign subsidiaries usually only hire Greek speakers. Many young people speak English, but you should generally initiate conversations in Greek.

Employment Regulations and Outlook for Americans

Americans do not need a visa to stay in Greece for less than 30 days, but you need a valid work and residence permit in order to accept a job in Greece. Your employer must obtain approval from the Greek government *before* you arrive in Greece. This approval requires your employer to demonstrate that no Greek citizen is qualified to fill the position. Greek employers are required by law to give hiring preference to Greek citizens, European citizens, people of Greek heritage, and foreigners with refugee status who legally reside in Greece. All work permits are issued for a specific employer, occupation, place of work, and time period. Keep in mind that most foreign subsidiaries in Greece are fairly small and have minor personnel needs. Greece also has an oversupply of university graduates in most fields, making it difficult for foreigners to find jobs.

Most employment recruiting takes place through advertisements or personal contacts. Writing a letter to a potential employer in Greece may prove beneficial. Greek employers tend to hire people with relevant degrees, even for general management positions. Few candidates with only bachelor's degrees will be hired without extensive work experience. Since very little training is available from most firms, employers expect job candidates to arrive with the necessary skills.

Americans may be able to find jobs teaching English, especially at private schools and service organizations. The fishing industry in Greece is large and constantly needs additional laborers. Various types of agricultural work, such as grape or olive picking, can also be found throughout Greece. Such agricultural employment should be sought in the *Athens News* and is usually advertised in local hostels and cafes.

Short–term and Temporary Work

The best bets for casual jobs are to work as an au pair or at a tourist resort See Chapter 9 for additional resources, especially for au pairs. Chapter 10 reports on opportunities to teach in private language schools. These jobs are frequently advertised in newspapers and via the Internet, but the organizations below may also be useful.

Agency Remarc
P.O.Box 77260
GR–17510 Athens, Greece
Tel.: [30] 210 9832955
Email: info@sunseafun.com
www.sunseafun.com
Recruits people for entertainment teams that perform in Greek resorts. The agency looks for people who can coach sports, act, dance or sing. Employees receive €500 per month and room and board.

Anglo–Hellenic
P.O. Box 263
GR–201 00 Corinth, Greece
Tel.: [30] 274 10 53511
Fax: [30] 274 10 85579
Email: info@anglo–hellenic.com
www.anglo–hellenic.com
Assists English–language teachers with finding placements throughout Greece. You can complete a single application available on its website to apply to multiple schools. TEFL certification is not required, but preferred.

Athenian Nanny Agency
P.O. Box 51181
GR–145 10 Kifissia Athens, Greece

Tel./fax: [30] 1 808 1005
Email: mskiniti@groovy.gr
Places experienced nannies and au pairs throughout Greece.

Au Pair Activities
P.O. Box 76080

GR–171 10 Nea Smyrni, Athens, Greece
Tel./Fax: [30] 1 932 6016
Email: porae@iname.com
Primarily places au pairs, but also assists people looking for positions in the tourist industry.

Internship Programs

For students interested in practical work experience or internships, the best opportunities are available through established organizations such as AIESEC and IAESTE, which are described in Chapter 9 along with other intership programs.

Volunteer Opportunities

Many of the organizations that manage service projects in Greece address issues associated with environmental protection. There are also a few groups that place volunteer English teachers in Greek schools. See Chapter 9 for additional resources, including information about the Council on International Educational Exchange, Global Volunteers, Civil Service International and Volunteers for Peace.

Archelon Sea Turtle Protection Society of Greece
Solomou 57
GR–10 432 Athens, Greece
Tel./Fax: [30] 1 523 1342
Email: stps@archelon.gr
www.archelon.gr
Recruits volunteers for work camps that complete sea turtle conservation projects. Some projects are in Zakynthos, Peloponnesus, and Crete, which are major nesting areas for sea turtles. Archelon also runs the only Sea Turtle Rehabilitation Center in Greece. Volunteers participate in projects such as protecting nests from wild animals, restoring sand dunes, maintaining nature trails, or running nature information centers. Projects last at least six weeks, and Archelon charges a $100 program fee. Volunteers are expected to cover travel and food expenses. Students may complete research during their volunteer assignments.

Conservation Koroni
Poste Restante, Koroni
GR–24 004 Messinia, Greece
Tel.: [30] 977 529224
Fax: [30] 725 22779
Recruits volunteers for at least one month in the summer to clean beaches and guard loggerhead turtles. Volunteers must be at least 18 years old.

Conservation Volunteers Greece
Omirou 15
GR–14 562 Kifisia, Athens, Greece
Tel.: [30] 210 62 31 120
Fax: [30] 210 80 11 489
Email: cvgpeep@otenet.gr
http://users.otenet.gr/~cvgpeep/
Recruits volunteers for work in protected landscapes, conservation of traditional buildings and work in archaeological sites. Volunteers are responsible for their own travel, but will receive room and board in exchange for their services. CVG charges a €120 fee.

Resources for Further Information

Newspapers in Greece

Athens News (English)
Tel.: [30] 1 333 3161
Fax: [30] 1 32 31 384
www.athensnews.gr

Eleftherotypia (daily)
Tel.: [30] 1 92 96 001
Fax: [30] 1 90 28 311
www.enet.gr

Kathimerini (daily)
Tel.: [30] 1 52 99 000
Fax: [30] 1 52 28 894
www.kathimerini.gr

Ta Nea (daily)
Tel.: [30] 1 333 3555
Fax: [30] 1 32 28 797
www.ta–nea.dolnet.gr/

Useful Websites for Job Seekers

The Internet is a good place to begin your job search. Although Greek employers are just beginning to use the Internet to list job vacancies, there are websites that provide general information about the job market.

Greek Classifieds
www.ads–in–greece.com
Lists what you'd expect in classified ads: housing, cars, professional services, and a few job listings.

Hellenic Resources
www.hri.org
A clearinghouse for other bulletin boards in Greece, this site features a comprehensive set of links to job listings in major Greek newspapers and magazines.

In Jobs Greece
www.injobs.gr
Features over 50 private sector jobs in Greece. It also includes a place to post your resume online.

Job Centers Hellas
www.jobcentres.gr
Caters to temporary, clerical and mid–management professionals in fields ranging from advertising and media to finance. Job listings are not extensive.

Manpower Greece
www.manpower.gr
Manpower is a recruitment agency. Its Greek site features a database of private sector jobs.

Payaway
www.payaway.co.uk
Geared toward short–term and holiday work. Most employers listed here are recruiting for help in resorts or on chartered boats.

2004 Olympics
www.athens.olympic.org
The official site for jobs related to the 2004 Olympics. Be forewarned, the application process for volunteering (there are virtually no paid jobs) is very competitive.

Embassies and Consular Offices

American embassies and consulates have commercial and/or economic sections that can provide you with business information and explain aspects of the local economy. Inquiries about business opportunities should be addressed either to "Commercial Officer" or "Commercial Section."

Representation of Greece in the United States

Embassy of Greece
2221 Massachusetts Avenue NW
Washington, DC 20008
Tel.: (202) 939-1300
Fax: (202) 939-1324
Email: greece@greekembassy.org
www.greekembassy.org

Consulates General of Greece:
Atlanta, (404) 261-3313; Boston, (617)
523-0100; Chicago, (312) 335-3915;
Houston, (713) 840-7522; Los Angeles,
(310) 826-5555; New Orleans, (504)
523-1167; New York, (212) 988-5500;
San Francisco, (415) 775-2102

Representation of the United States in Greece

American Embassy
91 Vasilissis Sophias Boulevard
GR-101 60 Athens, Greece
Tel.: [30] 210 721 2951
Email: usembassy@usisathens.gr
www.usembassy.gr

American Consulate General
43 Tsimiski, Seventh Floor
GR-546 23 Thessaloniki, Greece
Tel.: [30] 2310 242 905
Fax: [30] 2310 242 927
Email: amcongen@compulink.gr
www.usconsulate.gr

Chambers of Commerce

Chambers of commerce consist of member firms in both countries interested in international trade. These are appropriate companies to initially target in the job search.

American Hellenic Chamber of Commerce
16-18 Kanari Street, Third Floor
GR-106 74 Athens, Greece
Tel.: [30] 1 362 3231
Fax: [30] 1 361 0170
Email: s.yannopoulos@amcham.gr
www.amcham.gr

Hellenic-American Chamber of Commerce
960 Avenue of the Americas

Suite 1008
New York, NY 10001
Tel.: (212) 629-6380
Fax: (212) 564-9281

Union of Hellenic Chambers of Commerce
7 Academias Street
GR-10 671 Athens, Greece
Tel.: [30] 1 363 2702
Fax: [30] 1 362 2320
Email: hellas@uhcci.gr

World Trade Center in Greece

The world trade center usually houses many foreign companies that conduct business in Greece.

Athens World Trade Center
308 Messogion Avenue & 2 Arkadiou
GR-155 62 Holargos, Athens, Greece
Tel.: [30] 1 650 4300

Fax: [30] 1 654 1539
Email: contact@wtcathens.gr
www.wtcathens.gr

Other Informational Organization

Foreign government missions in the United States such as tourist offices can furnish visas and information on work permits and other important regulations. They may also offer economic and business information about the country.

Greek National Tourist Organization Tel.: (212) 421–5777
645 Fifth Avenue, 9th floor Fax: (212) 826–6940
New York, NY 10022 Email: info@greektourism.com

Business Directories

Although not always easy to find, business directories can prove invaluable in the international job search. Your best bet for locating these directories is to begin in the reference section of any public or university library. Most directories list company names, addresses, products, and phone numbers. Some directories include executive names and titles and financial information about the company. These sources provide you with the names of the people to contact for employment information as well as financial data, which can tell you how strong a company's position in a country may be.

American–Hellenic Chamber of Commerce–Business Directory of Members. American Hellenic Chamber of Commerce, 109–111 Messoghion Avenue, GR–115 26 Polita Business Center, Greece; email: info@amcham.gr; www.amcham.gr. Includes American subsidiaries in Greece and major Greek firms. 400 pages, $100, updated annually.

Greek Export Directory. Athens Chamber of Commerce and Industry, 7 Akadimias, GR–106 71 Athens, Greece; email: info@acci.gr; www.amcham.gr. Lists Greek firms engaged in export and chambers of commerce located in Greece. 544 pages, updated annually.

Greek Shipowners Register. Greek Shipping Publications Co. Ltd., 14 Skouze & Kolokotroni Street, GR–185 36 Piraeus, Greece. Listing of Greek ship–owning companies. 500 pages, $125, updated annually.

ICAP Financial Directory of Greek Companies. ICAP, 64 Queen Sophia Avenue, GR–115 28 Athens, Greece; email: icap@icap.gr. Distributed in the United States by EBSCO Subscription Services, P.O. Box 1943, Birmingham, AL 35201. Lists financial data on over 20,000 Greek companies. 3,300 pages, $450, updated annually.

Yearbook of the Athens Stock Exchange. Athens Stock Exchange, 10 Sophocleus Street, GR–105 59 Athens, Greece. Lists 196 companies quoted on the exchange and stockbrokers. 510 pages, updated annually.

American Companies in Greece

The following companies are classified by business area: Banking and Finance; Industrial Manufacturing; Retailing and Wholesaling; Service Industries; and Technology. Company information includes firm name, address, phone number, and specific business. Your chances of securing employment abroad are substantially better if you contact the subsidiary company in Europe rather than the parent company in the U.S. Keep in mind that the contact information for companies listed in this section can change pretty frequently. Confirm a company's address and phone number before writing to it.

Banking and Finance

The Chase Manhattan Bank
3 Korai Street
GR–102 10 Athens, Greece
www.chase.com

Cigna Insurance Co. (Hellas)
Phidippidou 2
Ampelokipi
GR–115 26 Athens, Greece
(Insurance)

Citibank
52–54 Syngrou Ave.
GR–117 42, Athens, Greece
Tel.: [30] 21 0924 5000
Fax: [30] 21 0924 3601
www.citibank.com

Merrill Lynch, Pierce, Fenner & Smith Hellas
17 Valaorithous Street
GR–106 71 Athens, Greece
Tel.: [30] 1 361 8916
Fax: [30] 1 364 8046
(Financial services)

Industrial Manufacturing

AlliedSignal
P.O. Box 65039
GR–154–10 Psychico, Athens, Greece
www.alliedsignal.com
(Aerospace and automotive products)

Baxter Hellas
34 Ethn. Makariou
GR–163 41 Ilioupoli, Greece
Tel.: [30] 21 099 87 000
Fax: [30] 21 099 5 9820
www.baxter.com
(Pharmaceuticals)

Bristol–Myers Squibb
102 Tatoiou Ave & Kolokotroni
GR–14671 Nea Erythraia, Greece
Tel: [30] 2106249300
Fax: [30] 2106249333
www.bms.com

(Pharmaceuticals)

Colgate–Palmolive (Hellas)
89 Athinon Street
GR–185 41 Piraeus, Greece
Tel.: [30] 21 0483 19 00–15
Fax: [30] 21 0483 1924
(Soaps and toiletries)

Dow (Hellas)
Thoriko
GR–195 00 Lavrio, Greece
Tel.: [30] 1 2292062200
Fax: [30] 1 2292025243
(Plastics and resins)

Goodyear Dunlop Tires Hellas
94 Kifissou Avenue
P.O. Box 41092
GR–122 10 Aigaleo, Greece
Tel.: [30] 2105625560–9
Fax: [30] 2105691244
www.goodyear.com
(Tires)

Johnson & Johnson Hellas
4 Epidavrou
GR–151 25 Maroussi, Greece
Tel.: [30] 2106875555
Fax: [30] 2106850309
www.wnj.com
(Health–care products)

Kodak (Near East)
10–12 Heimarras
GR–151 25 Maroussi, Greece
Tel.: [30] 2106189200
Fax: [30] 2106198635
(Photo chemical products)

Pharmaserve–Lilly
15 KM Athinon – Lamias National Rd
P.O. Box 51288
GR–14510 Kifissia, Greece
Tel.: [30] 21 0629 4600
Fax: [30] 21 0629 4610
www.lilly.com
(Pharmaceuticals)

Procter & Gamble Hellas
165 Syngrou Avenue
GR–171 21 Nea Smyrni, Greece
Tel.: [30] 21 0939 4000
Fax: [30] 21 0939 4801
www.pg.com
(Soaps and detergents)

Service Industries

Accenture
246 Avenue Kifissias
GR–152 31 Halandri, Greece
Tel.: [30] 2106776400–4
Fax: [30] 2106776405
(Management consulting)

Leo Burnett
6 Patroklou & Andromachis
GR–151 25 Maroussi, Greece
Tel.: [30] 2108112811
Fax: [30] 2106829040
www.leoburnett.com
(Advertising)

Deloitte & Touche
250–254 Avenue Kifissias
GR–152 31 Halandri, Greece
Tel.: [30] 2106781100
Fax: [30] 2106776221–2
(Accounting)

Hilton Hotel
46 Vassilissis Sofias Avenue
GR–115 28 Athens, Greece
(Hotels)

McCann–Erickson Advertising
1 Ag. Annis
GR–152 32 Halandri, Greece

Tel.: [30] 2108171100
Fax: [30] 2108171180
(Advertising)

Technology

Cisco Systems
Caravel Hotel, Suite 427
Vas. Alexandrou 2
Athens, Greece
www.cisco.com
(Computer hardware and networking systems)

Hewlett–Packard Hellas
62 Kifissias Avenue
GR–151 25 Athens, Greece
www.hp.com
(Computers and peripherals)

IBM Hellas
284 Kifissias Avenue
GR–152 32 Halandri, Greece
Tel.: [30] 21 0688 1111
Fax: [30] 21 0680 1300
(Data processing equipment)

Microsoft Greece
56 Kiffissias Avenue
GR–151 25 Maroussi, Greece
Tel.: [30] 21 06151200
Fax: [30] 21 06106780
www.microsoft.com
(Software)

Motorola Greece
22 Kifissias Avenue
GR–151 25 Maroussi, Greece
www.mot.com
(Semiconductors, cell phones)

European Companies in Greece

The following are major non–American firms operating in the country. These selected companies can be either Greek or based in another European country. Such companies will generally hire their own nationals first but may employ Americans.

Banking and Finance

Alpha Credit Bank
40 Stadiou Street
GR–102 52 Athens, Greece
Tel.: [30] 1 0 326 0000
Fax: [30] 1 0 326 5438

www.alpha.gr
(Commercial bank)

Commercial Bank of Greece
11 Sofokleous
GR–102 35 Athens, Greece
Tel.: [30] 21 0 321 0911

Fax: [30] 210 325 3746
www.combank.gr
(Commercial banking)

EFG Eurobank Ergasias
8 Othonos Street
GR–105 57 Athens, Greece
Tel.: [30] 21 0 333 7000
Fax: [30] 210 323 3866
www.efggroup.com
(Commercial banking)

National Bank of Greece
86 Eolou Street
GR–102 32 Athens, Greece
Tel.: [30] 33 41 00 0
Fax: [30] 33 46 51 0
www.nbg.gr
(Commercial banking)

Industrial Manufacturing

Aluminium de Grece
1 Sekeri Str.
GR–106 71 Athens, Greece
Tel.: [30] 1 369 3000
Fax: [30] 1 369 3615
www.alhellas.pechiney.com
(Aluminum)

Athenian Brewery
102 Kiffissou Avenue
GR–122 41 Aigaleo, Greece
Tel.: [30] 210 538 4911–60
Fax: [30] 210 538 4412
(Brewery)

Hellenic Petroleum
17th km., Athens–Corinth National
Road
GR–193 00 Aspropyrgos, Attikí Greece
Tel.: [30] 1 55 33 000
Fax: [30] 1 55 39 298
www.hellenic–petroleum.gr
(Oil and gas production)

Motor Oil (Hellas) Corinth Refineries
12a Irodou Attikou Street, Maroussi
GR–151 24 Athens, Greece
Tel.: [30] 10 809 4000
Fax: [30] 10 809 4444
www.moh.gr
(Oil and gas refining and marketing)

Nexans Hellas
15 Messoghion Avenue

GR–115 26 Athens, Greece
Tel.: [30] 1 749 2000
Fax: [30] 1 749 2199
www.nexans.gr
(Wire & cable manufacturing)

Petrola Hellas
59 Diligianni Street
GR–145 62 Kifissia, Athens, Greece
Tel.: [30] 10 55 36 000
Fax: [30] 10 55 48 509
www.petrola.gr
(Oil & gas refining & marketing)

Shell Company (Hellas) Ltd.
6–8 Ag. Kyriakis
GR–175 64 Palaio Faliro, Greece
Tel.: [30] 21 0 947 6000
Fax: [30] 21 0 940 0550
(Petroleum products)

Stelmar Shipping Ltd.
Status Center, 2A Areos Street,
Vouliagmeni
GR–166 71 Athens, Greece
Tel.: [30] 10 967 0001
Fax: [30] 10 967 0150
www.stelmar.com
(Shipping)

Tsakos Energy Navigation
367 Syngrou Ave.
GR–175 64 Athens, Greece
Tel.: [30] 10 940 770 13
Fax: [30] 10 940 7716
www.tenn.gr
(Shipping)

Viohalco
115 Kifissias Avenue
GR–115 24 Athens, Greece
Tel.: [30] 210 686 1111
Fax: [30] 210 686 1347
(Metals)

Unilever Hellas
92 Mar. Antypa
GR–141 21 Irakleio, Greece
Tel.: [30] 21 0 270 1500
Fax: [30] 21 0 271 9910
(Soaps, detergents, cosmetics)

Services

Antenna TV
Kifissias Ave. 10–12, Maroussi

GR–151 25 Athens, Greece
Tel.: [30] 1 688 6100
Fax: [30] 1 689 0304
www.antenna.gr
(Television production)

Royal Olympic Cruise Lines
Akti Miaouli 87
GR–185 38 Piraeus, Athens, Greece
Tel.: [30] 1 429 1000
Fax: [30] 1 429 0862
www.royalolympiccruises.com
(Cruise line)

Technology

Cosmote Mobile Telecommunications
44 Kifissias Avenue
GR–151 25 Maroussi, Greece
Tel.: [30] 210 617 7777
Fax: [30] 210 617 7578
www.cosmote.gr
(Wireless communications)

Hellenic Telecommunications Organization
99 Kifissias Avenue, Maroussi
GR–151 24 Athens, Greece
Tel.: [30] 1 8820 899
Fax: [30] 1 6810 899
www.ote.gr
(Telecommunications)

Panafon Hellenic Telecom Company
44 Kifissias Avenue
GR–151 25 Athens, Greece
Tel.: [30] 1 616 0061
Fax: [30] 1 616 0025
www.vodafone.gr
(Telecommunications)

STET Hellas Telecommunications
60 Kifissias Avenue, Maroussi
GR–151 25 Athens, Greece
Tel.: [30] 1 615 8585
Fax: [30] 1 610 8819
www.telestet.gr
(Wireless communications services)

International Nonprofit Employer In Greece

International Olympic Academy
4 Kapsali Street
GR–106 74 Athens, Greece

Tel.: [30] 01 724 9235–9
Fax: [30] 01 72 44813
www.sport.gov.gr

International Schools in Greece

American Community Schools of Athens
129 Aghias Paraskevis Street
GR–152 34 Halandri, Athens, Greece
Tel.: [30] 10 639 32 00
Fax: [30] 10 639 00 51
Email: acs@acs.gr
www.acs.gr
(U.S. curriculum, prekindergarten through grade 12)

TASIS Hellenic International School
P.O. Box 51025
145 10 Kifissia, Greece
Tel.: [30] 1 8081 426
Fax: [30] 1 8018 421
Email: bhani@hol.gr
www.tasis.com/TASIS/Hellenic/home.html
(U.S., U.K. curriculum, prekindergarten through grade 12)

Turkey

Major employment centers: Ankara, Istanbul, Izmir

Major business languages: Turkish, English, French

Language skill index: You can certainly get by in English, but a little Turkish will help.

Currency: Turkish lira

Telephone country code: 90

Time zone: Eastern Standard Time + 7 hours

Punctuality index: Punctuality is important.

Average daily temperature, high/low: January: 45°/36°; July: 81°/65° (Istanbul)

Average number of days with precipitation: January: 12 days; July: 3 days

Best bet for employment:

    For students: Internships with organizations such as IAESTE or AIESEC

    Permanent jobs: New businesses and trade

Chance of getting a job: Unless you are creating your own, slight chance

Useful tip: Nodding off during that morning meeting? Try a little Turkish coffee, considered by many to be the strongest in the world. Turkish hospitality requires that visitors always be offered coffee or tea, and it is impolite to refuse. Coffee is served both *sade* (without sugar) and *orta* (with sugar).

Turkey lies at the crossroads of Europe and Asia. The major part of its geographic area, the Anatolialies in far western Asia, consists of some 290,000 square miles. Separated from Asia by the Bosporus, the Sea of Marmara, and the Dardanelles (collectively known as the Straits) is the other 3 percent of Turkey's land area: the roughly 30,000–square–mile area of Eastern Thrace in far southeastern Europe. Taken as a whole, Turkey is bordered to the north by Bulgaria, the Black Sea, and Georgia; to the East by Armenia and Iran; to the south by Iraq, Syria, and the Mediterranean Sea, which along with Greece and the Aegean Sea defines Turkey's western limit. Turkey's total land area of just over 320,000 square miles makes it not quite the size of Oklahoma and Texas combined.

Despite rays of sunshine, most Turks say rising unemployment and inflation are crushing them.

Much of Turkey's terrain is mountainous. At the center is a wide plateau that rises to meet an interior ring of peaks, which in the east, south, and much of the north continue on to Turkey's borders. In the west, the mountains give way first to rolling plains then to coastal plains as the land bows to meet the sea.

Turkey's capital of Ankara, located in the central plateau, is home to over 2.5 million people. Istanbul is far larger, with a population nearing 7 million, and it perches on the eastern–most tip of Turkey's geographically European portion. The population of Turkey as a whole is just under 60 million, 60 percent of whom live in cities and towns. Turkey's population consists largely of ethnic Turks (80 percent). There is also a substantial Kurdish minority (18 percent), a fraction of which has been a source of tension since the mid–1980s: Kurdish separatists in the southeast have fought to create a Kurdish state.

The organization and outlook of modern Turkey is largely the product of Mustafa Kemal, or Ataturk, who led a war of independence against occupying British, French, Greek, and Russian armies after the defeat of the Ottoman Empire in World War I. Ataturk forged the Republic of Turkey from the remnants of the Ottoman Empire and strongly embraced for his foundling nation a policy of modernization, which he equated with Westernization. Ataturk imposed strict curbs on the civil power of Islam, instituted a roman alphabet, and guaranteed civil rights for women.

Turkey is a parliamentary democracy and a secular Muslim state. The military acts as an unofficial, although effective, guarantor of democracy and secularism. In 1960s, 1970s, and 1980s, the army stepped in to correct what it saw as a drift away from the principles set forth by Ataturk. In 1997, the military expressed its distrust of the government headed by Refah, the Islamic Welfare Party, and charges were brought that the party had engaged in unconstitutional, anti–secularist activities. The party was disbanded.

The overtly nationalist National Action Party, or MHP, was the clear winner in the 1999 elections. The MHP formed a coalition government with the DSP (Social Democratic Party) and ANAP, the right–of–center Motherland

Party, and installed Bulent Ecevit as prime minister. Ahment Necdet Sezer, a former judge, was elected president. The government succeeded in passing constitutional amendments to strengthen individual human rights; legislation to reform the banking sector and the social security system; and measures designed to enhance Turkey's role in regional security, including assuming control of the International Stability Assistance Force in Afghanistan in June 2002. Despite these reforms, Turkey was, once again, not admitted to the E.U. for which it has been an official candidate since 1999. This has been a source of frustration for the Turkish government. Official E.U. explanations are that its economic and human rights problems prohibit membership, but Muslim Turks suspect the real reason is because they are not a Christian nation. Turkey has been a member of NATO since 1952.

In 1999, two devastating earthquakes hit Turkey in less than three months. The first — with its epicenter at Izmit in Turkey's heavily populated northwest — registered 7.4 on the Richter scale and struck on August 17, 1999. Three months later, another earthquake struck farther to the east, centered on Duzce. The result was more than 17,000 known deaths and 29,000 injuries, with 800,000 left homeless. In addition, some 300,000 buildings were damaged or destroyed. These back–to–back disasters continue to have a significant impact on a region that accounts for one–quarter of Turkey's population and nearly half of its industry.

Turkey's coalition government collapsed in the summer of 2002. In November elections, voters soundly rebuffed the major governing parties in favor of the Justice and Development Party (AKP) led by Recep Tayyip Erdogan, the former mayor of Istanbul. After legislators amended the constitution to lift a ban that prohibited Erdogan from running for parliamentary office because of a conviction for "incitement to religious hatred" (he read a poem at a political rally), Erdogan was elected prime minister in March 2003. Prime Minister Erdogan is faced with the unenviable tasks of negotiating E.U. membership, reaching a settlement on Cyprus, and dealing with the United States' invasion of neighboring Iraq in 2003.

Regular weekday business hours are from 8:30 a.m. to 5:30 p.m. Lunch breaks are usually betweeen 1 p.m. and 2 p.m. Food shops generally open as early as 6 a.m. and close as late as 7 p.m.

Current Economic Climate

Turkey's economy is beginning a slow recovery from its last recession, yet remains very volatile: A bitter row between President Sezer and Prime Minister Ecevit triggered a run on the lira and a dramatic increase in interest rates. The result was rapid inflation, a severe banking crisis, a massive rise in domestic public debt, and a deep economic downturn. The GNP fell 9.4 percent in 2001. The government was forced to adopt a more ambitious economic reform program that included a very tight fiscal policy and unprecedented levels of lending by the International Monetary Fund.

Turkey's main economic problem remains inflation. Annual consumer price inflation has averaged 79 percent since 1988. The country is beginning to see economic improvements, however. An IMF–backed recovery plan has helped inflation plummet to 29.7 percent in 2002, and the Turkish government aims to further reduce it to 20 percent in 2003. Unemployment stands at roughly 9.9 percent. Yet despite these rays of economic sunshine, Turks say they are crushed between rising unemployment and inflation, caused in part by a currency devaluation that has driven up the price of imported goods and some rents by more than 50 percent.

Despite a slight decline over the past 20 years, Turkey remains a largely agrarian society, with 56 percent of its population engaged in agricultural work. Primary crops include tobacco, cereals, and cotton. Turkey's Black Sea region produces 70 percent of the world's hazelnuts. Industrial products emphasize metals and metal products, including iron, steel, machinery, and automobiles. A tourist boom in the 1980s has made tourism an important industry. Turkey's primary trading partners include E.U. nations and the United States.

Turks are well–known guest workers in other European countries, which has helped keep Turkey's unemployment rate in check. Economic troubles in Turkey traditionally result in more emigration. In 1998, 5 percent of the nation's population — 3.5 million people — worked abroad.

Turkey's 10 Largest Companies

(2001, based on market capitalization)

1. Turkiye Garanti Bankasi
2. Haci Omer Sabanci Holding
3. Koç Holding
4. Petrol Ofisi
5. Turkish Petroleum Refineries Corp.
6. Yapi ve Kredi Bankasi Anonim Sirketi
7. Akbank Turk Anonim Sirketi
8. Turk Hava Yollari
9. Petkim Petrokimya Holding
10. Anadolu Efes Biracilik Ve Malt Sanayi

Getting Around in Turkey

For local transportation, trains, buses, and *dolmus* (shared taxis) are likely your best options. Trains are the most economical but a bit slow. Buses are efficient, comfortable, and reasonably priced, although more expensive than trains. *Dolmus* follow set routes within and between cities, and users can get on or off as they please. For longer trips within Turkey, consider Turkish Airlines. Fares are reasonable and you may find a two– or three–hour flight preferable to hours on end in a bus.

Employment Regulations and Outlook for Americans

A residence permit is required by foreigners who wish to stay in Turkey for more than one month. The application must be made to the Turkish embassy or consulate. Those intending to work will need to present a work visa upon arrival. For work stays of less than six months, your visa application should include a copy of your employment contract plus a letter from your employer describing your position and its duration. Stays of more than six months require written approval from the State Planning Organization, which is submitted along with your employment contract when applying for a visa. Work permits are valid for two years and must be obtained before entering the country.

The weak condition of the Turkish economy means that jobs for Americans are scarce. Students may have luck with temporary jobs as au pairs or in tourist resorts. There are some opportunities to teach English, although your best opportunities will likely require that you have TEFL certification.

Merhaba from Turkey!

I worked in Istanbul in an internship arranged through AIESEC, and I can truly say I felt right at home. AIESEC Istanbul has the most amazing group of students who have devoted their entire summers to ensure that the 30 trainees who were here from around the world had a great time.

I worked at the Turkish education volunteer foundation, teaching about 50 children English, as well as doing sports with them. The school is located in a less developed part of the city, giving me a wide perspective of the different classes here. The kids were great. They either called me teacher or *Shirin habla*, meaning Sister Shirin! Even though the language barrier is a challenge, we worked daily to overcome it.

With a popluation of 7 million, Istanbul is truly a country of its own! Thanks to my poor sense of direction, I had the privilege of getting lost numerous times, allowing me to see nearly all of the city by bus! In the afternoons and on the weekends, the AIESEC group had many activities that trainees could participate in. I traveled to Troy (yes, I saw the wooden horse), islands near Istanbul, and of course all of the palaces, mosques, and numerous museums in the city.

AIESEC provided a wonderful opportunity. It's not just that I learned so much about Turkish culture, but living with people from Brazil, Denmark, Lithuania, Estonia, France, Colombia, Great Britain, Greece, Romania, and Poland made this trip much more meaningful than I had ever imagined. —*Shirin Hakimzadeh, Houston, TX*

Short–term and Temporary Jobs

The best bets for casual jobs are teaching English and working at resorts along the coast. There are some opportunities for au pair work in Istanbul and Ankara. See Chapter 9 for additional resources.

Intercultural Exchange Programs (ICEP Turkey)
Yuksel Cd 9/10
Kizilay–Ankara, Turkey
Tel.: [90] 312 418 44 60
Fax: [90] 312 418 44 61
Email: info@icep.org.tr
ICEP recruits women between the ages of 18 and 29 to work as au pairs for three to 12–month assignments. Most au pairs in Turkey earn about €250 per month, plus room and board.

Turkeng Recruitment
Ayanoglu Mah
1284 Sok No. 8
Antalya, Turkey
Tel.: [90] 242 325 2662
Fax: [90] 242 326 6778
Email: turkeng@angelfire.com
www.angelfire.com/biz/turkeng
Turkeng recruits native English speakers to teach in over 40 different schools in Istanbul, Bursa, Izmir, and Antalya. Turkeng does not charge a placement fee to teachers.

Internship Programs

Students looking for professional experience or internships in Turkey will find the best opportunities by working with established organizations such as AIESEC, IAESTE, and CDS International, described in Chapter 9.

Volunteer Opportunities

There are many workcamp opportunities in Turkey. Arrangements to participate can be made through organizations based in the United States, such as the Council on International Educational Exchange (CIEE) and Volunteers for Peace (VFP). See Chapter 9 for details and additional resources.

Gençtur
Istiklal Caddesi Zambak Sok. 15/A Kat 15/5 Taksim
TR–800 80 Istanbul, Turkey
Tel.: [90] 212 249 25 15
Fax: [90] 212 249 25 54
Email: workcamps@genctur.com.tr
www.genctur.com
Genctur's work camps provide opportunities for volunteers of all ages to meet people from other cultures, learn about traditional way of life in Turkey, and improve their foreign languages. Most of the camps are organized in small towns or villages. The work on the camps typically involves painting, renovation, basic construction, environmental development, nature protection, or beach cleaning. There are some opportunities to teach English or assist disabled people. Most programs last from two to three weeks. Volunteers should apply through partner organizations in the U.S., such as CIEE and VFP.

GSM Youth Services Centre
Bayindir Sokak, No 45/9
Kizilay
TR–06650 Kizilay–Ankara, Turkey
Tel.: [90] 312 417 1124
Fax: [90] 312 425 8192
Email: gsm@gsm–youth.org
www.gsm–youth.org
GSM manages about 15 work camps in Turkey. Projects typically last about two weeks and involve environmental preservation. Volunteers are expected to pay their own travel, but receive room, board, and limited insurance coverage.

Resources for Further Information

Newspapers in Turkey

Cumhuriyet
Tel.: [90] 512 05 05
www.cumhuriyet.com.tr

Ekonomist
Tel.: [90] 212 67 70 000

Fax: [90] 212 67 94 701

Milliyet
Tel.: [90] 212 506 61 11
www.milliyet.com.tr

Useful Websites for Job Seekers

The Internet is a good place to begin your job search. Although Turkish employers are just beginning to use the Internet to list job vacancies, there are websites that provide useful information about the job market.

Information on Turkey
www.turkey.com
While not specifically for the job seeker, this site is a useful source of information for anyone considering relocating to Turkey. It includes information on business, culture, travel, and sports.

Turkey Jobsite
www.turkeyjobsite.com

Job seekers can search positions by industry, geographic location, or key word. There is a place to post CVs online, and you can register to receive job announcements via email.

Seriilan
www.seriilan.com
Posts positions throughout the country. Written in Turkish.

Embassies and Consular Offices

American embassies and consulates have commercial and/or economic sections that can provide you with business information and explain aspects of the local economy. Inquiries about business opportunities should be addressed either to "Commercial Officer" or "Commercial Section."

Representation of Turkey in the United States

Embassy of the Republic of Turkey
2525 Massachusetts Avenue NW
Washington, DC 20008
Tel.: (202) 612–6700

Fax: (202) 612–6744
Email: turkish@erols.com
www.turkey.org

Representation of the United States in Turkey

American Embassy
110 Ataturk Bulvari
Kavaklidere, Ankara, Turkey
Tel.: [90] 312 455 5555
Fax: [90] 312 468 0019
ca–ankara@state.gov
www.usemb–ankara.org.tr

U.S. Consulate — Adana
Atatü Caddesi Vali Yolu

Bossa Apt. Kat 1
Adana, Turkey
Tel.: [90] 322 459 1551
Fax: [90] 322 457 6591
www.usconadana.org.tr

U.S. Consulate General — Istanbul
104–108 Mesrutiyet Caddesi
Tepebasi, Istanbul, Turkey
Tel.: [90] 212 251 3602

Fax: [90] 212 251 3218   www.usisist.org.tr

Chambers of Commerce

Chambers of commerce consist of member firms in both countries interested in international trade. These are appropriate companies to initially target in the job search.

Istanbul Chamber of Commerce

P.O. Box 377

TR–34378 Istanbul, Turkey

Tel.: [90] 212 511 4150

Fax: [90] 212 513 1565

Turkish–American Business Association
Barbaros Boulevard Eser Apt 48–14
TR–80700 Istanbul, Turkey
Tel.: [90] 212 274 2824
Fax: [90] 212 275 9316
Email: amcham@amcham.org
www.taba.org.tr

World Trade Centers in Turkey

These two world trade centers house many foreign companies that conduct business in Turkey.

World Trade Center Ankara
Tahran Caddesi No. 30
Kavaklidere
TR–067 00 Ankara, Turkey
Tel.: [90] 312 468 8750
Fax: [90] 312 468 8100
Email: wtcankara@wtcankara.org.tr
www.wtc.ankara.org.tr

World Trade Center Istanbul
Cobancesme Kavsagi P. K. 40
TR–34 830 Havalimani
Istanbul, Turkey
Tel.: [90] 212 663 0608
Fax: [90] 212 663 0564
Email: info@wtcistanbul.net
www.wtcistanbul.net

Other Informational Organization

Foreign government missions in the United States, such as tourist offices, can furnish visas and information on work permits and other important regulations. They may also offer economic and business information about Turkey.

Turkish Tourism Office
1717 Massachusetts Ave., NW,
Suite 306
Washington, DC 20036

Tel.: (202) 612–6800

Email: tourismdc@aol.com

www.turkey.org

Business Directories

Although not always easy to find, business directories can prove invaluable in the international job search. Your best bet for locating these directories is to begin in the reference section of any public or university library. Most directories list company names, addresses, products, and phone numbers. Some directories include executive names and titles and financial information about the company. These sources provide you with the names of the people to contact for employment information as well as financial data, which can tell you how strong a company's position in a country may be.

Directory of Exporting Industrialists. Istanbul Chamber of Industry, Mesrutiyet cad. 118 Tepebasi, TR–80050 Istanbul, Turkey. Lists approximately 700 exporting companies in Turkey. 430 pages, $8, updated annually.

Turkey's 500 Major Industrial Establishments. Istanbul Chamber of Industry, Mesrutiyet cad. 118 Tepebasi, TR–80050 Istanbul, Turkey. Lists the 500 leading Turkish industrial companies. 160 pages, updated annually.

American Companies in Turkey

The following companies are classified by business area: Banking and Financ, Industrial Manufacturing, Retailing and Wholesaling, Service Industries, and Technology. Company information includes firm name, address, phone and fax number, and specific business. In the case of American parent firms, your chances of securing employment abroad are substantially better if you contact the subsidiary company in Europe rather than the parent company in the U.S. Keep in mind that the contact information for companies listed in this section can change often. Confirm the firm's address and phone number before writing to it.

Banking and Finance

The Chase Manhattan Bank
Istanbul Branch
Emirhan Caddesi, No. 145
Atakule A Blok, Kat 11
TR–80700 Besiktas, Istanbul, Turkey
Tel.: [90] 2122279700
Fax: [90] 2122279727
www.chase.com
(Bank)

Marsh Sigorta ve Reasurans Brokerligli
Buyukdere Cad. Maya Akar Center
No.100/102 Kat:4
Esentepe
TR–80280 Istanbul, Turkey
Tel.: [90] 2123554300
Fax: [90] 2123554330
www.marshmac.com
(Insurance)

Turk Merchant Bank
Cevdetpasa Caddesi 288
TR–80810 Bebek, Istanbul, Turkey
Tel.: [90] 257 7684
Fax: [90] 212 257 7327
(Bank)

Industrial Manufacturing

Edison Mission Energy – Turkey
Merhaz Mah
Birlik Caddessi No. 36
TR–34850 Esenyurt, Istanbul, Turkey
Tel.: [90] 212 596 5415
Fax: [90] 212 596 5422
www.edisonx.com
(Power producer)

General Electrik Ticaret
Ve Servis AS
TR–80200 Nisantasi, Istanbul, Turkey
Tel.: [90] 212 230 81
Fax: [90] 212 230 9929
(Power production)

Goodyear Lastikleri
Buyukdere Caddesi 41
Maslak Meydomi, Levant
TR– 34330 Istanbul, Turkey
Tel.: [90]2123295000
Fax: [90]2123295055
(Tires and tubes)

Honeywell
Emirhan Caddesi 145
Barbaros Plaza C/18
Dikilitas
TR–80700 Istanbul, Turkey
www.honeywell.com
(Process control systems)

Johnson Wax
2 Tasocagi Caddesi
Urfali Is Hani No. 4, Kat–1
Mecidiyekoy
TR–80300 Istanbul, Turkey
www.scjohnsonwax.com
(Cleaning products)

Levi Strauss Istanbul
Buyukdere Caddesi
Yapi Kredi Plaza
C–Blok, Kat 9–10
TR–34330 Istanbul, Turkey
Tel.: [90] 212 279 8465
Fax: [90] 212 317 0539
www.levistrauss.com
(Apparel)

Marsa Kraft Jacobs Suchard Sabanci
Kisikli Cad. No: 90 Altunizade
TR–81190 Istanbul, Turkey
Tel.: [90] 216 325 5782
Fax: [90] 216 325 5790
(Food products)

Pfizer Ylaclari
TR–80840 Ortakoy, Istanbul, Turkey
Tel.: [90] 212 260 221
Fax: [90] 212 258 4297
www.pfizer.com
(Pharmaceuticals)

Procter & Gamble Tuketim Mallari Sanayi Ltd.
Eski Uskudar Caddesi NORA Ctr.S MZ
TR–81090 Icerenkoy, Istanbul, Turkey
Tel.: [90] 1 216 463 8000
Fax: [90] 1 216 410 9785
www.pg.com
(Personal care products)

Service Industries

Deloitte & Touche
Iran Caddesi No. 33/4
TR–06700 Gaziosmanpasa, Ankara, Turkey
(Accounting)

Korn/Ferry
Cumhuriyet Cad 30/19
Kervansaray Apt. B, Blok, Elmadag
TR–80200 Istanbul, Turkey

Tel.: [90] 212 231 3949
Fax: [90] 212 231 2250
www.kornferry.com
(Personnel recruitment)

PriceWaterhouseCoopers Ltd.
Mete Caddesi 34/6
TR–80090 Taksim, Istanbul, Turkey
Tel.: [90] 212 251 7454
Fax: [90] 212 251 2518
www.pwcglobal.com
(Audit services)

Technology

Computer Associates
Buyukdere Caddesi Oyal Is
Hani kat 5, No. 108–01
TR–80280 Esentepe, Istanbul, Turkey
Tel.: [90] 212 272 717
www.cai.com
(Computer consultants)

Hewlett–Packard Bilgisayar ve Olcum Sistemleri
19 Mayis Caddesi
Nova Baran Plaza, Kat. 17
TR–80220 Istanbul, Turkey
Tel.: [90] 212 224 5925
Fax: [90] 212 224 5939
www.hp.com
(Printers and computers)

IBM Turk Ltd. Sirketi
Buyukdere Caddesi
Yapi Kredi Plaza B Blok
Levent
TR 80613 Istanbul, Turkey
Tel.: [90] 212 280 0900
Fax: [90] 212 284 4520
www.ibm.com
(Data processing equipment)

Microsoft (Turkey) Bilgisayaar Yazlim Hizmetleri
Barbados Plaza Is Merkezi
145–C, Kat. 21
Emirhan Caddesi, Dikilitas, Besiktas
TR–80700 Istanbul, Turkey
Tel.: [90] 212 258 5998
Fax: [90] 212 258 5954
www.microsoft.com
(Computer software)

European Companies in Turkey

The following are major non–American firms operating in the country. They can be either Turkish or based in another European country. Such companies will generally hire their own nationals first but may employ Americans.

Banking and Finance

Akbank
Sabanci Center 4 Levent
Akbank Genel Mudurlugu
TR–80745 Istanbul, Turkey
Tel.: [90] 212 2702666
Fax: [90] 2122826575
www.akbank.com.tr
(Commercial bank)

Haci Omer Sabanci Holding
Sabanci Center, 4 Levent
TR–80745 Istanbul, Turkey
Phone [90] 212 281 6600
www.sabanci.com.tr
(Financial products)

Turkiye Garanti Bankasi
Buyukdere Cad. No: 63 Maslak
TR–80670 Istanbul, Turkey
Tel.: [90] 212 2854040
Fax: [90] 212 335 35 35
www.garantibank.com.tr
(Retail banking)

Turkiye Halk Bankasi
Istiklal Cad. No: 158 Beyoglu
TR–80090 Istanbul, Turkey
Tel.: [90] 2122511217
Fax: [90] 2122517296
(Bank)

Türkiye Is Bankasi Kultur Yayinlari
Ataturk Bulv. 191 K.13 Kav. Dere
TR–06700 Ankara, Turkey
Phone [90] 3124281140
(Commercial banking)

Yapi ve Kredi Bankasi Anonim Sirketi
Levent
TR–80620 Istanbul, Turkey
Tel.: [90] 212 339 7000
www.ykb.com.tr
(Commercial bank)

Industrial Manufacturing

BASF Turk
Defterdar Yokusu, Basf Han No: 3
Tophane–Istanbul, Turkey
Tel.: [90] 212 251 65 00
Fax: [90] 212 244 1673
(Plastics and resins)

Deva Holding
Barbaros Bulvari No 64
TR–80600 Zincirlikuyu Besiktas
Istanbul, Turkey
Tel: [90] 212 275 2700
www.devaholding.com.tr
(Pharmaceuticals)

Eczacibasi Ilac Sanayi ve T.A.S.
Buyukdere Caddesi
Ali Kaya Sokak No: 7
TR–80640 Leventk, Istanbul, Turkey
Tel.: [90] 212 350 8000
www.eczacibasi.com.tr
(Pharmaceuticals)

Haci Ömer Sabanci Holding
Sabanci Center 4 Levent
TR–80745 Istanbul, Turkey
Tel.: [90] 212 281 66 00
Fax: [90] 212 281 02 72
www.sabanci.com.tr
(Food products, consumer products, technology conglomerate)

Koç Holding
Nakkastepe Aziz Bey Sok.No:1
Kuzguncuk
TR–81207 Istanbul, Turkey
Tel.: [90] 216 531 00 00
Fax: [90] 216 531 00 99
www.koc.com.tr
(Automotive and consumer goods)

Petkim Petrokimya Holding
P.K. 12 Aliaga
TR– 35801 Izmir, Turkey
Tel.: [90] 232 616 3240
Fax: [90] 232 616 1248
www.petkim.com.tr
(Industrial chemicals and gases)

Petrol Ofisi
Bestekar sokak No: 8 Kavaklidere
TR–06680 Ankara, Turkey
Tel.: [90] 312 425 4453
Fax: [90] 312 425 2798
(Petroleum distribution)

Turk Pirelli Kablo ve Sistemleri
Buyukdere Caddesi no. 117, Gayrettepe
TR–34350 Istanbul, Turkey
Tel.: [90] 212 355 1500
Fax: [90] 212 217 5891
(Tires and tubes)

Turkish Petroleum Refineries
TR–41002 Korfez, Kocaeli, Turkey
Tel.: [90] 262 527 0660
www.tupras.com.tr
(Crude oil production)

Retailing and Wholesaling

Carsi Buyuk Magazacilik
Buyukdere Cad.
Noramin Is Merkezi No 5
Maslak Istanbul, Turkey
[90] 212 285 0520
www.carsi.com.tr
(Department stores)

Migros Turk
Caferaga Mah Damga Sok 23/25
TR–81300 Kadikoy, Istanbul, Turkey
Tel.: [90] 216 418 1910
www.migros.com.tr

(Grocery retailer)

Tansas Perakende Magacilik Ticaret
Ankara Asfalti
TR–35100 Bornova Izmir, Turkey
Tel.: [90] 232 462 1200
www.tansas.com.tr
(Consumer product superstores)

Service Industries

Turk Hava Yollari
Ataturk Hava Limani Yesilkoy
TR–34830 Istanbul, Turkey
Tel.: [90] 212 663 63 00
Fax: [90] 212 663 47 44
www.turkishairlines.com
(Airline)

Marmaris Marti
Kosuyolu Aksu Cad No: 3
TR–34730 Bakirkoy Istanbul, Turkey
Tel.: [90] 212 543 6050
www.marti.com.tr
(Resorts & hotels)

Technology

Turkcell Iletisim Hizmetleri
Turkcell Plaza, Mesrutiyet Cad. No. 153
TR–80050 Tepebasi, Istanbul, Turkey
Tel.: [90] 212 313 1888
Fax: [90] 212 292 9322
www.turkcell.com.tr
(Wireless communications)

International Schools in Turkey

Istanbul International Community School
Karaagac Koyu Hadimkoy
TR–34866, Istanbul, Turkey
Tel.: [90] 212 857 8264
Fax: [90] 212 857 8270
www.iics.k12.tr
(U.S. curriculum, kindergarten through grade 10)

The Koç School
Koç Özel Ilkög retim Okulu ve Lisesi
P.K. 60
TR– 34941 Istanbul, Turkey
Tel.: [90] 216 304 1003

Fax: [90] 216 304 1048
Email: chanjo@kocschool.k12.tr
www.kocschool.k12.tr
(U.S., Turkish curriculum, grades 6 through 12)

Robert College of Istanbul
Arnavutkoy P.K.1
TR–80820 Istanbul, Turkey
Tel.: [90] 212 265 3430
Fax: [90] 212 287 0117
Email: mdrons@robcol.k12.tr
www.robcol.k12.tr
(U.S., Turkish curriculum, grades 7 through 12)

Cyprus

Major employment center: Nicosia
Major business languages: Greek, Turkish, English
Language skill index: English is understood by many, but you'll get
   further with Greek.
Currency: Cypriot pound
Telephone country code: 357
Time zone: Eastern Standard Time + 7 hours
Punctuality index: Punctuality is expected.
Average daily temperature: January, 51° July, 83° (Nicosia)
Average number of days with precipitation: January, 10 days; July,
   none
Best bet for employment:
   For students: Technical work through the IAESTE
   Permanent jobs: Not much here
Chance of getting a job: Frankly, pretty slim
Useful tip: Despite the ongoing political unrest, many tourists still visit
   Cyprus because of the great ruins and beaches. Job seekers may have
   some luck looking for jobs in the tourist industry.

The Republic of Cyprus occupies the largest island in the eastern Mediterranean Sea and is located about 40 miles south of Turkey and 60 miles west of Syria. Cyprus covers just under 3,600 square miles, making it roughly two–thirds the size of Hawaii. Two mountain ranges span Cyprus from east to west and are separated by a broad, fertile plain. The capital city of Nicosia rests in the eastern central part of the plain and is home to 170,000 of the island's 700,000 inhabitants. The population of Cyprus consists largely of ethnic Greeks (almost 80 percent), with a Turkish minority (18 percent).

> **Your spouse cannot join you in Cypress unless you have a five–year work permit.**

Ethnic rivalries and questions of national sovereignty have, in recent decades, become a constant source of contention on the island. Violence broke out in the mid–1950s when the Greek majority urged union with Greece and the Turkish minority dissented. In 1959, Greek and Turkish interests agreed to disagree, in effect, and forged a republic with a permanent division of government offices upon ethnic lines, with constitutional guarantees for the Turkish minority. Not surprisingly, tensions continued over the years, resulting in violence during the 1960s and 1970s. After a 1974 attempt by the ruling Greek junta to assassinate the Cypriot leader and replace him with an extremist government, Turkey occupied Northern Cyprus in support of the Turkish minority living there. In 1975, Turkish Cypriots voted to form a separate Turkish Cypriot state. The government was officially installed in 1976, and 200,000 Greek Cypriots were expelled from the Turkish–controlled area. Turkey is the only nation that recognizes the Turkish Republic of Northern Cyprus.

Cyprus remains a divided island, and violence between the two sides erupts from time to time. The U.N. has overseen sporadic and largely unsuccessful peace talks. Cyprus' plans to enter the E.U., however, may provide the necessary incentive to finally reunify the divided country. The E.U. admitted Cyprus for membership beginning in 2004, a decision not without controversy. Several critics warned that admitting Cyprus without confronting the issue of reunification would provoke the wrath of Turkey. That did not happen. Instead E.U. membership renewed momentum behind the U.N.'s peace talks. The E.U. and U.N. set a March 2003 deadline for negotiators to recommend a reunification plan but the deadline was missed. Conservative Tassos Papadopoulos' surprise election as president of Cyprus in February 2003 is expected to make negotiations more complicated. Yet the desire to clinch a deal is unmistakable, largely due to the economic and political lure of joining the E.U.

Opening business hours vary according to the season, but are generally from 8 a.m. to 5 p.m., Mondays through Fridays.

Current Economic Climate

The economic divergence of the political divisions of Cyprus is becoming increasingly pronounced. The rebound of E.U. economies has translated into a tourism windfall for ethnic–Greek southern Cyprus, while the heavily subsidized Turkish Cypriot economy in the north is in crisis. The Greek Cypriot economy's full employment, rising standard of living, robust equity markets, and wave of corporate mergers, acquisitions, and start-ups stand in sharp contrast to the economic situation in the Turkish Republic of Northern Cyprus (TRNC). The Turkish Cypriot economy has about one-fifth the population and one-half the per capita GDP of the south. Because it is recognized only by Turkey, it has had much difficulty arranging foreign financing, and foreign firms have hesitated to invest there. Many of the state-owned enterprises in Turkish Cyprus are failing and the reliance on mainland Turkey subsidies is pervasive.

The service sector is the heart of the Cypriot economy, with more than two–thirds of the population working in service industries. Major industries include food, beverages, textiles, chemicals, metal products, tourism, and wood products. The economy is very dependent on tourism, problematic given the swings in tourist arrivals brought on by political instability and economic uncertainty. Major trading partners include the United States, the United Kingdom, Russia, and Bulgaria.

Getting Around in Cyprus

One attractive short–trip option in Cyprus is touring on rented mopeds and bicycles. Rates are reasonable, plus there is the advantage of flexibility: you can go where you like, when you like. Buses and shared taxis serve routes between major cities and towns, although tourists are prohibited from crossing between the Greek and Turkish sides of the island. Ferries and planes serve Cyprus and mainland European and Middle Eastern ports.

Employment Regulations and Outlook for Americans

For tourist stays in Cyprus of 90 days or less, U.S. citizens don't need a visa. As with most of the rest of Europe, Cyprus requires that people who intend to work in the country present a work permit upon arrival. Since preference in hiring is given to Cypriot nationals, legal employment can be difficult to find. Beginning in October 2000, an amendment to Cyprus immigration legislation made it more difficult for foreign workers to bring their spouses into the country. The new law required that foreigners must possess a work permit for a total duration of five years before they can be joined by their partners. This does not mean that you must work for five years before your spouse joins you — you simply have to possess the permit. Informal arrangements serving some aspect of Cyprus tourist industry, hotel or restaurant work for example, may be the only option available to some job seekers. Programs that provide young professionals with assistance in obtaining work visas, such as IAESTE and CDS International, will also make finding work in Cyprus possible.

Internship Programs

Students looking for practical work experience in Cyprus will have the best luck working with established organizations such as IAESTE and CDS International, described in Chapter 9.

Volunteer Opportunities

Volunteers for Peace offers opportunities on work camps in Cyprus. Prospective volunteers might consider contacting other international service organizations that coordinate projects in Turkey to inquire about opportunities in Cyprus. See Chapter 9 for contact information.

Resources for Further Information

Newspapers in Cyprus

The Cyprus Weekly (English)
Tel.: [357] 2 66 6047
Fax: [357] 2 66 8665
www.cyprusweekly.com.cy

I Simerini
Tel.: [357] 2 35 3532
Fax: [357] 2 35 22 37
www.simerini.com.cy

Useful Website for Job Seekers

The Internet is a good place to begin your job search. Although Cypriot employers are just beginning to use the Internet to list job vacancies, there are websites that provide useful information about the job market.

Cyprus Government Page
www.pio.gov.cy
The official website for the government of Cyprus, it is a good resource for general information. Includes links to most of the major media outlets in Cyprus.

Embassies and Consular Offices

American embassies and consulates have commercial and/or economic sections that can provide you with business information and explain aspects of the local economy. Inquiries about business opportunities should be addressed either to "Commercial Officer" or "Commercial Section."

Representation of Cyprus in the United States

Embassy of the Republic of Cyprus
2211 R Street NW
Washington, DC 20008–4017
Tel.: (202) 462–5772
Fax: (202) 483–6710
cypembpow@sysnet.net
http://cyprusembassy.org/

Representation of the United States in Cyprus

American Embassy
Metochiou and Ploutarchou Streets
CY–2407 Engomi, Nicosia, Cyprus
Tel.: [357] 2 776 400
Fax: [357] 2 780 944
www.amercanembassy.org.cy

Chambers of Commerce

Chambers of commerce consist of member firms in countries interested in international trade. These are appropriate companies to initially target in the job search.

Cyprus Chamber of Commerce and Industry
P.O. Box 21455
CY–1509 Nicosia, Cyprus
Tel.: [357] 2 44 95 00
Fax: [357] 2 44 90 48
Email: chamber@ccci.org.cy
www.ccci.org.cy

Cyprus Trade Centre
13 East 40th Street
New York, NY 10016
Tel.: (212) 213–9100
Fax: (212) 213–2918
www.cyprustradeny.org

Famagusta Chamber of Commerce
339 Ayiou Andreou Street
P.O. Box 3124
Limassol, Cyprus
Tel.: [357] 5 370165
Fax: [357] 5 370291

Larnaca Chamber of Commerce and Industry
P.O. Box 287
Larnaca, Cyprus
Tel.: [357] 4 624851
Fax: [357] 4 628281

World Trade Center in Cyprus

This world trade center usually hosts many foreign companies that conduct business in Cyprus.

Cyprus World Trade Center
Chamber Building
38 Grivas Dhigenis Avenue
P.O. Box 21455

CY–1509 Nicosia, Cyprus
Tel.: [357] 2 449 500
Fax: [357] 2 449 048
Email: wtccy@wtca.geis.com

Other Informational Organization

Foreign government missions in the United States, such as tourist offices, can furnish visas and information on work permits and regulations. They may also offer economic and business information about the country.

Cyprus Tourist Organization
13 East 40th Street
New York, NY 10016

Tel.: (212) 683–5280
Fax: (212) 683–5282
www.cyprustourism.org

Business Directory

Although not always easy to find, business directories can prove invaluable in the international job search. Your best bet for locating these directories is to begin in the reference section of any public or university library. Most directories list company names, addresses, products, and phone numbers. Some directories include executive names and titles and financial information about the company. These sources provide you with the names of the people to contact for employment information as well as financial data, which can tell you how strong a company's position in a country may be.

Cyprus Chamber of Commerce and Industry Directory. Cyprus Chamber of Commerce and Industry, 38 Grivas Dhigenis Avenue, P.O. Box 21455, CY–1509 Nicosia, Cyprus; email: chamber@ccci.org.cy; www.ccci.org.cy. Lists over 8,000 financial, commercial, and service companies in Cyprus, plus government offices. Available only as CD–ROM. $40; updated infrequently.

Major Companies in Cyprus

The company information below includes the firm's name, address, phone and fax number, and specific business. In the case of American parent firms, your chances of securing employment abroad are substantially better if you contact the subsidiary company in Europe rather than the parent company in the United States. Keep in mind that the contact information for these companies can change pretty often. Confirm the company's address and phone number before writing to it.

Bank of Cyprus
51 Stasinou Street, Ayia Paraskevi
CY–2002 Strovolos, Cyprus
Tel.: [357] 22 37 80 00
Fax: [357] 22 37 81 11
www.bankofcyprus.com
(Commercial banks)

Cyprus Airways
21 Alkeou Street
CY–2404 Engomi, Cyprus
Tel.: [357] 22 66 30 54
Fax: [357] 22 66 31 67
(Transportation, air)

Cyprus Telecommunications Authority
Telecommunications Street, Strovolos
CY–1396, Nicosia, Cyprus
Tel.: [357] 22 70 10 00
Fax: [357] 22 49 49 40
www.cyta.com.cy
(Telephone communications)

Gevo Ltd.
9 Meletiou Metaxaki Street
CY–1045 Nicosia, Cyprus

Tel.: [357] 22 34 30 45
Fax: [357] 22 34 30 65
(Electronics)

IBM Italia
42–44 Griva Digeni Avenue
CY–1080 Nicosia, Cyprus
Tel.: [357] 22 84 11 00
Fax: [357] 22 66 632
(Data processing equipment)

Johnson Company
8 Preveza Street
CY–1065 Nicosia, Cyprus
Tel.: [357] 22 36 05 00
Fax: [357] 22 36 06 10
www.scjohnson.com
(Home and personal care products)

Raychem Technologies
Memrb House 21
21 Akademias Avenue
CY–2107 Aglantzia, Cyprus
Tel.: [357] 22 66 28 22
Fax: [357] 22 66 2904
www.raychem.com
(Wires, cables, fiber optics)

International School in Cyprus

American International School in Cyprus
P.O. Box 23847
11 Kassos Street
CY–1086 Nicosia, Cyprus
Tel.: [357] 2 316 345

Fax: [357] 2 316 549
Email: aisc@aisc.ac.cy
www.aisc.ac.cy

Malta

Major employment centers: Birkirkara, Valletta
Major business languages: Maltese, English
Language skill index: Knowing English should be just fine.
Currency: Maltese lira
Telephone country code: 356
Time zone: Eastern Standard Time + 6 hours
Punctuality index: Punctuality is not a priority in Malta.
Average daily temperature: January, 55 July, 77 fact data
Average number of days with precipitation: January, 13 days; July, 1 day
Best bet for employment:
    For students: Technical work with IAESTE, resort work
    Permanent jobs: Business, trade
Useful tip: As the ancient home of the Knights of St. John, Malta has a history of internationalism and international diversity.

The Republic of Malta consists of three islands — Malta, Gozo, and Cominodue — south of Sicily in the Mediterranean Sea. The total area of the islands is only 122 square miles: a scant 11 square miles larger than Denver. Malta's terrain is uniformly hilly, making for a corrugated coastline where the hills meet the sea. The capital city is Valletta, although Birkirkara is the nation's largest city with over 20,000 inhabitants. Malta has a total population of more than 350,000.

> **Malta is only 11 square miles larger than Denver, Colorado.**

Malta has a colorful political history, having been governed at various times by Phoenicians, Romans, Arabs, Normans, the Knights of Malta, France, and Britain. The islands became independent in 1964 and declared a republic ten years later. Malta is currently governed by a parliamentary democracy, with 13 electoral districts. Malta follows a policy of international nonalignment and is one of the few countries to have good relations with the regime of Libyan dictator Col. Muammar Quadhafi, a relationship that slowed but did not halt the nation's efforts to become a member of the European Union. Malta was approved to join the E.U. beginning in 2004.

Roman Catholicism is established by law as the religion of Malta. The government guarantees full liberty of conscience and freedom of worship, and a number of people with practicing diverse religions have migrated to the island. There is a growing North African Muslim community of about 2,250, for example, married to Maltese nationals.

Typical weekday business hours are from 8:30 a.m. to 5:30 p.m., with most offices closing for lunch from 12:30 p.m. to 1:30 p.m. The best time to conduct a business visit is from October to May.

Current Economic Climate

The nation has a relatively strong economy, despite a shortage of fresh water and domestic energy supplies. Malta lacks virtually all agricultural, mineral, and energy resources and relies upon its geographical position in Mediterranean shipping lanes and its picturesque charm and historic appeal. Limestone is Malta's only mineral resource of any quantity while all energy inputs, in the form of coal and petroleum, must be imported. Agricultural potential is extremely limited due to population density and the poor quality of the soil. Service industries play an important role in Malta's economy, providing work for over 70 percent of the labor force. Tourism in particular is central to the Maltese economy. Major trading partners include Germany, France, the United Kingdom, and Italy.

Getting Around in Malta

Buses, reasonably priced and comfortable, service the entire island of Malta. For do–it–yourselfers, rented mopeds provide a more flexible option. Ferries provide transport among the islands of Malta, Gozo, and Comino and between Malta and several cities of southern Italy.

Employment Regulations and Outlook for Americans

For tourist stays of up to 90 days, U.S. citizens don't need a visa. Those planning to work in Malta must have received an offer of employment prior to arrival. Once this is achieved, a work permit is issued. As in much of Europe, though, official employment can be difficult to come by in Malta. Before the Director of Labor will issue a work permit to a foreign worker, a Maltese employer must demonstrate that the applicant possesses a skill that is both in demand and hard to come by in Malta, such as nurses or tour guides who speak a particular language.

Short–term and Temporary Work/Internship Programs

Students looking for practical work experience in Cyprus will have the best luck working with established organizations such as IAESTE and CDS International, described in Chapter 9.

Malta Youth Hostels Association
17 Triq Tal–Borg
PLA 06 Pawla, Malta
Tel./Fax: [356] 69 39 57

Email: myha@keyworld.net
Volunteers work in youth hostels for two weeks to three months in exchange for room and board.

Newspapers in Malta

L'Orizzont
Tel.: [356] 24 7687
Fax: [356] 2384 84
Email: l–orizzont@unionprint.com

The Times
Tel.: [356] 24 14 64 9
Fax: [356] 24 7901
www.timesofmalta.com

Useful Websites for Job Seekers

The Internet is a good place to begin your job search. Although Maltese employers are just beginning to use the Internet to list job vacancies, there are websites that provide useful information about the job market.

Jobs Malta
www.jobsmalta.com
Lists clerical, accounting, management, media, hospitality, and health care jobs and includes a place to post your CV online. At press time, this site was down for restructuring.

Search Malta
www.searchmalta.com
Not specifically for job seekers, this site offers information useful for anyone

planning to live and work in Malta. Includes links to specific Maltese employers and job search sites.

Travel and Business Information

www.malta.co.uk

The sections that describe Maltese culture, festivals, and special events will be useful to people considering working in the country.

Embassies and Consular Offices

American embassies and consulates have commercial and/or economic sections that can provide you with business information and explain aspects of the local economy. Inquiries about business opportunities should be addressed either to "Commercial Officer" or "Commercial Section."

Representation of Malta in the United States

Embassy of Malta
2017 Connecticut Avenue NW
Washington, DC 20008–6132
Tel.: (202) 462–3611
Fax: (202) 387–5470

Email: Malta_Embassy@
compuserve.com

http://www.foreign.gov.mt/ORG/ministry/missions/washington2.htm

Representation of the United States in Malta

American Embassy
Development House, 3rd Floor
St. Anne Street
Floriana, VLT 01Malta

Tel.: [356] 2561 4000
Fax: [356] 21 243229
http://usembassy.state.gov/posts/mt1/wwwhmain.html

Chamber of Commerce

Chambers of commerce consist of firms in both countries interested in international trade. These are appropriate companies to initially target in the job search.

Maltese Chamber of Commerce
Exchange Buildings
Republic Street
Valletta VLT05, Malta

Tel.: [356] 233 873
Fax: [356] 245 223
Email: admin@chamber.org.mt
www.chamber–commerce.org.mt

Business Directories

Although not always easy to find, business directories can prove invaluable in the international job search. Your best bet for locating these directories is to begin in the reference section of any public or university library. Most directories list company names, addresses, products, and phone numbers. Some directories include executive names and titles and financial information about the company. These sources provide you with the names of the people to contact for employment information as well as financial data, which can tell you how strong a company's position in a country may be.

Made in Malta. Malta External Trade Corp., P.O. Box 8, San Gwann SG N01, Malta; email: info@metco.net; www.metco.net. Lists 850 manufacturing firms located in Malta. 850 pages, free, updated annually.

Malta Trade Directory. Malta Chamber of Commerce, Exchange Buildings, Republic Street, Valletta, Malta; email: admin@chamber.org.mt. Includes company information, plus businesses, professional associations, and government offices. 600 pages, 10 Maltese lira, updated annually.

The Malta Year Book. De la Salle Brothers Publications, Street Benild School, Church Street, Sliema SLM 02, Malta; email: martin@kemmunet.net.met. Distributed in the United States by Paul E. Mifsud, Maltese–American Foundation, 2074 Ridgewood Road, Medina, OH 44256. Lists schools, banks, libraries, and trade unions in the Maltese islands. 550 pages, $27, updated annually.

Major Companies in Malta

Malta's economy depends heavily on tourism. The most effective way to secure employment in this field, which includes hotel and resort work, sports, and other entertainment, is to approach employers directly in the hope of striking some sort of informal arrangement. Information on a few other companies operating in Malta is given below. In the case of companies with American parent firms, you can improve your chances of getting hired abroad if you contact the subsidiary company in Europe rather than the parent company in the U.S. Keep in mind that the contact information for companies can change often. Confirm the company's address and phone number before writing to it.

Air Malta Company Ltd.
Air Malta
LQA 01 Luqa, Malta
Tel.: [356] 2169 0890
Fax: [356] 2167 3241
www.airmalta.com
(Air transportation)

Bank of Valletta
BOV Centre High Street
Sliema SLM 16, Malta
Tel.: [356] 313119
Fax: [356] 346160
(Commercial bank)

BJ Marine
Msida Road
Gzira GZR 03, Malta
[356] 213 46 461
[356] 213 32 234
www.bjmarine.com
(Shipping agents)

IBM
141 Old Bakery Street
P.O. Box 336
Valletta, Malta
www.ibm.com
(Information technology)

MGS
91, Triq Censu Busuttil
Iklin BZN 11, Malta
Tel.: [356] 214 37090
Fax: [356] 214 37324

www.mgs.com.mt
(Import/Export)

Mid–Med Bank
15 Republic Street
Valletta VLT 05, Malta
Tel.: [356] 485 713
Fax: [356] 489 425
(Commercial bank)

Petroil Engineering & Construction Group
A15A, Marsa Industrial Estate
Marsa LQA 06, Malta
Tel.: [356] 212 44 843
Fax: [356] 212 48 488
www.digigate.net/e&cgroup/index.htm
(Engineering & construction services)

Radisson
Street Georges Bay
St. Julians STJ02, Malta
Tel.: [356] 21 573 81/4
Fax: [356] 21 581 104
(Hotels)

Middle Sea Valletta Life Assurance
Floriana VLT 16, Malta
Tel.: [356] 226 414
Fax: [356] 226 429
(Insurance)

Maersk Sealand
Bianchi Trading & Shipping
Palazzo Marina

143 St. Christopher Street
Valletta VLT 02, Malta
Tel.: [356] 21 232 241–4
Fax: [356] 21 232 991
www.sealand.com
(Shipping and transport services)

Valletta Investment Bank Ltd.
144 St. Christopher Street
Valletta VLT 02, Malta
Tel.: [356] 235 246

Fax: [356] 234 419
(Bank)

Vodafone Malta
Vodafone House, Msida Road
B'Kara BKR 14, Malta
Tel.: [356] 214 82 820
Fax: [356] 214 46 166
www.vodafone.com.mt
(Wireless communications)

International School in Malta

Verdala International School
Fort Pembroke
St. Andrews STJ 14, Malta
Tel.: [356] 375133
Fax: [356] 372 387

Email: vis@verdala.org
www.verdala.org
(U.S., U.K. curriculum, prekindergarten
through grade 12)

Chapter 22

Resource Center

Because many of the affordable print resources described in *How to Get a Job in Europe* can be hard to find, we have arranged with some of their publishers to enable readers to conveniently order them from Planning/Communications by mail, phone, fax, or online. The descriptions of these resources tell you they are available from this Resource Center.

As a special thank you to readers of *How to Get a Job in Europe*, we are offering you the $65 directory, *American Jobs Abroad*, as a **free bonus.** See page 474 for full details on this still–valuable directory, and page 496 for instructions on obtaining your free copy while supplies last.

A brief bibliography of key resource books and software recommended in *How to Get a Job in Europe* follows. These books go into more depth to provide detailed guidance on selecting your international career and deciding if an international career is right for you; finding job vacancies abroad; applying for international jobs; preparing resumes and cover letters; interviewing; networking; identifying potential employers; and other details that go beyond the scope of *How to Get a Job in Europe*.

For detailed descriptions of these resources, visit our online "Job Quest Catalog" at http://jobfindersonline.com (click on the obvious link to the online *Job Quest Catalog)* and conduct a search for the title or part of the title.

> **Simply photocopy and use this page and the following page to order any of these resources by mail or fax.**

Resource Bibliography

____ *International Job Finder: Where the Jobs are Worldwide ($19.95)*
____ *Back Door Guide to Short–Term Job Adventures... ($21.95)*
____ *Best Resumes and CVs for International Jobs ($24.95)*
____ *Directory of Websites for International Jobs ($19.95)*
____ *e–Resumes ($11.95)*
____ *Flight Attendant Job Finder & Career Guide ($16.95)*

____ *The Global Etiquette Guide to Europe ($17.95)*
____ *Global Resume and CD Guide ($17.95)*
____ *Guide to Homeland Security Careers ($14.95)*
____ *How to Get a Job in Europe, 5th edition ($22.95)*
____ *How to Get a Job With a Cruise Line ($16.95)*
____ *International Directory of Executive Recruiters ($149.00)*
____ *Internships 2004 [Peterson's] (and subsequent years) ($26.00)*
____ *Job Surfing: Working Abroad ($14.95)*
____ *WinWay Resume for Windows ($55.96, 20 percent off retail)*
____ *Work Abroad: The Complete Guide... ($15.95)*
____ *Work Worldwide: International Career Strategies... ($14.95)*

**Simply photocopy and use the previous page and
this page to order any of these resources by mail or fax.**

$____.___ **Resources Total**
+ $____.___ **(Shipping) = $_____.___ Total Due**
(Illinois residents only: Add 7.75% sales tax)

Calculate Shipping:
Delivery in U.S: $5.50 for the first item plus $1 for each additional item.
Delivery outside U.S.: Email your order to order@planningcommunications.com
and we will email back the shipping cost before you finalize your order.

Ship to: **Please print clearly**

Name _____

Address _____

_____
Please supply a street address and apartment number so we can ship via UPS.
City–State–Zip Code _____

Phone number: ____ / _____ – _____ ❑ Home ❑ Work

Email address: _____

❑ Enclosed is my check or money order drawn on a U.S. bank for
US$ ____.___ (Total Due) payable to "Planning/Communications."

❑ Please charge US$ ____.___ (Total Due) to my VISA, MasterCard,
Discover Card, or American Express.

Card number _____ Expiration date ____ / _____
Signature on credit card _____
Print name on credit card _____
**Print address and zip (postal) code to which your monthly credit card
statements are sent if different than above** _____

_____

Send your order to:

Planning/Communications
7215 Oak Avenue River Forest, IL 60305 USA
You can also order online at http://jobfindersonline.com
Call within the U.S.: 888/366–5200 (toll–free) or from outside the U.S.:
708/366–5200, weekdays, 9 a.m. to 6 p.m. Central Time.
Email: order@planningcommunications.com   Fax: 708/366–5280

Free $65 Directory of International Employers

American Jobs Abroad may be the best affordable directory ever compiled of American companies, government agencies, and nonprofits with international positions. For each of 800 top employers, it provides contact information for the organization's main office and for its chief hiring officer, a company description, number of employees, number of U.S. employees located abroad, countries in which it places employees, job categories in which the company hires for positions abroad, and language requirements, if any.

Among its 882 pages are 250 pages that profile 111 nations. Each profile provides details on the country's:

- Pros and cons of living there
- Health care
- Requirements for work permits and visas
- Taxation
- Language and currency
- Climate

- Economy and resources
- Cost of living
- Principal international schools
- Crime
- Population, cities, and American residents

- Embassay and consultant contact information
- Additional sources of information
- Index of companies and organizations operating there

Use the unique "Job Category Index" to quickly find employers that hire people in your field. Also included are chapters on getting hired, making the move, and living abroad — filled with timeless insights.

Retailing for $65, this 882–page directory is available to you for free. You pay only the cost of shipping and handling. We are offering this free bonus book even though it was published in 1994 because so many of its insights are timeless, its country profiles are top notch, and the information on most of the employers profiled is still timely.

Available while supplies last. **Before ordering**: Please check to see whether copies are still available by visiting http://jobfindersonline.com and selecting *International Job Finder* on the home page. No refunds or returns on this directory. **To order: Photocopy and submit the form on page 496.**

You pay only shipping and handling (in U.S. dollars):

Destination: Remember each copy of this book weighs five pounds.
United States and Puerto Rico: $10 per copy
Canada: $19 per copy   Mexico: $25 per copy

Elsewhere: Visit http://ircalc.usps.gov/ and add $5 for handling to the amount the postal service reports for shipping 5 pounds via air mail to your country.

Index

H

I

N

O

P

About the Authors

Dr. Cheryl Matherly is Assistant Dean of Students for Career Services, Scholarships, and Fellowships at Rice University in Houston, Texas. Dr. Matherly currently directs Rice's International Internship Program, which has received national attention for placing undergraduate students into internships throughout Europe. Dr. Matherly, who has traveled and worked extensively in Europe, has advised hundreds of students and recent graduates about successfully finding work abroad. She is particularly interested in the impacts of globalization on the workplace. The recipient of two Fulbright grants for study of culture and higher education abroad, she holds a doctorate in education from the University of Houston.

Dr. Robert Sanborn is currently the Executive Director and CEO of the Education Foundation of Harris County, Texas. He is a recognized expert on international career opportunities, and has been a regular contributor to national magazines. Dr. Sanborn received his doctorate in International Education from Columbia University where he served as placement director for the School of International and Public Affairs. Dr. Sanborn was also Associate Dean at Rice University and Dean of the College at Hampshire College in Amherst, Massachusetts. The author of the first edition of *How to Get a Job in Europe* and other titles in the "How to Get a Job in …" series, Dr. Sanborn was among the first career education professionals in the U.S. to actively advise college students about opportunities to work abroad.

Free $65 Directory of International Employers

Probably the best affordable directory ever compiled of American companies, government agencies, and nonprofits with international jobs. For each of 800 top employers, it provides full contact information and everything else you need to know to decide if it is worth approaching the employer for an international job.

There's much more. Get full details on page 474.

To get your free copy:

Retailing at $65, you pay only for shipping and handling of this five–pound, 882–page resource. **Photocopy this page** and complete the information requested below. Limit: 10 copies per order. No refunds or returns on this item only. Do **not** use the order form on page 473 to get this free book. You must use a photocopy of this page (you can, however, mail the two forms together).

Send to: Planning/Communications, Dept. EJF, 7215 Oak Ave. River Forest, IL 60305 USA — **prepaid orders only**.

Please send _____ copies of *American Jobs Abroad* (10 copy limit) to:
Where did you buy or borrow your copy of *How to Get a Job in Europe?*

_____

Print your name   _____
Address   _____
City–State or Province   _____
Zip or Postal Code–Country _____
Email address: _____ Phone: _____

☐ Enclosed is a check or money order (U.S. funds only) payable to "Planning/Communications" for $_____ **(See page 474 for postage and handling)**.

　　Charge $_____ to my VISA, MasterCard, American Express, or Discover Card number   _____
Expiration Date _____ / _____ Signature _____
Print name on card if different than above   _____
Print address and zip (postal) code to which your monthly credit card statements are sent *if different than above:*

_____

496